THE PREHISTORIC SOCIETY

Bell Beaker Settlement of Europe

Bell Beaker Settlement of Europe

The Bell Beaker phenomenon from a domestic perspective

edited by
Alex M. Gibson

Prehistoric Society Research Paper No. 9
2019

THE PREHISTORIC SOCIETY
Series Editor: Michael J. Allen
Managing Editor: Julie Gardiner

Oxford & Philadelphia

Published in the United Kingdom in 2019 by
The Prehistoric Society

and

OXBOW BOOKS
The Old Music Hall, 106–108 Cowley Road, Oxford, OX4 1JE

and in the United States by
OXBOW BOOKS
1950 Lawrence Road, Havertown, PA 19083

Hardcover Edition: ISBN 978-1-78925-124-1
Digital Edition: ISBN 978-1-78925-125-8 (epub)

A CIP record for this book is available from the British Library

Library of Congress Control Number: 2019938768

Printed in Malta by Melita Press Ltd

For a complete list of Oxbow titles, please contact:

UNITED KINGDOM
Oxbow Books
Telephone (01865) 241249
Email: oxbow@oxbowbooks.com
www.oxbowbooks.com

UNITED STATES OF AMERICA
Oxbow Books
Telephone (610) 853-9131, Fax (610) 853-9146
Email: queries@casemateacademic.com
www.casemateacademic.com/oxbow

Oxbow Books is part of the Casemate Group

Front cover: Reconstructions at the Százhalombatta Archaeological Park, Hungary. Photograph: Alex Gibson
Rear Cover: Top: Giant beaker and cordoned vessels from Zwenkau (Leipzig), Germany (Chapter 13). Photograph: from Schunke 2017a, 64, Fig. 18 (Department of Archaeology, Saxony). *Middle right:* Entrance to the fortified settlement at Los Millares, Spain (Chapter 4). Photograph: Roy Loveday. *Bottom right:* Boat-shaped Beaker house at Albertfalva, Hungary (Chapter 12). Photograph: from Endrődi & Reményi (2016).

THE PREHISTORIC SOCIETY RESEARCH PAPERS

The Prehistoric Society Research Papers publish collections of edited papers covering aspects of Prehistory. These may be derived from conferences, or research projects; they specifically *exclude* the publication of single excavation reports. The Research Papers present the fruits of the best of prehistoric research, complementing the Society's respected *Proceedings* by allowing broader treatment of key research areas.

The Research Papers is a peer-reviewed series whose production is managed by the Society.

Further information can be found on the Society's website (www.prehistoricsociety.org)

THE PREHISTORIC SOCIETY

The Prehistoric Society's interests are world wide and extend from the earliest human origins to the emergence of written records. Membership is open to all, and includes professional, amateur, student and retired members.

An active programme of events – lectures, study tours, day- and weekend conferences, and research weekends – allows members to participate fully in the Society and to meet other members and interested parties. The study excursions cater for all preferences from the relatively luxurious to the more economical, including highly popular student study tours. Day visits to sites are arranged whenever possible.

The Society produces two publications that are included with most categories of membership: the annual journal, *Proceedings of the Prehistoric Society* and the topical newsletter, *PAST*, which is published in April, July and November. In addition the *Prehistoric Society Research Papers* are published occasionally on which members may have discount.

Further information can be found on the Society's website (www.prehistoricsociety.org), or via the Prehistoric Society's registered address: ℅ Institute of Archaeology, University College London, 31–34 Gordon Square, London, WC1H 0PY.

The Society is a registered charity (no. 1000567)

THE PREHISTORIC SOCIETY RESEARCH PAPERS

Other volumes in this series, available from Oxbow Books

No. 1. *From Bann Flakes to Bushmills – papers in honour of Professor Peter Woodman*
eds N. Finlay, S. McCartan, N. Milner & C. Wickham-Jones (2009)

No. 2. *Land and People – papers in memory of John G. Evans*
eds M.J. Allen, N. Sharples & T. O'Connor (2009)

No. 3. *Materialitas: working stone, carving identity*
eds B. O'Connor, G. Cooney & J. Chapman (2010)

No. 4. *Is there a British Chalcolithic? People, place and polity in the later 3rd millennium*
eds M.J. Allen, J. Gardiner, A. Sheridan & D. McOmish (2012)

No. 5. *Image, Memory and Monumentality: archaeological engagements with the material world*
eds A.M. Jones, J. Pollard, M.J. Allen and J. Gardiner (2012)

No. 6. *Settlement in the Irish Neolithic: new discoveries at the edge of Europe*
by Jessica Smyth (2014)

No. 7. *The Beaker People: isotopes, mobility and diet in prehistoric Britain*
eds M. Parker Pearson, A. Sheridan, M. Jay, A. Chamberlain, M. Richards & J. Evans (2019)

No. 8. *First Farmers of the Carpathian Basin: changing patterns in subsistence, ritual and monumental figurines*
by Eszter Bánffy (2019)

No. 9. *Bell Beaker Settlement of Europe: the Bell Beaker phenomenon from a domestic perspective*
ed. Alex M. Gibson (2019)

Volumes in production

No. 10. *Re-peopling La Manche: new perspectives on Neanderthals lifeways at La Cotte de St Brelade*
eds Beccy Scott & Andrew Shaw

No. 11. *The Social Context of Technology: non-ferrous metalworking in later prehistory*
by Leo Webley, Sophia Adams & Joanna Brück

CONTENTS

Open Access; the following chapters are also available in Open Access:
Chapter 8, Marie Besse, Eve Derenne, Lucas Anchieri, Aude Baumberger, Antoine Caminada & Martine Piguet.
https://books.casematepublishing.com/Bell_Beaker_settlement_of_Europe.pdf

LIST OF FIGURES

List of Figures

List of Tables

CONTRIBUTORS

VINCENT ARD
CNRS, UMR 5608 Traces, Université de Toulouse II le Mirail, Maison de la Recherche, 5, Allées Antonio Machado, F-31058 Toulouse cedex 9, France
vincent.ard@univ-tlse2.fr

LUCAS ANCHIERI
Laboratoire d'archéologie préhistorique et anthropologie, Département F.-A. Forel des sciences de l'environnement et de l'eau, Université de Genève,
Uni Carl-Vogt, 66 Boulevard Carl-Vogt, CH-1211 Genève 4, Switzerland
Lucas.Anchieri@etu.unil.ch

MARCO BAIONI
Museo Archeologico della Valle Sabbia, Gavardo (BS), Italy
baicop1@virgilio.it

ANA CATARINA BASÍLIO
ICArEHB Algarve University, Estr. da Penha 139, 8005–139 Faro, Portugal
catarinabasilio@gmail.com

AUDE BAUMBERGER
Laboratoire d'archéologie préhistorique et anthropologie, Département F.-A. Forel des sciences de l'environnement et de l'eau, Université de Genève,
Uni Carl-Vogt, 66 Boulevard Carl-Vogt, CH-1211 Genève 4, Switzerland
Aude.Baumberger@etu.unige.ch

MARIE BESSE
Laboratoire d'archéologie préhistorique et anthropologie, Département F.-A. Forel des sciences de l'environnement et de l'eau, Université de Genève,
Uni Carl-Vogt, 66 Boulevard Carl-Vogt, CH-1211 Genève 4, Switzerland
Marie.besse@unige.ch

ÉMILIE BLAISE
UMR 5140 ASM, Montpellier, France
emilie.blaise@gmail.com

STÉPHANE BLANCHET
Inrap, UMR 6566 CReAAH, 37, rue du Bignon CS 67737, F-35577 Cesson-Sevigné cedex, France
stephane.blanchet@inrap.fr

KATALIN T. BIRÓ
Hungarian National Museum, Archaeological Department, H-1088 Budapest, Múzeum krt. 14–16, Hungary
tbk@ace.hu

ANTOINE CAMINADA
Laboratoire d'archéologie préhistorique et anthropologie, Département F.-A. Forel des sciences de l'environnement et de l'eau, Université de Genève,
Uni Carl-Vogt, 66 Boulevard Carl-Vogt, CH-1211 Genève 4, Switzerland
antoine.caminada@etu.unige.ch

FABIEN CONVERTINI
Inrap Méditerranée, UMR 5140 ASM, Montpellier, France
fabien.convertini@inrap.fr

JANUSCZ CZEBRESZUK
Institute of Archaeology, Adam Mickiewicz University, Poznan, Poland
jancze@amu.edu.pl

EVE DERENNE
Laboratoire d'archéologie préhistorique et anthropologie, Département F.-A. Forel des sciences de l'environnement et de l'eau Université de Genève, Uni Carl-Vogt, 66 Boulevard Carl-Vogt, CH-1211 Genève 4, Switzerland
Eve.Derenne@unige.ch

KLET DONNART
Eveha, 23 Rue des Maréchales, F-35132 Vezin-le-Coquet, France
klet_donnart@yahoo.fr

Erik Drenth
Torenstraat 4, NL-3811 DJ Amersfoort, Netherlands,
drenth.erik@gmail.com

Anna Endrődi
Budapest History Museum, H-1014 Budapest, Szent György tér 2, Hungary
anna.endrodia@gmail.com

Quentin Favrel
University of Paris 1 Panthéon-Sorbonne, UMR 8215 Trajectoires, Maison de l'Archéologie et de l'Ethnologie 21, allée de l'université F-92023 Nanterre cedex, France
quentin.favrel@gmail.com

Nicolas Fromont
Inrap, 4, Rue du Tertre, F-44477 Carquefou, France
nicolas.fromont@inrap.fr

Robin Furestier
Cité de la Préhistoire d'Orgnac l'Aven, UMR 5140 ASM, Montpellier, France
r.furestier@orgnac.com

Rafael Garrido-Pena
Departamento de Prehistoria y Arqueología, Universidad Autónoma de Madrid, 28049, Madrid, Spain
rafael.garrido@uam.es

Alex M. Gibson
15 Alexandra Crescent, Ilkley, West Yorkshire, LS29 9ER, UK
AlexGibsonArchaeol@outlook.com

Christophe Gilabert
Ministère de la Culture, UMR 5140 ASM, Montpellier, France
christophe.gilabert@culture.gouv.fr

Ferenc Gyulai
Szent István University, H-2103 Gödöllő, Páter Károly u. 1, Hungary
gyulai.ferenc@mkk.szie.hu

Daniela Kern
Independent Researcher, Vienna, Austria
daniela-eve.kern@aon.at

J.P. (Jos) Kleijne
Graduate School 'Human Development in Landscapes', Christian-Albrechts Universität zu Kiel, Leibnizstrasse 3 room 126, 24118 Kiel, Germany
joskleijne@gmail.com

Matthieu Labaune
UMR 6298 ArTeHiS, Dijon, France
matthieu.labaune@gmail.com

Maria Lazarich
Departamento de Historia, Geografia y Filosofia, Universidad de Cadiz, Cadiz, Andalucia, Spain
maria.lazarich@uca.es

Olivier Lemercier
Université Paul Valéry, UMR 5140 Archeologie des Sociétés méditerranées (ASM), Route de Mende, 34 199 Montpellier Cedex 5, France
olivier.lemercier@univ-montp3.fr

Lorraine Manceau
Inrap, UMR 8215 Trajectoires, 7 Rue du Bac, F-49123 Ingrandes, France
manceau.lorraine@live.fr

Cyril Marcigny
Inrap, UMR 6566 CReAAH, Boulevard de l'Europe, F-14540 Bourguébus, France
cyril.marcigny@inrap.fr

Pablo Marticorena
Université populaire du Pays Basque, UMR 5608 Traces, Université de Toulouse II le Mirail, Maison de la Recherche, 5, Allées Antonio Machado, F-31058 Toulouse cedex 9, France
harriak@hotmail.fr

Fabio Martini
Università di Firenze, Dipartimento di Storia, Archeologia, Geografia, Arte e Spettacolo (SAGAS), Museo e Istituto Fiorentino di Preistoria, Firenze, Italy
fabio.martini@unifi.it

Rui Mataloto
Município do Redondo, Portugal
rmataloto@gmail.com

Maria Grazia Melis
Dipartimento di Storia, Scienze dell'Uomo e della Formazione, Università degli Studi di Sassari, Sassari, Italy
mgmelis@uniss.it

Günter Morschhauser
Archäologischer Dienst GesmbH, St. Pölten, Austria
g.morschhauser@ardig.at

Clément Nicolas
UMR 8215 Trajectoires, Maison de l'Archéologie et de l'Ethnologie 21, allée de l'université F-92023 Nanterre cedex, France
clement.nicolas@wanadoo.fr

Théophane Nicolas
Inrap, UMR 8215 Trajectoires, 37, Rue du Bignon CS 67737, F-35577 Cesson-Sevigné cedex, France
theophane.nicolas@inrap.fr

FRANCO NICOLIS
Provincia Autonoma di Trento, Ufficio Beni Archeologici, Italy
franco.nicolis@provincia.tn.it

YVAN PAILLER
Inrap, UMR 8215 Trajectoires, UMR 6554 LETG – Brest Géomer, IUEM Rue Dumont d'Urville, Technopôle Brest Iroise, F-29280 Plouzané, France
yvan.pailler@inrap.fr

MARTIN PENZ
Stadtarchäologie Wien, Vienna, Austria
martin.penz@stadtarchaeologie.at

MARTINE PIGUET
Laboratoire d'archéologie préhistorique et anthropologie, Département F.-A. Forel des sciences de l'environnement et de l'eau Université de Genève, Uni Carl-Vogt, 66 Boulevard Carl-Vogt, CH-1211 Genève 4, Switzerland
Martine.Piguet@unige.ch

RAFFAELLA POGGIANI KELLER
Former Archaeological Superintendent of Lombardy, Italy
rpoggianikeller@libero.it

M. PILAR PRIETO-MARTÍNEZ
Grupo de Investigación Sincrisis, Departamento de Historia, Facultad de Geografía e Historia, Universidad de Santiago de Compostela, Praza da Universidade, 1, 15702 Santiago de Compostela (A Coruña), Spain
pilar.prieto@usc.es

LÁSZLÓ REMÉNYI
Castle Headquarters, Integrated Regional Development Centre Nonprofit Ltd., H-1113 Budapest, Daróci u.1–3, Hungary
laszlo.remenyi73@gmail.com

JULIEN RIPOCHE
University of Paris ,
1 Panthéon-Sorbonne, UMR 8215 Trajectoires, Maison de l'Archéologie et de l'Ethnologie, 21, allée de l'université F-92023 Nanterre cedex, France

LOLITA ROUSSEAU
UMR 6566 CReAAH, France
lolita.rousseau@hotmail.fr

TORBEN SARAUW
Nordjyllands Historiske Museum, Vang Mark 25, DK-9380 Vestbjerg, Denmark
torben.sarauw@aalborg.dk

LUCIA SARTI
Università di Siena, Dipartimento di Scienze storiche e dei Beni culturali-Unità di Preistoria, Sienna, Italy
lucia.sarti@unisi.it

OLIVER SCHMITSBERGER
Institute for Oriental and European Archaeology, Austrian Academy of Sciences, Hollandstrasse 11–13, A-1020 Vienna, Austria
Oliver.Schmitsberger@oeaw.ac.at

TORSTEN SCHUNKE
Landesamt für Denkmalpflege und Archäologie Sachsen-Anhalt, Richard-Wagner-Straße 9, 06114 Halle (Saale), Germany
tschunke@lda.stk.sachsen-anhalt.de

ANDRÉ SPATZIER
Landesamt für Denkmalpflege Baden-Württemberg, Berliner Straße 12, 73728, Esslingen, Germany
andre.spatzier@rps.bwl.de

CHRISTIAN STRAHM
Ur- und Frühgeschichtliche Archäologie, Albert-Ludwigs-Universität Freiburg, 79085 Freiburg, Germany
Ch.strahm@t-online.de

MARZENA SZMYT
Institute of Eastern Studies, Adam Mickiewicz University, Poznań, Poland
marzena@amu.edu.pl

JAN TUREK
Center for Theoretical Study, Joint Research Institute of Charles University & the Czech Academy of Sciences, Prague 1, Husova 4, 110 00 Czech Republic
turekjan@hotmail.com

ANTÓNIO CARLOS VALERA
Era Arqueologia/ICArEHB-Algarve University, Portugal
antoniovalera@era-arqueologia.pt

ABSTRACT

At the transition from stone to bronze, the 'Bell Beaker People' have fascinated archaeologists for over 100 years. The distinctive pot, easily recognisable from Hungary to Portugal and from the Baltic to the Mediterranean, associated with distinctive burial rites and graves containing archery and martial equipment as well as items of personal adornment gave a degree of unity to the pan-European phenomenon. Round-headed warriors drank and fought their way across Europe. Modern research, however, has proved Bell Beakers to be much more complicated. Clear regional facies are identifiable. The period marked change in some aspects, but continuity in others and this also varied from region to region. Usually described as pan-European, in fact there are distinct pockets of denser Beaker activity within the overall distribution. Beaker burials have been well studied but their settlements remain more enigmatic, difficult to detect in terms of house plans despite considerable accumulations of domestic debris (middens) in some areas. This book attempts to draw together the available data from across Europe for Beaker settlement and, in particular, for Beaker domestic architecture. Each chapter is written by both new and established internationally recognised experts on the Beaker phenomenon and who belong to *Archéologie et Gobelets,* a loosely affiliated organisation devoted to the study of Bell Beakers in their regional settings. Despite local differences, common themes can be identified. There is, for example, a distinct geographical distinction between the oval houses of the Atlantic and Mediterranean distribution and the long houses of Northern and Central Europe. But in both areas, the settlement evidence represents a period of change when the Neolithic and Chalcolithic settlements enter a period of decline and even abandonment. The flimsy nature of many Beaker houses is in contrast to the effort invested on monument construction. The nomadic way of life in some areas seems to come to an end with a change to more robust timber structures that mark the genesis of the European longhouse tradition. There is a general increase in land clearance and in arable agriculture suggesting a period of economic surplus and growth and with a general appearance of stability within the settlement sphere. This in turn might lead to competition for economically viable land and the emergence of elites. The increasing permanence of the settlements and the agricultural surplus suggested by the palaeoenvironmental data herald the economic stability of the Bronze Age.

Résumé

À la transition entre le Néolithique et l'âge du Bronze, la « civilisation campaniforme » a fasciné les archéologues durant plus d'un siècle. Le gobelet campaniforme, facilement reconnaissable de la Hongrie au Portugal et de la Baltique à la Méditerranée, associé à des rites funéraires spécifiques et des tombes contenant du mobilier d'archerie, un équipement guerrier et des parures individuelles donne un semblant d'unité à ce phénomène paneuropéen. Ces faits ont longtemps accrédité l'image de guerriers brachycéphales buvant et se battant sur leur chemin à travers l'Europe. Toutefois, la recherche moderne a montré que le Campaniforme est nettement plus complexe. Des faciès régionaux sont clairement identifiables. Selon le point de vue que l'on adopte, la période est marquée par des changements ou des continuités, eux-mêmes variables d'une région à une autre. Habituellement décrit comme paneuropéen, le Campaniforme s'avère inégalement distribué avec des zones de forte densité et d'autres plus lâches. Les tombes campaniformes ont été abondamment étudiées, alors que les habitats sont plus énigmatiques. Les plans de maisons sont difficiles à repérer, bien que de larges accumulations de rejets domestiques soient connues dans certaines régions.

Cet ouvrage tente de rassembler les données disponibles en Europe sur les habitats campaniformes et, en particulier, sur leurs architectures. Chaque chapitre est écrit par des experts du phénomène campaniforme, jeunes ou de renommée internationale, membres d'Archéologie et Gobelets, une association dédiée à l'étude du Campaniforme dans ses dimensions régionales. Malgré des différences locales, des traits communs peuvent être identifiés. Il y a, par exemple, une opposition géographique entre des maisons ovales en Atlantique et en Méditerranée et des maisons longues en Europe centrale et septentrionale. Néanmoins dans ces deux aires, les occupations campaniformes témoignent d'une période de changements à un moment où les habitats néolithiques et chalcolithiques déclinent ou sont abandonnés. La structure légère de nombreuses maisons campaniformes contraste avec l'effort investi dans la construction de monuments. Dans certaines régions, le mode de vie nomade semble prendre fin avec le passage à des constructions en bois plus robustes marquant la genèse en Europe de la tradition des maisons longues. Il y a une augmentation générale du défrichement et des terres arables suggérant une période de croissance et de surplus économiques allant de pair avec une apparente stabilité dans la sphère domestique. Cela pourrait avoir conduit par la suite à une concurrence pour les terres fertiles et à l'émergence d'élites. La pérennité croissante des occupations et les excédents agricoles suggérés par les études paléoenvironnementales annoncent la stabilité économique de l'âge du Bronze.

Zusammenfassung

Die am Übergang von der Stein- zur Bronzezeit auftretenden „Glockenbecherleute" faszinieren Archäologinnen und Archäologen seit über hundert Jahren. Die leicht erkennbaren, namengebenden Gefäße sind von Ungarn bis nach Portugal und vom Baltikum bis in den Mittelmeerraum verbreitet und zeigen europaweit ebenso wie charakteristische Bestattungssitten und Gräbern mit Bogenschützenausrüstung und bestimmten persönlichen Schmuckgegenständen einen gewissen Grad an Übereinstimmung. Nichts desto trotz beweisen moderne Forschungen das die Glockenbecher weitaus komplizierter sind. Es sind klar ausgeprägte regionale Formen erkennbar. Der betreffende Zeitabschnitt ist geprägt von Veränderungen in einigen Bereichen, während in anderen Kontinuität feststellbar ist, was teilweise auch regional unterschiedlich ist. Gemeinhin wird von einer paneuropäischen Verbreitung gesprochen, doch muss festgehalten werden, dass Akkumulationen und Zentren vorhanden sind. Bisher waren vor allem die Gräber und die Bestattungssitten gut erforscht, während Siedlungsnachweise, besonders in Form von Hausgrundrissen fehlten, auch wenn in einigen Gebieten erstaunliche Anhäufungen von Hausabfall (middens) festgestellt werden konnten. Dieses Buch ist eine europaweite Zusammenstellung der derzeit greifbaren Daten betreffend die Bechersiedlungen im Allgemeinem und der Siedlungsarchitektur im Besonderen. Jedes Kapitel wurde von international anerkannten, etablierten oder neu hinzugekommenen Spezialistinnen und Spezialisten von „Archéologie et Gobelets", einer losen Gruppe von Archäologinnen und Archäologen, die sich der Erforschung der Glockenbecher in ihrer regionalen Ausprägung widmen, verfasst. Es zeigt sich, dass trotz regionalen Unterschieden auch Gemeinsamkeiten identifiziert werden können. Da ist z.B. eine klare geographische Trennung von Häusern mit ovalem Grundriss, wie sie am Atlantik und im Mittelmeerraum üblich sind, und den Langhäusern Mittel- und Nordeuropas. Aber in beiden Regionen ist eine Veränderung im Siedlungswesen feststellbar, die den Niedergang und das Ende der neolithischen bzw. chalkolithischen Siedlungsweise anzeigt. Die nachlässige Bauweise mancher Glockenbecherhäuser steht in erstaunlichem Gegensatz zur aufwendigen Konstruktion der Monumentalarchitektur. Die nomadische Lebensweise scheint in einigen Gebieten zu einem Ende zu kommen, was zu einer massiveren Holzbauweise bei den Wohnbauten beitrug, die am Beginn der europäischen, bronzezeitlichen Langhaustradition stehen. In dieser Zeit kommt es allgemein zu einer Ausweitung der landwirtschaftlichen Flächen, was zu einem Wachstum und dem Erwirtschaften von Überschüssen führt und, wie es scheint, auch zu mehr Stabilität innerhalb des Siedlungsgefüges. Das könnte auch zu mehr Konkurrenz um nutzbares Land und somit zur Entstehung von Eliten geführt haben. Diese zunehmende Stabilität der Siedlungen sowie der durch die paläoökologischen Daten belegte landwirtschaftliche Überschuss bilden die Grundlage für die ökonomische Stabilität der Bronzezeit.

Resumen

El "Pueblo Campaniforme", que vivió en la transición del Neolítico a la Edad del Bronce, ha fascinado a los arqueólogos de los últimos 100 años. Sus distintivas cerámicas, fácilmente reconocibles desde Hungría a Portugal y desde el Báltico al Mediterráneo, y asociadas con unos ritos funerarios y unas tumbas características, que contienen equipos de arquería y militares, así como elementos de adorno personal, proporcionaron una cierta unidad a este fenómeno paneuropeo. Unos guerreros braquicéfalos que habrían bebido y peleado a lo largo y ancho de Europa. Sin embargo, las modernas investigaciones han demostrado que el Campaniforme es algo mucho más complejo. Se pueden identificar claras variantes regionales. Es un periodo de cambio en algunos aspectos, pero de continuidad en otros, algo que también varía según las regiones. Aunque suele describirse como un fenómeno paneuropeo, existen, de hecho, diferentes focos más densos de actividad campaniforme dentro del mapa de distribución general. Se han estudiado muy bien las tumbas campaniformes, pero sus asentamientos siguen siendo más enigmáticos y difíciles de detectar, especialmente las plantas de las casas, a pesar de documentarse en algunas zonas considerables acumulaciones de desechos domésticos (basureros). Este libro intenta reunir los datos disponibles sobre el poblamiento campaniforme y, en particular, sobre la arquitectura doméstica campaniforme. Todos los capítulos están redactados tanto por nuevos como por consolidados expertos, internacionalmente reconocidos en el estudio del fenómeno campaniforme, que pertenecen al grupo "Archéologie et Gobelets", una organización dedicada al estudio del Campaniforme en sus diferentes escenarios regionales. A pesar de las diferencias locales se pueden identificar también patrones comunes. Hay, por ejemplo, una diferenciación clara entre las casas ovales de las zonas atlánticas y mediterráneas y las alargadas del Norte y Centro de Europa. Pero en ambas áreas, las evidencias del poblamiento indican un periodo de cambio en el que los poblados del Neolítico y Calcolítico entran en una fase dedecadencia o incluso abandono. La naturaleza endeble de muchas casas campaniformes contrasta con los esfuerzos invertidos en la construcción de monumentos. El modo de vida nómada de ciertas zonas parece finalizar, dando paso a un cambio hacia la aparición de unas estructuras de madera más robustas que marcan la génesis de la tradición europea de las casas alargadas. Se constata un incremento generalizado de la deforestación y la agricultura del arado, lo que sugiere un periodo de excedentes económicos y crecimiento, con la aparición generalizada de asentamientos estables. Por su parte, ello habría llevado a la competición por las tierras más viables económicamente y al surgimiento de las élites. La creciente estabilidad de los asentamientos y del excedente agrario indicados por los datos paleoambientales, anuncian la estabilidad económica de la Edad del Bronce.

ACKNOWLEDGEMENTS

The Prehistoric Society would like to add their thanks to Deborah Hallam for reading and commenting on an earlier draught of this volume, and to Clément Nicolas, Daniela Kern and Rafael Garrido-Pena for respectively the French, German and Spanish translations of the abstract. We also thank our referees and members of our Editorial Advisory Committee, and our reviewers for their expert advice and opinions. In particular I would like to offer my thanks to Oxbow Books and Julie Gardiner (Prehistoric Society Managing Editor), for their advice and assistance, and also to Julie Blackmore of Frabjous Books for typesetting yet another of our volumes with skill, proficiency, dexterity and great speed, and Mette Bundgaard (Oxbow Books) for assistance with proofing. This book received additional funding from AEA: Allen Environmental Archaeology towards colour reproduction in this volume.

Michael J. Allen

1

INTRODUCTION

Alex M. Gibson

First meeting in 1996, *Archéologie et Gobelets* is a loose-knit pan-European association devoted to the study of the Late Neolithic and Early Bronze Age cultures of Europe and especially the phenomenon that is represented by Bell Beakers. Annual meetings have ranged from Britain to Hungary and from Northern Germany to Sicily and comprise visits to relevant museum collections interspersed with formal lecture sessions largely devoted to new discoveries and on-going research. These meetings create an interactive platform for European debate and collaboration and important publications have already resulted from some of the colloquia, many of which are referenced throughout this book.

In the 18 or so years that I have been involved with the association, initially helping the late doyen of Beaker studies, Humphrey Case, lead the visit to southern England in 2000 and then organising an Edinburgh conference in 2010 (helped by Alison Sheridan), I have often been disappointed by the emphasis placed on funerary archaeology at these events as well as detailed artefactual analysis. Beaker settlements have been mentioned at some meetings but not at length, in detail or within their true contextual settings. It prompted me to coin the phrase 'the Beaker Veneer' as it seemed to me that attention was too often fixed on the prestigious artefacts that constitute the Beaker package to the detriment of what was happening in the contemporary archaeological background.

The trend was reversed at the tenth anniversary meeting in Florence and Tuscany (Baioni *et al.* 2008) when virtually the whole session was devoted to the study of the domestic aspects of Bell Beaker studies though with a heavy Italian weighting as might be expected. It was during this meeting that I was discussing domestic assemblages with the late Lawrence Barfield. When asked how much of the assemblage at Monte Covolo was Bell Beaker, Lawrence replied 'quite a lot.....some 6 or 7%'. Despite not being a mathematician, I was able to deduce that some 93–4% of the ceramic assemblage must therefore be 'something else' so was it really correct to call this a Beaker domestic site or a Beaker settlement? The Beaker Veneer was relevant once more.

Previously, in Poznań in 2002, the conference examined regional differences within the Bell Beaker complex (Czebreszuk 2004). Three important papers by Strahm, Besse and Leonini (all 2004) examined Beaker domestic pottery variously called Complimentary Ware, *Begleitkeramik,* and Common Ware. Besse was able to conclude that there were differences

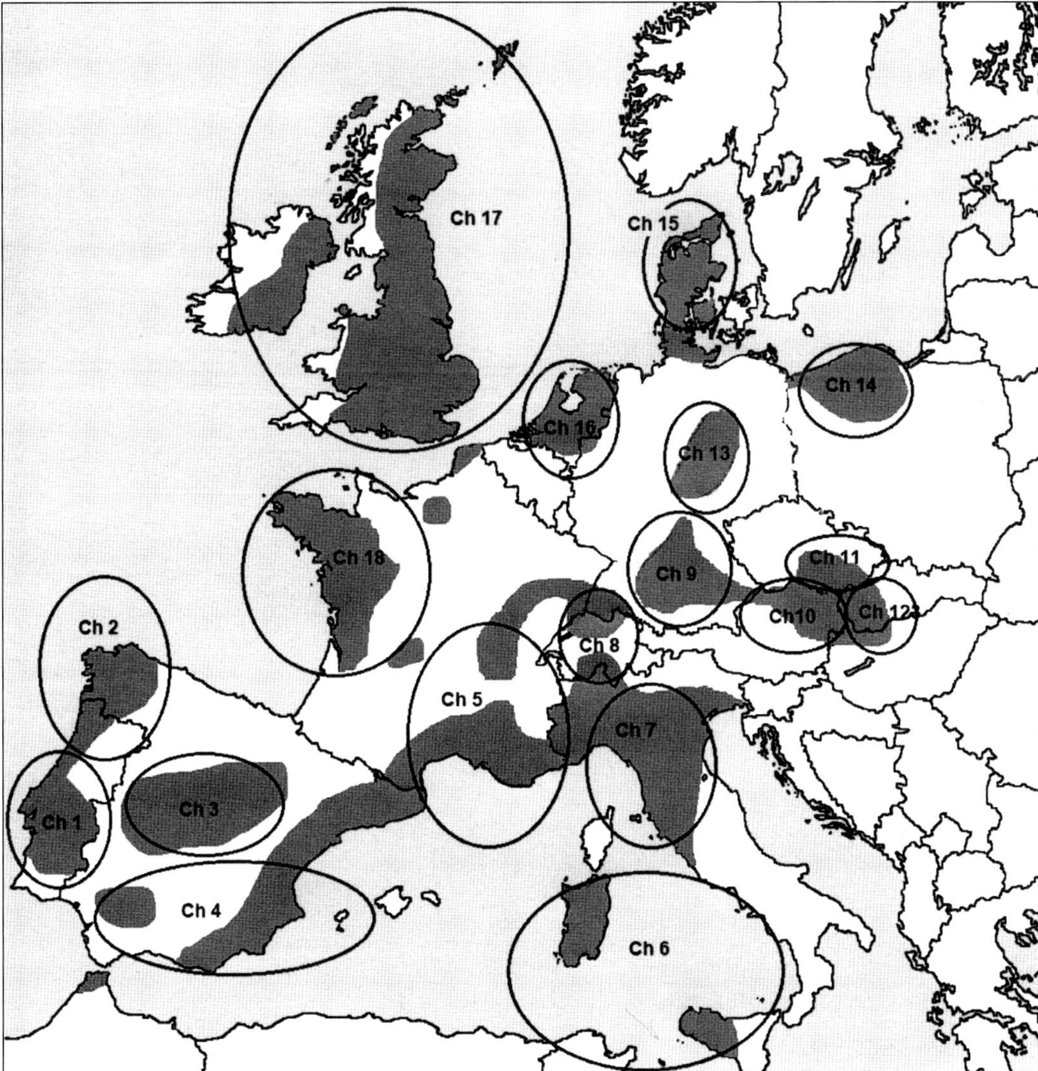

Figure 0.1: Schematic map of the major concentrations of Bell Beaker pottery in Europe. The Ch Nos refer to the chapters in this volume

within the Bell Beaker distribution and that in the Northern and Eastern parts of the network, local forms played an important part in the composition of the domestic assemblages whereas in the Southern and Western areas, the appearance of Beakers was more dramatic and radical with local pre-Beaker groups and Beakers keeping more distant. 'Bell Beaker pottery types are new; few of them originate from the cultures of the regional substrate …' (Besse 2004, 142). Some of the contributors to this volume might question the detail of this statement but it does highlight important differences that divide Beaker Europe diagonally from the Siene to the Tiber.

This is not to deny that some important settlement studies have taken place. In 2011, for example, an holistic approach was taken to the Beaker communities in Galicia (Prieto-Martínez & Salanova 2011) but this very important and detailed publication was regional in scope. Rather more encompassing was the current researches paper that followed the Pontevedra meeting in 2011 (Prieto-Martínez & Salanova 2013) but of the 20 chapters, only 2 dealt specifically with settlement.

Once again, at *Archéologie et Gobelets* meetings, Beaker settlements were examined in isolation. There were few studies that placed them in their regional settings. Few looked at what went before and what came afterwards and as a result the degree of continuity or fission was impossible to determine.

This volume is the first of its kind to deal specifically and in detail with the domestic sphere of the Bell Beaker phenomenon on a

European basis and to offer a comparative overview of how Bell Beaker settlements fit into or differ from existing traditions in each of the main focus areas of the Bell Beaker distribution. It also examines the artefactual background and notes instances of different ceramic facies being associated in a domestic context whereas they appear to have maintained a separation in graves. Beakers are not distributed uniformly over Europe (Fig. 0.1) but rather form pockets mainly in coastal and riverine areas and therefore a regional approach has been taken here. The broad foci for each chapter are shown on Fig. 0.1. The authors of these local syntheses, although often taking slightly different approaches as befits local needs and local states of knowledge, have all adopted a contextual approach identifying continuity and fission in relation to the appearance of Bell Beakers and the effect on local Late Neolithic or Chalcolithic groups. Interesting patterns emerge but one common trait is how Bell Beakers lay the foundations for the development of Early Bronze Age Europe.

Note on the Radiocarbon dates

Unless stated otherwise, all radiocarbon dates throughout the volume have been calibrated using the INTCAL13 calibration curve (Reimer *et al.* 2013), OxCal v4.3 (http://c14.arch.ox.ac.uk/) and the maximum intercept method (Stuiver & Reimer 1986). Radiocarbon results shown in the graphs have been calibrated by the probability method (Stuiver & Reimer 1993). Calibrated ranges are given 2σ (95–98%) confidence, with the end points rounded outwards to 10 years following Mook (1986).

References

Baioni, M., Leonini, V., Lo Vetro, D., Martini, F., Poggiani Keller, R. & Sarti, L. (eds), 2008. *Bell Beaker in Everyday Life. Proceedings of the 10th Meeting 'Archéologie et Gobelets' (Florence- Siena- Villanuova sul Clisi, May 12–15, 2006).* Firenze: Museo Fiorentino di Preistoria 'Paolo Graziosi'

Besse, M. 2004. Bell Beaker Common Ware during the third millennium BC in Europe. In J. Czebreszuk (ed.), 2004, 127–148

Czebreszuk, J. (ed.), 2004. *Similar but Different. Bell Beakers in Europe.* Poznań: Adam Mickiewicz University

Leonini, V. 2004. La ceramique domestique du Campaniforme de l'Italie Centrale et Septentionale. In J. Czebreszuk (ed.), 2004, 149–172

Mook, W.G. 1986. Business meeting: recommendations/resolutions adopted by the twelfth international radiocarbon conference, *Radiocarbon* 28, 799

Prieto-Martínez, P. & Salanova, L. (eds), 2011. *Las Comunidades Campaniformesen Galicia. Gambios Sociales en el III y II Milenios BC en el NW de la Península Ibérica.* Diputación de Pontevedra

Prieto-Martínez, P. & Salanova, L. (eds), 2013. *Current Researches on Bell Beakers. Proceedings of the 15th International Bell Beaker Conference: From Atlantic to Ural. 5th–9th May 2011. Poio (Pontevedra), Galicia, Spain.* Santiagio de Compostela: Galician Archaeopots

Reimer, P.J, Bard, E., Bayliss, A., Beck, J.W., Blackwell, P.G., Bronk Ramsey, C., Buck, C.E., Cgenge, H., Edwards, R.L., Friedrich, M., Grootes, P.M., Guilderson, T.P., Haflidason, H., Hajdas, I., Hatté, C; Heaton, T.J., Hoffmann, D. L., Hogg, A.G., Hughen, K.A., Kaiser, K.F., Kromer, B., Manning, S.W., Niu, M., Reimer, R.W., Richards, D.A., Scott, E.M., Southon, J.R., Staff, R.A., Turney, C.S.M. & van der Picht, J. 2013. Intcal 13 and marine 13 radiocarbon age calibration curves, 0–50,000 years cal BP. *Radiocarbon,* 55, 1869–87

Strahm, C. 2004. Die Glockenbecher Phänomen aus der Sicht der Komplimentär-Kramik. In J. Czebreszuk (ed.), 2004, 101–126

Stuiver, M. & Reimer P.J. 1986. A computer programme for radiocarbon age calculation. *Radiocarbon* 28, 1022–30

Stuiver, M. & Reimer, P.J. 1993. Extended 14C data base and revised CALIB 3.0 14C age calibration programme. *Radiocarbon* 35, 215–30

1

The South Portugal perspective. Beaker sites or sites with Beakers?

António Carlos Valera, Rui Mataloto and Ana Catarina Basílio

For many years 'the Beaker package' has been seen has a unitary phenomenon, in terms of its origins, diffusion processes or in the development of social inequalities based on the control of prestige goods. However, recent work has led to a growing awareness that the phenomenon is necessarily multiple, unequal, and dependent on local/regional constraints according to different pre-existing groups and their adaptive processes (Vander Linden 2004; Garrido-Pena 2005; Besse & Desideri 2005; Prieto-Martínez 2008; Valera & Rebuge 2011). This has led to new approaches to Bell Beakers, now perceived as a set of shared ideas, techniques, practices, interactions, and social developments, expressed through specific materials, dependent and relatable to regional social trajectories, where it can perform diversified social roles in a variety of contexts. Without ignoring the historical and social meanings inherent in large-scale phenomena, it is considered that the Bell Beaker phenomenon is also inherently plural due to its scale (Garrido-Pena 2005) and does not present the same expression and social agency in all areas. It is possible to find and individualise different versions as the result of local/regional processes of debate, acceptance, and rejection.

In Portugal, the identification of elements of the Beaker package in domestic and 'industrial' contexts, shows that the role of these artefacts is far from being limited to funerary contexts (Valera & Rebuge 2011; Valera & Basílio 2017; Mataloto 2017). The performance of Bell Beakers and associated materials is expanded to multiple social settings where it may have played diverse roles (Valera 2015a, 239). This contextual plurality also reveals integration into pre-existing practices, without corresponding to an abrupt change (Valera & Basílio 2017). On the contrary, it will simultaneously satisfy and incentivise an ongoing process of social complexification and mimetic behaviours in the context of social competition, that may be in part responsible for a sense of generalised standardisation and shared practices.

The face of Bell Beakers in Portugal

In Portugal, the first reference/representation of the Bell Beaker phenomenon dates to the 1960s. Since then research has traced the dispersion of these materials throughout the territory with 256 Bell Beaker sites recorded so far (Fig. 1.1). Of these, 146 sites are in Portuguese Estremadura and the Tagus Valley. This is noteworthy, not only due to the number of sites but also due to the typological diversity, the size of the assemblages and the variability of the decorative motifs (Figs 1.2–1.5). Adding to that, one can note the virtual absence of decorated Bell Beakers in the Algarve, with only two occurrences, coming from just one archaeological site: the ditched enclosure of Alcalar and the nearby *tholoi* structures (Morán 2017).

Decorated Beaker pottery outside of funerary contexts is common, although the contextual proportions vary from north to south (Fig. 1.1), suggesting that they may assume different roles in different regions. In the northern areas there is a prevalence of Beakers in funerary contexts (almost all megalithic monuments), although in the case of Beira Alta, one ceremonial walled enclosure (Fraga da Pena) has more Beaker pots than the rest of the sites of the region put together (Valera 2017a). In Estremadura and the Tagus Valley there is an equitable distribution between funerary and non-funerary contexts, but in the Alentejo decorated Bell Beakers predominate in non-funerary contexts, a fact that illustrates the multiplicity of roles that these artefacts can acquire.

This regional diversity is also visible in the distribution of Bell Beaker styles (Fig. 1.3). Vessels compatible with Maritime decorative motifs (Harrison 1977) have a significant presence in the Estremadura and Tagus/Sado Valleys, being also identified in the northernmost areas of Portugal and in the southern interior. The geometric dotted/incised patterns of the Palmela Group (Soares & Silva 1974–77) tend to have a similar distribution. Conversely, the vessels with Meseta influenced incised Ciempozuelos motifs (Harrison 1977) predominate in the Alentejo, with only two recorded in the northern margin of the Tagus river, and being rare or absent in central and north Portugal, especially in the more inland areas that form the natural limit of the northern Meseta, and where Ciempozuelos has a relevant presence (Valera 2017a).

These distributions result from processes of coexistence and confluence according to the type and size of the sites but also depend on acceptance, integration and rejection processes, conferring Beaker motifs a major role in regional identities. The same may be seen, at a regional scale, in the Alentejo, where the smallest sites with decorated Beakers present a monostylistic tendency and the large ditched enclosures present a plurality of styles (Valera & Rebuge 2011; Valera & Basílio 2017).

Other less frequent motifs and styles have also been identified in Beaker-shaped vessels, such as all-over corded patterns or vessels that result from regional reinterpretations (Fig. 1.4). In the case of AOC Beakers, it is notable that they only occur on five sites, only one of them funerary (Alcalar 7). They do not have a specific distribution pattern, being an element with almost no expression in Portuguese contexts. Other features, which represent processes of regionalised reinterpretation, are the combed incised vessels and pots with ungulated/pinched motifs ('crowsfoot' motif). The comb decorated pots have a significant concentration in the high basin of the Douro and Trás-os-Montes, while the finger-pinched vessels spread throughout the region. These distributions, mainly of the combed vessels, illustrate the processes of absorption and reconceptualisation of the Beaker-shaped vessels, receiving motifs and techniques from earlier traditions. Even so, this could also represent some type of resistance to a progressively shifting reality (Valera 2017a, 227). One can view the Palmela and Ciempozuelos complexes in a similar but opposite way since here the techniques and new motifs are applied to traditional regional pot styles (Soares & Silva 1974–7, 103).

Alongside the decorated Beakers, other associations are noteworthy. The cultural environment known as the 'Ferradeira' horizon, extending from the Algarve to the Central Alentejo, comprises a reduced set of individual and standardised graves from which only decorated Bell Beakers were excluded suggesting complex processes developing in the second half of the 3rd millennium (Mataloto 2006, 102). It contributes to the understanding of what seems to correspond to a distinct expression of identity and a regional resistance to decorated Beakers, establishing a stylistic frontier in the lower Alentejo (Fig. 1.5). This is expressed mainly in funerary practices and rituals associated with a package of copper weapons and undecorated pottery (with some Beaker shapes), which seems to define an area in the south of Portugal (Baixo Alentejo and Algarve), and which is part of the social trajectory of change marked by diversity (Valera 2014, 101; Basílio 2018, 26). This is also

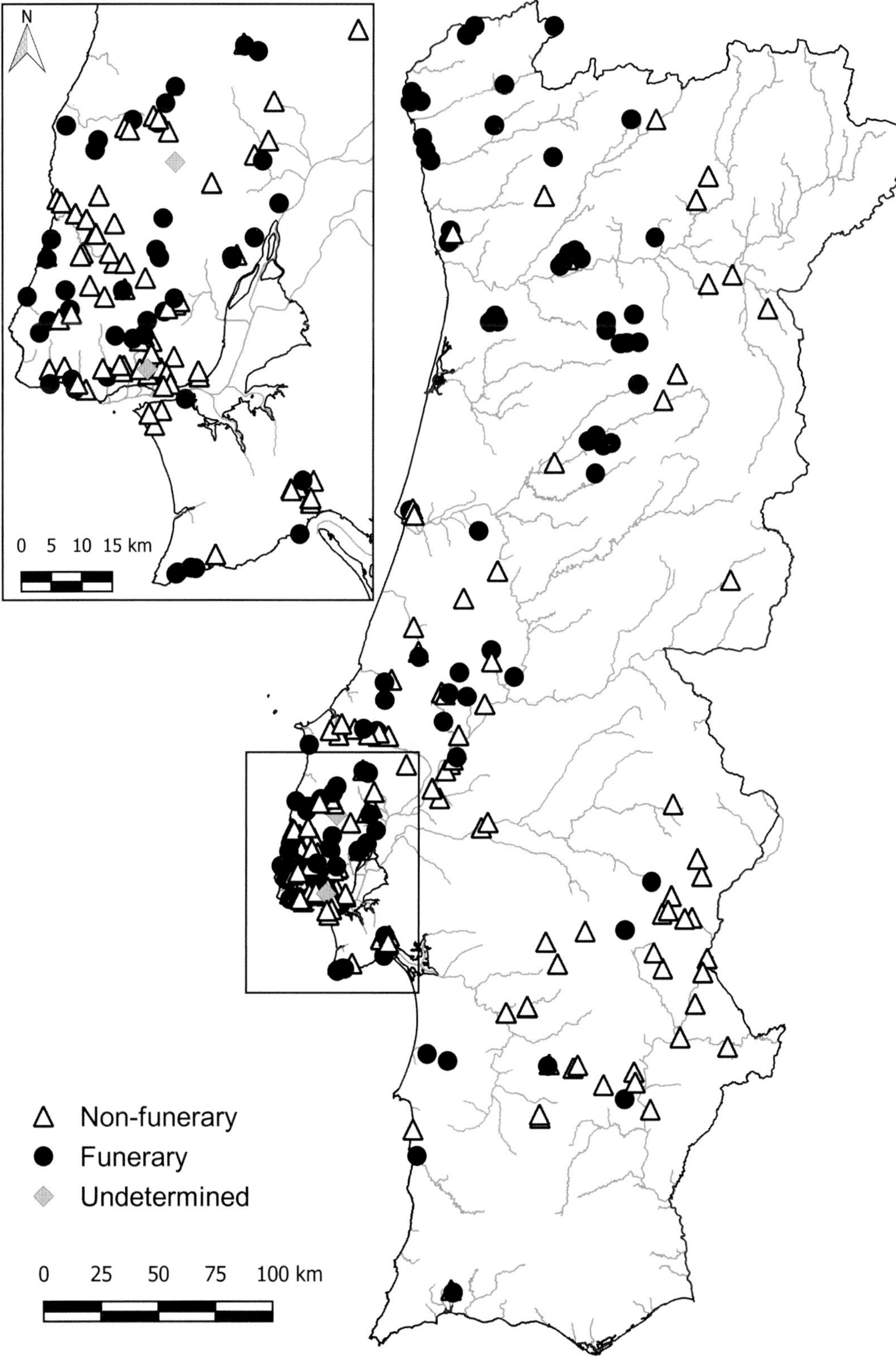

Figure 1.1: Type of contexts (funerary/non-funerary) with decorated Bell Beakers in Portugal

valid for the Montelavar Complex (a version of the 'Ferradeira' horizon), identified in the Portuguese Estremadura.

With this in mind, and merely referring to the ceramics, we are faced with a period in which resistance, adaptation and transformation processes coexisted, assumed diversified regional characteristics and accentuated the

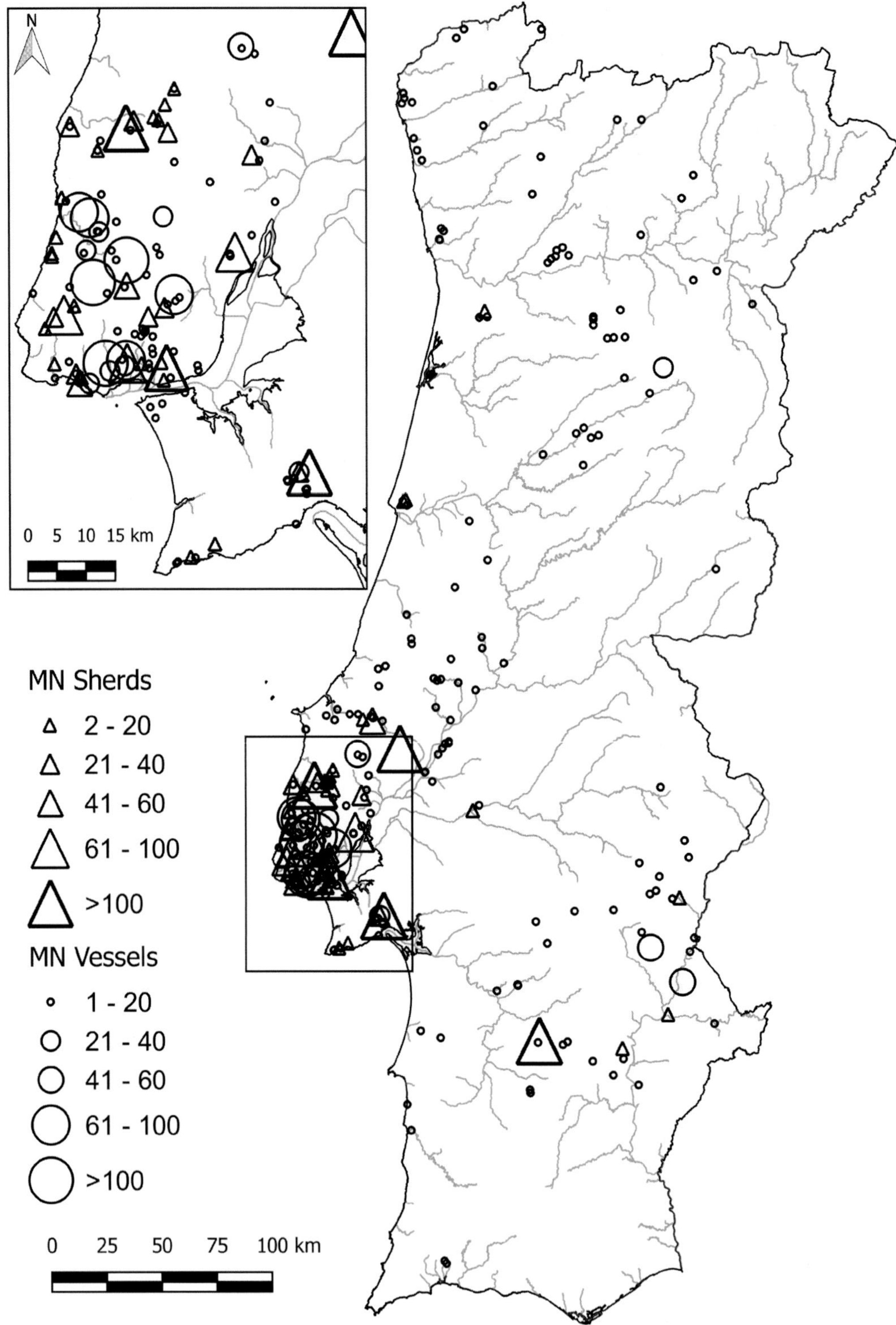

Figure 1.2: Minimum number of decorated Bell Beaker fragments and vessels per site in Portugal

plurality of meanings and social roles that Bell Beakers can incorporate, especially outside funerary contexts. Since this diversity is more striking in the south of Portugal, we will focus our analysis in this region.

The chronology of Bell Beakers in South Portugal

In the Alentejo region, Bayesian modelling of the dates from Porto das Carretas and Miguens 3 places the arrival of Bell Beakers

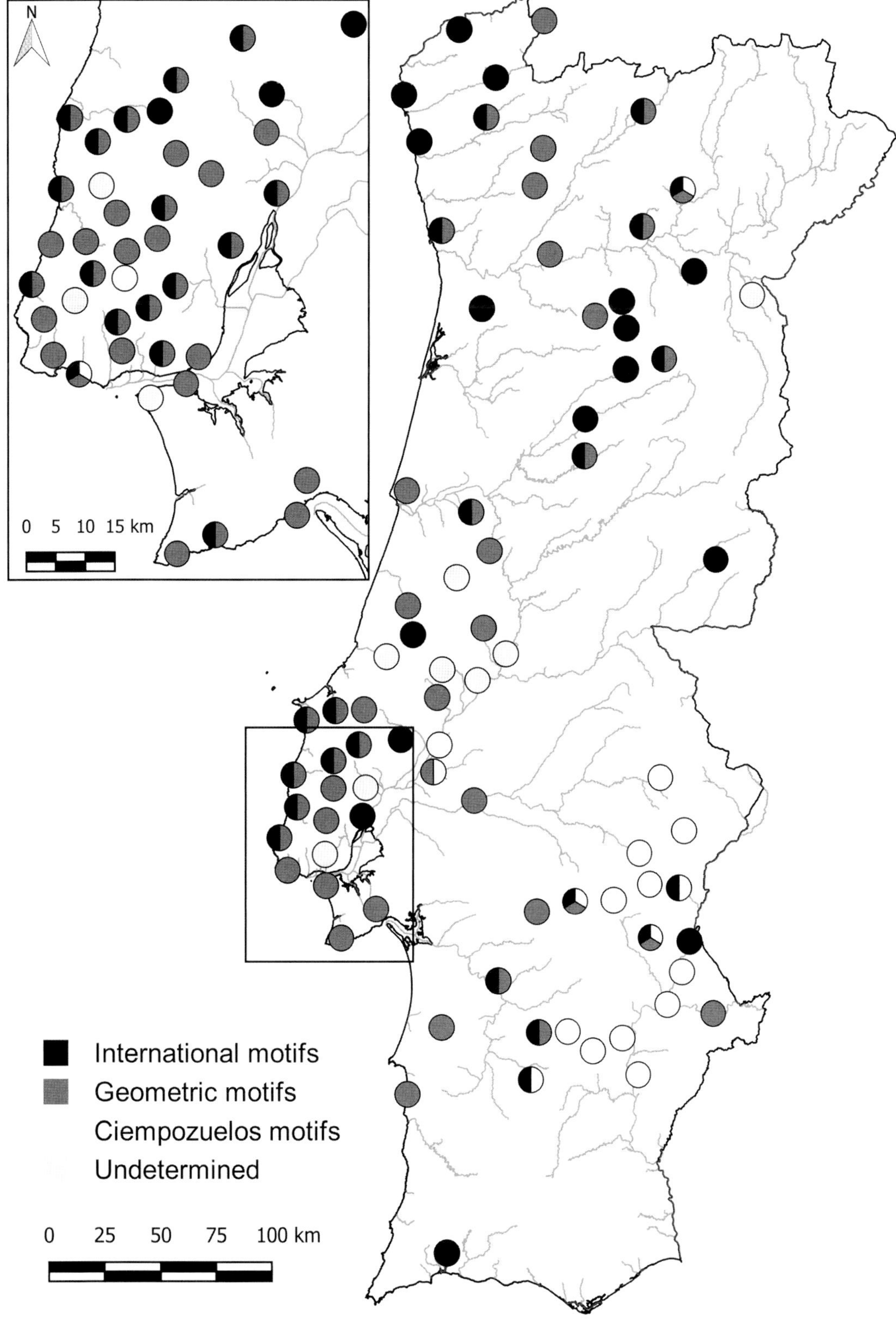

Figure 1.3: Distribution of the main Bell Beaker stylistic patterns in Portugal

between 2650–2430 cal BC (98% probability) (Mataloto & Boaventura 2009, 65; Mataloto *et al.* 2013) (Fig. 1.6). The dating programme at Perdigões, one of the most extensive radiocarbon sequences in Portugal (Valera *et al.* 2014a; Valera & Basílio 2017), confirms this chronology, contradicting the claim for an earlier appearence of Beakers based on shorter

Figure 1.4: Distribution of sporadic Bell Beaker stylistic patterns in Portugal

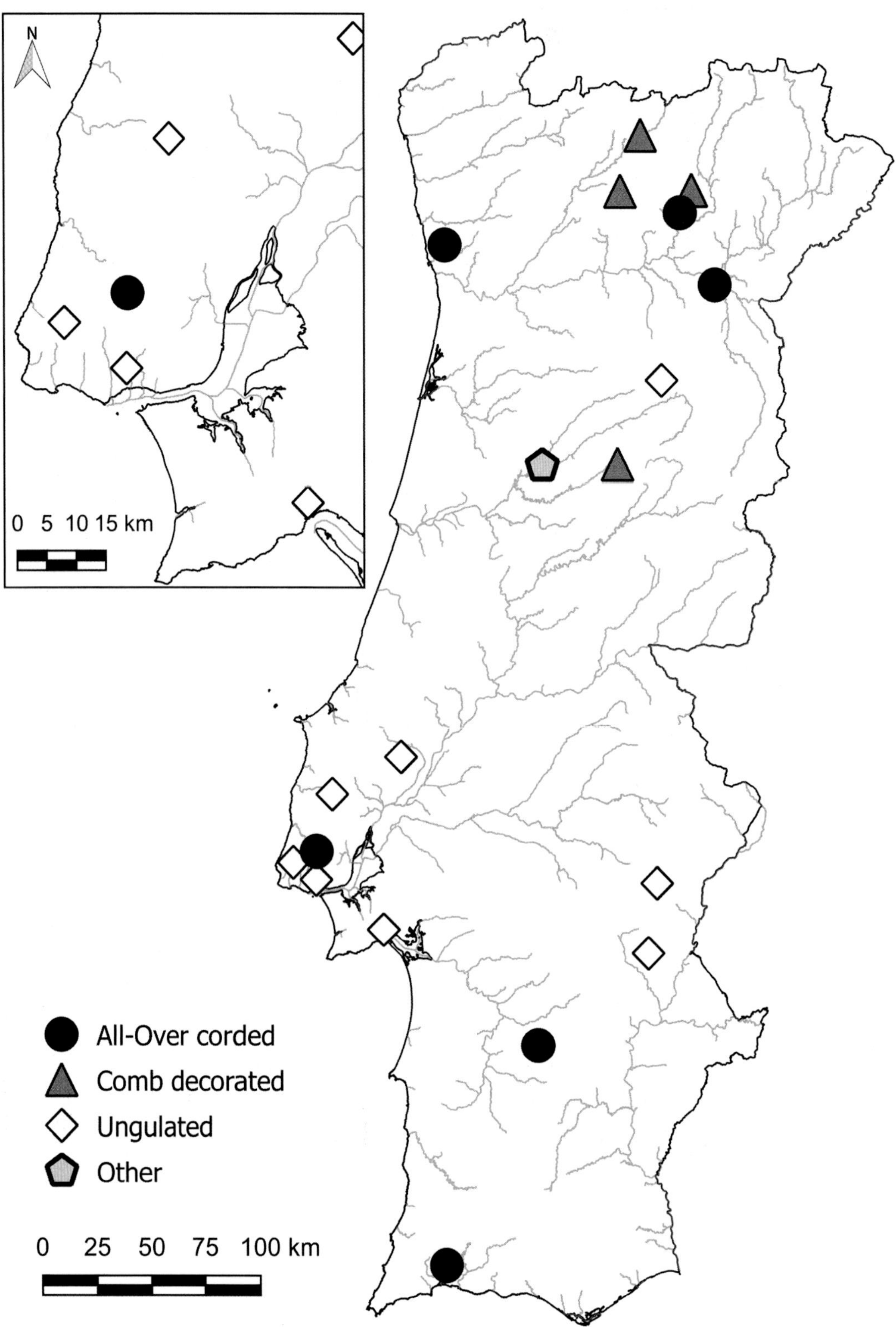

sequences that minimise the taphonomic noisiness characteristic of long and complex stratigraphies. The modelling has set the end of Bell Beakers in the early 2nd millennium (1950–1810 cal BC (98% probability)) and when modelled with the dates from Late Chalcolithic contexts without Bell Beakers and from Early Bronze Age contexts, we can

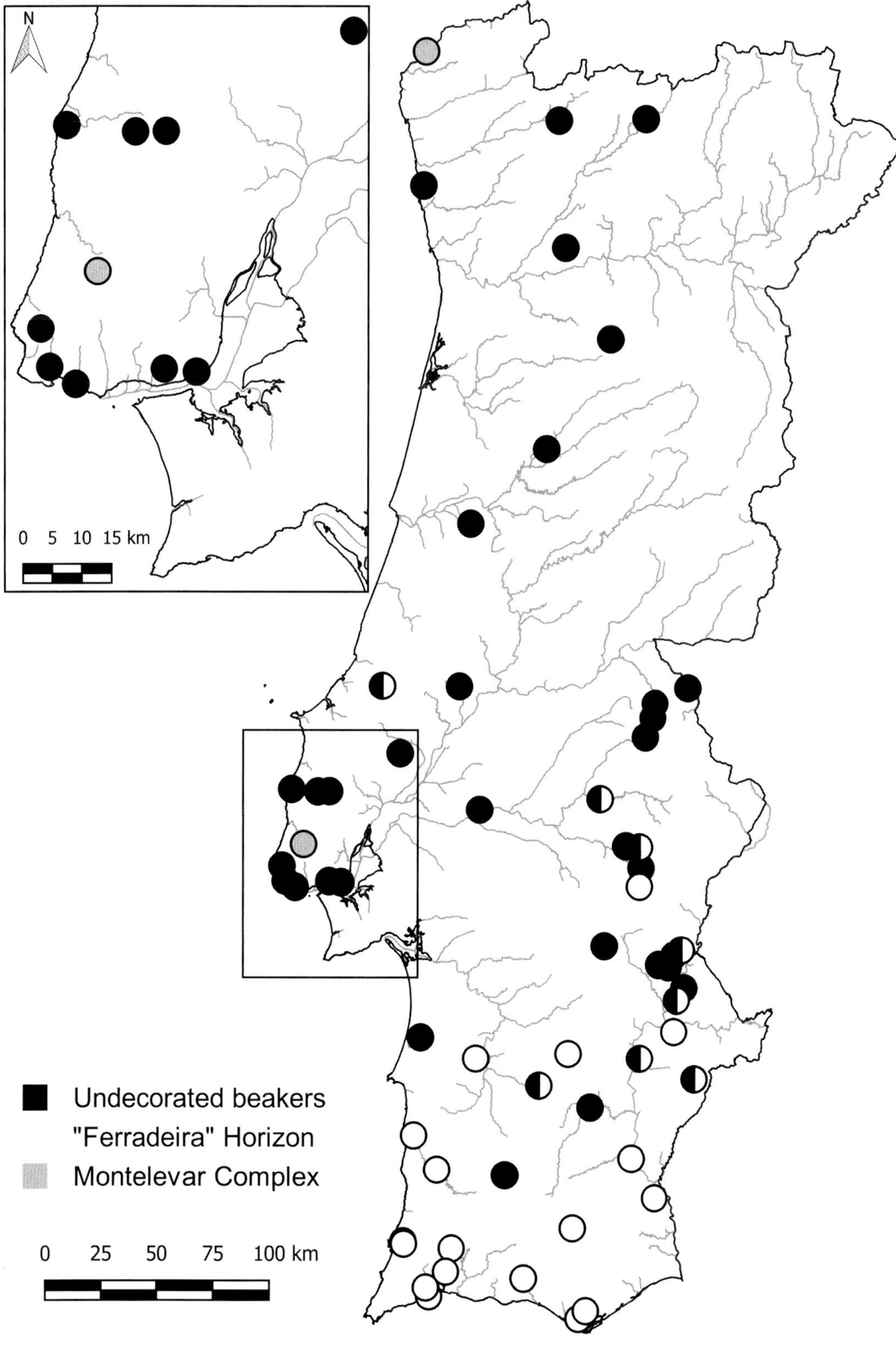

Figure 1.5: Distribution of undecorated Bell Beakers and of the 'Ferradeira' and 'Montelavar' horizons

suggest an earlier range of from 2130–2020 cal BC (98% probability) (Mataloto *et al.* 2013, 327) also confirmed at Perdigões.

The scarcer funerary data follow this trend. Two of the four funerary contexts in inner Alentejo that have decorated Bell Beakers have already been dated – Monte do Cardim 6 (Valera *et al.* 2014b), and Quinta do Castelo 1

(Valera *et al.* 2016). The pit burial of Quinta do Castelo 1 (Beja), a non-adult individual buried with a Maritime Beaker provided a date 2470–2290 cal BC (3890±30 BP: ICA 16B / 0304) and three other unpublished dates from this same context provide a similar range. Five unpublished dates from Monte do Cardim 6 produced a date range of 2490–2140 cal BC.

The 'Ferradeira' horizon has been recently dated at three funerary contexts: Monte da Velha 1 (Soares 2008), Tholos da Centirã (Henriques *et al.* 2013), Bela Vista 5 (Valera 2014) and Nossa Senhora da Conceição dos Olivais (Boaventura *et al.* 2014–15). The results show the 'Ferradeira' horizon coincides with the decorated Bell Beaker pottery in Southern Portugal in the third quarter of the 3rd millennium. The contemporaneity of predominantly non-funerary decorated Bell Beakers with the predominantly funerary 'Ferradeira' horizon, proves regional idiosyncrasies and adaptations, since the 'Ferradeira' set is also clearly integrated into the trans-European framework of the Bell Beaker phenomenon.

The dates from Bela Vista 5 or Nossa Senhora da Conceição dos Olivais, show the longevity of the 'Ferradeira' horizon into the last quarter of the 3rd millennium: a time of significant structural change (Valera 2015b; Mataloto 2017), but where some 'anachronic' behaviours and practices continue to occur.

Outside the graves: non-funerary Beaker contexts and architectures in South Portugal

Although the 'Ferradeira' horizon and non-funerary decorated Beakers are contemporary (Table 1.1 & Fig. 1.6), they have different distributions. The 'Ferradeira' contexts tend to concentrate in the Southern Alentejo and Algarve, where, except for Alcalar, no decorated Beakers are known. Furthermore, most sites with decorated Beakers are in the interior (32 contexts) of which only four are funerary sites (two megalithic monuments, one *tholos*, and one pit grave). Near the coast only four sites are known, three of which are funerary (two megalithic monuments and a possible *tholos* – Fig. 1.1). This means that along the southern coast, the general pattern seems to be similar to that in Estremadura and the more northern areas. Contrastingly, it is in the hinterland of the Alentejo, where one of the most significant concentrations of megalithic monuments and ditched enclosures is located, that the contextual pattern of decorated Beakers changes.

In this area, the quality of information on the 28 sites where decorated Beakers occur in non-funerary contexts is mostly varied and limited. Most (12) comprise surface finds or assorted layers without any detailed contextual information. In another seven cases, Beakers occur on open settlements, most located on hilltops, and in two concentrations of lowland pit structures. Specific Beaker architectonic features were rarely noticed.

Decorated Beaker sherds also appear in walled enclosures but, where stratigraphic information allows, only when the walls were already deactivated and, in some cases, abandoned. This is the case at Porto das Carretas (Soares 2013), S. Pedro (Mataloto *et al.* 2015), Monte da Tumba (Silva & Soares 1987), and Monte do Tosco 1 (Valera 2013). Beakers are associated with circular stone structures, sometimes with small radial walls, such as at Perdigões and Porto das Carretas and with evidence for copper working. Similar structures are also known at Miguens 3 (Calado 2002), a site that appears to be a Beaker foundation. The arrival of Beakers in these sites, therefore, seems to have been unrelated to the walled phases and at some ditched enclosures Beakers are contemporary with the later phases.

Although ditched enclosures are numerous in this region, decorated Beakers were stratigraphically recorded only at Porto Torrão and Perdigões, two of the larger sites (some fragments were also collected from the surface at Montoito and Pombal). It is interesting to note, however, that Porto Torrão has the highest number of decorated Beaker sherds in the region and one of the highest in western Iberia (over 400), followed by Perdigões (60 Beaker sherds), and both sites account for the highest Beaker stylistic variability of the region. At Porto Torrão, Beaker sherds occur in pits and in the ditch fills, but were also dispersed in occupation layers, both in central and peripheral areas of the enclosures (Valera & Filipe 2004). No specific Beaker features have been reported so far. At Perdigões, there was a concentration of Beakers in the central area (Valera & Basílio 2017) (Fig. 1.7,1), although some fragments also occur in the top fills of the outside ditch.

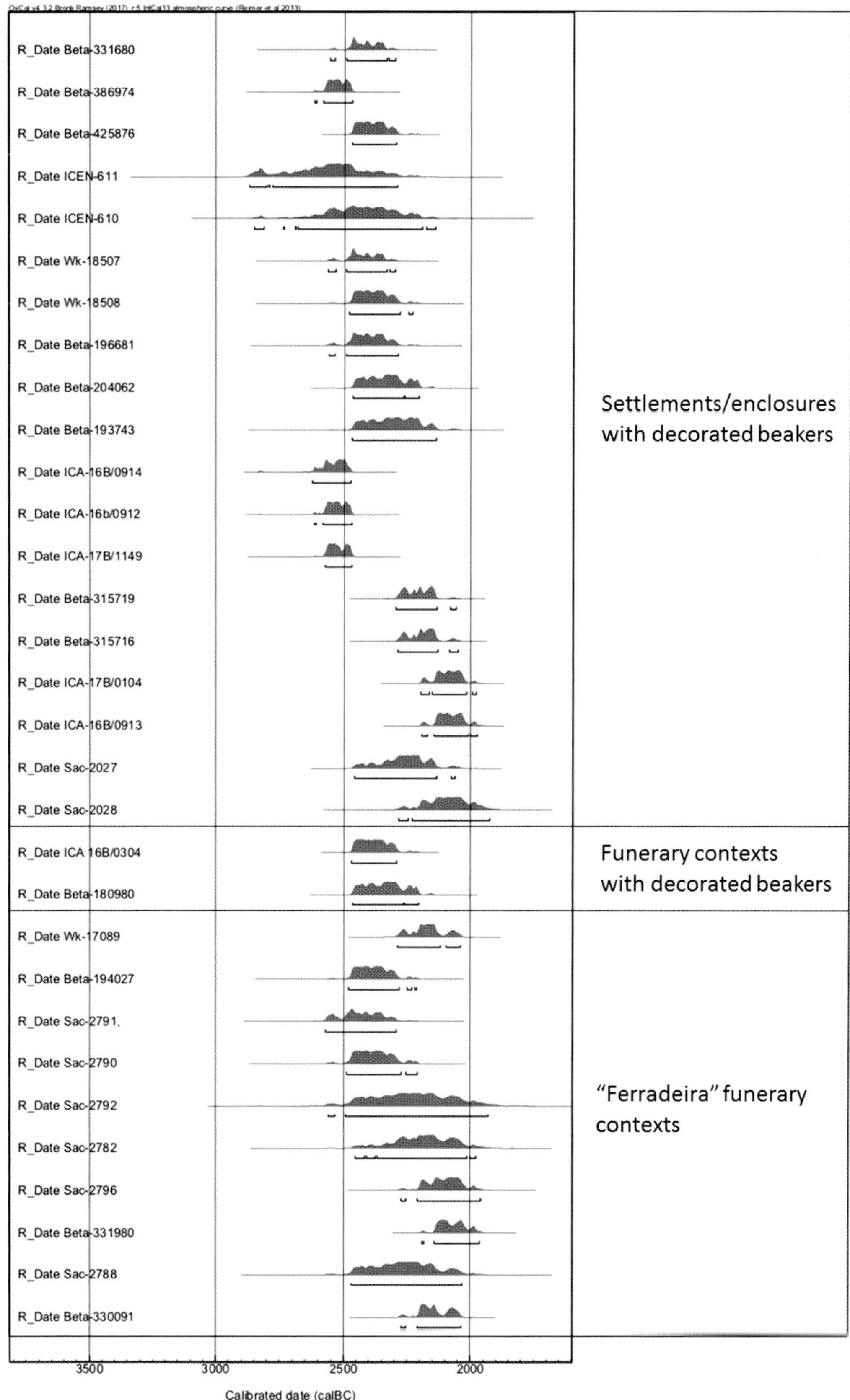

Figure 1.6: Radiocarbon dates for sites with Bell Beakers and sites of the 'Ferradeira' horizon in South Portugal

Table 1.1: Radiocarbon Dates for the 3rd Millennium BC in Southern Portugal

	Lab.	*Date BP*	*Cal BC (2 σ)*	*Context*	*Sample*	*Reference*
			Sites with decorated Beakers			
Barranco do Farinheiro	Beta-331680	3930±30	2430–1890	EU 3	Charcoal	Gonçalves *et al.* 2017, 115
	Beta-386974	4040±30	2620–2460	EU 4, A.5-17	Charcoal	
	Beta-425876	3900±30	2470–2290	EU 4, A.5-28	Charcoal	
Escoural	ICEN-611	4010±90	2880–2290	QD7/C.2	Animal bone	Gomes 1991
	ICEN-610	3940±90	2850–2140	QD7/C.1	Animal bone	
Miguens 3	Wk-18507	3934±33	2570–2300	EU 35	Charcoal: *Olea*	Mataloto & Boaventura 2009
	Wk-18508	3902±38	2480–2230	EU 55	Charcoal: *Olea*	
Porto das Carretas (Fase II)	Beta-196681	3920±40	2570–2290	C.2B Tower M13-fire C)	Charcoal: *Pinus pinea*	Soares *et al.* 2007
	Beta-204062	3860±40	2470–2200	C.2B Tower M13-fire B)	Charcoal: *Pinus pinea*	
	Beta-193743	3840±60	2470–2130	C.2B Tower M13-Fire A)	Charcoal: *Olea*	
Perdigões*	ICA-16B/ 0914	4030±30	2630–2470	After Hut 1 EU267	*Cervus elaphus*	Valera & Basílio 2017
	ICA-16b/ 0912	4010±30	2620–2470	Hut 1 EU393	*Sus sp.*	
	ICA-17B/ 1149	4000±30	2580–2470	Hut 2 EU421	*Big mammals*	
	Beta-315719	3780±30	2290–2140	Ditch 1 EU118	*Sus tooth*	
	Beta-315716	3770±30	2290–2060	Ditch 1 EU11	*Sus humerus*	
	ICA-17B/ 0104	3700±30	2200–1980	Pit 79/Cairn 488	Animal bone	
	ICA-16B/ 0913	3690±30	2200–1980	Pit 79/Cairn EU500	*Cervus elaphus*	
Porto Torrão	Sac-2027	3810±50	2460–2060	Ditch 2; EU 2056	Animal bone	Valera 2013
	Sac-2028	3700±60	2290–1920	Ditch 2; EU 2020	Animal bone	
			Sites without Beakers			
Cabeço do Pé da Erra	Beta-425879	4070±30	2860–2490	Phase 1	Charcoal	Gonçalves & Sousa 2017, 174
	Beta-427670	4050±30	2840–2470	Phase 2	Charcoal	
	Beta-386916	4050±30	2840–2470	Phase 2	Charcoal	
	Beta-386915	4040±30	2840–2470	Phase 2	Charcoal	
	Beta-425878	4020±30	2630–2470	Phase 2	Charcoal	
	Beta-425880	3930±30	2560–2300	Phase 2	Charcoal	
	Beta-394160	3960±30	2580–2340	Phase 2	Charcoal	
	Beta-361778	3830±30	2460–2150	Phase 2	Charcoal	
	Beta-331682	3850±30	2460–2200	Phase 2	Charcoal	
	Beta-361777	3830±30	2460–2150	Phase 2	Charcoal	
	Beta-361776	3800±30	2340–2130	Phase 2	Charcoal	
Horta do Albardão 3	Beta-261319	3990±40	2630–2350	Ditch-C.2	Cortiça: *Quercus suber*	Santos *et al.* 2009
	Beta-261320	3770±40	2340–2030	Ditch-C.5	Charcoal: *Quercus sp.*	
	Sac-2287	3730±190	2840–1630	Ditch-C.5	Cork: *Quercus suber*	
Moinho Valadares	Oxa-12715	3726±29	2210–2030	EU 83-top	Charcoal	Valera 2006
Mercador	Sac- 1933	3790±60	2460–2030	EU 1037	?	Valera 2006
	Sac- 1900	3720±80	2430–1890	EU 1039	?	
	Oxa-11982	3664±29	2140–1950	EU 327	?	
Monte Novo dos Albardeiros	ICEN-530	4060±80	2890–2350	Struture 2	Animal bone	Gonçalves 1988/89
	ICEN-529	3760±100	2470–1920	Structure 1	Animal bone	
São Pedro	KIA-33865	4043±35	2840–2470	Phase IV/V	Charcoal: *Quercus ilex*	Mataloto & Boaventura 2009
Outeiro Alto 2	Beta-339604	3920±30	2480–2300	Ditch	Fauna bone	Valera 2013

	Lab.	*Date BP*	*Cal BC (2 σ)*	*Context*	*Sample*	*Reference*
			Funerary monuments with decorated Beakers			
Quinta do Castelo 1	ICA 16B/0304	3890±30	2470–2290	Burial	Human bone	Unpublished
Alcalar 7	Beta-180980	3860±40	2470–2200	C.31/Fire 4	Charcoal	Móran & Parreira 2004
			Funerary monuments of 'Ferradeira' horizon			
Anta de N. Sra. da Conceição/ Estremoz 7	Wk-17089	3758±36	2290–2040		Human bone	Roch & Duarte 2009
Monte da Velha 1	Beta-194027	3900±40	2490–2210	Secundary burial	Human bone	Soares 2008
Centirã 2	Sac-2791,	3940±50	2580–2290	EU 12 Oss. 1	Human bone	Henriques *et al.* (2013)
	Sac-2790	3900±45	2570–2290	EU 13, Burial 2	Human bone	
	Sac-2792	3790±110	2570–1930	EU 14	Human bone	
	Sac-2782	3760±70	2460–1970	EU 14, Burial 4	Human bone	
	Sac-2796	3710±45	2280–1960	EU 12, Burial 1	Human bone	
	Beta-331980	3680±30	2190–1960	EU 12, Burial 1	Human bone	
	Sac-2788	3810±80	2480–2030	EU 7, Burial 1	Human bone	
Bela Vista 5	Beta-330091	3740±30	2270–2040	Funerary pit	Human bone	Valera 2014
			Funerary monuments without Beakers			
Anta 2 dos Cebolinhos	Beta-176899	3900±40	2490–2210	L.12-36a	Human bone	Gonçalves 2003a
	Beta-177471	3840±40	2470–2150	L.12-36b	Human bone	
Anta 3 de Santa Margarida	Beta-166418	3780±40	2350–2040	Strat. 3	Human bone	Gonçalves 2003b
	Beta-166417	3770±40	2340–2030	Strat. 2	Human bone	
	Beta-166420	3720±50	2290–1960	Underlying or within Strat. 3	Animal bone *Canis*	
	Beta-166421	3730±40	2290–1980	Strat. 4	Human bone	
Anta Grande Zambujeiro	Beta-243693	3910±40	2550–2230	C.2B exterior pit	Charcoal	Soares & Silva 2010a
Cortes 2	Beta-318382	4050±30	2830–2490	Hypogeum	Human bone	Valera *et al.* 2014c
	Sac-2574	3920±50	2570–2210	Hypogeum	Human bone	
	Sac-2575	3970±70	2880–2210	Hypogeum	Human bone	
Vale Rodrigo 2	Ua-10831	3905±75	2580–2150	Phase 4	Charcoal	Larsson 2000
Pedra Escorregadia	ICEN-844	4060±70	2880–2460		Human bone	Soares 2004
	ICEN-1028	3800±100	2550–1950		Human bone	
Perdigões	Beta-327750	4030±40	2830–2470	Tomb 1 chamber	Human bone	Valera *at al.* 2014a
	Beta-327748	4060±30	2830–2490	Tomb 1 chamber	Human bone	
	Beta-327747	4130±30	2870–2580	Tomb 1 chamber	Human bone	
	Beta-311480	3990±30	2580–2460	Tomb 1 chamber	Human bone	
	Beta-308791	4090±30	2860–2500	Tomb 2 chamber	Human bone	
	Beta-308792	3890±30	2470–2290	Tomb 2 chamber	Human bone	
	Beta-308793	3970±30	2570–2460	Tomb 2 atrium	Human bone	
	Beta-308789	3840±30	2460–2200	Tomb 2 atrium	Human bone	
	Beta-289262	3990±40	2580–2460	Pit 16	Human bone	
	Beta-308785	3970±30	2570–2460	Assemblage 1	Human bone	
	Beta-308784	3900±30	2470–2290	Assemblage 1	Human bone	
	Beta-313720	3850±30	2460–2200	Assemblage 1	Human bone	
	Beta-313721	4000±40	2620–2460	Assemblage 1	Human bone	

* Only dates from contexts producing decorated Bell Beakers

In that central area, Beakers occur in late occupation layers, in a pit filled with faunal remains and covered by a stone cairn, and in earlier occupation layers associated with a compound of stone huts and linear walls. In the surrounding necropolis, in *tholos* tomb 2, Beaker package items were found (ivory V-perforated button and some gold foil) but there was no Beaker pottery. Another three 'Beaker period' graves have been excavated within the enclosure, but again without Beaker pottery, reinforcing the idea that its stage of agency was non-sepulchral. Decorated Beakers were therefore added to an ongoing scenario in which no other significant changes are noticed other than the development and intensification of the previous site trajectory.

Huts and towers(?): stone constructions associated with Beakers and Beaker chronologies

Around 2500 BC, a change in house building seems to have occured in South Portugal, leading to a greater use of stone and sometimes associated with the presence of Bell Beaker pottery. These solid dwellings with stone bases supporting earth walls suggest a sense of permanence and stability, in contrast to those in the first half of the millennium that rarely use stone even though dry-stone building techniques were already present. In this period, dry-stone construction was mainly used in communal and defensive architecture such as perimeter walls or robust round buildings located in central areas. These have been interpreted as watchtowers, but in some cases (namely São Pedro) may also have had a domestic function. Multiple post-holes and alignments of small slabs around these rotunda (at least at São Pedro) might suggest that numerous constructions or huts of perishable materials could have co-existed. The construction of *tholoi* also utilised circular stone walls similar to those of the later houses. So, this change in domestic architecture merely represents a new application of an already existent knowledge. It is the new arrangement of space that represents the main change.

The later 3rd millennium in the region sees the abandonment of walled enclosures and these new types of dwelling emerge over the ruined walls, or in new locations. These new buildings are marked by some powerful circular structures (huts and possibly towers), with strong stone bases, that are sometimes surrounded by smaller buildings, frequently linked by stone walls. They tend to form homesteads. Further research is needed to establish a coherent standard definition of a tower as opposed to a circular hut especially with regard to the inner diameter of the building in proportion to the thickness of the wall. For now, we might consider that structures with thicker walls and smaller inner diameters allow higher construction. In the Alentejo region, these circular stone structures are associated with Bell Beaker ceramics, at Perdigões (Valera & Basílio 2017), Miguens 3 (Calado 2002), Porto das Carretas (Soares 2013), São Pedro (Mataloto *et al.* 2015), Monte do Tosco 1 (Valera 2013) and Monte da Tumba (Silva & Soares 1987) (Table 1.2), but also at other sites of the same general period without decorated Beakers (eg, Mercador).

The large complex enclosure at Perdigões is well-researched with a number of important publications. It had a complex sequence of multiple ditches and pits from the mid-4th millennium to the end of the 3rd. The recent excavations in the central area have produced well-preserved stone structures (Fig. 1.7,2). Hut 2 was a solid circular construction with a double-faced wall 0.7 m thick and with an inner diameter of 3 m. The entrance faces east (90º). This hut is part of a compound of stone structures that was partially dismantled in prehistory. Three walls radiate from this structure: what seems to be the beginning of a wall at the north-east; another one heading west and connecting with what seems to be two circular structures located by geophysics (one partially dismantled); a third wall runs south to another wall running east into the section of the excavated area. Immediately south of this wall there are two overlapping circular structures, also partially dismantled. This compound was built in the centre of the enclosures, where the higher concentration of Beaker sherds can be found (Fig. 1.7,1) and in the lower part of the natural amphitheatre in which Perdigões is situated. According to the available radiocarbon dates, it was contemporary with the filling of the outer and the innermost ditch and with two funerary pits used for the deposition of the cremated human remains of more than 200 individuals (Fig. 1.7,2).

Miguens 3, located 20 km north-east of Perdigões on a small spur overlooking the River

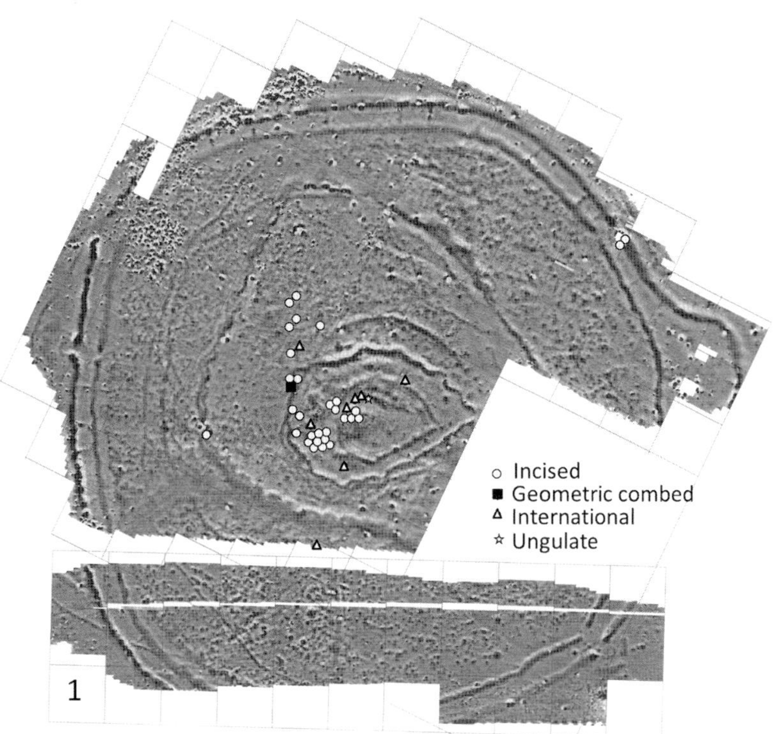

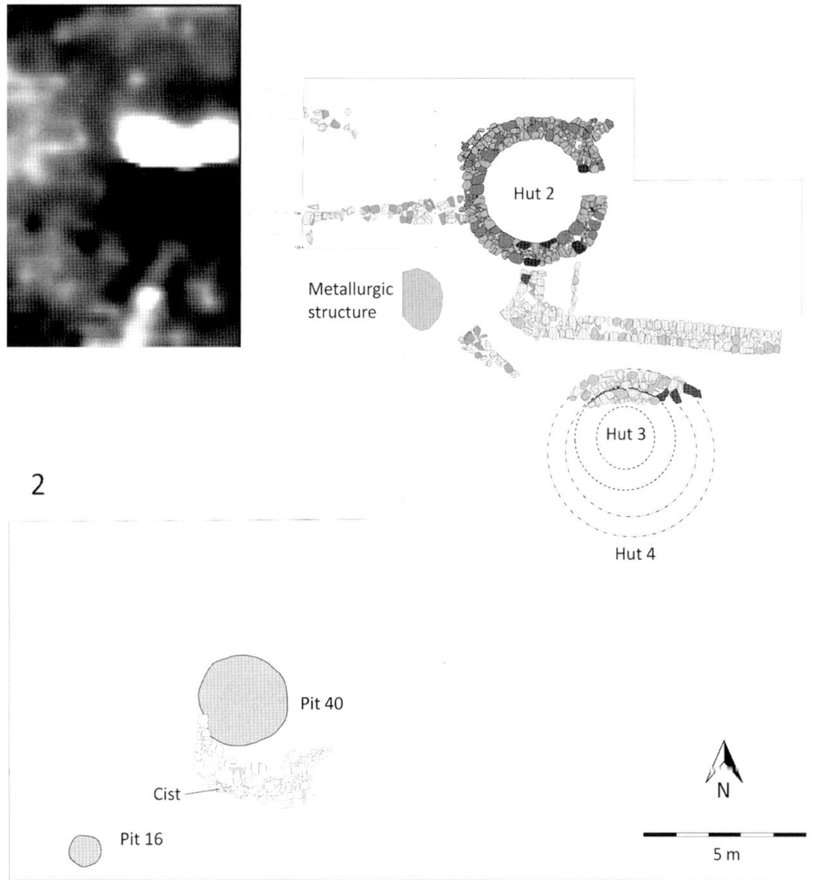

Figure 1.7: Perdigões. 1 – Distribution of decorated Bell Beaker sherds at Perdigões; 2 – Stone structures in the central area of Perdigões, associated with Bell Beaker pottery

Table 1.2: Stone structures from the middle or second half of the 3rd millennium BC in southern Portugal

Site	*Structure*	*Plan*	*Inner diam. (m)*	*Wall thickness (m)*	*Opening orientation*	*Building method*	*Decorated BB*
Perdigões	Hut 2*	Circular	3	0.7	E	1	×
Miguens 3	Structure 1*	Circular	3.88	0.8	SE	1	×
	Structure 2	Circular	5.3	0.65	–	1	–
Porto das Carretas	M3	Circular	6	0.7	–	1	×
	N7*	Circular	5.7	0.9	NW & SE	1	×
	M13*	Circular	4.2	1.1	SE	1	–
	R5	Circular	4.3	0.75	NW	1	–
São Pedro	[53]	Circular	3	1.2	–	1	–
	[127]	Circular	6.2	0.8	–	1	–
	[62]	Circular	3	0.7	–	1	–
	[491]	Circular	3.9	0.85	–	1	–
Monte do tosco 1	Hut 1	Circular	4.3	0.6	–	2	×
Mercador	Hut 1	Circular	6.5	0.74	–	1	–
	Hut 2	Circular	5	0.7	–	1	–
Moinho Novo de Baixo 1	Structure 1	Circular	5.3	0.7	–	1	–
Monte da Tumba	Structure 1	Sub-circular	9.6	1.2	–	1	×

Building method: 1 – Double row of stones with internal filling; 2 – Double row of stones

Guadiana, has fairly peculiar characteristics, being a paradigm for the architectural layouts under analysis. In its centre, there is a circular double-faced stone structure, 0.8 m thick and with an internal diameter of 3.88 m. It is surrounded by a small walled enclosure that, in plan, has clear affinities with the large fortified walled layouts of the earlier 3rd millennium, but on a much smaller scale, with an internal diameter of just 12 m (Fig. 1.8,2). The central building is open to the south-east whilst the enclosure has an entrance passage leading east-north-east. The space between them was divided by radial walls, presumably related to different uses. The central building must have preceded the construction of the outer enclosure, which is flattened on the southern side, in order to accommodate the external enclosure of another circular structure. Half of the latter was dismantled but would have had an inner diameter of 5.3 m, larger than Hut 1 but with a less robust wall (0.65 m thick). A third similar structure lay to the north.

Miguens 3 therefore seems to begin as a set of at least three stone-built huts possibly with adobe or wattle and daub superstructures. Each was at some time surrounded by a thick perimeter wall that isolated the household. This process, which took place within the third quarter of the 3rd millennium BC, can be related to the individualisation of kinship groups suggested by the new spatial organisation, or even to an expression of an emerging individual distinctiveness recognised throughout Europe, particularly in funerary practices. Despite the robustness and density of the structures, this site seems short-lived and was undoubtedly abandoned before the end of the 3rd millennium. Only the central building produced Bell Beaker pottery, representing just two or three vessels.

Further south, the site of Porto das Carretas (10 km from Miguens 3 and 17.5 km east of Perdigões), is also located on a spur overlooking the Guadiana (Soares 2013). In its initial phase of occupation, the architecture of the site is characterised by a walled enclosure and huts built from perishable materials and small slabs of stones. The site is then abandoned and, over the ruined walls, a compound of circular

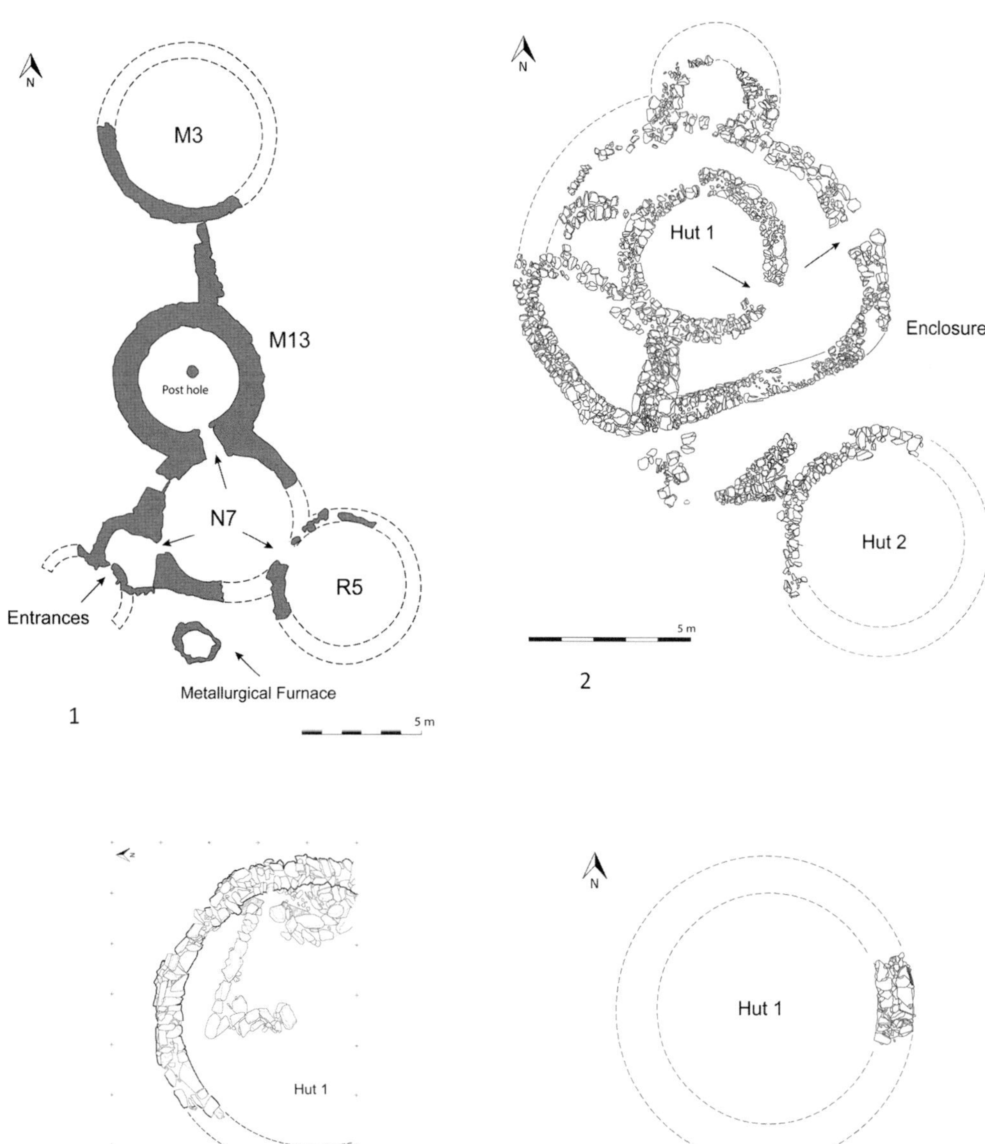

Figure 1.8: 1 – Porto das Carretas compound (adapted from Soares 2013); 2 – Miguens 3 (adapted from Calado 2002); 3 – Monte do Tosco 1 (adapted from Valera 2013); 4 – Moinho Novo de Baixo

structures of varying sizes was built in the second half of the 3rd millennium (Fig. 1.8,1). In the centre of the area, towers M13 and N7 were built, with internal diameters of 4.2 m and 5.4 m respectively. These were linked and interconnected by a strongly built doorway and with walls of 1.1 m and 0.9 m, which gave rise to their interpretation as towers. Linked to N7, to the south-east, was structure R5, with an internal diameter of 4.3 m and walls 0.75 m thick, therefore slightly less robust than M13 and N7. Also attached to N7, by a possible doorway, was the small hut K5. It is not evident whether this was an independent living space or merely some sort of porch. To the north of this complex, was Hut M3, larger (6.2 m diameter) but with less robust walls (0.7 m thick), linked to M13 by a wall. Only 14 Bell Beaker fragments were found here, mainly in structures M13 and N7.

Porto das Carretas shows, in a unique way, the trend of consolidation of stone construction and monumentalising of the domestic buildings in the later 3rd millennium. The linking of the structures also indicates an early process of the division of domestic space. These compounds seem to have dynamic biographies that are deeply bonded to the dynamics of the group and express its social structure and relations between members, activities and prescriptions, recalling the small compounds of some African communities (Hansen 1998). Once again, these robust household buildings demonstrate the importance that these small dispersed communities assume in the later 3rd millennium BC.

São Pedro is located about 30 km north-west from Porto das Carretas and 23 km north of Perdigões, and presents a slightly different situation. It is on a hilltop and was occupied throughout the 3rd millennium by consecutive different settlements, with two distinct walled enclosures and three phases of open occupation. In this sequence, the two main walled phases (II and IV) were characterised by imposing circular stone structures in the central area. In the first of these phases, a smaller circular structure was also documented. In addition to these, many flimsier structures were built as shown by the substantial number of post-holes and alignments of small vertical slabs. However, in the last phase of occupation, Phase V, built over the ruins of the later walled enclosure, circular stone structures seem to dominate the domestic contexts, at a time when collective structures, like the enclosures, were entirely abandoned.

These circular stone constructions spread over the hilltop (Fig. 1.9,2). In a seemingly central position, a robust circular structure was recorded, with an internal diameter of only 3 m and a wall about 1.2 m thick. This structure was largely dismantled, but it also overlapped with and reused part of the previous circular structure from Phase IV, which in turn overlapped the circular structure of Phase II, creating a sequence of overlapping circular structures in the central area of the hill. Near this central structure were at least four huts, less robust and quite damaged. Hut [127] was situated at the east side of the excavated area, and had an internal diameter of 6.2 m and a wall 0.8 m thick, while Hut [62], closer to the central area, and overlapping the ruins of the previous enclosure, had an internal diameter of 3 m, and a wall 0.7 m thick. The huts [492], with a probable internal diameter of 3.9 m and a wall 0.85 m thickness, and another near the central area, were poorly preserved, but showed similar building characteristics. Flimsier structures were still being built in this final phase. After the abandonment and collapse of these structures, a stone pavement was built, 30 m long by 4 m wide, which incorporated a large part of the ruin, and which produced all the small Bell Beaker fragments.

Monte do Tosco 1 is also on a hilltop about 15 km south of Porto das Carretas. There are two phases of occupation during the 3rd millennium BC: the first comprising a walled enclosure and the latter a circular stone hut. This hut (Fig. 1.8,3) (4.3 m internal diameter and with a 0.6 m thick wall) was located in a prominent position near the top of the hill. The most extensive southern Portuguese assemblage of Ciempozuelos Bell Beaker associated with a domestic context was found in this hut. Another earlier stone hut was recorded but had been partially dismantled.

These stone structures increasingly seem to characterise the second half of the 3rd millennium BC in Southern Iberia, being often associated with the presence of Bell Beaker pottery. The available data for San Blás (Spain), located on the left bank of the Guadiana, a few kilometres north of Miguens 3, also illustrates this trend, with the construction of stone huts H22, J27 and K7 (Fig. 9.4) over a set of timber-built constructions (Hurtado 2004, 151). All the later huts are associated with Bell Beaker ceramics of distinctive styles (García-Rivero 2008, 268).

The frequency of Bell Beakers in these huts suggests an association between Beakers and these specific architectures, suggesting the existence of a 'Beaker hut'. However, in some contemporary sites, the same architecture is present but not associated with Beakers. This is the case at Mercador, just 2 km south of Porto das Carretas (Valera 2013) (Fig. 1.9,1) and at Moinho Novo de Baixo 1, located between Miguens 3 and San Blás, where a heavily destroyed possible circular stone structure was recorded, (Fig. 1.8,4), but again with no trace of Beaker pottery. Similar structures (Fig. 1.9,3), again without but contemporary with Beakers were also recently found at Cabeço do Pé da Erra, a ditched enclosure in the Tagus basin, between the Alentejo and Estremadura regions (Gonçalves & Sousa 2017). So, rather than Beaker houses, we have houses using deep rooted techniques built when Beaker pottery was circulating in the region and in which Beaker sometimes appears.

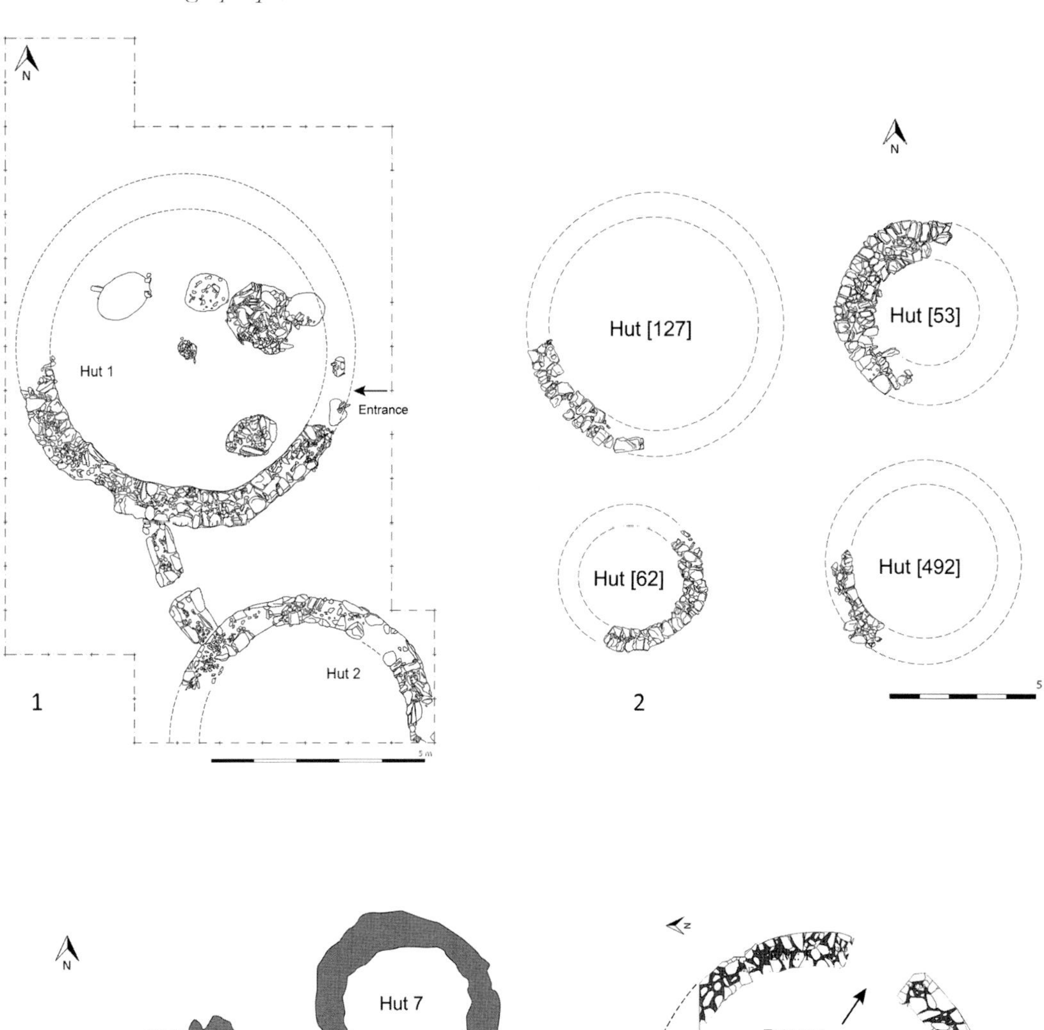

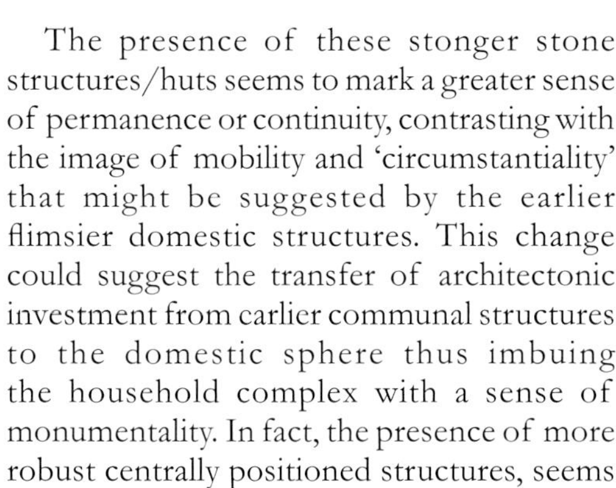

Figure 1.9:
1 – Mercador (adapted from Valera 2013);
2 – S. Pedro (adapted from Mataloto, et al. *2015); 3 – Pé da Erra (adapted from Gonçalves & Sousa 2017);*
4 – San Blás (adapted from Hurtado 2004)

The presence of these stonger stone structures/huts seems to mark a greater sense of permanence or continuity, contrasting with the image of mobility and 'circumstantiality' that might be suggested by the earlier flimsier domestic structures. This change could suggest the transfer of architectonic investment from earlier communal structures to the domestic sphere thus imbuing the household complex with a sense of monumentality. In fact, the presence of more robust centrally positioned structures, seems to perpetuate previous monumental dialogues. If walled enclosures seem to disappear in the Alentejo by the middle of the 3rd millennium BC, the investment in large-scale collective monumentality does not disappear, as demonstrated by the construction and use of large ditched enclosures at Perdigões and Porto Torrão, or smaller ones maintaining previous designs in Outeiro Alto 2, Horta do Albardão or Bela Vista 5. These document a trajectory in the continuity of architecture and landscape organisation.

Along with the living: social plurality of Beakers

The Alentejo region presents three clear Beaker stylistic borders (Figs 1.3 & 1.5): two of them spatial and one contextual. One of the spatial boundaries is the already mentioned 'south border', located in the south of the Alentejo, where the distribution of decorated Beakers seems to end. The other can be seen in the distribution of the influences of the Ciempozuelos style of central Iberia, and of the Palmela group originating in Portuguese Estremadura (Valera & Rebuge 2011). The Ciempozuelos style has its presence in the more interior area of the Guadiana basin, and the Palmela style in the more littoral area of the Sado basin. The Maritime style, however, seems to have crossed this boundary. These stylistic boundaries show that the region was subjected to two main influences and the Alentejo hinterland functioned as an intermediary between the Portuguese Estremadura, Spanish Extremadura and western Andalusia. Bell Beakers seem to have been used as a means of identity management between the groups that were more related to central Iberia (through the Guadiana basin) and the groups more connected to the Estremadura, (through the Sado basin). The 'south border', therefore, could correspond to a phenomenon of resistance to decorated Beaker pottery and its social implications and roles. That the 'Beaker border' is coincident with other boundaries, such as the ditched enclosures whose distribution also ends here, and with a significant change in the geology which gives way to the Pyrite Belt, where the settlement network seems to be sparser and archaeologically invisible. Contrastingly, this is an area where several funerary contexts of the 'Ferradeira' horizon are known, associated with undecorated Beaker shapes and 'Beaker weapons'.

The tendency for different monothematic styles in the smaller clustered sites – only International style Beakers at Porto das Carretas and Miguens 3 and only incised Ciempozuelos Beakers at S. Pedro and Monte do Tosco 1 – also suggests the use of Beaker styles as agents in identity strategies and at a local scale. Beakers were, therefore, involved in multi-scaled emblematic forms of expression of the complex network of communities and respective webs of social interaction. At another level, in a contextual scenario, some associations of Beaker pottery with specific production areas have recently prompted ideas of other possible social roles.

In the central area of Perdigões, Beaker is associated with stone structures in an area where there is significant evidence of copper working. This was also the case at Porto das Carretas. This association of Beakers with metallurgy was recently interpreted as a way of reinforcing the ideological value of metal production through the ritualisation of the production procedures, namely through propitiatory ceremonies intended to ensure a good outcome (Valera & Basílio 2017). Metallurgy, as a transformative process, has the potential to necessitate the ritualisation of the production procedures and use the techniques themselves as elements of social differentiation. A similar interpretation was proposed for the association of Beaker pottery with salt production in the Northern Meseta (Delibes de Castro *et al.* 2016), in that salt is also a product that involves a metamorphosis. Furthermore, the contemporary pits with human cremated remains in the central area of Perdigões also reference practices that involve the transformation through fire. We then find ourselves in the presence of linked contexts and scenarios that are usually considered separately. This constitutes a complex frame for the social practices that were carried out in this area and for the variability of social roles that Beakers might have assumed there.

Also significant is the amount and state of preservation of Beaker pottery in many of these sites. Leaving Porto Torrão aside, the number of sherds is 60 at Perdigões, 44 at Monte do Tosco 1, 16 at S. Pedro, 14 at Porto das Carretas and always fewer than 10 in the other sites. We can also note the high degree of fragmentation of the sherds and whilst no complete Beakers are known in the Alentejo outside funerary structures, the same cannot be said about other pottery types. In some cases, like Monte do Tosco 1, where almost all the Beaker sherds were inside hut 1, at Porto das Carretas and at S. Pedro most of the sherds represent different pots and very little refitting was possible. This raises the question of what was circulating: the vessels or just sherds? The potential social agency of fragments in establishing bonds, facilitating mobility, sharing, and even exchange, particularly if they are fragments of 'special things', should be considered when studying Beaker pottery in most of the non-funerary contexts in South Portugal. This process of fragmentation has been noted in other contemporary materials like the lunulae of tomb 2 at Perdigões (Valera 2010) and might also be suggested for many of the circular stone structures described here. Most of these structures appear to have been partially dismantled, resulting in the preservation of just a segment of their plans. This circumstance is a recurrent pattern suggesting a specific social practice. We can observe this at Perdigões (three cases), Porto das Carretas and S. Pedro (four cases each), Mercador (two cases) and at Monte do Tosco 1 (one case). The structures revealed different amounts of dismantled walls, although the potential towers, seem to survive better than the huts. This suggests a recurrent social practice and stratigraphy indicates that it still occurred during the 3rd millennium BC.

Two interpretative approaches may be developed to explain this circumstance. One more functionalistic approach may favour the reuse of raw materials. The other may integrate this dismantling activity in the broader context of social practices of segmentation, closure and memorisation. This could also be related to the rhythms of the compounds' biographies, expressing the dynamics of the groups, like fissioning and re-forming (Hanson 1998). This might suggest deconstructive activity as being as socially powerful as the construction phases and to the awareness that dismantling could be a deliberate act of closure. This practice can also end the active life of a space while simultaneously providing materials that may be reused as memories and links to the past. This dismantling process could easily be related to a fractal and fragmentation perspective that has been mainly applied to objects, but that could be extended to bodies, or to architecture. At São Pedro, the presence of several stones with multiple cupmarks, in one structure, suggests practices related to ancestry, meanings, and perceptions. They help to root and to strengthen the group identity of those newly established or revisited sites, once again developing a sense of continuity.

Epilogue: Beaker sites or sites with Beakers?

In south Portugal decorated Bell Beaker has its main social stage outside funerary contexts. This can be extended to all south-west Iberia, integrating Spanish Extremadura and western Andalusia (Hurtado 2005; Lazarich González 2005; Garcia Rivero 2006; Lazarich this volume). It is a situation that contrasts with other Iberian regions, such as the Portuguese Estremadura, central Iberia, northern Meseta, northern Portugal or Galicia (Criado Boado & Vazquez Varela 1993; Garrido-Pena 2005; Cardoso 2014; Valera 2017a; Sanchez *et al.* 2017; Lettow-Vorbeck 2017; Bueno-Ramírez *et al.* 2017), where funerary contexts with decorated Beakers are well represented and sometimes predominant. This situation is of historical significance because it does not seem to be related to insufficient research. A paradigmatic example comes from the Perdigões enclosures. Here, several funerary contexts dated to the middle and second half of the 3rd millennium (the Beaker period in this region) were excavated and, although containing large and diversified assemblages of exogenous and exotic materials (Valera 2017b), did not produce Beaker pottery. Beakers are only present in several non-funerary contexts inside the enclosure.

Except at Porto Torrão, Beaker pottery is always relatively scarce in non-funerary contexts, even in those with large archaeological assemblages which tend to maintain earlier elements. The appearance of Beaker sherds in settlements is not accompanied by significant changes in the background material culture, except for the advent of copper (daggers and Palmela points) that occur mainly in 'Ferradeira' burials. In architectonic terms, the walled enclosures seem to decay by the middle of the 3rd millennium BC, but large and small ditch enclosures continued to be built and used during the second half of the millennium (Perdigões, Porto Torrão, Outeiro Alto 2, Horta do Albardão 3, Bela Vista 5, Montoito). The same happens in the neighbouring regions of Extremadura and western Andalusia, in enclosures such as Pijotilla, San Blás, Valencina de la Concepción, Loma del Tesoro (Hurtado 2004; Mederos Martín 2016; Escudero Carrillo *et al.* 2017). What the archaeological record is suggesting is an intensification, during the middle and third quarter of the 3rd millennium BC, of the social trajectory that was being developed from the end of the 4th millennium. This is expressed through the complexification and expansion of interaction networks, the growth in demand for and consumption of exotic materials, the increase of social emulation practices and the development of settlement networks marked by asymmetry regarding size, monumentality, complexity, and duration.

This period seems to reveal an intensity and an exuberance of social display emphasised by diverse and contradictory behaviours and practices. This is especially visible in funerary contexts. While in the 'Ferradeira' tombs individuality and body integrity is underlined (following the pattern of the Bell Beaker graves of Continental Europe and other Iberian regions), the funerary practices associated with large ditched enclosures are the opposite. Perdigões only has the collective secondary deposition of bones, or parts of bodies and cremated remains, where no sense of individuality or corporeal integrity can be perceived. Even so, these contexts are full of exotic prestigious materials but not Bell Beakers (Valera 2017a). At Porto Torrão, primary and secondary collective depositions occur in the surrounding graves, but again do not express individuality. If these contexts were differentiating something, it would be group identities, not individual ones. The old practices of manipulating and depositing human remains outside of funerary contexts seem to increase and occur in many of these ditched enclosures and this reinforces the social importance of segmentation and possibly the idea of a resistance to an increasing social differentiation. In fact, the data do not legitimise any intra-group social stratification, as presumed at other places (Soares 2013, 376), but rather social organisations of transegalitarian type (Hayden 1995) developing increasing emulative relations.

Decorated Bell Beaker pottery appears during these times of intensification before the collapse detectable at the end of the 3rd millennium BC (Valera 2015b). Even so, they are not present in all arenas of social display, suggesting that they have a varied social role and are just part of a diversified set of alternative and complementary forms of power negotiation, identity management and symbolic agency. Only if we focus on some particular innovations, like Bell Beaker pottery and metal weapons, do we get a perception of significant social transformation. This tends to generate an inflation of the social agency of Beaker pottery in the socio-political structural changes in the region. However, innovations are not necessarily synonymous with structural social transformation and might very well be aligned with the intensification of a current social path. This idea, that Bell Beakers represent an addition to an ongoing social trajectory, has also been upheld for other regions of the Portugual (Sanches *et al.* 2017) based on the argument for the early appearance of Beakers dating from the first half of the 3rd millennium BC in the north and in Estremadura. Although the available data for the early emergence of Bell Beakers in these regions are far from indisputable, this idea of diversified forms of absorption in regionalised social trajectories is supported, in the Alentejo, by the overall picture provided by the archaeological record: continuity in social practices (showing a tension between collectiveness and individuality expressed in the funerary contexts); permanence and construction of new enclosures; maintenance of the logics of landscape organisation; growing need for monumental and iconographic forms of expression, keeping the same general symbolic framework (that also appears in Beaker decoration in some regions – the solar and deer motifs); continuity of the basic features of the material culture; and development and intensification of earlier interaction networks. Approached through a broader contextualisation, where all these variables are considered, the decorated Bell Beaker pottery in the Alentejo is one more ideotechnic contribution to what seems to be an increasing need for diversified forms of ideological display, having its social exhibition stages mainly in (some) settlement and monumental contexts. There are sites with Beakers but not Beaker sites.

Acknowledgements

Dates obtained for the project 'Beyond migration and diffusion: exploring the movement of people, practices and technologies in the Prehistoric world', were kindly financed by the Australian Research Council.

References

Bartleheim, M., Bueno Ramírez, P. & Kunst, M. (eds), 2017. *Key Resources and Socio-cultural Developments in the Iberian Chalcolithic*. Tübingen: Tübingen Library Publishing

Basílio, A.C. 2018. Dinâmicas ocupacionais na segunda metade do 3º milénio a.C. nos Perdigões: Continuidades e descontinuidades. Unpubl. Master thesis. University of Algarve. https://www.researchgate.net/publication/323999608_Dinamicas_ocupacionais_na_segunda_metade_do_3_milenio_aC_nos_Perdigoes_Continuidades_e_Descontinuidades

Besse, M. & Desideri, J. 2005. Bell Beaker diversity: settlements, burials and ceremonies. In Rojo-Guerra, *et al.* (eds), 2005, 89–105

Boaventura, R., Mataloto, R., Nukushina, D. & Andrade, M. 2014–15. E*stremoz 7* ou a Anta de Nossa Senhora da Conceição dos Olivais (Estremoz, Évora). *O Arqueólogo Português* 5, 4–5

Bueno-Ramírez, P., Bermejo, R. & Balbín-Behrmann, R. 2017. Redefining Ciempozuelos: Bell Beaker culture in Toledo? In Gonçalves, V.S. (ed.), 2017, 324–41

Calado, M. 2002. Povoamento pré e proto-histórico da margem direita do Guadiana. Almada. *Al-Madan* 2 (11), 122–27

Cardoso, J.L. 2014. Absolute chronology of the Beaker phenomenon north of the Tagus estuary: demographic and social implications. Madrid: *Trabajos de Prehistoria* 71 (1), 57–76

Criado Boado, F. & Vázquez Varela, J.M. 1993. *La Cerâmica Campaniforme en Galícia*. Corunha: Cuadernos do Seminario de Sargadelos, 42

Delibes de Castro, G., Guerra Doce, E., & Abarquero Moras, J. 2016. Rituales campaniformes en contextos no funerarios: la factoría salinera de Molino Sanchón II (Villafáfila, Zamora). *Arpi Arqueologia y Prehistoria del Interior Peninsular* 4, 286–97

Escudero Carrillo, J., Díaz-Zorita, B., Bartelheim, M. & García Sanjuán, L. 2017. Chalcolithic enclosures in the lower Guadalquivir Basin. La Loma del Real Tesoro (Carmona, Seville, Spain) and its resources. In Bartelheim *et al.* (eds), 2017, 257–72

García Rivero, D. 2006. Campaniforme y territorio en la cuenca media del Guadiana. *SPAL – Revista de Prehistoria y Arqueología de la Universidad de Sevilla*, 15, 71–102

García Rivero, D. 2008. *Campaniforme y rituales estratégicos en la Cuenca Media y Baja del Guadiana (Suroeste de la Península Ibérica)*. Oxford: British Archaeological Reports International Series, 1837

Garrido-Pena, R. 2005. El Laberinto Campaniforme: breve historia de un reto intelectual. In Rojo-Guerra, *et al.* (eds), 2005, 29–44

Gomes, M.V. 1991. Les corniformes de deux sanctuaires rupestres dans le Sud du Portugal. Chronologie et interpretation. *Colloque International le Mont Bego. Une Montagne Sacrée de l'Age du Bronze*. 434–96. Tende

Gonçalves, V.S. 1988/89. A ocupação pré-histórica do Monte Novo dos Albardeiros (Reguengos de Monsaraz). *Portugalia* 9 (10) 49–61

Gonçalves, V.S. 2003a. A Anta 2 da Herdade dos Cebolinhos (Reguengos de Monsaraz, Évora): sinopse das intervenções de 1996–97 e duas datações de radiocarbono para a última utilização da câmara ortostática. *Revista Portuguesa da Arqueologia*, 6 (2), 143–66

Gonçalves, V.S. 2003b. STAM-3, a Anta 3 da Herdade de Santa Margarida (Reguengos de Monsaraz). Lisboa: Instituto Português de Arqueologia. *Trabalhos de Arqueologia*. 32

Gonçalves, V.S. (ed.), 2017. *Sinos e Taças. Junto ao Oceano e mais longe. Aspectos da presença campaniforme na Península Ibérica*. Lisboa: Estudos & Memórias 10

Gonçalves, V.S. & Sousa, A.C. 2017. The shadows of the rivers and the colours of copper. Some reflections on the Chalcolithic farm of Cabeço do Pé da Erra (Coruche, Portugal) and its Resources. In Bartleheim *et al.* (eds), 2017, 143–66

Gonçalves, V.S., Sousa, A.C., Andrade, M.A. 2017. O Barranco do Farinheiro (Coruche) e a presença Campaniforme na Margem Esquerda do Baixo Tejo. In Gonçalves, V. S., (ed.), *Sinos e Taças. Junto ao Oceano e mais longe. Aspectos da presença campaniforme na Península Ibérica*, 98–125. Lisboa: Estudos & Memórias 10

Hanson, J. 1998. *Decoding Homes and Houses*. Cambridge: Cambridge University Press

Harrison, R. 1977. *The Bell Beaker cultures of Spain and Portugal*. Harvard: Peabody Museum

Hayden, B. 1995. Pathways to Power. Principles for Creating Socioeconomic Inequalities. In Price, T.D. & Feinman G.M. (eds), *Foundations of Social Inequality*, 15–86. New York: Plenum Press

Henriques, F.R., Soares, A.M., António, T.F., Curate, F., Valério, P. & Rosa, S. 2013. O Tholos Centirã 2 (Brinches, Serpa): construtores e utilizadores; práticas funerárias e cronologias. In Jiménez Ávila, J., Bustamante Álvarez, M. & García Cabezas, M. (eds.), *Actas del VI Encuentro de Arqueología del Suroeste Peninsular*, 319–55. Villafranca de los Barros: Ayuntamiento

Hurtado, V. 2004. El asentamiento fortificado de San Blas (Cheles, Badajoz). III Milenio A.C. *Trabajos de Prehistoria* 61 (1), 141–55

Hurtado, V. 2005. El Campaniforme en Extremadura: valoración del proceso de cambio socioeconómico en las cuencas medias del Tajo y Guadiana. In Rojo-Guerra, *et al.* (eds), 2005, 321–36

Larsson, L. 2000. Symbols in stone: ritual activities and petrified traditions. In Jorge, V.O. (ed.), *Actas do 3.º Congresso de Arqueologia Peninsular*, 445–58. Porto, ADECAP

Lazarich González, M. 2005. El Campaniforme en Andalucía (Bell Beakers in Andalucía). In Rojo-Guerra, *et al.* (eds), 2005, 351–87

Lettow-Vorbeck, C. 2017. Campaniforme y Ciempozuelos en la región de Madrid. In Gonçalves, V.S., (ed.), 2017, 302–41

Mataloto, R. 2006. Entre Ferradeira e Montelavar: um conjunto artefactual da Fundação Paes Teles (Ervedal, Avis). *Revista Portuguesa de Arqueologia* 9 (2), 83–108

Mataloto, R. 2017. We are ancients, as ancient as the sun: Campaniforme, antas e gestos funerários nos finais doIII milénio a.C. no Alentejo Central. In Gonçalves, V.S., (ed.), 2017, 58–81

Mataloto, R. & Boaventura, R. 2009. Entre vivos e mortos nos IV e III milénios a. n. e. do Sul de Portugal: um balanço relativo do povoamento com base em datações pelo radiocarbono. *Revista Portuguesa de Arqueologia* 12 (2), 31–77

Mataloto, R., Martins, J.M. & Soares, A.M. 2013. Cronologia absoluta para o Bronze do Sudoeste. Periodização, base de dados, Tratamento estatístico. *Estudos Arqueológicos de Oeiras* 20, 303–38

Mataloto, R., Costeira, C. & Roque, C. 2015. Torres, Cabanas e Memória: a Fase V e a cerâmica campaniforme do povoado de S. Pedro (Redondo, Alentejo Central). *Revista Portuguesa de Arqueologia* 18, 81–100

Mederos Martín, A.F. 2016. La cronología actual de los sistemas de fosos del poblado calcolítico de Valencia de La Concepción (Sevilla) en el contexto del Sur de la Península Ibérica. *ARPI Arqueología y Prehistoria del Interior Peninsular* 4, 298–323

Morán, E. 2017. O Campaniforme de Alcalar no contexto do extremo sul. In Gonçalves, V.S. (ed.), 2017, 28–37

Morán, E. & Parreira, R. (eds), 2004. *Alcalar 7. Estudo e Reabilitação de um Monumento Megalítico*. Lisboa: Ministério da Cultura, IPPAR

Prieto-Martinez, M.P. 2008. Bell Beaker communities in Thy: the first Bronze Age society in Denmark. *Norwegian Archaeological Review* 41 (2), 115–158

Rocha, L. & Duarte, C. 2009. Megalitismo funerário no Alentejo Central: Os dados antropológicos das escavações de Manuel Heleno. In Polo-Cerdá, M. & García-Poósper, E. (ed.), *Investigaciones histórico-médicas sobre salud y enfermedad en el Pasado*, 763–781. Congreso Nacional de Paleopatologia, 9, Morella (Castellón). Valencia: Grupo Paleolab & Sociedad Española de Paleopatologia

Rojo-Guerra, M.A., Garrido-Pena, R. & Garcia-Martínez de Lagrán I. (eds), 2005. *Bell Beakers in the Iberian Peninsula and their Euroepean Context*. Valladolid: Universidad de Valladolid

Sanches, M.J., Barbosa, H. & Vieira, A. 2017. Bell Beaker contexts in Portugal: the northern and the Douro region basin. In Gonçalves, V.S., (ed.), 2017, 238–57

Santos, F.J.C., Soares, A.M., Rodrigues, Z., Queiroz, P., Valério, P. and Araújo, M. 2009. A Horta do Albardão 3: um sítio da Pré-História Recente, com fossos e fossas, na encosta do Albardão (S.Manços, Évora). *Revista Portuguesa de Arqueologia,* 12, 1, 53–71

Silva, C.T. & Soares, J. 1987. O povoado fortificado calcolítico do Monte da Tumba. I Escavações arqueológicas de 1982–86 (resultados preliminares). *Setúbal Arqueológica,* 8, 29–79

Soares, A.M. 2004. Variabilidade do 'Upwelling' costeiro durante o Holocénico nas Margens Atlânticas Ocidental e Meridional da Península Ibérica. Unpubl. PhD thesis. University of Algarve

Soares, A.M. 2008. O monumento megalítico Monte da Velha 1 (MV1) Vila Verde de Ficalho, Serpa). *Revista Portuguesa de Arqueologia* 11 (1), 33–51

Soares, A.M., Soares, J. & Silva, C.T. da. 2007. A datação pelo radiocarbono das fases de ocupação do Porto das Carretas: algumas reflexões sobre a cronologia do Campaniforme. *Revista Portuguesa de Arqueologia* 10 (2), 127–34

Soares, J. 2013. Transformações sociais durante o III milénio AC no Sul de Portugal: O povoado do Porto das Carretas. Lisboa: Empresa de Desenvolvimento e Infra-Estruturas do Alqueva, Direcção Regional de Cultura do Alentejo, Museu de Arqueologia e Etnografia do Distrito de Setúbal. M*emórias d'Odiana*

Soares, J. & Silva, C.T. da. 1974–77. O Grupo de Palmela no quadro da cerâmica campaniforme em Portugal. *O Arqueólogo Português* 7 (9), 102–12

Soares, J. & Silva, C.T. da. 2010. Anta Grande do Zambujeiro – arquitectura e poder. Intervenção arqueológica do MAEDS, 1985–87. 83–129. Setúbal: Fórum Intermuseus do Distrito de Setúbal/ Museu de Arqueologia e Etnografia do Distrito de Setúbal. *MUSA, museus, arqueologia & outros patrimónios* 3

Valera, A.C. 2006. A margem esquerda do Guadiana (região de Mourão), dos finais do 4º aos inícios do 2º milénio AC, Lisboa: *Era Arqueologia* 7, 136–210

Valera, A.C. 2010. Marfim no recinto calcolítico dos Perdigões (1): Lúnulas, fragmentação e ontologia dos artefactos. *Apontamentos de Arqueologia e Património* 5, 31–42

Valera, A.C. 2013. Cronologia dos recintos de fossos da Pré-História Recente em território português, 335–43. *Arqueologia em Portugal 150 anos*, Actas do I congresso da Associação dos Arqueólogos Portugueses, Lisboa, AAP

Valera, A.C. 2014. Bela Vista 5: Um recinto do Final do 3º milénio a.n.e. (Mombeja, Beja). Lisboa: *Era Monográfica*. 2

Valera, A.C. 2015a. The Diversity of Ideotechnic Objects at Perdigões Enclosure: A First Inventory of Items and Problems. *Arpi Arqueologia y Prehistoria del Interior Peninsular* 3, 238–56

Valera, A.C. 2015b. Social change in the late 3rd millennium BC in Portugal: the twilight of enclosures. In Meller, H., Arz, H. W., Jung, R. & Risch, R. (eds), 2015. *2200 BC – Ein Klimasturz als Ursache für den Zerfall der Alten Welt? 7. Mitteldeutscher Archäologentag vom 23. bis 26. Oktober 2014 in Halle (Saale),* 409–27. Tagungen des Landesmuseum für Vorgeschichte 12/II. Halle/ Saale: Landesamt für Denkmalpflege und Archäologie Sachsen-Anhalt

Valera, A.C. 2017a. Beakers in Central Portugal: social roles, confluences, and strange absences. In Gonçalves, V.S., (ed.), 2017, 214–29

Valera, A.C. 2017b. The 'Exogenous' at Perdigões: Approaching interaction in the Late 4th and 3rd Millennium BC in Southwest Iberia. In Bartelheim *et al.* (eds), 2017, 201–24

Valera, A.C. & Basílio, A.C. 2017. Approaching Bell Beakers at Perdigões enclosures (South Portugal): Site, local and regional scales. In Gonçalves, V.S., (ed.), 2017, 82–97

Valera, A.C. & Filipe, I. 2004. O povoado do Porto Torrão (Ferreira do Alentejo). *Era Arqueologia* 6, 28–61

Valera, A.C. & Rebuge, J. 2011. O Campaniforme no Alentejo: contextos e circulação. Um breve balanço. *Arqueologia do norte alentejano: Comunicações das 3as Jornada*s, 111–21. Fronteira: Câmara Municipal de Fronteira

Valera, A.C., Silva, A. M. & Márquez Romero, J.E. 2014a. The temporality of Perdigões enclosures: absolute chronology of the structures and social practices. *SPAL – Revista de Prehistoria y Arqueología de la Universidad de Sevilla.* 23, 11–16

Valera, A.C. Santos, H., Figueiredo, M. & Granja, R. 2014b. Contextos funerários na periferia do Porto Torrão: Cardim 6 e Carrascal 2. 4.º Colóquio de Arqueologia do Alqueva. O plano de rega (2002–2010). *Memórias d'Odiana* 2 (14), 83–95

Valera, A.C., Godinho, R., Clavo, E., Berrequero, F.J.M.,

Filipe, V. & Santos, H. 2014c. Um mundo em negativo: fossos, fossas e hipogeus entre o Neolítico Final e a Idade do Bronze na margem esquerda do Guadiana (Brinches, Serpa), 4º Colóquio de Arqueologia do Alqueva. O plano de rega (2002–2010), *Memórias d'Odiana*, 2 (14), 55–73

Valera, A.C., Calvo, E. & Simão, P. 2016. Enterramento campaniforme em fossa da Quinta do Castelo 1 (Salvada, Beja). *Apontamentos de Arqueologia e Património* 11, 13–20

Vander Linden, M. 2004. Polythetic networks, coherent people: A new historical hypothesis for the Bell Beaker phenomenon. In Czebreszuk, J. (ed.), *Similar but different. Bell Beakers in Europe*. 33–60. Poznan: Adam Mickiewicz University

2

Settlement in the north-west Iberian peninsula in the 3rd and 2nd millennia BC

M. Pilar Prieto-Martínez

From the Chalcolithic to the start of the Middle Bronze Age important changes took place in this region with increasing social division and complexity, transformations in pottery production, new artefacts and objects testifying to a social hierarchy and complex exchange systems. These changes are wide-ranging and can also be seen in the settlement record, the use of natural resources, the sepulchro-ritual record and even palaeo-environmentally. In this study we will focus on how these changes occurred, exploring the differences between the cultures of a region that includes Asturias, Galicia, and northern Portugal as far south as the northern bank of the River Duero over a period of nearly 1500 years. Our knowledge is variable since the available information is fragmented, partial, widely dispersed, and little published. Nevertheless, this region can no longer be regarded as marginal, as we now have more than 200 sites, although the record for Bell Beakers is unevenly distributed (Table 2.1, Fig. 2.1a–c).

The current status

Bell Beaker pottery has long been seen as a significant material element, considered to have appeared around 2800/2600 cal BC (Prieto 2011a; Sanches *et al.* 2017) while the date of its disappearance varies more widely from region to region.

In the north of Portugal, Bell Beaker sites are only considered such if they actually produced Beaker pottery. The Bell Beaker culture is considered to be a continuation of the previous tradition, dating from the latter stage of the Chalcolithic, clearly separated from contemporary non-Bell Beaker producing sites that date to the Bronze Age, from 2300–2200 BC onwards (Bettencourt 2011). The pottery studies are typological, something that is a limiting factor when attempting to compare pottery that was contemporary with the Bell Beaker style. Recent summaries have placed more emphasis on providing an inventory of Bell Beaker sites (Bettencourt 2011; Sanches *et al.* 2017) and Bettencourt highlights projects that focus on the Bronze Age in the coastal region, compared to a growing number of projects concentrating on Chalcolithic sites in the interior.

In Galicia, Bell Beaker studies currently focus on the study of the *chaîne opératoire*, in which typology is only a complementary element. The pottery is considered as simply one of many elements of a more complex assemblage and which was deposited selectively

Table 2.1: List of known contexts in the NW Iberian Peninsula and types of pottery that have been found in each of them, by periods

		Pottery types	*Settlements*	*Fortified sites*	*Rural sites*	*Caves/ Shelter*	*Barrows*	*Pits*	*Cists*	*Production places*
Late Neolithic	Early & Middle Chalcolithic	Undecorated pot	G P	P	G P	–	–	–	–	–
		Penha type	G P	P	–	P	G P	–	–	–
		Bell Beaker imitation	G	P	–	P	G	–	–	–
Early & Middle Bronze Age	Late Chalcolithic	International Bell Beaker	G	P	G	–	G P	–	–	A
		Geometric Bell Beaker	G	P	G P	–	G P	–	–	–
		Incised Bell Beaker	G	P	–	–	–	–	–	–
		Regional Bell Beaker	G	–	G	–	–	–	–	–
		Palmela/Ciempozuelos Bell Beaker	–	P	P	–	P	–	–	–
		Brittany style Bell Beaker	G P	–	G	–	G P	–	–	–
		Epicampaniforme*	G	–	–	–	–	P	–	A
Galicia	Portugal Asturias	Undecorated pot	G	–	G	–	–	G P	G P	–
		Decorated non-Bell Beaker	–	–	G	–	–	–	–	–

* = Later Bell Beaker with grooved decoration, G: Galicia; P: Portugal, A: Asturias

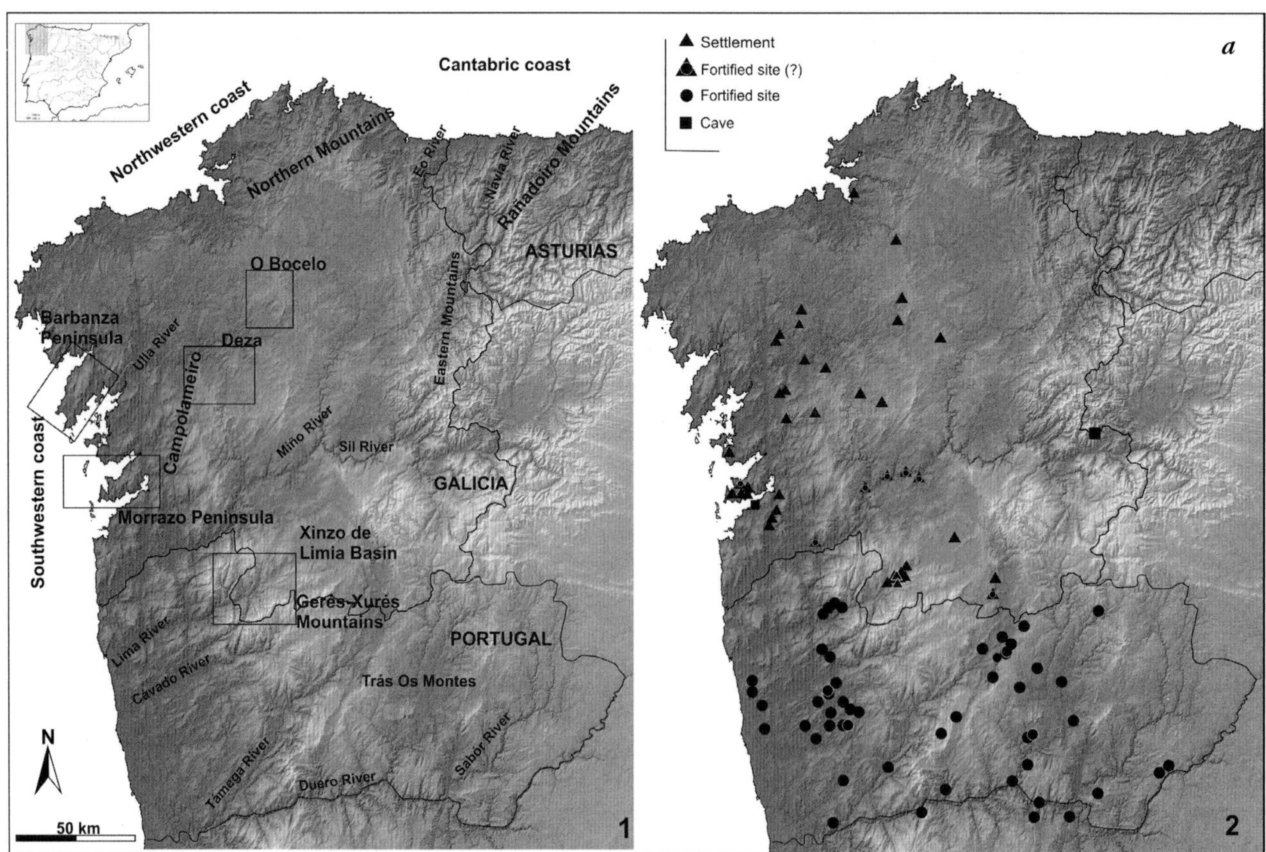

Figure 2.1: Distribution maps. a) 1: Areas mentioned in the text; 2: Sites with Penha-type pottery (pre-Bell Beaker) (Prieto 2009; Jorge 1986). b) 1: Open air sites with Bell Beaker pottery (Prieto 2011a; 2013a); 2: Sites probably used for ritual activities with Bell Beaker pottery (Seoane et al. *2013. c: 1: Burials with Penha-type and Bell Beaker pottery (Prieto 2009; Jorge 1989); 2: Burials from the 3rd and 2nd millennia BC excavated without Penha-type or Bell Beaker pottery (Nonat 2017)*

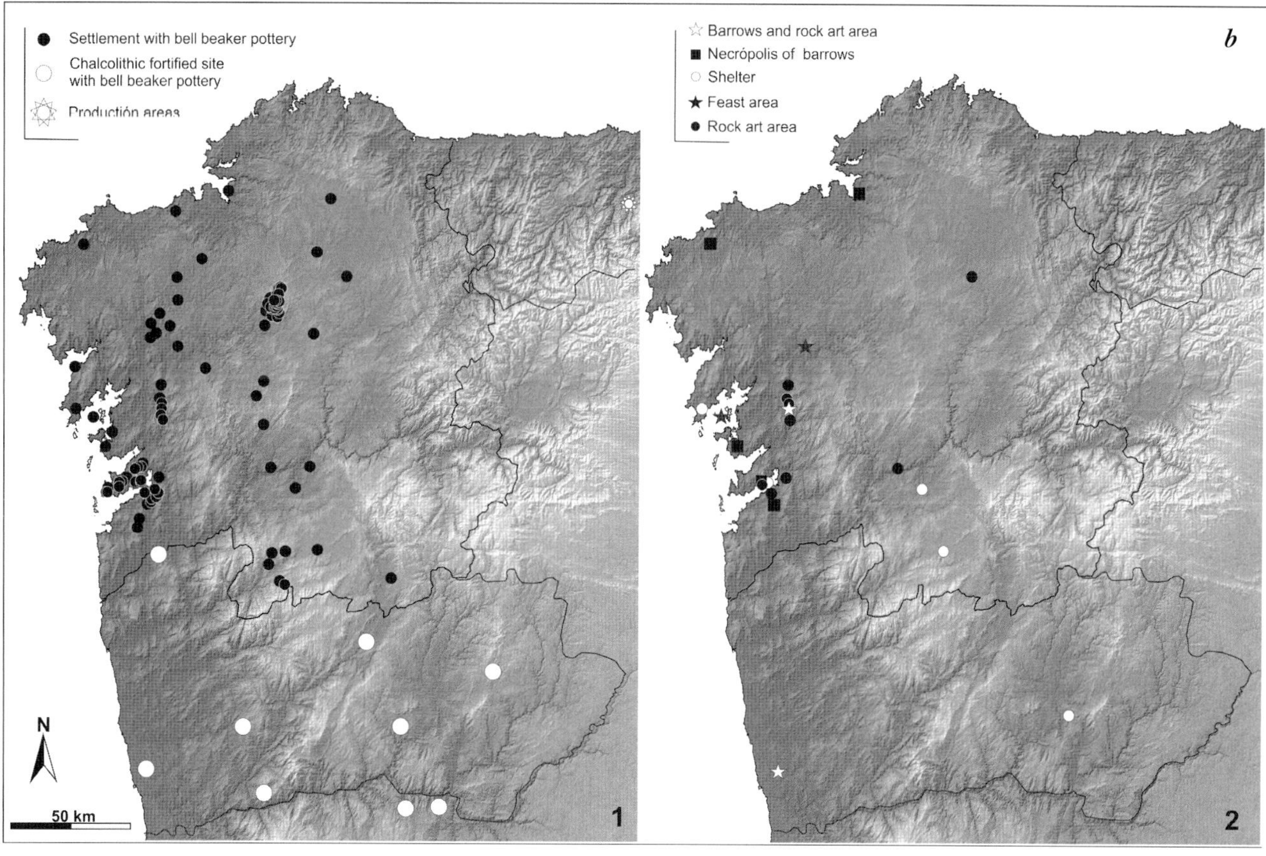
Settlement with bell beaker pottery
Chalcolithic fortified site with bell beaker pottery
Productión areas
N
50 km
1
Barrows and rock art area
Necrópolis of barrows
Shelter
Feast area
Rock art area
b
2

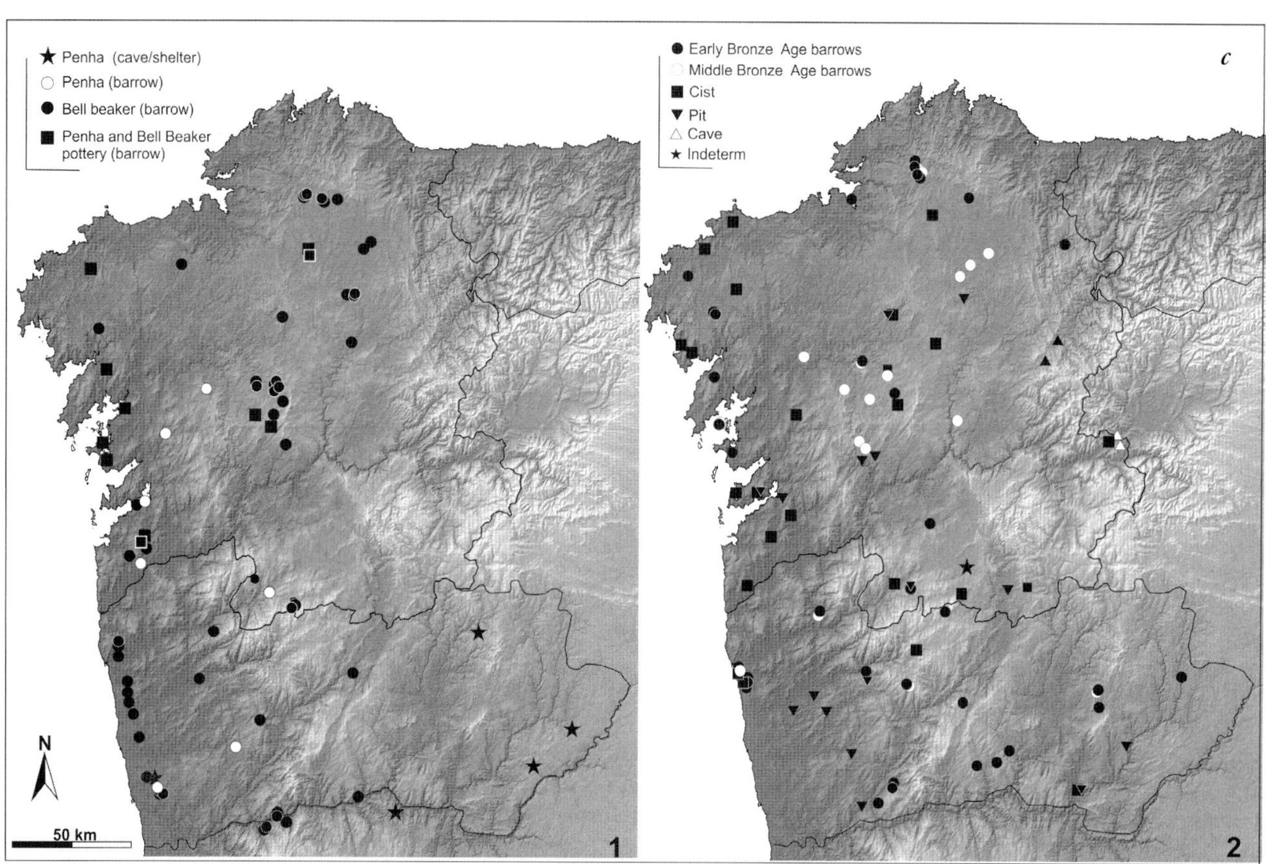
Penha (cave/shelter)
Penha (barrow)
Bell beaker (barrow)
Penha and Bell Beaker pottery (barrow)
N
50 km
1
Early Bronze Age barrows
Middle Bronze Age barrows
Cist
Pit
Cave
Indeterm
c
2

depending on the contexts of use and the function. Consequently, it is logical that some sites without Bell Beaker pottery still form a part of a Bell Beaker *savoir faire*. As a whole, the Bell Beaker phenomenon is considered as representing a break in the archaeological record, lasting perhaps as late as 1600 BC and heralding the Bronze Age (Prieto 2011a).

Only a few summary articles have been published for this region. As well as for the north of Portugal generally (Criado & Vázquez 1982; Prieto 2011a; Prieto & Salanova 2011) there are four local syntheses that deal with areas producing large Bell Beaker sites namely the Morrazo Peninsula (Criado & Cabreras 2005), the Baixa Limia (Eguileta 1999), Bocelo (Criado *et al.* 1991) and Deza (Prieto & Criado 2010). Unfortunately, there are no current research programmes aimed at understanding the archaeological problems affecting the sites from this period. In Asturias, the first and only discovery of Bell Beaker pottery was made quite recently, it was interpreted as an import and was dated to the last third of the 3rd millennium BC (Blas & Rodríguez 2015).

Proposals and objectives

The notion of continuity between the pre-Bell Beaker and Bell Beaker Chalcolithic has hampered research from data collection to publication. Assemblages have been dealt with as uniform collections resulting from the same historical and physical process, making it impossible to distinguish between phases. This means that there is a lack of good contextual information from the most important sites and few sites can be used as references to help interpret future discoveries. As recording systems become more refined, we can see differences between the Bell Beaker and pre-Bell Beaker elements and some sites were occupied and re-occupied, as is the case with A Romea (Prieto 2007), and Zarra de Xoacín (Aboal *et al.* 2004–5) in Galicia, and Crasto de Palherios (Sanches 2008), and Castelo Velho in Portugal (Jorge 2004).

In this study we see the Bell Beaker culture, and all of the processes associated with it, as embodying a change that was probably on a greater scale than we can identify through the archaeological record (Prieto 2008). Chronological complexity has been verified in all of the recently excavated sites and it has been shown that the material changes that took place in all of the different spheres of evidence (settlements, structures, tombs, pottery, metals, stone tools, etc.) did not occur at the same rate. We see Bell Beaker pottery as a physical element reflecting a profound change and a break with Chalcolithic societies. As a result, we believe that the society in which the Bell Beaker was used did not form a part of the Late Chalcolithic, but instead marked the start and development of another type of socio-cultural phenomenon which had its own characteristics and was the prelude to the Bronze Age (Prieto 2008; 2011a).

In order to be able to understand the settlement sites of this period, we first offer a general summary of the contexts that have been identified, and we then explore the pre-Bell Beaker sites in order to identify instances of continuity and dramatic change.

Palaeoenvironmental information

In terms of climate, the 3rd and 2nd millennia BC correspond to the second half of the Neoglaciation, one of the coldest parts of the Holocene. However, around 3100 cal BC there may have been a warmer phase, with temperatures possibly 2° higher than the current average, which would correspond to the time when part of the sedimentary zones of the south-western coast of Galicia were disturbed, possibly due to a momentary rise in sea levels. Around 2800–2700 cal BC the climate rapidly cooled (Martínez Cortizas *et al.* 1999) and this phase continued until the temperature finally recovered around 1300–1200 cal BC. During this period, however, there were two phases of more intense cold, between 2800–2200 cal BC (with temperatures 2° lower than at present), and between 1600–1400 cal BC (with temperatures around 1.5° lower than present). Between 2000–1600 cal BC (López *et al.* 2011) there was a phase of relative recovery which coincided with the time from which the largest number of sites have been recorded. This colder phase was combined with a damp environment with precipitation values that were substantially higher than in the preceding periods, and slightly higher than today, with two slightly higher peaks at the start and end of the Bell Beaker period (López *et al.* 2011). This period was also marked by strong winds that lasted until 2200 cal BC after which windspeeds dropped significantly (Fábregas *et al.* 2003).

Coinciding with this sudden cooler and wetter climate, between 4000–3000 cal BC the sea level rose, altering the shape of the coastline in an alternating process in which sediments were deposited and removed. Around 2500 cal BC, we find evidence of hill-slope erosion associated with anthropogenic activity, which led to the formation of alluvial deposits of considerable thickness and accumulated layers of stone especially at the mouths of rivers. Between 2500–1330 cal BC, the rising sea level caused cliffs to crumble resulting in continental sedimentary events (Blanco Chao *et al.* 2002).

There was also a general change in forestry dynamics as a result of anthropogenic activities in the 3rd millennium BC with evidence for increased human impact on the landscape represented by concentrations of charcoal in paleosoils resulting from the cutting and burning of woodland to create new opportunities for agriculture. This is particularly noticeable between 2500–1200 cal BC and coincides with the arrival of the first Bell Beaker communities (López *et al.* 2011). Although the erosion caused by deforestation began in the Neolithic (Martínez Cortizas *et al.* 2009a), there is accelerated change at this time to the point where saprolites and unaltered rock surfaces were becoming exposed (López *et al.* 2011). This can be seen very clearly in the area of Campo Lameiro, where three phases of increased erosion can be identified, the most intense of which was between 2400–2150 cal BC (Martínez Cortizas *et al.* 2009b). This led to a redistribution and reduction of soil resources and there was probably a greater demand for their control. This intensification of agriculture resulted in a landscape of cleared woodlands dominated by extensive stretches of pasture and arable fields throughout the entire region (López *et al.* 2011). Despite this, palynology confirms that there was still a presence of oak-dominated forests, particularly near the coast, and woodland and shrub species were exploited on settlements (Martín *et al.* 2017). Finally, the first signs of heavy metal contamination have been detected from around 1500 cal BC in Galicia (López *et al.* 2011) and late Bell Beaker pottery has been found on some of those sites.

Pottery styles, *chaînes opératoires*, contexts, chronology

Pre-Bell Beaker and native pottery in Galicia and North Portugal

Around 3100–3000 cal BC a type of pottery was manufactured in north-west Iberia with its own unique features that would last for some 600–700 years, to around 2500–2400 cal BC. Known as Penha-type pottery, this was named after Monte da Penha in Portugal (Jorge 1986; Sanches 1997) and went on to characterise the pottery style that extended throughout the western half of the Peninsula (Prieto 2009) (Fig 2.2). It mainly consists of undecorated pottery and is found in funerary and domestic contexts and caves. It is a uniform type of pottery, with simple forms in a wide variety of sizes. The vessels have rough or medium finishes and have dull reddish or black surfaces. Both the undecorated and decorated pottery used the same manufacturing process, following on from earlier traditions, which means it is difficult to differentiate the undecorated pottery from the different phases of the Neolithic.

There are different variations in the designs, although they follow a well-defined scheme. The decoration covers the outer top third of the vessel, incision is more common than impression, the designs are large and clumsy and geometric motifs feature straight horizontal lines, zig-zags or herringbone patterns, grids, and in exceptional cases, symbolic or eye motifs. In Galicia, the decorated pottery varies according to the context. For example, metope designs appear in both settlements and tombs, although pottery with complex metopes is more often found in sepulchral contexts. The designs with friezes are less common and are only found on settlements (Prieto 2009). In Portugal, there seems to be a geographical distinction because pottery with metope designs predominates in the western zone, while designs with friezes or comb incisions are predominant in the east (Bettencourt 2011).

Finally, a new and different *chaîne opératoire* has been recently defined for a small group of pottery, which due to its rarity and anomalous appearance has been interpreted as imitation Bell Beaker pottery. These imitations combine the features of Penha-type and Bell Beaker pottery (Prieto & Vázquez-Collazo 2011; Prieto & Lantes 2017) and were identified for the first time in Buraco da Pala (Sanches

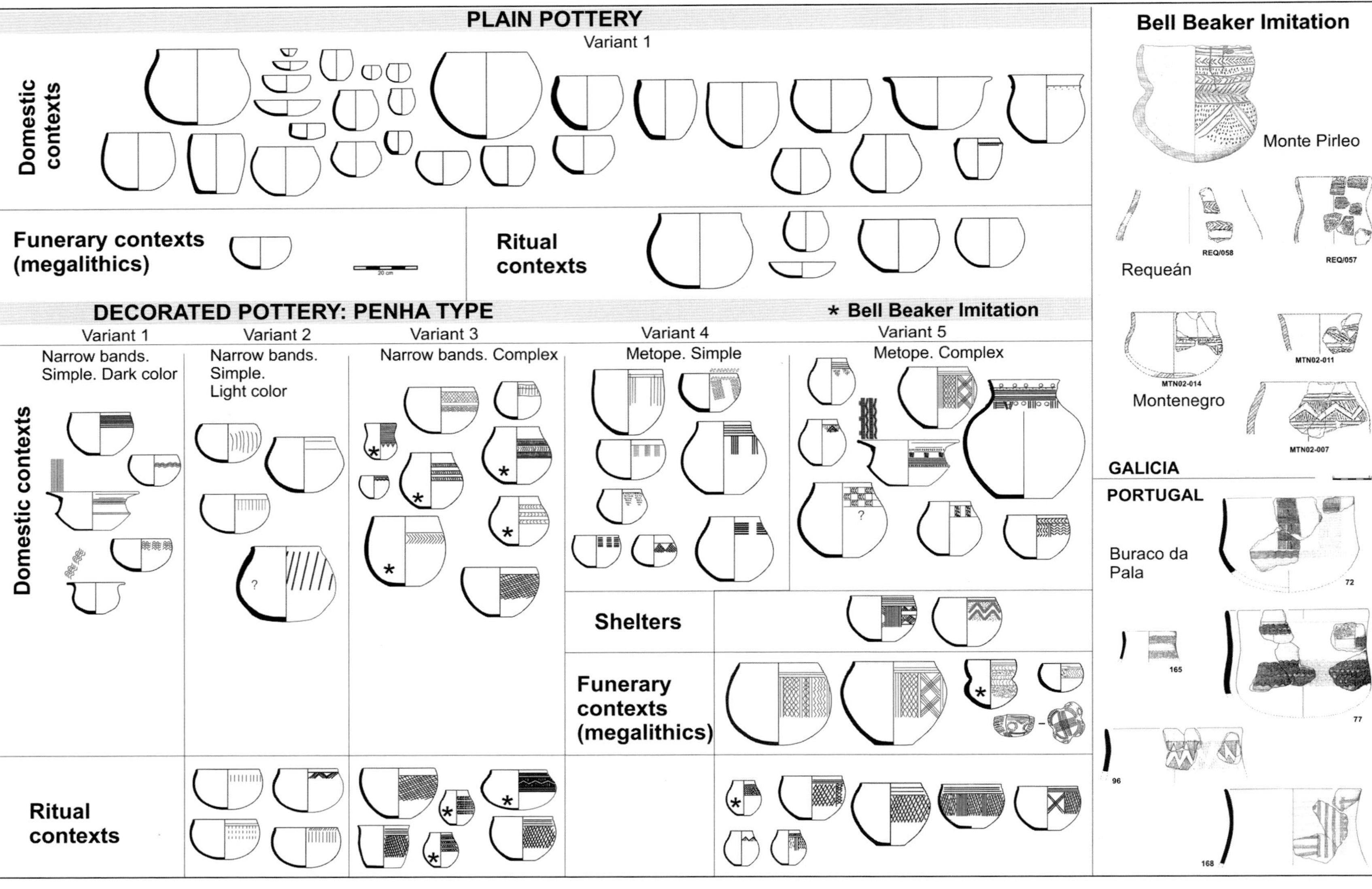

Figure 2.2: Penha-type pottery grouped by contexts. Example of the Galician zone from Prieto 2009. On the right, illustrations of some of the imitation Bell Beaker vessels (based on Prieto & Vázquez Collazo 2011)

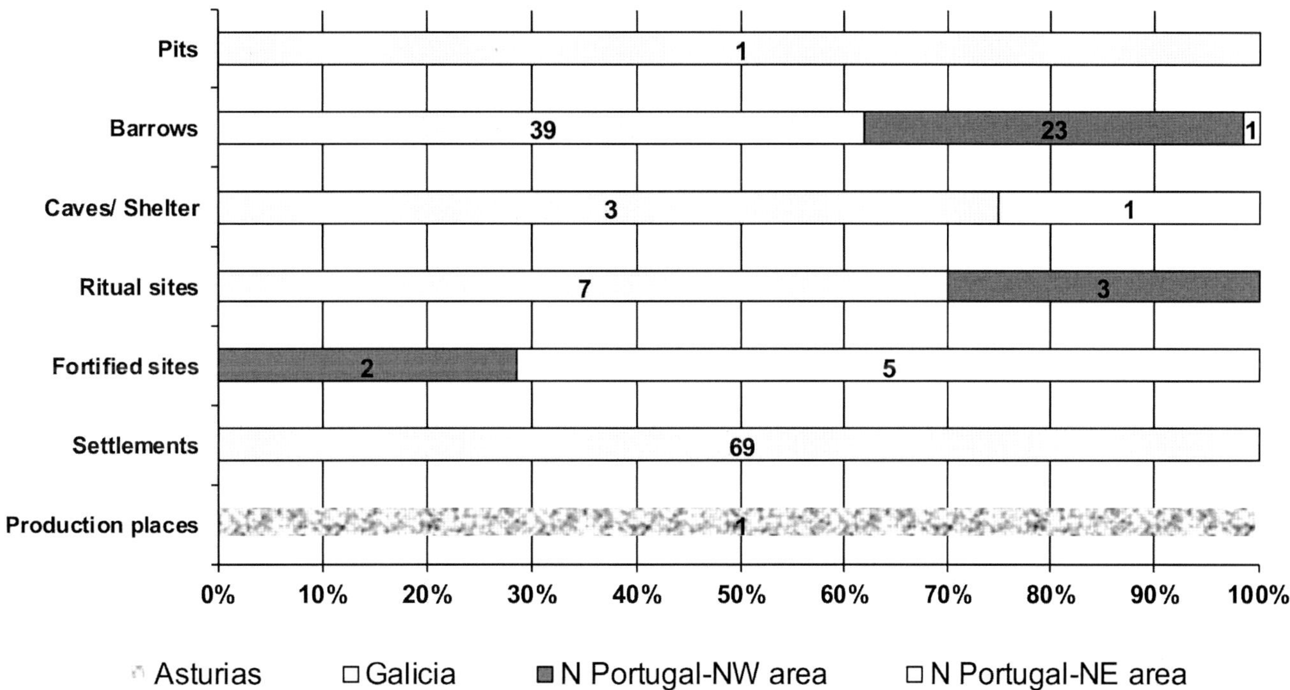

Figure 2.3: Sites and contexts with Bell Beaker pottery: graph showing distribution according to regions

1997). More sites with this pottery have been identified in Galicia (Prieto & Vázquez-Collazo 2011) and in the north of Portugal (Sanches *et al.* 2017).

Bell Beaker pottery in Galicia and the north of Portugal

The earliest Bell Beaker pottery from the region has been found in tombs, with the earliest dates (2800–2500 BC) coming from the re-use of the Neolithic dolmen of Dombate (Bello *et al.* 2013). The Beaker types that have been recorded are the international (Maritime) style, the herringbone variety, corded and geometric types, and in exceptional cases undecorated Bell Beakers have also been found. Beakers also come from the fortified sites of northern Portugal, associated with early dates as, for example, from A Forca (Bettencourt 2011), and Crasto de Palheiros (Sanches 2008).

In Galicia, regional variations have been found in a variety of different contexts, and dated to later periods. These regional styles are predominant in the settlements, and it has still not been possible to accurately define their chronology (Prieto 2011a). In Portugal, regional Bell Beaker pottery has still not been classified, and although a study of the Bell Beaker phenomenon in the region is still pending, Ciempozuelos or Palmela-type Bell Beakers have been found (Sanches *et al.* 2017; Valera *et al.* this volume), indicative of long-distance exchanges in Iberia.

Finally, a grooved type of late Bell Beaker (*epicampaniforme*) has also been found in Galicia, and there are rare cases of Bell Beakers decorated with fish bone impressions, a technique common in Atlantic France, indirectly associated with dates from the middle of the 2nd millennium BC. There is no late Bell Beaker pottery as such in Portugal (Figs 2.3 & 2.4).

Recent studies have shown that the most frequent decorative technique used for Bell Beaker pottery is a shell impression which is a technique found extensively throughout Galicia (Prieto & Salanova 2009; 2011) and which would seem to be of Atlantic inspiration (Salanova 2000). No specific identification studies have been carried out in Asturias and northern Portugal, although this technique has been found on some sites, such as in association with the corded Bell Beaker pottery from A Forca. Bell Beaker and Penha-type pottery were contemporary for two centuries or more but were used by different communities and this suggests that Bell Beaker pottery marks a social break in Neolithic and Chalcolithic societies.

There are three pottery categories, with different degrees of internal variation, which can

Figure 2.4: Bell Beaker pottery grouped by contexts. Example of the Galician zone (based on Prieto 2011a; 2013a)

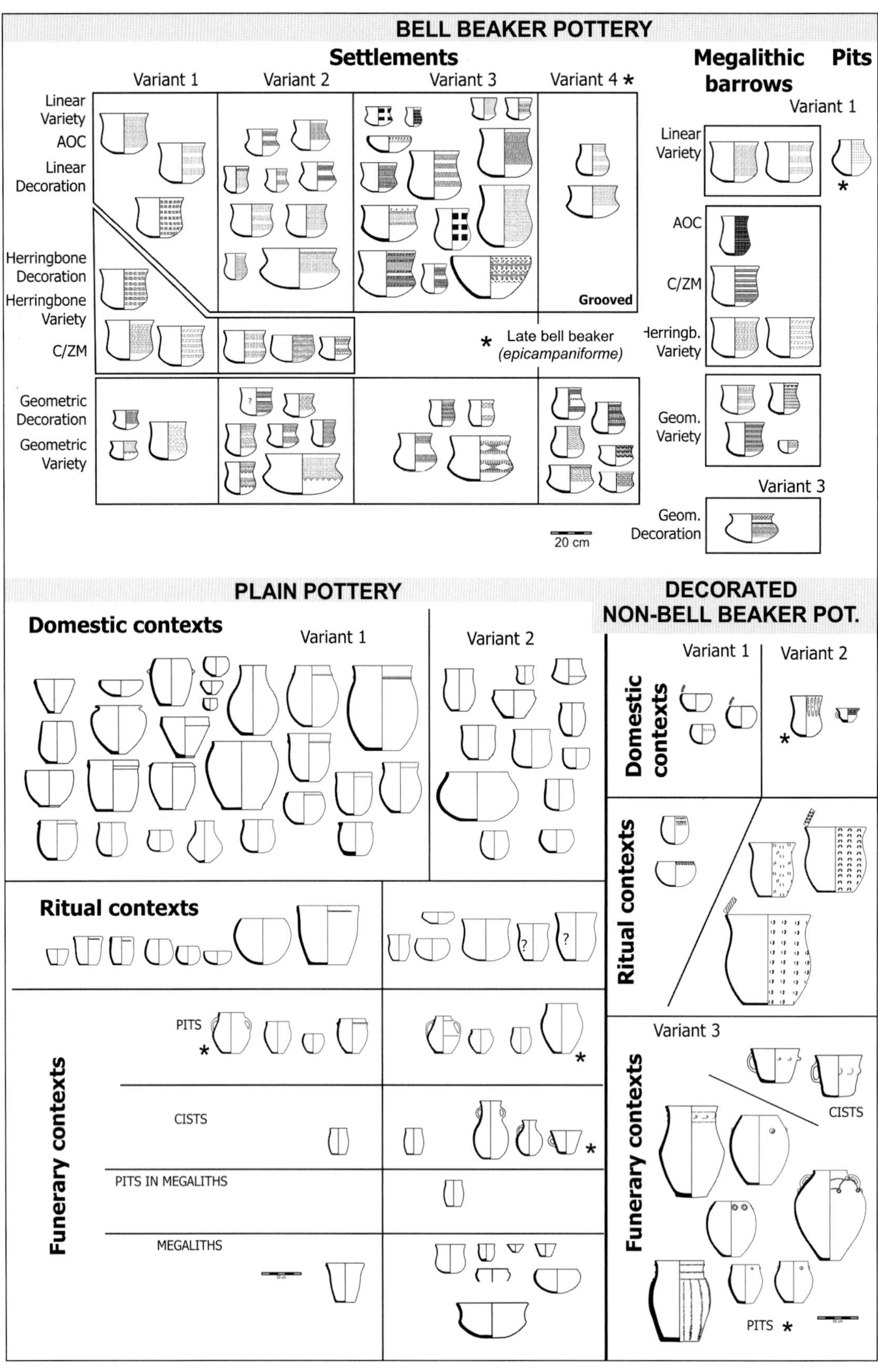

be identified in all of the manufacturing stages (morphological, technical, and decorative). These comprise a decorated Bell Beaker type, a widespread type of undecorated pottery (incorrectly known as 'accompanying' pottery), and another decorated, non-Bell Beaker type. The increased variability in the production of this pottery is an important change, but even more important is the selective contextual use of each category and variant. Regional Bell Beaker pottery was deposited at settlements, the international versions at the re-used megaliths, and late Bell Beakers in exceptional cases in pits (Prieto 2011a).

In the north of Portugal, very few assemblages have been documented, there are no references to undecorated pottery, and the Bell Beaker pottery mainly belongs to the international varieties. It is most commonly found in re-used tumuli, rock shelters, and on some fortified settlements and is associated with periods of reconstruction or destruction, such as at Pastoría or Crasto de Palheiros (Sanches *et al.* 2017). These activities were probably associated with the secondary use of these sites, after they had been abandoned by the original Chalcolithic population.

The analyses carried out on this pottery show that it was manufactured locally from materials occurring within a radius of 7 km from the find spots. If we consider the contexts, the pottery that has been analysed from tombs and ceremonial sites tends to have a greater lithological variety, indicating that the materials may have come from distances of up to 30 km away (Martínez-Cortizas *et al.* 2011). These studies allow us to identify with greater certainty the connections between Galicia and northern Portugal (Prieto & Salanova 2009; Prieto & Lantes 2017) or Asturias and other more distant regions.

Post-Bell Beaker pottery in Galicia and northern Portugal

From 2300/2200 cal BC onwards, the appearance of Bronze Age pottery coincided with the decline and disappearance of Bell Beaker pottery in northern Portugal (Bettencourt 2011), although in recent studies this chronology has been extended a little further to 1900/1800 cal BC (Sanches *et al.* 2017). In Galicia, it is thought that the pottery that was produced at this time overlapped for possibly more than 600 years with Bell Beakers (Prieto 2011a). The majority of vessels are undecorated and of a form and manufacture inherited from and shared with the undecorated wares that 'accompanied' the Bell Beaker pottery.

Asturias and the northern Iberian Peninsula

Asturian ceramics are different to Galicia and the north of Portugal. Here we find what is known as Trespando-type pottery, which is also found in Cantabria (Los Avellanos) and the Basque Country (Santimamiñe). This was initially thought to date from the end of the Chalcolithic period and Early Bronze Age, although it has also been documented in Cantabria in the Mid-Late Bronze Age (Toledo 1999). This pottery has simple profiles, well-finished clays, metope decoration made using incisions and impressions, and designs based on dots and lines (Vega 2011). This pottery has only been found in caves (Ontañón & Armendáriz 2005).

As previously stated, we only know of one site with Bell Beaker pottery in Asturias (Blas & Rodríguez 2015) which has very similar features to the regional Galician pottery, although only a few fragmented pieces have been found. In the east of Cantabria corded Bell Beaker pottery is associated with settlements, while the cord-impressed ware is associated with tombs. The incised Bell Beaker pottery extends towards the west in funerary contexts yet is absent in the central and virtually absent in the western zones. A duality has been recently observed in the distribution of this pottery, with Bell Beaker pottery being concentrated in the eastern zone and ending at Santander, with Trespando-type pottery (and Palmela points) in the western zone, reaching as far as Guernica (Vega 2011).

Stone tools

Stone tools have not been studied in any real detail in the region, probably because the most abundant raw material used for chipped stone tools was quartz and it is difficult to define any typologies in this medium. Also, until the 1980s, quartz was not collected from excavations as it was not considered anthropogenic. The studies that have been carried out are mainly typological rarely including microspatial and contextual analyses. This means that it is currently impossible to identify the existence of diachronic morpho-typological and technological changes from the 4th to 2nd millennium BC. Despite this, the elements that were used in pre-Bell Beaker and Bell Beaker sites can be defined in general terms.

As well as quartz, quartzite, slate, or schist, rock crystal, tourmaline and flint were utilised. The latter is very rare and is normally considered to have been imported. They constitute artefact types that are long-lived and so far unsuited to typo-chronology (Rodríguez & Fábregas 2011). Re-worked artefacts, such as knives, scrapers, and microliths are rare. Arrowheads are also found in the settlements mainly from the middle of the 3rd millennium BC, made of quartz, quartzite, or slate. The most representative types have a straight or concave base, with rarer convex or triangular based types. These are closely associated with funerary contexts and are rarely found in Galicia (Rodríguez & Fábregas 2011). A few technological studies have identified bipolar knapping from the Early Neolithic in Regueiriño (Prieto *et al.* 2005b), although it has also been identified in pre-Bell Beaker sites such as Montenegro (Tabares & Baqueiro 2005) and Bell Beaker sites such as A Devesa de Abaixo-Os Torradoiros (Prieto *et al.* 2005a) and Zarra de Xoacín, which was occupied in both the pre-Bell Beaker and Bell Beaker periods (Aboal *et al.* 2004–5).

There is greater variety amongst polished stone tools (Fig. 2.5), although these are generally fewer in number. The main raw materials are granite, schist, and amphibolite, with a predominance of tools such as axes, maceheads, adzes and hoes, which were associated with individual burials prior to the arrival of Bell Beaker pottery (Rodríguez & Fábregas 2011; Bettencourt 2011). The Marabiu macehead found in Asturias is interesting as its raw material originates in Galicia (Blas & Corretgé 2001).

Artefacts associated with processing foodstuffs such as grinding stones are common on settlements but are also found in cist tombs mixed with the rubble fill. Other artefacts such as abrasive wood-working tools, adornments, or small stelae are also found deposited in tombs, together with artefacts of unknown purpose such as stone balls.

In the tombs, unlike in the domestic sites, artefacts seem to be more opulent, often imported, with fewer chipped elements (except arrowheads), and a preference for polished tools such as axes or hammers (Fábregas 1991–2; Rodríguez & Fábregas 2011; Sanches *et al.* 2017). During the 2nd millennium BC, the number of stone artefacts found in funerary contexts drastically decreased, with grave goods now being limited to certain types of ornaments or polished artefacts, such as bracers (Rodríguez & Fábregas 2011).

Models of occupation of inhabited spaces. The early phases of monumentality of the habitat and its diversity

The 3rd millennium BC in this region is characterised by three domestic models, although to a different degree in different areas. Caves and rock shelters continued to be occupied. Unenclosed settlements continued to be built, and, as a new element of the Chalcolithic period, two new types of fortified settlement appear: some walled and built of stone, and others comprising palisades and ditches (Fig. 2.6). Studies have mainly focused on the environmental setting of the settlement and on a description of the structures found (pits, hearths, trenches, houses, storage areas) but no information is available on the internal organisation of these sites, as few large-scale excavations have been carried out, there are few publications, and access to the data is limited.

'Walled' fortified settlements

From the Chalcolithic period, settlements became more important and grew significantly in size (Jorge 1986) resulting in the fortified settlements that are known throughout much of the Iberian Peninsula. It is inevitable that attention continues to be focused on these iconic sites that made it possible to identify territories, with the paradigmatic examples of Los Millares, Vila Nova de São Pedro and Zambujal (Jorge 1994). The fortified settlements, also known as 'walled areas' in Portugal, appeared in the first half of the 3rd millennium BC, and comprise monumental settlements with fortifications of varying size and complexity. They are also known as hill forts, as they are located on hilltops that command spectacular views. They are the prototype of the settlements that characterises the Chalcolithic period, and the only known settlement model for the north of Portugal, especially the north-east (Bettencourt 2011). This is the area where the first examples were discovered and excavated, and some

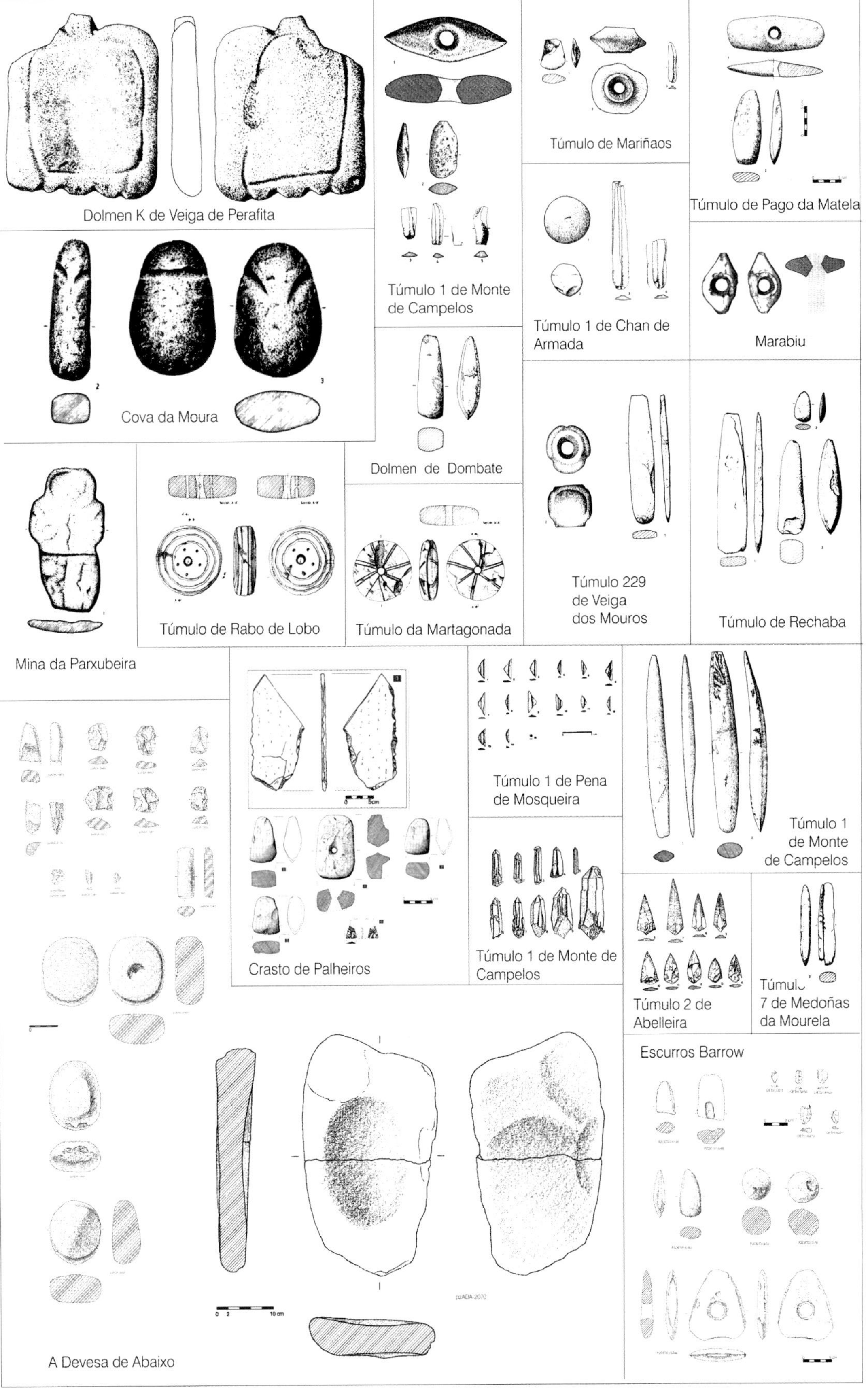

Figure 2.5: Selection of stone items from north-west Iberia. Devesa de Abaixo (Prieto et al. *2005a); Escurros (based on Parga & Prieto 2010); Crasto de Palheiros (based on Sanches* et al. *2017); Marabiu (based on Blas & Corretgé 2001); and the remaining elements (based on Fábregas 1991–2)*

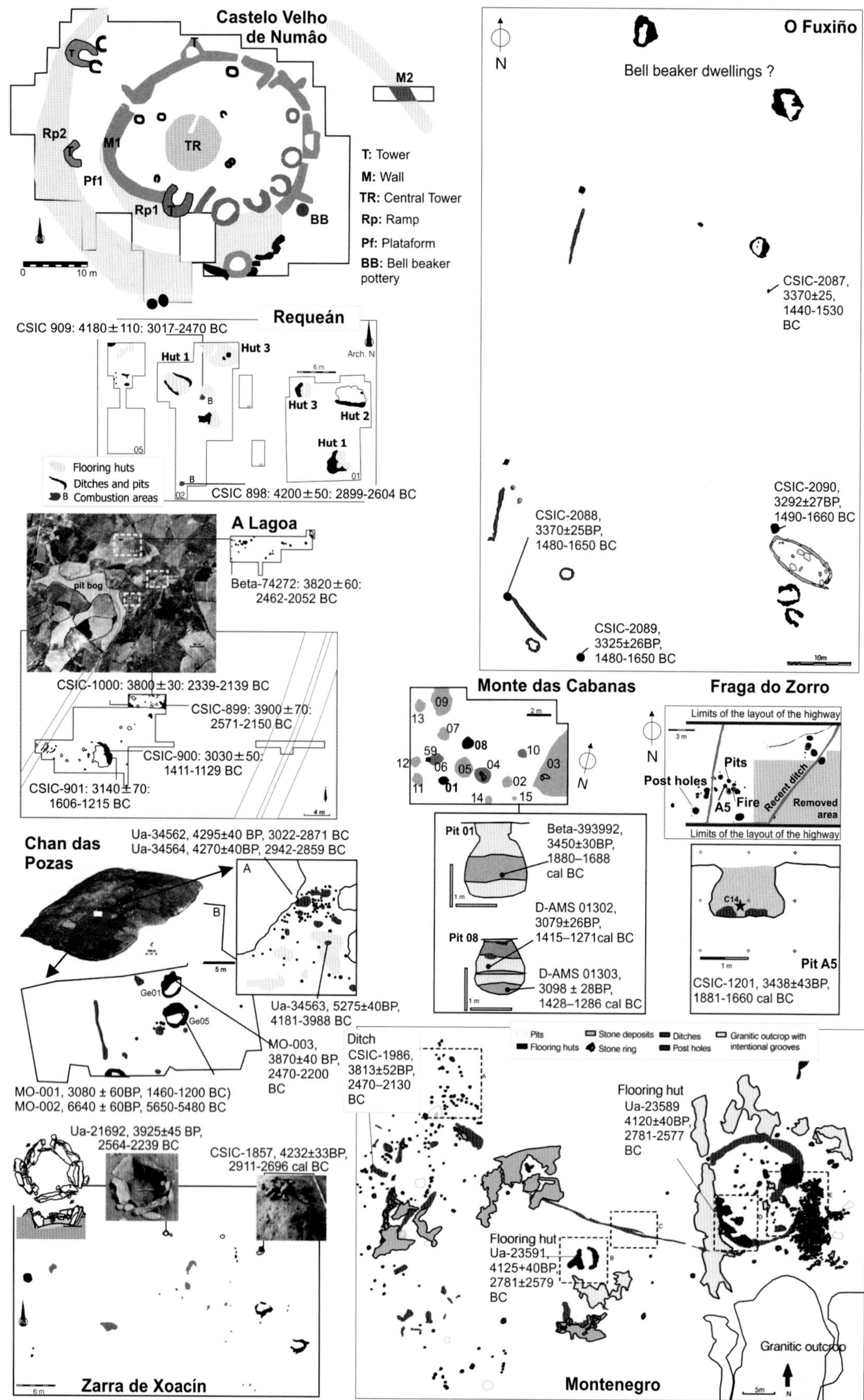

Figure 2.6: Plans showing settlements in the north-western Iberian Peninsula. Castelo Velho (based on Jorge 2004); Galician sites (based on different studies by Prieto 2011a; 2013a; Gianotti et al. *2011, Vidal 2011)*

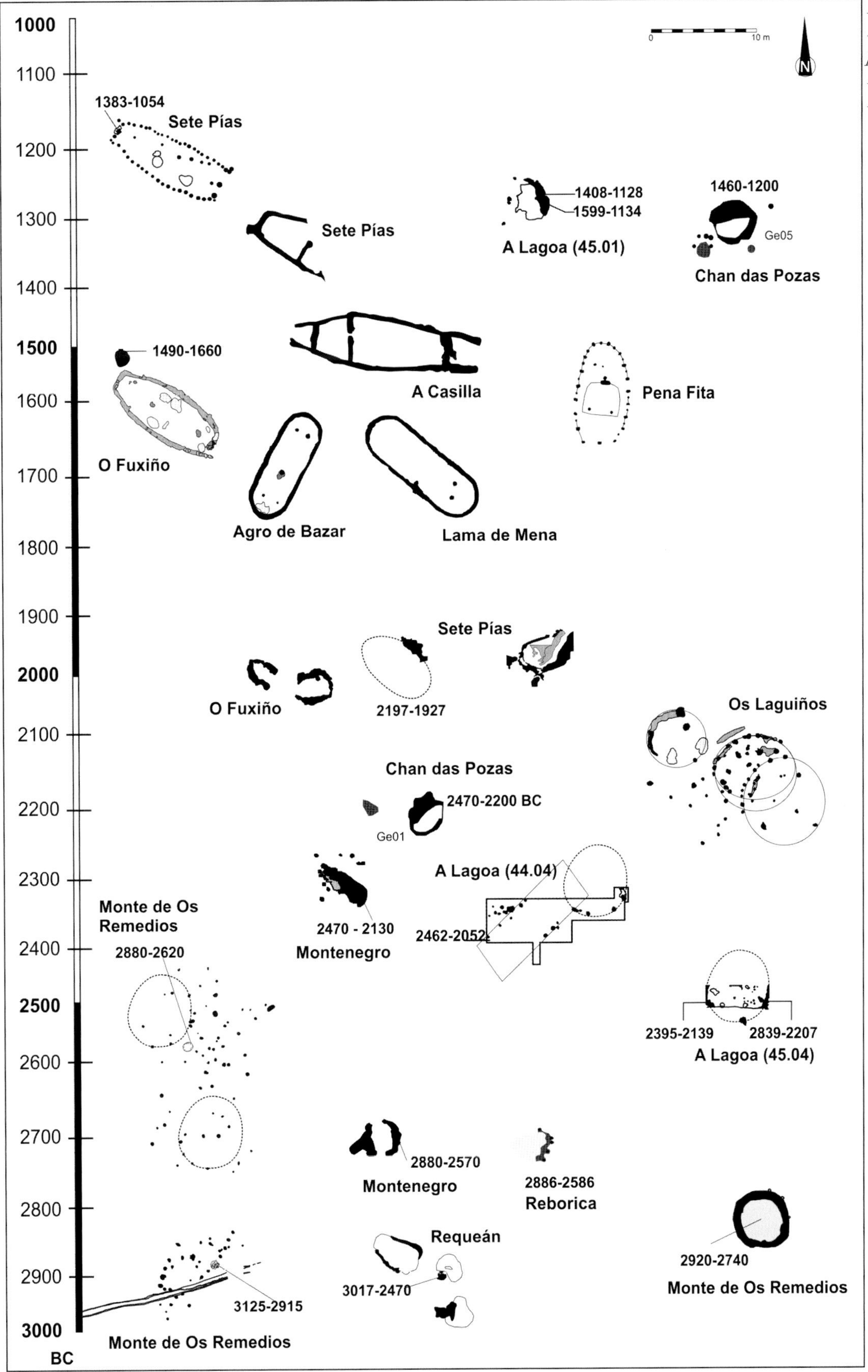

Figure 2.7: Evolutionary sequence of the ground plan of dwellings from Late Neolithic to Late Bronze Age

produced Bell Beaker pottery from their construction phases such as Castelo Velho de Freixo de Numão, or Crasto de Palheiros. The earliest dates from the upper platform of the enclosure of Crasto de Palheiros, with 18 Bell Beaker vessels of different kinds fall between 2800–2400 cal BC (Sanches 2008). The houses were made of stone, like the rest of the settlement, although they have not been described in reports.

In Galicia, similar sites have begun to be identified. They are found on the banks of the River Miño, close to the Portuguese border, and possibly in the Morrazo Peninsula (the site of Mesa de Montes). Only trial trenching has been carried out, and none of them have yet been excavated on a large scale.

Ditched settlements

These well-known megasites are becoming increasingly common in the centre and south of the Iberian Peninsula (see Garrido-Pena, and Valera *et al.* this volume). They first appear in the first half of the 3rd millennium BC, with several palisades that enclose and protect large, collective buildings, tombs, and areas used for different purposes. They date from the pre-Bell Beaker Chalcolithic in the central Duero valley (Delibes *et al.* 2014), the Central Plateau (Díaz del Río 2006) and south-western Iberia. In north-west Iberia, only one Chalcolithic context is known from the area of Forca, where a fragment of Bell Beaker pottery was found in pit 46, and which was dated to between 2630–2330 cal BC (3980±50 BP, Beta-258088, 2580–2460 cal BC 68.3%, 2630–2300 cal BC 95.4%) (Bettencourt 2011).

A Galician site that might be included in this group is Montenegro, in the Morrazo Peninsula. This is a site that has been interpreted as a ceremonial enclosure dating from the first half of the 3rd millennium (Gianotti *et al.* 2011), as it seems to have been inspired by tumulus architecture. It also has a substantial ditch. Foundations of timber buildings have been found both within and outside the enclosure and they are similar to those described below at Requeán. Sites are being found in Galicia with palisades that enclosed habitation areas, and although the only one that has been dated so far is from the Middle Neolithic, it is most likely that this type of settlement continued in use, as is the case in other areas. This site contains large amounts of Penha-type pottery, together with a large amount of imitation Bell Beaker (Prieto & Lantes 2017), which suggests contacts between the groups.

Caves and rock shelters

In Portugal, the most important cave is in Buraco da Pala (Sanches 1997), where activity has been recorded since the Neolithic, although the most important discovery is associated with Penha-type pottery and imitation Bell Beaker (Prieto & Vazquez 2011). In Galicia, there is still no published Bell Beaker pottery from caves, although some has been found in rock shelters, such as Os Pericos (Vilaseco & Fábregas 2008) or O Cepo (Parga *et al.* 2017). In both cases, only 3–4 fragments have been found, and most of the occupation evidence dated to the Iron Age. Other important sites are Arca dos Penedos (Criado & Vázquez 1982) and O Regueiriño (Prieto 2010) where large numbers of fragments were recovered from two very unusual Bell Beakers. Production areas might also be associated with these sites. In Asturias basins and hearths used for copper extraction have been found in the vicinity of caves as well as more conventional settlements (Blas & Rodríguez 2015).

Unenclosed settlements

In Galicia these sites date from the start of the 3rd millennium BC. Around 30 are known and they are located in rich agricultural valleys. They are almost unknown in Portugal, with the exception of Crasto de Palheiros and Pastoría (Jorge 1986), where fragments of Bell Beaker were found in a destroyed part of the site. These settlements have a certain degree of complexity, and this is the first time that we can refer to organised settlements and house-like structures. We find settlements with groups of two or three houses clustered around a central hearth, such as at Requeán, and the methods of construction that would persist throughout the millennium were introduced at this time (Fig. 2.7). Small spaces with different levels were enclosed using posts or bedding trenches (Figs 2.7 & 2.8). There also appears to be a shape-size ratio, as the smallest structures are circular in shape (4 m^2), the medium sized are oval (between 8–15 m^2), and other boat-shaped structures have started to come to light, for example in Os Remedios, and these represent the largest structures (*c.* 32 m^2) (Fig. 2.8). The chronology of these houses still

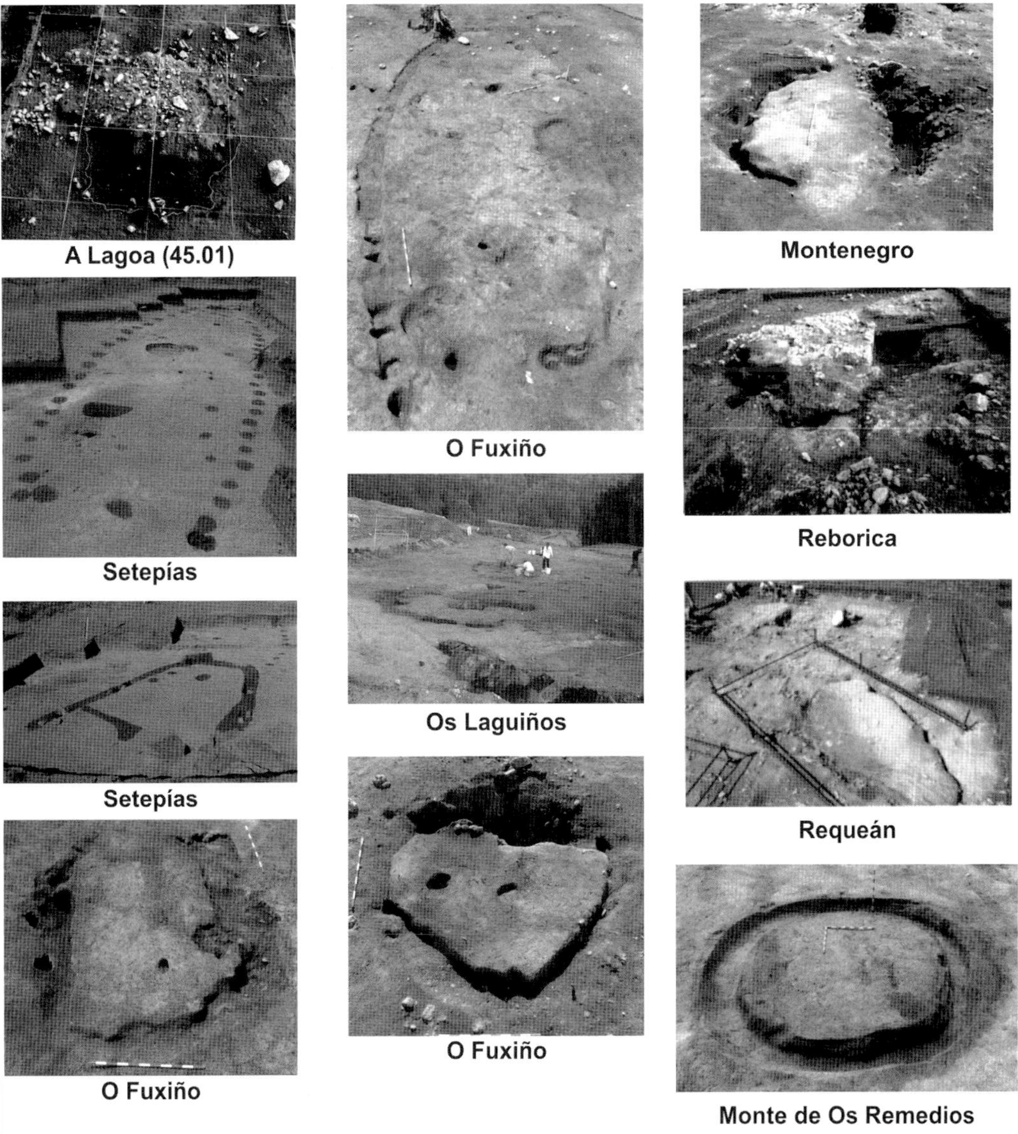

Figure 2.8: Photographs of examples of dwellings from 3rd and 2nd millennia BC in Galacia

has to be refined and they are normally not found together in the same site. There are at least 86 such sites associated with Beaker pottery, although only 17 have been dated by a total of 23 radiocarbon dates. Once again, the majority are in Galicia, and they are quite rare in Portugal.

The settlements that we know from this period comprise small hamlets, which were occupied over long periods of time although we do not know if they were occupied on a seasonal basis, cyclically, or simply sporadically. These numerous but small-sized sites may be the result of a mobile lifestyle (Prieto 2008). They are located in mountainous areas and around wetlands and were involved in the control of livestock. The most typical site in the region is A Lagoa.

Despite a change in the layout, post-hole and bedding trench houses continued to be built although we find a greater variety of shapes and sizes and the size of the houses tends to increase slightly. The circular structures had an area of 7 m^2, while the oval buildings were the same standard size as the Late Neolithic examples, between 8 and 16 m^2 (Figs 2.7 & 2.8).

As previously stated, these sites are difficult to interpret or define precisely as we have hardly any dates, or any clear understanding of their stratification or sequence, however, towards the end of the period, with the late Bell Beaker culture, we have started to identify larger settlements, suggesting greater stability. The houses were larger and more complex and had separate storage spaces, as is the case of Monte das Cabanas in Galicia (Martín *et al.* 2017) and possibly Tapado da Caldeira in Portugal (Jorge 1980).

Apart from the obvious settlements, some similar sites do not seem to have had a strictly domestic function, despite the discovery of apparently domestic assemblages and these are new types of site to the region. Their common denominator is the presence of Bell Beaker pottery that acts as a relative chronological indicator within a site that has produced evidence for repeated human activity over hundreds of years. In the Bell Beaker phase there seems to have been less intense activity at these sites, as structures are absent or limited or highly dispersed, meaning it is impossible to estimate their chronological relationship with the Bell Beaker culture in the absence of absolute dates. Some of these settlements seem to have been locations where festivals or banquets were held, such as at A Devesa do Rei (Vedra, A Coruña) (Aboal *et al.* 2005; Prieto 2011b; Prieto 2011c), or the rubbish dump found in the cemetery of Guidoiro Areoso (Vilagarcía de Arousa) (Rey & Vilaseco 2012), or possibly in the cemetery of A Devesa de Abaixo – Os Torradoiros (Vázquez & Prieto 2015).

Others seem to comprise or incorporate funerary locations that were significant for the Neolithic or Chalcolithic societies. By carrying out activities in these locations, Bell Beaker communities may have helped to strengthen the new social order and they comprise complex archaeological sites. They include As Mamelas (Cano *et al.* 2017), a site with a tumulus that was built in the 4th millennium BC, re-used during the Bell Beaker period, and surrounded by two areas of occupation that were used to different degrees. In both areas, Bell Beaker and Penha-type pottery from the Late Neolithic has been found, and there are numerous associated structures that form a complex palimpsest (hut floors, pits with pottery deposits, hearths, post holes, and bedding trenches). The funerary complex of the dolmen of Dombate is another example (Bello *et al.* 2013; Cebrián *et al.* 2011). This comprised two funerary structures of the 4th millennium BC that were re-used at least twice by Beaker users in the second half of the 3rd millennium. In the surrounding area there are numerous hearth-type structures and other activity areas associated with Bell Beakers, dated to around the end of the 3rd millennium (Pérez *et al.* 2016). This may be associated with a possible settlement enclosed by a substantial ditch which though undated was probably constructed around the start or middle of the 2nd millennium BC (Cebrián *et al.* 2011).

Another type of archaeological complex consists of barrow cemeteries where, at a later stage, the rocks were carved with different types of designs, creating genuinely ritual landscapes. Materials associated with the Bell Beaker period have been found scattered around the vicinity of these monuments. These sites are better known in Galicia and were probably established after the Bell Beaker activity (Seoane *et al.* 2013), although Bouça da Cova da Moura is a recently discovered site in Portugal (Bettencourt *et al.* 2012). Finally, at Saídos das Rozas, tumuli and rock art are arranged within the same area, and Bell Beaker pottery has been found on the surface. It seems that human activity in these locations was short-lived, sporadic, and of varying intensity, with only a very small number of artefacts being found. The archaeological site at Pena Fita (in Lugo) is exceptional, as here Bell Beaker pottery and pottery from later periods has been recovered close to a single petroglyph depicting the ground plan of a longhouse (Vázquez *et al.* 2015).

Finally, there are locations with rock art from the Bell Beaker period, but without any associated artefacts or dates. There are rock carvings with images of weapons (daggers, halberds, and swords), or sites with anthropomorphic stelae or representations of human figures, such as at the site of Peñatú in Asturias. These are probably related to the anthropomorphic stelae that have been documented elsewhere in Europe (Prieto 2013b).

Conclusions

On the basis of this summary, we can no longer accept that Bell Beaker pottery represents an element of continuity that added to the spread of the Chalcolithic in the region, or of the associated processes in economy and social organisation. It is important to understand this in order to prevent the deductive presumption of continuity affecting the way in which the data are recorded because, by considering a uniform whole as being pre-Bell Beaker or Bell Beaker in nature, the studies fail to identify the existence of changes in the archaeological record.

The domestic and funerary spheres changed throughout the 3rd millennium BC, combining a re-interpretation of old formulas with very different new ones. It seems that different types of settlement were preferred in different areas. In Galicia, unenclosed settlements were preferred but the location of these varied between the pre-Bell Beaker and Bell Beaker periods. Northern Portugal is almost exclusively predominated by fortified settlements, although any Bell Beaker settlements *per se* have yet to be discovered. The houses and domestic structures changed little during the whole of the millennium, although some new designs appeared and with a more marked period of change around the middle of the 2nd millennium when longhouses and late Bell Beaker pottery appear. There are also regional differences in construction techniques, as wood was preferred in Galicia, while in Portugal the preferred material was stone.

This change can also be seen in the pottery, where there were not only major differences in the manufacture of Penha-type and Bell Beaker vessels, but also their use seems to have been based on opposing strategies. Even ceremonial sites, which are rare in the first half of the 3rd millennium, multiplied with the arrival of Bell Beaker communities. These changes were also accompanied by significant and powerful environmental transformations that may have brought about a change in the location and internal organisation of the settlements. These now became more oriented towards livestock farming, became smaller than they were in the Late Neolithic, and populations seem to have become more mobile within the territory that they controlled. A change in economic strategies has been tenuously identified one or possibly two centuries prior to the introduction of Bell Beakers in other parts of Europe, though the related settlement changes appear to become more accelerated with the arrival of Bell Beaker communities in this and other regions (Prieto 2008)

One of the key elements that helped support the Bell Beaker socio-political system in time and space must have been based on social, economic, political, and symbolic strategies that gave meaning to this way of life. In the end, the key lay in controlling the mechanisms of power that linked these strategies and made them interdependent, and by developing and reinforcing these mechanisms through the creation of new ways of appropriating space at all levels of social life.

Despite only dealing with a limited number of topics, this study has made it clear that the social processes that developed in the north-west Iberian Peninsula may seem to have been quite different between Asturias, Galicia, and northern Portugal, although as we have discovered more sites these regional differences have become less evident, especially in the latter two regions.

Acknowledgements

I am extremely grateful to Alex M. Gibson for his hard work in compiling the texts for this volume, and especially his help in improving this article. This study is included in the project titled *A study of social change in the third and second millennia BC in the north-west Iberian Peninsula, based on mixed context sites* (HAR2012-34029), part of the National R+D+I Plan of the Spanish Ministry of Economy and Competitiveness.

References

Aboal Fernández, R., Ayán Vila, X., Criado Boado, F., Prieto Martínez, M.P. & Tabarés Domínguez, M. 2005. Yacimientos sin estratigrafía: Devesa do Rei, ¿un sitio cultual de la Prehistoria Reciente y la Protohistoria de Galicia? *Trabajos de Prehistoria* 62 (2), 165–80

Aboal Fernández, R., Baqueiro Vidal, S., Castro Hierro, V., Prieto Martínez, M.P. & Tabarés Domínguez, M. 2004–5. El yacimiento del III milenio BC de Zarra de Xoacín (Lalín, Pontevedra). *Lancia* 6, 37–58

Barceló, J.A., Bogdanovic, I. & Morell, B. (eds), 2017. *Actas del Congreso de Cronometrías Para la Historia de la Península Ibérica (IberCrono 2016), Barcelona, Spain, September 17–19, 2016. CEUR-WS*, Vol 2024 (urn:nbn:de:0074-2024-4). http://ceur-ws.org/Vol-2024/

Bello Diéguez, J.M., Lestón Gómez, M. & Prieto Martínez, M.P. 2013. The Dolmen of Dombate in its Bell Beaker phase. Ceramic styles and occupation of space. In Prieto Martínez & Salanova 2013, 21–30

Bettencourt, A.M.S. 2011. El vaso campaniforme en el Norte de Portugal. Contextos, cronologías y significados. In Prieto Martínez & Salanova 2011, 363–74

Bettencourt, A.M.S., Alves L.B., Ribeiro, A.T. & Menezes, R.T. 2012. Gravuras rupestres da Bouça da Cova da Moura (Ardegães, Maia, Norte de Portugal), no contexto da Pré-historia Recente da bacia do Leça. *Gallaecia* 31, 47–62

Blanco Chao, R., Costa Casais, M., Martínez Cortizas, A., Pérez Alberti, A. & Vázquez Paz, M. 2002. Holocene evolution on Galician coast (NW Spain): an example of paraglacial dynamics. *Quaternary International* 93–4, 149–59

Blas Cortina, M.A. & Corretgé Castañon, L.G. 2001. El origen geológico, galaico, del ejemplar de Marabiu (Teverga, Asturias) y consideraciones culturales sobre los útiles-arma, calificados de 'hachas nórdicas', del noroeste ibérico. *Trabajos de Prehistoria* 58 (2), 143–58

Blas Cortina, M.A. & Rodríguez del Cueto, F.G. 2015. La cuestión campaniforme en el Cantábrico Central y las minas de cobre prehistóricas de la sierra del Áramo. *CuPAUAM* 41, 165–79

Cano Pan J., Prieto Martínez, M.P. & Vázquez Liz, P. 2017. El yacimiento de As Mamelas (Sanxenxo, Pontevedra): las fases de actividad en la prehistoria reciente. In Barceló, Bogdanovic & Morell 2017, 67–87

Cebrián, F., Yañez, J., Lestón, M., Vidal, F. & Carrera, F. 2011. *El dolmen de Dombate. Arqueología, restauración, arquitectura.* A Coruña: Diputación de A Coruña

Criado Boado, F. & Cabreras Domínguez, E. (coords.). 2005. *Obras públicas e patrimonio: Estudio arqueolóxico do Corredor do Morrazo* (TAPA 35). Santiago de Compostela: CSIC

Criado Boado, F. & Vázquez Varela, X.M. 1982. *La cerámica campaniforme en Galicia.* A Coruña: Edicións O Castro

Criado Boado, Felipe (dir.), Bonilla Rodríguez, A., Cerqueiro Landín, D., Díaz Vázquez, M., González Méndez, M., Infante Roura, F., Méndez Fernández, F., Penedo Romero, R., Rodríguez Puentes, E. & Vaquero Lastres, J. 1991. *Arqueología del paisaje, el área del Bocelo-Furelos entre los tiempos paleolíticos y medievales (campañas de 1987, 1988 y 1989).* Santiago de Compostela: Dirección Xeral do Patrimonio Histórico e Documental

Delibes de Castro, G., García García, M., Olmo Martín, J. & Santiago Pardo, J. 2014. *Recintos de fosos calcolíticos del valle medio del Duero. Arqueología aérea y espacial.* Valladolid: Studia Archaeologica 100-Universidad de Valladolid

Díaz del Río, P. 2006. Chapter 6. An appraisal of social inequalities in Central Iberia (*c.* 5300–1600 cal BC). In Diaz del Río, P. & García Sanjuán, L. (eds), *Social Inequality in Iberian Late Prehistory*, 67–79. Oxford: BAR International Series 1525

Eguileta Franco, J.M. 1999. *A Baixa Limia galega na Prehistoria Recente: arqueoloxía dunha paisaxe da Galicia interior.* Ourense: Diputación Provincial de Ourense.

Fábregas Valcarce, R. 1991–1992. *Megalitismo en el Noroeste de la Península Ibérica. Tipología y secuencia de los materiales líticos.* Madrid: Universidad Nacional de Educación a Distancia

Fábregas Valcarce, R., Martínez Cortizas, A., Blanco Chao, R. & Chesworth, W. 2003. Environmental change and social dynamics in the second–third millenuium BC in NW Iberia. *Journal of Archaeological Sciences* 30, 859–71

Gianotti, C., Mañana-Borrazás, P., Criado-Boado, F. & López-Romero, E. 2011. Deconstructing Neolithic Monumental Space: the Montenegro Enclosure in Galicia (Northwest Iberia). *Cambridge Archaeological Journal* 21 (3), 391–406

Jorge, S.O. 1980. A Estação Arqueológica do Tapado da Caldeira (Baião), *Portugália* NS, I, 29–50

Jorge, S.O. 1986. *Povoados da Pré-história Recente (III.º – inícios do II.º Milénios AC) da Região de Chaves – V.ª P.ª de Aguiar.* Porto: Instituto de Arqueologia da Faculdade de Letras da Universidade do Porto

Jorge, S.O. 1994. Colónias, fortificaçôes, lugares monumentalizados. Trajectória das concepçôes sobre um tema do calcolítico peninsular. *Revista da Facultade de Letras de Porto* XI, 447–546

Jorge, S.O. 2004. O sítio como mediador de sentido. Castelo Velho de Freixo de Numão: um recinto monumental pré-histórico do Norte de Portugal. In *Estudos em Homenagem a Luís António de Oliveira Ramos*, 583–611. Porto: Facultade de Letras da Universidade do Porto

López Sáez, J.A., Carrión Marco, Y., López Merino, L., Kaal J., Costa Casáis, M. & Martínez Cortizas, A., 2011. Cambios ambientales en el Noroeste peninsular durante el campaniforme (2800–1400 cal. BC). In Prieto Martínez & Salanova 2011, 375–81

Martín Seijo, M., Tereso, J.P., Bettencourt, A.M.S., Sampaio, H.A., Abad Vidal, E. & Vidal Caeiro, L. 2017 Socio-ecology of Early and Middle Bronze Age communities in the northwest Atlantic region of Iberia: Wood resources procurement and forest management. *Quaternary International* 437, 90–101

Martínez Cortizas, A., Pontevedra Pombal, X., García-Rodeja, E., Nóvoa Muñoz, J.C. & Shotyk, W. 1999. Mercury in a Spanish peat bog: archive of climate change and atmospheric metal deposition. *Science* 284, 939–42

Martínez Cortizas, A., Costa Casais, M. & López Sáez, J.A. 2009a. Environmental change in NW Iberia between 7000 and 500 cal. BC. *Quaternary International* 200, 77–89

Martínez Cortizas, A., Kaal, J., Costa Casais, M. & Chesworth, W. 2009b. Human activities and Holocene environmental change in NW Spain. In Sánchez Díaz, J. & Asíns, S. (eds), *Control de la Degradación de los Suelos y Cambio Global. Centro de Investigaciones sobre Desertificacion*, 193–208. Valencia: CSIC, Universitat de València, Generalitat Valenciana

Martínez Cortizas, A., Lantes Suárez, O. & Prieto Martínez, M.P. 2011. Cerámica campaniforme del NW de la Península Ibérica. Indagando en sus materias primas, elecciones tecnológicas y procedencia. In Prieto Martínez & Salanova 2011, 309–27

Nonat, L. 2017. Monde funéraire de l'Âge du Bronze Ancien et Moyen de la Façade Nord de l'Espagne jusqu'au Sud-Ouest de la France: Identités et espaces. Unpubl. PhD thesis, L'Université de Pau et des Pays de l'Adour and Universidad de Santiago de Compostela

Ontañón, R. & Armendáriz, A. 2005. Cuevas y megalitos: los contextos sepulcrales colectivos en la Prehistoria reciente cantábrica. *Munibe* 57, 275–86

Parga Castro, A., Prieto Martínez, M.P. & Sánchez Blanco, F. 2017. Datación de un yacimiento de la Edad del Hierro no fortificado en Galicia: el caso de O Cepo (San Cibrao de Viñas, Ourense). In Barceló, Bogdanovic & Morell 2017, 260–71

Pérez Díaz S., López Sáez, J.A. & Lestón Gómez, M. 2016. Paisajes del megalitismo. Paleambiente y antropización en el entorno del conjunto arqueológico de Dombate (A Coruña). *Arpi* 5: 27–46

Prieto Martínez, M.P. 2007. Volviendo a un mismo lugar: recipientes y espacios en un monumento megalítico gallego (Noroeste de España). *Revista Portuguesa de Arqueologia* 10 (2), 101–25

Prieto Martínez, M.P. 2008. Bell Beakers communities in Thy. The first Bronze Age society in Denmark. *Norwegian Archaeological Review* 41 (2), 115–58

Prieto Martínez, M.P. 2009. From Galicia to the Iberian Peninsula: Neolithic ceramics and traditions. In D. Gheorghiu (ed.), *Early farmers, Late Foragers and Ceramic traditions. On the beginning of pottery in Europe*, 116–49. Cambridge: Cambridge Scholar Press

Prieto Martínez, M.P. 2010. La cerámica de O Regueiriño (Moaña, Pontevedra). Nueva luz sobre el neolítico en Galicia. *Gallaecia* 29, 63–82

Prieto Martínez, M.P. 2011a. La alfarería de las comunidades campaniformes en Galicia. Contextos, cronologías y estilo. In Prieto Martínez & Salanova 2011, 345–61

Prieto Martínez, M.P. 2011b. Devesa do Rei, contribución del estudio cerámico a la interpretación de la ocupación campaniforme. In Prieto Martínez & Salanova 2011, 163–9

Prieto Martínez, M.P. 2011c. Vasos troncocónicos y cerveza en contextos campaniformes de Galicia. La cista de A Forxa como ejemplo. In Prieto Martínez & Salanova 2011, 119–125

Prieto Martínez, M.P. 2013. What underlies behind the homogeneity of Galician Bell Beaker style? In Prieto Martínez & Salanova 2013, 209–250

Prieto Martínez, M.P. & Criado Boado, F. (eds), 2010. *Reconstruyendo la historia de la comarca del Ulla-Deza (Galicia, España). Escenarios arqueológicos del pasado.* TAPA 41. Madrid: Closas-Orcoyen S.L

Prieto Martínez, M.P. & Lantes Suárez, O. 2017. Mobility in late Prehistory in Galicia: a preliminary interpretation from pottery. In Besse, M. & Guilaine, J. (eds), *Materials, productions, exchange network and their impact on the societies of Neolithic Europe, Proceedings of the XVII UISPP World Congress (1–7 September 2014, Burgos, Spain), vol. 13/Session A25a*, 51–67. Oxford: Archaeopress Archaeology

Prieto Martínez, M.P. & Salanova L. 2009. Coquilles et Campaniforme en Galice et en Bretagne: mécanismes de circulation et stratégies identitaires. *Bulletin de la Société Préhistorique Française* 106 (1), 73–93

Prieto Martínez, M.P. & Salavona, L. (eds), 2011. *Las Comunidades Campaniformes en Galicia. Cambios sociales en el III y II milenios BC en el NW de la Península Ibérica.* Pontevedra: Diputación de Pontevedra

Prieto Martínez, M.P. & Salavona, L. (eds), 2013. *Current researches on Bell Beakers. Proceedings of the 15th International Bell Beaker Conference: From Atlantic to Ural. 5th–9th May 2011, Poio-Pontevedra, Galicia, Spain.* Santiago de Compostela: Copynino-Centro de Impresión Digital

Prieto Martínez, M.P. & Vázquez Liz, P. 2011. La cerámica campaniforme de la medorra 2 de Roza das Aveas (Outeiro de Rei, Lugo). In Prieto Martínez & Salanova 2011, 101–4

Prieto Martínez, M.P., Tabarés Domínguez, M. & Baqueiro Vidal, S. 2005a. Estudio de la cultura material de A Devesa de Abaixo-Os Torradoiros. In Criado & Cabrejas 2005, 120–4

Prieto Martínez, M. P., Tabarés Domínguez, M. & Baqueiro Vidal, S. 2005b. Estudio de la cultura material del yacimiento de O Regueiriño. In Criado & Cabrejas 2005, 113–8

Prieto Martínez, M.P. & Vázquez Collazo, S. 2011. Campaniformes singulares ¿imitación u ocultación (diferenciación) de la identidad?. In Prieto Martínez & Salanova 2011, 267–74

Rey García J.M. *&* Vilaseco Vázquez, X.I. 2012. Guidoiro Areoso. Megalithic cemetery and prehistoric settlement in the Ría de Arousa (Galicia, NW Spain). In Campar Almeida, A., Bettencourt, A.M.S., Moura, D., Monteiro-Rodrigues, S. and Caetano Alves M.I. (eds), *Environmental changes and human interaction along the western Atlantic edge. Mudanças ambientais e interação humana na fachada atlântica ocidental*, 243–58. Coimbra: Coimbra Associação Portuguesa para o Estudo do Quaternário

Rodríguez Rellán, C. *&* Fábregas Valcarce, R. 2011. La industria lítica en el Noroeste de la península Ibérica durante el III y II milenios BC. In Prieto Martínez & Salanova 2011, 249–57

Salanova, L. 2000. *La question du campaniforme en France et dans les Iles anglonormandes: productions, chronologie et rôles d'un standard céramique.* Paris: Coédition Société Préhistorique Française et Comité des Travaux Historiques et Scientifiques.

Sanches, M.J. 1997. *Préhistória Recente de Trás-os-Montes e Alto Douro.* Porto: Sociedade Portuguesa de Antropologia e Etnologia

Sanches, M.J. 2008. *O Crasto de Palheiros Fragada do Crasto, Murça, Portugal.* Rga: Municipio de Murça

Sanches, M.J., Barbosa, M.H.L. & Vieira A.M.F. 2017. Bell Beaker contexts in Portugal: the Northern and the Douro región basin. In Victor S. Gonçalves (ed.), *Sinos e taças. Junto ao océano e mais longe. Aspectos da presença campaniforme na Península Ibérica*, 239–57. Lisboa: Estudos e Memorias 10

Seoane-Veiga, Y., Prieto Martínez, M.P. & Dal Zovo, C. 2013. Bell Beaker findings in rock art contexts. In Prieto Martínez & Salanova 2013, 31–40

Tabarés Domínguez, M. & Baqueiro Vidal, S. 2005. Estudo da cultura material do xacemento de Montenegro. In Criado & Cabrejas 2005, 117–9

Toledo Cañamero, C. 1999. Las decoraciones en la producción cerámica de la Edad del Bronce en Cantabria. *Nivel Cero* 6–7, 85–99

Vázquez Liz, P., Prieto Martínez, M.P. & Núñez Jato, J.F. 2015. El pasado olvidado: El sitio del II y I milenio BC de Pena Fita (Adai, Lugo) en el contexto de las 'longhouses' del NW peninsular. *Gallaecia* 34, 9–56

Vega Maeso, C. 2011. La cerámica calcolítica en la región cantábrica. Los restos de la cueva de la Llana, Andrín, Asturias. *Estrat Critic* 5 (2), 335–9

Vidal Lojo, M.P. 2011. O Fuxiño: un asentamiento de la Edad del Bronce con campaniforme. In Prieto Martínez & Salanova 2011, 31–8

Vilaseco Vázquez, X.I. & Fábregas Valcarce, R. 2008. Dos finais do II milenio A.C. á Segunda Idade do Ferro: o asentamento fortificado de Os Pericos (Ribeira, A Coruña). *Gallaecia* 27, 89–112

3

Living with Beakers in the interior of Iberia

Rafael Garrido-Pena

'serán ceniza, mas tendrán sentido;
polvo serán, mas polvo enamorado'.

To my father, in loving memory

What is a 'Beaker settlement'?

The traditional 'cultural' view of Bell Beakers saw them as the remains of a singular culture, an ethnic group, or even a racial variety: the famous 'Beaker folk'. Just a few decorated potsherds amongst thousands of material items were enough to ensure the 'cultural' identification of a tomb or settlement as 'Beaker'. However, since Clarke (1976) this vision of Beakers has been criticised (Garrido-Pena 2000, 12–16), and an alternative social perspective has been argued, considering them as prestige items, exchanged and consumed by elites to reinforce their position. Beakers can therefore be viewed as a symptom of certain processes leading towards the emergence of social ranking in different parts of Western Europe. This hypothesis established the new standard and widespread interpretation of Beakers, notably successful in recent years (Garrido-Pena 2014a; 2014b) In fact, Clarke (1976, 472–74) established two broad categories of settlements based on the abundance of Beaker finds. Type A settlements had a high density of Beakers sherds (15–30% of the ceramic assemblage), usually found in regions with both a large concentration of Beaker sites and long chronological sequences, which presumably represented the core areas of origin. Type B habitats, where Beakers only represented 1–10% of the assemblage are located in regions with a lower density of sites. This may be tentative or simplistic but in his vision of Beakers as luxury products, it was necessary to distinguish the core production areas from the other regions where they were acquired.

Since Sherratt (1987), Beaker pottery has also been connected with the consumption of alcoholic beverages. Beakers were interpreted as special vessels involved in the consumption of food and drinks, in significant ceremonial contexts of social value such as funerals (*inter alia* Garrido-Pena *et al.* 2011). Case (1995) criticised this stereotypic vision stressing that many Beakers, especially in domestic contexts, had very large volumes incompatible with drinking rituals and the great range of pot sizes might suggest a wide range of functions.

Nevertheless, it is important to note that rituals were also part of everyday life in prehistoric societies, even in mundane subsistence tasks (Bradley 2005). It is also obvious that ritual commensality ceremonies

Figure 3.1: (opposite page) Pre-Bell Beaker Chalcolithic domestic structures: 1 – The enclosure and ditch section at Casetón de La Era (Matallana, Valladolid) (after Crespo et al. *2015); 2 – Fuente de la Mora (Leganés, Madrid) and; 3 – Gózquez de Arriba (San Martín de la Vega, Madrid) (after Díaz del Río 2003)*

were not exclusive to burials (hospitality rituals, feasts, marriages, rites of passage, etc.). Settlements, therefore, are a potential scenario for these rituals, and Beaker vessels could be found amongst other domestic evidence, as they were used for the dead and by the living. Moreover, the scarcity of Beaker materials in most of these habitats may be an indication of the regular but exceptional character of the activities deployed with them, probably far from the usual tasks of everyday subsistence (Rojo *et al.* 2008).

Consequently, those groups were more likely people 'with Beakers' than 'Beaker peoples', and not 'Beaker settlements', but 'settlements with Beakers' (See Valera *et al.* this volume). Domestic Beakers could then be interpreted as just the remains of regular and important ceremonial activities. In fact, the recent ancient DNA studies across Western Europe showed no signs of a genetically homogeneous population compatible with 'migrant folk' (Olalde *et al.* 2018), but a diversity of traits and origins.

Settlement patterns and domestic structures during the Late Neolithic – Early Copper Age in the Spanish Meseta (*c.* 3000–2500 BC)

It was commonly held that in the 3rd millennium BC there were still mobile populations practising a pastoral economy, with scarce and fragile settlement structures. These were also in intensively cultivated areas where sites were severely damaged by modern ploughing and where less archaeological research had been undertaken: research has been focused on peripheral regions with more spectacular finds such as the south-eastern fortified villages of Los Millares type. The few sites so far discovered had produced materials with parallels in south-eastern Iberia (Martínez 1984) and especially Portugal (Delibes *et al.* 1995), but in terms of structural evidence, there were only a few circular pits of unclear function, and almost no signs of permanent structures, palisades or any other means of site delimitation.

Research in the Duero Basin began to change this picture through both excavations, such as at the famous site of Las Pozas (Zamora), and aerial photography that located new types of monument such as large circular enclosures (Delibes *et al.* 2014) that have also been discovered in the Tagus Basin (Díaz del Río 2003) (Fig. 3.1). It became clear that Chalcolithic societies in central Iberia were fully sedentary as already noted in earlier related studies (Delibes *et al.* 1995; Garrido-Pena 2006). The archaeological inventories developed in different areas have listed several hundred surface sites clustered beside the main rivers and streams. We now know that the area was densely populated during the 3rd millennium (Fig. 3.2), with settlement patterns lacking signs of clear centralisation or hierarchy, but rather comprising small autonomous agro-pastoral villages connected through extensive exchange networks.

Settlements are located mainly in fertile lowlands near water courses, but also occur on gentle slopes and hills. They are extensive open areas with negative structures excavated into the bedrock, mainly numerous circular pits (sometimes hundreds) containing domestic debris. We can also identify different chronological phases in those settlements across the 3rd and 2nd millennia BC, and in occupation spreads (Delibes *et al.* 2014, 8), sometimes of several hectares, where pits from various periods appear in close proximity. This is a clear indication of the continuity of settlement patterns during the Copper and Bronze Ages.

Amongst these accumulations of pits, other domestic structures are occasionally discovered comprising mainly huts and enclosures. The enclosures have circular singular or multiple concentric ditches of enigmatic form and rarely delimit the whole site given that the pits are usually found both inside and outside the perimeters (Fig. 3.1). This sort of enclosure is also known in other parts of Iberia, such as in the south-west, where they are much larger, extending to hundreds of hectares in the case of Valencina de la Concepción or Marroquíes Bajos. Our examples are much more modest, exceptionally over one hectare, such as the Madrid sites of Fuente de la Mora, Gózquez de Arriba, Las Matillas, Humanejos, Polvoranca-M50, Los Badenes, La Cuadrá, El Juncal, etc. (Díaz del Río 2003, Balsera 2017, 213–14), or El Casetón de la Era in Valladolid (Crespo *et al.* 2015, Delibes *et al.* 2014) (Fig. 3.1). Perhaps the only exception is Camino de las

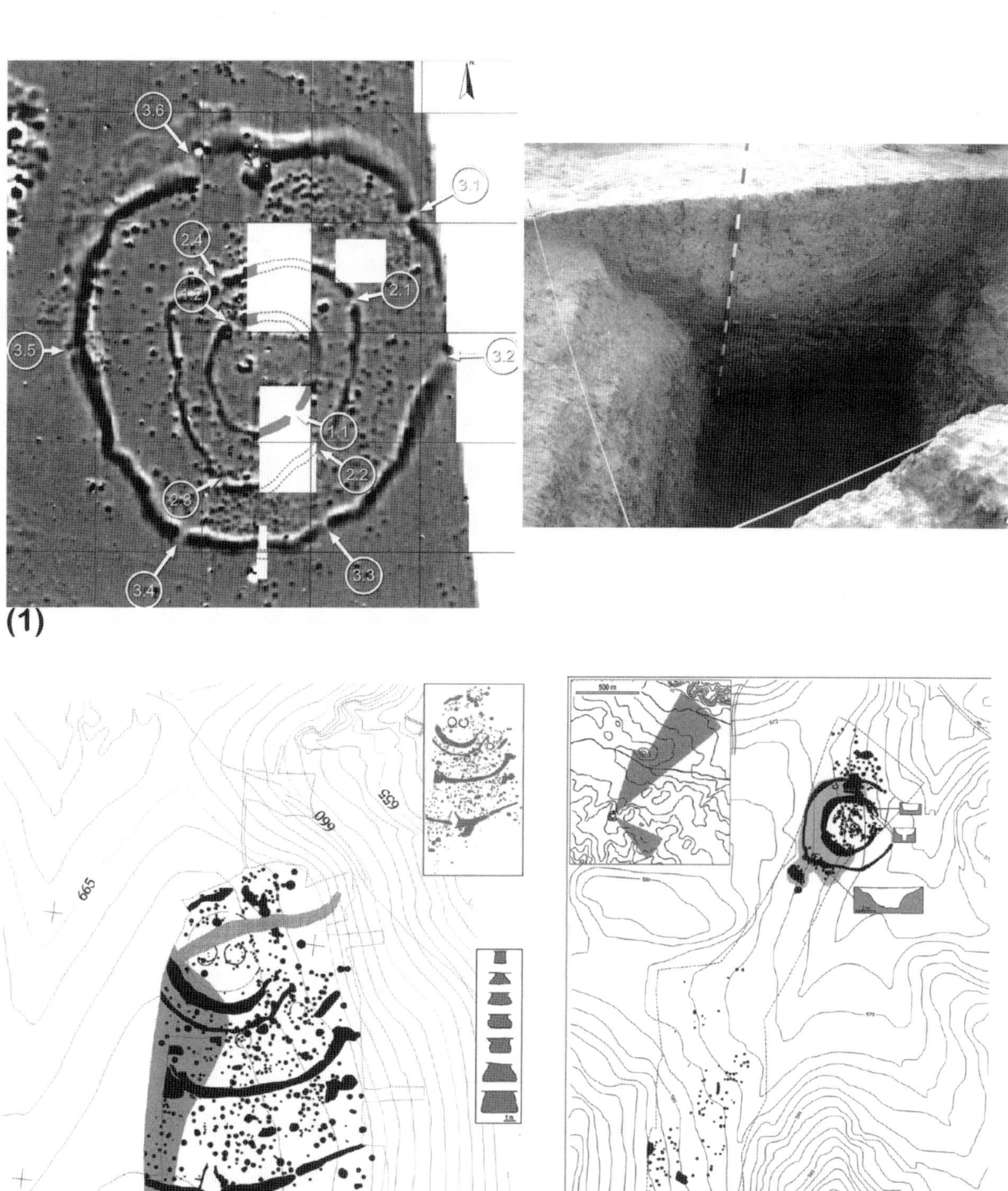
3.6
3.1
2.4
2.1
1.2
3.5
3.2
1.1
2.2
2.3
3.4
3.3
(1)
665
660
655
Fase 2
Fase 1
N
0
50 m
(2)
500 m
100 m
(3)

Figure 3.2: Bell Beaker sites in the interior of Iberia

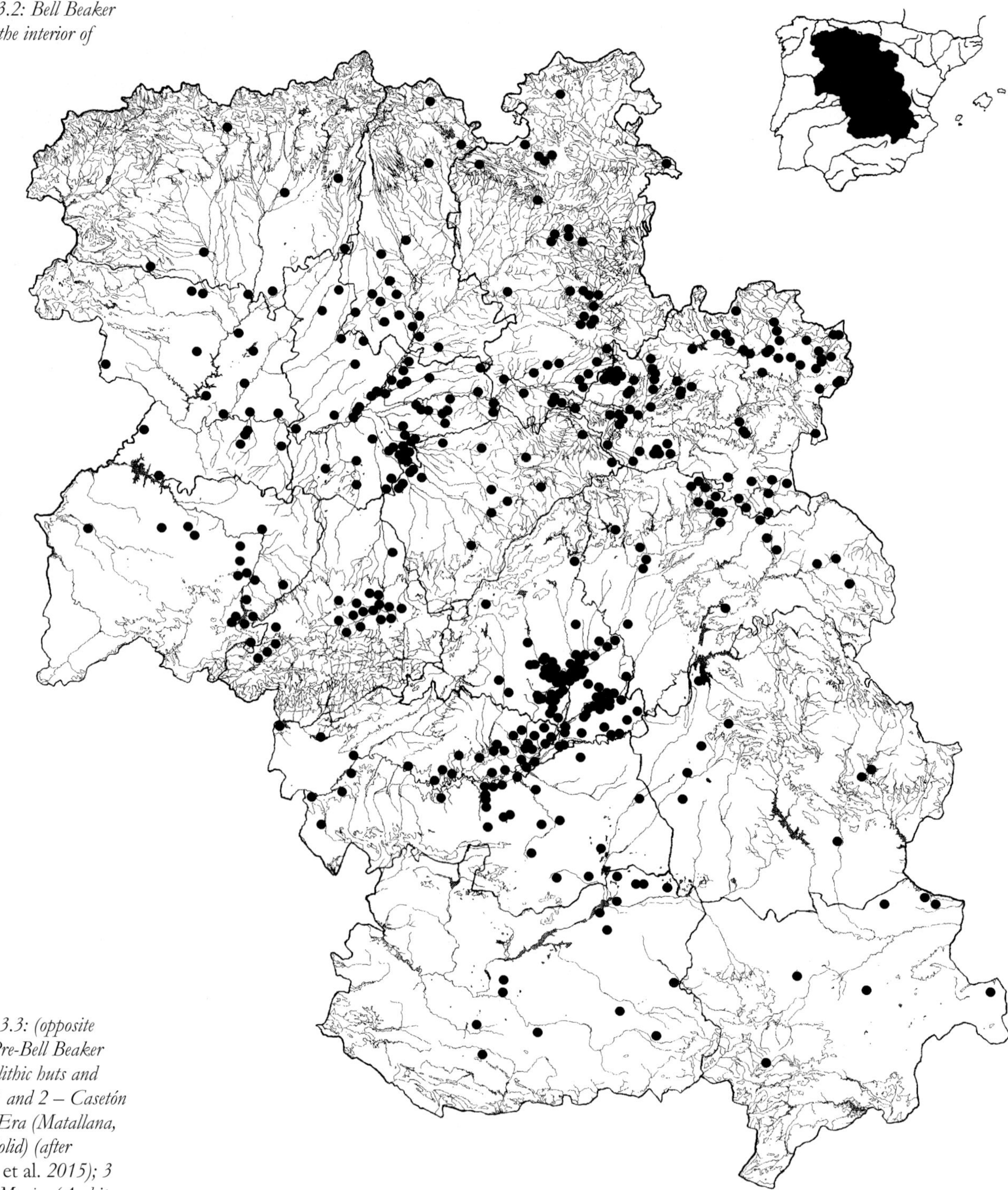

Figure 3.3: (opposite page) Pre-Bell Beaker Chalcolithic huts and finds: 1 and 2 – Casetón de La Era (Matallana, Valladolid) (after Crespo et al. *2015); 3 – Los Monjos (Ambite, Madrid) (after Balsera 2017); 4 – Casetón de La Era (Matallana, Valladolid) (after Gibaja* et al. *2012); 5 – Different types of huts inferred from typical negative structures (after Ríos* et al. *2016)*

Yeseras, where several concentric enclosures have been detected, the outermost enclosing over 10 hectares (Liesau *et al.* 2008, 100).

Huts are rarely encountered, but recent excavations have added to the few scattered examples already known (Fig. 3.3). In the southern Meseta (Tagus and Guadiana basins) huts are abundant in sites such as Fuente de la Mora or Camino de las Yeseras and less frequent in others like Ambite or Barranco del Herrero. They are mostly oval and range from substantial structures of 50 m^2 (Los Monjos, Camino de las Yeseras, Fuente de la Mora, El Espinillo, etc) (Fig. 3.3,3), to more common

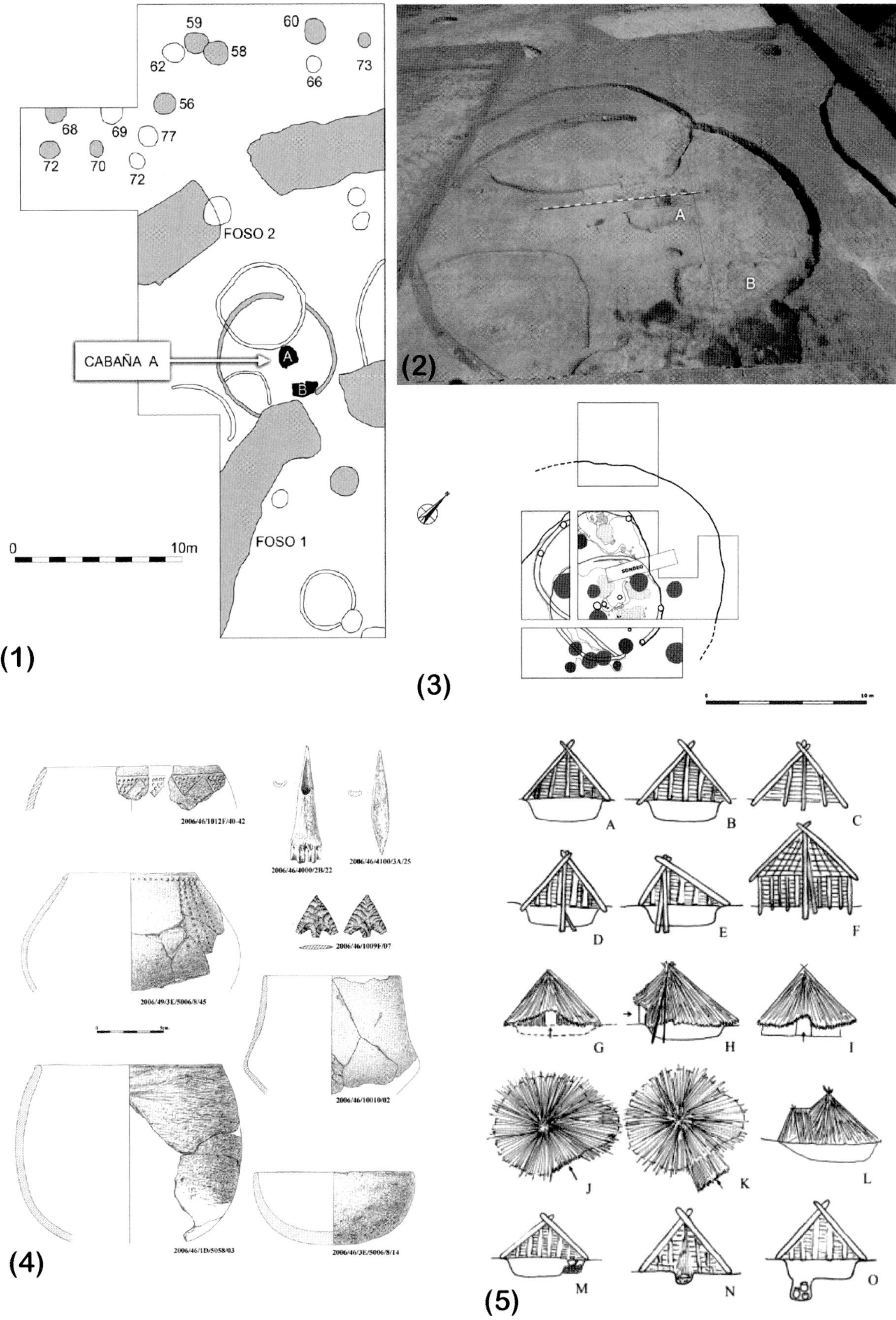
59
60
62
58
73
66
56
68
69
77
72
70
72
FOSO 2
CABAÑA A
A
B
0
10m
FOSO 1
(1)
A
B
(2)
SONDEO
(3)
(4)
A
B
C
D
E
F
G
H
I
J
K
L
M
N
O
(5)

houses of 20–40 m^2 (El Juncal, Camino de las Yeseras, Fuente de la Mora, El Espinillo, etc.) and finally to the most common structures of less than 20 m^2 (El Capricho, Barranco del Herrero, Gózquez, etc.). At sites like Ambite or Barranco del Herrero, different stratigraphic sequences were identified in individual huts indicating several phases of use and alteration (Ríos *et al.* 2016, 95–6; Balsera 2017, 215–17).

In the Northern Meseta (Duero Basin) a few sites have produced *c.* 20 huts. Mostly oval or circular rock-cut structures, there are also some rare examples of rectangular houses such as at Los Cenizales (2.85 × 2.50 m) (Sacristán 1990, 253). The most interesting and numerous huts have been recently found in the site of Casetón de la Era in Valladolid (Crespo *et al.* 2015) where 8 circular structures range from 2.5 m (hut H) to 10.5 m (hut C) in diameter. Hut A has a surface area of 34 m^2, has five post-holes and is delimited by a small ditch measuring 6.6 m in diameter (Fig. 3.3,1 & 2).

There are a few examples of defensive structures. Some from the southern Meseta, such as El Castrejón and other sites of the La Jara region in Toledo (Carrobles & Méndez 1991), or la Huerta del Diablo also in Toledo (Rojas 1987) are dubious and known only from surface finds. The most convincing examples are in the Duero Basin, the most famous being El Pedroso, to the west of Zamora, that is clearly related to the Portuguese sites (Delibes *et al.* 1995, 50–1, figs 7–8). A very recent find, currently under excavation, has been discovered at El Pico de la Mora in Valladolid (Villalobos & Roriguez-Marcos 2018). It is located on top of a small rise and has a defensive wall, *c.* 100 m long by 2.5 m wide, enclosing the more accessible side of the hill. It was also occupied during the Beaker phase.

Contemporary pottery comprises simple globular forms and a restricted but typical range of decoration (incised, impressed and painted motifs) that largely disappear during Beaker times, with the exception of the so called 'symbolic pottery' with its schematic figurative motifs such as cervids, 'suns/stars' and 'eye-idol motifs', all of which also appear on other ritual objects (bone or stone idols) as well as in the rock-art of this period. Some of these special motifs endured in the so-called Symbolic Bell Beakers, a unique Iberian type with clear local roots (Garrido-Pena & Muñoz 2000). The lithic industry is dominated by blades, sometimes of considerable size, and arrowheads of different types (rhomboid, leaf-shaped and even barbed and tanged ones that become the typical projectile point of the Beaker period) (Fig. 3.3,4). The simple copper tools are rare, mainly from tombs, and comprise awls, flat axes or small daggers/knives. Ornaments made from exotic materials such as stone beads (variscite) also circulated amongst these groups illustrating the intensification of exchange systems during the 4th and the first half of the 3rd millennia (Odriozola *et al.* 2017).

Domestic Bell Beakers

The settlement patterns and the environmental/economic context

Over 200 domestic sites with Beakers are known in the interior of Iberia (Fig. 3.2), most of them through surface finds (80%). In the 20% that have been excavated, some structures such as huts (25%) but mostly circular pits (75%) have been located. There is obvious pattern to the 'Beaker occupation', but it is important to note that the majority (around 70%) are located in open places with wide vistas, mostly beside rivers or streams, both on top of the ridges, on the gentle slopes or fluvial terraces. Fewer than 25% of Beaker-producing sites occupy flat areas and fewer than 5% are in caves or rock-shelters. On a wider scale they cluster around the main rivers and streams which provided natural communication routes in this generally rough terrain (Garrido-Pena 2000, figs 45, 97).

Beaker materials appear in settlements with exactly the same features as those described above: aglomerations of hundreds of circular pits of different phases spanning the 3rd–2nd millennia BC, with the occasional presence of huts. Moreover Beaker materials (mostly sherds) have been discovered in very small quantities (normally less than 1% of the total amount of pottery) in just a few of those pits or huts. Beakers appear in different taphonomic conditions, as do the rest of the ceramics, but many of them are eroded and some are partially burned (Blanco & Chapman 2014), suggesting that they were discarded some time before being definitively and intentionally deposited (Fig. 3.4). It is always very difficult to reconstruct complete pots and the various sherds usually belong to several different vessels.

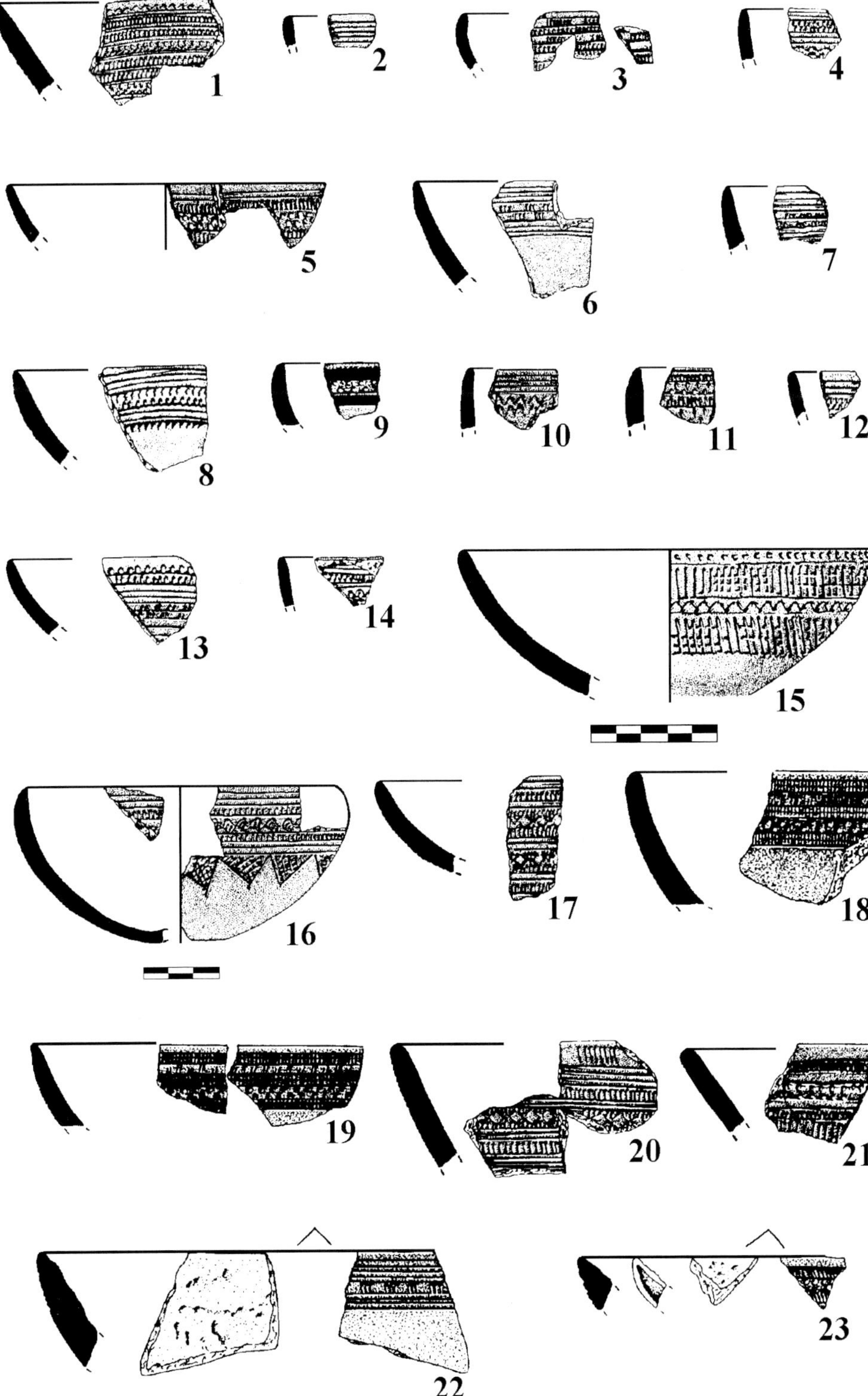

Figure 3.4: Bell Beaker bowls from the El Ventorro settlement (Madrid) (after Priego & Quero 1992)

'Beaker settlements', therefore are more likely to have been complex occupation spaces where different activities took place over several periods and just a few of those activities involved Beaker pottery. Unless we have radiocarbon dates for every pit, we cannot be sure which of them were absolutely contemporary with those that produced Beaker sherds, given that their contents are usually chronologically undiagnostic. This produces a more difficult and complex, but also a more realistic, picture of the place of Bell Beakers in Spanish Chalcolithic settlements.

Given this problem it is impossible to estimate the total size of Beaker-associated settlements, and to compare them with those of the first half of the 3rd millennium to determine continuity or change. It is, however, common to find Beaker materials at sites both previously occupied by local populations as well as later Middle Bronze Age sites suggesting clear continuity of both settlement and population. For the same reason, it is very difficult to research the economic basis of Bell Beaker using groups: 'Beaker pits', always represent a minority of the features on each site, and probably do not represent the whole economic pattern. The only alternative is to try to trace any process of economic and social change across the whole 3rd millennium.

Regional studies point to an important intensification of Chalcolithic farming economies compared to previous periods (Garrido-Pena 2000, 193; 2006, 84; López-Sáez *et al.* 2017, 132). Cattle and pig become more important and herds seem to be larger. There are indications of increased human pressure suggested by increased grazing activities, crop cultivation and forest clearance. This process seems to stop and change at the end of the Chalcolithic and coincides with an important climatic event (4200 ka cal BP, 2200–2000 cal BC), an aridity crisis, leading to the more pastoralist Bronze Age economies (Delibes *et al.* 2015; López-Sáez *et al.* 2017, 133–6). Those economic and environmental dynamics set the scenario for the appearance, development and transformation of the important social changes that explain the widespread use of Beakers in central Iberia during the second half of the 3rd millennium.

The chronological framework

Mainly from graves, Maritime Beakers date to *c.* 2500–2300 BC, and the slighty later Ciempozuelos style to *c.* 2400–1900 BC (there is considerable overlap due to the irregularity of the calibration curve during this period). Most Beaker settlements belong to the Ciempozuelos type, with just a few examples with Maritime or Geometric Comb Beaker, such as El Castillo (Burgos), Poste de la Luz de Preresa (Madrid) or more recently in Salmedina/Yacimiento 1 (Madrid) (Flores & Berzosa, 2003). These could be dated to *c.* 2500–2300 BC but they lack radiocarbon dates and it is common to find Maritime and Ciempozuelos potsherds mixed in domestic contexts as, for example, in Soto del Henares pit 21680 (Galindo & Sánchez 2010). The only radiocarbon dates for Maritime/Comb Geometric Beakers in domestic contexts are those from Cerro del Bu (Toledo) of 2870–2200 (I-13.959, 3970±100) and 2570–1980 cal BC (I-14416, 3830±100) (De Álvaro & Pereira 1990, 205). Unfortunately, these lack contextual integrity between the two Beaker sherds discovered as surface finds and the charcoal samples from the Early Bronze Age settlement (Fernández 2014, 146).

More radiocarbon dates are available from recent fieldwork at domestic contexts producing the Ciempozuelos style. Charcoal from El Pico del Castro (Valladolid) was dated to 2400–1970 cal BC (GrN 15897; 3750±60 BP) (Rodríguez 2005) and charcoal from the salt-production centre of Molino Sanchón (Zamora), produced four dates: 2460–2150 cal BC (PoZ-35252; 3835±35 BP), 2460–2150 cal BC (PoZ-35227, 3830±35 BP), 2490–2280 cal BC (PoZ-35226, 3910±35 BP), and 2300–2040 cal BC (PoZ-35223, 3765±35 BP) (Abarquero *et al.* 2012, 218–19).

Faunal samples from Beaker-associated pits provide more modern dates, in the late part of the Beaker period (2200–1900 BC), such as La Mata, Burgos, 2140–1960 cal BC (UGA-7557, 3670±25 BP) and Rompizales I, Burgos, 2200–1980 cal BC (UGA-7558, 3690±25 BP) (Carmona 2014, 32). In a ritual pit in Almenara de Adaja (Valladolid), with Ciempozuelos ceramics, two radiocarbon dates were obtained: one from a charcoal sample from the base of the pit 2350–1880 cal BC (GrN-27817, 3700±80 BP) and another from an aurochs bone from the fill 2460–2200 cal BC (Poz-43076, 3845±35 BP) (Liesau *et al.* 2014, 90, 92). The first has a large standard deviation and spans 463 years in calibrated chronology, but the one from the bone is much better and falls in the older section of the late Beaker period.

The domestic structures: pits, huts, enclosures and barrows

Of over 200 Beaker domestic sites, most comprise surface finds, only about 20 of them have been excavated to any degree, and several rescue excavations remain unpublished. They mostly comprise circular pits (75%), mainly of around 1m in diameter and less than 1m deep and contain Beaker sherds mixed with undecorated pottery and the usual domestic debris. Huts are exceptional (25%), and are always rock-cut oval structures, occasionally delimited by post-holes suggesting wattle-and-daub construction and many clay lumps preserved wood impressions (Fig. 3.5). This is a very similar picture to that of the Pre-Beaker period, except that the large ditched enclosures cease to be built in the northern Meseta (Delibes *et al.* 2015, 18), although they continue in the South at sites such as Soto del Henares, Madrid (Galindo & Sánchez 2010, 952–70). New types of structure also appeared in this period, such as small cenotaph barrows and complex salt production centres.

The northern Meseta

Pits with Beakers have been documented in several sites such as El Castillo (Burgos), Tierras Lineras (Salamanca), Cuéllar (Segovia), Montuenga (Soria) (Garrido-Pena 2000, 40–2), with recent finds in Valladolid such as Almenara de Adaja (Liesau *et al.* 2014) and Prado Esteban (Delibes *et al.* 2017), or Burgos, such as Manantial de Peñuelas (Villanueva *et al.* 2014), La Mata, Los Rompizales I (Carmona 2011, 304, 323–56) or Fuente Buena (Carmona 2013, 163–7).

Remains of huts with Beaker pottery of the Ciempozuelos style are known from early excavations such as those of Schulten in El Molino de Garrejo where two large storage vessels with Beaker decoration were found *in situ*. Also, at El Perchel (Soria), part of a structure was found with an important concentration of Beaker artefacts including large decorated storage vessels (Garrido-Pena 2000, 41–5). More recent fieldwork has located other examples of huts such as at Mojabarbas (Burgos), where there was an extensive habitation area but where it was not possible to identify any complete structure, however, a large decorated Beaker storage vessel appeared to have been broken *in situ* (Fig. 3.11,4) beside an accumulation of stone pebbles interpreted as the remains of a hearth. In Villafría V (Burgos), several Beaker sherds appeared in the excavation of a complete oval hut (5.8 × 1.28 m) with two hearths on one side (Garrido-Pena 2000, 41) (Fig. 3.5,1). Below the stone walls of a medieval tower, a circular hut, 8m across and 0.6 m deep and delimited by eight post-holes, was also discovered associated with Beaker at El Pico del Castro (Valladolid), (Rodríguez, 2005; Delibes *et al.* 2015, 8) (Fig. 3.5,3). A recent rescue excavation at Los Rompizales (Burgos) uncovered several Beaker-associated structures, mainly pits but also a possible hut 4 m in diameter, 12 m^2 in area and delimited by post-holes (Carmona 2011, 332).

Recent fieldwork in the Duero Basin has discovered a very peculiar type of small non-sepulchral stone barrow or cairn containing Beakers for example at El Morcuero (Blanco & Fabián 2010) and Los Tiestos (Blanco & Fabián 2011), both in Ávila, and El Alto I and III, La Perica and Las Cuevas/El Morrón in Soria (Rojo *et al.* 2014). It is clear that the construction of these barrows marked a very special place worthy of commemoration, and sometimes with excellent views as in El Alto III, where perhaps certain singular activities and ceremonies took place. In all these sites the lack of any human bone could not be attributed to taphonomic factors, since they were all in environments were bone would have been preserved, and the excavations were done to modern standards.

Perhaps the most spectacular example is El Alto III given the quality and abundance of the finds. They comprised two complete Beaker vessels, a bowl and a carinated bowl of Ciempozuelos style, and three gold ornaments deposited on the natural bedrock. Other Beaker pots, fragmented perhaps as part of a mound-building ceremony, were included in the mound material. They curiously belonged to reduced sets of incomplete vessels (eight pots represented by 1/2 or 1/3 of their complete profile). Each of them was intentionally broken, and sherds were carefully collected and later deposited in a certain area of the barrow, during its construction.

Abundant Beaker sherds of the Ciempozuelos style have been found in a settlement near the Villafáfila saline lagoons at Molino Sanchón II (Zamora) (Fig. 3.6). This site produced evidence for salt-making by boiling brine. Beaker sherds, both fine ware and decorated storage pots, were discovered in all salt-processing areas. They have been interpreted as a way of claiming property rights over this crucial activity in the same or in a similar way to Beaker pottery clusters at metal-working sites in Iberia (Guerra *et al.*

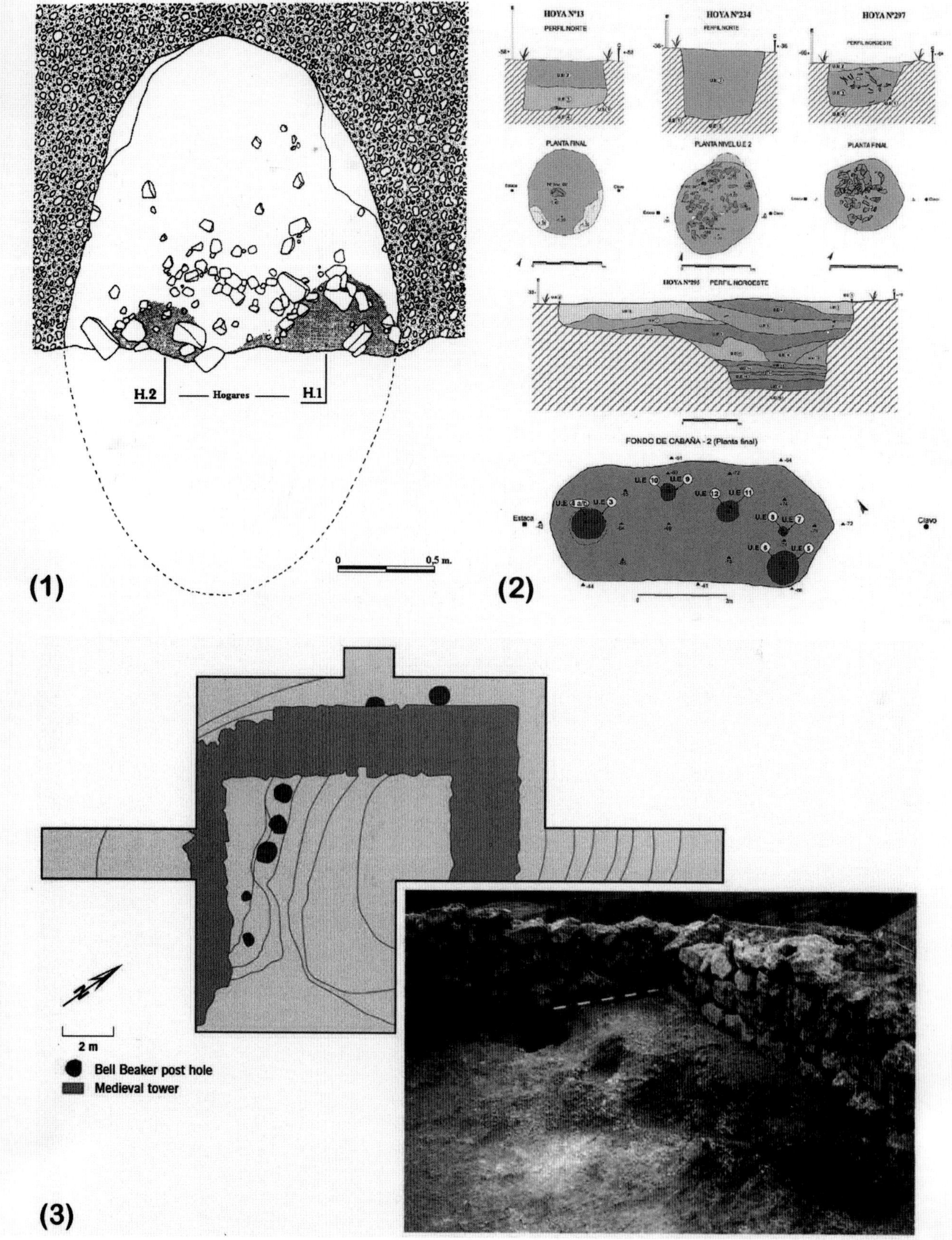

Figure 3.5: Huts associated with Bell Beakers: 1 – Villafría (Burgos) (after Uribarri & Martínez 1987); 2 – Alto del Romo F C2 (Tarancón, Cuenca) (after Vicente et al. *2007); 3 – El Pico del Castro (Quintanilla de Arriba, Valladolid) (after Delibes* et al. *2015)*

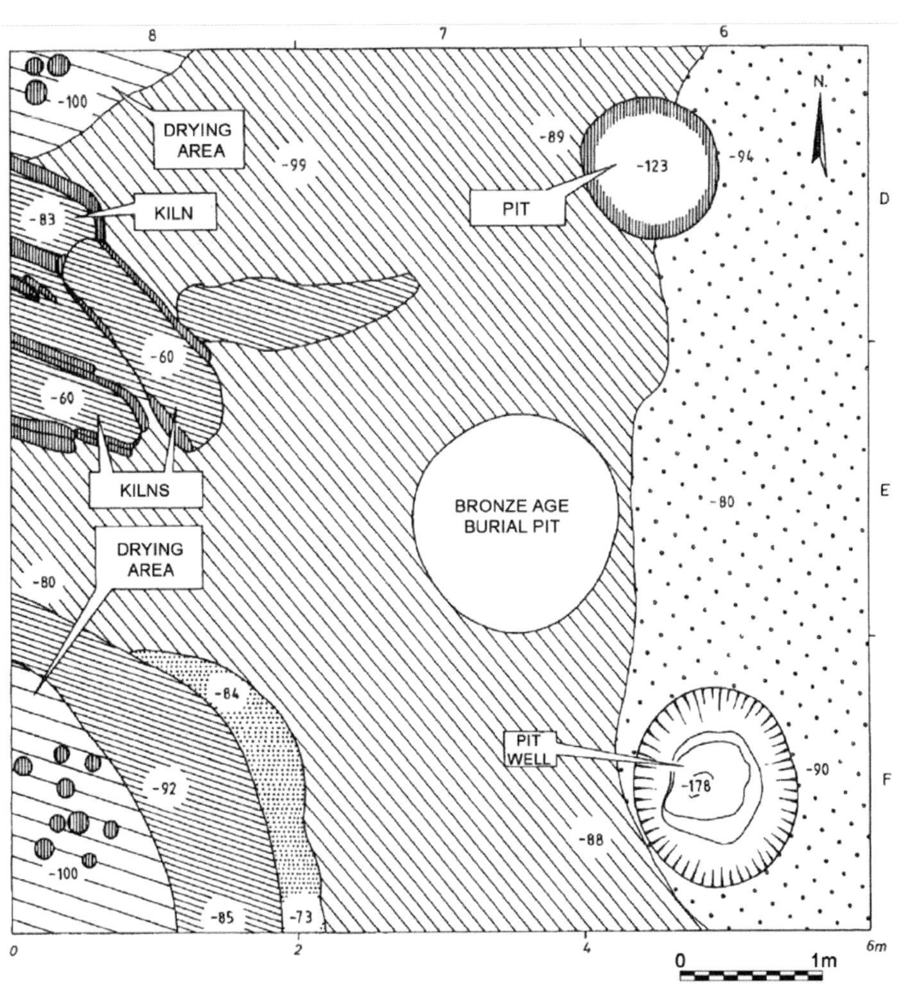

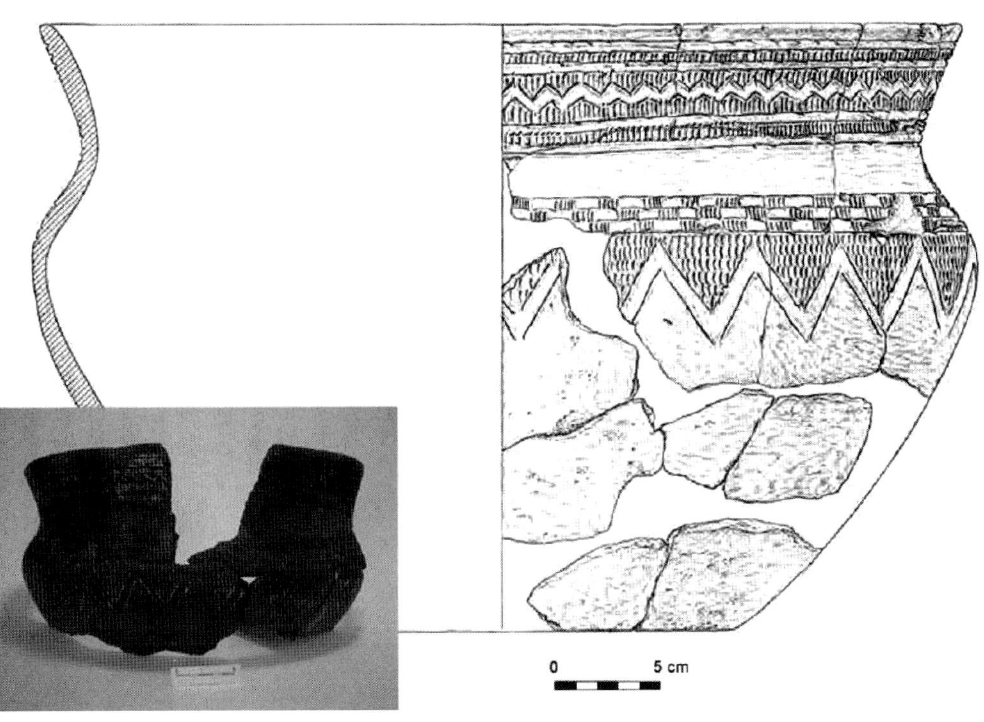

Figure 3.6: Molino Sanchón (Zamora) salt production centre: archaeological structures and domestic Beaker storage vessel (after Guerra et al. *2011)*

2015). Recent excavations are discovering more examples of this curious association of Beaker with salt-production activities at sites such as Prado Esteban (Valladolid) (Delibes *et al.* 2017).

The southern Meseta

Here pits were already known at sites such as Arenero de Soto I, II, Fábrica de Preresa, Fábrica Euskalduna, Loma de Chiclana, Ventorro, Pedazo del Muerto in Madrid, or Arenales I in Toledo (Garrido-Pena 2000, 41–4), but many other finds have been recently discovered in rescue excavations, such as, for instance, La Cuesta in Torrejón de Velasco, Madrid with nearly 20 pits containing 73 Ciempozuelos Beaker sherds (Flores *et al.* 2014) and Soto del Henares (Galindo & Sánchez 2010). Still mainly unpublished, this site has produced several pits mainly with Ciempozuelos style sherds, but also occasionally mixed with Maritime ceramics (pit 21680). In El Alto del Romo in Cuenca (Vicente *et al.* 2007) nearly 400 pits and two huts have been discovered (Fig. 3.5,2), several of them with Ciempozuelos pottery, but this excavation is still only partially published. Interestingly amongst the Beaker sherds recovered was at least one from a decorated pedestalled cup (Vicente *et al.* 2007, 70) which is a very rare form but with good parallels in central Portugal (Garrido-Pena 2000, 97) and of a type that has previously only been found in central Iberia at El Ventorro (see below). More recently a spectacular complete example was discovered in a tomb in the Humanejos cemetery (Flores & Garrido-Pena 2014). In Varas del Palio and Casa de Antoñón II (Camuñas, Toledo) (Gómez *et al.* 2010) Beaker sherds were also discovered inside circular pits, associated with hearths and burning. Interestingly in Varas del Palio the 11 pits formed a curious circular pattern, and in the westernmost pit amongst a layer of charcoal and ashes, a complete Maritime Bell Beaker was discovered. The discovery of a complete Beaker in a domestic context is exceptional and suggests an intentional deposit.

The settlement of El Ventorro (Madrid) is still the best known and published (Priego & Quero 1992), even though the number of structures uncovered was not very great: 23 pits and two huts (Fig. 3.7). The circular pits have an average 0.6–1.3 m in diameter and two of them were perhaps roofed, since several post-holes were located around their perimeter. Ciempozuelos Beaker sherds appeared in 10 of the pits mixed with domestic debris. Pit number 025 contained a very special deposit of three nearly complete Beaker vessels (two Bell Beakers and a carinated bowl) and the exceptional fragment of the decorated foot of a pedestalled cup. Beaker represented just the 2.5% of the total amount of pottery recovered from this site.

Beaker-associationed huts are also rare in the Southern Meseta, with well known finds from sites in Madrid such as Poste de la Luz de Preresa, where part of the floor of a hut was found, or Pedazo del Muerto where a large oval hut of 22 m^2 was defined by the distribution of finds and several post-holes both inside and outside the structure (Garrido-Pena 2000, 41–4). At El Ventorro three oval huts were found having semi-circular sections, post-holes and several daub fragments from the superstructure. They produced most of the finds comprising plain and Beaker pottery, faunal remains, stone and bone tools, and traces of metallurgical activity. Interestingly at this site Beaker bowls were exceptionally used as crucibles (Priego & Quero 1992). This agglomeration of material is especially clear in huts 013 and 021, which both have rammed earth floors with clear signs of burning. Structure 021 is where most metallurgical remains were discovered (57 pieces), especially in the northern corner, and has a semi-circular hearth or possible furnace delimited by stones (Fig. 3.7). In hut 013 the copper smelting traces (17 pieces) were found concentrated in half of the structure, within a space of 4m. Near this hut another metallurgical structure was located and comprised a circular pit broadly associated with metalworking debris such as five crucible fragments, several pieces of copper slag, two incomplete copper awls and a complete grinding stone of granite. Finally, it was also in hut 013 where most of the faunal remains were located (around 82%).

A recent find at El Alto del Romo in Cuenca provides two more examples of Beaker-associated huts which have only been partially published (Vicente *et al.* 2007, 47–8). FC-1 was an oval structure of 32 m^2 (8 × 5 m) with a trapezoidal section but which was severely eroded (just 0.2 m deep) and lacked any archaeological finds. FC-2 was a smaller hut

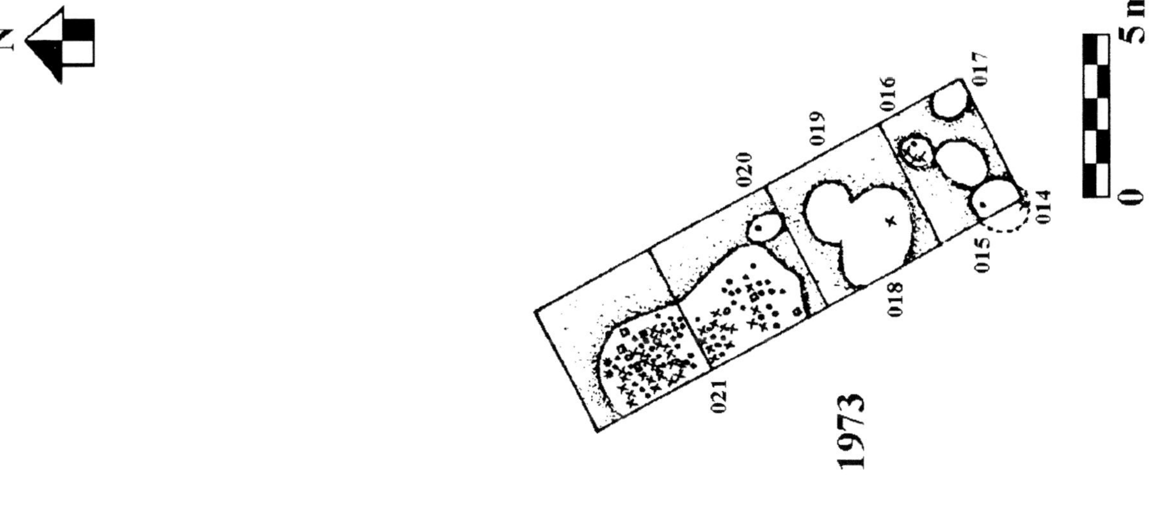

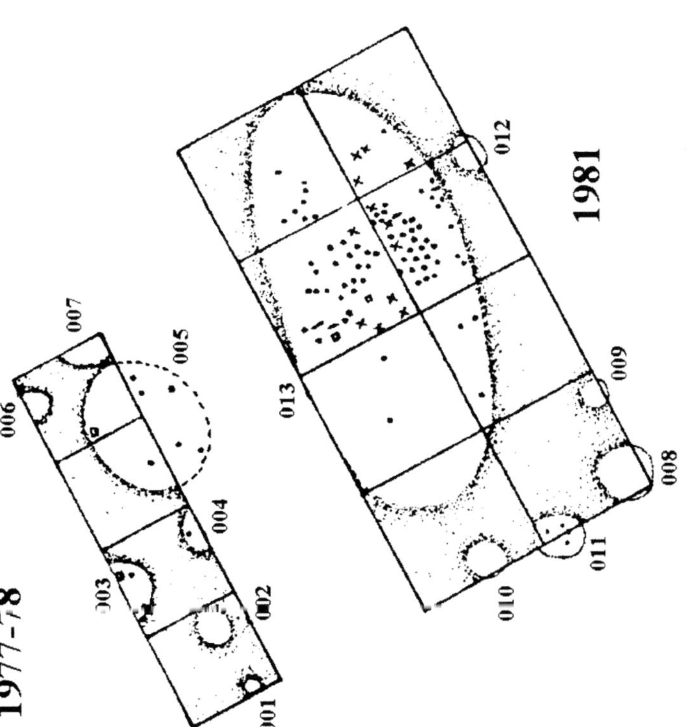

Figure 3.7: Domestic structures of El Ventorro (Madrid) Beaker-associated settlement (after Priego & Quero 1992)

of 15 m^2 (6 × 2.5m) with a single occupation layer sealed by the collapse of adobe walls (Fig. 3.5,2). Several pits and post-holes were found inside this structure perhaps representing roof supports.

The recent discovery of a very extensive settlement at Soto del Henares (Madrid), has located intense activity associated with the construction and sealing/infilling of ditched enclosures during the Beaker period, in contrast to the northern Meseta where this type of site was no longer in use. At this site nearly 400 Beaker sherds, mostly of the Ciempozuelos style, appeared inside substantial ditches belonging to two different circular enclosures of quite different sizes (Galindo *et al.* 2009, 54; Galindo & Sánchez 2010, 1577–83). The larger ditch cuts other previous enclosures of pre-Beaker origin, one of them Neolithic (Blasco *et al.* 2016). The smaller enclosure, circular and interrupted by different 'entrances', has a very interesting and homogeneous fill of sediment mixed with abundant small to medium-sized stone blocks, and which contained considerable amounts of archaeological finds such as faunal remains and lithics, but mainly sherds, and amongst them an important assemblage of Beaker fragments (Galindo & Sánchez 2010, 952–70).

In the southern Meseta clear evidence for the close association between Beakers and salt-production has also been very recently published (Barroso *et al.* 2017). The two main sites are Salinas de Espartinas (Madrid) which lies close to the famous Beaker cemetery of Ciempozuelos, and here Ciempozuelos Beaker sherds were uncovered in the same areas where salt processing activities were taking place. Secondly, at the site of Pontón Chico (Toledo), numerous remains of salt production were uncovered associated with a Ciempozuelos Beaker bowl.

Beaker materials in their domestic contexts

The artefact assemblages usually associated with Beakers in central Iberia are not very different from those from pre-Beaker sites. The lithic and bone industries comprise the same types and basic composition, and the undecorated pottery consists of a set of very simple forms, mostly bowls of different sizes and profiles (Fig. 3.8,1–4). In addition, there are other spherical forms, such as globular or ovoid pots with round bases (Fig. 3.8,5–8, 11–14, 17–19), rarely with handles, and also cylindrical vessels (Fig. 3.8,9–10) and vessels with a slightly sinuous profile (Fig. 3.8.15–16). Large storage jars are also occasionally present (Fig. 3.8,19), usually with simple plastic decoration and occuring in a range of sizes appropriate to the diverse functions that they performed. Occasionally cheese strainers are also encountered (Fig. 3.8,22–4), but these were more intensely produced and used during the 2nd millennium BC.

A very special and interesting type of decorated pottery associated with Beakers, mostly in the southern Meseta, and especially in the area of Madrid, is one with ungulate (paired fingernail or 'crowsfoot') impressions all over the external surface of the pot. It was originally identified at sites such as Almenara de Adaja (Valladolid) (Liesau *et al.* 2014, fig 2) in the northern Meseta, but mostly in Barranco de la Peña del Agua, Arenero de Pedro Jaro II, Fábrica Euskalduna, Tejar de Don Pedro, or El Ventorro, in the area of Madrid (Garrido-Pena, 2000, 40) (Fig. 3.8,18). At this last site, Priego and Quero (1992, 272) have already pointed out that this type of pot always appeared in the same structures as Beakers. Moreover, we have further confirmation of this association in the form of a Beaker burial from Humanejos (Madrid) where a complete sinuous vessel with this kind of fingernail rustication was recently discovered amongst the grave goods. This pottery could have a western origin, since it has been found in pre-Beaker Chalcolithic sites in Portugal, mainly in the Estremadura region, and also as a rare type in Penha Verde, Leceia, Rotura, Penedo (Cardoso *et al.* 1993) or Fraga da Pena and Moita da Ladra (Valera 2017, 226–7, fig. 4).

The analysis of Beaker assemblages from domestic contexts exhibits certain differences to those from tombs (Garrido-Pena 2000, 74–9), expecially in the form of the ceramics. Bell Beakers are much more standardised in tombs, and those from settlements tend to be larger, since those of more than 200 mm in diameter make up about 30% of the total sample studied. By contrast, Bell Beakers recovered in tombs are rarely more than 200 mm in diameter and are mostly (77%) between 110–65 mm. The only vessels with a capacity of over 3000 cc. come from domestic sites (Perchel and Preresa). Nevertheless, it is not that simple, because all the vessels with a

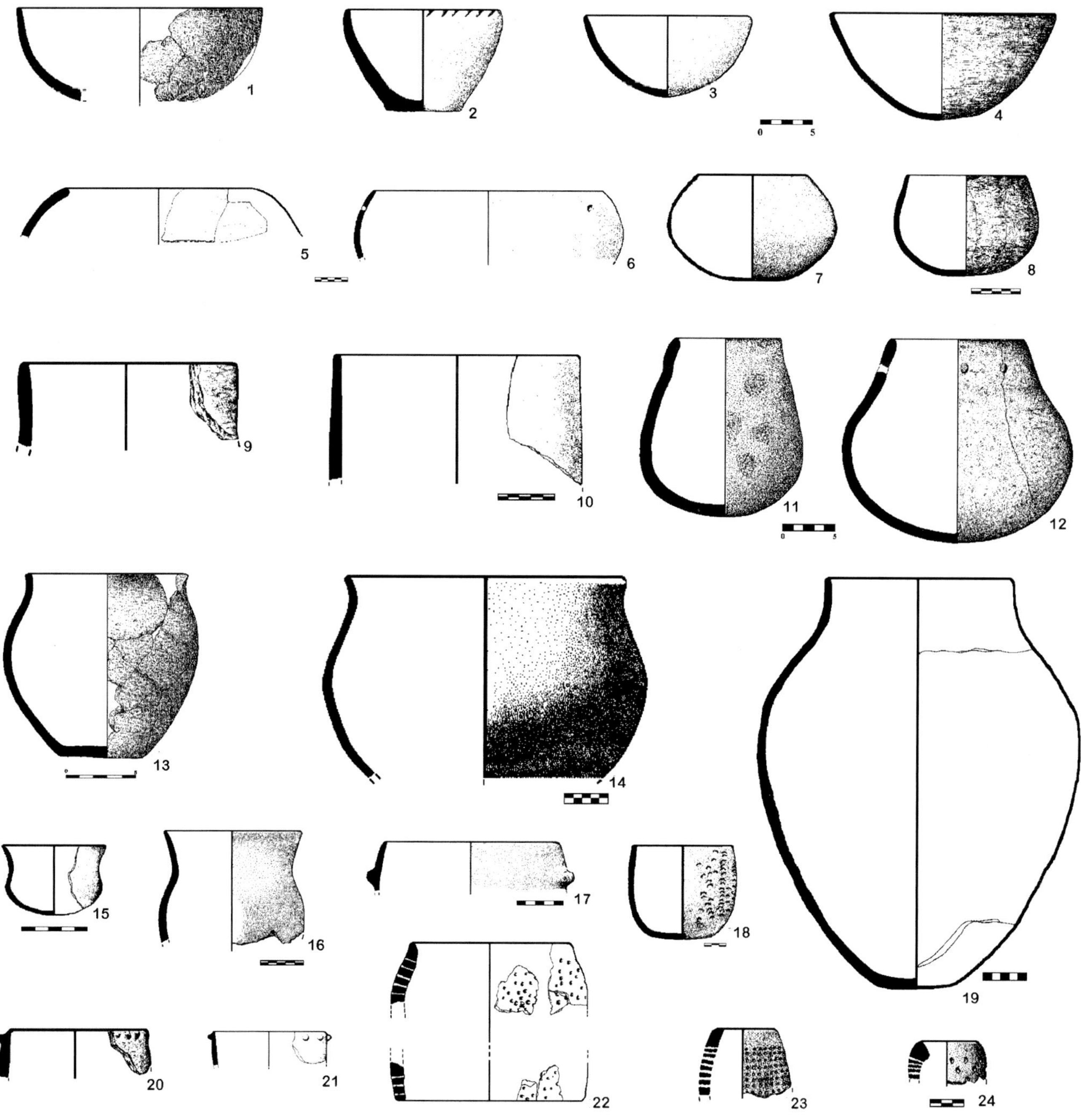

Figure 3.8: Selection of pottery types accompanying Bell Beakers in the interior of Iberia (after Garrido-Pena 2000)

capacity of between 2000–2500 cc came from graves (Pajares de Adaja, Galisancho, Veguilla, Palencia, Valdilecha) whilst there are several examples of small Beakers (450–1250 cc) from settlements (Somaén, Camino de la Yesera, Vascos, Ventorro).

Carinated bowls also exhibit differences that could be context related. The statistical correlation (Pearson coefficient) between the dimensions of the rim diameter and the total height shows striking differences between those of tombs (0.71) and settlements (0.33), which is a clear indication that those deposited in tombs were much more standardised. If we analyse just the rim diameter of carinated bowls a much larger sample (39 vessels) also clearly demonstrates this pattern since 80% of sepulchral pots cluster between 195–300 mm, in contrast to only 43% from settlements. However, the larger examples are more

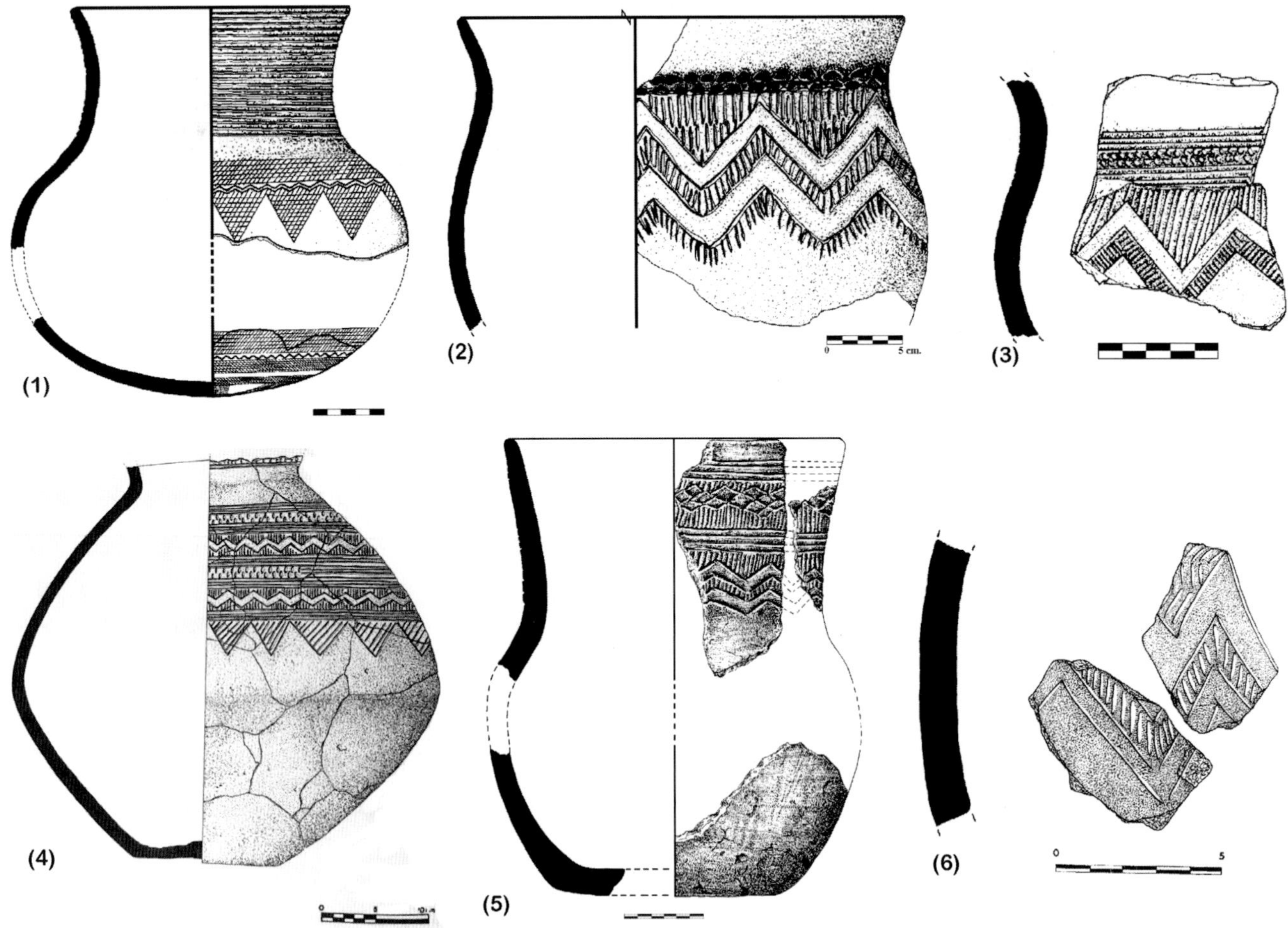

Figure 3.9: Beaker domestic storage vessels from different sites of the interior of Iberia. 1 & 2 – Cueva de La Mora (Somaén, Soria) (after Cajal 1981); 3 – El Ventorro (Madrid) (after Priego & Quero 1992); 4 – Mojabarbas (Burgos) (after Carmona 2011); 5 – Cueva de Arevalillo de Cega (Segovia) (after Fernández-Posse 1981); 6 – Los Molodros (Orgaz, Toledo) (after Garrido-Pena 2000)

frequently found in tombs (70% of carinated bowls over 225 mm in rim diameter) compared to those from domestic contexts (35%).

Beaker bowls also exhibit differential patterns between tombs and settlements, because they are clearly the most predominant Beaker form in settlements whilst in burials they play an auxiliary role to Bell Beakers and carinated bowls (Garrido-Pena, 2000, 72–3; Garrido-Pena *et al.* 2011, 118–19). In fact, bowls are the most distinctive Beaker form in settlements. This is the case, for instance, at Alto del Romo (Cuenca) (Vicente *et al.* 2007, 53), and Soto del Henares (Madrid) where 40% of the Beaker forms are bowls whilst just 8% are Bell Beakers and 5% are carinated bowls (Galindo & Sanchez 2010, 1583, 1632). Bowls over 200 mm in diameter (large dishes) are almost exclusively found in settlements, with some rare exceptions (Valdeprados grave), and again this phenomenon is confirmed by the most recent discoveries at Soto del Henares (Galindo & Sánchez 2010, 1347, 1459).

Large Beaker storage jars are almost exclusive to settlements with the notable exception of some recent finds in the Humanejos cemetery where they were deposited not as grave goods but as 'ceremonial pottery kits' probably associated with the closing ceremonies of certain tombs. They are large vessels with thick walls (10–15 mm) and with poorly finished surfaces, which have Beaker decoration comprising both comb impressions (Comb Geometric Style) and especially impressed Ciempozuelos style motifs (Figs 3.5 & 3.11). These vessels have been documented in the whole interior of Iberia, with more than 70 sites currently known (Fig. 3.10) and, clearly, they are a domestic variant of the standard Bell Beaker styles (Garrido-Pena 2000, 99–100). Those decorated with comb impressions (domestic variant of the Comb Geometric Style) are present in only a few sites such as Perical (Guadalajara), Aldehuela, Poste de la Luz Preresa, Casa del Cerro, Pedro Jaro II or Tejar de Pedro Ugarte (Madrid), Tarascona cave

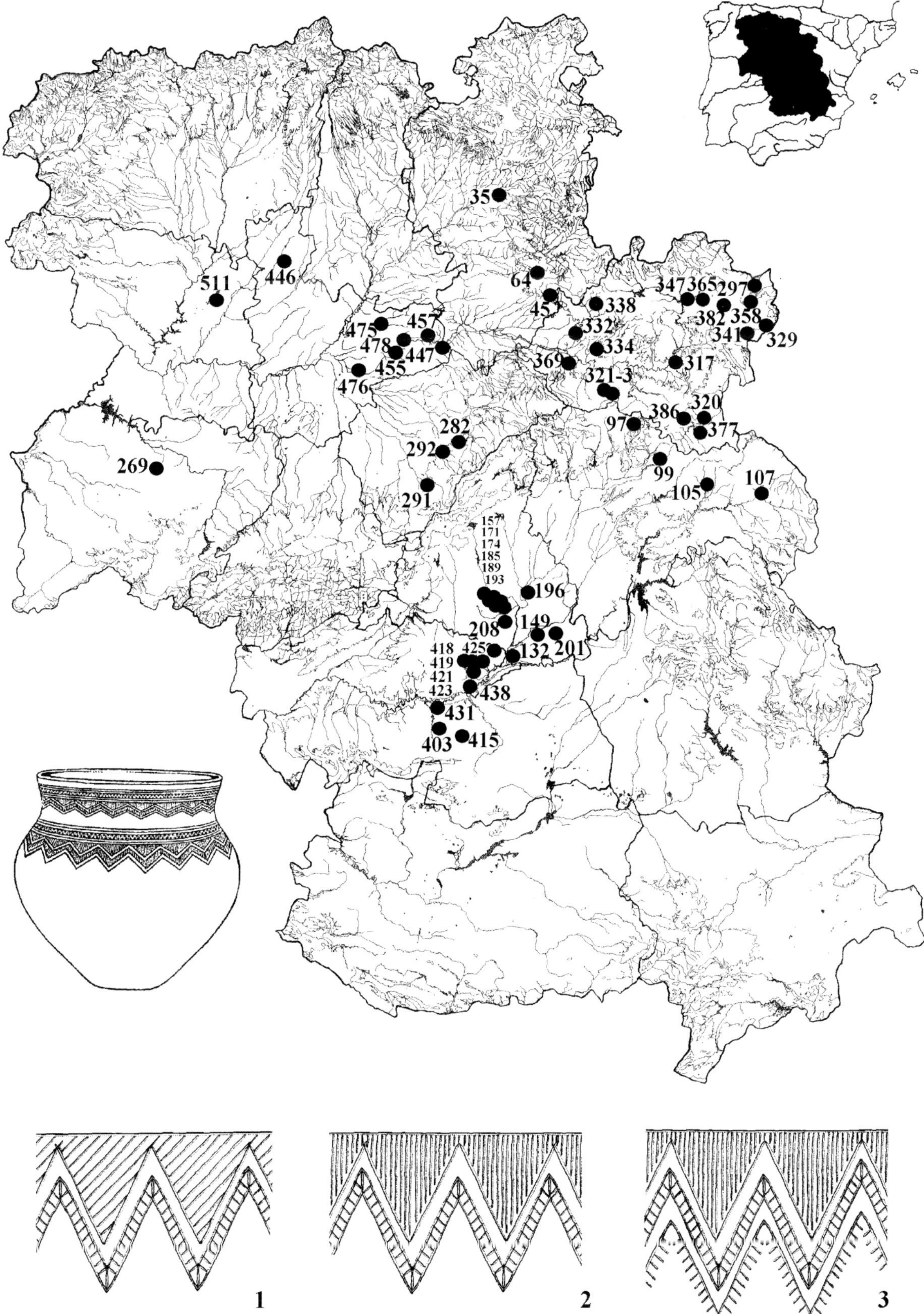

Figure 3.10: Distribution of sites with domestic Bell Beaker storage vessels in the interior of Iberia

(Segovia), Carratiermes (Soria) or Abardiales II (Toledo) and they are mostly fragmentary.

Much more abundant are Ciempozuelos Beakers with several complete vessels, and pots of different types, sizes and profiles (Fig. 3.9). There are sinuous pots reproducing the classic form of Bell Beakers but larger in size from Arevalillo cave (Segovia), Somaén cave (Soria), Piña de Esgueva (Valladolid), Molino Sanchón (Zamora) or Arenero de Soto III/Nicomedes (Madrid). There are also pots with large ovoid or spherical bodies with long and straight necks (Perchel and Somaén (Soria)), and finally there are large ovoid bodies with short necks and flat base (Renieblas and Molino de Garray (Soria), Mojabarbas (Burgos)). The volume range of these vessels is also diverse, from 1.7 litres in the smallest example (Somaén) to over 21 litres in the case of the well-known vessels of Molino de Garray (Soria) though most of them contained between 2 and 8 litres. It is quite clear that they were large closed vessels intended to process or store large quantities of liquid.

The regular and standardised decoration of these vessels is noteworthy. The frequent combination of the same motifs in the same parts of the vessels appears in the western part of the northern Meseta (Molino Sanchón, Zamora), and in the southern Meseta, for instance in the large assemblage of El Ventorro (Madrid), as well as at other sites such as Arenero de Soto III (Madrid), Los Molodros and La Bóveda in Toledo (Garrido-Pena 2000, 127–8) (Fig. 3.10).

These characteristic decorative schemes were perhaps signalling that those vessels were special and had a peculiar function. They also comprise a minority of vessels when compared with the rest of the large (undecorated) storage jars discovered in those settlements, associated, as it happens, with standard Beaker pots. This points to a restricted use or function that could be related to the production or storage of a special drink as was confirmed by the chemical analysis of a sherd from a Beaker storage vessel of the Carlos Álvarez rock-shelter (Soria) which contained wheat beer (Garrido-Pena *et al.* 2011, 115).

As a rule, the decorative patterns from Beaker vessels from domestic sites show less richness, diversity and complexity of designs than those from burials (Garrido-Pena 2000, 77, fig 20). But we can also observe striking differences between the Beaker domestic assemblages compared to those from graves if we examine the rest of the items of the 'Beaker package'. They are hardly found in settlements, especially copper objects (20% compared to 80% from graves), and they are mostly awls, flat axes and Palmela points. This can be explained by the fact that copper items were presumably used and recycled several times, and just stop circulating when they were deliberately deposited. Nevertheless, recent discoveries of non-funerary barrows in the interior of Iberia, such as that of El Alto III (Soria) with two small gold ornaments (Rojo *et al.* 2014) show that occasionally and in very special circumstances this type of precious object could also be deposited in non-funerary contexts.

Everyday routines? What were Beakers for?

In central Iberia, domestic Beakers seem to represent special vessels, used in singular occasions of social and ceremonial relevance, and which were specifically made for those purposes following certain rules regarding their size, functionality, etc. This is the reason why they were both highly standardised and extraordinarily scarce within the assemblages of the settlements of this period. This is particularly relevant in the case of Beaker pottery, given that Bell Beaker rarely represents more than 4–5% of the total amount of the ceramics recovered from those sites. As Liesau (2017, 308) has recently pointed out Beaker comprises only 0.1% in Camino de las Yeseras, and around the 2% in Perales del Río, Pedazo del Muerto or El Ventorro.

The type of ceremonial activity associated with Beakers is more difficult to determine. It has long been proposed that Beaker pottery had a strong connection with the consumption of alcoholic beverages, other drinks and solid foods in diverse social contexts: hospitality rituals, collective feasts, political pacts, marriage exchanges, and so on (Garrido-Pena 2000, Garrido-Pena *et al.* 2011, 114–20). Beaker pots met certain rules especially in decoration and the variation of capacity and proportions between different forms: Bell Beakers were probably used as drinking vessels, carinated bowls for serving foods, and small bowls as ladles or cups (Garrido-Pena 2000, 70–4, 208–10). Moreover, in the Ciempozuelos style graves, it is common to find bowls deposited inside carinated bowls associated with Bell Beakers.

The use of alcohol in a ceremonial context must be particularly useful to social elites in groups lacking stable or strongly hierarchical political institutions. Power must be negotiated and is always difficult to maintain and reinforce. One of the means to protect those tentative social privileges could be the gathering of followers, as a sort of military support in times of social conflict for power or political pre-eminence or forming marriage bonds and so on. Competitive feasting activities have been extensively documented in the ethnographic record as a social practice for just such purposes (Sherratt 1987, 98; Dietler 1996, 2001; Hayden 1996, 2001). Funerals may provide just one arena for these commensality rituals, houses and private spaces might be another hence the finding of Beakers with faunal remains in house sites. Beakers in open areas and pits may reflect larger open rituals such as work-party feasts or communal feasting. Moreover, the appearance of omphalos bases on Beakers may be related to new ways of consumption involving flat surfaces and an element of formality.

In some domestic contexts Beakers seem to be connected with the celebration of religious ceremonies, which may or may not be related to commensality rituals: we have no archaeological proof for these through chemical analyses, but they were most probably connected with special commemorations. This could also be the case for the 'symbolic' Beakers (Garrido-Pena & Muñoz 2001) found in several domestic sites in central Iberia (Carolinas, Almenara de Adaja, La Escarapela, El Ventorro, etc). These combine typical geometric Beaker decoration with religious imagery (sun/stars, cervids, etc) (Fig. 3.11). Finally, perhaps also related with those evocative ceremonies are several small barrows discovered on the tops of hills with spectacular views, where Beaker pottery including complete finely decorated pots, was carefully deposited, accompanied by other exceptional items such as gold ornaments as at El Alto III (Rojo *et al.* 2014). Perhaps the presence of those sorts of items, normally only discovered in tombs, points to the celebration of special rituals, later marked in the landscape by those overlying cairns, in commemoration of singular ritual acts possibly connected with the remembrance of the dead, already gone but still strongly present in the memory and the heart of the living.

Figure 3.11: Beaker bowl with 'symbolic' decoration from Las Carolinas (Madrid). Photograph by the Museo Arqueológico Regional de Madrid

References

Abarquero, F.J., Guerra, E., Delibes, G., Palomino, A.L. & Del Val, J. 2012. *Arqueología de la Sal en las Lagunas de Villafáfila (Zamora): Investigaciones sobre los cocederos prehistóricos.* Valladolid: Arqueología en Castilla y León, Monografías 9, Junta de Castilla y León

Balsera, V. 2017. *Demografía y Poblamiento en La Meseta Sur entre el 5500 y el 1200 BC. Una perspectiva desde el radiocarbono.* Tesis Doctoral. Universidad Autónoma de Madrid

Barroso, R., Bueno, P., De Balbín, R. & Lancharro, M.A. (2017): Production and Consumption of Salt in the Inland Tagus Valley in Prehistory (Spain). In Bartelheim *et al.* 2017, 89–105

Bartelheim, M., Bueno, P. & Kunst, M. (eds), 2017. *Key Resources and Sociocultural Developments in the Iberian Chalcolithic.* Tübingen: Tübingen University

Blanco, A. & Chapman, J. 2014. Revisiting the Chalcolithic site of El Ventorro (Madrid, Spain). Ceramic Refitting and Taphonomy, *Proceedings of the Prehistoric Society* 80, 87–103

Blanco, A. & Fabián, J.F. 2010. Un hito de la memoria: el túmulo de El Morcuero (Gemuño, Ávila), *Munibe (Antropologia-Arkeologia)* 61, 183–212

Blanco, A. & Fabián, J.F. 2011. ¿Monumentos evocativos? Los túmulos de Los Tiesos (Mediana de Voltoya, Ávila) en su contexto prehistórico, *Munibe (Antropologia-Arkeologia)* 62, 251–82

Blasco, C., Galindo, L., Sánchez, V.M., Ríos, P. & Liesau, C. 2016. Ampliando el registro del Neolítico en el interior peninsular: ocupaciones inéditas en tres yacimientos de la región de Madrid'. In *Del neolític a l'edat del bronze en el mediterrani occidental: Estudis en homenatge a Bernat Martí Oliver*, 257–67. Valencia: *TV SIP 119*. Diputación Provincial de Valencia

Bradley, R. 2005. *Ritual and Domestic Life in Prehistoric Europe*. London: Routledge.

Cajal, N. 1981. Materiales de la Cueva de la Mora de Somaén (Soria) en el Museo Arqueológico Nacional, *Trabajos de Prehistoria* 38, 193–224

Cardoso, J.L., Roque, J., Da Veiga Ferreira, O. 1993. Cerâmicas unguladas do Povoado Calcolítico da Penha Verde, *Al-madan IIa série. Arqueologia Património e História Local*, nº 2. Centro de Arqueologia de Almada, 35–8

Carmona, E. 2011. *Las comunidades campesinas calcolíticas en el valle medio del Arlanzón (cal. 3000–1900 a.C.): transformaciones y procesos históricos*. Tesis doctoral. Universidad de Burgos

Carmona, E. 2013. *El Calcolítico en la Cuenca Media del Arlanzón (Burgos, España): Comunidades campesinas, procesos históricos y transformaciones*. Oxford: BAR International Series 2559

Carmona, E. 2014. Dataciones radiocarbónicas de contextos calcolíticos al aire libre en la cuenca media del Arlanzón (Burgos, España), *SPAL Revista de Prehistoria y Arqueología* 23. Universidad de Sevilla, 27–48

Carrobles, J. & Méndez, M. 1991. Introducción al estudio del Calcolítico en la Jara toledana, *Anales Toledanos* XXVIII, 7–23

Case, H.J. 1995. Beakers: loosening a stereotype. In Kinnes, I. & Varndell, G. (eds), *Unbaked Urns of Rudely Shape,* 55–67. Oxford: Oxbow Monographs 55

Clarke, D. 1976. The Beaker network-social and economic models. In Lanting, J. N. & Van der Waals J. D. (eds), *Glockenbecher Symposium, Oberried, 1974*, 459–77. Bossum/Haarlem: Fibula-van Dishoeck

Crespo, M., Rodríguez, J.A., Delibes, G., & Becker, H. 2015. Prospección magnética en el recinto de fosos calcolítico de 'El Casetón de la Era' (Villalba de los Alcores, Valladolid): representación gráfica e interpretación arqueológica, *Boletín del Seminario de Estudios de Arqueología* LXXXI, 55–84

De Álvaro, E. & Pereira, J. 1990. El cerro del Bu (Toledo), *Actas del Primer Congreso de Arqueología de Toledo*, 199–213

Delibes, G., Herrán, J.I., De Santiago, J. & Del Val, J. 1995. Evidence for social complexity in the Copper Age of the Northern Meseta. In Lillios, K.T. (ed.), *The origins of complex societies in late prehistoric Iberia.* 44–63, International Monographs in Prehistory 8. Ann Arbor

Delibes, G., García, M., Del Olmo, J. & Santiago, J. 2014. *Recintos de fosos calcolíticos de valle medio del Duero. Arqueología aérea y espacial.* Valladolid: Studia Archaeologica, 100. Ediciones Universidad de Valladolid

Delibes, G., Abarquero, F.J., Crespo, M., García, M., Guerra, E., López, J.A., Pérez, S. & Rodríguez, J.A. 2015. The archaeological and palynological record of the Northern Plateau of Spain during the second half of the 3rd millennium BC. In *Tagungen des Landesmuseums for Vorgeschichte.* Halle 12 (1), 1–20

Delibes, G., Guerra, E., Abarquero, J., Moreno, M. & Sanz, F.J. 2017. Sobre el binomio vaso campaniforme/ paisajes de sal: nuevos documentos de Pedrajas de San Esteban (Valladolid) y Poza de la Sal (Burgos), *Oppidum. Cuadernos de Investigación* 13, 7–26

Díaz-Del-Río, P. 2003. Recintos de fosos del III milenio AC en la Meseta peninsular, *Trabajos de Prehistoria* 60 (2), 61–78

Dietler, M. 1996. Feasts and commensal politics in the political economy. Food, power and status in prehistoric Europe. In P. Wiessner and W. Schiefenhovel (eds), *Food and the status quest*, 87–125: Providence: Berghahn Books

Dietler, M. 2001. Theorizing the Feast: Ritual of Consumption, Commensal Politics, and Power in African Contexts. In Dietler& Hayden (eds), 65–114

Dietler, M. & Hayden, B. (eds), 2001. *Feasts: Archaeological and Ethnographic Perspectives on Food, Politics, and Power.* Washington DC: Smithsonian Institution Press

Fernández, J. 2014. *Aproximación al conocimiento de la Edad del Bronce en la Cuenca Media del Tajo. El Cerro del Bu (Toledo).* Toledo: Auditores de Energía y Medio Ambiente S.A

Fernández-Posse, M.D. 1981. La Cueva de Arevalillo de Cega (Segovia), *Noticiario Arqueológico Hispánico* 12, 45–84

Flores, M. & Berzosa, R. 2003. Informe definitivo de la excavación arqueológica efectuada en el Yacimiento 1, Finca 'La Salmedina' (Distrito Villa de Vallecas, Madrid). Unpubl. report. Dirección General de Patrimonio Histórico, Comunidad de Madrid

Flores, R. & Garrido-Pena, R. 2014. Campaniforme y conflicto social: Evidencias del yacimiento de Humanejos (Parla, Madrid), 159–67. *Actas de las IX Jornadas de Patrimonio arqueológico en la Comunidad de Madrid.* Madrid: Dirección General de Patrimonio Histórico, Comunidad de Madrid

Flores, R.,Sanabria, P.J. & Garrido-Pena, R. 2014. Materiales campaniformes en 'La Cuesta', Torrejón de Velasco, 379–84. *Actas de las IX Jornadas de Patrimonio arqueológico en la Comunidad de Madrid.* Madrid: Dirección General de Patrimonio Histórico, Comunidad de Madrid

Galindo, L. & Sánchez, V.M. 2010. Memoria final de la excavación arqueológica en el yacimiento 'Soto del Henares' Torrejón de Ardoz. Unpubl. Report. Comunidad de Madrid. Servicio de Patrimonio Histórico

Galindo, L., Marcos, V. & Lorente, M. 2009. Soto del Henares: Aproximación a un poblado de recintos, 263–71. *Actas de las IV Jornadas de Patrimonio arqueológico en la Comunidad de Madrid.* Madrid: Dirección General de Patrimonio Histórico, Comunidad de Madrid

Garrido-Pena, R. 2000. *El Campaniforme en la Meseta Central de la Península Ibérica* (c. *2500–2000 A.C.).* Oxford: BAR International Series 892

Garrido-Pena, R. 2006. Transegalitarian societies: an ethnoarchaeological model for the analysis of Copper Age Bell Beakers using groups in Central Iberia. In Díaz-Del-Río, P. and García-Sanjuán, L. (eds), *Social Inequality in Iberian Late Prehistory,* 81–96. BAR International Series, S1525

Garrido-Pena, R. 2014a. Entre el consenso y la incertidumbre: perspectivas actuales en el estudio del fenómeno campaniforme, 87–104. *Actas IX Jornadas de Patrimonio Arqueológico en la Comunidad de Madrid (Alcalá de Henares, 15–16 Noviembre 2012).* Alcalá de Henares (Madrid)

Garrido-Pena, R. 2014b. Bell Beakers in Iberia. In M. Almagro (ed.), *Iberia. Protohistory of the far west of Europe: from Neolithic to Roman conquest*, 113–24. Burgos: Universidad de Burgos. Fundación Atapuerca

Garrido-Pena, R. & Muñoz, K. 2000. Visiones sagradas para los líderes, *Complutum* 11, 285–300

Garrido-Pena, R., Rojo, M.A., García, I. & Tejedor, C. 2011. Drinking and eating together: the social and symbolic context of commensality rituals in the Bell Beakers of the interior of Iberia (2500–2000 BC). In Aranda, G. Montón, S. & Sánchez, M. (eds), *Guess Who's Coming to Dinner: feasting Rituals in The Prehistoric Societies Of Europe and the Near East*, 109–29. Oxford: Oxbow Books

Gibaja, J.F., Crespo, M., Delibes, G., Fernández, J., Fraile, C., Herrán, J.I., Palomo, A. & Rodríguez, J.A. 2012. El uso de trillos durante la Edad del Cobre en la Meseta española. Análisis traceológico de una colección de denticulados de sílex procedentes del 'recinto de fosos' de El Casetón de la Era (Villalba de los Alcores, Valladolid). *Trabajos de Prehistoria* 69 (1): 133–48

Gómez, A., Rojas, J.M., Cáceres, Y. & De Juan, J. 2010. Los asentamientos del III Y II Milenio a.d.C. en la Autovía de los Viñedos. Tramo: Consuegra – Tomelloso (P.K. 0+000 A 74+600). La Serna, Casa de Antoñón I, Casa de Los Castos, Santa Lucía, Varas del Palio, Casa de Antoñón II y Casa del Montón. *Actas de las II Jornadas de Arqueología de Castilla La Mancha (Toledo 2007),* 1–49. Diputación de Toledo. Junta de Comunidades de Castilla La Mancha

Gonçalves, V.S. (ed.), 2017. *Sinos e Taças. Junto ao Oceano e mais longe. Aspectos da presença campaniforme na Península Ibérica.* Estudos and memórias 10. Lisboa: UNIARQ

Guerra, E., Delibes, G., Abarquero, F.J., Del Val, J. & Palomino, A.L. 2011. The Beaker salt production centre of Molino Sanchón II, Zamora, Spain, *Antiquity* 85, 805–818

Guerra, E., Abarquero, F.J., Delibes, G., Palomino, A.L. & Del Val, J. 2015. Bell Beaker pottery as a symbolic marker of property rights: the case of the salt production centre of Molino Sanchón II, Zamora, Spain. In Prieto P.M. & Salanova, L. (eds), *The Bell Beaker Transition in Europe: Mobility and local evolution during the 3rd millennium BC*, 169–81. Oxford: Oxbow Books

Hayden, B. 1996. Feasting in prehistoric and traditional societies. In Wiessner, P. & Schiefenhovel, W. (eds), *Food and the status quest*, 127–47. Providence: Berghahn Books

Hayden, B. 2001. Fabulous feasts: A prolegomenon to the importance of feasting. In Dietler & Hayden (eds), 2001, 23–64

Liesau, C. 2017. Campaniforme y Ciempozuelos en la región de Madrid. In Gonçalves 2017, 302–23

Liesau, C., Blasco, C., Ríos, P., Vega, J., Menduiña, R., Blanco, J. F., Baena, J., Herrera, T., Petri, A. & Gómez, J.L. 2008. Un espacio compartido por vivos y muertos: El poblado calcolítico de fosos de Camino de las Yeseras (San Fernando de Henares, Madrid), *Complutum* 18 (1), 97–120

Liesau, C., Guerra, E. & Delibes, G. 2014. Casual or ritual: The Bell Beaker deposit of La Calzadilla (Valladolid, Spain), *Quaternary International* 330, 88–96

López-Sáez, J.A., Blanco, A., Pérez, S., Alba, F., Luelmo, R., Glais, A. & Núñez, S. 2017. Landscapes, Human Activities and Climate Dynamics in the South Meseta of the Iberian Peninsula during the 3rd and 2nd Millennia cal BC. In Bartelheim *et al.* 2017, 129–42

Martínez, Mª.I. 1984. El comienzo de la metalurgia en la provincia de Madrid: La cueva y cerro de Juan Barbero (Tielmes, Madrid), *Trabajos de Prehistoria* 41, 17–91

Odriozola, C.P., Villalobos, R., Bueno, P., Barroso, R., Flores, R. & Díaz-Del-Río, P. 2017. Late Prehistory Body Ornaments Exchange and Social Dynamics in the Middle Tagus Basin. In Bartelheim *et al.* 2017, 59–87

Olalde, I. *et al.* 2018. The Beaker Phenomenon and The Genomic Transformation of Northwest Europe, *Nature* 555, 190–6

Priego, M.C. & Quero, S. 1992. *El Ventorro, un poblado prehistórico de los albores de la metalurgia.* Madrid: Estudios de Prehistoria y Arqueología Madrileñas 8

Ríos, P., Daza, A., Ortiz, I., de Chorro, M.A. & Liesau, C. 2016. La Cabaña 'E' del yacimiento de Camino de las Yeseras. Nuevos datos sobre el espacio doméstico en un Poblado de Hoyos. *Anejos a Cuadernos de Prehistoria y Arqueología 2: Homenaje a la Profesora Concepción Blasco Bosqued*: 73–105

Rodríguez, J.A. 2005. Una cabaña de época campaniforme. El yacimiento de Pico del Castro (Quintanilla de Arriba, Valladolid). In Iglesias, L.S., Payo, R. J. & Alonso, P. (eds), *Estudios de Historia y Arte. Homenaje al profesor D. Alberto C. Ibáñez Pérez*, 81–6. Burgos: Universidad de Burgos

Rojas, J.M. 1987. La Huerta del Diablo: Un posible asentamiento calcolítico con muralla circular. *Trabajos de Prehistoria* 44, 271–82

Rojo, M.A., Garrido-Pena, R. & García, I. 2008. Everyday routines or special ritual events?: Bell Beakers in domestic contexts of Inner Iberia. In Baioni, M., Leonini, V., Lo Vetro, D., Martín, F., Poggiani-Keller, R. & Sarti, L. (eds), *Bell Beaker in Everyday Life*, 321–26. Firenze: *Proceedings of the 10th Meeting 'Archéologie et Gobelets' (Florence – Siena – Villanuova sul Clisi, May 12–15, 2006). Millenni. Studi di Archeologia Preistorica 6.* Museo Fiorentino di Preistoria 'Paolo Graziosi'

Rojo, M.A., Garrido-Pena, R., García, I. & Tejedor, C. 2014. Beaker Barrows (not) for the dead: El Alto I and III, Las Cuevas/El Morrón and La Perica (Soria, Spain), *Cuadernos de Prehistoria y Arqueología de la Universidad Autónoma de Madrid* 40, 31–40

Sacristán, J.D. 1990. Arqueología Preventiva y de Gestión (1984–1988): Burgos, *Numantia. Arqueología en Castilla y León* III, 251–8

Sherratt, A. 1987. Cups that Cheered. In Waldren, W.H. & Kennard, R.C. (eds), *Bell Beakers of the Western Mediterranean. Definition, interpretation, theory and new site data,* 81–114. Oxford: *British Archaeological Reports International Series S*331

Uribarri, J.L. & Martínez, J.M. 1987. Primeros asentamientos humanos en el término municipal de la ciudad de Burgos, *Caesaraugusta* 64, 135–56

Valera, A.C. 2017. Beakers in Central Portugal: social roles, confluences and strange absences. In Gonçalves 2017, 214–29

Vicente, A., Rojas, J.M., Pérez, J. & Sánchez, F. 2007. El yacimiento campaniforme del 'Alto Del Romo' (Tarancón, Cuenca). Asentamiento calcolítico en la Mancha Alta, *ARSE (Boletín del Centro Arqueológico Saguntino)* 41, 37–73

Villalobos, R. & Rodríguez-Marcos, J.A. 2018. El Pico de la Mora (Peñafiel, Valladolid). Un nuevo asentamiento amurallado del Calcolítico Inicial normeseteño, *Trabajos de Prehistoria* 75 (1): 155–62

Villanueva, L., Carmona, E., Arnaiz, M.A. & Delgado, M.E. 2014. La articulación del espacio en el 'campo de hoyos' de Manantial de Peñuelas (Celada del Camino, Burgos). *II Jornadas de jóvenes investigadores del valle del Duero: del Neolítico a la Antigüedad Tardía*, 109–127

4

Bell Beaker settlements in Andalusia

María Lazarich

The choice of settlements for this Andalusian study is based on the presence or absence of certain items that are classified according to the traditional tripartite division of the peninsular Chalcolithic, in which the final stage is characterised, almost exclusively, by Bell Beaker pottery and related elements. This can cause problems because the pottery and accompanying artefacts can be found in various contexts and not just settlements (Lazarich 1999; 2000; 2004). There is also an imbalance in research in the different regions. In western Andalusia macro-spatial studies are missing and so it is necessary to consider a broader area not only including Lower Andalusia, but also the entire Baetic Depression (Arteaga *et al.* 1995; Lazarich 1999). We also have little information on the internal organisation of settlements, given that none have been extensively studied. With few exceptions, only some limited and dispersed trenches have been excavated as at Valencina de la Concepción (Vargas, 2003; Wheatley *et al.* 2012; García-Sanjuan 2012) and consequently most of the information used for delimiting the occupation area is based on surface finds rather than on a knowledge of their true limits. Furthermore, it is difficult to assess the distribution or density of settlements due to the lack of detailed prospection in the region, and this is exacerbated when dealing with specifics, such as chronology and contemporaneity.

More extensive settlement excavations have been carried out in eastern Andalusia providing more detailed information on their defensive systems, their limits and their distribution, as well as their construction materials (Almagro & Arribas 1963; Arribas *et al.* 1983; Molina-González *et al.* 2004; Molina & Cámara 2005). Worthy of mention is the 'Campiñas' project in the Upper Guadalquivir Basin (Nocete 1994a; 1994b) which has provided important information on sites such as Alcores, Albalate, Cazalilla, Los Pozos, Cerro de la Horca, Sevilleja, Atalayuelas, Puente Tablas and Peñalosa (Nocete 1994a; Nocete *et al.* 2010).

Bell Beaker settlements

When defining or referring to the different domestic sites we face the problem of knowing what criteria must be used to classify the nature and status of settlements. Terms such as 'towns', 'villages' and 'farms' are commonly used in Iberian prehistory, where the former would include those settlements that contain a greater number of inhabitants, covering a large area, with complex structural elements and accommodating specialist artisans and merchants. The second might constitute nucleated settlements whose population was mostly or exclusively dedicated to agriculture but with some part-time artesans. Finally, the farms consist of a single house, normally with several rooms (Wells 1989). This definition is probably too simple as the real situation is much more complex and it is often difficult to integrate them with the more or less permanent settlements related to various extraction industries (quarries, mines, salt mines), as well as with seasonal temporary camps for fishing, hunting, and grazing.

Location, visibility and status of the settlements of the 3rd and 2nd millennia BC in Andalusia

Of the five climatic phases that were defined for the Holocene period (Lumley *et al.* 1976) the Bell Beaker horizon would correspond to the Subboreal (*c.* 2500–700 BC) characterised by a warm climate, similar to today, and with reduced rainfall compared to the previous period. As the climate became drier there was a progressive lowering of sea level.

In southeast Andalusia the climatic conditions were more humid than today as evidenced by the fauna from Granada and extensive forest cover but despite this, the aridity factor has been used by some researchers as one of the fundamental causes of cultural change in the Chalcolithic societies of the area (Gilman & Thornes 2014; Chapman 1990). Likewise, in the period from 7000 to 2700 BC, the first phase of Mediterranean delta formation takes place. Conditions of relative aridity occur in the Chalcolithic *c.* 2000 BC (Cacho *et al.* 2010) and at the beginning of the Bronze Age, (Cámara *et al.* 2016).

Various geoarchaeological projects (Arteaga *et al.* 1987; 1995; 2016; Arteaga & Hoffmann 1999; Schubart *et al.* 1990; Schulz *et al.* 1996) have also been fundamental in reconstructing the ecosystem and locating settlements and broadly speaking, with the information that we currently have, we can confirm that there is a total Bell Beaker preference for good, open agricultural land near secondary (and occasionally primary) waterways. There is also a preference for locally prominent hills, near constant streams of water and with natural defences (Lazarich 1999; 2005).

From the early 3rd millennium some places are occupied by increasingly stable settlements to the extent that one of the defining characteristics of the settlement of the Lower Guadalquivir is its stability or permanence. This definitive sedentism is closely related to new agricultural practices and leads, as the population grows, to an expansion of cultivation areas and eventually to competition for arable land and territorial control. Visibility is also important in relation to the location of settlements. Preferred locations commanded good local views and, if possible, had good natural defences and a reliable water supply. They overlook the local countryside and/or control natural routes, especially along the courses of the rivers and their estuaries, bays and the Gulf of the Guadalquivir (Fig. 4.1). In addition, there is a preference for easily worked soils.

In the regions of the Sierra Morena of Cordoba, Huelva and Andévalo, it has been possible to verify the existence of stable settlements such as Cabezo de los Vientos (Chinflón) prior to the metallurgical exploitation of the area, together with small villages that are located nearby (Nocete *et al.* 2010). Towards the end of the 3rd and the beginning of the 2nd millenium BC there was an increase in population marked by new settlements devoted to ore exploitation, leading to technical and territorial divisions as at Los Castillejos, El Peñón, La Longuera and Sierra Palacios (Córdoba) and Cabezo Juré (Huelva) (Nocete 2004; 2006). The preponderance of these copper mining sites in the southwestern pyrite belt decreases from 2500 to 2300 BC while, *c.* 2200–2000 BC, the metallurgical centres of the upper Guadalquivir River acquire greater importance (Nocete *et al.* 2010).

In certain regions, such as Los Alcores, El Aljarafe, in the southern sector of what was once the Gulf of the Guadalquivir, and in the countryside of Cordoba and Cadiz, a high concentration of finds have been recovered suggesting some central towns around which lie small hamlets or farms dedicated to agriculture. Thus, during the 3rd millennium there is an increasing nuclearisation of the territory which reaches its full development at the beginning of the 2nd millennium. This means that the regions of Los Alcores and Aljarafe whose fundamental nuclear centres are the towns of El Gandul and Valencina de la Concepción, are considered to be part of the same territory. This hypothesis is based on the complexity of the population seen in these two centres and on the identification of

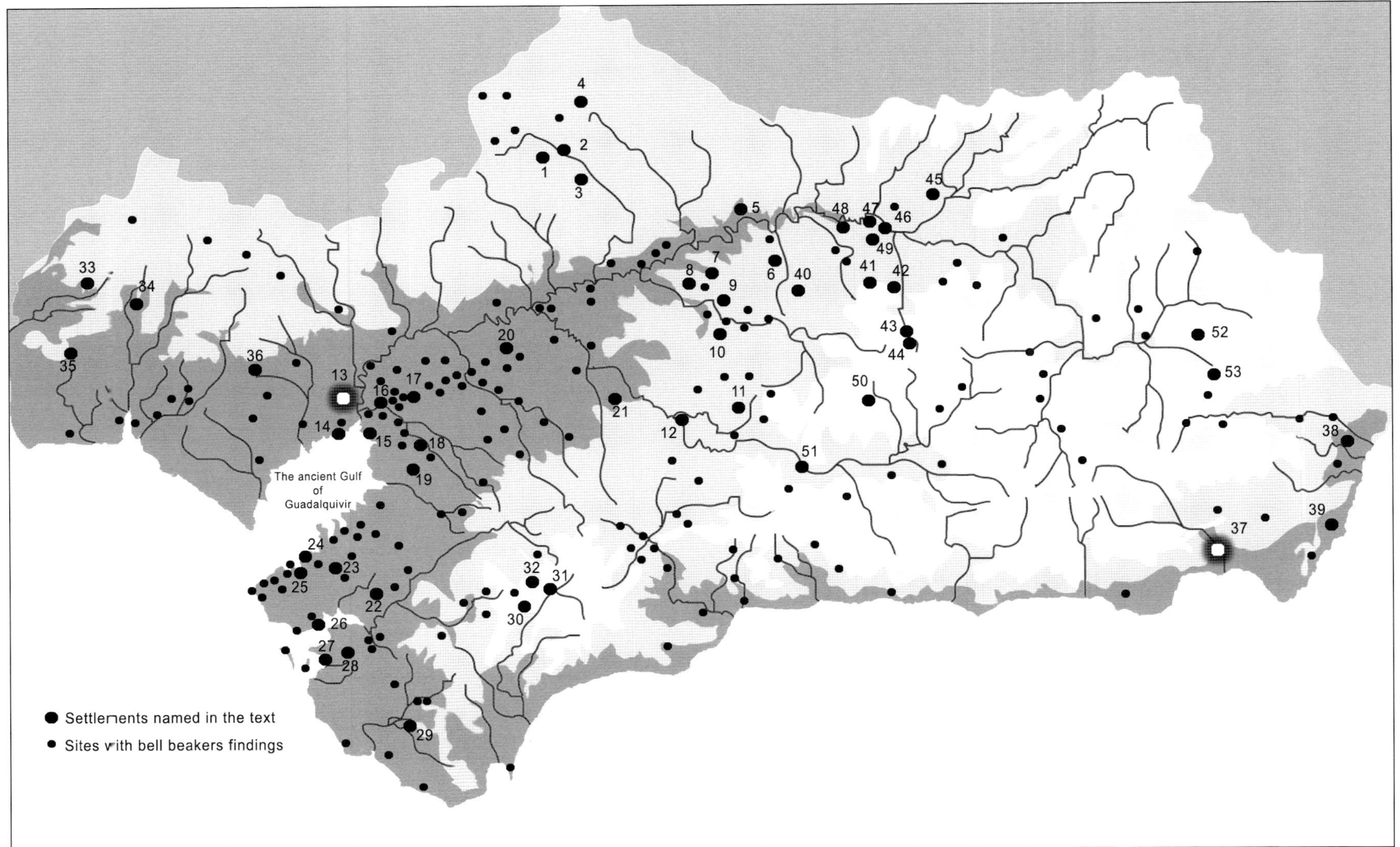

Figure 4.1: Settlements named in the text. Province of Córdoba: 1 – Los Castillejos; 2 – El Peñón; 3 – Sierra Palacios; 4 – La Longuera; 5 – Llanete de los Moros; 6 – Cerro de Jesús; 7 – Prádena; 8 – Ategua; 9 – Los Carambolos; 10 – Guta; 11 – Monturque; 12 – Cerro del horcado. Province of Sevilla; 13 – Valencina; 14 – Cerro de San Juan; 15 – Universidad Laboral; 16 – Mesa deª Gandul; 17 – El Acebuchal; 18 – El Amarguillo; 19 – Las Aguzaderas; 20 – Cerros de San Pedro; 21 – Marinaleda. Province of Cádiz; 22 – Jadramil; 23 – Cuervo Grande; 24 – Haza de la Torre; 25 – Mesas de Asta; 26 – Castillo de Doña Blanca; 27 – La Mesa; 28 – El Berrueco; 29 – Los Charcones, Province of Málaga; 30 – Silla del Moro; 31 – Acinipo o Ronda la Vieja; 32 – Ronda Casco Urbano. Province of Huelva; 33 – Cabezo de los Vientos; 34 – Cerro Juré; 35 – La Junta; 36 – Cerro de la Matanza, Province of Almería; 37 – Los Millares; 38 – Almizaraque; 39 – Las Pilas. Province Jaén; 40 – Albalate; 41 – Cerro de los Alcores; 42 – Marroquíes Bajos; 43 – Sevilleja; 44 – Puente Tablas; 45 – Cástulo; 46 – Talayuelas; 47 – Cazalilla; 48 – Los Pozos; 49 – Cerro de la Horca, Province Granada; 50 – Los Castillejos de Montefrío; 51 – El Manzanil; 52 – Cerro de la Virgen de Orce; 53 – El Malagón

other towns located in different landscapes and sharing the same 'socio-historical relationship' (Arteaga & Hoffman 1999).

Estuarine studies have determined that the changes that the mouths of the principal rivers have undergone from the 3rd millennium to the present day are striking. This is especially the case in the Guadiana and the Gualdalquivier, but also in some minor rivers, such as the Tinto, Odiel, Guadalete, Guadalhorce, Andarax and Almanzora amongst others (Arteaga & Hoffman 1999; Arteaga *et al.* 1995).

Activity areas and structural elements

Although we have very little information regarding the urban characteristics of the towns due to the lack of extensive excavations, especially in certain areas of western Andalusia, an augmented population can be observed throughout the entire region by the increased number of inhabited sites. The houses, which are mainly circular or oval, have stone foundations and mud walls and were more permanent than in the previous period. Storage structures, water management systems, together with defensive constructions, also indicate greater social organisation towards the mid-3rd millennium BC. The different structures and associated artefacts provide information on different community activities implying that there is a logic to the organisation of subsistence, techno-economic, social and ideological areas. Study of these specific areas allows us to define production, consumption and distribution processes.

Production areas

Production areas are spaces where certain specific manufacturing processes are undertaken at a higher level than the purely domestic. These specialised workshops correspond to settlements which have reached a high degree of socio-economic complexity. These activities were carried out in different areas of the towns, either in the open or inside structures. Sometimes they occur in places of non-related function such as the pottery kiln in bastion 1, C.A of the citadel of Cabezo de los Vientos (Piñón 1995; 2004).

In many settlements we have proof of metallurgy sometimes near to the extraction sites in the southwestern pyrite belt. In the province of Huelva, metallurgy took place in Masegoso, with the remains of a possible bowl-furnace, and in Chinflón, Cuchillares, Río Corumbel and Cueva del Monje where slag was found (Blanco & Rothenberg, 1981). Extensive metallurgical activity was found at Cerro Juré, where the smelting furnaces are situated within the fortifications (Nocete 2004). In the Sierra Morena of Cordoba, at Castillejos, El Peñón (Murillo 1986) and possibly at La Longuera (Murillo *et al.* 1991), as far as we know, metallurgy was undertaken both close to the extraction sites and further afield. At Valencina de la Concepción, remnants of slag, ore and crucibles were found, indicating reduction and smelting tasks (Fernández-Gómez & Oliva 1983), especially in what is known as the 'metallurgical district' with evidence for very important and varied metallurgical activity (Nocete *et al.* 2008). The El Amarguillo II settlement provided vestiges of smelting with the presence of ore and fragments of copper, tuyères and a crucible (Cabrero 1990). At El Acebuchal, fragments of copper oxide (malachite) and slag were found around Bell Beaker huts and a fragment of Bell Beaker had slag deposits adhering to its interior suggesting that this pot had been used in smelting (Bonsor 1899; Lazarich *et al.* 1995). The hut floors belonging to the Universidad laboral de Sevilla (Alcalá de Guadaira) have also produced fragments of crucible and tuyères (Lazarich 1999).

The collapse of the mining-metallurgical nuclei of the pyrite belt takes place *c.* 2300 BC. Some two hundred years later, a specialised industry of copper workshops and distribution centres had been created in the upper Guadalquivir basin such as at Peñalosa, in the mining district of Linares-La Carolina. These settlements were smaller than those of the southwest (Valencina), and more like like Castulo, Marroquíes or Úbeda (Nocete *et al.* 2010). There are four around Córdoba, El Cerro del Ahorcado, Guta, Prádena and Cerro de Jesús, providing evidence of similar activities, although At El Cerro del Ahorcado there is as yet no evidence for metallurgy *per se*. By contrast, the remaining three, in the Guadajoz valley and therefore distant from the copper sources, have provided evidence of metalworking. In Guta, traces of metalworking, as well as finished products, are so numerous that they led Carrilero and Martínez (1985) to interpret it as a metal production and recycling centre. A smelting site was also located in the town centre of Ronda (Malaga) where a crucible with the remains of smelted copper, furnace slag and some metal awls were found (Aguayo *et al.* 1987). In eastern Andalusia metallurgical activities have also been found at Los Millares (Almizaraque) (Delibes *et al.* 1989), at Las Pilas (Almeria) (Murillo-Barroso *et al.* 2017) and at El Malagón, El Cerro de la Virgen de Orce (Granada) and Cerro Minado-Santa Barbara (Huercal-Overa, Almería).

Lithic working was also carried out on most of the excavated sites either in the open or inside the huts. In eastern Andalusia, the Los Gallumbares and Malaver-Lagarín quarries are noted for the production of blades supplemented by imported items from lesser quarries in the valleys of the Turón and the Guadalhorce, in Alto Vélez and the Granada-Loja mountains and basin (Morgado 2002; Morgado & Lozano 2009). We also find other specialised settlements located close to the sources, such as those of the Sub-Baetic system that exploited siliceous outcrops, the specialised exploitation of tuff quarries in Pulpito, the dacite quarries of El Cerrajón (Linares *et al.* 1998) and obsidian outcrops in Huelva (Morgado *et al.* 2011). The exploitation and distribution of silicified oolitic limestone started in the 4th millennium BC but it is not until the 3rd millennium that the distribution of blades expands throughout the whole area of the lower Guadalquivir with its distribution point being Valencina de la Concepción. This material is found over 500 km from its source and comprises important elements of grave assemblages in the most outstanding tombs of the upper and lower Guadalquivir valleys. The circulation of lithics and metals is not considered to be commercial but rather part of a distribution system for prestige goods. These products therefore constitute elements of social differentiation and symbols of elite power (Nocete *et al.* 2005).

Textile production is confirmed by the presence of spindle whorls and crescentic, rectanguar or round loom weights in some of the huts. At Los Millares, Cerro de la Virgen in Orce, Castillejos de Montefrío, Valencina de la Concepción, and in the Ronda region and Monturque (Cordoba), the quantity of such artefacts suggests something more than simple domestic production.

Dwelling and consumption areas

These domestic activities take place in the houses and in consumption areas that are established either inside or outside the huts and close to hearths. In the huts we can identify sleeping areas, food preparation areas, workshop areas and areas where weaving took place. The remains of construction materials such as wattle and daub fragments, stone foundations and beaten earth hut floors containing abundant organic material are commonly found in the majority of the settlements.

The floor plans of these huts tend to be circular or oval. Some floors can reach almost 10 m in diameter, such as those at El Acebuchal (Carmona, Seville) (Lazarich *et al.* 1997), Cuervo Grande 1A and Haza de la Torre 7 and 8 (Jerez de la Frontera, Cadiz) (Ramos Muñoz & González Rodriguez 1992) and at Marinaleda (Sevilla) (Caro Gómez *et al.* 2004). There are also smaller structures, such as those excavated at El Amarguillo, measuring 2 m in diameter (Cabrero 1990), or the 2.5 m diameter floors found in the Universidad Laboral de Sevilla. At El Amarguillo both structures with sunken floors and others with stone foundations and adobe walls, some with a false-dome roof, are also observed (Cabrero 1990). Sunken-floored structures also occur at Gilena and Valencina de la Concepción (Cruz-Auñón *et al.* 1993). In Cabezo de los Vientos, vestiges of modest circular huts, partially excavated into the earth or the slate, were found in the area immediately adjacent to the citadel while in the interior there were huts with stone foundations measuring between 3–3.5 m in diameter and with the floor excavated between 0.2–0.3 m into the slate (Piñón, 1995). This same duality of construction appears in other settlements such as La Dehesa (El Puerto de Santa María, Cadiz) and probably in the nearby site of El Castillo de Doña Blanca, with stone and adobe-walled huts partially excavated into the ground (0.4–0.5 m) associated with simple windbreaks. (Ruiz Mata & Pérez 1994). Of the seven or eight huts excavated at El Acebuchal, hut M, which provided some complete Bell Beaker vessels, had a stone foundation while huts N, O, P and Q, were defined by mud walls and some type of organic framework indicated by large quantities of daub with reed impressions (Lazarich *et al.* 1997).

Figure 4.2: Hearth, grinding structure and stone socket in a hut at Los Millares (Santa Fé de Mondujar, Almería) (Molina & Cámara 2005)

In the province of Cordoba, only circular structures with stone foundations and mud walls are found, such as those located at Monturque (where Bell Beaker fragments were found in the rubble) (López Palomo 1993), el Llanete de los Moros and at Sierra Palacios (Gavilán 1989). They are similar to the circular huts with adobe foundations found at Cerro de la Virgen (Orce, Granada) both during is pre-Bell Beaker and Bell Beaker phases (Schüle 1980). In the same way, at Castillejos de Montefrío, with a long occupation sequence, the Bell Beaker presence does not coincide with a change in hut design.

Hearths are frequently found in settlements both in or outside the houses and are rich in artefactual and ecofactual data. Numerous activities and work processes related to consumption (Fig. 4.2), or the repair and manufacture of lithic tools took place around these hearths.

Depending on their location, hearths can also provide social information such as whether they belong to a nuclear family (individual homes) or to larger groups (larger collective homes). The concentration of hearths in the centre of the citadel of El Cabezo de los Vientos were each surrounded by stones, reaching diameters of between 0.5–1.2 m but were difficult to associate with the houses. In contrast, the huts found outside the citadel each had their own hearth (Piñón 1989). In Monturque, a hearth delimited by stones was associated with the remains of adobe and abundant organic matter but was not related to any house (López Palomo 1993). In El Acebuchal, hearths defined by stones were located inside some of the huts, while in others the hearths were defined by fire-hardened mud rings (Lazarich *et al.* 1997).

Water management

Constructions for water management include both those intended for the supply of drinking water as well as those for agricultural irrigation: 'acequias' or irrigation channels. The construction and maintenance of these structures implies a complex degree of social organisation.

The most common water supply features are wells. At Valencina de la Concepción they are circular in shape with a diameter of just over 1 m and up to 11 m deep (Fernández-Gómez & Oliva 1983). At El Jadramil (Arcos de la Frontera, Cadiz) (Lazarich 2003). The wells were concentrated in two areas (zones 1 and 2) the first at an elevation of between 116–17 m and the other a little lower at 109–113 m. In zone 1 they vary between 1–1.4 m in diameter to just over 4 m deep. Of the wells excavated in zone 2, 11 had circular wellheads while two others were square but it has not been possible to determine their depths since, for safety reasons, the excavation was halted at 4 m. The exception was well E-III (Fig. 4.3), which was excavated to 9 m but without reaching the base. Around 100 of these wells were counted before almost all of this site was destroyed by quarrying. They were dug through layers of sandstone that make up the solid geology of the region and which permit the formation of a concentration of aquifers along a layer of blue-grey clay and that emerge as springs (Gracia 2003). The walls of the wells are not regular but have small opposed cavities or openings to facilitate the descent and ascent during their construction and some of which were later partly blocked by stone walls (Lazarich 2003). All these structures were filled in using various layers of sand and sandstone blocks and some of these levels contained rare flint artefacts, some grooved dolerite fragments from the miners' hammers and fragments of decorated

Beakers. Some of these structures may have been for the capture and filtering of rainwater.

At Cerro de la Virgen (Orce) an irrigation channel was found (Schüle 1966) and Siret (1893) also mentions the existence of a large cistern near the citadel of Los Millares that was served by a long aqueduct that supplied water to the settlement (Molina & Cámara 2013). There is another example in western Andalusia at Cabezo Juré (Nocete 2004).

Storage structures

Silos are one of the most characteristic settlement features in Western Andalusia, specifically in the Guadalquivir valley. There are many such structures but they cannot be attributed to any specific period given the chronological depth of the archaeological materials found in them. Within the Bell Beaker horizon they have been found at Marinaleda and El Acebuchal (Lazarich *et al.* 1997) and, above all, at El Jadramil (Lazarich 2003). It is believed that functional variability is a factor that must be considered when trying to understand the importance of these features to their communities. The term 'silo' should only be used for those structures that we can be certain were built for the storage of cereals or legumes or, at the most, for the conservation of other foodstuffs. In this way we can avoid misunderstandings and erroneous conclusions about the importance of agriculture in these communities (Lizcano *et al.* 1993). To this end, pollen analysis is essential, as are associated tools related to such activities. They usually appear in limestone and sandstone areas, where the bedrock is easy to dig, impermeable and well-drained (Lazarich 2003).

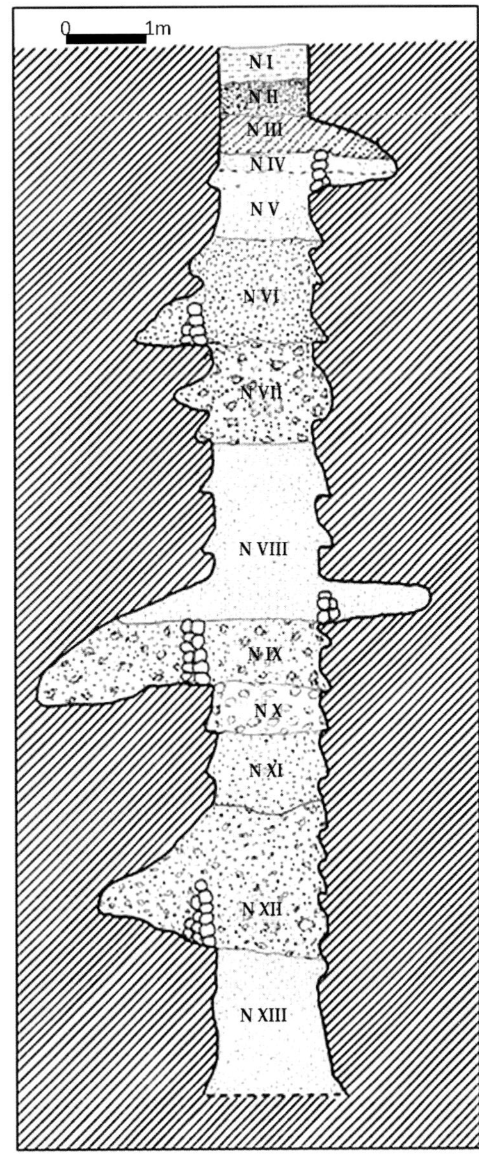

Figure 4.3: Example of one of the wells of El Jadramil (Arcos de la Frontera, Cádiz). Section of Well E-III (Lazarich 2003)

At El Jadramil, pits come in various types and sizes. There are some concentrations of small silos, which have been dated to the transition of the 4th to the 3rd millennium (Molina Carrión 1996). However, some of these structures changed their function over time, either because they were considered too small for the new needs, or because they were in a poor state of repair and some were eventually reused as burial sites or as depositories for ritually charged materials, as discussed below.

Generally speaking, Bell Beaker pits were larger with some being formed of several large silos joined together at the bottom, although these communication openings were normally blocked by masonry walls. They have openings of between 1–1.4 m in diameter which progressively increases as they gain depth, reaching maximum diameters of around 4 m at their lowest levels. Depths vary from 1.45–3.80 m (Lazarich 2003). We assume that these large structures indicate the storage of an agricultural surplus greater than that generated by a small peasant community and they seem to be designed to supply a population or work force employed for collective specialist construction or production tasks.

As well as these underground structures evidence for cereal storage in the rooms of some of the huts is also starting to emerge such as that at Monturque which was made of wattle and daub and contained an esparto basket with charred wheat, as well as some broad beans. Accompanying these foods were fragments of sickles, debitage, circular and rectangular loom weights, fragments of globular vessels, bowls with inverted rims, abundant spherical cups and some medium size dishes and bevelled-edged plates. There were also fragments of Maritime and incised Bell Beakers. Huts used for storage have also been found at Acinipo (Aguayo *et al.* 1988) and in the excavations in the urban area of Ronda, where huts containing abundant large earthenware jars and pots were located, together with numerous fragments of denticulate sickles and mortars and pestles (Aguayo *et al.* 1987).

Structures for the deposit of offerings and/or commensality and cult rituals

Other underground structures have been located in various Andalusian Chalcolithic settlements which, due to the archaeological deposits they contain, have led many researchers to interpret them as having a ritual function. These are sometimes re-used silos or shallow pits or wells with a circular ground plan and with narrow wellheads (<1m). The fact that many of them are filled with organic matter along with abundant lithics and ceramics initially suggested that they were rubbish dumps and it is reasonable to assume that any redundant underground structure would be backfilled with all kinds of remains, or simply with earth, so that they would not pose a danger to people or animals. It is very unlikely that they were principally constructed as rubbish pits. A review of Bonsor's excavation diaries for El Acebuchal revealed that in the 22 wells located during the 1896 excavations near barrow H, there were ivory buttons, idols, Beakers, carinated bowls and almost complete plates with Bell Beaker decoration. In addition, there were selected animal remains such as deer hooves and antlers, remains of the skull and jaws of pigs or wild boar, and even the presence of metal objects such as Palmela points, chisels, and a large number of awls. Together, these deposits suggest ritual deposition (Bonsor 1899) and, possibly, the remains of a banquet or feast (Lazarich *et al.* 1995; Lazarich 1999). In support of this hypothesis, it should be noted that Bonsor records in his diary that many of these wells were inside a large hut of about 10 m in diameter in which he found a burial as well as complete Bell Beakers (General Archive of Andalusia, Bonsor, File. 12. P.1. Sheets: 1, 2, 6, 8, 9). This tradition appears on many other Andalusian settlements and cemeteries prior to the Bell Beaker horizon.

Finally, mention must be made of a large underground structure with a horizontal double entrance (Structure A-3), found in Zone 3 at El Jadramil. Excavated entirely into the sandstone bedrock, the main entrance had a carved portico with a large 4.5 m long and 1.7m high arch. After negotiating a step of about 0.5 m, access was gained to a corridor or anteroom in which there were two small secondary chambers, and where a silo-like structure had been constructed but this could not be completely excavated. Continuing down the corridor, and after negotiating a step, access was gained to the main chamber which had an irregular shaped floor plan, measured 4 m–3.8 m and had a vaulted ceiling. Off one of its sides, within its central axis, entrance was gained to another chamber or corridor but this could not be explored as the ceiling collapsed. Entrance could also be gained to the main chamber through another opening situated further North. This had a corridor approximately 3 m long and 1.5 m wide which, also after negotiating a step, accessed the chamber. What is significant about this structure, which was unfortunately quarried away, is that its access entrances had been blocked up with stone walls and the structure partly filled with very clean yellow sand. Only a very small number of finds were recovered among which were flint debitage and retouched artefacts, fragments of plates with a thickened rim, smooth hemispherical bowls, and a fragment of comb-decorated Bell Beaker. There was also a fragment of a cylindrical sandstone idol and a heavily used grooved miner's maul (Lazarich 2003). Although the true purpose of this structure is currently unknown it is very likely that it may have been a hypogeum or sanctuary devoted to worship.

Defensive systems

These reflect the degree of development of the communities that built them. They clearly arise from the need to defend the inhabitants and their belongings but they also display prestige and power and demonstrate a degree of control over their locales. In Andalusia structures range from simple single-walled enclosures, to the most complex settlements that have several lines of walls, bastions and even exterior fortifications.

An example of the latter type is Los Millares (Almería) which was founded around

3200 BC. According to Cámara and Molina (2013) the settlement was at its height when Bell Beakers arrived (2600–2400 BC) and comprised three lines of concentric walls and a fortified 'citadel' in the centre of the settlement (Fig. 4.4) (Molina-González *et al.* 2004). The great 'barbican' or main gate built towards the end of the Copper Age also had loophole arrow-slits (Cámara and Molina 2013) (Fig. 4.5). During the second period (2400–2200 BC) which coincides with the expansion of the local Bell Beaker style, the walls are abandoned and only the citadel is occupied coinciding with recurrent fires in the fortifications. Other researchers, however, have suggested that the construction of the forts was later and that during this last stage of Los Millares they were inhabited by decentralised and hostile populations (Lull *et al.* 2010).

Another fortified settlement in the southeast of the Peninsula is El Malagón (Cullár, Granada) with several sections of curtain wall and a fort situated on a rocky crest in the extreme eastern part of the site (Torre & Sáez 1984). Equally remarkable are the fortifications at Cerro de la Virgen de Orce (Granada) where the main timber-laced wall of the acropolis was built by superimposing rows of layers of mud and well-worked stones in a 'herringbone' fashion (Schüle 1980). Added to this is a series of parallel curtain walls and intermediate trenches that totally enclose the site which is situated on a rocky escarpment. At los Castillejos de Montefrío, despite its extensive occupation from the 5th millennium, there is no evidence for defences until the transition from the 3rd to the 2nd millennia (Period VIII, Chalcolithic 2400–2000 BC) when the eastern access to the town is closed by a stone wall. To the north it has been possible to define strata attesting a great fire that affected the whole site. The absence of defences up until this time was possibly due to the rough topography making the site difficult to access (Cámara *et al.* 2016).

We have little information regarding fortified sites in western Andalusia mainly due to the lack of archaeological excavations but in the literature there are numerous references to the possibility of walls at many of the settlements contemporary with Bell Beakers based simply on the morphology of the hill where the site is located or on the presence of accumulations of more or less regular stones in specific areas. However, it is unwise to attribute the construction of these walls to specific periods as many of these sites have protohistoric or historical phases, and some are even still occupied.

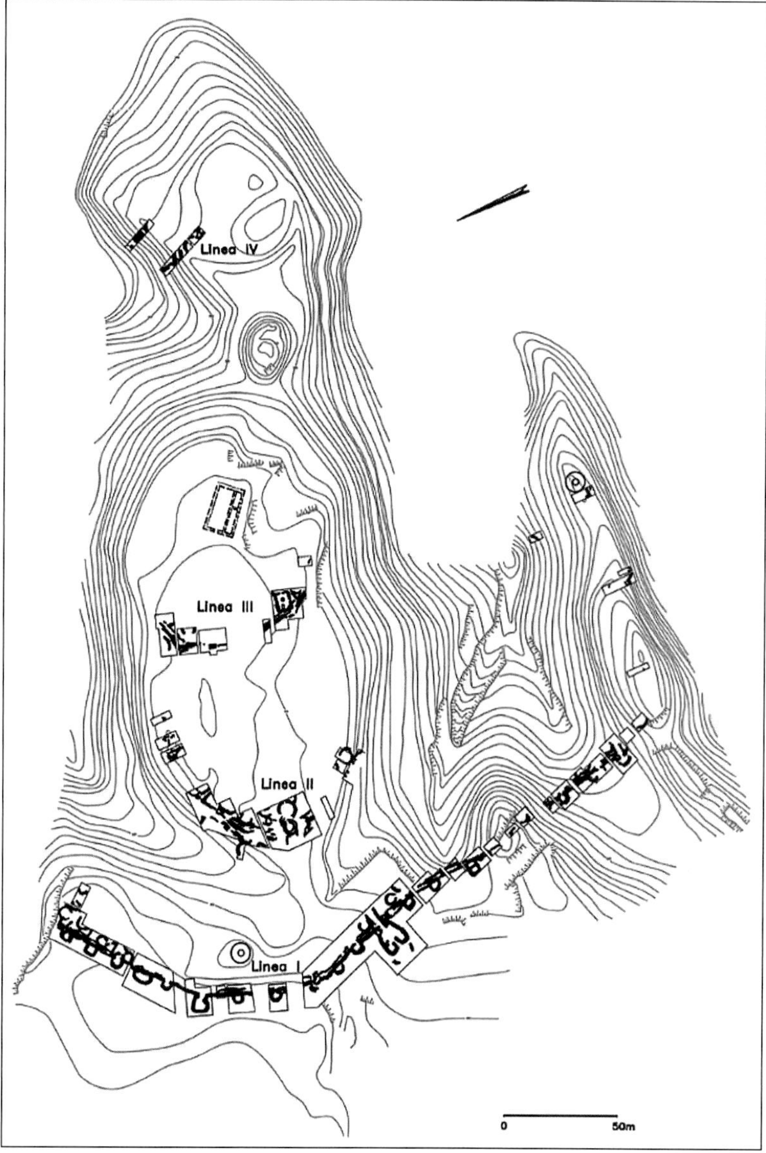

Figure 4.4: Plan of Los Millares, showing the layout of the walls (Cámara & Molina 2013, fig. 1).

We have references, substantiated to varying degrees, to the existence of defensive systems at Chinflón (Nocete 1993), at el Cerro de la Matanza (Campos *et al.* 1996) and without doubt at Cabezo Juré and La Junta (Huelva). At this last site, the defensive wall was more than 2 m wide and some 50 m long, and may have been as much as 4 m high. Likewise, the citadel of Cabezo de los Vientos (Huelva) encloses an oval area 30–20 m respecting the shape of the ridge on which it stands. The hollow bastions

Figure 4.5: Photograph of the main gate through the outer wall at Los Millares (Molina & Cámara 2005)

and towers, located in places that, apparently, offered the greatest vulnerability, are integrated into its walls. In the Guadalquivir valley there are other examples, although less numerous than in the mountains, situated on ridges. These include Cerros de San Pedro (Fernández Caro 1992), Mesa del Gandul (Pellicer & Hurtado 1987) and Marinaleda (Caro Gómez *et al.* 1994) (all in Seville) and Los Castillejos and El Peñon (Cordoba) (Gavilán & Vera 1990). Further sites are found at Mesas de Asta (Esteve 1971) and La Mesa (Cadiz) (Ramos Muñoz *et al.* 1994) and La Silla del Moro in the mountain range of Ronda (Aguayo *et al.* 1987; 1988).

Defences, of course, do not always have to be made of stone. Wood could also be used for palisades and in this regard it is important to remember the numerous references to trenches and ditches in many Chalcolithic settlements. Unfortunately, in most of these instances, the exact relation of the ditch to the settlement is unknown. In Valencina de la Concepción the ditches vary from almost 4 m wide and 2–7 m deep and with U- and V-shaped profiles. The total length is unknown. Within the last 10 years it has recently been confirmed that at least one of the ditches in Valencina constitutes part of the defensive network of this extensive enclosure. In certain areas of the Lower Guadalquivir Valley, building stone is not very abundant and some areas such as the area of Aljarafe, suffer from mass land movements (Díaz del Olmo & López Reguero 1983) neither being conducive to stone construction and possibly accounting for the ditches at Valencina de la Concepción, where stone walls would have needed constant labour-intensive reconstruction.

Many questions remain unanswered at Valencina. Situated on a large elevated plateau overlooking the former Guadalquivir estuary (Fig. 4.1) and about 6 km from present-day Seville, we do not know if the 400 hectares from which surface finds were recovered represents simultaneous occupation of the entire area. A residential zone and an industrial zone (storage structures and metallurgical activities) occupy the northern part of the settlement and there is a burial area including both an important megalithic cemetery (Matarrubilla, Ontiveros, La Pastora, Montelirio, etc.) associated with smaller tombs (Vargas 2003). This settlement is interpreted as a great centre of power and the main nucleus of the first Mediterranean Atlantic civilisation in Western Europe (Arteaga & Cruz-Auñón 1999; Arteaga 2000).

Although the 'symbolist' interpretation of certain enclosures is fashionable there are still those who see the enclosures as primarily defensive though the two hypotheses are not exclusive (Cámara & Molina 2013).

Conclusions

Bell Beakers in Andalusia do not merely represent a chronological stage, nor a simple introduction by exchange or trade of a prestige package. Its presence is linked to a whole series of economic and social transformations that have been in development since the end of the Neolithic period and ultimately lead to a more complex social structure motivated by internal factors, such as the accumulation of surpluses and the expansion of productive forces. Thus, at the beginning of the 3rd millennium, we can perceive a series of innovations in settlement patterns, closely related to the new and emerging social needs for the environment's resources.

Settlement features do not change with the advent of Bell Beakers. The fortifications and the variety of structures (ditched enclosures, silos, wells, etc.) have been present since the end of the 4th millennium (some even before) and undergo considerable development during the 3rd millennium BC and it is only after this population expansion in the middle of the 3rd millennium that the first International or Maritime Bell Beaker complex appears but always accompanied by so-called 'regional' styles of pottery with incised and comb impressed decoration (Carrilero 1992; Lazarich 1999; 2000; 2005). However, it is also the Maritime style that is the first to disappear with no recorded finds after 2000 BC. Stratigraphic information from Los Millares, Los Castillejos de Montefrío, Cerro de la Virgen de Orce, Malagón, El Manzanil, Monturque, Cerro de San Juan and Valencina de la Concepción, shows that it also appears with other types of pottery with combed and metopic decoration and of these, Bell-shaped forms survived the longest (*c.* 2000–1800 BC) with the greatest number of discoveries being made on occupation sites (80%).

In Andalusia there is a wide variety of ceramic forms decorated with Bell Beaker techniques (beakers, bowls, plates, dishes, casseroles, cups and supports). This includes the classic S-profiled Maritime Beaker but there are also other manifestations such as bowls, goblets and casseroles with or without carinations (Carrilero 1992; Lazarich 1999). Scanning Electron Microscopy on 28 ceramic samples from various sites in the Lower Guadalquivir has shed light on the composition of the clays and the comparative analysis of another 30 undecorated and contemporary samples, as well as those corresponding to other historical periods (60 samples from the Neolithic to the Roman era) indicate the exploitation of local clay sources (Lazarich 1999). Likewise, there are no differences in the composition of the ceramic pastes between the different styles, so we can consider them all to be locally made products. These results coincide with those from X-ray diffraction, petrographic and thermal analysis carried out on fragments from Monturque (Barrios *et al.* 1991a; 1991b), and new analyses at Valencina de la Concepción (Inácio *et al.* 2012) and Cerro de la Virgen in Orce (Molina *et al.* 2017) only confirm the previously obtained data.

Since Clarke (1976) considered Bell Beakers to be symbols of rank and prestige few have questioned it. Here in Andalusia, finds were concentrated in the most monumental tombs or in those in which they were accompanied by other prestigious items such as gold, amber, variscite beads and ivory. In the settlements, Bell Beakers also appear in the central areas of citadels or in structures containing more valuable items. Bell-shaped vessels are present in a great variety of funeral structures, from the reuse of megalithic graves, in particular *tholoi*, to the more or less complex artificial caves, pits, and cists. They are also found in burials in natural caves. Because many graves were the result of antiquarian activity we lack physical anthropological studies regarding gender or age nevertheless, we can affirm from what evidence that we do have that Bell Beakers were associated with both sexes.

As mentioned above, paleoclimatic studies show that the weather at the beginning of the Bell Beaker period in Andalusia was more humid than at present but that the beginning of the 2nd millennium saw the start of an arid trend that became more pronounced towards the middle of this millennium, coinciding with the regional demise of Bell Beakers.

It is also at the transition from the 3rd to the 2nd millennium BC when we observe settlement changes such as houses with straight walls, changes in subsistence strategies, the production of objects and funeral practices for example burials below the houses in the settlements. New non-decorated ceramic forms emerge and more sophisticated metalwork appears (Lull *et al.* 2015). Fire levels can be detected in many settlements and some are conspicuous such as at Castillejos de Montefrío (2150–2000 BC) coinciding with the construction of a wall on the most unprotected flank of the hill (Cámara *et al.* 2016). Population reduction can be seen at sites such as Los Millares, when only the citadel was inhabited (Cámara & Molina 2013) and some settlements such as Cabezo Juré and El Jadramil were even abandoned.

These changes start with the advent of rain-irrigated agriculture when the vegetation cover was cleared in order to cultivate new lands and to generate a greater surplus, especially in the areas that specialised in providing food to an increasingly centralised population with an increased artesan class. At the same time there is a need to supply those peripheral areas responsible for obtaining certain raw materials. This, possibly aggrevated by adverse climatic factors, would see the progressive abandonment of the less fertile agricultural land and the excessive deforestation would result in greater water run-off leading to soil erosion and the loss of the humic topsoil during the increasingly torrential rainy season resulting in population pressure to control the most productive soils.

Acknowledgements

I would like to express my gratitude to Alex M. Gibson for his invitation to contribute to this monograph, as well as for his suggestions and help with writing this article. I would also like to thank Gómez and Gleghorn for the initial English translation of the text.

References

Aguayo, P., Lobato, R. & Carrilero, M. 1987. Excavaciones arqueológicas en el casco antiguo de Ronda (Málaga). Agosto de 1984, *Anuario Arqueológico de Andalucía*, 1985 III, 236–39

Aguayo, P., Carrilero, M. & Martínez, G. 1988. Excavaciones en el yacimiento pre y protohistórico de Acinipo: (Ronda, Málaga). *Anuario Arqueológico de Andalucía* 1986, II, 333–7

Almagro, M. & Arribas, A. 1963. *El poblado y la necrópolis megalítica de Los Millares (Santa Fe de Mondújar, Almería)*, Biblioteca Praehistorica Hispanica III, Madrid

Arteaga, O. 2000. El proceso histórico en el territorio argárico de Fuente Álamos. La ruptura del paradigma del sudeste desde la perspectiva atlántica-mediterránea del extremo occidente. In Schubart, Pingel y Arteaga: *Fuente Álamos. Las excavaciones arqueológicas de 1977–1991 en el poblado de la Edad del Bronce*, 117–44. Sevilla. Consejería de Cultura de la Junta de Andalucía.

Arteaga, O. & Cruz-Auñón, R. 1999. Una valoración del Patrimonio Histórico en el campo de silos de la finca El Cuervo-RTVA (Valencina de la Concepción, Sevilla). *Anuario Arqueológico de Andalucía,* 1995, 608–16

Arteaga, O. & Hoffmann, D. 1999. Dialéctica del proceso natural y sociohistórico en las costas mediterráneas de Andalucía. *Revista Atlántica-Mediterránea de Prehistoria y Arqueología Social* 2, 13–121

Arteaga, O. & Roos, A.Mª. 1996. El Proyecto Geo-arqueológico de las Marismas del Guadalquivir. Perspectivas arqueológicas de la Campaña de 1992. *Anuario Arqueológico de Andalucía* 1992, 329–39

Arteaga, O., Nocete, F., Ramos, J., Recuerda, & Roos, A.Mª. 1987. Excavaciones sistemáticas en el Cerro de Albalate (Porcuna, Jaén). *Anuario Arqueológico de Andalucía* 1986, II, 395–400

Arteaga, O., Schulz, H.D. & Roos, A.M. 1995. El Problema del 'Lacus Ligustinus'. Investigaciones Geoarqueológicas en torno a las Marismas del Bajo Guadalquivir. *Tartessos 25 años después 1968–1993. Jerez de la Frontera,* 99–135

Arteaga, O., Barragan, D., Roos, A.Mª & Schulz, H.D. 2016. Primicia cartográfica del río Guadalquivir hace 6500 años. *Revista atlántico-Mediterránea de Arqueología Social*, 18, 139–61

Arribas, A., Molina, F., Saez, L. de la Torre, F. Aguayo, P. Bravo A. & Suarez, A. 1983. Excavaciones en Los Millares (Santafé de Mondujar, Almería). Campañas de 1982 y 1983, *Cuadernos de Prehistoria Universidad de Granada* 8, 123–147

Barrios, J., López Palomo, J.A., Montealegre, L. & Najas, J.J. 1991a. Materiales cerámicos de la campiña de Córdoba y su posible uso en la fabricación de vasos campaniformes. *XXXI Congreso Nacional de Cerámica y Vidrio*, 87–8

Barrios, J., López Palomo, J.A., Montealegre, L., Najas, J.J. 1991b. Características estructurales y mineralógicas de cerámicas campaniformes procedentes de Monturuque (Córdoba)». *Boletín de la Sociedad española de Cerámica y Vidrio*, 30, 3, 187–193

Blanco, A. & Rothenberg, B. 1981 *Exploración arqueometalúrgica de Huelva (EAH).* Río Tinto Minera S.A. Labor, S.A. Barcelona

Bonsor, G. 1899. Les colonies agrícoles preromaines de la Vallée du Betis. *Revue Archéologique, XXXV* (3 serie). Paris

Cabrero, R. 1990. El poblado de la Edad del Cobre denominado Amarguillo II (Los Molares, Sevilla). Informe preliminar tras la excavación sistemática de 1987. *Anuario Arqueológico de Andalucía* 1987, II, 276–7

Cacho, I., Valero B. & González Samperiz, P., 2010. Revisión de las reconstrucciones paleoclimáticas en la Península Ibérica desde el último periodo glacial. In Pérez, F.F. & Bóscolo, R. (eds), *Clima en España: Pasado, presente y futuro.* Ministerio de Ciencia e Innovación, Madrid, 9–24

Cámara, A. & Molina, F. 2013. Indicadores de conflicto bélico en la prehistoria reciente del cuadrante sudeste de la Península Ibérica: El caso del calcolítico. *Cuadernos de Prehistoria y Arqueología de la Universidad de Granada* 23, 99–132

Cámara, J.A., Afonso, J.A. & Molina, F. 2016. La ocupación de las Peñas de los Gitanos (Montefrío, Granada) desde el Neolítico al mundo romano. Asentamiento y ritual funerario. In Pedregosa Megías, R.J. (ed.), *Arqueología e Historia de un paisaje singular. La Peña de los Gitanos, Montefrío (Granada)*, 17–121. Montefrío: Ayuntamiento de Montefrío/Ministerio de Cultura

Caro Gómez, J.A., Cruz-Auñón Briones, R., García Sanjuan, L. 2004. Excavación de Urgencia en el asentamiento de la Edad del Cobre de Marinaleda (Marinaleda, Sevilla). *Anuario Arqueológico de Andalucía* 2001, 2, 920–8

Carrilero, M. 1992. *El fenómeno campaniforme en el sureste de la Península Ibérica.* Tesis doctoral microfilmada. Granada

Carrilero, M. & Martínez, G. 1985. El yacimiento de Guta (Castro del Río, Córdoba), y la Prehistoria reciente de la Campiña cordobesa. *Cuadernos de Prehistoria Universidad de Granada* 10, 187–223.

Campos, J.M., Gómez Toscano, F., Borja, F., Castiñeira, J. & García Rincón, J.M. 1996. Prospección arqueológica superficial en la Campiña de Huelva. Sector Guadiamar-Candon, *Anuario_Arqueológico de Andalucía 1992*, 231–6

Chapman, R. 1990. *Emerging complexity: The later prehistory of south-east Spain, Iberia and the west Mediterranean.* Cambridge. Cambridge University Press

Clarke, D.L. 1976. The Beaker network. Social and economic models, In Lanting, J.N. & Van der Waals J.D. (eds), *Glockenbecher Symposium, Oberried, 1974*, 459–76. Bussum/Haarlem: Fibula-van Dishoeck

Cruz-Auñón, R., Moreno, E. & Cáceres, P. 1993. Proyecto: Estudio del hábitat calcolítico en el pie de sierra del Bajo Valle Guadalquivir. *Proyectos 1985–1992*, 373–82, Consejería de Cultura. Junta de Andalucía

Delibes, G., Fernández-Miranda, M., Fernández Posse, M., Martín Morales, C., Rovira, S. & Sanz, M. 1989. Almizaraque (Almería): Minería y metalurgia calcolíticas en el sureste de la Península Ibérica, in *Minería y metalurgia en las antiguas civilizaciones mediterráneas y europeas*. I. Ministerio de Cultura, 81–96

Díaz del Olmo, F. & López Reguero, C. 1983. La provincia de Sevilla. Aspectos físicos configuradores de su territorio. *Sevilla y su Provincia*, 97–203. Sevilla: Ed. Gever

Esteve, M. 1971. *Historia de unas ruinas: Mesas de Asta Jerez.* Instituto de Estudios Gaditanos. Diputación de Cádiz

Fernández Caro, J.J. 1992. *Carta arqueológica del Término de Fuentes de Andalucía (Sevilla).* Écija. Ayuntamiento de Fuentes de Andalucía

Fernández-Gómez, F. & Oliva, D. 1983. Las Edades del Metal, In *Sevilla y su Provincia*, 35–65. Ediciones Gever. Sevilla

García Sanjuán, L. 2012. El asentamiento de la Edad del Cobre en Valencina de la Concepción estado actual de la investigación, debates y perspectivas, in García Sanjuán, L., Vargas Jiménez, J.M., Hurtado Pérez, V., Ruiz Moreno, T. & Cruz-Auñón Briones, R. (eds), *El Asentamiento Prehistórico de Valencina de la Concepción. Investigación y Tutela en el 150 Aniversario del descubrimiento de La Pastora,* Sevilla, Universidad de Sevilla, 21–60

Gavilán, B. & Vera, C. 1990. La Edad del Cobre en el alto Valle del Guadiato (Tramo Fuente Obejuna. Bélez, Córdoba). *Cuadernos de Prehistoria Universidad de Granada* 14–15, 137–55

Gilman, A. & Thornes, J. B. 2014. *Land-use and Prehistory in South-East Spain.* London. Rouletledge library edition

Gracia, F.J. 2003. Condicionantes geológicos del yacimiento de 'El Jadramil' (Arcos de la Frontera, Cádiz), in Lazarich, *El Jadramil (Arcos de la Frontera). Estudio arqueológico de un asentamiento agrícola en la campiña gaditana.* Cadiz: Ayuntamiento de Arcos de la Frontera

Inácio, N., Nocete Calvo, F., Nieto Liñán, J.M., López Aldana, P.M., Pajuelo, A., Rodríguez Bayona, M. & Abril, D. 2012. Cerámica común y campaniforme en Valencina de la Concepción (Sevilla): Indagando su precedencia través del análisis arqueométrico. *Estudos Arqueológicos de Oeiras, 19. Actas del IX Congresso Ibérico de Arqueometria, 2011*, 95–104

Lazarich, M. 1999. *El campaniforme en Andalucía Occidental,* Servicio de Publicaciones Universidad de Cádiz, Cádiz

Lazarich, M. 2000. Estado actual de la investigación sobre el campaniforme en Andalucía occidental, *Madrider Mitteilungen* 41, 112–38

Lazarich, M. 2003. *El Jadramil (Arcos de la Frontera) Estudio Arqueológico de un asentamiento agrícola en la campiña gaditana.* Ayuntamiento de Arcos de la Frontera. Cádiz

Lazarich, M. 2005. El campaniforme en Andalucía. In Rojo Guerra, M.; Garrido Pena, R. & García Martínez de Lagrán, I. (eds), *El campaniforme en la Península Ibérica y su contexto europeo. Bell beakers in the Iberian Peninsula and their European context.* Valladolid: Universidad de Valladolid (Serie Arte y Arqueología 21), 351–70

Lazarich, M., Ladrón de Guevara, I., Rodríguez de Zuloaga, M. & Sánchez, M. 1995. El yacimiento de El Acebuchal (Carmona, Sevilla): Análisis de las estructuras calcolíticas a través de los escritos inéditos de J. Bonsor e Historiografía. *SPAL* 4, 81–100

Lazarich, M., Ladrón De Guevara, I., & Sánchez, M. 1997. El Campaniforme de El Acebuchal (Carmona, Sevilla). Nuevos datos e interpretaciones, *XXIV Congreso Nacional de Arqueología*, (Cartagena, Octubre de 1997), 155–61

Lizcano, R., Gómez, E., Cámara, J.A., Aguayo, M., Araque, D., Bellido, I., Contreras, L., Hernández, M., Izquierdo, M. & Ruiz, J. 1993. 1ª Campaña de excavaciones de urgencia en el Pabellón polideportivo de Martos (Jaén). *Anuario Arqueológico de Andalucía*, 1991, III, 278–91

López Palomo, L.A. 1993. *Calcolítico y Edad del Bronce al Sur de Córdoba. Estratigrafía de Monturque.* Córdoba: Monte de Piedad y Caja de Ahorros de Córdoba

Lull, V., Micó, R., Rihuete, C. & Risch, R. 2010. Las relaciones políticas y económicas de El Argar, *Menga. Revista de Prehistoria de Andalucía* 1, 11–36

Lull, V., Micó, R., Rihuete, C. & Risch, R. 2015. Transitional and conflict at the end of the 3rd millennium BC, in south Iberia. In Meller, H., Arz, H. W., Jung, R. & Risch, R. (eds), 2015. *2200 BC – Ein Klimasturz als Ursache für den Zerfall der Alten Welt? 7. Mitteldeutscher Archäologentag vom 23. bis 26. Oktober 2014 in Halle (Saale).* Tagungen des Landesmuseum für Vorgeschichte 12/II, 365–408. Halle/Saale: Landesamt für Denkmalpflege und Archäologie Sachsen-Anhalt

Lumley, H., Renault, J., Miskovsky, J.C. & Guilaine, J. 1976. Le cadre chronologique et Paleoclimatique du postglaciaire'. *Prehistoire Francaise.* T. II, 3–16. París: C.N.R.S.

Molina Carrión, M. 1996. Excavaciones de urgencias en el cerro de 'El Palmar' (El Jadramil, Arco de la Frontera). *Anuario Arqueológico de Andalucía* III, 1992, 78–9.

Molina-González, F. & Cámara, J.A. 2005. *Los Millares. Guía del yacimiento arqueológico*, Dirección General de Bienes Culturales. Sevilla

Molina-González, F., Cámara, J.A., Capel, J.; Nájera, T., Sáez, L. 2004. Los Millares y la periodización de la Prehistoria Reciente del Sureste. *III Simposio de Prehistoria de la Cueva de Nerja*, II-III, 142–58. Nerja

Molina-González, F., Cámara Dorado, A. & Villarroya, M. 2017. El fenómeno campaniforme en el Sudeste de la Península Ibérica: el caso del Cerro de la Virgen (Orce, Granada). In Victor S. Gonçalves (ed.), *Sinos e taças junto ao oceano e mais longe. Aspectos da presença Campaniforme na Península Ibérica*, 258–75

Morgado, A. 2002. Transformación social y producción de hojas de sílex durante la Prehistoria Reciente de

Andalucía oriental. La estrategia de la complejidad, Unpubl. PhD thesis, Universidad de Granada, Granada (electronic edition, 2008), Granada

Morgado, A. & Lozano Rodríguez, J.A. 2009. Geological Factors and Flint Mining in the Betic Cordillera (Southern Spain, 4th – 3rd mill. BC): *The Case of the Large Blades Production, The 2nd International Conference of the UISPP Comission on Flint Mining in Pre- and Protohistoric Times* (Madrid, October 14–17, 2009), 45–6

Morgado, A., Lozano Rodríguez, J.A. & Pelegrin, J. 2011. Las explotaciones prehistóricas del sílex de la Formación Milanos (Granada, España). *Menga, Revista de Prehistoria de Andalucía* 2, 261–9

Murillo-Barroso, M., Martinón, M., Camalich Mª D., Martín Socas, D. & Molina- González, F. 2017. Early metallurgy in SE Iberia. The workshop of Las Pilas (Mojácar, Almería, Spain) *Archaeological and Anthropological Sciences* 9 (7), 1539–69

Murillo Redondo, J.F. 1986. Nuevos yacimientos calcolíticos en el sector noroccidental de la provincia de Córdoba. *Estudios de Prehistoria Cordobesa* I, 77–94.

Murillo Redondo, J.F., Araque, F., Ruiz López, A. & Ruiz Gómez A. Mª. 1991. Materiales calcolíticos procedentes de la Longuera (El Viso, Córdoba). *Anales de Arqueología Cordobesa* 2, 53–92

Nocete, F. 1993. Primera sesión de trabajo: Limites culturales-fronteras políticas. *En Frontera. Arqueología Espacial* 14. Teruel

Nocete, F. 1994a *La formación del estado en la Campiñas del Alto Guadalquivir (3.000 1.500 a.n.e.).* Universidad de Granada

Nocete, F. 1994b. Space as coercion: the transition to the state in the social formations of la Campiña, Upper Guadalquivir Valley, Spain. *c.*1900–1600 B.C. *Journal of Anthropological Archaeology* 13, 171–200

Nocete, F. 2004. *Odiel. Proyecto de investigación arqueológica para el análisis del origen de la desigualdad social en el Suroeste de la Península Ibérica.* Arqueología Monografías 19, Sevilla. Consejería de Cultura. Junta de Andalucía

Nocete, F. 2006. The first specialised copper industry in the Iberian Peninsula: Cabezo Juré (2900–2200 BC) *Antiquity* 80, Issue 309, 1 September 2006, 646–57

Nocete, F., Sáez, R., Cabrero, R., Cruz-Auñón, R. & Nieto, J. M. 2005. Las relaciones centro/periferia en el Valle del Guadalquivir del III milenio ANE: La circulación de hojas de caliza oolítica silicificada, *Tabona: Revista de prehistoria y de arqueología* 14, 33–62

Nocete, F., Sáez, R., Nieto, J.M., Inácio, N., Bayona, M.R., Peramo, A., Vargas, J.M., Cruz-Auñón, R., Gil-Ibarguchi J.I. & Santos J.F. 2008. The smelting quarter of Valencina de la Concepción (Seville, Spain): the specialised copper industry in a political centre of the Guadalquivir Valley during the Third millennium BC (2750–2500 BC). *Journal of Archaeological Science* 35 (3), 717–32

Nocete, F., Lizcano, R., Peramo, A. & Gómez, E. 2010. Emergence, collapse and continuity of the first political system in the Guadalquivir Basin from the fourth to the second millennium BC: The long-term sequence of Úbeda (Spain). *Journal of Anthropological Archaeology* 29, (2), 219–37

Pellicer, M. & Hurtado, V. 1987. Excavaciones en la Mesa de El Gandul (Alcalá de Guadaira, Sevilla). *Anuario Arqueológico de Andalucía* 1986, II, 338–41

Piñón, F. 1989. El proceso de poblamiento del sector noroccidental de la provincia de Huelva durante la Edad del Cobre. *III Jornadas del Patrimonio de la Sierra de Huelva*, 93–155

Piñón, F. 1995. Los Vientos de la Zarcita (Santa Bárbara de la Casa). Un asentamiento calcolítico fortificado en el sector noroccidental de la provincia de Huelva, in Kunst, M. (Coord) *Orígenes, Estructuras y Relaçoes das Culturas Calcolíticas da Península Ibérica. Actas da I Jornadas Arqueológicas de Torres Vedras (3–5 de Abril de 1987),* 169–87. Lisboa: Patrimonio Cultural

Piñón, F. 2004. *El horizonte cultural megalítico en el área de Huelva.* Sevilla. Consejería de Cultura

Ramos Muñoz, J. & González Rodríguez, R. 1992. Prospección arqueológica superficial en el término municipal de Jerez de la Frontera, Cádiz. Campaña 1990. *Anuario Arqueológico de Andalucía* 1990, 64–75

Ramos Muñoz, J., Castañeda, V.; Pérez, M., Lazarich, M., Martínez, C., Montañés, M., Lozano, J.M. & Calderón, D. 1994. La secuencia prehistórica del poblado de La Mesa (Chiclana de la Frontera). Su contribución a la ordenación del territorio de la Campiña Litoral y Banda Atlántica de Cádiz. *Boletín del Museo de Cádiz* 4, 23–41

Ruiz Mata, D. & Pérez, C. 1994. El Bronce en el Bajo Guadalquivir, Edad del Bronce: *Actas del curso de verano de la Universidad de Vigo (Xinzo de Limia, 1993)*, 235–76

Schubart, H., Arteaga, O., Hoffmann, G., & Kunst, M. 1990. Investigaciones geológico-arqueológicas sobre la antigua línea de costa en Andalucía. Campaña 1988. *Anuario Arqueológico de Andalucía* 1988, II, 185–9

Schüle, W. 1966. El poblado del Bronce antiguo en el Cerro de la Virgen de Orce (Granada) y su acequia de regadío. *IX Congreso Nacional de Arqueología* (Valladolid 1965), 113–26

Schüle, W. 1980. *Orce und Galera.* Zwei Siedlungen aus dem 3. bis I. Jahrtausend v. Chr. im Sudösten der Iberischen Halbinsel: I. Übersicht über die Ausgrabungen 1962–1970

Schulz, H.D., Felis, T., Hagedorn, Ch., Von Lüthrte, R., Reiners, C., Sander, H., Schneider, R., Schubert, J. & Schulz, H. 1996. La línea costera Holocena en el Curso bajo del Río Guadalquivir entre Sevilla y su desembocadura en el Atlántico. Informe preliminar sobre los trabajos de Campo realizados en Octubre y noviembre de 1992. *Anuario Arqueológico de Andalucía* 1992, II, 323–8

Siret, H. 1893. *L'Espagne préhistorique.* Imprimerie Polleunis et Ceuterick. Bruxelles.

Torre, F. de la & Sáez, L. 1984. Nuevas excavaciones en el yacimiento de la Edad del Cobre de 'El Malagón' (Cúllar Baza,Granada). *Homenaje a Luis Siret* 1934–1984, 221–6. Sevilla: Junta de Andalucía

Vargas, J. M. 2003. Elementos para la definición territorial del yacimiento prehistórico de Valencina de la Concepción (Sevilla). *SPAL* 12, 125–144

Wells, P.S. 1989. *Farms, villages, and cities: commerce and urban origins in late prehistoric Europe.* Cornell U.P, Ithaca and London

Wheatley, D., Strutt, K. García Sanjuán, L., Mora Molina, C. & Peinado Cucarella, J. 2012. New Evidence on the Spatial Organisation of the Valencina de La Concepción Copper Age Settlement: Geophysical Survey between La Pastora and Montelirio. *Trabajos de Prehistoria* 69 (1), 65–79

5

Beaker settlements in Mediterranean France in their cultural context

Olivier Lemercier, Émilie Blaise, Fabien Convertini, Robin Furestier, Christophe Gilabert and Matthieu Labaune

---

The proposed study area (Fig. 5.1) corresponds to a wide arc extending from the Pyrenees to the western Alps including the French Mediterranean coastline for a total area of approximately 110,000 km^2. This zone is in contact with the Iberian Peninsula in the West and the Italian Peninsula in the East and is located at the confluence of two great diffusion corridors: the valleys of the Aude/Garonne and the Rhone. The first allows contacts with the Atlantic cultural sphere, while the second accesses the interior of the European continent. The issues that concern Bell Beaker domestic settlements are as old as the history of research on this culture and go back to the 19th century (Lemercier 2015) but some of the major archaeological excavations of the 1950s and 1960s have raised the issues of habitat and common ware (Taffanel & Taffanel 1957; Guilaine 1967).

One of the greatest problems for this research is the lack of radiocarbon dates. The radiocarbon dates are still very few when compared to the number of sites that we have from the beginning of the 3rd to the 2nd millennium but nevertheless, when old dates with large standard deviations are excluded it possible to place Bell Beakers between 2550/2500–1950/1900 cal BC: a period of six or seven centuries. Sometimes considered as marking the end of the Neolithic or the beginning of the Bronze Age (Lemercier forthcoming), Bell Beakers in fact begin in the final Neolithic or Chalcolithic (depending on regional terminologies) and end in the Early Bronze Age. It is also now well established that Bell Beakers appear in Mediterranean France in the context of regional Late Neolithic cultures. Although some local cultures remained for a few centuries after the arrival of the Bell Beaker phenomenon, most were replaced before the beginning of the early Bronze Age. This, however is a very complex period and all artefacts or sites dated between 2500–2000 BC are not necessarily related to the Bell Beaker culture. In Mediterranean France, the classic periodisation comprises four phases and was proposed by Jean Guilaine in 1967. More recently, we have proposed an alternative theory, merging the first two phases of Guilaine's periodisation and based on the evolution of ceramic styles, detailed contextual analysis, the associations of various artefacts and radiocarbon dates (Lemercier 2004; 2012; 2018; Lemercier *et al.* 2014b). This new periodisation therefore comprises

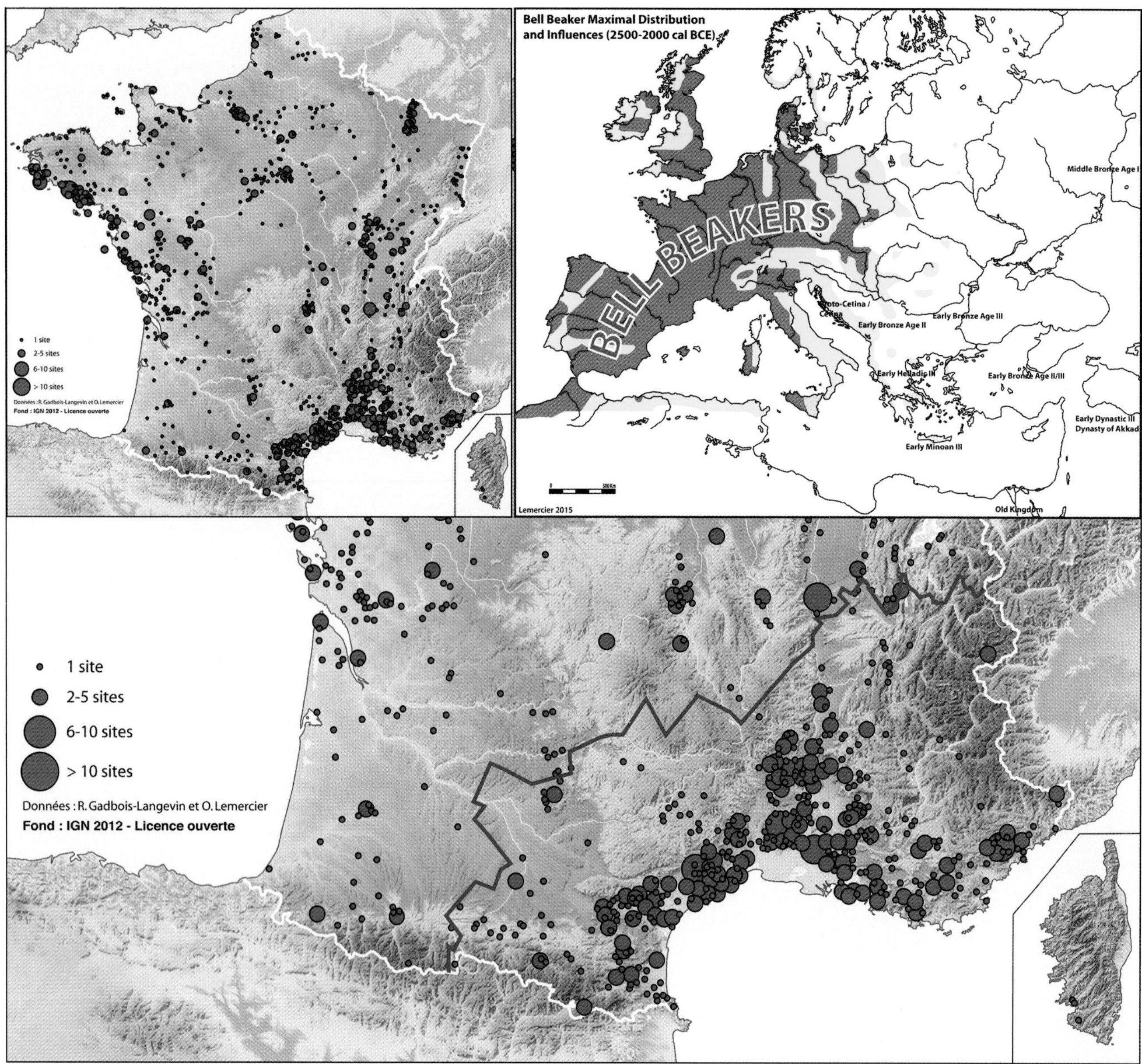

Figure 5.1: Beaker sites in Mediterranean France in their context (CAD R. Gadbois-Langevin & O. Lemercier)

three main phases (Fig. 5.2), articulated around a so-called middle or recent phase marked by regional Bell Beaker groups (the Pyrenean and Rhodano-Provençal groups, in the Mediterranean Midi) and dating to between 2400/2350–2150 cal BC. The earliest phase concerns everything that happened before 2550/2500–2400/2350 cal BC and includes Maritime styles, AOC and mixed-style Beakers, but also the geometric comb-zoned decorated vessels that probably developed very quickly after the initial appearance of Beakers. The late phase is best dated between 2150–1950 cal BC (Vital *et al.* 2012) and is marked by incised and barbed wire-decorated pottery.

An important observation is that Bell Beakers do not replace the local cultures of the Late Neolithic but instead represent an introduced type in its initial, early phase, before developing as a complete culture in the middle phase. Again, in this phase, there is considerable evidence, in certain regions, to demonstrate that the local cultures of the Late Neolithic have not disappeared but rather they evolved in parallel with the regional Beaker groups. We must therefore clearly identify the cultural components of the pre-Beaker traditions in order to identify any changes that were affected by the arrival of Bell Beakers.

There are some 632 archaeological sites

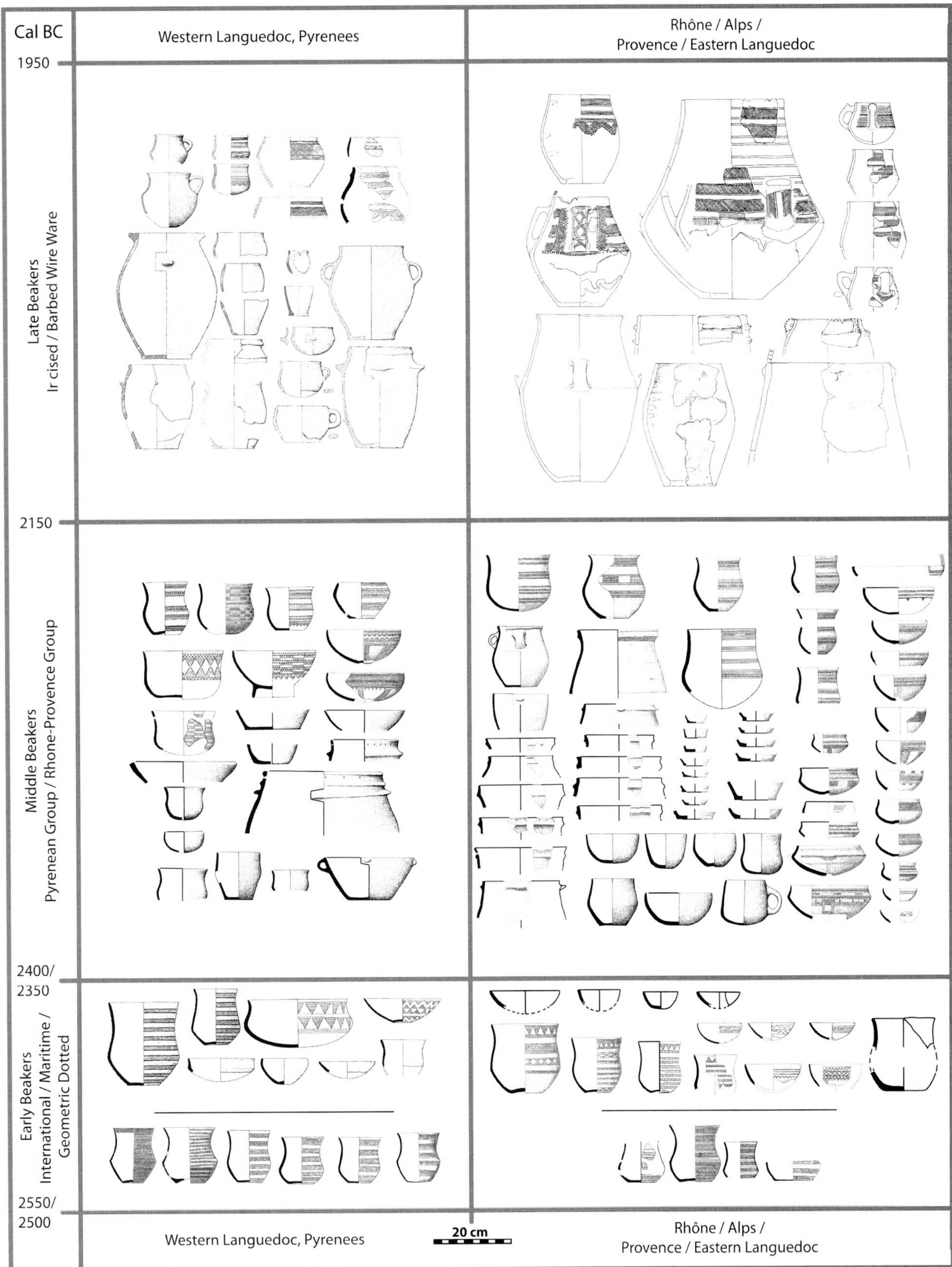

Figure 5.2: Periodisation of the Bell Beaker pottery in Mediterranean France (detailed Legends in Lemercier (2012) and Vital et al. *(2012), CAD O. Lemercier)*

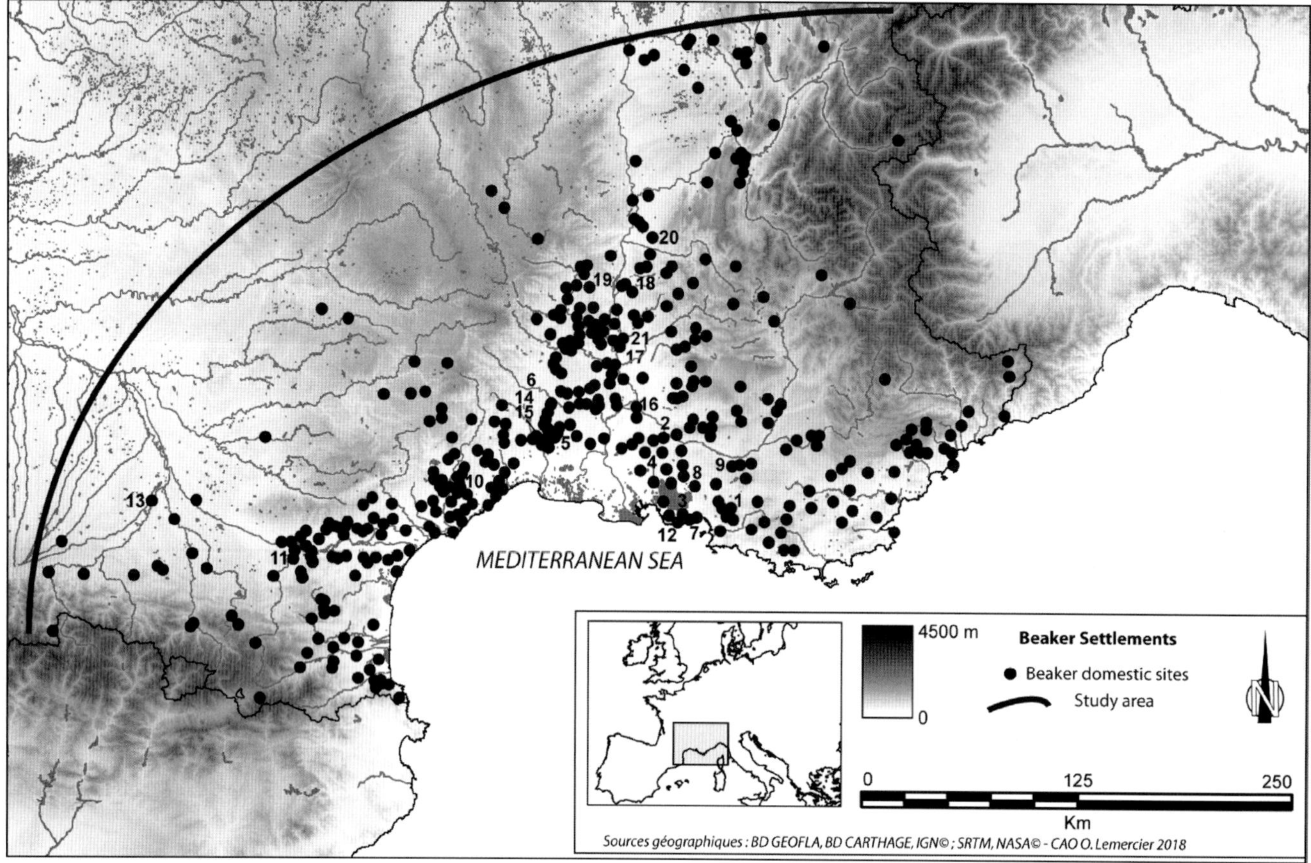

Figure 5.3: Beaker settlements (domestic sites) in Mediterranean France. Main sites mentioned in the text: 1 – Le Col Sainte-Anne (Simiane-Collongue, Bouches-du-Rhône); 2 – Les Calades (Orgon, Bouches-du-Rhône); 3 – Le Fortin du Saut (Châteauneuf-les-Martigues, Bouches-du-Rhône); 4 – Les Barres (Eyguières, Bouches-du-Rhône); 5 – Le Mas de Vignoles IV (Nîmes, Gard); 6 – Le Vignaud 3 – Chemin du Puits Neuf (Langlade, Gard); 7 – Le Camp de Laure (Le Rove, Bouches-du-Rhône); 8 – le Clos Marie-Louise (Aix-en-Provence, Bouches-du-Rhône); 9 – La Plaine (Meyrargues, Bouches-du-Rhône); 10 – Mas de Garric (Mèze, Hérault); 11 – Roc d'en Gabit (Carcassonne, Aude); 12 – Le Collet-Redon, Martigues (Bouches-du-Rhône); 13 – Lapeyrère and Moulin de Garonne (Muret, Haute-Garonne); 14 – Maupas (Calvisson, Gard); 15 – Bois Sacré (Saint-Côme-et-Maruéjols, Gard); 16 – La place du Palais (Avignon, Vaucluse); 17 – Les Ribauds (Mondragon, Vaucluse); 18 – Le Serre 1 (Roynac, Drôme); 19 – Rue du Bouquet (Montélimar, Drôme); 20 – Les Vignarets (Upie, Drôme); 21 – Les Juilléras (Mondragon, Vaucluse). (CAD O. Lemercier)

producing Bell Beakers and associated artefacts in this region. Within this corpus, 304 sites can be considered as likely domestic sites or settlements (Fig. 5.3), 196 as burials and 136 as indeterminate sites or stray finds (Gadbois-Langevin 2013; Lemercier 2014).

Mediterranean France before Bell Beakers (3000–2550/2500 cal BC)

Cultural framework

In the first half of the 3rd millennium, Mediterranean France was marked by a strong cultural fragmentation defined by ceramic cultures recognised successively during the second half of the 20th century. These cultures also seem to change over time during this period (Lemercier 2007; Jallot & Gutherz 2014).

Between 3200 and 2800/2600 cal BC, depending on the regions and dates selected, the situation in the far east of the study area remains unknown. The *Couronnien* group has been identified in central and western Provence and is mainly defined by features that are absent from the *Chasséen* of the Middle Neolithic. In eastern Languedoc, between 3300/3200 and 2900 cal BC there is the *Ferrières* group and the *Bruyères* in the Rhône Valley. Between 2900 and 2700/2650 cal BC a new group emerges called the *groupe des Vautes* or *Epiferrières*. In central Languedoc, the '*Vallée de l'Hérault B*' group has been identified and in western Languedoc and Roussillon an ancient *Vérazien*. The *Treilles* group can be found to the north of these cultures, on the limestone plateaus of the Causses.

From 2700/2650 cal BC, the *Fontbouisse* group developed in eastern Languedoc, replacing the *Epiferrières or Vaute* groups and the groups of the other regions are also replaced (the *Rhône-Ouvèze* group replacing the *Couronnien* group in Provence), or undergo important evolutions in their pottery styles (recent *Vérazien*, recent *Treilles* groups). In the extreme east of the region, ceramics with metopic decoration with Italian affinities are present. The *Fontbouisse* group seems to last until the 23rd century BC.

The first half of the 3rd millennium BC has a great variety of ceramic traditions both typologically and technically. The defined major cultures are composed of numerous distinct micro-regional facies with ceramics decorated to a lesser or greater extent, but a general evolution of morphologies from simple to segmented forms is universally visible throughout the period.

Recent studies of the Late Neolithic lithic industries (Briois 2005; Furestier 2007; Briois *et al.* 2008; Piatscheck 2014) agree in identifying a break in the previous circulation networks in the different regions of Mediterranean France which are replaced by an increased consumption of local resources, a technological simplification of the industries, now mainly utilising flakes, and also the parallel development of high status products (large blades, daggers and elaborated arrowheads).

Apart from rare metallic elements that have been circulating from probably as early as the middle of the 4th millennium, metal artefacts appear in some regions from the beginning of the 3rd millennium with some well-known production centres, such as the district of Cabrières-Péret (Hérault) (Ambert 1995) and others either suspected or currently under study (Ardèche, Aveyron). Metal production, based on the use of specific and local raw materials (copper with antimony and silver) is limited to small objects, such as beads and awls and some flat axes and daggers (Gutherz & Jallot, 2005; Labaune, 2016).

The funerary practices are characterised by a great diversity both in the places and modes of burial. Rock shelters and open sites are utilised and monuments such as dolmens or hypogea are constructed. From the last third of the 4th millennium BC, the majority of burials were collective although individual burials are also known (Schmitt *et al.* 2017). Inhumations predominate but cremations also exist as does evidence for the post-mortem manipulation of human remains and the variability in quantity and type of funeral furniture (Sauzade 2011).

While specific studies on the agricultural economy remain rare, the available data point to a developed agriculture with a bias towards cereals. Animal husbandry is based on the breeding of sheep, goats and cattle (for meat and milk) supplemented by pigs (Blaise 2010; Blaise *et al.* 2010). Hunting is almost non-existent at the end of the Neolithic (usually only small game such as rabbit). The fleeces of domestic caprines were used and cattle were probably widely exploited for their labour (Blaise 2010; Helmer *et al.* 2018).

Habitat and house

Settlement in the 3rd millennium is a subject that has been largely covered since the 1970s and 1980s. Several syntheses have been produced in recent years and allow this short summary (for more details see: Lemercier & Gilabert 2009; Gilabert & Jallot 2018). Pre-Beaker domestic sites show very dense settlement patterns with the exploitation of all regions of Mediterranean France. The total number of sites currently remains unknown but a recent evaluation carried out on the Vaucluse department (Lemercier *et al.* 2004) has shown that Late Neolithic sites were four times more numerous than those of the Middle Neolithic. It remains difficult to determine if this is the result of demographic factors or of changes in the patterns of land use. Nevertheless in certain sectors such as in the Rhône Valley and the plains around Nîmes and Montpellier in Languedoc, important rescue excavations have revealed a remarkable density of Late Neolithic occupation and additionally all the geographical and topographical situations seem to have been used from the littoral zones to the massifs by way of the plains and hilly areas. The occupation of caves and rock-shelters persisted but only represents 15% of the total domestic sites known in Provence (Lemercier & Gilabert 2009). Lowland and elevated sites were known in equal proportion in Provence in the early 2000s (Lemercier & Gilabert 2009) but this observation might change given the recent increase in large rescue excavations in the lowlands, which have revealed a significant density of sites as seen in Languedoc. The size of the settlements can usually only be estimated but tend to show a great variability from a few hundred square metres at la Citadelle (Vauvenargues, Bouches-du-Rhône, Fig. 5.4,J) to tens of hectares at le Mas de Vignoles IV (Nîmes, Gard, Fig. 5.5,J) or les Fabrys (Bonnieux, Vaucluse).

Our understanding of the forms of the settlements, and especially the houses, remains very patchy. To the east of the Rhône, some sites attributable to the *Couronnien* group revealed the remains of enclosures dating from the end of the 4th to the beginning of the 3rd millennium. These enclosures are of different shapes and sizes and are constructed from different materials but they are often poorly preserved. Stone walls with single or double facings are the most common type such as la Barre du Pommier (Saint-Savournin Bouches-du-Rhône), Miouvin (Istres, Bouches-du-Rhône, Fig. 5.4,H), la Citadelle (Vauvenargues, Bouches-du-Rhône, Fig. 5.4,J), Ponteau-Gare (Martigues, Bouches-du-Rhône, Fig. 5.4,L), la Brémonde (Buoux, Vaucluse) and les Lauzières (Lourmarin, Vaucluse, Fig. 5.4,I). Ditched enclosures are also known at La Fare in Forcalquier (Alpes-de-Haute-Provence, Fig. 5.5,M) and at Payennet (Gardanne, Bouches-du-Rhône, Hasler *et al.* 2016). Wooden palisades have also been identified on several sites. In Languedoc, circular or sub-rectangular enclosures developed at the end of the 4th or the beginning of the 3rd millennium, at le Puech-Haut (Paulhan, Hérault, Fig. 5.5,C), at Mourral-Millegrand (Trèbes, Aude, Fig. 5.5,K) and Peirouse Ouest (Marguerittes, Gard, Fig. 5.5,F). Eastern Languedoc especially sees the development of enclosures a little later in the context of the *Fontbouisse* group from 2700–2600 cal BC. In the plains around Nîmes and Montpellier, large conglomerated enclosures appear composed of sinuous ditch networks enclosing areas of 1000 to 3000 m^2 but forming parts of sites that can extend over 15 hectares in some cases, such as in le Mas de Vignoles IV (Nîmes, Gard, Fig. 5.5,J). This type of site can also be seen at Moulin Villard (Caissargues, Gard, Fig. 5.5,I), Richemont (Montpellier, Hérault, Fig. 5.5,E), le Stade Richter (Montpellier, Hérault, Fig. 5.5,G) and la Capoulière (Mauguio, Hérault, Fig. 5.5,H). At Mitra (Garon, Gard, Fig. 5.5,L), an enclosure made up of several concentric ditches is so far unique in the area. Several of these enclosures have some sort of outwardly projecting 'bastions' as in Puech Haut (Paulhan, Hérault, Fig. 5.5,C), Richemont (Montpellier, Herault, Fig. 5.5,E), la Capoulière (Mauguio, Hérault, Fig. 5.5,H), Mitra (Garon, Gard, Fig. 5.5,L) or Pascale et Bérange (Mudaison, Gard), which recall the better-known circular structures on stone walled enclosures. In the hilly areas (the scrubland), especially behind Nîmes and Montpellier, is a well-known set of stone-built sites. Several of these have dry stone wall enclosures fairly evenly spaced circular structures such as Boussargues (Argelliers, Hérault, Fig. 5.4,B), les Tailladettes (Rouet, Hérault, Fig. 5.4,C), le Lebous (Saint-Mathieu-de-Tréviers, Hérault, Fig. 5.4,D) and le Vignaud 3 – Chemin du Puit Neuf (Langlade, Gard). The site of le Rocher du Causse (Claret, Hérault, Fig. 5.4,E) is the same broad architecture type but encloses a promontory.

The sites, enclosed or not, generally have many structures, pits and cisterns of varying shapes and sizes, such as Plaine de Chrétien (Montpellier, Hérault, Fig. 5.5,B), le Puech Haut (Fig. 5.5,C), la Capoulière (Fig. 5.5,H), Moulin Villard (Fig. 5.5,I), Mas de Vignoles IV (Fig. 5.5,J), La Fare (Forcalquier, Alpes-de-Haute-Provence, Fig. 5.5,M), le Mourre du Tendre (Courthézon, Vaucluse, Fig. 5.5,N) or les Martins (Roussillon, Vaucluse, Fig. 5.5,O). They sometimes have remarkably dense distributions as at les Compasses-Labro (Hospitalet-du-Larzac, Aveyron, Fig. 5.5,A). Special hollowed out structures such as cellars, sometimes walled, are also known.

Houses of the period are rare in Mediterranean France and the example often given is that of the houses of the *Fontbouisse* group located in Languedoc, in the sector of Nîmes and north of Montpellier. These oval or rectangular houses with apsidal facades are found at Cambous (Viols-en-Laval, Hérault, Fig. 5.4,A), Boussargues (Argelliers, Hérault, Fig. 5.4,B), les Tailladettes (Rouet, Hérault, Fig. 5.4,C), le Lebous (Saint-Mathieu-de-Tréviers, Hérault, Fig. 5.4,D), le Rocher du Causse (Claret, Hérault, Fig. 5.4,E), le Bois de Martin (Les Matelles, Hérault, Fig. 5.4,F), Conquette (Saint-Martin-de-Londres, Hérault, Fig. 5.4,G), la Capitelle du Broum (Péret, Hérault) or le Vignaud 3 – Chemin du Puit Neuf and have varying dimensions. The house foundations are made of stone, but their superstructures are a matter of debate. Earthen structures are also known on several sites, such as at la Capoulière (Fig. 5.5,H), where the mud buildings partly reproduce the forms of the dry-stone structures complete with apsidal facades. Rectangular post-built structures with probable walls of mud are geographically widespread from western Languedoc (Mourral-Millegrand (Fig.

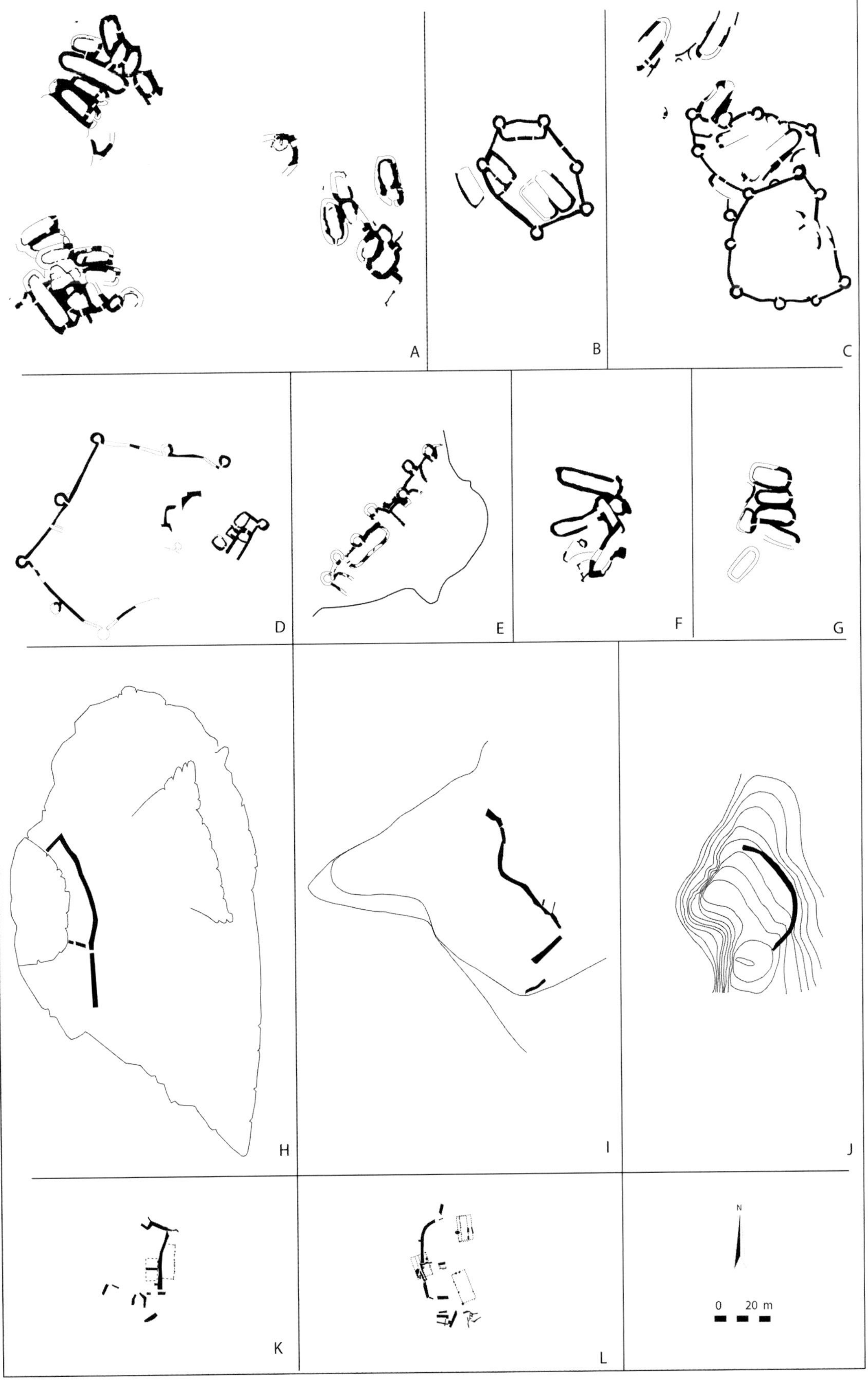

Figure 5.4: Final Neolithic settlements (domestic sites) in Mediterranean France. Stone architecture. A – Cambous (Viols-en-Laval, Hérault); B – Boussargues (Argelliers, Hérault); C – les Tailladettes (Rouet, Hérault); D – le Lébous (Saint-Mathieu-de-Tréviers, Hérault); E – le Rocher du Causse (Claret, Hérault); F – le Bois de Martin (Les Matelles, Hérault); G – Conquette (Saint-Martin-de-Londres, Hérault); H – Miouvin (Istres, Bouches-du-Rhône); I – les Lauzières (Lourmarin, Vaucluse); J – la Citadelle (Vauvenargues, Bouches-du-Rhône); K – le Collet-Redon (Martigues, Bouches-du-Rhône); L – Ponteau-Gare (Martigues, Bouches-du-Rhône) (after Gilabert & Jallot in press; CAD O. Lemercier)

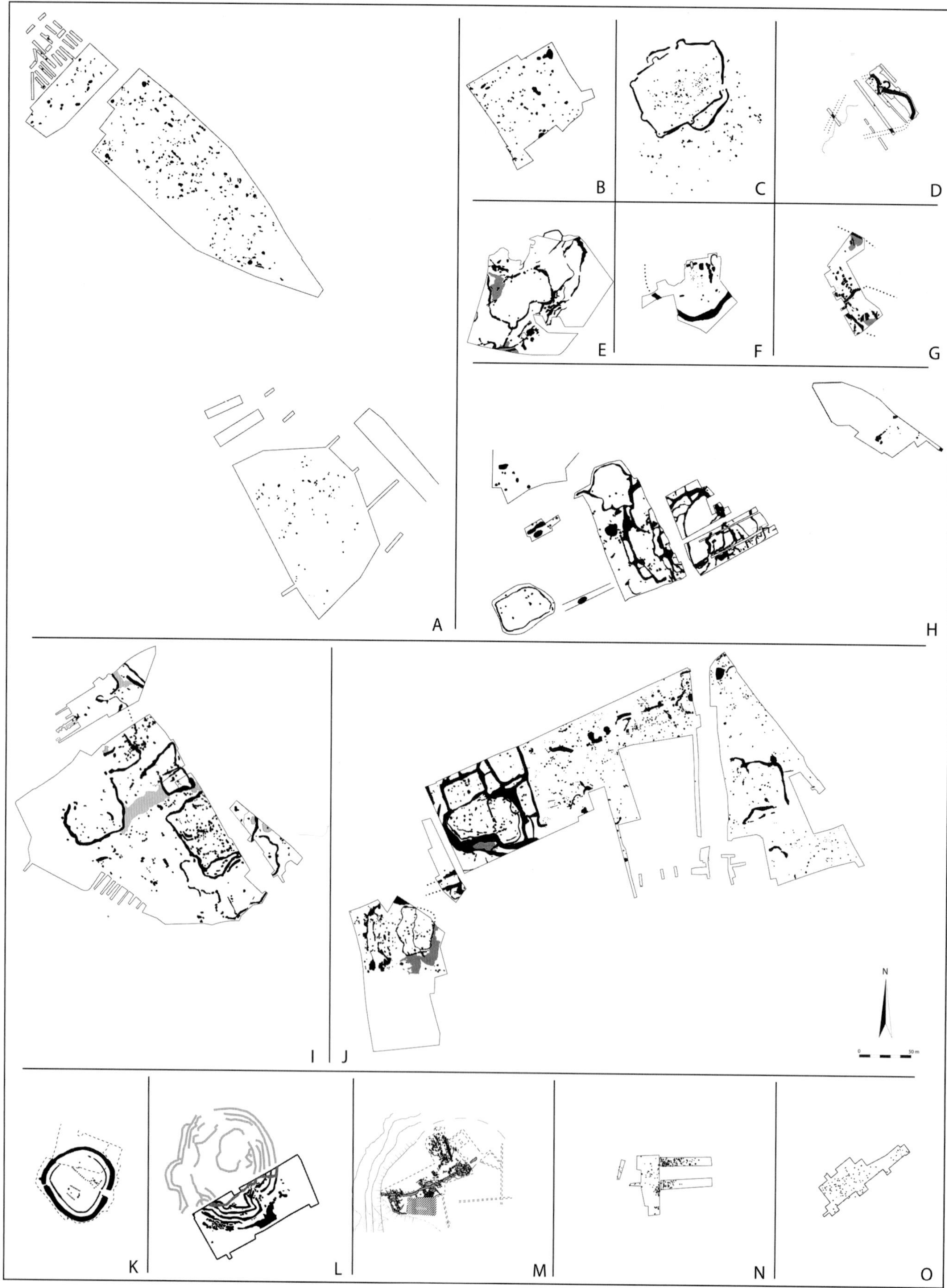
A
B
C
D
E
F
G
H
I
J
N
0
50 m
K
L
M
N
O

5.5,K) to Provence (Ponteau-Gare, Martigues, Bouches-du- Rhône (Fig. 5.4,L).

In summary, the pre-Beaker settlements in Mediterranean France show a great diversity according to different regional developments and trajectories with specific features and styles adapted to the local environmental conditions.

Bell Beakers in Mediterranean France (2550/2500–1950 BC)

Cultural framework

When Bell Beakers appeared in Mediterranean France, several Late Neolithic cultures were still in existence such as the *Fontbouisse* group in eastern Languedoc or the *Rhône-Ouvèze* group in Provence. The situation is less clear in western Languedoc, where the Bell Beakers are systematically later than the *Vérazien* group though the hypothesis of a region totally empty of population seems unlikely. That certain local Late Neolithic groups persisted is now more likely because the association of *Fontbouisse* and *Rhône-Ouvèze* style ceramics with middle Bell Beakers of the *Rhodano-Provençal* style is now well documented. Some sites in central Provence, contemporary with the Bell Beaker phenomenon but with no Bell Beaker artefacts, have very evolved ceramic styles.

One of the peculiarities of Mediterranean France is the variety of Bell Beaker pottery styles. As mentioned in the introduction, there are Beakers of Maritime or International Style, mixed style and geometric dotted styles that together present a range of important forms. The Beakers with geometric dotted decoration may have developed from the others at an early stage in the Beaker period. The *Rhodano-Provençal* and *Pyrénéen* styles that share Mediterranean France in the middle phase are marked by the presence of a specific domestic ware (Lemercier 2004) and an incised and barbed-wire style herald Early Bronze Age type morphologies (Vital *et al.* 2012) (Fig. 5.2). From the technical point of view, different tempering choices also appear to have been made (Convertini 1996; 2009; 2017). The flint industry is marked by the use of local raw materials and the appearance and significant increase in production of a very specific type of arrowhead: the tanged and square-barbed arrowhead that was widely used at the time in western European Beaker contexts (Furestier 2007). With regard to metallurgy, two major changes occur during the Bell Beaker period namely the use of a non-local raw material (arsenical copper) that probably comes from the Iberian Peninsula (see the lead isotopes analysis in Labaune 2016) and the diffusion of new types of copper objects such as the Palmela points and tanged daggers. The individual burials are rare (Lemercier & Tcheremissinoff 2011) and collective burial in megalithic monuments or in caves and shelters remains the rule.

Little is known of the agricultural economy. A few studies show the presence of both milling equipment and the remains of cereals, mainly barley and wheat (Lemercier 2004). Stock farming remained largely based on domesticated livestock and the exploitation of their produce and services. There is also a marked increase hunting, even if it remains marginal in the food economy. This activity, especially the hunting of big game, which hardly existed in the local cultures of the Late Neolithic (Blaise 2010; Blaise *et al.* 2010; 2014), persists into the middle Bell Beaker phase.

Habitat and house

Knowledge of Bell Beaker settlements or, at least, Bell Beaker domestic activity remains patchy despite numerous examples (Appendix1). A great number of archaeological projects have often been restricted to surface collection or the excavation of extremely small areas. Of a total of more than 600 sites surveyed, half are settlements or deemed to have had domestic activity. The distribution of the sites is very unequal, due partly to the intensity of current economic development and developer-funded archaeology, but probably also to a certain prehistoric reality. In considering all types of evidence (domestic, funerary, etc), they are concentrated in the coastal departments of Hérault (122 sites, 19%) and Gard (91 sites, 14.5%), then in the Bouches-du-Rhône (67 sites) and Aude (63 sites) and secondarily in the Rhône Valley, while the peripheries of the Alps and the Massif Central have only revealed a few sites. The distribution of domestic sites is roughly the same in Hérault (71 sites, 23.5%), Gard (47 sites, 15.5%), Bouches-du-Rhône (39 sites), Vaucluse (28 sites) and Drôme (25 sites). Together, these five departments of eastern Languedoc and the lower Rhône Valley total 69% of the Bell Beaker domestic sites currently known. The concentration of sites along the

Figure 5.5: (previous page) Final Neolithic settlements (domestic sites) in Mediterranean France. Earth and wood architecture. A – les Compasses-Labro (Hospitalet-du-Larzac, Aveyron); B – Plaine de Chrétien (Montpellier, Hérault); C – le Puech Haut (Paulhan, Hérault); D – Font de Mauguio (Mauguio, Hérault); E – Richemont (Montpellier, Hérault); F – Peirouse Ouest (Marguerittes, Gard); G – Stade Richter (Montpellier, Hérault); H – la Capoulière (Mauguio, Hérault); I – Moulin Villard (Caissargues, Gard); J – le Mas de Vignoles IV (Nîmes, Gard); K – le Mourral (Trèbes, Aude); L – Mitra (Garons, Gard); M – La Fare (Forcalquier, Alpes-de-Haute-Provence); N – le Mourre du Tendre (Courthézon, Vaucluse); O – les Martins (Roussillon, Vaucluse) (after Gilabert & Jallot, in press, Sendra et al. *2016, Vaquer 1998; CAD O. Lemercier)*

coast and the main river valleys is also worthy of note.

In Provence, at least, a certain return to the use of caves and shelters, compared to their frequency in the pre-Beakers groups has been noticed (Lemercier & Gilabert 2009) but their domestic use remains, in all cases, limited in relation to the number of known open air sites.

Bell Beaker users seem to have used all topographical situations but in certain sectors, such as in western Provence, it has been possible to identify a tendency towards elevated positions for the domestic sites of the ancient phase of Bell Beakers. This siting, on hillsides or hilltops is particularly pertinent to sites with large Bell Beaker assemblages such as le Col-Sainte-Anne in Simiane-Collongue (Bocquenet 1995; Bocquenet *et al.* 1998; Bocquenet & Müller 1999), les Calades in Orgon (Barge-Mahieu 1987; 1995), le Fortin du Saut in Châteauneuf-lès-Martigues (Courtin 1978; Courtin & Onoratini 1977; Furestier *et al.* 2007) all in the Bouches-du-Rhône. This is in contrast to sites of the local Final Neolithic which are found in all topographic locations even if they have an element of Beaker on site.

In general, Bell Beaker settlements are small in area, from a few tens to a few hundred square metres. On the few elevated sites mentioned above, they most often occupy small terraces (le Col Sainte-Anne or les Calades) or peaks that offer only a few tens of square metres of exploitable surface. This is usually enough for a single building and even then it may be partly terraced. Some open air sites, often in lowland areas, that contain Bell Beaker elements, can be much larger. Some may be contemporary with Bell Beaker (les Barres in Eyguières in the Bouches-du-Rhône for example – Barge 2000), whilst others may have been re-occupied by Bell Beaker groups (generally in the middle phase) (le Mas de Vignoles IV for example, – Convertini *et al.* 2004). On these sites, Bell Beaker remains are invariably located on only a small part of the site.

It has often been difficult to recognise Bell Beaker settlements. The case of the Vignaud 3 – Chemin du Puits Neuf (Hayden *et al.* 2011) is a case in point. The site is a typical settlement of the *Fontbouisse* group with its oval houses and its dry-stone enclosure. The occupation levels produced fragments of two or three early Bell Beakers which are probably contemporary with this occupation. A second occupation phase can be attributed to the Rhodano-Provençal Bell Beakers with a small series of decorated ceramics, but this occupation overlies the ruins of the *Fontbouisse* group houses, and no associated structures can be clearly recognised.

In addition to the few elevated sites which are difficult to access and have a limited area for construction, some other sites are enclosed. These enclosures are typically connected to the late phase of the Bell Beakers, with incised and barbed-wire ware such as le Camp de Laure in le Rove (Courtin 1975; 1978; Vital *et al.* 2012), le Clos Marie-Louise in Aix-en-Provence (Vignaud 2002) in Bouches-du-Rhône, Mas de Garric in Mèze (Hérault) (Laroche *et al.* 2012), Roc d'en Gabit in Carcassonne (Aude) (Vaquer & Remicourt 2008). The presence, in Languedoc especially, of Bell Beaker elements of the early and middle phases on enclosed sites typically represents a phase of reoccupation. Beaker only appears in the upper levels of the already-silted ditches as is the case at Mas de Vignoles IV (Convertini *et al.* 2004). Similarly, on some stone-walled enclosures that date to the beginning of the Late Neolithic, Beakers have only a minimal presence such as on the site at les Lauzières in Lourmarin (Vaucluse).

The enclosures dating to the late Bell Beaker phase comprise several types. A stone wall, or at least stone foundations for a wall of unknown height, is attributed to the late Beaker phase at le Camp de Laure. The site sits on a small spur, 150 m long, (Fig. 5.6,B1) that is closed by a stone wall with a complex entrance system (Fig. 5.6,B2) and has at least two circular structures. A similar and contemporary structure can be found at le Collet-Redon in Martigues (Bouches-du-Rhône) (Durrenmath *et al.* 2004). Located on a small plateau, the wall extends for about 30m and describes a right angle but it only partially survives so cannot be fully reconstructed. Another if smaller defended spur is known at the site of le Clos Marie-Louise in Aix-en-Provence (Bouches-du-Rhône). The structure consists of clay and stone structures (Fig. 5.6,A) and mostly belongs to the Iron Age, but the excavators proposed that a structure had been in existence from the late Beaker phase.

Although ditched enclosures attributed to this same late phase are known from several sites, it remains unclear whether they involved more elaborate defence systems involving palisades, stone or clay walls. This is the case at le Mas del Garric where a section of ditch probably forms part of the enclosure of the summit of a small hill (Fig. 5.6,C). Another ditched enclosure at Roc d'en Gabit (Fig. 5.6,D) lies on a spur cut off by a ditch and palisade attributed to the late Beaker phase. These enclosed sites are few, however, and all date to the late Bell Beaker phase. They are also rather exceptional in this area and at this time.

Domestic structures are generally rare on Bell Beaker settlements. In addition to pits and post-holes, some hearths and heated stones are known on such sites as Moulin de Garonne and Lapeyrère in Muret (Haute-Garonne) (Jolibert 1988). As for Bell Beaker houses, excluding the obvious cases of the reoccupation of earlier structures, Mediterranean France has very few examples and they vary greatly in form. In the current state of research, it is possible to distinguish three domestic zones. In the eastern part of Languedoc, two previously excavated sites produced oval- or roughly oval-shaped paved structures. At Maupas in Calvisson (Gard), the oval pavement is 12 × 2.5–4 m (Fig. 5.7,B) (Roger 1988; 1989; Roger *et al.* 1988). At le Bois Sacré in Saint-Côme-et-Maruéjols (Gard), the partially destroyed structure is roughly oval shaped and reaches 12 m in length but is only 2.5 m wide (Fig. 5.7,A) (Roudil *et al.* 1974). This type of structure may also be present on the left bank of the Rhône, in the Vaucluse, at the site of la Place du Palais in Avignon where Sauzade described 4 'huts' with stone pavements and abundant fragments of daub. This is also the case at the site of les Ribauds in Mondragon where a probable but irregular stone pavement is partially visible (Margarit *et al.* 2002). In Provence, buildings with a perimeter wall and post-holes are known on several sites. On the elevated site of les Calades, two terraces yielded structures 8–10 m long and surviving to 6 m wide. Cabin 2 (Fig. 5.8,C) is probably oval in shape with a very degraded peripheral wall, a central line of post-holes and a hearth. Similarly, on le Col Sainte-Anne site, 'terrace I' has a partially preserved structure with a line of post-holes and peripheral stone banks. It is truncated but survives to 6.5 m long and at least 4.5 m wide (Fig. 5.8,A). On 'terrace XI' there was a structure that partially used the natural rock in its perimeter supplemented by a wall of blocks and post-holes measuring 4 m by 3 m and was largely occupied by a hearth arranged on a clay foundation (Fig. 5.8,B). In the same region, les Barres in Eyguières (Bouches-du-Rhône) (Barge-Mahieu 1995; Barge 2000) produced a series of 4 to 5 structures built with peripheral stone banks and with oval or rectangular forms. There were also numerous pits including 3 or 4 probable 'cellars' (Fig. 5.8,D). However, if Bell Beaker remains are abundant on this site, their precise place in the site chronology has not yet been fully published.

In the Rhône Valley, in North-Vaucluse and Drôme, several sites yielded excavated structures including a number of post-holes, sometimes associated with significant amounts of daub. Le Serre 1 site in Roynac (Drôme) (Vital 2005; Vital *et al.* 1999; 2002) produced the plan of a rectangular building with two naves and an area of over 60 m^2 (Fig. 5.9,A). Most recently, la Rue du Bouquet in Montélimar (Drôme) (Néré *et al.* 2016) produced a set of post-holes where several hypothetical building outlines could be proposed (Fig. 5.9,B). Even more complex, and in several sectors, les Vignarets in Upie (Drôme) (Lurol 2002) produced important sets of post-holes where a certain number of alignments can be observed but without any convincing building plans (Fig. 5.9,C). Finally, the site of les Juilléras in Mondragon (Vaucluse) (Lemercier *et al.* 2002) did not produce the plan of a building but nevertheless exhibits a highly structured space (Fig. 5.9,D). To the south, a set of fairly deep pits (> 1m) is isolated from the rest of the site by an alignment of elongated depressions interpreted as the remains of a fence structure. Beyond this, an almost empty space is occupied by four hearths arranged in a rectangle. In the northern part, a set of small, shallow circular depressions yielded abundant archaeological remains associated with late Bell Beakers. In a later phase, but still in the late Beaker period, the eastern part was occupied by 9 burials.

Breaks and continuities in Mediterranean France

Cultural framework

In a recent article (Lemercier *et al.* 2014a), it was possible to highlight all the changes that characterise the appearance and development of Bell Beakers in Mediterranean France. These changes seem to concern all aspects of material culture, but also certain aspects of the economy, rituals and environment. These

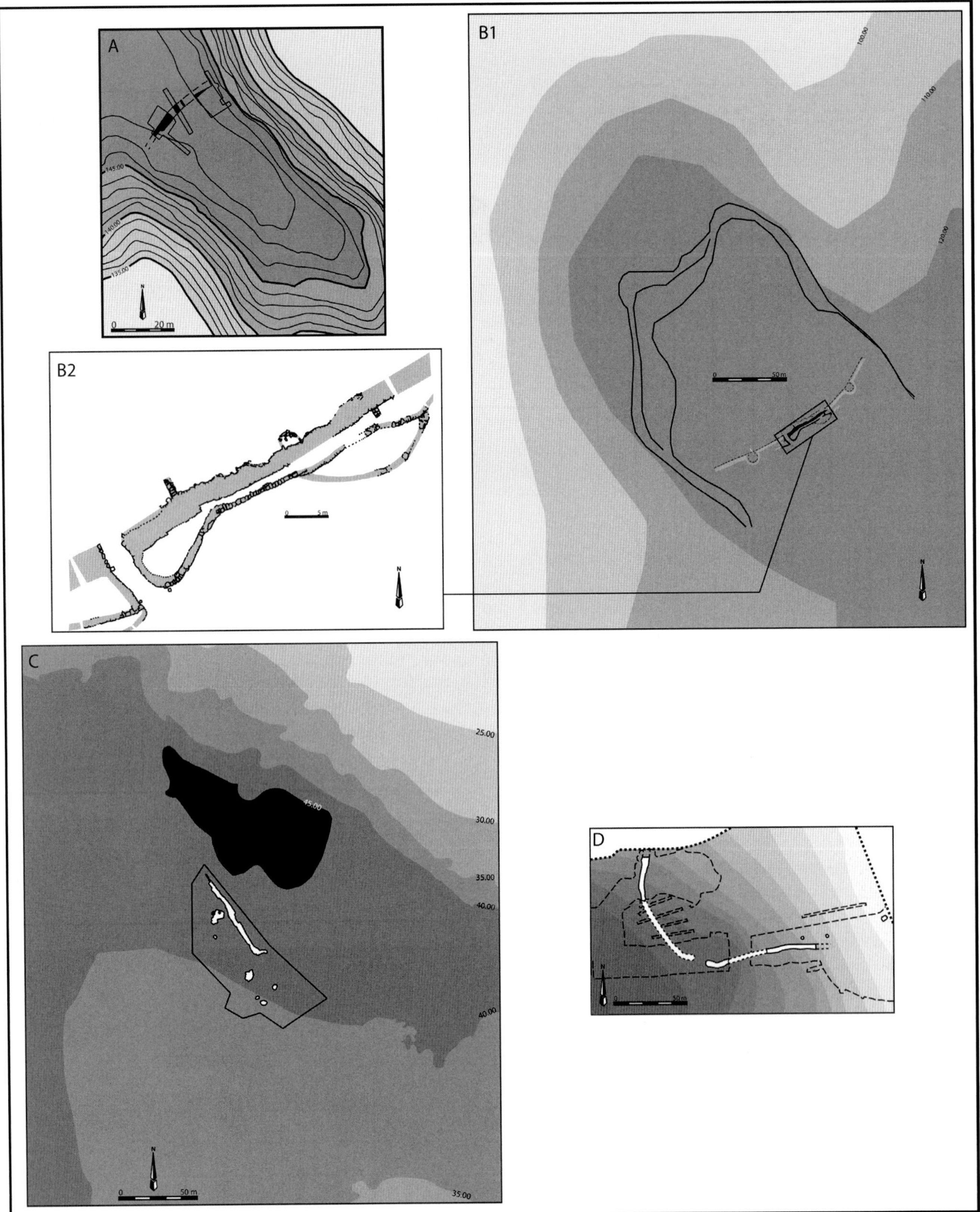

Figure 5.6: Late Beaker enclosures in Mediterranean France. A – le Clos Marie Louise (Aix-en-Provence, Bouches-du-Rhône; after Vignaud 2002); B – le Camp de Laure (Le Rove, Bouches-du-Rhône; after Lemercier 2004); C – Mas de Garric (Mèze, Hérault; after Laroche et al. *2012); D – Roc d'en Gabit (Carcassonne, Aude; after Vaquer & Remicourt, 2008) (CAD O. Lemercier)*

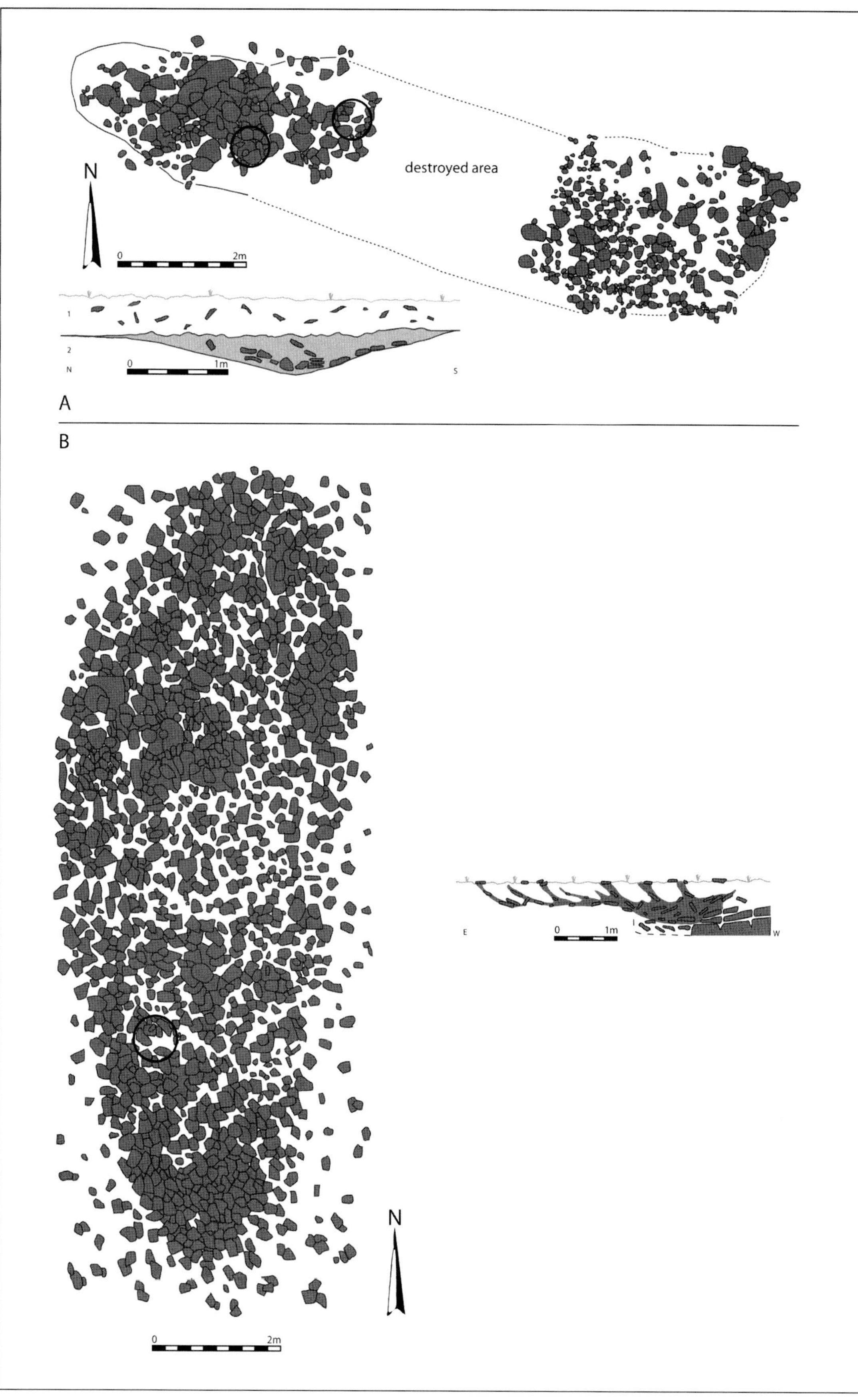

Figure 5.7: Beaker houses in Mediterranean France: Languedoc. A – le Bois Sacré (Saint-Côme-et-Maruéjols, Gard); B – Maupas (Calvisson, Gard) (after Roger 1988) (CAD O. Lemercier)

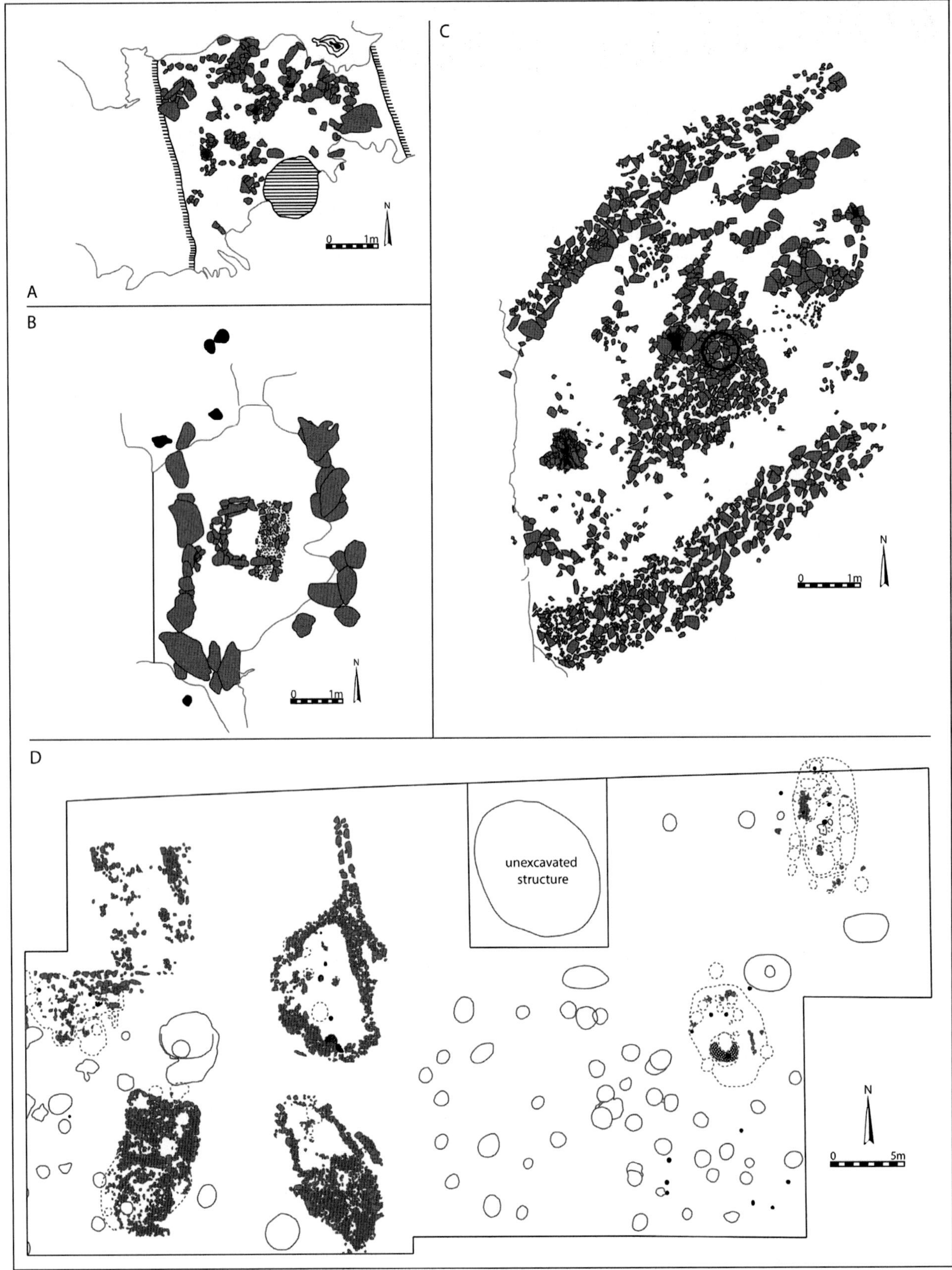

Figure 5.8: Beaker houses in Mediterranean France: Provence. A – le Col Sainte-Anne – Terrasse I (Simiane-Collongue, Bouches-du-Rhône; after Bocquenet et al. *1998); B – le Col Sainte-Anne – Terrasse XI (Simiane-Collongue, Bouches-du-Rhône; after Bocquenet 1995); C – les Calades 2 (Orgon, Bouches-du-Rhône; after Barge-Mahieu 1995); D – les Barres (Eyguières, Bouches-du-Rhône; after Barge-Mahieu 1995) (CAD O. Lemercier)*

profound transformations have led us to look outside the region for their origins, and the evidence for a small displacement of artefacts (with the exception of certain metallic objects) seemed also to plead for a displacement of individuals or groups of individuals rather than entire populations.

Settlement and house

The image we currently have of the settlement of the Late Neolithic in Mediterranean France is largely due to the many sites that have been discovered by developer-funded and rescue archaeology. The famous small stone-walled sites in the scrubland around Nîmes and Montpellier, which have long been regarded as representative of this region, can now be supplemented by radically different types of site. On the left bank of the Rhône, many small lowland settlements are contemporary with the hilltop enclosures. In the coastal plains of Languedoc, numerous very large sites have shown, in recent years, a massive use of earth or daub in their constructions (Sénépart *et al.* 2016; 2018). However, the data remain mainly confined to the coastal strip and the large valleys and to a lesser extent to the hilly areas. Sites are still poorly known in the mountainous areas and the borders of the region.

It is in this context and in a rather densely populated world that Bell Beakers appear, in the middle of the 3rd millennium BC in Mediterranean France. The standard Maritime beakers are discovered in isolated burials but also on domestic sites of the local Late Neolithic groups such as the *Fontbouisse* group and the *Rhône-Ouvèze* group and so on. These Maritime beakers are also associated, always with *Fontbouisse* or *Rhône-Ouvèze* ceramics, with a much larger series of geometric dotted style Beakers that are found on particular sites in Western Provence such as small hilltop sites and with difficult access such as les Calades, le Col Sainte-Anne, le Fortin du Saut amongst others. The only buildings certainly attributable to this phase are those of les Calades. The recoverable floor plan of the oval hut 2, measuring 10 × 6 m and with an area of about 60 m^2 is not a real novelty in the region because this size of house is similar to the houses of the *Fontbouisse* group. The main difference, in this case, is the location of the houses on small terraces perched above cliffs overlooking the valley.

For the middle Bell Beaker phase, with the *Rhodano-Provençal* and *Pyrénéen* groups, the data are a little more numerous and diversified. The settlements that are purely Bell Beaker are known in all the topographic contexts previously used by the local Neolithic groups. Hilltop sites are still known, sometimes still situated on an isolated rock peak or outcrop like Château-Virant in Lançon de Provence (Bouches-du-Rhône). Domestic occupation is located in small caves and shelters in remote canyons in Haute-Provence, such as those in the Verdon canyon, in the Var and the Alpes-de-Haute-Provence, including some well-known sites such as la grotte Murée in Montpezat and the shelter of le Jardin du Capitaine in Sainte-Croix-du-Verdon (Alpes-de-Haute-Provence). There are, however, also many lowland sites throughout the region. In general, these settlements are always small and there does not seem to be the very large sites like those known in the *Couronnien* or *Fontbouisse* groups. The buildings are more varied with oval and paved structures known in eastern Languedoc at sites such as Maupas and le Bois Sacré. There are buildings with peripheral walls and a central line of post-holes in Provence as at terrace I at le Col Sainte-Anne (although this may have already been present in an earlier phase) and there are the post-constructed buildings of the Rhône Valley as at le Serre 1, Rue du Bouquet and probably les Vignarets. The double-aisled rectangular house of le Serre 1 measures 63 m^2 while the stone structures of the Languedoc measure 30–50 m^2.

Houses dating to the end of the Bell Beaker period, marked by vessels with incised and barbed wire decoration are less well known. The small structure on terrace XI at le Col Sainte-Anne is probably attributable to this late phase but is very small and largely occupied by a large structured hearth that one would not expect in a normal house: it would be better placed in an annexe to a larger and more overtly domestic structure. The latest development in this phase is the discovery of enclosures. Enclosure is a well-known phenomenon at the beginning of the Late Neolithic in Provence and lasts until the middle of the 3rd millennium in eastern Languedoc although enclosures appear to be absent in the early and middle Bell Beaker phases. These enclosures seem fairly diverse both in their topographic layout and in the nature of the perimeter comprising stone

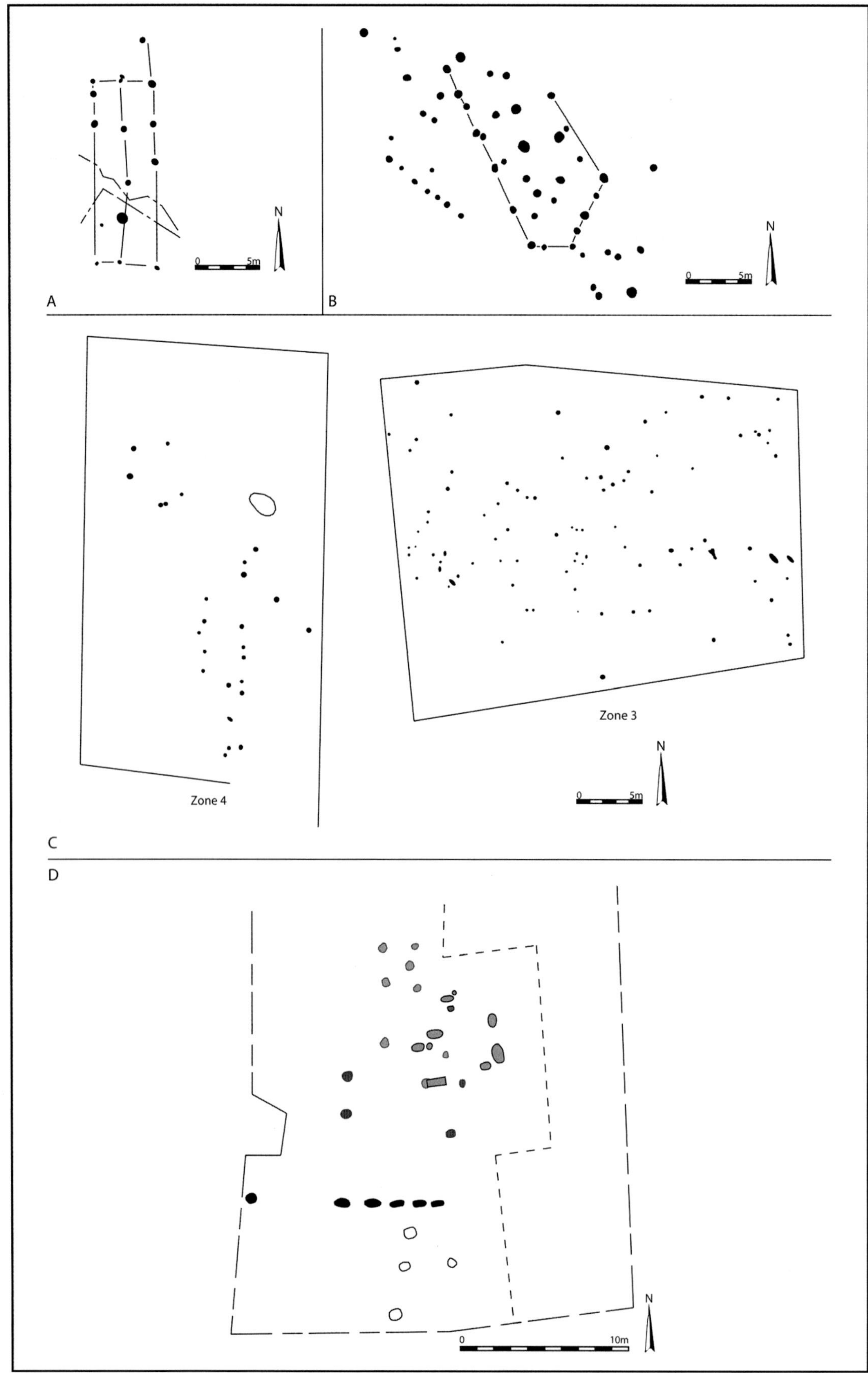

Figure 5.9: Beaker houses in Mediterranean France: Rhone Valley. A – le Serre (Roynac, Drôme; after Vital 2005); B – Rue du Bouquet (Montélimar, Drôme; after Néré et al. *2016); C – les Vignarets (Upie, Drôme; after Lurol 2002); D – les Juilléras (Mondragon, Vaucluse; after Lemercier 2002) (CAD O. Lemercier)*

walls, earthworks, ditches and palisades. These remarkable structures remain scarce in the region but are widespread from low Provence to the Aude valley.

Conclusions

In Mediterranean France, the settlements of the Late Neolithic are becoming better known and therefore are highlighting our lack of knowledge of Bell Beaker settlements. Although 'domestic' sites are numerous, extensive excavations are rare and the nature of Bell Beaker domestic activity is still poorly understood. It is obvious that on certain sites Bell Beaker objects have been discovered but without any obvious or specific structures but rather directly over the ruins of the dwellings of the previous occupation.

For the few known structures, as elsewhere in Europe, but with the exception of certain specific areas (British Isles, Netherlands, Hungary), there is a general continuity of architectural traditions and a continuity of regional or local choices in dimensions, shapes and building materials. The appearance with Bell Beakers of oval or apsidal structures in regions where they had not previously existed is the most remarkable change (Lemercier & Strahm 2018).

Mediterranean France is at the border between the two great building traditions that are known in Bell Beaker Europe (Lemercier & Strahm 2018). The littoral zone belongs to a southern and western European tradition generally characterised by oval or apsidal plans and the use of both wood and stone as the main building materials (though see chapters by Garrido-Pena, Melis, and Baioni *et al.* this volume). The Rhône valley, however, can be viewed as a southern extension of northern and eastern European traditions characterised by post-built structures with rectangular or boat-shaped ground-plans.

It remains unclear whether the low investment in Bell Beaker settlements is more of a state of knowledge or a prehistoric reality that might underlie the idea of more mobile Bell Beaker groups in keeping with pastoral and/or cynegetic activities. In the current state of the research, the paucity of data on Bell Beaker settlements is not very different from that observed for other periods and other cultures of late prehistory. It is in comparison with the remarkable sites and structures of the *Fontbouisse* group that Bell Beaker investment seems extremely weak. Finally, even if this low Bell Beaker investment is proven in the future, nevertheless a renewed dynamism can be seen at the end of the period, associated with late Bell Beakers around 2150/2100 BC, with the building of substantial enclosures in all parts of the region.

References

Alix, S. 2009. Saint-Victor-La-Coste, La Tuilerie (Gard), *Bilan Scientifique Régional Languedoc Roussillon 2008*. Montpellier: DRAC, SRA, 96–7

Ambert, P. 1995. Les mines préhistoriques de Cabrières (Hérault) : quinze ans de recherches. État de la question. *Bulletin de la Société préhistorique française,* 92 (4), 499–508

Ambert, P. 2003. Contribution à l'étude du Campaniforme du Languedoc central méridional, *Bulletin de la Société préhistorique Française* 100 (4) 715–32

Barge, H. 2000. Le site des Barres à Eyguières. Un exemple d'habitat chalcolithique entre les Alpilles et la Crau. In P. Leveau and J.-P. Saquet (eds), *Milieux et sociétés dans la vallée des Baux*, 129–38. Revue Archéologique de la Narbonnaise, supplément 31, Travaux du Centre Camille Julian, 26

Barge-Mahieu, H. 1987. L'habitat campaniforme des Calades à Orgon (Bouches-du-Rhône), Découverte d'un nouveau décor céramique en Provence. In Waldren, W.H. & Kennard, R.C. (eds), *Bell beakers of the western Mediterranean, Definition, Interpretation, Theory and new site Data, The Oxford International Conference 1986*, 483–93. Oxford: British Archaeological Reports International Series 331

Barge-Mahieu, H. 1995. Les structures d'habitat chalcolithiques dans les massifs des Alpilles et du Deffends (Bouches-du-Rhône). In Guilaine, J. & Vaquer, J. (eds), *L'habitat néolithique et protohistorique dans le sud de la France, Séminaires du Centre d'Anthropologie*, 41–8. Toulouse: Ecole des Hautes Etudes en Sciences Sociales

Besse, M. (ed.), 2014. *Around the Petit-Chasseur Site in Sion (Valais, Switzerland) and New Approaches to the Bell Beaker Culture*, 181–204. Oxford: Archaeopress Archaeology

Bevilacqua, R. (ed.), 2015. *La Pièce d'Alquier à Fontiès d'Aude. Un nouveau jalon pour l'étude du Campaniforme pyrénéen.* Toulouse: Archives d'Ecologie Préhistorique

Blaise, E. 2010. *Economie animale et gestion des troupeaux au Néolithique final en Provence: approche archéozoologique et contribution des analyses isotopiques de l'émail dentaire.* Oxford: British Archaeological Reports International Series 2080

Blaise, E. Brehard, S. Carrere, I. Favrie, T. Gourichon, L. Helmer, D. Riviere, J. Tresset, A. & Vigne, J.-D. 2010. L'élevage du Néolithique moyen 2 au Néolithique final dans le Midi méditerranéen de la France: état des données archéozoologiques. In Lemercier, O., Furestier, R. & Blaise, E. (eds), *4è Millénaire. La transition du Néolithique moyen au Néolithique final dans le sud-est de la France et les régions voisines*, 261–84. Lattes: Monographies d'Archéologie Méditerranéenne 27

Blaise, E. Helmer, D. Convertini, F. Furestier, R. & Lemercier, O. 2014. Bell Beaker herding and hunting in south-eastern France: technical, historical and social implications. In Besse, M. (ed.), 163–80

Bocquenet, J.P. 1995. *Espaces domestiques et structures d'habitat épicampaniformes au Col Sainte-Anne (Simiane-Collongue, Bouches-du-Rhône).* In J. Guilaine & J. Vaquer (eds), *L'habitat néolithique et protohistorique dans le sud de la France, Séminaires du Centre d'Anthropologie*, 49–55. Toulouse: Ecole des Hautes Etudes en Sciences Sociales

Bocquenet, J.P. & Müller A. 1999. Structures d'habitat épicampaniformes au Col Sainte-Anne (Simiane-Collongue, Bouches-du-Rhône). In Beeching, A. & Vital, J. (eds), *Préhistoire de l'espace habité en France du sud. Actes des 1eres Rencontres Méridionales de Préhistoire récente*, 101–8. Valence: Travaux du CAP 1

Bocquenet, J.P. Lemercier, O. & Müller A. 1998. L'occupation campaniforme du site perché du Col Sainte-Anne (Simiane-Collongue – Bouches-du-Rhône – France) Séries céramiques, structures d'habitat et espaces domestiques. In *Proceedings of the XIII International Congress of Prehistoric and Protohistoric Sciences, Forli (Italia) 8–14 september 1996, Section 10: The Copper Age in the Near East and Europe*, 159–66. Forli: Abaco

Bocquet, A. Ballet, F. Bintz, P. Castel, R. & Ginestet J.-P. 1987. Nouveaux témoins de la civilisation campaniforme dans les Alpes françaises du Nord, *Bulletin d'Études Préhistoriques Alpines* XIX, 9–22

Bourgueau, R. Mougin, P. & Rouleau, R. 2009. Poussan, Les Clachs 2M, *Bilan Scientifique Languedoc Roussillon 2008*. Montpellier: DRAC, SRA, 157–8

Briois, F. 2005. *Les industries de pierre taillée néolithiques en Languedoc occidental.* Lattes: Monographies d'Archéologie Méditerranéenne 20

Briois, F. Furestier, R. Léa, V. & Renault, S. 2008. Les industries lithiques du midi méditerranéen français et de ses marges aux IVème et IIIème millénaires. In Dias-Meirinho, M.-H., Léa, V., Fouéré, P., Gernigon, K., Bailly, M. & Briois, F. (eds), *Les industries lithiques des IVème et IIIème millénaires av. J.-C. en Europe occidentale, Actes du colloque de Toulouse, 7–8 avril 2005*, 207–30. Oxford: British Archaeological Reports International Series 18845

Brochier, J.-E. & Livache, M. 2006. Apt, Abri du Centre 2 (Vaucluse), *Bilan Scientifique Régional PACA 2005.* Aix-en-Provence: DRAC, SRA, 191–2

Carozza, L. (ed.) 2005. *La fin du Néolithique et les débuts de la métallurgie en Languedoc central: les habitats de la colline du Puech Haut (Paulhan-Hérault).* Toulouse: Archives d'Ecologie Préhistorique

Claustre, F. & Mazière, F. 1998. La céramique campaniforme des Pyrénées Orientales, *Bulletin de la Société Préhistorique Française* 95 (3), 383–92

Convertini, F. 1996. *Production et signification de la céramique campaniforme à la fin du 3ème millénaire av. J.C. dans le Sud et le Centre-Ouest de la France et en Suisse occidentale.* Oxford: British Archaeological Reports International Series 656

Convertini, F. 2009. Céramiques campaniformes et sépultures collectives de l'Aude: origine et statut du standard. In *De Méditerranée et d'ailleurs. Mélanges offerts à Jean Guilaine*, 221–234. Toulouse: Archives d'Écologie Préhistorique

Convertini, F. 2017. Les dégraissants des céramiques des sites d'Avignon (Vaucluse): nouvelles données, nouvelles visions de l'implantation du Campaniforme dans le Midi de la France. *Bulletin de la Société Préhistorique Française* 114 (4), 691–710

Convertini, F. & Georjon C. (eds), 2018. *Le Champ du Poste (Carcassonne, Aude). Une succession d'occupations du début du Néolithique moyen à l'âge du Bronze ancien.* Toulouse: Archives d'Ecologie Préhistorique

Convertini, F. Furestier, R. Astruc, L. Forest, V. & Jallot, L. 2004. Le Mas de Vignoles IV à Nîmes (Gard). Résultats préliminaires des fouilles d'un fossé à occupation campaniforme. In H. Dartevelle (ed.), *Auvergne et Midi, actualité de la recherche*, Actes des 5ème Rencontres Méridionales de Préhistoire récente de Clermont-Ferrand, (8 et 9 novembre 2002), 493–507. Cressensac: Préhistoire du sud-ouest, supplément 9

Courtin, J. 1975. Un habitat fortifié du Bronze ancien en Basse-Provence: Le Camp de Laure, *Bulletin du Museum d'Histoire Naturelle de Marseille* XXXV, 218–40

Courtin, J. 1978. Quelques étapes du peuplement de la région de l'Étang de Berre au Post-glaciaire, *Bulletin Archéologique de Provence* 1, 1–36

Courtin, J. & Onoratini, G. 1977. L'habitat campaniforme du 'Fortin du Saut'Châteauneuf-les-Martigues (Bouches-du-Rhône). In *Congrès Préhistorique de France, XXe session, Provence 1974*, 109–21. Paris: Société Préhistorique Française

Durand, E. (ed.), 2005. *Route départemental 104, déviation de Lachapelle-sous-Aubenas (Ardèche, Rhône-Alpes).* Rapport de diagnostic. Lyon: Inrap

Durrenmath, G. Luzi, C. Furestier, R. Gilabert, C. Pellissier, M. Lazard, N. & Provenzano N. 2004. Les occupations du Collet-Redon (Martigues, Bouches-du-Rhône): l'enceinte de l'âge du Bronze. In J. Gasco, X.Gutherz, and P.A. De Labriffe (eds) , *Temps et espaces culturels du 6e au 2e millénaire en France du Sud,* Actes des IVe Rencontres Méridionales de Préhistoire récente, Nîmes 28 et 29 octobre 2000, 263–70. Lattes: Monographies d'Archéologie Méditerranéenne

Escallon, G. Furestier, R. Lachenal, T. Convertini, F. & Forest V. 2008. Le Parc Georges Besse II: un site du Bronze ancien épicampaniforme à Nîmes (Gard), *Bulletin de la Société Préhistorique Française* 105 (3), 517–37

Furestier, R. 2007. *Les industries lithiques campaniformes du sud-est de la France.* Oxford: British Archaeological Reports International Series 1684

Furestier, R. Cauliez, J. Lazard, N. Lemercier, O. Pellissier, M. & Courtin, J. 2007. 1974–2004: Le site du Fortin-du-Saut (Châteauneuf-lès-Martigues, Bouches-du-Rhône) et le Campaniforme 30 ans après. In J. Evin (ed.), *Un siècle de construction du discours scientifique en Préhistoire.* Actes du XXVIe Congrès Préhistorique de France, 297–310. Paris: Société Préhistorique Française

Gadbois-Langevin, R. 2013. *Le Campaniforme en France: étude spatiale de l'évolution d'un territoire.* Mémoire de Master. Dijon: Université de Bourgogne

Gilabert, C. & Jallot, L. 2018. L'habitat du Néolithique final en Provence et en Languedoc (IVe–IIIe millénaire av. n. è.), systèmes techniques, organisation spatiale, évolution architecturale et dynamique de peuplement. In Lemercier, *et al.* (eds), 319–34

Guilaine, J. 1967. *La civilisation du vase campaniforme dans les Pyrénées françaises.* Carcassonne: Gabelle

Guilaine, J. Vaquer, J. Coularou, J. & Treinen-Claustre, F. (eds), 1989. *Médor / Ornaisons. Archéologie et écologie d'un site de l'Age du Cuivre, de l'Age du Bronze final et de l'Antiquité tardive.* Toulouse: CASR, Carcassonne: Archéologie en Terre d'Aude

Guilaine, J. Sacchi, D. & Vaquer J. 1994. *Aude des origines.* Carcassonne: Archéologie en Terre d'Aude

Guilaine, J. Barthès, P. Coularou, J. Briois, F. & Vaquer J. (eds), 1997. *La Poste-Vieille, de l'enceinte néolithique à la bastide d'Alzau.* Toulouse: CASR, Carcassonne: Archéologie en Terre d'Aude

Guilaine, J. Claustre, F. Lemercier, O. & Sabatier P. 2001. Campaniformes et environnement culturel en France méditerranéenne. In Nicolis, F. (ed.), *Bell Beakers today: Pottery, people, culture, symbols in prehistoric Europe. Proceedings of the International Colloquium, Riva del Garda (Trento, Italy), 11–16 May 1998*, 229–75. Trento: Provincia Autonoma di Trento, Servizio Beni Culturali. Ufficio Beni Archeologici

Gutherz, X. & Jallot, L. 2005. Âge du cuivre et changements sociaux en Languedoc méditerranéen. In Ambert, P. & Vaquer, J. (eds), *La première métallurgie en France et dans les pays limitrophes. Actes du colloque de Carcassonne 2002*, 119–30. Paris: Mémoires de la Société Préhistorique Française 37

Guyon, M. 1999. Voiron, la Brunerie (Isère), *Bilan Scientifique Régional Rhône-Alpes 1997.* Lyon: DRAC, SRA, 118–19

Hasler, A. Chevillot, P. Rodet-Belarbi, I. & Sargiano, J.-P. 2016. Le Néolithique final de Payennet à Gardanne (Bouches-du-Rhône). In Cauliez, J., Sénépart, I., Jallot, L., de Labriffe, P.-A., Gilabert, C. & Gutherz, X. (eds), *De la tombe au Territoire and actualité de la recherche.* Actes des 11e Rencontres méridionales de Préhistoire récente, Montpellier 2014, 551–65. Toulouse: Archives d'Écologie Préhistorique

Hayden, C. Blaise, E. Furestier, R. Lemercier, O. Linton, J. Perez, M. Smith, W. & Todisco, D. 2011. Le Vignaud 3, Chemin du Puits Neuf (Langlade, Gard): du Fontbouisse au Campaniforme. In Sénépart, I., Perrin, T., Thirault, E. & Bonnardin, S. (eds), *Marges, frontières et transgressions. Actualité de la recherche.* Actes des 8e Rencontres Méridionales de Préhistoire Récente, 439–48. Toulouse: Archives d'Écologie Préhistorique

Helmer, D. Blaise, E. Gourichon, L. & Saña-Segui, M. 2018. Using cattle for traction and transport during the Neolithic period. Contribution of the study of the first and second phalanxes, *Bulletin de la Société Préhistorique Française* 115 (1), 71–98

Jallot, L. & Gutherz, X. 2014. Le Néolithique final en Languedoc oriental et ses marges: 20 ans après Ambérieu-en-Bugey. In Sénépart, I., Leandri, F., Cauliez, J., Perrin, T. & Thirault, E. (eds), *Chronologie de la Préhistoire récente dans le sud de la France: Acquis 1992–2012. Actualité de la recherche.* Actes des 10e Rencontres Méridionales de Préhistoire Récente, 137–58. Toulouse: Archives d'Écologie Préhistorique

Jolibert, B. 1988. *Le gisement campaniforme de Muret*, Toulouse: Archives d'Écologie Préhistorique

Labaune, M. 2016. *Le métal et la métallurgie campaniforme en Europe occidentale. Usage et circulation dans la 2e moitié du IIIe millénaire av. n. è.* Thèse de Doctorat. Dijon: Université de Bourgogne

Lachenal, T. 2010. *L'âge du Bronze en Provence: productions céramiques et dynamiques culturelles.* Thèse de Doctorat. Aix-en-Provence: Université de Provence

Laroche, M., Duny, A. & Piatscheck, C. 2012. Les occupations de la fin du Néolithique du Mas de Garric (Mèze, Hérault): résultats préliminaires. In Perrin, T., Sénépar, I., Cauliez, J., Thirault, E. & Bonnardin, S. (eds), *Dynamismes et rythmes évolutifs des sociétés de la Préhistoire récente. Actualité de la recherche. Actes des 9e Rencontres Méridionales de Préhistoire Récente (Saint-Georges-de-Didonne – 8–9 octobre 2010),* 257–69. Toulouse: Archives d'Écologie Préhistorique

Lemercier, O. 2004. *Les Campaniformes dans le sud-est de la France.* Lattes: Monographies d'Archéologie Méditerranéenne 18

Lemercier, O. 2007. La fin du Néolithique dans le sud-est de la France. Concepts techniques, culturels et chronologiques de 1954 à 2004. In Evin, J. (ed.), *Un siècle de construction du discours scientifique en Préhistoire, Actes du XXVIe Congrès Préhistorique de France, Avignon, 21–25 septembre 2004*, I, 485–500. Paris: Société Préhistorique Française

Lemercier, O. 2012. The Mediterranean France Beaker Transition. In Fokkens, H. & Nicolis. F. (eds), *Background to Beakers. Inquiries into the regional cultural background to the Bell Beaker complex*, 81–119. Leiden: Sidestone Press

Lemercier, O. 2014. Bell Beakers in Eastern France and the Rhone-Saone-Rhine axis question. In Besse, M. (ed.), 181–204

Lemercier, O. 2015. *'I did not entirely understand your argument, yet I disagree.' Histoire et perspectives de la recherche campaniforme.* Mémoire d'HDR. Dijon: Université de Bourgogne

Lemercier, O. 2018. La question campaniforme. In Guilaine, J. & Garcia, D. (eds), *La Protohistoire de la France,* 205–17. Paris: Hermann

Lemercier, O. forthcoming. Campaniforme: fin du Néolithique et/ou début de l'âge du Bronze? In Buchez, N., Lemercier, O., Praud, I. & Talon, M. (eds), *La fin du Néolithique et la genèse du Bronze ancien dans l'Europe du nord-ouest.* Paris: Société Préhistorique Française

Lemercier, O. & Gilabert, C. 2009. Approche chronoculturelle de l'habitat de la fin du Néolithique en Provence. In Beeching, A. & Senepart, I. (eds), *De la Maison au village. L'habitat Néolithique du sud de la France et du nord-ouest méditerranéen, Actes de la table ronde de Marseille, 23–24 mai 2003*, 255–66. Paris: Société Préhistorique Française, Mémoire de la Société Préhistorique Française 48

Lemercier, O. & Strahm, C. 2018. Nids de coucous et grandes maisons. L'habitat campaniforme, épicampaniforme et péricampaniforme en France dans son contexte européen. In Lemercier, *et al.* (eds), 459–78

Lemercier, O. & Tchérémissinoff Y. 2011. Du Néolithique final au Bronze ancien: les sépultures individuelles campaniformes dans le sud de la France. In Salanova, L. & Tcheremissinoff, Y. (eds), *Les sépultures individuelles campaniformes en France.* 177–94. Paris: Gallia Préhistoire, Supplément XLI

Lemercier, O. with the collab. of: Berger, J.-F. Düh, P. Loirat, D. Lazard-Dhollande, N. Mellony, P. Nohe, A.-F. Pellissier, M. Renault, S, Seris, D. and Tcheremissinoff, Y. 2002. Les occupations néolithiques de Mondragon – Les Julliéras (Vaucluse). In *Archéologie du TGV Méditerranée, Fiches de Synthèse. Tome 1: La Préhistoire*, 147–72. Lattes: Monographies d'Archéologie Méditerranéenne, 8

Lemercier, O. Blaise, E. Cauliez, J. Furestier, R. Gilabert, C. Lazard, N. Pinet, L. & Provenzano, N. 2004. La fin des temps néolithiques. In Buisson-Catil, J. *et al.* (eds), *Vaucluse Préhistorique*, 195–246. Avignon: Editions A. Barthélémy

Lemercier, O. Blaise, E. Cattin, F. Convertini, F. Desideri, J. Furestier, R. Gadbois-Langevin, R. & Labaune, M. 2014a. 2500 avant notre ère: l'implantation campaniforme en France méditerranéenne. In Mercuri, L., Villaescusa, R.G. & Bertoncello. F. (eds), *Implantations humaines en milieu littoral méditerranéen: facteurs d'installation et processus d'appropriation de l'espace (Préhistoire, Antiquité, Moyen-Age)*, actes des XXXIVe Rencontres internationales d'Archéologie et d'Histoire d'Antibes, 191–203. Antibes: APDCA

Lemercier, O. Furestier, R. Gadbois-Langevin, R. & Schulz Paulsson, B. 2014b. Chronologie et périodisation des campaniformes en France méditerranéenne. In Sénépart, I., Leandri, F., Cauliez, J., Perrin, T. & Thirault, E. (eds), *Chronologie de la Préhistoire récente dans le sud de la France: Acquis 1992–2012. Actualité de la recherche.* Actes des 10e Rencontres Méridionales de Préhistoire Récente, 175–95. Toulouse: Archives d'Écologie Préhistorique

Lemercier, O., Sénépart, I., Besse, M. & Mordant, C. (eds), 2018. *Habitations et habitat du Néolithique à l'âge du Bronze en France et régions voisines. Actes des Deuxièmes Rencontres Nord-Sud de Préhistoire Récente, Dijon, 19–21 novembre 2015.* Toulouse: Archives d'Écologie Préhistorique

Loison, G. Gandelin, M. Vergély, H. Gleize, Y. Tchérémissinoff, Y. Haurillon, R. Marsac, R. Remicourt, M. Torchy, L. & Vinolas, F. 2011. Dynamiques d'occupation des sols à la Préhistoire récente dans la basse vallée de l'Hérault: les apports de l'A75, tronçon Pézenas-Béziers. In Sénépart, I., Perrin, T., Thirault, E. & Bonnardin, S. (eds), *Marges, frontières et transgressions: Actualité de la recherche: Actes des 8e Rencontres Méridionales de Préhistoire Récente, Marseille, 7–8 novembre 2008,* 317–44. Toulouse: Archives d'Ecologie Préhistorique

Lurol, J.-M. 2002. Upie – Les Vignarets (fiche 2). In *Archéologie du TGV Méditerranée: fiches de synthèse – Tome 1 – La Préhistoire*, 23–34. Lattes: Monographies d'Archéologie Méditerranéenne 8

Machu, P. Mano, L. Magnardi, N. Sandrone, S. & Strangi, J.-M. 2004. Haute-Roya, Tende, La Brigue, Fontan (Alpes-Maritimes), *Bilan Scientifique Régional PACA 2003.* Aix-en-Provence: DRAC, SRA, 83–4

Margarit, X. Renault, S. & Loirat, D. 2002. L'occupation campaniforme du site des Ribauds à Mondragon (Vaucluse). In *Archéologie du TGV Méditerranée: fiches de synthèse – Tome 1 – La Préhistoire*, 189–93. Lattes: Monographies d'Archéologie Méditerranéenne 8

Montjardin, R. 1996. L'habitat campaniforme (pyrénaïque) du Travers des Fourches, Veyrac (Villeveyrac – Hérault) dans le cadre de la chronologie campaniforme. In Duhamel, P. (ed.), *La Bourgogne entre les bassins rhénan, rhodanien et parisien: Carrefour ou frontière? Actes du XVIIIe Colloque interrégional sur le Néolithique, Dijon, 25–27 octobre 1991,* 483–502. Dijon: Revue Archéologique de l'Est, quatorzième supplement

Néré, E. Cousseran-Néré, S. Nordez, M. & Notier, F. 2016. Un vaste habitat à niveaux de sol conservés de l'âge du Bronze à Montélimar (Drôme), *Bulletin de la Société préhistorique Française* 113, 155–7

Noret, C. 2010. Nîmes, Mas de Mayan 5, *Bilan Scientifique Régional Languedoc Roussillon 2009*. Montpellier: DRAC, SRA, 79–80

Piatscheck, C. 2014. *Production et consommation des outils de pierre taillée à la fin du Néolithique en Provence: caractérisation pluridisciplinaire et renouvellement méthodologique*, Thèse de Doctorat. Aix-en-Provence: Aix-Marseille Université

Roger, J.-M. 1988. Le Campaniforme en Vaunage: vestiges diffus et structures évidentes. In A. Beeching (ed.), *Le Campaniforme: 5e Rencontres Néolithiques Rhône-Alpes*, 80–109. Valence: CAP, ARENERA 5

Roger, J.-M. 1989. La transition du chalcolithique bronze ancien en Languedoc oriental: Campaniforme et Epicampaniforme en Vaunage (Gard). In *Hommages à Henri Prades*, 73–86. Lattes: Archéologie en Languedoc 4

Roger, J.-M. Ferrier, C. & Valette, P. 1988. La structure campaniforme de Maupas (Calvisson, Gard*), Bulletin de la Société d'Etude des Sciences Naturelles de Nîmes et du Gard* 58, 91–5

Roudil, J.-L. Bazile, F. & Soulier, M. 1974. L'habitat campaniforme de Saint-Côme-et-Maruéjols (Gard). *Gallia Préhistoire,* 17 (1), 181–213

Sargiano, J.-P. & Lachenal, T. 2008. Velaux, La Bestide Neuve 2 (Bouches-du-Rhône), *Bilan Scientifique Régional PACA 2007.* Aix-en-Provence: DRAC, SRA, 176

Sauzade, G. 2011. Caractérisation chronoculturelle du mobilier funéraire en Provence au Néolithique final et au Bronze ancien. Évolution des rites funéraires liés à l'inhumation individuelle ou collective et distribution chronologique des sépultures, *Préhistoires Méditerranéennes,* 2, 71–104

Schmitt A., Remicourt, M. & D'Anna, A. 2017. Inhumations individuelles en contexte domestique au Néolithique final en France méridionale. Une alternative à la sépulture collective? *Bulletin de la Société Préhistorique Française,* 114 (3). 469–96

Sendra, B. Lachenal, T. Michel, J. & Moquel, J. 2016. La cellule funéraire du Bronze ancien 3 de Mitra à Garons (Gard, France). In Cauliez, J., Sénépart, I., Jallot, L., De Labriffe, P.-A., Gilabert, C. & Gutherz, X. (eds), *De la tombe au territoire and Actualités de la recherche, Actes des 11e Rencontres Méridionales de Préhistoire Récente (Montpellier 25–27 septembre 2014)*, 363–83 Toulouse: Archives d'Écologie Préhistorique

Sénépart, I. Wattez, J. Jallot, L. Hamon, T. & Onfray M. 2016. La construction en terre crue au Néolithique. Un état de la question en France, *Archéopages*, 42, 6–19

Sénépart, I. Hamon, T. Jallot, L. Laporte, L. Wattez, J. Onfray, M. Bailleux, G. & Coussot C. 2018. De l'usage d'un matériau éphémère? Bilan et actualités de l'habitat en terre crue du Néolithique à l'âge du Bronze en France. In Lemercier *et al.* (eds), 2018, 479–94

Sohn, M. Ambert, P. Laroche, M. Houlès, N. & Grimal, J. 2008. Les indices campaniformes du district minier de Cabrières-Péret dans leur contexte régional de la basse vallée de l'Hérault, *Bulletin du Musée d'Anthropologie Préhistorique de Monaco* 48, 73–103

Souville, S. 1994. *La céramique à décor barbelé du Bronze ancien dans le midi de la France*. Mémoire de DEA. Toulouse: EHESS

Taffanel, O. & Taffanel, J. 1957. La station Préhistorique d'Embusco (Commune de Mailhac, Aude). *Cahiers Ligures de Préhistoire et d'Archéologie,* 6, 53–72

Thevenin, E. 2008. Pierrelatte. Les Tomples, les Planchettes, *Bilan Scientifique Régional Rhône-Alpes 2006*. Lyon: DRAC, SRA, 73

Vaquer, J. 1990. *Le Néolithique en Languedoc Occidental.* Paris: CNRS

Vaquer, J. 1998. Le Mourral, Trèbes (Aude). A fortified languedocian late Neolithic site reoccupied by Bell Beakers. In Benz, M. & Van Willigen, S. (eds), *Some New approaches to The Bell Beaker Phenomenon, Lost Paradise? Proceedings of the second Meeting of the 'Association Archéologie et Gobelets', Feldberg (Germany), 18th–20th avril 1997*, 15–21. Oxford: British Archaeological Reports IS 690

Vaquer, J. & Remicourt, M. 2008. La série céramique du Bronze ancien 1 au Roc d'en Gabit, Carcassonne (Aude), *Bulletin de la Société Préhistorique Française,* 105(3), 501–16

Vermeulen, C. 2009. Montélimar, rue André Malraux, Le Bouquet. In *Bilan Scientifique de la Région Rhône-Alpes 2008*, 68. Lyon: Direction Régionale des Affaires Culturelles

Vial, J. 2006. Fabrègues, l'Estagnol (Hérault), *Bilan Scientifique Régional Languedoc Roussillon 2005.* Montpellier: DRAC, SRA, 130–1

Vignaud, A. 2002. L'éperon du Clos Marie Louise. L'âge du Bronze ancien. In *Archéologie du TGV Méditerranée, Fiches de Synthèse. Tome 2: La Protohistoire*, 573–6. Lattes: Monographies d'Archéologie Méditerranéenne, 9

Vital, J. 2005. Modalités et contextes d'évolution des formes architecturales à la fin du Néolithique et au début de l'âge du Bronze en moyenne vallée du Rhône. In Buchsenschutz, O. & Mordant, C. (eds), *Architectures protohistoriques en Europe occidentale du Néolithique final à l'âge du Fer. Actes des congrès nationaux des sociétés historiques et scientifiques, 127e congrès, Nancy (2002),* 365–87. Paris: CTHS

Vital, J. Brochier, J.-L. Durand, J. Prost, D. Reynier, P. & Rimbault, S. 1999. Roynac le Serre 1 (Drôme): Une nouvelle séquence holocène en Valdaine et ses occupations des Âges des métaux, *Bulletin de la Société Préhistorique Française* 96 (2), 225–40

Vital, J. Brochier, J.-L. Durand, J. Prost, D. Reynier, P. Rimbault, S. & Sidi Maamar, H. 2002. La séquence holocène et les occupations des âges des Métaux de Roynac – Le Serre 1 (Drôme). In *Archéologie du TGV Méditerranée: fiches de synthèse – Tome 2 – La Protohistoire*, 411–26. Lattes: Monographies d'Archéologie Méditerranéenne 9

Vital, J. Convertini, F. & Lemercier, O. (eds), 2012. *Composantes culturelles et premières productions céramiques du Bronze ancien dans le sud-est de la France. Résultats du Projet Collectif de Recherche 1999–2009.* Oxford: British Archaeological Reports 2446

Appendix 5.1: List of Bell Beakers settlements

Town	*Site*	*Periodisation phase*	*Reference*
Cavanac	Station de Pébril-la-Gravette	undet.	Guilaine 1967
Conilhac-Corbières*	Station de la Foun den Peyre II	undet.	Guilaine 1967
Conques-sur-Orbiel	Abri de Font-Juvénal	M/L	Guilaine *et al.* 1994
Gaja-et-Villedieu	Las Gravas	E?/L	Vaquer 1990
Ladern-sur-Lauquet	Station de la Condamine	E/M?	Guilaine 1967
Ladern-sur-Lauquet	Ribos de Bila	M	Guilaine *et al.* 2001
Ladern-sur-Lauquet	Station de Pech-Régal	undet.	Guilaine 1967
Mailhac	Station I d'Embusco	E/M	Guilaine 1967
Mailhac	Station II d'Embusco	M	Guilaine 1967
Mailhac*	La Careirasse	L	Souville 1994
Carcassonne	Roc d'En Gabit	E/L	Vaquer 1990
Ornaisons	Médor	M	Guilaine *et al.* 1989
Ouveillan	plusieurs sites	undet.	Unpublished data, P. Barthès
Pennautier	Station de Font-Bonne	M	Vaquer 1990
Pennautier	Station d'Huniac	M	Vaquer 1990
Pezens*	La Poste Vieille	M	Guilaine *et al.* 1997
Sallèles-Cabardès*	Grotte de Gazel	E	Guilaine 1967
Trausse	Station de Frigoulas	undet.	Guilaine 1967
Trèbes*	Le Mourral Millegrand	E	Vaquer 1998
Carcassonne	Champ du Poste	E?	Convertini & Georjon 2018
Mailhac*	Le Traversant	M	Unpublished data, E. Gailledrat
Monze*	Laval de la Bretonne	M	Unpublished data, E. Gailledrat
Fontiès d'Aude*	Domaine de la Pièce d'Alquier	undet.	Bevilacqua 2015
Bages	Station de los Matés III	M	Claustre & Mazière 1998
Laroque-des-Albères	Station du Bosc de Villeclare	M?	Claustre & Mazière 1998
Passa	Pedra Blanca	L	Claustre & Mazière 1998
Saint-André-de-Sorrède	Station de Saint Michel	M	Claustre & Mazière 1998
Saint-Génis-des-Fontaines	Station du Mas Coste	M	Claustre & Mazière 1998
Saleilles	Mas Couret	M/L	Claustre & Mazière 1998
Le Soler	Station des Campellanes	M	Claustre & Mazière 1998
Campoussy	Station de Cayenne	E	Claustre & Mazière 1998
Eyne	Abri de lo Pla del Bach	undet.	Claustre & Mazière 1998
Aigne	Station d'Embusco III	M	Montjardin 1996; Guilaine 1967
La Livinière	Parignoles	E/L	Montjardin 1996
Pardailhan	Grotte Tournié	L	Guilaine *et al.* 2001
Paulhan	Le Puech Haut	E/M	Carozza *et al.* 2005
Gorniès	Grotte du Claux	E	Montjardin 1996
Vailhauquès	Station de Vailhauquès	undet.	Montjardin 1996
Claret	Rocher du Causse	L	Montjardin 1996
Valflaunès	Grotte de l'Hortus	E	Montjardin 1996
Saint-Mathieu de Tréviers	Château du Lébous	E	Montjardin 1996
Buzignargues	Station du Pont de Buzigargues	undet.	Montjardin 1996
Grabels	Station de la Paillade	undet.	Montjardin 1996
Le Crès	Station I des Faysses	undet.	Montjardin 1996
Le Crès	Station du Mas Reinhardt	undet.	Montjardin 1996
Le Crès	Château Juvénal	undet.	Montjardin 1996
Montpellier	Richemont	L	Montjardin 1996
Villeneuve-les-Maguelonne	L'Eau Périe	undet.	Montjardin 1996
Villeneuve-les-Maguelonne	Grotte de la Madeleine	M	Montjardin 1996
Fabrègues	Station de la Chicane	undet.	Montjardin 1996
Mireval	Station du Creux de Canet	M	Montjardin 1996
Mireval	Station du Creux de Miège	E/M	Montjardin 1996
Vic-la-Gardiole	Station III de la Roubine de Vic	undet.	Montjardin 1996

Town	*Site*	*Periodisation phase*	*Reference*
Frontignan	Caramus	undet.	Montjardin 1996
Mèze	Station de Font Mars II	L	Montjardin 1996
Méze	Station de Saint-Paul le Haut	E/L	Montjardin 1996
Mèze	Station de Raffègues	L	Montjardin 1996
Mèze	Station de Farlet	undet.	Montjardin 1996
Mèze	Station de Pioch Badieu	E	Montjardin 1996
Loupian	Station du Plescat	undet.	Montjardin 1996
Villeveyrac	Station du Serre des Fourches	M	Montjardin 1996
Villeveyrac	Station du Puech Argentié	undet.	Montjardin 1996
Villeveyrac	Station des Peyrals	M?/L	Montjardin 1996
Gignac	Station de Pioch Courbi	E	Montjardin 1996
Gignac	Station des Trés Vents	undet.	Montjardin 1996
Le Pouget	Station des Crozes	undet.	Montjardin 1996
Plaissan	Station 1 de Rouviège	E/M	Montjardin 1996
Saint-Bauzille de la Sylve	Station de la Vigne Plantier	undet.	Montjardin 1996
Saint-Pons de Mauchien	Station de Montredon	E/L	Montjardin 1996
Saint-Pons de Mauchien	Roquemengarde	E/L	Montjardin 1996
Aumes/Montagnac	Oppidum de Puech Balat	E/L	Sohn *et al.* 2008
Florensac	Station de Saint-Apolis de Fontenille	M	Montjardin 1996
Marseillan	Station submergée de l'étantg de Thau	undet.	Montjardin 1996
Mourèze	Station de Mourèze (cirque ?)	E	Montjardin 1996
Cabrières	Site ancien de Cabrières	undet.	Montjardin 1996
Cers	Station de Montloubat	undet.	Montjardin 1996
Portiragnes	Station de l'Habitarelle	undet.	Montjardin 1996
Portiragnes/Vias	Les Mourguettes	E/M	Montjardin 1996
Espondeilhan	La Croix de Fer	undet.	Montjardin 1996
Pomerols	La Donne II	undet.	Montjardin 1996
Montpellier	Richter	E?	Guilaine *et al.* 2001
Montpellier	Port Marianne	undet.	Montjardin 1996
Cessenon	Aumet	E	Ambert 2003
Cessenon	Viala	M	Ambert 2003
Ferrières-Les-Verreries	Ferrières-Les Verreries	E	Guilaine *et al.* 2001
Villeveyrac	Le Travers des Fourches	M	Montjardin 1996
Villeveyrac*	L'Olivet 2	E	Montjardin 1996
Florensac*	Les Carreiroux	M	Montjardin 1996
Florensac*	Montredon	E	Montjardin 1996
Florensac*	Le Pinier	undet.	Sohn *et al.* 2008
Plaissan	Station 2 de la Rouviège	M?	Sohn *et al.* 2008
Gignac*	Rieu-Salat	M	Sohn *et al.* 2008
Péret*	Capitelle du Broum	L	Sohn *et al.* 2008
Agde*	Station d'Escarpes	E?	Sohn *et al.* 2008
Le Pouget*	Station de Pouzets	undet.	Sohn *et al.* 2008
Le Pouget*	Station de Vigne-Debru	E?	Sohn *et al.* 2008
Valros-Montblanc	Champ Redon	L	Loison *et al.* 2011
Valros	Rec de Ligno 2	L	Loison *et al.* 2011
Mèze	Mas de Garric	L	Laroche *et al.* 2012
Aumes-Montagnac	Puech-Auby	M	Sohn *et al.* 2008
Aumes-Montagnac	Les Mazes	L	Sohn *et al.* 2008
Poussan	Les Clachs 2M	M/L?	Bourgueau *et al.* 2009
Fabrègues	L'Estagnol	undet.	Vial 2006
Muret	Moulin de Garonne	M	Jolibert 1988
Muret	La Peyrère	M	Jolibert 1988
Baziège	Pont de la Route nationale	undet.	Vaquer 1990
Ganties-les-Bains	La Spugo	M	Vaquer 1990
La Balme	Grande Cave	M	Bocquet *et al.* 1987
Sollières-Sardières	Les Balmes	L	Vital, *et al.* 2012
Conjux*	Lac du Bourget	undet.	Bocquet *et al.* 1987

Town	*Site*	*Periodisation phase*	*Reference*
Esparron-de-Verdon*	Aven de Vauclare	M	Lemercier 2004
Esparron-de-Verdon*	Baume de l'Eau	M	Lemercier 2004
Forcalquier	La Fare	M	Lemercier 2004
La Brillanne	Le Champ du Roi	M	Lemercier 2004
Manosque	Vallon de Gaude	L	Lemercier 2004
Méailles*	Grotte du Pertus II	M	Lemercier 2004
Montpezat	Grotte Murée	M	Lemercier 2004
Sainte-Croix du Verdon	Abri du Jardin du Capitaine	M	Lemercier 2004
Chabestan*	Chaumiane 3	M	Vital *et al.* 2012
Lazer*	Ferme des Aros	M	Unpublished
Antibes	Antibes	M	Lemercier 2004
Castellar	Abri Pendimoun	E/M	Lemercier 2004
Grasse	Usine Chiris	M	Lemercier 2004
Greolières	Abri Martin	M	Lemercier 2004
Greolières	Baou dou Draï	undet.	Lemercier 2004
Tende	Gias del Ciari	M	Lemercier 2004
Villeneuve-Loubet*	Site du Rééméteur	M?	Lemercier 2004
Fontan*	Abri Gilbert	M	Machu *et al.*2004
Bourg-Saint-Andéol	Le Bois de Sorbier	L	Lemercier 2004
Bourg-Saint-Andéol	Le Bois de Sorbier 2	L	Furestier, unpublished
Chateaubourg*	Grotte Billon	M	Lemercier 2004
Chauzon	Beaussement	M	Lemercier 2004
Grospierres	Grotte des Conchettes	M	Lemercier 2004
Lagorce	Combe Obscure	undet.	Lemercier 2004
Cros de Géorand	Les Trémoulèdes	M	Lemercier 2004
Saint-André-de-Cruzières	Grotte de Chazelles	E	Lemercier 2004
Soyons	La Brégoule	M	Lemercier 2004
La Chapelle-sous-Aubenas*	RD 104/Lachamp	undet.	Durand 2005
Lussas*	Aven Jacques	M	Furestier, unpublished,
Niaux	Petite grotte de Niaux	E	Guilaine 1967
Aix-en-Provence	Le Clos Marie Louise	L	Lemercier 2004
Aix-en-Provence	Abri des Fours	M	Lemercier 2004
Alleins	La Coste	L	Lemercier 2004
Bouc-Bel-Air	Baou Roux	E/L	Lemercier 2004
Châteauneuf-les-Martigues	Le Fortin du Saut	E	Lemercier 2004
Châteauneuf-les-Martigues*	Grotte du Déboussadou	E	Lemercier 2004
Ensuès-la-Redonne	Abri du Cap Méjean	M	Lemercier 2004
Eygalières*	Station du Château	L?	Lemercier 2004
Eyguières	Les Barres	E/M/L	Lemercier 2004
Fontvieille	Station de la Calade	E/L	Lemercier 2004
Fontvieille	Station du Castellet	L	Lemercier 2004
Fontvieille	Station d'Estoublon	L	Lemercier 2004
Gémenos	La Grande Baume	M/L	Lemercier 2004
Grans	Toupiguières	M	Lemercier 2004
Grans	Station du Baou Majour	E?/M	Lemercier 2004
Istres	Miouvin	M/L	Lemercier 2004
Jouques*	Le Mourre de la Barque	E/M	Lemercier 2004
Lançon-de-Provence	Château Virant	M	Lemercier 2004
Le Rove	Le Camp de Laure	L	Lemercier 2004
Les Baux	Escanin 1	M	Lemercier 2004
Les Baux	Escanin 2	E	Lemercier 2004
Les Baux*	Station du Rocher	E	Lemercier 2004
Marseille	Saint-Joseph Fontainieu	undet.	Lemercier 2004
Marseille*	Saint-Marcel	M	Lemercier 2004
Marseille*	Louis Armand	L	Lachenal 2010
Martigus	Le Collet-Redon	M/L	Lemercier 2004
Martigues	Ponteau-Gare	M/L	Lemercier 2004
Martigues	Saint-Pierre	M/L	Lemercier 2004
Meyrargues	La Plaine	L?	Unpublished data, M. Remicourt

Town	*Site*	*Periodisation phase*	*Reference*
Orgon	Les Calades	E	Lemercier 2004
Pélissanne	Saint-Laurent	M/L?	Lemercier 2004
Peyrolles	La Bastide Blanche	M/L?	Lemercier 2004
Saint-Chamas	Le Collet du verdon	L?	Lemercier 2004
Saint-Martin-de-Crau*	La Carougnade	M	Unpublished
Saint-Mitre-les-Remparts*	Saint-Blaise	M/L	Lemercier 2004
Simiane-Collongue	Le Col Sainte-Anne	E/M/L	Lemercier 2004
Velaux*	La Bastide Neuve II	L	Sargiano & Lachenal 2008
Saint-Martin de Crau*	Redorcamin/Etang des Aulnes	M	Gadbois-Langevin 2013
Ventabren*	Chateaublanc	L	Vital *et al.* 2012
Beauvallon*	Station de Beauvallon (Fiancey)	M?	Lemercier 2004
Boulc-en-Diois	La Tune de la Varaime	M/L?	Lemercier 2004
Chabrillan	La Prairie	L	Lemercier 2004
Chabrillan*	Saint-Martin 2	M	Lemercier 2004
Chabrillan	Saint-Martin 3	M/L	Lemercier 2004
Châteauneuf-sur-Isère*	Beaume	M	Lemercier 2004
Donzère	Baume des Anges	E	Lemercier 2004
Donzère	Grotte de la Chauve-Souris	E	Lemercier 2004
Espeluche*	Lalo	M	Lemercier 2004
Le Pegue*	Oppidum de Saint-Marcel	undet.	Lemercier 2004
Francillon	Baume Sourde	M	Lemercier 2004
Montélimar	Le Gournier	M	Lemercier 2004
Montmaur-en-Diois*	Grotte d'Antonnaire	L	Lemercier 2004
Montségur-sur-Lauzon*	Le Plateau du Laboureau	M/L	Lemercier 2004
Pierrelatte	Les Malalones – Pylone 30	M	Lemercier 2004
Portes-les-Valence*	Ferme Beaumont	undet.	Lemercier 2004
Roynac	Le Serre 1	M/L	Lemercier 2004
Saou	Cissac	M/L	Lemercier 2004
Upie	Les Vignarets	M	Lemercier 2004
Vercoiran	Sainte-Luce	E/M	Lemercier 2004
Chantemerle-Lès-Grignans*	Village	L	Vital *et al.* 2012
Montségur-sur-Lauzon	Daillers	L	Vital *et al.* 2012
Montélimar	Rue André Mlraux-Le Bouquet	M	Vermeulen 2009
Pierrelatte	Les Tomples - Les Planchettes	L?	Thevenin 2008
Sauzet	A7 Section 2	M	Gadbois-Langevin 2013
Allègre-Les Fumades*	Les Fumades	M	Lemercier 2004
Aubussargues*	Mas de Juston	M	Lemercier 2004
Beaucaire*	Triple Levée	L	Lemercier 2004
Caissargues	Moulin Villard	M	Lemercier 2004
Calvisson	Largellier	E/M?/L	Lemercier 2004
Calvisson	Maupas	M	Lemercier 2004
Calvisson	Bois de Calvisson	M	Lemercier 2004
Castillon*	Grotte d'Embaraude	M	Lemercier 2004
Caveirac*	Cagonson	M/L	Lemercier 2004
Chusclan*	Station de la Dent de Marcoule	undet.	Lemercier 2004
Collorgues*	Station du Mas Cornet	M	Lemercier 2004
Congenies	Le Pesquier	E/L	Lemercier 2004
Congenies	Font de Lissac	L	Lemercier 2004
Congenies	Puech de la Fontaine	M?	Lemercier 2004
Congenies	Grange de Jaulmes	E/M/L	Lemercier 2004
La Capelle-Masmolène*	Station de l'Etang de la Capelle	M	Lemercier 2004
Méjannes-le-Clap	Grotte de Théris	E	Lemercier 2004
Montclus	Grotte du Travès	M	Lemercier 2004
Montfaucon*	Station de Montfaucon	undet.	Lemercier 2004
Montpézat	Station de Font de Figue	M/L	Lemercier 2004
Nages-et-Solorgues	Oppidum des Castels	L	Lemercier 2004
Nîmes	Mas de Vignoles 4	M	Convertini *et al.* 2004
Nîmes	Mas de Mayan	L	Noret 2010
Nîmes	Georges Besse 2	L	Escallon *et al.* 2008

Town	Site	Periodisation phase	Reference
Nîmes*	Mas de Cheylon	L	Unpublished
Remoulins*	Grotte de la Sartanette	E/L	Lemercier 2004
Rochefort-du-Gard*	Station des Fontaines	undet.	Lemercier 2004
Sabran	Le Gardonnet	M	Lemercier 2004
Saint-Bauzély	Station des graou	L	Lemercier 2004
Saint-Côme-et-Maruejols	Le Bois Sacré	M	Lemercier 2004
Saint-Dionisy	Oppidum de Roque de Viou	L	Lemercier 2004
Saint-Geniès-de-Malgoire	Station de Bernirenque	M	Lemercier 2004
Saint-Mamert*	Station de Robiac	L	Lemercier 2004
Saint-Paulet-de-Caisson*	Station de Saint-Paulet-de-Caisson	undet.	Lemercier 2004
Sainte-Anastasie*	Abri du Cheval	E	Lemercier 2004
Sanilhac et Sagriès	Baume Raymonde	L	Lemercier 2004
Sauzet	Station de Rouveirolles	L	Lemercier 2004
Uzès	Station de Carrignargues	M	Lemercier 2004
Villevieille	Fontbouise	L	Lemercier 2004
Sommières*	Station du Frigoulier	undet.	Lemercier 2004
Langlade	Le Vignaud	E/M	Hayden *et al.*2011
Saint-Chaptes*	Roque Penat II	L	Vital *et al.* 2012
Aubais	Les Pins	L	Vital *et al.* 2012
Bagnols-sur-Cèze	Euze	L	Vital *et al.* 2012
Congenies*	Fontanes – Sud	L	Vital *et al.* 2012
Saint-Victor-la-Coste*	La Tuilerie	undet.	Alix 2009
Garons	Mitra 3	E?	Gadbois-Langevin 2013
Choranche	Grotte de la Balme Rousse	M/L	Lemercier 2004
Saint-Bernard-du-Touvet*	L'Aulp du Seuil	E	Lemercier 2004
Sassenage	Abri de la grande Rivoire	M	Lemercier 2004
Voiron	La Brunerie	undet.	Guyon 1999
L'Albenc	Les Faverges	undet.	Unpublished
Baudinard	Grand Abri de la Plage	M	Lemercier 2004
Brignoles*	Le Plan Saint-Jean	M?	Lemercier 2004
Cabasse*	La Grande Pièce	M?	Lemercier 2004
Correns	Abri de Sous-Ville	M	Lemercier 2004
Evenos	Station de Saint-Estève	E	Lemercier 2004
Evenos*	Grotte de Saint-Martin 1	M?	Lemercier 2004
Evenos*	Grotte de la Stalagmite	undet.	Lemercier 2004
Le Castellet*	Abri de la Roche Ronde	M	Lemercier 2004
Le Cannet-des-Maures*	Les Blaïs	M?	Lemercier 2004
Mazaugues	Baume des Drams	undet.	Lemercier 2004
Saint-Tropez	La Moutte	undet.	Lemercier 2004
Salernes*	Baume Fontbrégoua	M	Lemercier 2004
Signes*	Grotte du Vieux Mounoï	M?	Lemercier 2004
Signes	Bergerie des Maigres	E/M	Lemercier 2004
Tourtour*	Station de Saint-Pierre	M	Lemercier 2004
Saint-Maximin-la-Sainte-Baume	Chemin de Barjols	L	Lachenal 2010
Avignon	La Balance	E/M	Lemercier 2004
Avignon	La Place du Palais	E	Lemercier 2004
Bédoin	Abri de la Madeleine	M	Lemercier 2004
Blauvac	Station des Aubes	undet.	Lemercier 2004
Bollène	Les Bartras 4	M	Lemercier 2004
Bonnieux	Les Fabrys	M?	Lemercier 2004
Buoux	La brémonde	L	Lemercier 2004
Cheval Blanc	Grande grotte de Vidauque	E	Lemercier 2004
Goult	Irrisson	L	Lemercier 2004
Grillon	Hypogée du Capitaine	M	Lemercier 2004
Lamotte-du-Rhône	Les Petites Bâties	M	Lemercier 2004
Lamotte-du-Rhône	Le Chêne	E?	Lemercier 2004
La Roque-sur-Pernes	Station Ouest du Fraischamp	undet.	Lemercier 2004
La Roque-sur-Pernes	Abri de la Source	E/M/L	Lemercier 2004

Town	*Site*	*Periodisation phase*	*Reference*
La Roque-sur-Pernes	La Clairière	M/L	Lemercier 2004
La Roque-sur-Pernes*	Station du Lauvier	M?/L	Lemercier 2004
Le Beaucet*	Station de la Rouyère	L	Lemercier 2004
Lourmarin*	Les Lauzières	M/L	Lemercier 2004
Mazan*	Station du Banay	M	Lemercier 2004
Menerbes*	Abri Soubeyras	M	Lemercier 2004
Mondragon	Le Duc	L	Lemercier 2004
Mondragon	Les Juilléras	E?/M?/L	Lemercier 2004
Mondragon	Les Ribauds	M	Lemercier 2004
Venasque*	Grotte de l'Ascle	E	Lemercier 2004
Venasque*	Station du Colombier	M/L	Lemercier 2004
Villes-sur-Auzon*	Le Redon	M	Lemercier 2004
Apt*	Abri du Centre 2	M?	Brochier & Livache 2006

* Denotes sites that are not certainly domestic; E = Early; M = Middle; L = Late; undet = undetermined

6

Bell Beaker evidence in the domestic sphere of island contexts: Sardinia and Sicily

Maria Grazia Melis

Regarding the Bell Beaker phenomenon, the current tendency is to focus attention on analysis of the variations in its characteristics in different regions, its relationships with local cultures and its diverse possible significations and social effects. We must also keep in mind the observation made by Vander Linden that we should regard 'human mobility, not as a 'natural state' or as 'migration', but as a way to continually create and maintain social relationships' (Vander Linden 2007, 350).

Sardinia and Sicily occupy a peculiar position in Beaker Europe as they are island territories situated on the southern margins of the Bell Beaker sphere. In the south of peninsular Italy, Bell Beakers are found sporadically in Calabria and Campania and Barfield proposed the existence a 'Tyrrhenian Bell Beaker *koinè*', a 'culture that avoids the Adriatic' (Barfield 1994, 450). This idea still holds true yet there are signs in southern Italy, towards the end of the Chalcolithic, of interaction with central European, Balkan and Aegean complexes (Aurino & Mancusi forthcoming). In Campania, cases of hybridisation including Beaker, Laterza and Cetina cultural elements have recently been recognised in the necropolis of Gaudello near Acerra (Arcuri *et al.* 2016). A cultural dynamism in southern Italy and the islands emerges during the later phases of the Chalcolithic (second half of the 3rd–early 2nd millennia cal BC), in which the areas of influence of the different cultural *facies* are connected through a network of exchange and circulation of models of raw materials and ritual behaviour.

The aim of this contribution is to focus attention on Bell Beaker settlement, on its interaction with other local *facies* and on territorial dynamics. This research also embodies an opportunity to analyse two insular environments and to highlight any similarities and differences in the impact that Bell Beakers had. The starting point was the creation of maps showing the distribution of sites (Figs 6.1 & 6.7) and including an indication of their typology. In the same way, in order to accurately compare the two islands, Tables 6.1 and 6.2 also show the dates relating to the 3rd and early 2nd millennia BC (from Melis 2013; Giannitrapani 2009; Maniscalco 2013; Martinelli 2013).

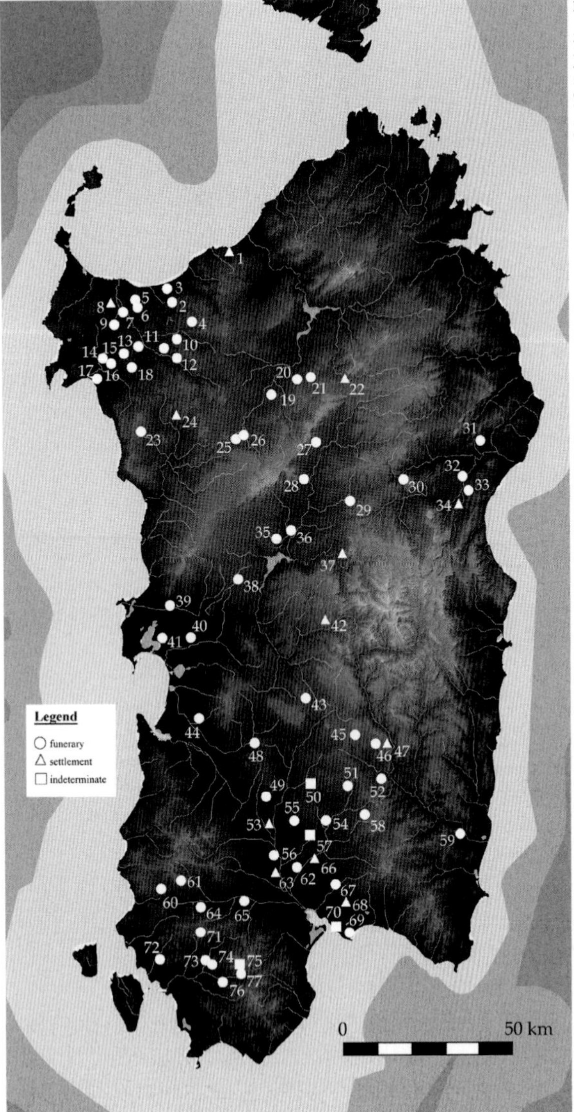

Figure 6.1: Map of Sardinian Bell Beaker sites (graphics C. Caradonna)

Sardinia

Before Bell Beakers

In Sardinia the transition from the Neolithic to the Chalcolithic takes place during the mid-4th millennium, in the sphere of the Ozieri *facies*. It involved a gradual technological development accompanied by the persistence of Neolithic traditions relating to settlements and ritual behaviour (Melis 2013). Regarding material culture, several trends that began in the Early Chalcolithic continue in the 3rd millennium, including limited technical investment in pottery, bone and stone tool production (with the exception of some classes of artefact), the preference for type SC Monte Arci obsidian and the growth of metallurgy. At the same time the seemingly intrusive Monte Claro *facies* emerges and evolves, apparently unrelated to the preceding phases. At the beginning of the millennium there is a notable change in land-use strategies and increasing territorial competition.

Bell Beaker and local cultures

Radiocarbon dates show that Bell Beakers arrived in Sardinia during the development of the Abealzu and Monte Claro cultural *facies*. The former is to be found in a few sites, one of which is Hut p-s at Monte d'Accoddi (Fig. 6.2). The hut was destroyed by fire, thus conserving intact its last phase of use, including a rich collection of pottery and stone tools. With regard to the production of the ceramics, compared to the previous Filigosa phase, the sporadic use of decoration is noticeable, together with the demise of carinated vessels in favour of long-necked, deeper forms. The Monte Claro pottery was completely different showing a marked preference for geometric decoration. There is evidence for differing metallurgical techniques being employed by the Filigosa and Abealzu *facies* compared to Monte Claro. The former share a taste for silver and copper and, less frequently, lead, while the latter use more copper than silver and use lead more frequently, even to repair pottery (Melis 2014). Monte Claro material was present on previously occupied sites, on open ground, in natural caves and rock cut tombs, although these groups also built their own funerary monuments (cists and hypogea) as well as domestic structures.

According to the three or four phase models of development (Atzeni 1996; Lemercier *et al.* 2007) the Beaker phenomenon in Sardinia gradually acquires regional characteristics. It is represented by numerous elements of the 'Beaker package' and in addition to the pottery we find triangular daggers, completely different to those of the other *facies*, the barbed and tanged arrowhead with squared barbs, crescent microliths, bone and stone jewellery and the armlet which is also found in the Bonnanaro *facies* of the Early Bronze Age. Impressed ring decorations are present in both Monte Claro and Bell Beaker spheres and some of the cups from Tomb I at Filigosa and from the Abealzu phase vaguely resemble Beaker profiles (Melis 2000).

Chronology

Radiocarbon dates are limited (Table 6.1). The date from layer 3 in the Filiestru cave, was

Site, Context	Lab. no.	BP	Cal BC (95.4%)	Cultural facies
Serra Cannigas	AA72151	4289±47	3090–2710	Filigosa
Scaba 'e Arriu	AA72793	4278±42	3020–2750	Filigosa
Scaba 'e Arriu	AA64828	4202±45	2910–2630	Filigosa
Scaba 'e Arriu	unavailable	unavailable	2900–2480*	Filigosa
Gannì	OxA-25343	unavailable	2469–2293*	Monte Claro
Sedda de Daga	AA64830	4091±41	2870–2490	Monte Claro
Bau su Matutzu	LTL4197A	4121±45	2880–2570	Monte Claro
Nuraghe Noeddos, squares Ed(3)5	Q-3069	4030±50	2860–2460	Monte Claro (?)
Scaba 'e Arriu	AA64829	3989±41	2630–2340	Monte Claro
Mind'e Gureu	AA64826	3957±56	2620–2280	Abealzu
Padru Jossu	AA72790	3912±42	2560–2230	Monte Claro
Padru Jossu A	AA72152	3845±41	2470–2200	Bell Beaker
Padru Jossu A	AA72153	3843±41	2470–2200	Bell Beaker
Padru Jossu B	AA72791	3837±41	2470–2150	Bell Beaker
Filiestru, Layer 3, trench B	Q-3030	3805±40	2460–2130	Bell Beaker, Monte Claro
Padru Jossu B	AA72792	3790±41	2430–2040	Bell Beaker
Grotta Sisaia	Stocc. (?)	3800±100	2550–1950	Bonnanaro
Is Calitas	AA72149	3738±42	2290–2020	Bonnanaro
Is Calitas	Beta-107558	3700±70	2300–1900	Bonnanaro
Concali Corongiu 'Acca II	AA72150	3699±42	2203–1965	Bonnanaro

*Table 6.1: Radiocarbon dates of the Sardinian cultural facies, calibrated with OxCal 4.3.2 and the IntCal 13 calibration curve (except where indicated *)*

associated with Monte Claro and Bell Beaker artefacts. The tomb at Padru Jossu provided four dates ranging from 2470–2040 cal BC. The earliest section of this range is partially contemporary with some of the Abealzu and Monte Claro dates. Stratigraphically Bell Beakers often overlap with the Monte Claro, however in some cases it is possible to identify the contemporaneity of elements of both *facies*.

The last two centuries of the Bell Beaker range coincide with the beginning of the Bonnanaro *facies* of the initial Early Bronze Age. These data are consistent with the close, perhaps genetic, relationship between these two *facies* as represented by hybrid artefacts distinguished by Bell Beaker decoration on Bonnanaro forms (Fig. 6.3). The acquisition of elements that become typical of the Early Bronze Age, such as the angular profiled handle (*a gomito*) has its precedent in contexts that remain typically Bell Beaker.

Pre-Bell Beaker settlements

During the Early Chalcolithic (later 4th millennium BC) settlements were sited and employed building styles akin to those of the Late Neolithic. Substructures were dug into the subsoil with the walls and a roof made from raw earth and plant materials. With the exception of Monte Claro, settlements of the 3rd millennium *facies* are rare. Regarding the Filigosa *facies* a settlement in north-western Sardinia, is surrounded by a defensive wall (San Giuseppe). For the succeeding Abealzu phase, probably partially contemporary with the Beaker culture, the village that grew around the shrine at Monte d'Accoddi is of great interest. In particular, Hut p-s (Fig. 6.2) which was destroyed by fire as mentioned above. It was trapezoidal in plan (6.90 × 5 m) and was built from medium-sized polygonal stone blocks. The external wall was double-faced only on the long sides and the internal spaces had been divided into small rooms with differing functions such as food storage, and larger domestic rooms with a hearth.

Settlements with Bell Beakers

Large Monte Claro settlements were built on the plains, with smaller villages on middle to high ground in order to control the landscape. Defensive structures are mainly represented in northern Sardinia. At Monte Baranta (Moravetti 2004) a wall protected the settlement while a semicircular tower overlooked the surrounding territory (Fig. 6.4,1). A similar settlement has been identified at Monte Ossoni (Fig. 6.4,2) where Monte Claro and Bell Beaker elements were found close to the walls. The most diffuse architectural model, not dissimilar to Hut p-s at Monte d'Accoddi, is that of the rectangular hut (often trapezoidal) with single-faced dry-stone walling and having one or more rooms, with stone or beaten earth floors and hearths.

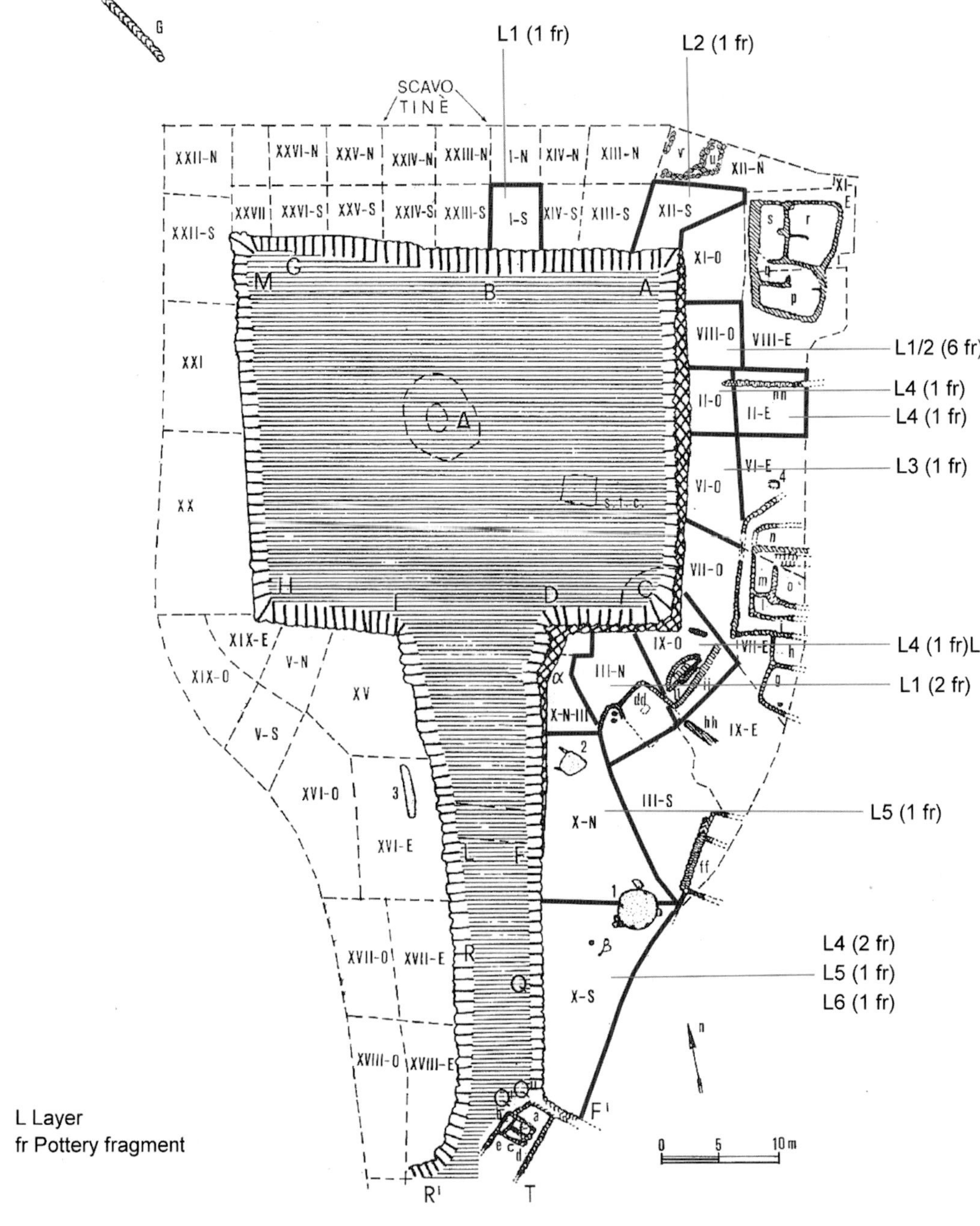

Figure 6.2: Plan of the Monte d'Accoddi shrine and village (graphics C. Caradonna)

The village at Monte Prano (Manunza *et al.* 2014), exclusively occupied by the Monte Claro *facies*, covered an area of roughly 40,000 m², within which were 50 mostly trapezoidal buildings (5.9/7.4 × 4.8/7.7m) of which some were larger and had more complex plans (Fig. 6.5,5). The settlement at Biriai, in central-eastern Sardinia (Fig. 6.5,1–3), also exclusively Monte Claro, is rather different and comprises rectangular huts with one curved end and double-faced walls. The dimensions of these vary from 4.10 × 6 m to 5.50 × 15.30 m. In the village at Monte d'Accoddi, 23 Bell Beaker fragments (Fig. 6.6) were found belonging to polypod vessels, carinated vases, beakers, a hemispherical bowl and other indeterminate forms. They were discovered in the part of the village to the east of the shrine (Fig. 6.2), chiefly in the upper layers (1 and 2), and less frequently in deeper levels (3–6). It seems likely that Bell Beakers were at least partially contemporary with the developing Abealzu and, maybe, Filigosa *facies*. The Abelalzu context in Hut p-s is to be found in Level 3 of Trench

VIII. A Beaker presence has occasionally been attested in inhabited caves (Filiestru) and rock shelters (San Basilio, Frattale) though the occupation was probably brief (Melis 2010).

Finally, Bell Beaker artefacts have also been recorded in uncertain contexts in open settlements which, in southern Sardinia, were typified by substructures in the Neolithic tradition: Monte Olladiri, Palaggiu and Sant'Iroxi (Melis 2010). The extremely rare finds of Bell Beaker pottery are present in the Monte Claro huts at Monte Olladiri and Palaggiu. Sant'Iroxi was a multi-layered settlement, occupied from the Late Neolithic to the Early Bronze Age and the Chalcolithic finds are related to Ozieri II, Monte Claro and Bell Beaker. Not much is known about the settlement that grew near the menhir alignments at Bidu'e Concas (Puddu 2014). In the village, occupied during the Final Neolithic (Ozieri I) and Chalcolithic (Abealzu, Monte Claro,

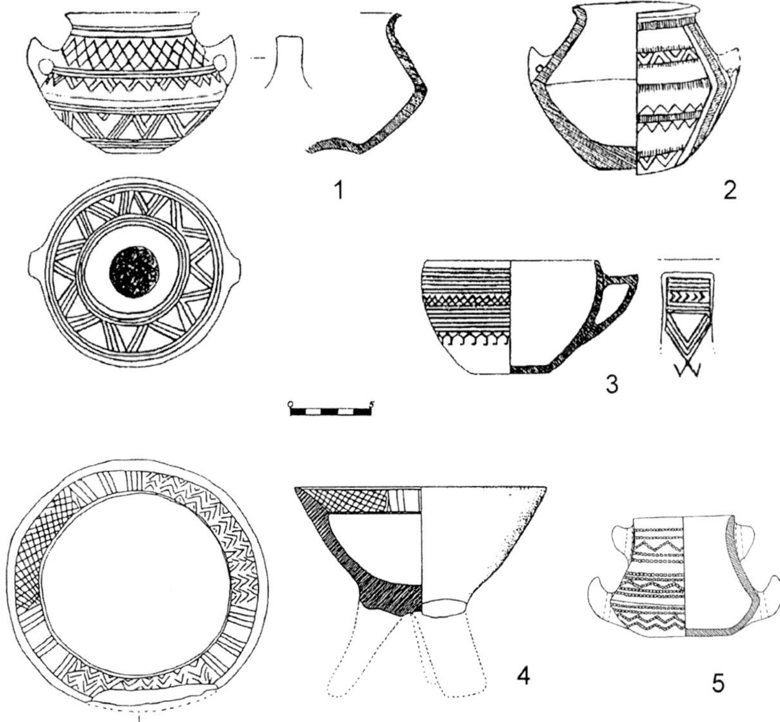

Figure 6.3: (above) Pottery with Bell Beaker and Sardinian Early Bronze age characteristics: 1 – Grotta della Volpe; 2 – Seurru; 3 – unknown; 4–5 – Locci Santus (by Atzeni 1996)

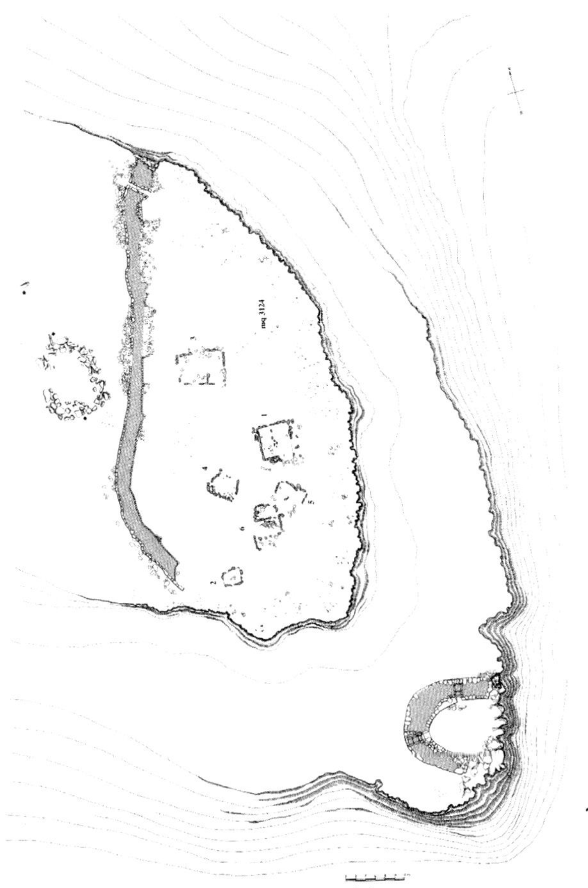

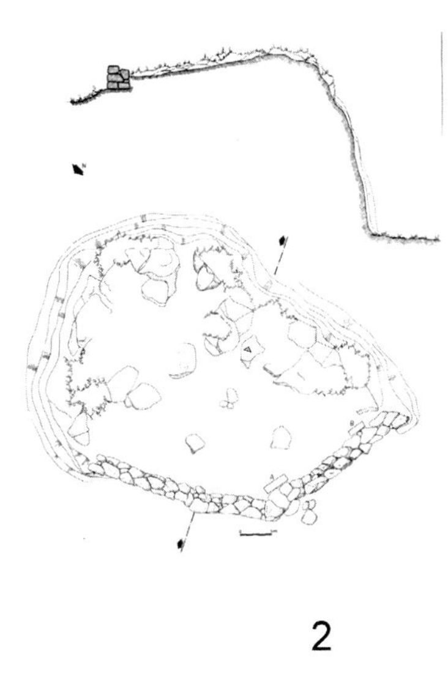

Figure 6.4: (left) Monte Baranta; (1) and Monte Ossoni; (2) defensive walled villages (by Moravetti 2004)

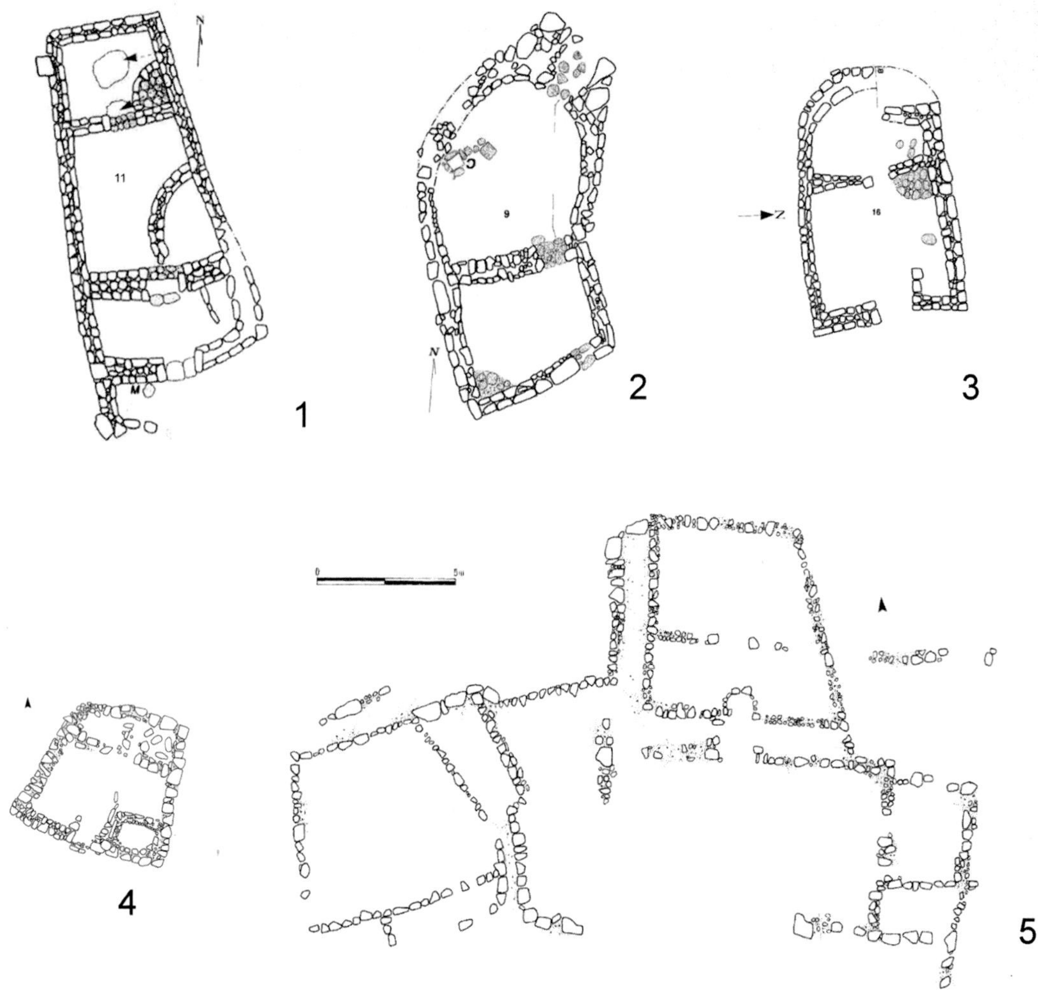

Figure 6.5: Plans of Monte Claro huts (by Moravetti 2004)

Bell Beaker), the Bell Beaker finds came from contexts associated with Monte Claro. The possible Bell Beaker origin of several pottery fragments found close to the settlement at Lerno remains unproven.

Palaeo-environmental and palaeo-economic data

During the Sardinian Chalcolithic the most sudden and evident cultural transformations take place at the beginning of the 3rd millennium (the Ozieri II-Filigosa transition and the first appearance of Monte Claro) and at the end of the period (Monte Claro, Bell Beaker–Early Bronze Age transition). Palynological analyses suggest that these transformations were not caused by climate changes, as pollen diagrams show no reduction that corresponds to these periods (Di Rita & Melis 2013; Beffa *et al.* 2015). The scarcity of domestic data from the various cultural phases of the 3rd millennium limits any conjecture regarding economic organisation. In Hut p-s at Monte d'Accoddi, and in other areas of the village, the high number of querns and grinders underlines the intensity of work relating to the processing of agricultural produce, which is further confirmed by the presence of numerous large storage jars or *dolia* for conserving foodstuffs. Spindle whorls and loom weights attest to the importance of spinning and weaving. Cattle breeding is indicated by the discovery of a bovine tibia, although the lack of analyses on other bone assemblages makes it impossible to know how widespread the raising of other livestock may have been. An antler fragment, a boar tooth and various mollusc fragments suggest hunting and harvesting shellfish (Melis 2000). In order to supplement these limited data, archaeo-zoological results from funerary contexts as well as data from carbon and nitrogen stable isotope analyses have been taken into consideration.

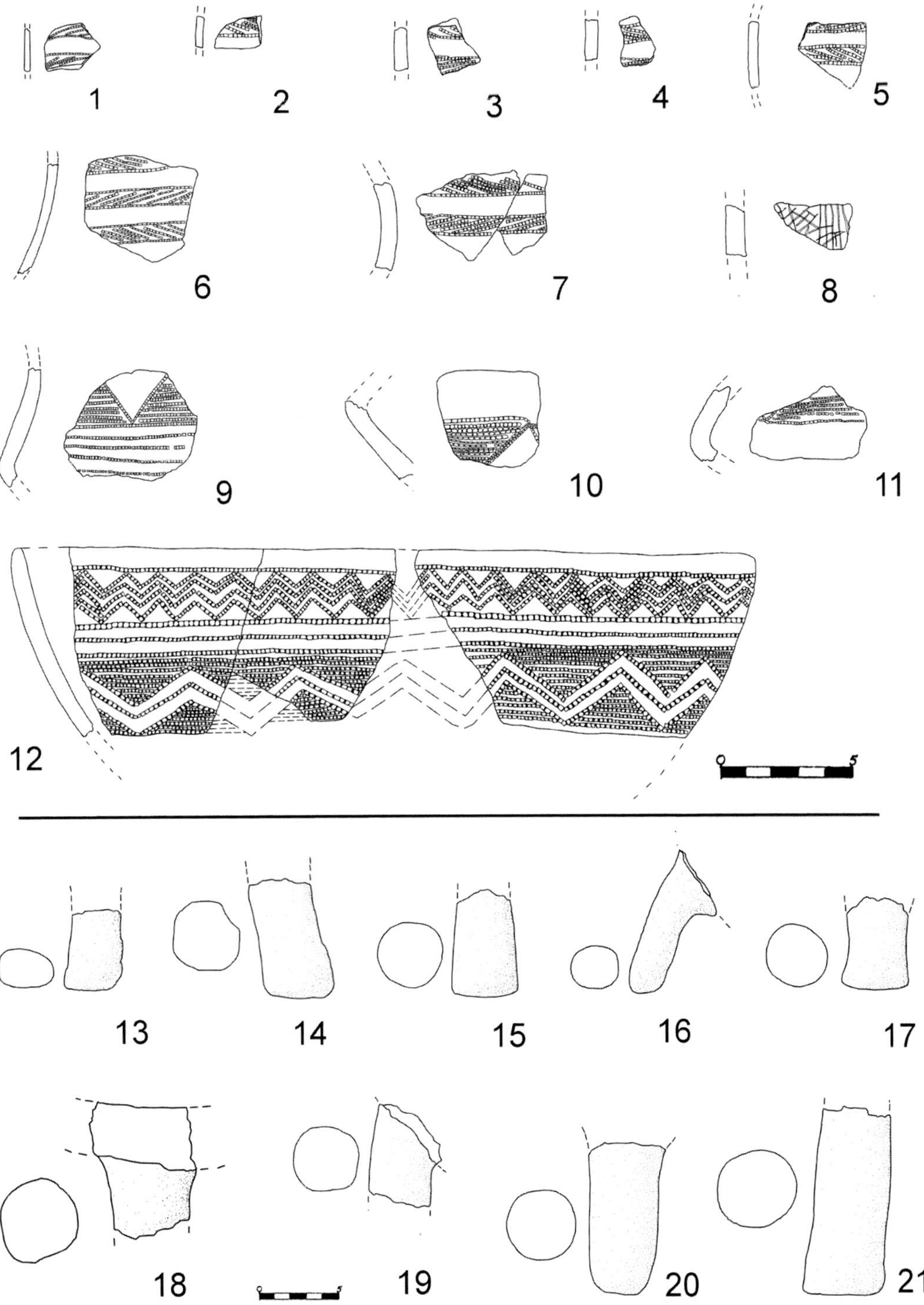

Figure 6.6: Bell Beaker pottery from Monte d'Accoddi (graphics C. Caradonna and M.G. Melis)

Hunted wild fauna are well represented in Bell Beaker contexts, (boar, deer and foxes), and the bones are often used for ornamental objects. Other artefacts (made from ivory and hippopotamus teeth) were imported. Domestic animals appear in Bell Beaker burials and at Padru Jossu both young and mature examples of *Ovis aries* suggest the consumption of both meat and milk. There were also the remains of *Bos*, *Canis familiaris* and, among undomesticated animals, two adult examples of *Sus scrofa* (Ugas 1998). Both land and marine molluscs are also represented among the ornamental objects found in the grave goods (Manca 2010; Pau

2013). Most of the shells were collected *post mortem*, and therefore not as food.

The isotope data from Bingia 'e Monti reveals a chiefly land-based diet (Floris *et al.* 2011). The high readings of $\delta^{15}N$ suggest a large intake of animal protein, which decreases in the Early Bronze Age and this can be confirmed at other sites (Lai *et al.* 2013). The isotopic data from Padru Jossu confirms that Bell Beaker groups shared the same type of diet as the contemporary community at Bingia 'e Monti (Lai *et al.* 2007) and it is interesting to note that a diet based predominantly on animal protein was also shared by Monte Claro. In contrast, the isotopic readings from the tomb at Scaba 'e Arriu reveal a more plant-based diet for the groups of the Filigosa *facies* when compared to the more recent Monte Claro community (Lai *et al.* 2011). The analyses made of Beaker skeletal remains at Iloi/Ispiluncas (L. Lai & M. G. Melis, unpublished research) have provided only partial results due to the absence of collagen but the $\delta^{13}C$ of apatite suggests a moderate consumption of animal protein, with a higher incidence amongst males.

Sicily

Before Bell Beakers

Summarising the essential characteristics of the cultural *facies* present in Sicilian pre-Bell Beaker Chalcolithic phases is not simple, considering the various complex geographical and chronological connections. This peculiarity is probably due to greater external influxes originating from the eastern Mediterranean, from Italy and Malta. This is very likely caused by its geographical position at the centre of the Mediterranean and its easier accessibility from Italy. The Sicilian Chalcolithic seems to occur earlier than in Sardinia. In the areas that were later affected by Bell Beakers, the contexts relating to the San Cono and Piano Notaro *facies* and the painted Conzo-style products develop from the early 4th millennium, showing similarities with the Maltese Zebbug and Mgarr *facies* (Cazzella & Maniscalco 2012). Simultaneously, in the north-western part of the island the Conca d'Oro *facies* appears, which embraces a wider chronological arc. Production in the Serraferlicchio-style appears in a mid-Chalcolithic horizon in which painted pottery is predominant.

Bell Beaker and local cultures

Up until a few years ago almost all the known sites were funerary, as was also the case in Sardinia (Tusa 1998). More recently, Bell Beaker evidence in domestic sites has restored homogeneity to the cultural overview and provided important information especially for central Sicily (Fig. 6.7). Bovio Marconi (1963) subdivided the Sicilian material into two groups. Group A, was distinguished by the absence of painted decoration and through its similarities with Iberia, it was considered as a probable import. Group B, on the other hand, showed evident signs of mixing with local cultures, and for this reason was judged to be of local production. This schematically highlights a process of regionalisation which, when compared to Sardinia, leads to greater contamination and integration with the local *facies*. Tusa (1997) considers impressed decoration (*pointillé*) either simple or bichrome, simple incised decoration, red painting, polypod vessels and V-perforated buttons as distinctive elements of Bell Beaker production however the V-perforated button can also sometimes be found in older contexts, such as in the Zebbug phase in Malta. In Sicily it is associated with material in the Serraferlicchio style, found in Tomb II at Uditore, however here we also find boar-tooth pendants which share similarities with approximately ten Sardinian Bell Beaker contexts (Pau 2013). The same class of artefact is found at Mozia, in the Puleri cave (Bovio Marconi 1944) and in the cave at Pergole 2 (Carnieri *et al.* 2012).

The period of greatest Bell Beaker diffusion comes at the same time as the development of the Malpasso and Sant'Ippolito *facies*. The Malpasso contains some innovative elements and there was a growing tendency towards pottery forms tied to specific uses: oval mouthed vases for the slow pouring of liquids such as oil, and bowls with internal ribbing, perhaps linked to the processing of milk (Cazzella & Maniscalco 2012). These data, together with the archaeo-zoological results, reaffirms the important role of raising livestock. The ceramic production of the S. Ippolito *facies* has some morphological and technological analogies with the Malpasso *facies*, with which it often shares settlement strategies. These similarities have led some scholars to consider these two aspects as one unitary cultural horizon, each distinguished by regional differences (Alberghina & Gullì 2011).

N	Site and function
1	Maiorana Cave, funerary (?)
2	Uzzo Cave, indeterminate
3	Carini, funerary
4	Casa Galati, Cozzo dell'Aquila Cave, funerary (?)
5	Cozzo Palombaro Cave, funerary (?)
6	Malatacca (or di Mezzo?) Cave, indeterminate
7	Uditore, funerary
8	Villagrazia, funerary
9	Torrente Cannizzaro, funerary
10	Moarda, funerary
11	Bagni di Cefalà Diana, indeterminate
12	Chiaristella (caves), funerary
13	Puleri Cave, funerary
14	Geraci Cave, indeterminate
15	Caccamo, indeterminate
16	Fico Cave, funerary
17	Chiusilla Cave, funerary
18	Segesta, funerary
19	Pietralunga, settlement
20	Montagna Vecchia, settlement
21	Caputo, settlement
22	Montagna Grande, funerary
23	Posillesi, funerary
24	Gattolo, funerary
25	Mokarta, funerary
26	Mozia, indeterminate
27	Pergola (Contrada), funerary
28	Torrebiggini, funerary
29	Cisternazza-Vallesecco, funerary
30	Stretto, funerary
31	Pileri, funerary
32	Torre Donzelle, funerary
33	Marcita, funerary
34	Vallone S. Martino, funerary
35	Torre Cusa, funerary
36	Manicalunga, funerary
37	Malophoros, settlement
38	Santa Margherita Belice, funerary
39	Castello di Venaria, funerary
40	Chiappetta (Contrada), funerary
41	Caselle (Contrada), funerary
42	Kronio Cave, ritual
43	San Bartolo, funerary
44	Ribera, funerary
45	Terravecchia di Cuti, Contrada Cammareri, indeterminate
46	Cuti, settlement
47	Cuti, funerary
48	Case Bastione, settlement
49	Mezzebi, settlement
50	La Fastuchera, settlement (?)
51	Tornambè, settlement
52	Marcato del Re, settlement (?)
53	Serraferlicchio, indeterminate
54	Favara, funerary
55	Val Paradiso, settlement
56	Naro, funerary
57	La Muculufa, settlement
58	Manfria, settlement (?)
59	Manfria, funerary
60	Settefarine, settlement
61	Predio Iozza, funeray
62	Palombara Cave, funerary/ritual
63	Conzo Cave, indeterminate

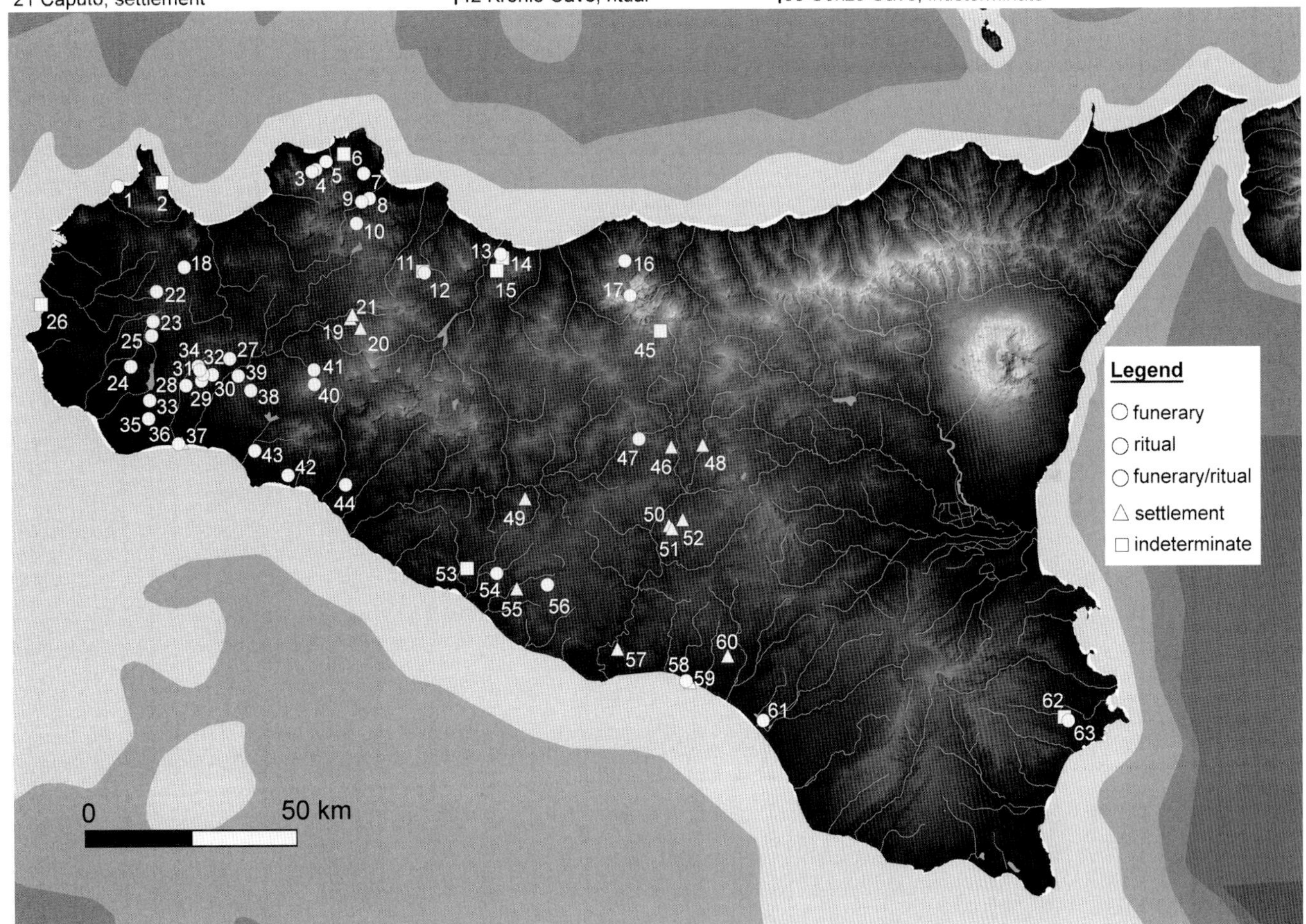

Figure 6.7: Map of Sicilian Bell Beaker sites (graphics C. Caradonna)

At the end of the Chalcolithic, during the final centuries of the 3rd and the beginning of the 2nd millennia BC, relationships become apparent between Bell Beaker, the Castelluccio *facies* and its western variant the Naro-Partanna (Nicoletti & Tusa 2012). In this phase elements of cultural syncretism appear (Fig. 6.8), as demonstrated for example at Marcita by the adoption of Bell Beaker decoration in the formal repertoire of Naro-Partanna ceramics (Tusa 1998). The so-called Moarda-style in the Sicilian north-west, appears to be the result of a process of hybridisation with the local cultures. In this context they coexist, but do not seem to

*Table 6.2: Radiocarbon dates for the Sicilian cultural facies, calibrated using OxCal 4.3.2 and the IntCal 13 calibration curve (except where indicated *). ** Layers with Bell Beaker or contemporary material. US = context (Unità Stratigrafica/ Stratigraphic Unit)*

Site, context	*Lab. no.*	*BP*	*Cal BC (95.4%)*	*Cultural facies*
Venetico, US 14, carbon n. 4	LTL-3518A	4476±50	3360–2940	Malpasso
Venetico, US 4, square M23	LTL-3517A	4330±50	3100–2880	Malpasso
Rocchicella, Sector FA VIII, US 376	LTL124		3090–2870*	Early Chalcolitic
Case Bastione, Area alfa, US 1008	LTL-3650A	4131±50	2880–2570	Malpasso, S. Ippolito, Campaniforme**
Grotta Zubbia, S89/2	A-?	4010±55	2860–2340	Malpasso
La Muculufa, hut 3, floor	A-6547	3990±60	2840–2290	S. Ippolito, Campaniforme**
La Muculufa, hut 3, upper level	A-6546	3960±70	2840–2200	S. Ippolito, Campaniforme**
Rocchicella, Sector FA VIII, US 376			2570–2230*	Malpasso
Case Bastione, Area alfa, US 1024	LTL-3651A	3893 ±45	2480–2200	Malpasso, S. Ippolito, Campaniforme**
Case Bastione, Area alfa, US 1106	Rome-2054	3830±40	2460–2140	Malpasso, S. Ippolito, Campaniforme**
Rocchicella, Sector FA VIII, US 360	LTL12422A		2460–2060*	Malpasso, Early Castelluccio
Tornambè, hut 1, US 1003	LTL-3639A	3798±45	2460–2050	Malpasso, S. Ippolito, Campaniforme**
La Muculufa, Nord hut 2	A-5283	3790 ±60	2460–2030	S. Ippolito, Campaniforme**
Case Bastione, Area alfa, US 1045	Rome-2058	3780±40	2350–2040	Malpasso, S. Ippolito, Campaniforme**
Case Bastione, Area alfa, US 1111	LTL-3649A	3765±45	2340–2030	Malpasso, S. Ippolito, Campaniforme**
Tornambè, hut 1, US 1014	LTL-3641A	3732±35	228–2020	Castelluccio
Tornambè, hut 1, US 1017	LTL-3643A	3709±40	2270–1970	Castelluccio
La Muculufa, F102, bd. –1.38 to –1.52	A-5284	3680±100	2440–1770	Castelluccio

integrate, with elements of the Capo Graziano *facies* (Nicoletti & Tusa 2012).

Chronology

The presence in north-western Sicily of Bell Beakers with Maritime characteristics suggests that this area sees the earliest appearance of the phenomenon (Tusa 1997a). This appears to be confirmed by the so-called Carini Beaker (*bicchiere di Carini*), which some suggest was of Bell Beaker influence, and a V-perforated button from Tomb II at Uditore. Further proof appears to be a Beaker fragment found in the Kronio cave, with impressed cord decoration in the Maritime style (Barfield 1994).

The radiocarbon dates (Table 6.2) offer a reasonably detailed picture of the evolution of the Sicilian Chalcolithic. The Late Chalcolithic, the period in which Bell Beakers occur, can be placed between 2600–2300 cal BC, during the development of the Malpasso and Sant'Ippolito *facies*, that proceeds in some areas into the first phases of the Early Bronze Age (Giannitrapani 2009). The extension of some Late Chalcolithic dates towards the end of the 3rd millennium, and therefore overlapping with the Early Bronze Age, underlines the continuity between the two phases, which is confirmed by the uninterrupted occupation seen at some sites. If 2600 cal BC is given as the upper limit of the Bell Beaker phase, the comparison between Sicilian and Sardinian radiometric data

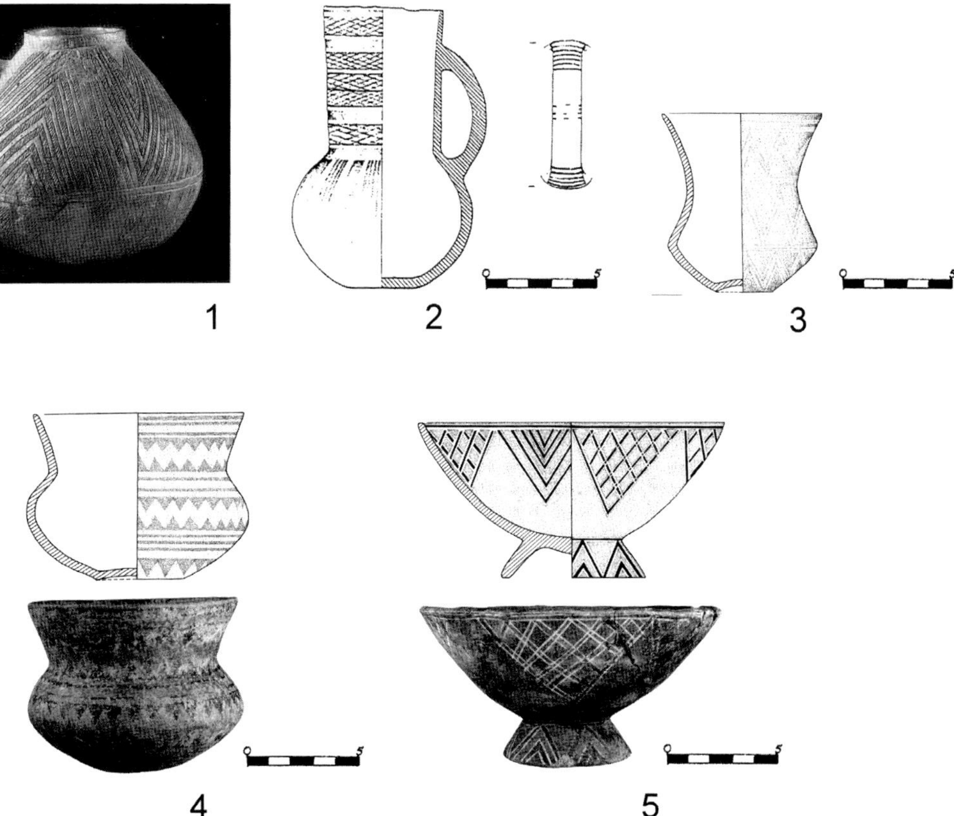

Figure 6.8: Sicilian Bell Beaker with hybrid characteristics: 1 – Moarda; 2 – Partanna; 3–5 – Veneroso collection (1–2 by Tusa 1998; 3–5 by Guilaine 2009)

highlights an important issue and given that the limited Sardinian dates do not extend beyond 2500 cal BC, it would appear that Bell Beakers appeared in Sicily before Sardinia. If this is the case, Guilaine's hypothesis that Bell Beakers arrived in Sicily via Iberia through land routes across the Maghreb, appears to be reinforced (Guilaine 2009).

The sites

The sites known so far are chiefly funerary such as rock cut tombs and cave burials, occasionally frequented for possible ritual reasons (Fig. 6.7). Open settlement sites are less common. Hypogea are mostly present in western Sicily. The addition of dolmen corridors occurs during the final phase of the Chalcolithic and is connected the arrival of Bell Beakers (Tusa 2014). As mentioned above, the use of caves in the Sicilian Chalcolithic is mainly funerary and occasionally ritual (Gullì 2014) and recent studies have shown how these are part of an integrated system of the use of territory, combining open settlements and funerary monuments (Battaglia 2014). The intensive use of caves is particularly evident in relation to the Malpasso *facies* (Cazzella & Maniscalco 2012).

The data for pre-Bell Beaker phases

Early Chalcolithic villages often have traditional Neolithic characteristics. At Roccazzo (Fig. 6.9,1) the settlement comprises large rectangular structures (maximum length 16 m) outlined by foundation trenches with post-holes at regular intervals. Some also have a line of internal axial roof supports. The rebuilding and enlargement of several structures is evidence of a growing demographic over time (Tusa 1997b). The settlement model seen at Roccazzo, typified by small groups of huts placed close to each other, is repeated in other contemporary localities (Conca d'Oro and Custonaci; Tusa 2001).

The numerous sites surrounding Palma di Montechiaro (Agrigento), among which is the multi-layered settlement of Piano Vento, are generally typified by small circular or elliptical huts with stone foundations and sometimes surrounded by a fence. At Piano Vento a central post supported a conical roof, however on other sites, such as Predio Rinollo, the elliptical huts were much larger (7 × 5 m) and were surrounded by a semi-circular fence

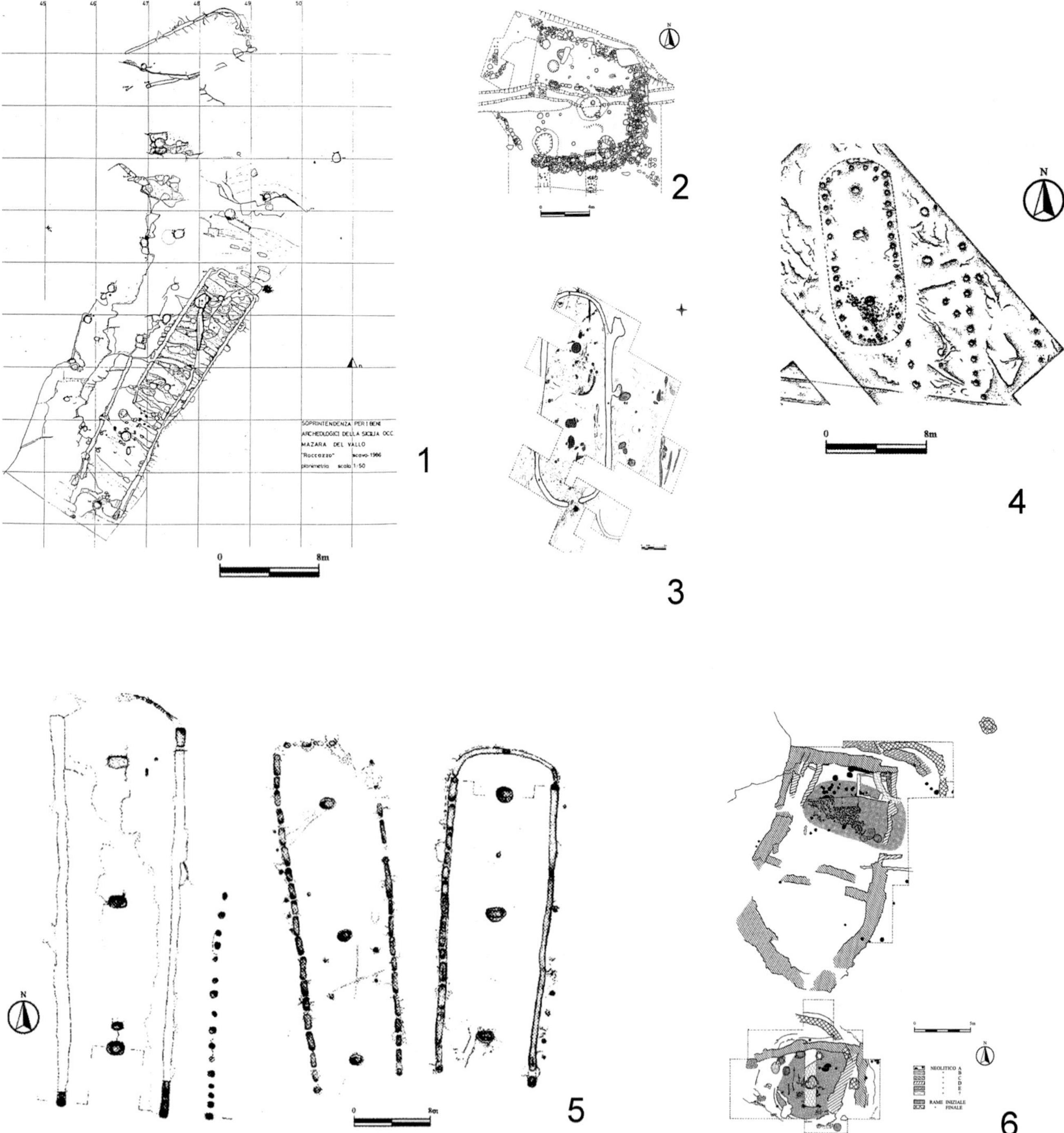

Figure 6.9: Plans of huts of the Sicilian Early Chalcolithic: 1 – Roccazzo; 2 – Casa Sollima; 3 – Cozzo Matrice; 4 – Gisira; 5 – Fildidonna; 6 – Serra di Palco (1 by Tusa 2000; 3 by Giannitrapani 2012; 2, 4–6 by Cazzella & Maniscalco 2012)

(Giannitrapani *et al.* 2014a).

The middle Chalcolithic site at Serraferlicchio consisted of a long natural gallery which ran along the crest of the hill. It contained niches, hut-like structures and a rock cut tomb (Arias 1938) but Orsi (1928) did not think that it could have served as a stable settlement on the grounds that its form, the views that it commanded and finds of complete vases suggested a ritual function. The structures share similar characteristics to those in the Palma di Montechiaro area (Giannitrapani *et al.* 2014a).

In eastern Sicily, at Militello val di Catania, the model of a longhouse with curved ends is affirmed. The settlement of Casa Sollima (Fig. 6.9,2), located on the edge of a small plateau, can be placed in the same chronological horizon as the Serraferlicchio site, and it also contained ceramics comparable to the Malpasso and Conzo *facies* (Ashley *et al.* 2007). The hut was elliptical, the lower part built with small stone blocks, possibly within a foundation trench, while the standing portion of the wall was formed of larger blocks. Inside, it was divided lengthwise by a partition wall and contained a hearth surrounded by small stone slabs and stake-holes. Outside it boasted a fence, hearths and silos (Malone & Stoddart 2000). Analysis of the stone finds revealed that roughly 20% were not of local origin including obsidian from Pantelleria and Lipari, and flint from the Peloritani mountains. The bio-archaeological data reveal subsistence based on the cultivation of wheat, barley and legumes accompanied by livestock, mainly small ruminants, and by deer-hunting (*Sheep/goat* 62.7%, *Cow* 16.1%, *Pig* 11.5%, Canid 7.9%, *Deer* 1.1%, *Cat* 0.4%, *Horse* 0.4%). Finds of small strainers and boiling pans are perhaps related to milk processing (Ashley *et al.* 2007; Ayala 2012).

Recent discoveries in central Sicily have provided important data on Chalcolithic settlements and the evolution of territorial relationships (Giannitrapani & Iannì 2011a). Starting with the beginning of the period there is a gradual growth in the number of sites, probably representing a population increase. From the later 3rd millennium settlements stabilise and there is an intensification in agriculture as illustrated by signs of deforestation. Settlements also generally become sited on hill slopes, whereas later more defensive positions are preferred (Giannitrapani 2013). An example of Early Chalcolithic domestic architecture can be found at Cozzo Matrice (McConnell 2003), in the form of an elongated hut with curved ends (Fig. 6.9,3). Its perimeter is formed of a bedding trench cut into the rock, while inside, three axial posts supported the roof. The finds of Lipari obsidian blades and Spatarella ceramics proves that these internal territories rapidly became part of a network of contact and exchange. The plan of the hut, which is replicated in eastern Sicily at Gisira and Fildidonna (Fig. 6.9,4 & 5), has been compared to dwellings in northern Italy and Montenegro (Cultraro 2013). If the earliest Chalcolithic sees the development of villages following Neolithic architectonic traditions, there is sometimes a noticeable break with the final phases, such as at Serra di Palco (Fig. 6.9,6), where there is a change from the Neolithic-type hut with a curved end to smaller elliptical buildings (La Rosa 1994).

Settlements frequented by Bell Beakers

As in Sardinia, Sicily has no villages that are exclusively occupied by Bell Beakers rather Bell Beaker material occurs in specific contexts. Some such settlement sites remain dubious given that many are represented by surface collections or were discovered around a century ago. At Manfria (Fig. 6.10,3) the Bell Beaker presence is represented by a deposit found close to the Early Bronze Age village (Orlandini 1962). A Beaker fragment was found with material from the Castelluccian *facies* close to a large stone embankment of unknown purpose, however the decoration in the international style raises doubts about its possible association with Early Bronze Age material. Surveys in the Valle del Salso (central-southern Sicily) have located wide areas of surface finds, possibly relating to settlements. A Bell Beaker fragment with incised decoration was found at La Fastuchera (Fig. 6.11,7) where there is evidence of occupation from the early Chalcolithic to the start of the Early Bronze Age. Another Bell Beaker sherd was recovered with Late Chalcolithic and Early Bronze Age material at Marcato del Re (Fig. 6.11,8) (Iannì 2016).

The most interesting and informative sites are those that have been excavated such as Case Bastione (Fig. 6.10,1) (Giannitrapani *et al.* 2014b) where material relating to the Malpasso, Sant'Ippolito, Capo Graziano I and Bell Beaker *facies* was found in the Late Chalcolithic occupation (Fig. 6.11,9–15). The extensive settlement had an occupation sequence starting in the Final Neolithic and lasting through to Late Antiquity. The first Late Chalcolithic phase contained domestic and workshops consisting of a building outlined by a double-faced limestone wall, a sub-circular structure 4 m across, a circular well 1.40 m in diameter surrounded by a circle of stones, an oval well (1–0.5 m wide) and part of a structure from which a straight wall, a beaten earth floor, post-holes and irregularly-shaped baked clay slabs

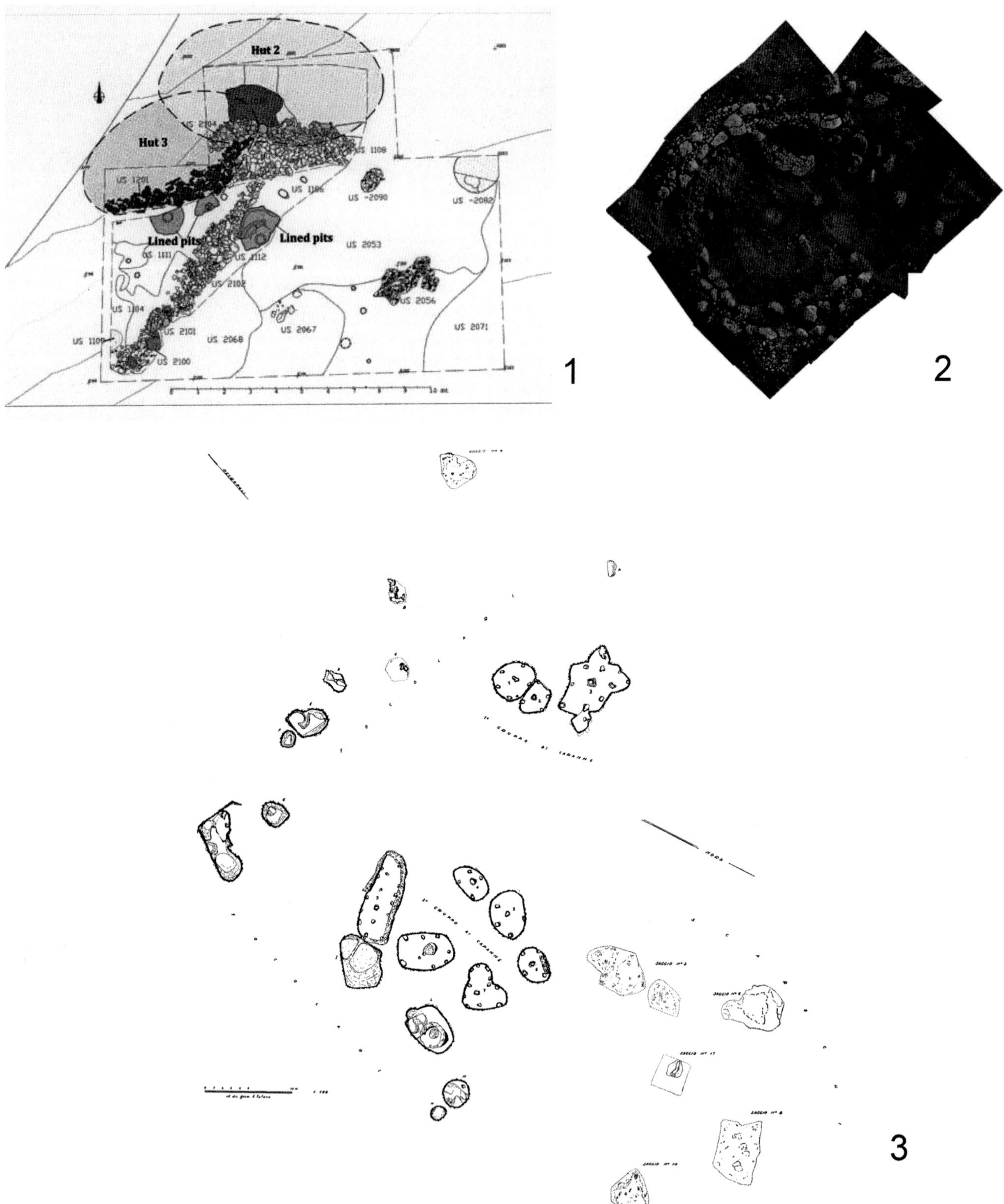

Figure 6.10: Plans of huts of the Sicilian Late Chalcolithic and Early Bronze Age: 1 – Case Bastione; 2 – Tornambè; 3 – Manfria (1 by Giannitrapani 2009; 2 by Giannitrapani, Iannì 2011a; 3, by Orlandini 1962)

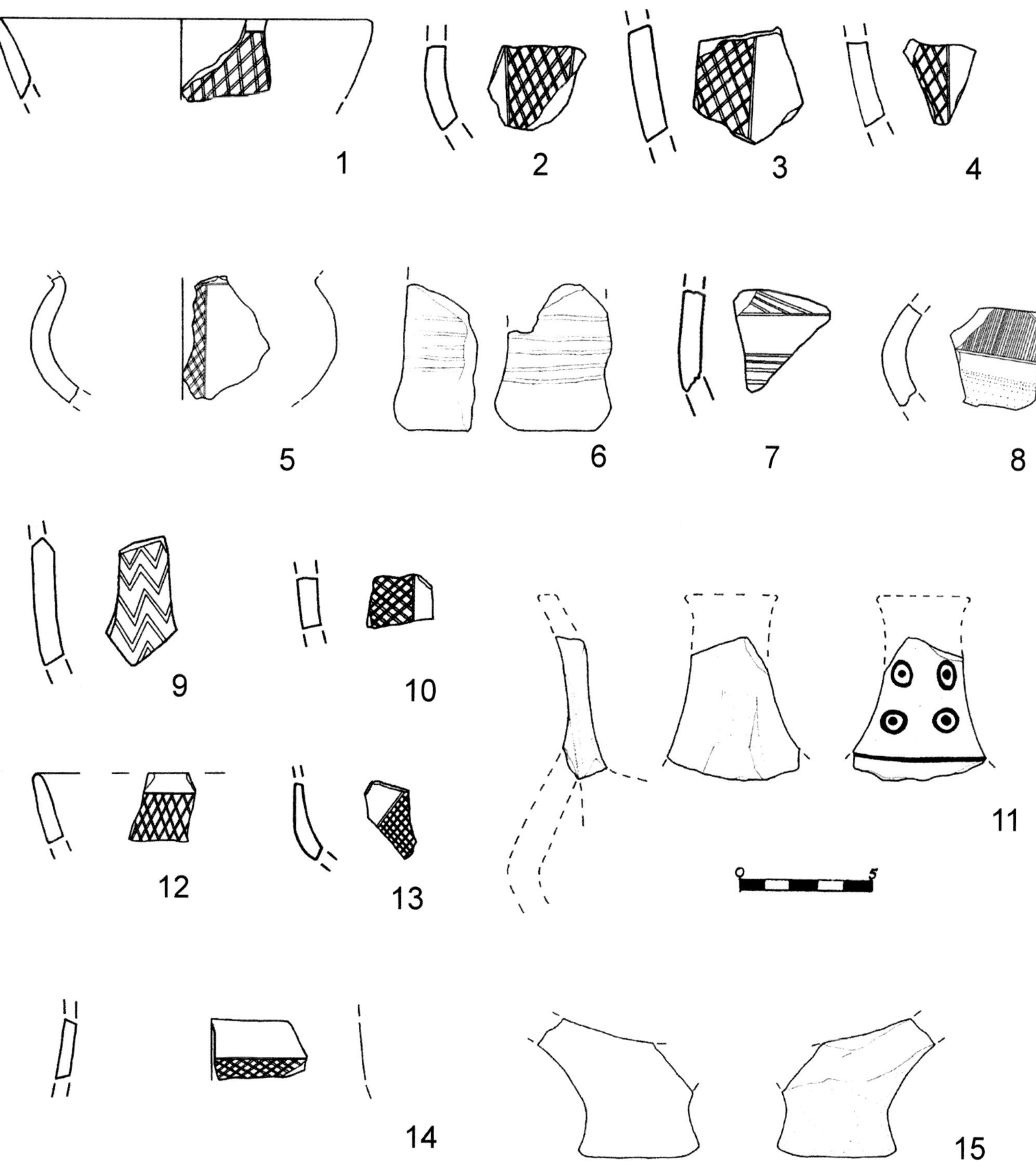

Figure 6.11: Bell Beaker pottery found in Sicilian settlements: 1–6 – Tornambè; 7 – La Fastuchera; 8 – Marcato del Re; 9–15 – Case Bastione (1–6, 9–15 by Giannitrapani, Iannì 2011a; 7–8 by Iannì 2016)

survive and which was later covered by a cairn. The second Late Chalcolithic phase corresponded to a period of disuse and/or partial reuse. This phase contained two silos, surrounded by stones and a circular terracotta slab associated with a central lined pit that had traces of burning and vitrified clay. In the Early Bronze Age, the settlement was visited by the Castelluccio groups who built elliptical, sub-circular and circular huts.

Tornambè is another key site that is particularly valuable for understanding the domestic character of Bell Beakers, the technological changes and the social groups of the Late Chalcolithic (Fig. 6.10,2). The village (Giannitrapani & Iannì 2011b) is located in a valley between two rocky outcrops and was occupied from the Final Neolithic to the Late Chalcolithic. In the Early Bronze Age the settlement relocated to the summit of one of the crests where and was occupied until the Middle Bronze Age. The Late Chalcolithic witnessed the construction of larger round huts 8–10 m in diameter. These had foundations of double-faced outer limestone walls with a superstructure of clay-clad wood and with internal clay floors and roof-supports. Hut 1 contained Malpasso, Sant'Ippolito and Bell Beaker material (Fig. 6.11,1–6), had a small circular annex and contained a stone bench and two hearths. The ceramics demonstrate both continuity and innovation in technology (Fragnoli *et al.* 2013). The Malpasso ceramics, in red slipware, are mainly represented by ovoid beakers with ribbon-shaped handles. The pottery repertoire of Sant'Ippolito contained both undecorated and red painted ceramics and the most common type were small, single-handled ovoid flasks. Among the Bell Beaker finds were classic Beakers with Maritime style decoration, a fragment of a polypod bowl with impressed linear decoration and a greenstone armlet. Scientific analyses of the ceramics demonstrate a certain technological homogeneity and the local sourcing of clays but with some differences in petrographic composition between the Malpasso and Sant'Ippolito ceramics on the one hand and Bell Beakers on the other. Beakers had a greater affinity with the ceramics of the following Early Bronze Age phase.

A very similar settlement pattern can be found at La Muculufa, a Late Chalcolithic village (S. Ippolito, Malpasso, Bell Beaker) which was positioned on the slopes of a rocky crest at the southern end of the Imera valley and which, during the Early Bronze Age relocated to the summit of the outcrop. The settlement at Mezzebi also comprised circular huts and here Bell Beakers were associated with S. Ippolito ceramics (Privitera 1997). S. Ippolito material was associated with the two Bell Beaker fragments from the village of Settefarine (Giannitrapani 2009) which was a multi-layered Chalcolithic and Early Bronze Age site in which the proto-Chalcolithic model of the sub-rectangular hut seems to appear (Orsi 1910; Giannitrapani *et al.* 2014a). Pietralunga (Corleone) is notable amongst the settlements of western Sicily. It was occupied from the Chalcolithic to the Early Bronze Age with various facies represented including Beaker (Scuderi *et al.* 1997; Nicoletti & Tusa 2012). The settlement was surrounded by agricultural land and was home to a natural spring. Some 2 km to the south of Corleone, in the area around the imposing hill of Montagna Vecchia, some settlement areas with Bell Beaker material have also been identified (Scuderi *et al.* 1997).

The palaeo-environmental and palaeo-economic data

The dense occupation of central Sicily in the Late Chalcolithic is probably due to topography, the abundance of water sources and important communication routes between inland and coastal areas. The pollen sequences of Lake Pergusa show an episode of aridity during the later 4th and earlier 3rd millennium, followed by a humid period with a consistent presence of both cultivated and wild plant species and with a reduction in *Quercus* pollen from around 2000 cal BC (Sadori *et al.* 2013; Giannitrapani 2017).

Central Sicily also exploited its rich natural resources (Giannitrapani 2017). The region is home to flint, quartzarenite and granite for tools and to rock salt deposits one of the most important of which is close to the settlement of Case Bastione. Furthermore, the area has reserves of sulphur and although there is no direct evidence, the proximity settlements such as Tornambè and La Muculufa to these deposits suggests a possible ancient exploitation of the mineral (Panvini 2012). The use of sulphur in the Late Chalcolithic is attested at the Grotta dell'Infame Diavolo (Cultraro 2007) as well as in Early Bronze Age sites such as Ticchiara and Monte Grande (Castellana 1997; 1998).

Away from the domestic buildings at Case Bastione, work areas have been identified for weaving, clay processing and for stone tool production. The hypothesis that a possible furnace could have been used for copper smelting, as implied by the presence of crucibles and a mould, remains so-far unproven despite archaeometric analyses (Giannitrapani *et al.* 2014b). In fact, the Sicilian Chalcolithic has a limited development of metallurgy, probably due to the scarcity of raw materials (Giardino 1997; Giardino *et al.* 2012).The earliest evidence of metalworking at Lipari in the Early Chalcolithic is relatively ancient, but it never reaches the levels of production in contemporary Sardinia.

Chalcolithic settlements had a preference for high ground and in eastern Sicily there is a notable change from the flat agricultural lands of the Final Neolithic to highland in the Early Chalcolithic such as the site at Fildidonna, adapted as it was to a subsistence based on stock rearing (Cazzella & Maniscalco 2012). The Late Chalcolithic sees an increase in the number of sites and also signs of greater stability. These data suggest a growing population and this trend continues into the Early Bronze Age (Leighton 2005; Giannitrapani 2017). Settlements were also frequently positioned close to water courses or springs and the higher and more defensive sites of the Early Bronze Age probably attest the growing need to control territory and natural resources (Giannitrapani 2013).

The Late Chalcolithic sees the intensification of agriculture and the importance of livestock and increased specialisation is exemplified by the presence of pottery used for dairy processing. The results of zoo-archaeological analyses at Case Bastione (Giannitrapani *et al.* 2014b) allow the comparison of the phases of the Late Chalcolithic and the Early Bronze Age. In both these phases the exploitation of small domestic ruminants is most common and bovines seem to have been exploited for both meat and for agricultural work. The most significant difference is in hunting, which is considerably reduced in the Early Bronze Age. The importance of agriculture from the mid 3rd millennium is attested by the numerous *Campignano* tools used for clearing woodland, and the pollen sequences from Lake Pergusa, document the appearance of cultivated cereal pollen in the Late Chalcolithic, while carbon data reveal traces of widespread burning, perhaps relating to forest clearance to create space for crops and livestock.

Sicily and Sardinia: a comparison of insular territories

There are visible similarities in the spheres of substantially diverse cultural developments in Sardinia and Sicily. Some similarities could simply be coincidental but in other cases they may result from the earlier or contemporary contacts with the spread of Bell Beakers. The geographical and geolithological differences between the two islands and the availability of natural resources evidently led to distinct cultural paths and differing courses of interaction with the outside world. Sardinia, further from the continent and placed at the centre of the western basin of the Mediterranean, made use of mainly maritime routes that favoured the Tyrrhenian seaboard of Italy, Corsica and the French Midi. This network saw the development on the island of western megalithic traditions and of metallurgy, the latter under central Italian influence (Melis 2014; 2018). Sicily, closer to the mainland and a halfway point between the eastern and western Mediterranean, became part of a network that included the eastern Mediterranean and the Adriatic coast of peninsular Italy.

Several similarities also emerge regarding settlement strategies (including a growth in territorial competition) and in some categories of monument, such as hypogeic-megalithic burials. The Sicilian monuments have been compared to Sardinian rock cut tombs with dolmen-type corridors, which can be placed approximately between the advanced Chalcolithic and the Early Bronze Age. Their construction in Sardinia is not attributable to Bell Beaker users who, however, often reuse them. This does not disprove the theory, but makes it less likely, that the introduction of megaliths to Sicily from Sardinia was connected to Bell Beaker diffusion (Tusa 2014) but probably during the Malpasso *facies*, a period that preceded Bell Beakers (Veneroso 2014).

The pre-Bell Beaker longhouses with one or both of the short sides curved, together with some similarities between the pottery of the Sardinian Abelazu and Monte Claro and the Sicilian Malpasso and Sant'Ippolito are not in themselves sufficient to demonstrate the existence of intense and stable relationships between the two islands. In the field of ceramic decoration, there is limited evidence for the use of colour in the Sardinian Early Chalcolithic yet in Sicily a richness of decoration on painted ceramics emerges in various Sicilian *facies*. This influenced the production of Bell Beakers which later developed a taste for polychrome decoration.

The paucity of dates is currently the principal obstacle in understanding the interactional dynamics of the two islands with regard to Beakers. The presence, while sporadic, of ceramics with impressed cord decoration in Sardinia (Corongiu Acca I) and Sicily (Grotta del Kronio) implies that the arrival of Bell Beaker elements could be relatively early. The international style is poorly represented in Sardinia but well documented in Sicily (Guilaine 2009). During the transition to the Early Bronze Age and during the Initial Early Bronze Age, the islands acquire regional characteristics that appear more pronounced in Sicily such as the adoption of colour which is a decorative technique unrelated to Bell Beakers. Despite these differences, various authors have illustrated numerous analogies between Sardinian and Sicilian ceramic production. Where archaeometric studies of the ceramics has been undertaken, differences between the Bell Beakers and the pottery of the other *facies* have been identified especially in the Monte Claro in Sardinia (at Iloi/Ispiluncas; Melis 1998) and the Malpasso and Sant'Ippolito in Sicily (at Tornambè; Fragnoli *et al.* 2013). This perhaps implies the existence of distinct cycles of production, possibly attributable to different individual potters. The extension of these analyses to other contexts could eventually confirm this hypothesis.

Similarities relating to other elements of the Beaker 'package' are less evident. The poverty of data regarding Sicilian metallurgy compared to the wealth of Sardinian finds has already been stated (Melis 2014) probability due to the contrasting availability of raw materials. Furthermore, the two islands share a lack of settlements that are exclusively Bell Beaker but rather a limited number of villages where there is a Bell Beaker presence.

Conclusions

The absence of exclusively Bell Beaker settlements in both Sardinia and Sicily turns our attention to the ways in which the phenomenon arrived on each island and how it interacted with the respective local *facies*. Over the years, the traditional 'diffusionist' approach has given way to the models that envisage a system where exchange revolved around the acquisition of elements of the Bell Beaker 'package' regarded as status symbols by emerging elite. Accepting that the phenomenon is multi-faceted and involved multi-directional dynamics, it is possible to speculate that the development of the phenomenon on the two islands was the result of exchange over long and medium distances, repeated over time and sometimes following convergent paths.

In Sardinia the appearance of Bell Beakers does not seem to correspond to a phase of change in cultural, social or economic aspects though significant transformations did occur in the preceding period, starting in the early 3rd millennium. Bell Beakers appear at a time marked by the conflict between the *facies* of a Neolithic tradition (Filigosa and Abealzu) and Monte Claro. This conflict seems to be seen, in the territories of central-northern Sardinia, in the contrast between the megalithic tombs and menhir statues of the Filigosa-Abealzu groups and the walls of the Monte Claro *facies,* which disappeared during the Beaker period. Less well defined, given the presence of only a single radiocarbon date, is the precise time at which the Abealzu *facies* ceased. Currently there are insufficient data to interpret meaningfully the similarities between the Filigosa-Abealzu and Bell Beakers, or between the Abealzu and the Bonnanaro of the initial Early Bronze Age (Melis 2000). This latter *facies* has sufficient similarities to Bell Beaker to be able to suggest a possible genetic connection as implied by hybrid ceramic production.

But how did Bell Beakers really come into contact with the local *facies*? While there is evidence of the presence of Bell Beaker elements in sites occupied by Monte Claro, there are rarely any stratigraphic relationships. In the cases where there is reliable stratigraphy Bell Beaker overlaps with Monte Claro. Unpublished data from Monte d'Accoddi provide important indications as to the possible relationships with the Filigosa and Abealzu and demonstrate a Bell Beaker presence at the village during the Abealzu phase and possibly also during the Filigosa. With that said and pending new discoveries and fresh radiocarbon dates we can speculate with due caution that in this situation of social, economic and political instability, created or aggravated by the spread of the Monte Claro, the Filigosa-Abealzu groups acquired elements of the Bell Beaker 'package' though at what precise time remains uncertain. In that eventuality, the similarity of some daggers represented on menhir statues with those of Bell Beakers rather than with those of the Filigosa-Abealzu *facies*, would gain in significance. If this reconstruction is confirmed, it would lend weight to the idea that

Bell Beakers and the Abealzu both contributed to the creation of the Bonnanaro.

Unlike Sardinia, the appearance of Beakers in Sicily coincides with a period of profound transformation, clearly seen in the settlements. The study of central Sicily has provided an important contribution to the understanding of the dynamics of Beaker diffusion and the social and cultural changes occurring between the Chalcolithic and Early Bronze Age. Bell Beaker appears in the Malpasso and S. Ippolito *facies* which represent a cultural and social break from the previous phases (Giannitrapani 2009). The transformations that took place between the Early and Late Chalcolithic are evident in domestic buildings, with large rectangular houses with apses being replaced by circular huts. The growth in the number of sites in this area is probably related to the increased exploitation of natural resources. The increasing population and the intensification of agriculture and stock rearing in the Late Chalcolithic possibly led to greater territorial competition, both for the control and use of these resources. These transformations were perhaps connected with increasing social complexity and the rise of ruling classes. In this scenario of social and economic change Bell Beakers may have played a role, explicit in the ownership of artefacts and the creation of monumental tombs, aimed at the acquisition and ostentatious display of social status. The scarcity of Bell Beaker elements in domestic contexts suggests that the preferred way of expressing this was in funerary customs.

The evidence from Sardinia and Sicily illustrates partly analogous models of interaction between Bell Beakers and local *facies*, which was probably dependant on the mobility of small groups or individuals (Vander Linden 2007). These relationships do not seem to be the cause, but rather a component, of the socio-economic transformations of the Late Chalcolithic. At the end of the period both islands display the influence of Bell Beakers in the formation of initial Early Bronze Age society. The further gathering of new data on settlement contexts, more radiocarbon dates, continuing technological and archaeometric analyses of artefacts and isotopic analyses are all indispensable to the confirmation of the reconstruction presented here, and will serve to complete the picture of the complex interchanges of the 3rd millennium BC, in which the diffusion of Bell Beakers played an important, if not yet entirely clear, role.

References

Alberghina, F. & Gullì, D. 2011. L'età del rame finale in Sicilia: considerazioni per una facies unitaria di Malpasso – Sant'Ippolito. IIPP 3, 129–34

Arias, P.E. 1938. La stazione preistorica di Serraferlicchio presso Agrigento. *Monumenti Antichi dei Lincei* 36, 693–838

Arcuri, F., Livadie, C., Di Maio, G., Esposito, E., Napoli, G., Scala, S. & Soriano, E., 2016. Influssi balcanici e genesi del Bronzo antico in Italia meridionale: la koinè Cetina e la facies di Palma Campania. *Rivista di Scienze Preistoriche* 66, 77–95

Ashley, S., Bending, J., Cook, G.T., Corrado, A., Malone, C., Pettitt, P., Puglisi, D., Redhouse, D. & Stoddart, S. 2007. The resources of an Upland community in the Fourth Millenium BC. In M. Fitzjohn (ed.), Uplands of Ancient Sicily and Calabria: The Archaeology of Landscape Revisited, 59–80. London: Accordia Research Institute Publishers

Atzeni, E. 1996. La cultura del vaso Campaniforme e la facies di Bonnanaro nel Bronzo Antico sardo. Proceedings of the International Congress *L'antica età del Bronzo in Italia,* 397–411. Firenze: Octavo

Aurino, P. & Mancusi, V.G. forthcoming. Irradiazione, propagazione e rielaborazione nel bacino mediterraneo degli aspetti puri e ibridi degli orizzonti Campaniforme e Cetina. In IIPP 51

Ayala, G., 2012. Recovering the hidden landscape of Copper Age Sicily. *Journal of Mediterranean Archaeology* 25 (2), 175–96

Barfield, L.H. 1994. Vasi Campaniformi nel Mediterraneo centrale: problemi attuali. In S. Tusa (ed.) 1994, 439–60

Battaglia, G. 2014. Contestualizzazione delle grotte nell'archeologia del paesaggio della provincia di Palermo prospettive di ricerca. In D. Gullì (ed.), 2014, 115–26

Beffa, G., Pedrotta, T., Colombaroli, D., Henne, P.D., Van Leeuwen, J.F.N., Süsstrunk, P., Kaltenrieder, P., Adolf, C., Vogel, H., Pasta, S., Anselmetti, F.S., Gobet, E. & Tinner, W. 2015. Vegetation and fire history of coastal north-eastern Sardinia (Italy) under changing Holocene climates and land use. *Vegetation History and Archaeobotany* 25 (3), 271–89

Bovio Marconi, J. 1944. La cultura tipo Conca d'Oro nella Sicilia Occidentale. *Monumenti Antichi dei Lincei* 60, 1–170

Bovio Marconi, J. 1963. Sulla diffusione del Bicchiere Campaniforme in Sicilia. *Kokalos* 9, 93–128

Carnieri, E., Lentini, L., Levi, S., Mandò, P.M., Valenti, A. & Zanini A. 2012. La tomba a grotticella artificiale di 'Pergole 2', Partanna (Trapani), Contrada Pergola. In *IIPP* 41, 611–21

Castellana, G. 1997. *La Grotta di Ticchiara ed il Castellucciano Agrigentino.* Palermo: Museo Archeologico Regionale

Castellana, G. 1998. *Il Santuario Castellucciano di Monte Grande e l'Approvvigionamento Dello Zolfo nel Mediterraneo dell'età del Bronzo.* Agrigento: Assessorato Beni Culturali ed Ambientali

Cazzella, A. & Maniscalco, L. 2012. L'età del rame in Sicilia. In *IIPP* 41, 57–80

Cocchi Genick, D. (ed.), 2013. *Cronologia Assoluta e Relativa dell'età del Rame in Italia.* Verona: QuiEdit

Cultraro, M. 2007. Evidence of amber in Bronze Age Sicily: local sources and the Balkan-Mycenaean connection. In Galanaki, I., Tomas, H., Galanakis, Y. & Laffineur, R. (eds), *Between the Aegean and Baltic Seas. Prehistory across borders,* 377–89. Liège: Université de Liège

Cultraro, M. 2013. L'Eneolitico in Italia centro-meridionale e Sicilia attraverso la prospettiva delle nuove ricerche nel mondo egeo-balcanico. In Cocchi Genick (ed.), 2013, 213–32

Di Rita, F. & Melis, R. T. 2013. The cultural landscape near the ancient city of Tharros (central West Sardinia): vegetation changes and human impact. *Journal of Archaeological Science* 40, 4271–82

Floris, R., Mascia, F., Sonedda, E., Sarigu, M., Lai, L., O'Connell, T., Montisci, M. & Zuncheddu, M. 2011. Bioanthropological Analysis of the Individuals Buried in the Multi-Layered Tomb of Bingia 'E Monti (Gonnostramatza – Or – Sardinia): First Results. *Journal of Biological Research* 84 (1), 186–9

Fragnoli, P., Manin, A.L., Giannitrapani, E., Iannì, F. & Levi, S.T. 2013. La composizione della ceramica preistorica e protostorica di Tornambè (EN). In G. Vezzalini & P. Zannini (eds), *Proceedings of the VII National Congress of Acheometry*, 137–49. Bologna: Patròn Editore

Giannitrapani, E. 2009. Nuove considerazioni sulla diffusione del Bicchiere Campaniforme in Sicilia. *Rivista di Scienze Preistoriche* 58, 219–42

Giannitrapani, E. 2013. Dalla capanna alla casa. L'architettura domestica nella preistoria della Sicilia centrale. In C. Bonanno & F. Valbruzzi (eds), *Mito e Archeologia degli Erei. Museo Diffuso Ennese: Itinerari Archeologici,* 69–75. Palermo: Regione Siciliana

Giannitrapani, E. 2017. Paesaggi e dinamiche del popolamento di età preistorica nella Sicilia centrale. In F. Anichini & M. L. Gualandi (eds), *Mappa Data Book 2*, 43–64. Roma: Edizioni Nuova Cultura

Giannitrapani, E. & Iannì, F. 2011a. Nuovi dati sulla presenza del Bicchiere Campaniforme nella Sicilia centrale. In *IIPP* 43, 477–82

Giannitrapani E. & Iannì F., 2011b. La tarda età del Rame nella Sicilia centrale. L'Età del Rame in Italia. In *IIPP* 43, 271–8

Giannitrapani, E., Grillo, F. M. & Speciale, C. 2014a. Household Archaeology nella preistoria siciliana. In Sposito, A. (ed.), *Agathòn. RFCA & RCAPIA* (Recupero e Fruizione dei Contesti Antichi. *Recupero dei Contesti Antichi e Processi Innovativi nell'Architettura*) *PhD Journal,* 3–8. Palermo: ARACNE editrice

Giannitrapani, E., Ianni, F., Chilardi, S. & Anguilano, L. 2014b. Case Bastione: a prehistoric settlement in the Erei uplands (central Sicily). *Origini,* 36, 181–211

Giardino, C. 1997. La metallotecnica nella Sicilia pre-protostorica. In S. Tusa (ed.), 1997, 405–10

Giardino, C., Spera, V. & Tusa, S. 2012. Nuovi dati sulla metallurgia della Sicilia occidentale nell'età del Bronzo. In *IIPP* 41, 697–708

Guilaine, J. 2009. La Sicile et l'Europe campaniforme. In Guilaine, J., Tusa, S. & Veneroso, P. (eds), *La Sicile et l'Europe Campaniforme. La collection Veneroso à Sciacca,* 135–95. Toulouse: Archives d'écologie préhistorique

Gullì, D. 2014. The meanings of caves in the prehistory and protohistory of the Agrigento territory, 73–80. In D. Gullì (ed.), 2014, *From Cave to Dolmen. Ritual and Symbolic Aspects in the Prehistory between Sciacca, Sicily and the central Mediterranean.* Oxford: Archaeopress

Iannì, F. 2016. L'età del Rame nella Sicilia centro-meridionale: nuovi dati dalla valle del Salso, *Rivista di Scienze Preistoriche* 66, 61–76

IIPP 43, 2011. XLIII Riunione Scientifica *dell'Istituto Italiano di Preistoria e Protostoria* L'età del rame in Italia, L'età del rame in Italia. Firenze: Istituto Italiano di Preistoria e Protostoria

IIPP 41, 2012. XLI Riunione Scientifica dell'Istituto Italiano di Preistoria e Protostoria, Dai Ciclopi agli Ecisti. Società e territorio nella Sicilia preistorica e protostorica. Firenze: Istituto Italiano di Preistoria e Protostoria

IIPP 51 forthcoming. LI Riunione Scientifica dell'Istituto Italiano di Preistoria e Protostoria, Italia tra Mediterraneo ed Europa: mobilità, interazioni e scambi. Firenze: Istituto Italiano di Preistoria e Protostoria

Lai, L., Fonzo O., Tykot R.H., Goddard E. & Hollander D. 2011. Le due comunità di Scaba 'e Arriu (Siddi). Risorse alimentari nella Sardegna del III millennio a.C. indagate tramite analisi isotopiche di tessuti ossei. Studio antropologico dei reperti umani. In *IIPP* 43, 401–8

Lai, L., Tykot, R.H., Beckett, J. F., Floris, R., Fonzo, O., Usai, E., Manunza, M.R., Goddard, E. & Hollander, D. 2007. Interpreting stable isotopic analyses: case studies on Sardinian prehistory. In Glascock, M.D., Speakman, R.J. & Popelka-Filcoff, R.S. (eds), *Archaeological chemistry: analytical techniques and archaeological interpretation,* 114–36. Washington, DC: ACS Symposium Series 968, American Chemical Society

Lai, L., Tykot, R.H., Usai, E., Beckett, J.F., Floris, R., Fonzo, O., Goddard, E., Hollander, D., Manunza, M.R., Usai A. 2013. Diet in the Sardinian Bronze Age: models, collagen isotopic data, issues and perspectives, *Préhistoires Méditerranéennes,*4, 139–154

La Rosa, V. 1994. Le nuove indagini nella media valle del Platani. In Tusa (ed.), 1994, 287–97

Leighton, R. 2005. Later prehistoric settlement patterns in Sicily: old paradigms and new surveys. *European Journal of Archaeology* 8 (3), 261–87

Lemercier, O., Leonini, V., Tramoni, P. & Furestier, R. 2007. Campaniformes insulaires et continentaux de France et d'Italie méditerranéennes. Relations et échanges entre Corse, Sardaigne, Toscane et Midi français dans la seconde moitié du troisième millénaire avant notre ère. In D'Anna, A., Cesari, J., Ogel, L. & Vaquer, J. (eds), *Corse et Sardaigne préhistorique. Relation et échanges dans le contexte méditerranéen*, 241–52. Paris: Éditions du Comité des travaux Historiques et Scientifiques (CTHS)

Malone, C.A.T. & Stoddart, S.T.K. 2000. A house in the Sicilian hills. *Antiquity* 74, 471–2

Manca, L. 2010. Gli oggetti d'ornamento in conchiglia. In Melis (ed.), 2010, 237–49

Maniscalco, L. 2013. Cronologia assoluta della tarda età del rame nella Sicilia orientale: nuovi dati dal Santuario dei Palici presso Mineo. In Cocchi Genick (ed.), 2013, 194–5

Manunza, M.R., Fenu, P. & Nieddu, F. 2014. Approcci allo studio delle architetture domestiche di facies Monte

Claro: l'abitato del lago di Monte Pranu – Tratalias/ Villaperuccio (CI). *Quaderni della Soprintendenza Archeologica per le province di Cagliari e Oristano* 25, 33–56

Martinelli, M.C. 2013. Cronologia assoluta della tarda età del rame nella Sicilia orientale tirrenica e Isole Eolie, In Cocchi Genick (ed.), 2013, 192–3

McConnell, B.E. 2003. Insediamenti dell'altopiano Ibleo e l'architettura dell'età del Rame in Sicilia. In *XXXV* Riunione Scientifica dell'Istituto Italiano di Preistoria e Protostoria, Le comunità della Preistoria Italiana: Studi e Ricerche sul Neolitico e le Età dei Metalli, 225–38. Firenze: Istituto Italiano di Preistoria e Protostoria

Melis, M.G. 1998. *La tomba n. 3 di Iloi.* Villanova Monteleone: Soter

Melis, M.G. 2000. *L'età del Rame in Sardegna: origine ed evoluzione degli aspetti autoctoni.* Villanova Monteleone: Soter

Melis, M.G. 2010. Capitolo quinto. Sintesi dei risultati, 287–98 In Melis (ed.), 2010, *Usini Ricostruire il passato, una ricerca internazionale a S'Elighe Entosu*, 237–49. Sassari: Carlo Delfino

Melis, M.G. 2013. Problemi di cronologia insulare. La Sardegna tra il IV e il III millennio BC. In Cocchi Genick (ed.), 2013, 197–211

Melis, M.G., 2014. Silver in Neolithic and Eneolithic Sardinia. In Meller, H., Risch, R. & Pernicka, E. (eds), *Metalle der Macht – Frühes Gold und Silber.* 6. Mitteldeutscher Archäologentag vom 17. Tagungen des Landesmuseums für Vorgeschichte Halle, Band 11/I, 483–94

Melis, M.G. 2018. Modelli di sfruttamento e circolazione delle materie prime nel Mediterraneo occidentale durante il IV millennio BC. I dati della Sardegna. In Proceedings of the International Workshop *La Préhistoire et la Protohistoire des îles de Méditerranée Occidentale. Matières premières, circulation, expérimentation et traditions techniques,* Quaderni del LaPArS 3. Sassari: Università di Sassari – LaPArS, 99–124

Moravetti, A. 2004. *Monte Baranta e la cultura di monte Claro.* Sassari: Carlo Delfino

Nicoletti, F. & Tusa, S. 2012, L'età del Bronzo nella Sicilia occidentale. In *IIPP* 41, 105–30

Nicolis, F. & Mottes, E. (eds), 1998. *Simbolo ed Enigma. Il bicchiere campaniforme e l'Italia nella preistoria europea del III millennio a.C.* Trento: Provincia Autonoma di Trento

Orlandini, P. 1962. *Il villaggio preistorico di Manfria, presso Gela.* Palermo: Banco di Sicilia

Orsi, P. 1910. Due villaggi del primo periodo siculo. *Bullettino di Paletnologia Italiana* 36, 159–93

Orsi, P. 1928. Miscellanea sicula. *Bullettino di Paletnologia Italiana* 48, 44–98

Panvini, R. 2012. *L'età del Bronzo nella Sicilia centro-meridionale.* In *IIPP* 41, 131–56

Pau, C. 2013. Cuentas y colgantes campaniformes y epicampaniformes de Cerdeña, *Lucentum* 32, 9–30

Privitera, F. 1997. La stazione di Mezzebi nel contesto del Bronzo antico del territorio di Milena. In La Rosa, (ed.), *Dalle Capanne alle Robbe. La storia lunga di Milocca-Milena,* 85–92. Milena: Pro Loco

Puddu, L., 2014. Il complesso megalitico di Biru 'e Concas (Sorgono NU): lo scavo del 1994, *Fasti On Line Documents & Research* http://www.fastionline.org/docs/FOLDER-it-2014-310.pdf.

Sadori, L., Ortu, E., Peyron, O, Zanchetta, G., Vannière, B., Desmet, M. & Magny, M. 2013. The last 7 millennia of vegetation and climate changes at Lago di Pergusa (central Sicily, Italy). *Climate of the Past* 9, 1969–1984

Scuderi, A., Tusa, S. & Vintaloro, A. 1997. La preistoria e la protostoria nel Corleonese e nello Jato nel quadro della Sicilia occidentale. In Tusa (ed.), 1997, 503–10

Tusa, S. (ed.), 1994. *La preistoria del basso Belice e della Sicilia meridionale nel quadro della preistoria siciliana e mediterranea.* Palermo: Società Siciliana per la Storia Patria

Tusa, S. (ed.), 1997. *Prima Sicilia. Alle origini della società siciliana.* Palermo: Ediprint

Tusa, S. 1997a. Il fenomeno del bicchiere campaniforme in Sicilia. In Tusa (ed.), 1997, 317–332

Tusa, S. 1997b. Nuovi dati sull'Eneolitico nella Sicilia occidentale: insediamenti di Roccazzo (Mazara del Vallo) e Grotta del Cavallo (Castellammare del golfo). Atti delle *Seconde giornate internazionali di studi sull'area elima*, Pisa – Gibellina, 1305–17

Tusa, S. 1998. Prospettiva mediterranea e integrità culturale del bicchiere campaniforme siciliano. In Nicolis & Mottes (eds), 1998, 205–19

Tusa, S. 2000. L'ipogeismo in Sicilia. In Melis, M.G. (ed), Proceedings of the International Congress *L'ipogeismo nel Mediterraneo. Origini, sviluppo, quadri culturali*, 267–312. Sassari

Tusa, S. 2001. Nuovi dati dal territorio di Custonaci sul processo di aggregazione insediamentale nell'eneolitico nella Sicilia occidentale. In Martinelli, M.C. & Spigo, U. (eds), *Studi di Preistoria e protostoria in onore di Luigi Bernabò Brea*, 145–56

Tusa, S. 2014. Apporti megalitici nelle architetture funerarie e abitative della Preistoria siciliana, 237–46. In Gullì (ed.), 2014, *From Cave to Dolmen. Ritual and Symbolic Aspects in the Prehistory between Sciacca, Sicily and the central Mediterranean.* Oxford: Archaeopress

Ugas, G. 1998. Facies campaniformi dell'ipogeo di Padru Jossu (Sanluri-Cagliari). In Nicolis & Mottes (eds), 1998, 261–80

Vander Linden, M. 2007. What linked the Bell Beakers in third millennium BC Europe? *Antiquity* 81, 343–352

Veneroso, P. 2014. Il fenomeno del Bicchiere Campaniforme in rapporto alle culture della Sicilia centro-occidentale. In Gullì (ed.), 2014, 231–6

7

Bell Beaker settlements in northern and central Italy

Marco Baioni, Fabio Martini, Franco Nicolis, Raffaella Poggiani Keller and Lucia Sarti

Italy fully participated in the Bell Beaker phenomenon, although to varying degrees in the peninsula. There are concentrations of sites, especially in central northern Italy including eastern Lombardy, western Veneto and central Emilia (Nicolis 1998; Baioni *et al.* 2008), and on the Tyrrhenian side of central Italy (Sarti 1998; Leonini & Sarti 2008a). Scarce Bell Beaker remains are also known from the Adriatic and southern central Italy, (Fugazzola *et al.* 1998, Leonini & Sarti 2008b). In this contribution the territory has been divided into three macro-areas:

- North-western Italy (Valle d'Aosta, Piedmont, Liguria, Lombardy)
- North-eastern Italy (Veneto, Trentino-Alto Adige, Emilia Romagna, Friuli Venezia Giulia)
- Tyrrhenian central Italy (Tuscany, Lazio)

An overview of each area is followed by a synthesis, and a concluding statement.

West-central northern Italy – Valle d'Aosta, Piedmont, Liguria, Lombardy (MB, RPK)

Our knowledge of Bell Beakers in northern Italy (notwithstanding recent funerary discoveries in Emilia in Bernabò Brea & Mazzieri 2013) is largely based on settlement sites (Nicolis 1998, Baioni & Poggiani Keller 2008). This distinguishes this area from other areas of Europe, and sometimes makes it difficult to see the Italian data clearly in the more general European Bell Beaker studies. The evidence is not spread uniformly over this area. There are areas that – either due to a greater number of sites or more intensive research – provide more information than others. The quality of the evidence also varies. While there are some well excavated sites, some with extensive excavated areas, others are known from small excavations, or finds scatters.

The archaeological contexts

Bell Beaker finds come from a wide range of domestic contexts. In Liguria (Maggi 1998, 26) they are recorded from rock shelters and underground caverns and seems to be connected with domestic use (Loreto in the Argentina Valley, Arma di Nasino in the Pennavaira Valley, Grotta Arma delle Anime, Grotta Pollera). Use of the Cà dei Grii cave in eastern Lombardy is less certain, since the deposit had been greatly reworked and it is uncertain if the human bones found were associated with the Bell Beaker levels or not (Biagi & Marchello 1970).

In western Lombardy Bell Beakers come from marshland settlements near the lakes in the Province of Varese (settlements built on reclaimed land and pile dwellings with Neolithic and Bronze Age phases in Biandronno – Isolino Virginia, Bardello-Stoppani, Monate and Laveno Mombello). Unfortunately, detailed information on stratigraphy is usually lacking (Banchieri 1988).

The most common settlement type is on open, well-drained land (Baioni & Poggiani Keller 2008). In the alluvial plains and the bordering piedmont hills, settlements seem more frequent in the foothills (Brescia – S. Polo), the upper and middle Po Plain river terraces, and the lower plain sand dunes (Curtatone – Montanara, Fontanella Grazioli, Isorella, Montalbano of Cadimarco, Malpensata di Fiesse and Calcinate – Campo Musna). They are usually near watercourses, but protected from floods.

In upland areas Bell Beaker sites are found in essentially three different environments: in valley bottoms or low terraces near rivers (Trescore Balneario; Cividate Camuno/Malegno, Aosta – Nuovo Ospedale), on quite steep slopes (Monte Covolo; Ponte Pier), and on hilltops or plateaux (Brescia – S. Anna; Lovere; Breno Castle; Puegnago – Castello; Rocca and Sopra Sasso of Manerba). Most of these locations seem to have been chosen either due to the presence of resources or because they controlled the local territory and communication routes. Some settlements exploited particular raw materials, such as flint at Monte Covolo and Trescore Balneario – Canton, soapstone in Pianaccia di Suvero, and metal ores in Lovere – Colle del Lazzaretto.

There are also multi-period sites, where the Bell Beaker phase follows earlier phases, and is often the last occupation at the location, as well as geographically and structurally distinctive single-period sites. In the former, building types and certain aspects of the material culture show continuity with the preceding phases. In the latter, the Bell Beaker culture is clearly dominant and particular features are present.

Cultural evolution and radiometric data

Bell Beaker sites are principally identified by their decorated pottery. Unfortunately, these sherds are often small and poorly preserved making reconstruction complicated. The dominant form is undoubtedly the S-profile beaker, either with a convex or flat base. Frequently handled forms have been found and there are examples of angular handles that herald Early Bronze Age forms.

The pottery is decorated with various types of impression, sometimes combined, made with fine or thick cords, a toothed comb or (rarely) a *Cardium* shell and are often accompanied by various linear incisions. Styles are often difficult to reconstruct. The accepted sequence of northern Italian Bell Beaker remains generally valid. All Over Corded and All Over Ornamented forms are present as are vessels in the Maritime style. Barfield's (1977) Italian style, distinguished by broader bands, is rarer. The sequences at Monte Covolo and Lovere show a progression from simpler horizontally banded decoration to a more complicated scheme, but the assemblage is small and fragmentary.

Common ware is constantly associated with Bell Beakers and different ceramic traditions appear contemporary as well as there being a development from Chalcolithic traditions towards styles with incipient Early Bronze Age features. Although the relative chronology of the Monte Covolo and Lovere Bell Beaker levels is unproblematic, being clearly stratified between Chalcolithic and Early Bronze Age layers, and therefore belonging to one of the final phases of the Copper Age, recent radiocarbon dates from Monte Covolo, Trescore and Lovere are not all reliable whilst other dates demonstrate that Bell Beakers overlapped with the early Polada Culture (Nicolis 1998, 65; Baioni & Poggiani Keller 2008, 163–7).

The best documented sites

A survey of the best preserved and documented sites reveals a concentration in central and eastern Lombardy. This is certainly a bias in research, but may also partly derive from a greater density of Bell Beaker sites, and the area has long been known for its funerary sites (Cadimarco, Santa Cristina di Fiesse). The marked presence of Bell Beaker sites along the course of the River Chiese, perhaps related to an important trans-Alpine communication route suggests territorial organisation (Nicolis 1998, 50–1).

Starting with sites on high ground and steep slopes, that of Rocca of Manerba del Garda excavated between 1995–2001, was a terraced settlement founded in the Late Neolithic and occupied until Bell Beaker times (Fig. 7.1,2–3). While the Neolithic terrace is well preserved, potential Chalcolithic levels were severely damaged by the subsequent medieval castle (Fig. 7.1,1). The Bell Beaker layers are superficial and disturbed with no structural remains (Barfield 1998, Barfield *et al.* 2002, Barfield & Borrello 2006). Better preserved remains are found at Villanuova sul Clisi – Monte Covolo which was founded in the Late Neolithic and lasted until the early Middle Bronze Age (Fig. 7.1,5) (Poggiani Keller *et al.* 2006a; Poggiani Keller & Baioni 2008). The area comprises a series of natural terraces that were extended and joined to create artificial terraces with drystone retaining walls. No structures can be attributed to the Bell Beaker phase, but it seems that the pre-existing terraces were used. Bell Beaker occupation layers were quite near the surface and had been disturbed by subsequent occupation and slope erosion (Fig. 7.1,4).

On one of the better-preserved terraces, the Bell Beaker structural remains were less substantial than those of middle Chalcolithic houses which were solidly built with drystone walls, post-holes and foundation trenches and were partly sunken. The general shape of the Bell Beaker dwellings is indicated by the sub-rectangular terrace areas available and the spread of occupation deposits. One house measured *c.* 7 × 5 m. Only two shallow irregular post-holes were identified belonging to a central row of posts (Fig. 7.1,6). The lower side of the structure was destroyed and there were no post-holes on the upslope side, where the roof probably rested on the terrace behind (Poggiani Keller & Baioni 2008). Of particular interest was a large two-phased hearth on the eastern edge of a slight depression (Fig. 7.1,7). The deposits associated with the use of this dwelling correspond to the two phases of the hearth and contained numerous sherds of Bell Beaker and common ware of both Beaker-associated and local types.

Terrace organisation seems to have been present on both the nearby site of Ponte Pier di Villanuova sul Clisi (Barfield 2006), and at Breno Castle in Valle Camonica, where redeposited Bell Beaker material was found. The settlement was founded in the Neolithic and continued in intermittent use until Later Prehistory (Fedele 2003). At Lovere – Colle del Lazzaretto, a hilltop settlement occupied from the Late Neolithic, the Bell Beaker phase was associated with copper metallurgy that had started in an earlier period. Unfortunately, the site had been destroyed (Poggiani Keller 2000; Poggiani Keller *et al.* 2006b. At Cividate Camuno – Malegno, the settlement was founded in the Middle/Late Neolithic and continued uninterruptedly through the entire Iron Age and later. The Bell Beaker evidence comprises largely redeposited material but suggests contemporary settlements on both banks of the River Oglio (Poggiani Keller 2006a). *In situ* evidence for Chalcolithic wooden structures was found in the Via Cavour excavations but the Bell Beaker material here was redeposited.

At Trescore Balneario – Canton (BG) two distinct but interconnected complexes were found, with separate functions and a partly overlapping chronology (Poggiani Keller 1998; Poggiani Keller 2006b). They date from the Middle Neolithic to the Copper Age and lie to the north of a Middle Neolithic funerary-cult complex (Poggiani Keller 2004) (Fig. 7.1). The Chalcolithic buildings of the pre-Bell Beaker phase were circular in plan, or sometimes composite (circular with a rectangular 'corridor'), oriented N–S (Fig. 7.2,4) and have sunken floors some 0.1–0.6 m. deep. The Bell Beaker phase occupied the northernmost strip of the settlement at the foot of the hillside (Poggiani Keller 2006b). During the Late Copper Age, the village was centred on the well-preserved road that crossed it in a NW–SE direction, running safely along the edge of a terrace. The road was 1.6–1.7 m. wide, bordered on both sides by a channel, 0.2–0.3 m. wide which would have held horizontal timbers to contain the gravel and small stones forming the road surface (Fig. 7.2,2). In one area the road surface preserved wheel ruts produced by four-wheeled carts similar to those represented in the Chalcolithic rock engravings in nearby Valle Camonica (Poggiani Keller 2006b, figs 6–7).

The laying of the road was followed by the construction of two rectangular houses the perimeters of which were marked by post-holes (Fig. 7.2,5). In House 1, a sequence of three hearths was found, each with a base of small

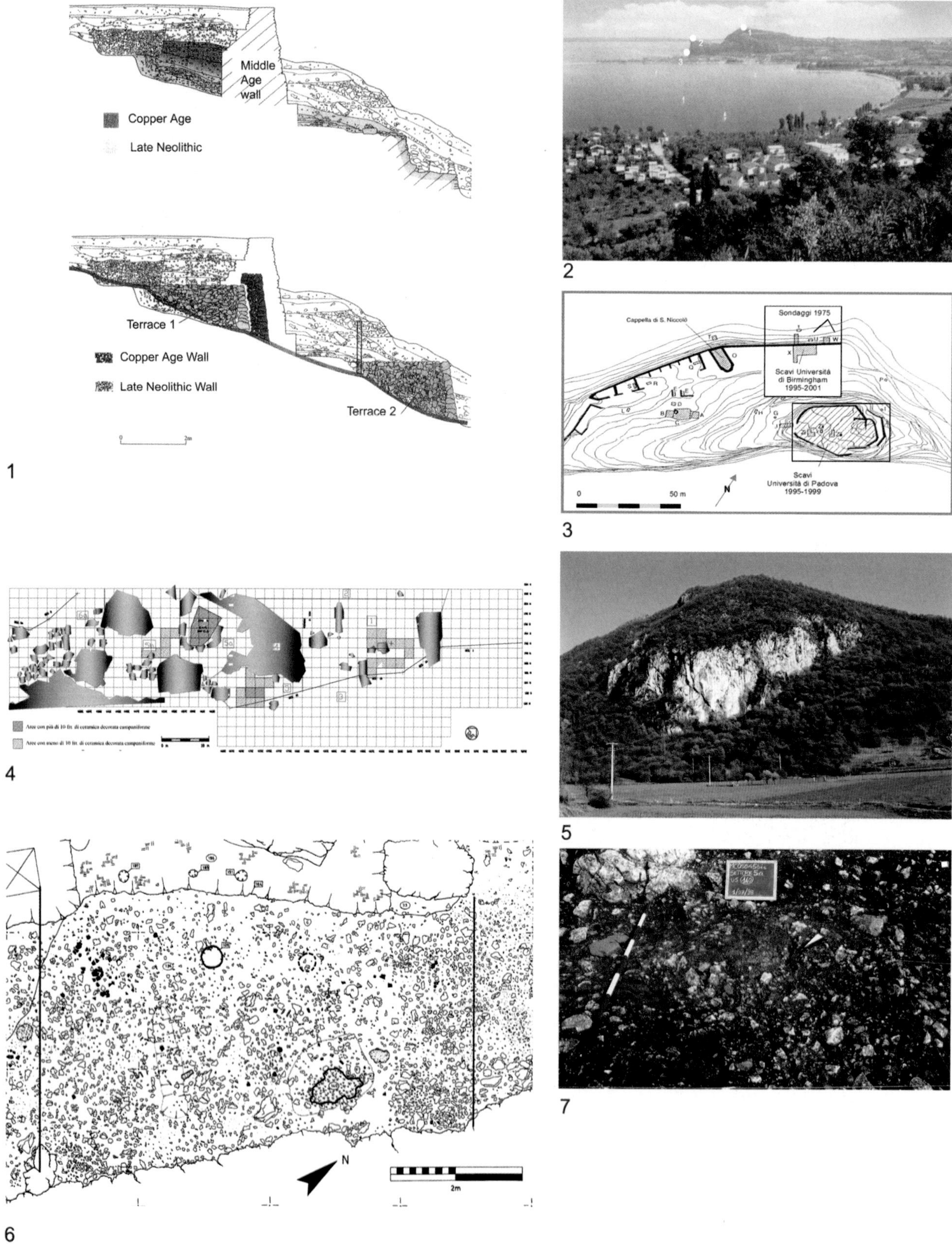

Figure 7.1: 1 – Rocca of Manerba del Garda, Section of stratigraphic sequence showing the different terraces; 2 – Rocca of Manerba del Garda, panoramic view; 3 – Rocca of Manerba del Garda, location of the excavated areas; 4 – Villanuova sul Clisi – Monte Covolo, distribution of Bell Beaker pottery; 5 – Villanuova sul Clisi – Monte Covolo, panoramic view of the settlement area at the foot of the mountain; 6 – Villanuova sul Clisi – Monte Covolo, house plan with hearth and post-holes; 7 – Villanuova sul Clisi – Monte Covolo, hearth with different layers of clay

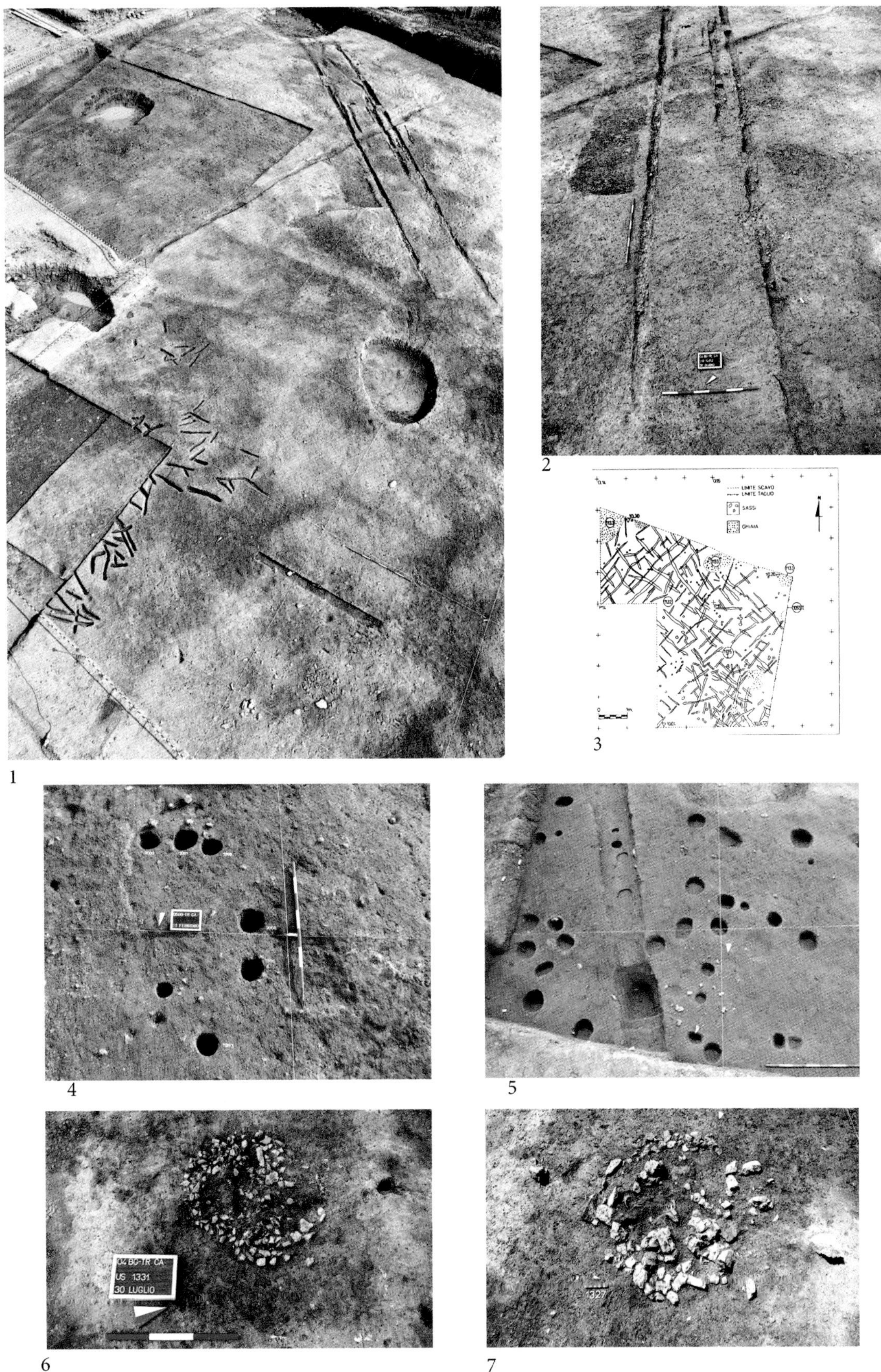

Figure 7.2: Trescore Balneario – Canton: 1 – an aerial view of the settlement; 2 – the well-preserved road; 3 – cultivated fields with cross-ploughing; 4 – Pre-Bell Beaker circular houses; 5 – Bell Beaker rectangular house marked by post-holes; 6–7 – Sequence of different hearths on clay and stone bases

stones covered by a layer of clay (Fig. 7.2,6–7). The most recent hearth was dated to 3580±30 BP (Poz-15089, 2030–1820 cal BC). Trodden surface layers in the two houses contained Bell Beaker sherds. The excavation also showed that the settlement organisation was less regular during the Bell Beaker phase with the zones occupied by wooden huts, fences and small wooden structures interspaced with cultivated fields (Fig. 7.2,3).

Recent excavations in the plain have revealed a number of single-phased sites. Cascina Urbana in Solero, located in Piedmont, revealed a preserved palaeosol with the remains of lightly-built dwellings with post-holes and daub fragments with wattle impressions (Sannella 1998). At the Lombard site of Brescia – San Polo (Poggiani Keller *et al.* 2006c), an area of about 1200 m² was excavated between 1995 and 2000, and the remains of three houses (A, B and C) were found, each with a different orientation (Fig. 7.3,2.). The buildings were sub-oval in plan and similar in size, with post-holes defining their perimeters (Fig. 7.3,4). House A (reconstructed in the Val Senales Archaeological Park, Fig. 7.3,3), measured 5.6 × 3.4 m. House B measured 5.3 × 3.6 m. House C extended into the unexcavated area and the full measurements could not be recovered. The maximum depth of the perimeter post-holes was 0.25–0.35m (Fig. 7.3,6). Neither floors nor hearths were preserved but a further single post-hole was present on the longitudinal axis. The discovery of daub and clay fragments, in particular around the perimeter of House C, suggests that the walls were, at least in part, covered with clay (Fig. 7.3,5). The existence of a central pole may indicate that there was an internal dividing wall and the door was probably on one of the short sides. The presence of post-holes, sometimes aligned, in the open areas around the huts suggests the presence of fences or enclosures.

More recently, in Calcinate – Campo Musna, an extensive settlement on a palaeoterrace of the River Serio was found, near a Middle Neolithic village and an area with traces of occupation datable to the Chalcolithic (De Stefani 2016, Poggiani Keller 2016). The settlement belongs to the final part of the Bell Beaker period, from the end of the Copper Age to the onset of the Early Bronze Age ('epicampaniforme'). The general organisation of the settlement is not known due to the limited excavations which also meant that several large buildings dug 0.4–0.5 m. into the ground, and of unknown function, were not fully excavated. The site featured three sunken oval and circular buildings measuring 7.8 m wide by more than 8 m long and 0.45 m deep; 16 × 4.5 m; and 3.6 × 2.3 m. The circular structure measured 4 m in diameter but lacked trodden surfaces and structural components. They were associated with charcoal-rich deposits containing pottery, worked stone, rare metal finds, and animal bones.

Settlement and house features

A distinctive feature of this settlement type was its layout on terraces, involving both the use of small natural flat areas and the construction of regular artificial terraces with retaining walls. These terraces may also have had a defensive function. At both Monte Covolo and Trescore it seems that there was no regular layout of the settlement area. In both cases zones with the remains of houses (or, more generally, with signs of human activity, such as activity areas and small ill-defined constructions) seem to alternate with larger areas lacking in structural remains and with few finds. At Trescore these areas were cultivated.

In Monte Covolo the sparse nature of the occupation, with large open areas, contrasts with the extensive Neolithic artefactual evidence though this may be due to the greater length of this phase and the relatively brief Early Bronze Age presence. In general, no enclosures delimiting the settlements have ever been found, and even at Monte Covolo large boulders at the settlement's lower limit are of glacial origin. At Monte Covolo the palaeobotanical data suggest that certain plants might have been used as boundary hedges and at San Polo, lines of post-holes suggest fences or enclosures. At Trescore, the road that crossed the settlement must have been of great importance.

In no cases can the actual limits of a settlement be precisely defined, and on long occupied sites it is difficult to understand the horizontal stratigraphy of the various phases, to identify periods of expansion and contraction and especially in riverside, hill-base and plain locations where human natural activities have been detrimental to the survival of the Bell Beaker settlement remains. At Trescore, as at Castenaso near Bologna, the dwellings were rectangular in plan, with perimeters marked by post-holes. The houses found in San Polo were rather different, being decidedly sub-oval in shape.

North-eastern Italy – Veneto, Emilia Romagna, Trentino Alto Adige, Friuli Venezia Giulia (FN)

The current state of knowledge regarding Bell Beaker settlements in north-eastern Italy (Trentino, Veneto, Friuli Venezia Giulia, Romagna) is not greatly different from that outlined nearly 20 years ago (Nicolis 2001a). However, new data acquired in recent years, particularly from the rescue excavations in Emilia and Romagna, have improved our knowledge regarding both funerary and settlement aspects. There seems no pattern to the geographical settings of Bell Beaker sites. They are found on the alluvial plain, close to old river channels and pools, and on river terraces. There is a large group of sites situated along the hilly Alpine piedmont strip and in the Apennine valleys. Sites may be in the open, or in caves or rockshelters. Bell Beaker users were also present in mountainous areas, although the sites are almost always in the principal valleys (Monte Mezzana, Doss Trento, Montesei di Serso, Velturno).

Neither are the sites evenly distributed, but form concentrations of varying size. One of the areas with the highest concentration is the Veronese piedmont belt, from the Adige to the Chiampo Valleys. Minor groupings occur in Emilia and Romagna in the Po Plain and at the foot of the Apennines, and in the Trentino-Alto Adige area. An interesting observation is the distribution of several sites along the course of certain rivers, some on the plain and others in the valley or near the valley mouth. Along the Secchia, for example, we find a site at Rubiera on the plain and another at Pescale, where the river flows through the Apennines. Along the Enza there is the Sant'Ilario site on the plain and that at Bismantova in the high Apennines, right on the Enza-Secchia watershed. If these sites were contemporary, this suggests riverine communication between the Bell Beaker settlements. Most of the sites in north-eastern Italy where Bell Beaker pottery has been found were probably settlements.

Trentino, Veneto and Friuli Venezia Giulia

In the Trentino area (Nicolis 2001b), the currently available evidence does not permit a Bell Beaker phase to be distinguished stratigraphically, but the archaeological data from a number of sites in the Trento basin and Alta Valsugana indicate the existence of a formative phase of the Early Bronze Age, generally associated with Chalcolithic cultural traditions, in particular Bell Beakers, and metalwork of Danubian ancestry. An example of this chronological horizon is Montesei di Serso in Valsugana, which clearly demonstrates close connections between Slovenia and north Italy. Here (although unfortunately redeposited) two Bell Beaker sherds and other pottery linked to central Europe, were discovered along with copper alloy awls, flint daggers and a casting mould for a socketed axe that closely resemble items from the Ljubljana marshes. At Montesei several pottery fragments were also found that have been linked with the Vučedol Culture, although now appearing more closely associated with the Cetina Culture and it seems that the connections between north Italy and the Cetina Culture utilised the Trieste Karst area. Evidence for the strong influence of this culture is supported by the Montesei di Serso finds, to which can be added other objects such as the Bell Beaker bowl from Monte Castello di Gesso (Bologna) and a fragment from the Tanaccia di Brisighella (Ravenna).

Interesting information has emerged from Monte Baone (Arco), not far from where six statue-steles were found. The archaeological deposit, partly disturbed by clandestine digging and animal burrows, is located inside a small rockshelter at the foot of the cliff and behind a large fallen block. The lower portion of the deposit, probably Later Neolithic or Chalcolithic is associated with the sheltering of ovicaprids, as attested by dung-burning and litter layers revealed through soil micromorphology and in common with other north Italian caves. The Bell Beaker finds discovered during the excavation (eight sherds from at least three different combed vessels,) are almost all from disturbed layers. It is difficult to explain the presence of so many Bell Beaker fragments in such a small space and it seems rather unlikely that they were associated with the herding activity although one sherd did come from these levels. It is possible that one or more Beaker-associated burials had been disturbed in

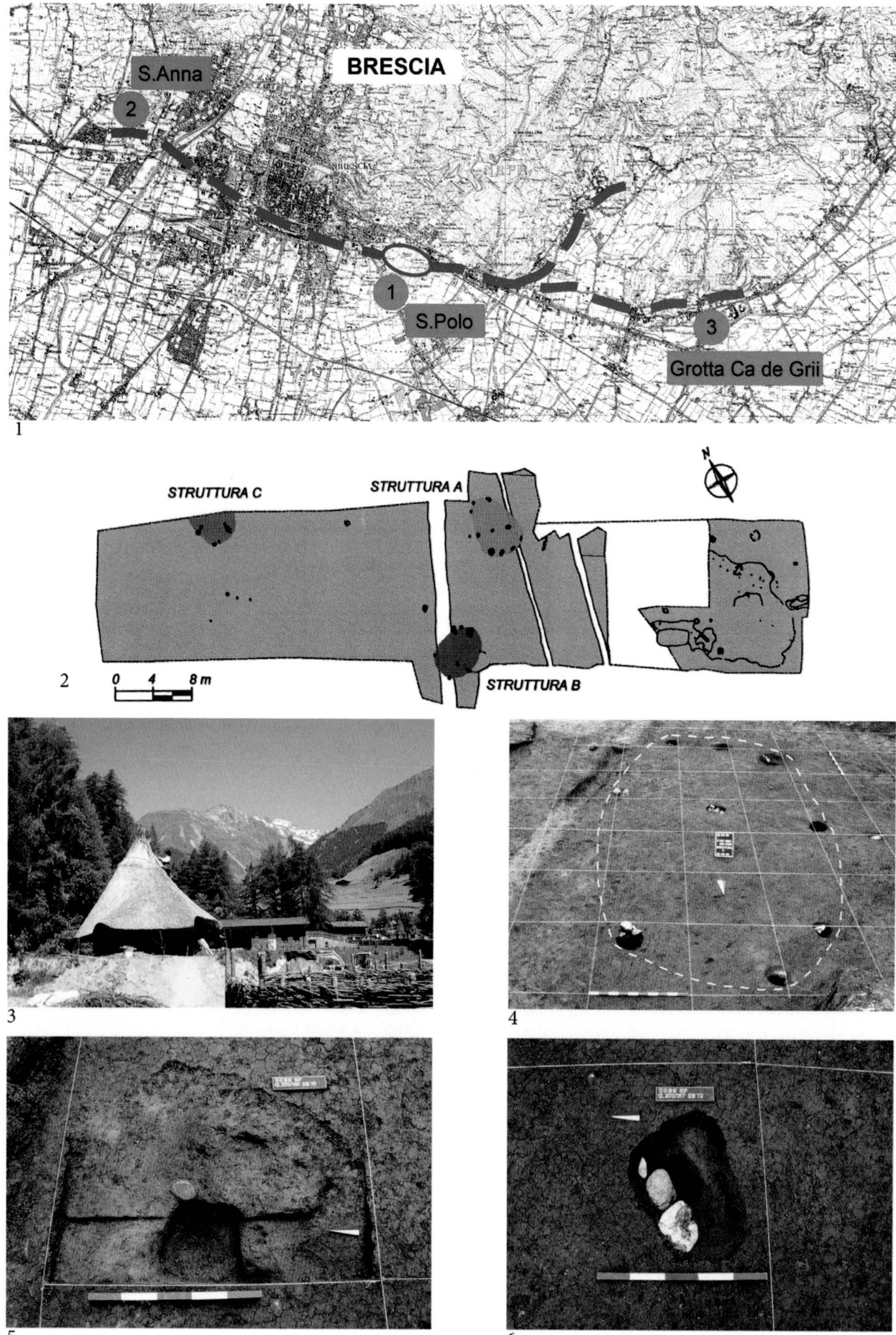

Figure 7.3: Brescia – San Polo: 1 – The settlement situated in a plain at the foot of the mountains, and its connection with other Bell Beaker sites; 2 – the excavation area containing three sub-oval houses; 3 – Reconstruction of House A in the Val Senales Archaeological Park; 4 – The post-holes defining the sub-oval plan of a house; 5 – Clay fragments; 6 – Limestone used for post-packing

antiquity however, no human skeletal remains have yet been found.

In Veneto, the highest concentration of sites occurs along the Veronese Alpine foothills, with an east–west distribution between the Adige and Chiampo valleys (Nicolis 2002). As for northern Italy in general, it is probable that most of the Veneto sites are associated with settlements and in just a few cases have buildings been found indicating the overall poverty of such structures and of the settlements themselves.

Bell Beaker Culture finds from Veneto consist above all of decorated but fragmentary pottery which makes it difficult to reconstruct shapes and decorative schemes. In general, though, the decoration seems little different from the most common patterns and 'styles' found throughout the Bell Beaker area. The decoration was produced using comb and cord impressions and incision, while 'barbelé' (barbed wire) pottery seems likely to have appeared at the end of the Bell Beaker era.

A partly sunken hut divided into four rooms was found near Gazzo Veronese – Il Cristo, and produced several Bell Beaker sherds, together with large ovoidal vases decorated with applied cordons (Salzani 1998). The association between the dry-stone hut remains found during excavations in Colombare di Negrar and the Bell Beaker pottery in the same site, is uncertain. On the basis of surface evidence only, it is possible that the settlement at Cerro Veronese – La Nasa was linked to the working and distribution of flint, given the large quantity of tools and production waste found there. However, the presence of numerous Campigny-type tools (picks and tranchets) might instead indicate that the surrounding woodland was cleared and farmed.

Emilia Romagna

The Bell Beaker presence in Emilia Romagna is better documented than in other north Italian regions and archaeological discoveries in Emilia allow certain early cultural features to be recognised, as well as later developments found in the same phases in other parts of the country, especially in Tuscany. These help us to understand the emergence of the earliest Early Bronze Age cultures.

In Emilia, a recent excavation at Strada Santa Margherita, on the south-east margin of Parma, has yielded new information which may be added to that from the Reggio Emilia sites of Rubiera and Sant'Ilario d'Enza. A 30 m long trench revealed two pits and a NE–SW aligned concentration of post-holes 0.2–0.3 m. in diameter that seemed to define rectangular buildings associated with late Bell Beaker finds (Bernabò Brea & Mazzieri 2013, 512–13). On the south-west margin of Parma, in Via Guidorossi, two Bell Beaker 'mortuary house' tombs were found, respectively containing two and three individuals. Typologically, the finds resemble those from Rubiera, whereas close parallels are not present in eastern Emilia or Tuscany. A radiocarbon date from bone (2200–1930 cal BC 95% probability) dates to the onset of the Early Bronze Age. In the same area, Parma – Via Guidorossi, structures of a single-phase settlement belonging to the pre-Beaker 'scale pottery' facies were investigated (Alfieri *et al.* 2011). The settlements of Sant'Ilario d'Enza and Rubiera were both located next to river channels and near woodland but structural evidence is scarce in both cases (Barfield *et al.* 1975; Bermond Montanari *et al.* 1982) and the small excavations do not allow the estimation of settlement size. At Sant'Ilario d'Enza the excavation covered less than 100 m² but produced two pits, some post-holes, and concentrations of grinding stones and river pebbles.

The collective evidence suggests short-lived occupation phases with woodland clearance, intense crop cultivation and animal raising. The settlements seem to have been rather unsophisticated with farming-based economies tied to extensive slash-and-burn deforestation (Cremaschi *et al.* 2011, 230).

In the Spalletti gravel pit, Montecchio Emilia, a sequence of Chalcolithic soils interleaved with alluvial deposits was recently investigated. In one of these soils, in which brush-decorated and scaled potsherds were found, a shallow subrectangular, flat-bottomed pit measuring 3.5 × 1.8 m was excavated. Although much smaller in size, this feature resembles in some respects the sunken hut dug in Gazzo Veronese – Il Cristo (Steffè *et al.* 2017). A recent discovery on the floodplain at Castenaso – Stellina, near Bologna produced three rectangular structures in the uppermost level. These were orientated NW–SE and one measured 15 × 7 m, another 12.5 × 6 m and the third was not fully excavated. The huts' perimeters were marked by posts and bedding trenches. The finds date to a fairly late Bell Beaker period (Tanaccia style) and two radiocarbon dates obtained from bone from Building 1 date to 2150–1910 and 2030–1870 cal BC (Ferrari & Steffè 2008; Cadeddu *et al.* 2011; Steffè *et al.* 2017).

In Romagna a recent excavation yielded particularly significant results at a settlement in Provezza di Cesena (Steffè *et al.* 2017) distinguished by a complex stratigraphic sequence and a detailed series of phases featuring diverse building types proving that it had been occupied for a lengthy period. The settlement was located in a wetland environment in an area crossed by two watercourses and several canals. Phase 2 of the settlement contained scaly pottery, Laterza-type pottery of southern ancestry and pottery with 'timber-frame' engravings. In Phase 3 the first Bell Beaker items appear, and show significant contacts with central Italy, especially the Florence area. The chronological framework for Phases 2–3 is provided by three radiocarbon dates: 3050–2850 cal BC, 2880–2620 cal BC, and 2840–2570 cal BC (all at 95% probability). Finds from phases 4 and 5 are predominantly typical of the late Chalcolithic/Early Bronze Age transition, occasionally with late Bell Beaker ornament present on Early Bronze Age forms. Occupation of the settlement came to an end during the first phase of the Early Bronze Age.

Phase 2 was characterised by a construction with a curved end (*alpha*) and with a ditch running round the perimeter, central weight-bearing posts and an internal hearth. There were also two other buildings (*gamma* and *delta*). In Phase 3 a complex, stable settlement was constructed, with the partial rebuilding of *alpha*. In an area that had previously been cleared and used for agricultural purposes, a large rectangular building with an apsidal end (*eta*) was erected and measured 16 × 12 m. The perimeter posts lay inside a double ditch, and the roof was supported by two large central posts. The internal hearths were sunken and bordered by stakes. A second building (*mu*) measuring 6 × 5 m. resembled the former in plan and structural details, but lacked hearths.

In Phase 4 the water-management system ceased to function due to lack of maintenance of the ditches resulting in the slow collapse of the buildings. The new buildings (*beta*, *kappa* and *nu*) all had curved ends, but were smaller than those of the preceding phase (*kappa* 7.5 × 5 m). Internal hearths were absent. By Phase 5 the ditches had filled, and hut *sigma* was built, rectangular in plan and orientated N–S, unlike the previous buildings. It measured 16 × 3.5 m, was of post construction and was divided internally by ditches. In the zone where building *eta* and the Phase 4 constructions had stood, the land was given to arable agriculture. Set in a basin crossed by watercourses, Provezza is unusual in that settlements are normally found on low hills near rivers. Here, the water flow had to be constantly controlled and the ditches kept clear. The end of water management led to the demise of the settlement itself.

Central Italy (FM, LS)

In central Italy Bell Beaker remains are mainly found on the Tyrrhenian coast and at present the major concentration lies between Versilia and the area north of the River Tiber (Fig. 7.4,A). These comprise domestic and funerary contexts both in caves and in the open. The boundaries of the 'Middle-Tyrrhenian' Bell Beaker group can be identified as the areas south of the River Po and those north of the Tiber, and follow the Apennine ridge, which forms the eastern limit. Three main areas of diffusion are distinguishable: north-western Tuscany, inland north-eastern Tuscany connected to the Bologna-Ravenna zone, and southern Tuscany and Lazio, including the Fucino basin. Each of these areas contains distinctive settlement and funerary features, and unique production traits although with common characteristics. Comparisons with the local Chalcolithic contexts show these to be similarly differentiated (Leonini & Sarti 2008a and b).

The archaeological contexts

Domestic sites are found in the area around Florence (Leonini & Sarti 2008a; Pizziolo & Sarti 2008; 2011), concentrated along the River Arno in low-lying wetland areas with the exception of Poggio La Croce and perhaps Fiesole that lie on modest elevations. In north-western Tuscany, Bell Beaker remains consist above all of burials in caves or natural recesses, and more rarely of sheltered dwelling sites, such as the La Romita di Asciano Shelter. Settlement remains are most frequently found around Florence and less so in southern Tuscany and

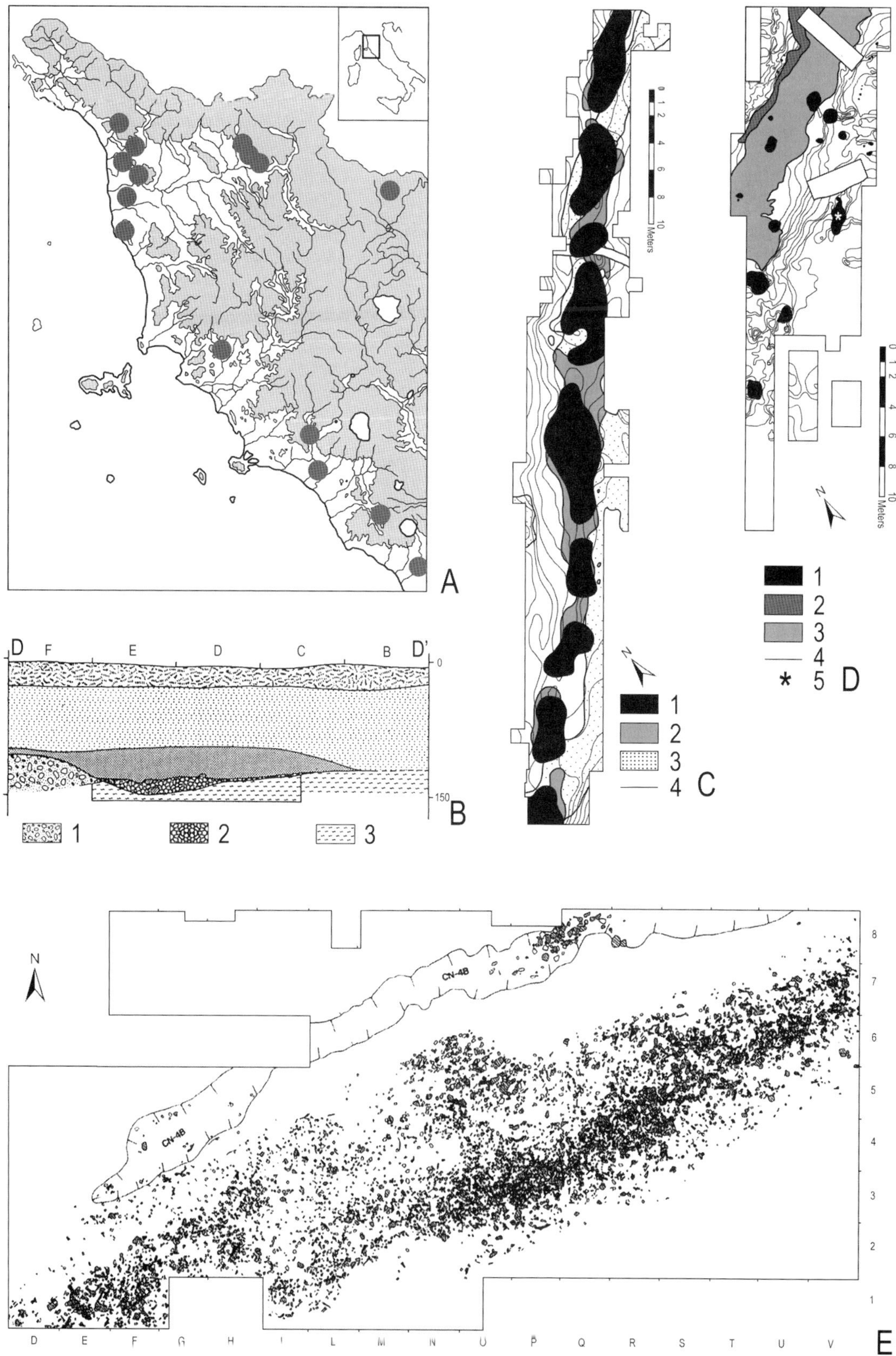

Figure 7.4: A – location of the Bell Beaker sites in Central Italy (Tuscany and Latium); B – Querciola. Stratigraphic section, 1 – Pebbles to facilitate drainage, 2 – Artificial drainage, 3 – Clay layer covering the drains of the occupation level (grey); C – Querciola: 1 – Structures, 2 – Artificial drainage, 3 – Natural drainage, 4 – Contour lines; D – Semitella, 1 – Post-holes and hollows, 2 – Small gully, 3 – Artificial drainage, 4 – Contour lines, 5 – Ox burial; E – Lastruccia 3, distribution of the archaeological remains (bones, pottery, lithic industry) on the epi-Bell Beaker occupation surface (layer 8)

Lazio. These are stratified settlement sites on both slight elevations and flat ground. A ceramic fragment from Grotta Polesini suggests that occasional visits were made to the cave. The probable identification of an Early Bell Beaker find in Lazio (Quadrato di Torre Spaccata) might indicate the wider diffusion of Evolved and Final Bell Beaker at a time when the Rinaldone facies was becoming less widespread but the scarcity of radiometric dates dictates caution.

A few sporadic instances are found on the Adriatic coast, including Apulia, where large Bell Beaker groups were absent, but there is evidence for contacts along the eastern coast of the peninsula. The Apennine peaks may have constituted a rather well-defined western boundary to Bell Beaker diffusion. It should be emphasised that recent discoveries of funerary contexts and open settlements in the eastern Po Valley seem to confirm close relations with central Italy as do rare cave sites (eg Grotta Tanaccia di Brisighella).

In central Italy, burials contain Bell Beaker objects among the grave goods, but without substantial changes in the funerary practices of local pre-Bell Beaker Chalcolithic facies (Leonini & Sarti 2006) such as collective burials in caves (Riparo La Romita di Asciano, Grotta del Fontino and Grotta Tanaccia di Brisighella in the Tuscan-Emilian Apennines). In the middle of the Rinaldonian area Beaker elements are present in the artificial cave structure at Fontanile di Raim. The local tradition of the Florence area comprises burial pits, so the barrow in Via Bruschi (where no bones were found in the partially excavated pit) was an innovative structure (Sarti *et al.* 2011). It resembles certain European contexts, especially in the Rhine-Main area where there are numerous structural and detailed similarities. At Fosso Conicchio in Lazio there is a striking cult site that exhibits Sardinian contacts, also indicated by the pottery from Grotta del Fontino.

Central Italian Bell Beaker cultural evolution and radiometric data

The evolutionary model for Bell Beakers in north-eastern Tuscany applies to the other central Italian complexes as a working hypothesis but only a limited number of radiometric measurements is available (Leonini *et al.* 2013), and multi-phase stratified sites in Tuscany and Lazio are very rare, except around Florence (Sarti 1995–6; 2004; Sarti & Martini 2001; Leonini *et al.* 2013). Nevertheless, we can identify four stages, the first representing the oldest Bell Beaker presence in the Florence area (Neto – via Verga). The local Evolved Bell Beaker constitutes stages 2 and 3 (Olmi, Ambrosetti, Querciola, Semirella, Lastruccia) and the Epi-Bell Beaker, Stage 4, sees Bell Beakers developing into the Early Bronze Age (Lastruccia, Neruda).

All available dates are for the Evolved Bell Beaker only but dates from seeds are consistent the model, in which the Olmi and Ambrosetti sites are placed at the beginning of the Evolved Bell Beaker period (2490–2200 cal BC) with Querciola being slightly later (2200–1980 cal BC both 95% probability).

The Bell Beaker Culture in Tuscany exhibits wide-ranging relationships and influences, probably involving well-known routes in those areas already linking earlier cultures. Understanding the relationships between human groups in central Italy in the various micro- and macro-areas is mainly based on pottery and lithic production and the framework employed here makes use of established interpretations (Leonini & Sarti 2008a; 2008b) supported by archaeological sequences that link pre-Beaker episodes to an evolutionary process seen in various stages of the Early Bronze Age. The most recent studies have enabled the local Evolved Bell Beaker to be examined in greater detail (Sarti 1998).

Production

The oldest local Bell Beaker evidence comes from horizon 3 at Neto – Via Verga and is related to a brief visit, rather than a stable settlement. The ceramic production is made up of small rather deep vessels with sinuous profiles, decorated with bands of close parallel comb or cord lines. Better known are the Evolved Bell Beakers, with regional styles that include a variety of characteristic pottery forms and various impressed or incised motifs organised in horizontal bands filled with dashes or triangles. Lithic production (Martini 2008) shows standardised characteristics. The pottery and lithic industries indicate relationships with, at different times, the Mediterranean area (southern France), Central and Eastern Europe (Bohemia, Moravia), and Central Europe (southern Germany and northern Austria).

The relationship between the Bell Beaker and preceding Chalcolithic facies around Florence is complex. Ceramic and lithic production in the early Bell Beaker phases demonstrates a break with the previous traditions but subsequently local traditions appear in the lithics and in the common-ware pottery (Leonini 2004; Leonini & Sarti 2008a). These are also associated with forms linked to Western European Bell Beaker elements. As far as settlements in the Florence area are concerned, although some sites have Chalcolithic layers and stratigraphically later Bell Beaker deposits, the Evolved Bell Beaker building types appear to be innovative features that continue into the Bronze Age (Sarti & Martini 2001; Pizziolo & Sarti 2008).

Metallurgy in the Florence area, as in other parts of central Italy, was present at the beginning of the 4th millennium BC (Leonini *et al.* 2013; Sarti 2014). A few finished artefacts and limited traces of metalworking have been found in Middle Chalcolithic residential areas (second half of the 4th millennium), associated with more varied Bell Beaker artefacts. In the Via Bruschi burial mound some animal bones have butchering marks from metal artefacts (Mascaro *et al.* 2012).

Bell Beaker settlements

The most data for domestic activity in central Italy come from the Florence area, and Evolved Bell Beaker settlement strategies. The first evidence, from Neto – Via Verga, consists of a simple ephemeral structure. In the Lazio area (as in Emilia Romagna, not far from Tuscany) the settlement models seem to be the same as in the previous period. The recurring and innovative aspect of Bell Beaker settlements is the building of simple, slightly sunken structures, as in some earlier periods, but exploiting palaeostreams in an almost systematic manner, and especially using secondary channels rather than the main river course. Activity areas were created and drained using pebbles mixed with ceramic fragments and faunal remains. The hypothetical workspaces and structures probably had light roofs, and were sometimes rebuilt on the same sites (Pizziolo & Sarti 2011).

In some settlements (Lastruccia, Olmi, Querciola-Semitella-Campo del Sorgo) large-scale excavation has uncovered various forms of settlement organisation but with a preference for the same palaeostream exploitation (Fig. 7.4,B). Marginal, even isolated, areas (possible secondary and satellite zones), hosted functional structures (Sarti 2014) (Fig. 7.4,C & D). Settlements seem to have been occupied continuously and future research may well demonstrate continuous evolution within a more detailed and refined chronological model.

Some large Evolved Bell Beaker settlements, such as that of Lastruccia (3200 m^2 excavated stratigraphically of a potential area of 31,000 m^2), seem to indicate that palaeostream exploitation lasted for a long period of time, involving repeated and readapted systems (Fig. 7.4,E). The large settlements became reference points in the territory and tended to become permanent. The initial settlers seem to have selected slightly higher ground now under alluvium as a result of the river dynamics in the Florence plain.

When trying to analyse the internal organisation of the settlements we have assumed that the roofed structures are not easily identifiable and have left little trace. They have been reconstructed on the basis of the distribution of post-holes (though these are not always present) (Fig. 7.6,1), the concentration and typology of finds, and the presence of hearths or other cut features such as ditches, wells and pits. However, at the Evolved Bell Beaker sites of Querciola and Semitella, the layout of the inhabited space is better understood.

At Querciola the structures are elliptical in shape, more or less regular, and form three size groups: one structure of over 20 m^2 (area E), five structures covering 10–16 m^2 (areas A, B, D, G, H), and two structures of 5–6 m^2 (areas C and F). The width seems to be standardised at between 2 and 4 m. The settlement would have been made up of several close nuclei, arranged neatly along the palaeostream. There seem to have been two more important areas recognised by their larger area, increased density of finds (Fig. 7.6,2), and their more elaborately constructed hearths. At Semitella, only one large dwelling was investigated, which abutted an outside living area (Fig. 7.5,1 & 2). The presence of a covered surface is inferred mainly by the number of post-holes, which are more or less equidistant from a wide, deep central hole: a conical roofed structure is envisaged but full details are not currently available. Of particular interest is the inclusion

1

2

Figure 7.5: Semitella: 1 – view of the excavation;. 2 – View of a large hollow

Figure 7.6: 1, 2 – Querciola; post-holes and the Bell Beaker occupation surface; 3 – Lastruccia 3, layer 8; 4 – Lastruccia 3, layer 8, palaeostream and stratigraphic section

in the settlement of the inhumation of a bovine, located in the northern zone outside the structure. In the same area numerous other animal bones were present, sometimes partially articulated suggesting a slaughtering area.

The most significant Epi-Bell Beaker settlements are those of Lastruccia, Fosso di Lumino and Termine East. In this final Bell Beaker phase the same construction methods were maintained, sited by palaeostreams and with stone, gravel, pot and bone fragments drainage facilities. The largest settlements were sited alongside several palaeostreams. The concentrations of material interpreted as the remains of buildings are well defined, with considerably elongated elliptical shapes aligned on the nearby riverbeds. The use of small ditches around the structures continues but adjacent pits and small ditches seem to be less numerous.

The Lastruccia 2 structure measures 15 × 5 m and of the two other distinct structures found, one measured more than 8 × *c.* 4 m while the second was only partially excavated. Lastruccia 1 and 3 and Termine East demonstrate the stratigraphic overlap of several Bell Beaker and Epi-Bell Beaker phases in the use of the same palaeostreams over time, even when these appear to have been practically blocked. The various phases of re-use of these sites in the Early Bronze Age were followed by periods of abandonment linked to flooding episodes that sealed the different occupation horizons with layers of silt. Dwellings were refurbished with new flooring surfaces within the same palaeostream. Later modest drainage structures connected to slightly sunken structures are also found in the early Middle Bronze Age. At Petrosa, for example, at Lastruccia 1 – horizon C and at Val di Rose (Sarti, unpublished data), the dwelling area is located near, but not within, a palaeostream. This palaeostream utilisation began with the Evolved Bell Beaker, continued in the Epi-Bell Beaker (the initial Early Bronze age), was weaker in the later Early Bronze Age, and was definitively abandoned at the beginning of the Middle Bronze Age.

Settlements and the environment

The considerable number of variously sized Evolved Bell Beaker settlements might point to an increase in population density from the middle of the 3rd millennium BC to the beginning of the 2nd millennium BC. Palaeobotanical studies indicate a populated landscape with plants indicative of disturbed environments. The accumulation of organic and inorganic remains seems to indicate deforestation, probably for expanding agriculture. The production of cereals seems to have increased, combined with the collection of wild plants (partly for animal feed) and the use of *Vitis vinifera,* features which suggest that these settlements were long-lived (Carra 2008).

Sheep and goats were the animals exploited most in the pre-Bell Beaker Chalcolithic and cattle were only minimally present. During the Evolved Bell Beaker cattle were more common with an increase in pig raising. Hunting (wild boar, roe and other deer) remained a supplementary activity. The Bell Beaker period saw the reintroduction of the horse (rare remains from the Querciola site) as a result of external contacts and perhaps also social changes (Perusin *et al.* 2008).

The Bell Beaker Culture exploited existing supply areas as, for example, for the raw materials for pottery manufacture (these come from the ophiolite areas, not far from the sites, where there are also copper ores), and some local rock types used for stone tools (Agostini *et al.* 2008). Artefacts made of imported materials (eg, 'Scaglia rossa'), which arrived as finished or semi-finished products are also found (Martini *et al.* 2006).

The reasons for the consolidation of the Evolved Bell Beaker Culture in the central Tyrrhenian area may have been multiple. The local landscape may have had an important role as it included large well-watered valleys and plains with rivers connecting to the sea. It had estuarine landing areas that facilitated penetration into areas with potential for mining, and it had easy north–south communication routes, and eastward paths, which had already been utilised in previous periods. The Tyrrhenian Bell Beaker evidence must be evaluated in the context of relations between the central-northern Tyrrhenian area and the surrounding regions in various periods of prehistory. Since the 5th millennium, southern Tuscany and the Lazio region had played an active role in adopting and reworking cultural elements from southern Italy, which became more evident during the Chalcolithic. The entire Florence plain appears to have constituted a privileged communication route. Hypothetical routes would have run along the Arno Valley, both towards Pisa and Versilia (lower Valdarno) and towards the Tiber Valley (Upper Valdarno); the Apennine area linked up with the Emilia area. This framework supports the interpretation that sees the spread of the Bell Beaker Culture as having been associated with the development of a network of pre-existing relationships (Salanova 2005). Subsequently, in some cases only, Bell Beaker growth appears connected to the emergence of new traditions and the social systems of the Early Bronze Age.

Conclusions

From this overview for northern Italy, it can be seen that it is difficult to define Bell Beaker settlements precisely. For example, in long-lived terraced sites the Bell Beaker period continues previous traditions, both in house forms and village organisation. The only common element is the poor preservation of the archaeological evidence, perhaps attesting the presence of less substantial houses. The most authentically Bell Beaker characteristics are more evident in single-phased lowland sites, especially now that large pre-Bell Beaker villages of very different forms have started to come to light, as at Parma – Via Guidorossi (Alfieri *et al.* 2011).

In central Italy Bell Beaker settlements, funerary structures, pottery, worked stone and metal production indicate that diverse cultural dynamics were combined, from both pre-Bell Beaker and Early Bronze Age traditions. Thus Bell Beaker elements were occasionally introduced into local traditional contexts (funerary practices in north-western Tuscany), and Bell Beaker groups changed over time.

In the region of Florence, the Bell Beaker Culture has a local style which lasted until the Epi-Bell Beaker Early Bronze Age (late 3rd millennium), as seen in artefact production, settlements, and funerary rites. More is known about the later developments when artefacts exhibit regionally distinct characteristics representing modifications of the preceding Chalcolithic traditions. The use of landscape and local resources also had traditional bases. The Florence area had long had inter-regional contacts with northern and southern Italy and also Sardinia but in the Bell Beaker period it expanded to a European network, confirming its role as a communication hub that was maintained until historical times. The Florence area's high Bell Beaker population density may be explained by its favourable geographical position for north–south and east–west communications, together with its natural resources (wetlands, open areas, useful minerals).

In southern Tuscany and Lazio the more scarce data point to the presence of Bell Beaker groups who were in contact with inland northern Tuscany. The eastern Emilia area (northern Italy) was well connected with central Italy during the Bell Beaker Culture, and also in pre-Bell Beaker Chalcolithic.

Acknowledgements

We thank Jim Bishop for the partial translation of the text.

References

Agostini, L., Briani, F., Pallecchi, P. & Sarti, L. 2008. Notes about Bell Beaker pottery raw material in Sesto Fiorentino (Florence). In Baioni *et al.* 2008, 81–7

Alfieri, A., Bernabò Brea, M., Bronzoni, L. & Mazzieri, P. 2011. L'insediamento eneolitico di via Guidorossi a Parma, *Atti della XLIII Riunione Scientifica IIPP*, 593–604

Baioni, M., Leonini, V., Lo Vetro, D., Martini, F., Poggiani Keller, R. & Sarti, L. (eds), 2008. Bell Beaker in everyday life, Proceedings of the 10th Meeting 'Archéologie et Gobelets' (Florence – Siena – Villanuova sul Clisi, May 12–15, 2006), *Millenni* 6, Firenze

Baioni, M. & Poggiani Keller, R. 2008. Bell Beakers in Lombardy: sites and settlement strategies. In Baioni *et al.* 2008, 151–70

Banchieri, D. G. 1988. L'eneolitico delle prealpi varesine, *Atti Congresso Internazionale 'L'età del Rame in Europa'*, Viareggio 1987, *Rassegna di Archeologia* 7, 626–7

Barfield, L.H. 1977. The Beaker Culture in Italy. In R. Mercer (ed.), *Beakers in Britain and Europe: Four Studies*, 27–49. Oxford: British Archaeological Reports Supplementary Series 26

Barfield, L. H. 1998. I siti campaniformi del Garda occidentale. In Nicolis & Mottes (eds), 1998, 80–2

Barfield, L. H. 2006. Villanuova sul Clisi (BS) – Ponte Pier. Sito Pluristratificato con sepoltura, *Annali del Museo* (2003–2006) 20, 117–19. Gavardo

Barfield, L. H. & Borrello, M.A. 2006. Manerba del Garda (BS). Località Rocca, Sopra Sasso e Riparo Valtenesi, *Annali del Museo* (2003–2006) 20, 69–77. Gavardo

Barfield, L.H., Borrello, M.A., Buteux, S. & Ciaraldi, M. 2002. Scavi preistorici sulla Rocca di Manerba, Brescia, In Ferrari, A. & Visentini, P. (eds), *Il declino del mondo neolitico. Ricerche in Italia centro-settentrionale fra aspetti peninsulari, occidentali e nord-alpini*, Atti del Convegno (Pordenone, 2001), *Quaderni del Museo Archeologico del Friuli Occidentale* 4, 291–309

Barfield, L.H., Cremaschi, M. & Castelletti, L. 1975. Stanziamento del vaso campaniforme a Sant'Ilario d'Enza (Reggio Emilia), *Preistoria Alpina* 11, 155––99

Bermond Montanari, G., Cremaschi, M. & Sala, B. 1982. Rubiera: insediamento del vaso campaniforme, *Preistoria Alpina* 18, 79–109

Bernabò Brea, M. & Mazzieri, P. 2013. Nuovi dati sul campaniforme in Emilia. In De Marinis R.C. (ed.), *L'Età del Rame. La pianura padana e le alpi al tempo di Ötzi*, 503–24. Brescia

Biagi, P. & Marchello, G. 1970. Scavi nella cavernetta Cà dei Grii (Virle-Brescia), *Rivista di Scienze Preistoriche* XXV 1, 253–99

Cadeddu, F., Dalla Casa, G., Ferrari, A., Lucianetti, M. & Steffè, G. 2011, Strutture abitative di età tardocampaniforme a Castenaso (Bologna), *Atti della XLIII Riunione Scientifica IIPP*, 633–7

Carra, M. 2008. Plant Macroremains from Olmi 1 (Sesto Fiorentino, Florence). Preliminary study. In Baioni *et al.* 2008, 59–66

Cremaschi, M., Nicosia, C. & Salvioni, M. 2011, L'uso del suolo nell'Eneolitico e nel Bronzo antico, nuovi dati dalla Pianura Padana centrale, Atti della XLIII Riunione Scientifica *IIPP*, 225–31

De Stefani, M. 2016. L'insediamento campaniforme di Campo Musna 1, 2 e 3 tra età del Rame e Bronzo Antico. In Fortunati & Poggiani Keller 2016, 69–70

Fedele, F. (ed.), 2003. Ricerche archeologiche al castello di Breno, Valcamonica. I. Notizie generali. Ceramica neolitica e calcolitica, *Notizie Archeologiche Bergomensi* (2000) 8

Ferrari, A. & Steffè, G. 2008. Castenaso (Bologna), Stellina Area. In Baioni *et al.* 2008, 379–83

Fortunati, M. & Poggiani Keller., R. (eds.), 2016, *Dal Serio al Cherio. Ricerche archeologiche lungo il canale di irrigazione del Consorzio di Bonifica della Media Pianura Bergamasca, 2005–2009*, Bergamo

Fugazzola Delpino, M. A. & Pellegrini E. 1998. Presenze 'campaniformi' nell'Italia centro-meridionale. In Nicolis & Mottes (eds), 1998, 155–60

Leonini, V., 2004. La ceramique domestique du Campaniforme de l'Italie centrale et Septentrionale. In J. Czebreszuk (ed.), *Similar but different. Bell Beakers in Europe*, 149–72. Poznan: Adam Mickiewicz University

Leonini, V. & Sarti, L. 2006. Sepolture e rituali funerari nell'Eneolitico e al passaggio del Bronzo in Italia. In F. Martini (ed.), *La cultura del morire nelle società preistoriche e protostoriche italiane. Dal Paleolitico all'età del Rame*, 129–60, Origines, Progetti 3, Firenze

Leonini, V. & Sarti, L. 2008a. Bell Beaker pottery in the Florentine area. In Baioni *et al.* 2008, 87–102

Leonini, V. & Sarti, L. 2008b. Bell Beaker pottery in Central Italy. In Baioni *et al.* 2008, 119–28

Leonini, V., Sarti, L. & Volante, N. 2013. La cronologia dell'Età del Rame in area fiorentina nel quadro dell'Italia centrale tirrenica. Stato dell'arte e nuove datazioni. In Cocchi Genick, D. (ed.), *Cronologia assoluta e relativa dell'età del Rame in Italia*, 67–80, Preistoria e Protostoria, 1, Verona: QuiEdit

Maggi, R. 1998, 1-Storia della Liguria fra 3.600 e 2.300 anni Avanti Cristo (Età del Rame). In Del Lucchese, A., & Maggi, R. (eds.), *Dal diaspro al bronzo. L'Età del rame e del Bronzo in Liguria: 26 secoli di storia fra 3600 e 1000 anni Avanti Cristo*, 7–28. La Spezia: Luna Editore

Martini, F. 2008. Bell Beaker lithic industries in the Florentine area. In Baioni *et al.* 2008, 103–19

Martini, F., Ghinassi, M. & Moranduzzo, B. 2006, Caratterizzazione degli areali e modalità di raccolta della materia prima litica in area fiorentina dal Paleolitico all'età del Bronzo. In *Materie prime e scambi nella preistoria italiana: nel cinquantenario della fondazione dell'Istituto italiano di Preistoria e Protostoria,* Atti XXXIX Riunione Scientifica Istituto Italiano di Preistoria e Protostoria, 299–314, Firenze 2004

Mascaro, I., Perusin, S. & Sarti, L. 2012. La 'quotidianità' del metallo: analisi al SEM delle tracce di macellazione dei reperti faunistici del sito campaniforme di Via Bruschi a Sesto Fiorentino. In De Grossi Mazzorin, J., Saccà, D. & Tozzi, C. (eds), Atti 6°Conv. Naz. Archeozoologia, 7–9, 2009, Lucca

Nicolis, F. 1998. Alla periferia dell'impero: il bicchiere campaniforme nell'Italia settentrionale. In Nicolis, Mottes 1998, 47–67

Nicolis, F. 2001a. Some observations on the cultural setting of the Bell Beakers of northern Italy. In Nicolis, F. (ed.) *Bell Beakers today. Pottery, people, culture, symbols in prehistoric Europe.* Proceedings of the International Colloquium, Riva del Garda, 11–16 May 1988, Vol II, 207–227. Trento

Nicolis, F. 2001b. *Il fenomeno del bicchiere campaniforme tra età del Rame e età del Bronzo*, Lanzinger M., Marzatico F., Pedrotti A. (eds.), *Storia del Trentino. I. La preistoria e la protostoria*, Il Mulino, 255–83. Bologna

Nicolis, F. 2002, *Il fenomeno del bicchiere campaniforme nel Veneto*, in Aspes A., (ed.), *Preistoria veronese. Contributi e aggiornamenti*, Memorie del Museo Civico di Storia Naturale di Verona, 2a serie, Sezione Scienze dell'Uomo, 5, 98–101

Nicolis, F. & Mottes, E. (eds.) 1998. *Simbolo ed Enigma. Il Bicchiere campaniforme e l'Italia nella preistoria europea del III millennio a.C.*, Catalogo mostra, Trento

Perusin, S., Di Giuseppe, Z., Corridi, C. & Mazza, P. 2008. The Sesto Fiorentino Fauna. Subsistence strategies from the late third millennium to the early second millennium BC: preliminary data. In Baioni *et al.* 2008, 67–74

Pizziolo, G. & Sarti, L. 2008. Prehistoric landscape, peopling process and Bell Beaker settlements in the Florentine area. In Baioni *et al.* 2008, 39–59

Pizziolo, G. & Sarti, L. 2011. A prehistoric hidden landscape in an alluvial plain. Investigations in the Florentine area. In M. Leusen van, G. Pizziolo, L. Sarti (eds), Hidden Landscapes of Mediterranean Europe, 17–27, Oxford: British Archaeological Reports International Series 2320

Poggiani Keller, R. 1998. Trescore Balneario (Bergamo). Il sito del Canton tra Neolitico VBQ e Campaniforme. In Nicolis, Mottes 1998, 87–91

Poggiani Keller, R. 2000. Lovere (Bergamo): una sequenza stratigrafica esemplare dal Neolitico Antico al Bronzo Finale in area prealpina, Rivista di Scienze Preistoriche L (1999–2000), 261–95

Poggiani Keller, R. 2004. Il sito del Canton di Trescore Balneario (BG) fra Neolitico medio ed età del Rame. In E. Bianchin Citton (ed.), *L'area funeraria e cultuale dell'età del Rame di Sovizzo nel contesto archeologico dell'Italia settentrionale*, Quaderni di Archeologia Vicentina, 1, 103–22. Vicenza: Museo Naturalistico Archeologico

Poggiani Keller, R. 2006a. Cividate Camuno – Via Palazzo. Malegno – Via Cavour (Valle Camonica – BS). Abitato pluristratificato dal Neolitico Medio/Recente ad Epoca Romana. Annali del Museo, 20 (2003–2006), 149–54

Poggiani Keller, R. 2006b. Trescore Balneario (BG) – Canton. Insediamento pluristratificato dal Neolitico VBQ al Campaniforme. Annali del Museo, 20 (2003–2006), 179–99

Poggiani Keller, R. 2016. I reperti ceramici. In Fortunati, Poggiani Keller 2016, 71–6

Poggiani Keller, R. & Baioni, M. 2008. The Bell Beaker at Monte Covolo: structures and decorated pottery. In Baioni *et al.* 2008, 171–82

Poggiani Keller, R., Degasperi, N., Piancastelli, M. & Simonotti, F. 1998, Il sito campaniforme di Brescia-S. Polo. In Nicolis, Mottes 1998, 83–6

Poggiani Keller, R., Baioni, M., Leonini, V. & Lo Vetro, D. 2006a. Villanuova sul Clisi (BS) – Monte Covolo. Insediamento pluristratificato dal Neolitico tardo alla Media età del Bronzo. *Annali del Museo* 20 (2003–2006), 79–115. Gavardo

Poggiani Keller, R., Castiglioni, E. & Leonini, V. 2006b. Lovere (BG) – Colle del Lazzaretto, via Decio Celeri. Insediamento pluristratificato dal Neolitico tardo/prima età del Rame al Bronzo Finale. *Annali del Museo* 20 (2003–2006), 155–77

Poggiani Keller, R., Cottini, M., Fusco, V., Leonini, V., Massari, A. & Simonotti, F. 2006c. Brescia – S. Polo. Abitato campaniforme. *Annali del Museo* 20 (2003–2006), 121–48

Salanova, L. 2005. The origins of the Bell Beaker phenomenon: breakdown analysis mapping. In Rojo-Guerra, M.A., Garrido-Pena, R. & Garcia-Martínez de Lagrán I. (eds), 2005. *Bell Beakers in the Iberian Peninsula and their European Context,* 19–28. Valladolid: Universidad de Valladolid

Salzani, L. 1998, *Capanna dell'età del rame a Gazzo Veronese*, in Nicolis & Mottes 1998, 77–9

Sannella, A. 1998. *Testimonianze campaniformi a Solero località Cascina Urbana*, Atti della XXXII Riunione Scientifica dell'IIPP, 167–79

Sarti, L. 1995–96. Cronostratigrafia del Campaniforme in area fiorentina. Dati preliminari dall'insediamento di Lastruccia. 239–60. Firenze: *Rivista di Scienze Preistoriche* XLVII

Sarti, L. 1998. Aspetti insediativi del Campaniforme nell'Italia Centrale. In Nicolis & Mottes 1998, 136–53

Sarti, L. 2004. L'Epicampaniforme en Italie Centrale: stratigraphie, datations radiométriques, productions lithiques et céramiques. In J. Czebreszuk (ed.) *Similar but different. Bell Beaker in Europe,* 205–22. Poznan: Adam Mickiewicz University

Sarti, L. 2014. Archeologia preistorica in area fiorentina: ricerche, documenti, ricostruzione storica. In G. Poggesi & L. Sarti (eds.), Passaggi a Nord-Ovest. 35–80. Firenze: Millenni 10

Sarti, L., Fenu, P., Leonini, V., Martini, F., Perusin, S. & Zannoni, M. 2011. The Bell Beaker mound in Via Bruschi-Sesto Fiorentino (Florence, Tuscany). New research. In E. La Borgna & S. Muller Celka (eds). *Ancestral Landscapes: burial mounds in the Copper and Bronze ages, Central and Eastern Europe-Balkans-Adriatic-Aegean, 4th–2th millennium BC.* Proceedings of the International Conference, 231–38. Lyon: Série Recherches Archéologiques, 58

Sarti, L. & Martini, F. 2001. Strategie insediative del Campaniforme nell'Italia centrale tirrenica. In Nicolis, F. (ed.) 2001, 187–98

Steffè, G., Bernabò Brea, M. & Miari, M. 2017. L'Eneolitico dell'Emilia Romagna. In Bernadò Brea (ed.) 2017. Preistoria e Protostoria dell'Emilia Romagna – I. IIPP, Firenze, pp. 139–58

8

Continuity or rupture? Investigating domestic structures during the Final Neolithic and the Bell Beaker culture in central-eastern France and western Switzerland

Marie Besse, Eve Derenne, Lucas Anchieri, Aude Baumberger, Antoine Caminada and Martine Piguet

The region comprising central-eastern France and western Switzerland is particularly interesting when considering the transition between the final Neolithic and Bell Beaker periods, around 2500 BC. Indeed, the modalities of this transition are diverse, and depend on whether one observes domestic or funerary structures, technical expertise, economic networks, ideologies, or population movements. These are the many nuances that one must take into account when adopting a holistic approach to Neolithic societies. In this research, the authors identified over a hundred Bell Beaker sites, from tenuous traces to domestic architecture, from isolated objects to funeral complexes. Only sites with domestic structures definitely attributed to the Bell Beaker culture are considered here. We will attempt to understand the modalities of the final Neolithic to Bell Beaker transition through the perspective of domestic structures and their function and roles within the landscape. First, domestic structures belonging to the final Neolithic are presented, followed by those associated with Bell Beakers, and concluding with a synthesis of the observations made on the importance of the Neolithic substrate in the establishment of the Bell Beaker culture.

Before the Bell Beaker culture: central-eastern France and western Switzerland

In central-eastern France and western Switzerland the final Neolithic phase, preceding the Bell Beaker culture, was characterised by six cultural groups (Fig. 8.1), 'Chassey niveau 5', Saône Group, Chalain Group, Auvernier-Cordé, 'Néolithique final valaisan' and Lüscherz. They are presented here, following their geographical location from west to east.

The 'Chassey niveau 5' Final Neolithic

The 'Chassey niveau 5' Final Neolithic

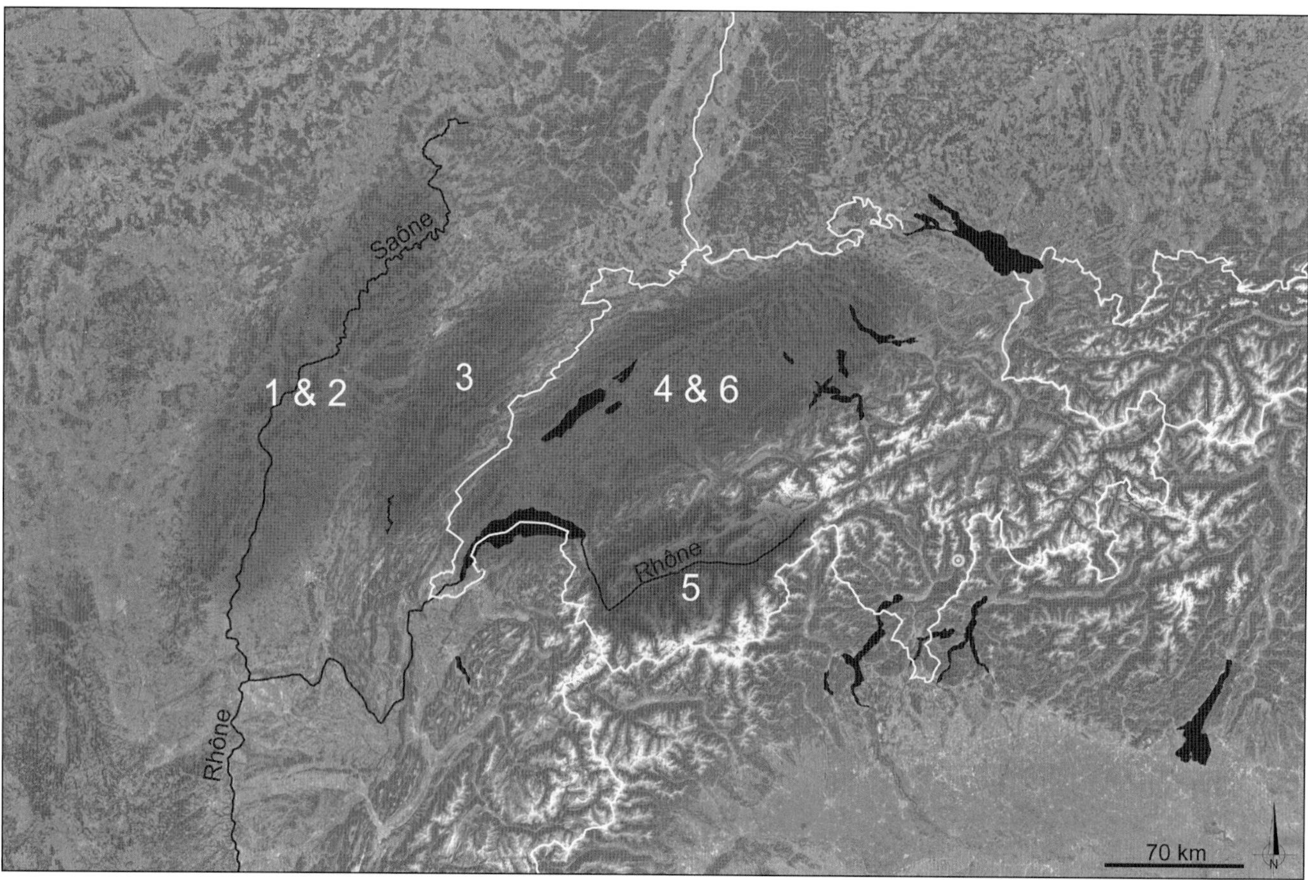

Figure 8.1: Location map of the pre-Bell Beaker cultures of central-eastern France and western Switzerland. 1 – 'Chassey niveau 5' Final Neolithic; 2 – Saône group; 3 – Chalain group; 4 – Auvernier-Cordé; 5 – Néolithique final valaisan; 6 – Lüscherz

(Fig. 8.1,1) lasted between *c.* 3000–2400 cal BC (Thevenot *et al.* 2015), although some researchers narrow its time span to 2800–2350 cal BC (Lemercier *et al.* 2015). Most of the sites linked to this culture are found on the limestone hills located alongside the Saône valley, between the Dijon and Mâcon regions (Thevenot *et al.* 2015).

To this day, very little is known about the architecture and organisation of 'Chassey niveau 5' settlements. Even the eponymous fifth level of Chassey-le-Camp 'La Redoute' site only revealed scarce traces of structures. These included two post-holes and fragments of burnt daub with wattle impressions but no structure plan could be reconstructed (Thevenot 2005). The lithic assemblages linked to this group revealed contacts with northern and central France, as some raw materials have been proven to have come from the Grand-Pressigny, Berry, Oise valley and Sens regions (Thevenot *et al.* 2015). The majority of the pottery has rounded rims and open forms including hemispherical vases (some with a carination) and more cylindrical forms with a flattened base. Oval-shaped lugs were quite common (Thevenot 2005).

Saône Group – Saône drainage basin (F)

The Saône group (Fig. 8.1,2) appeared around 2900–2800 BC and lasted until 2400–2300 BC (Thevenot *et al.* 2015). The settlement sites attributed to this group were mostly located on river banks, close to fords, tributaries or small islands, but it appears that they were not pile dwellings (Jeunesse *et al.* 1998; Thevenot *et al.* 2015). As with 'Chassey niveau 5' their architecture is almost unknown (Lemercier *et al.* 2015) although a few rectangular structures have been identified at Ouroux-sur-Saône 'Le Grand Bois'/'Le Taillis', the main archaeological site for this group (Thevenot *et al.* 2015).

Southern influences can be observed in the lithic assemblages, in the form of diamond-shaped arrowheads with lateral indentations. Other lithic types such as barbed and tanged arrowheads and Grand-Pressigny daggers, have been found in Saône group sites and indicate contacts with Bell Beaker groups

(Jeunesse *et al.* 1998). In terms of pottery, the assemblages mostly have cylindrical shapes with open mouths, rounded bases, and horizontal lugs (Jeunesse *et al.* 1998; Thevenot *et al.* 2015).

Chalain Group – western Jura plateaux (F)

Sites from the Chalain group (Fig. 8.1,3) date from 2700–2650 BC to around 2400 BC (Giligny *et al.* 1995). These pile dwellings were situated on the shores of Lakes Chalain and Clairvaux in the Jura (Pétrequin 1998). The three typical sites for this group are Clairvaux III, La Motte-aux-Magnins (Clairvaux-les-Lacs), and Chalain 2 Fontenu (Jeunesse *et al.* 1998). The material culture from these sites revealed a cultural background rooted in the preceding Clairvaux group, as well as influences from the Auvernier-Cordé group (see below) (Giligny *et al.* 1995; Pétrequin 1998).

The architecture of Chalain settlement structures is well-preserved thanks to their location in wetland areas. The rectangular houses, of around 8 × 4 m, were built on three rows of piles and had raised floors (Jeunesse *et al.* 1998). The associated lithic assemblages are diverse, with 14 types of arrowheads, the two most frequent being diamond-shaped with an elongated tang, and the second a larger arrowhead with short barbs, both of which are linked to the preceding Clairvaux group. Auvernier-Cordé influences are most clear in the pottery assemblages, with rounded- or flat- based jars with horizontal lugs decorated with a smooth or impressed cordon (Giligny *et al.* 1995; Jeunesse *et al.* 1998).

Auvernier-Cordé – western Swiss plateau (CH)

The Auvernier-Cordé culture (Fig. 8.1,4) appeared around 2700 BC in the Trois-Lacs region, in the western part of the Swiss Plateau (Pétrequin 1998). The pile dwellings that make up the majority of sites concentrated on lake shores and some bays appeared to have been occupied by several villages at the same time (Arnold 2012). Like the Chalain settlements on the western side of the Jura mountains, Auvernier-Cordé villages are particularly well preserved and the house plans and architecture are almost identical to the Chalain group with the rectangular structures supported by three rows of piles and with raised floors (Winiger 2008; Arnold 2012). The houses were built on both sides of a central wooden walkway with several perpendicular rows running off. The villages themselves, located in floodplains, were often enclosed by fences (Winiger 2008) and the most iconic settlement was discovered in Concise 'Sous-Colachoz' (Vaud) (Winiger 2008).

Auvernier-Cordé pottery is characterised by Lüscherz roots (see below) and influences from the Corded Ware Culture (Pétrequin 1998) and comprises in particular hemispherical vases (Giligny *et al.* 1995).

'Néolithique final valaisan' – Upper Rhône Valley (CH)

The fifth cultural group in our research area, the 'Néolithique final valaisan' (Fig. 8.1,5), existed from *c.* 3300–2500 cal BC (Besse 2012) and was present in the Upper Rhône Valley (Valais and Vaud, CH). Settlements were established below 1000 m on small hills alongside the Rhône, or on alluvial fans as at Collombey-Muraz 'Barmaz I', Savièse 'Château de la Soie', Sion 'La Gilière' and 'Sous-le-Scex', Saint-Léonard 'Les Champlans', and Bramois 'immeuble Pranoé D' (Mottet *et al.* 2011).

Few of these sites have produced structural remains, the exception being Bramois 'Immeuble Pranoé D', where sub-rectangular, partly subterranean houses were discovered. Lithic assemblages mostly comprise imported flint and the most frequent pottery type is a cylindrical or slightly barrel-shaped vase with horizontal lugs and a smooth cordon (Mottet *et al.* 2011).

Lüscherz – western Switzerland

The final group was the Lüscherz (Fig. 8.1,6), which spanned the period 2900–2700 BC (Stöckli 1995). Settlements from this group were located in Western Switzerland and were mainly pile dwellings. The main sites are at Auvernier ('Port', 'Tenevières', 'Ruz Chatru', 'Brise-Lames', 'La Saunerie'), Concise 'Sous-Colachoz', Delley 'Portalban II', Genève 'Parc la Grange', Saint-Blaise 'Bain-des-Dames', Thielle-Wavre 'Pont-de-Thielle', Vinelz 'Strandboden' and Yverdon 'Avenue des Sports' (Pugin & Corboud 2006).

The architecture is characterised by rectangular houses built on three rows of piles, their longest side parallel to the lakeshore. The known examples from Delley 'Portalban II' had a standard width of 4 m, while their

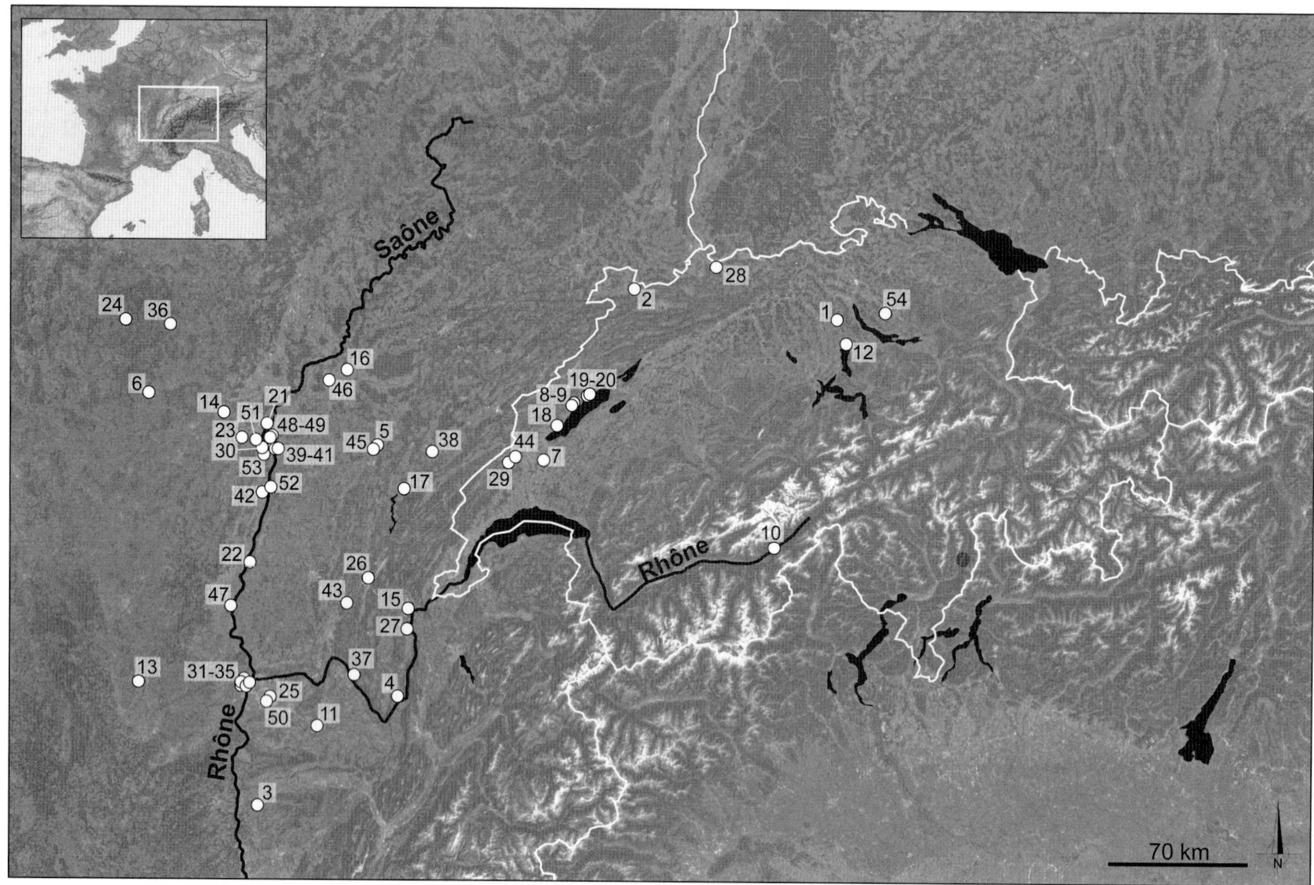

Figure 8.2: Location map of the Bell Beaker settlements of central-eastern France and western Switzerland. The numbers refer to Table 8.1

length could vary between 10–20 m (Danérol *et al.* 1991). The later Chalain and Auvernier-Cordé groups used similar building techniques.

Lüscherz lithic assemblages were the first in Switzerland in which Grand-Pressigny flint was found showing clear links with central France (Stöckli 1995). Most of the arrowheads are diamond-shaped (Pugin & Corboud 2006) whilst most of the pottery consists of cylindrical-shaped vessels with a round or slightly flattened base. Decoration includes small buttons and lugs, sometimes accompanied by smooth cordons (Giligny & Michel 1995).

The Bell Beaker culture in central-eastern France and western Switzerland

Within this study area, the Bell Beaker culture seems to appear with a slight chronological lapse depending on the region concerned. For the Saône valley, radiocarbon dates indicate an appearance *c.* 2600 cal BC (Lemercier *et al.* 2015) whilst in Switzerland researchers argue for an appearance nearer *c.* 2500 cal BC (Besse 2012). The end date of this phenomenon, on the other hand, is agreed at around 2200 cal BC (Besse 2012; Lemercier *et al.* 2015). Some 54 settlement sites with domestic structures belonging to the Bell Beaker culture have been identified (Fig. 8,2). Of these, 24 are located in the Saône valley or slightly more to the east, 15 are in the High Rhône valley, downriver from Lake Geneva, one is in the same valley but high in the Alpine massif, two are on the western Jura plateau, and 12 are on the Swiss plateau.

The sites concentrate in three zones. The first, and most densely occupied, is situated in the Saône valley around Chalon-sur-Saône, and includes the sites of Marnay, Ouroux-sur-Saône, Lux, Saint-Rémy, Saint-Marcel, Dracy-le-Fort, and Crissey. The second follows the Rhône River with the sites of Injoux/Génissiat, Châtillon-en-Michaille, Arbignieu, Montagnieu, as well as the five sites situated within the city of Lyon. The third concentration is localised on the northern shore of Lake Neuchâtel, on the western Swiss Plateau, and includes the sites of

Table 8.1: The Bell Beaker settlements of central-eastern France and western Switzerland

No.	*Name of site*	*Département/Canton*	*Country*
1	Affoltern 'Zwillikon-Weid'	Zurich (ZH)	Switzerland
2	Alle 'Noir-Bois'	Jura (JU)	Switzerland
3	Anneyron	Drôme	France
4	Arbignieu 'Site de plein air'	Ain	France
5	Arlay 'Champ-Joly'	Jura	France
6	Autun 'Les Grands Champs'	Saône-et-Loire	France
7	Bavois-en-Raillon	Vaud (VD)	Switzerland
8	Bevaix 'Le Bataillard'	Neuchâtel (NE)	Switzerland
9	Bevaix 'Treytel-A Sugiez'	Neuchâtel (NE)	Switzerland
10	Bitsch 'Massaboden'	Valais/Wallis (VS)	Switzerland
11	Bourgoin-Jallieu	Isère	France
12	Cham 'Oberwil-Hof'	Zoug/Zug (ZG)	Switzerland
13	Chambéon	Loire	France
14	Chassey-le-Camp 'le Camp de Chassey'	Saône-et-Loire	France
15	Châtillon-en-Michaille 'En Chatanay'	Ain	France
16	Choisey/Damparis 'Les Champins'	Jura	France
17	Clairvaux-les-Lacs 'La Motte aux Magnins'	Jura	France
18	Concise 'Courbes-Pièces'	Vaud (VD)	Switzerland
19	Cortaillod 'Sur les Rochettes-Est'	Neuchâtel (NE)	Switzerland
20	Cortaillod 'Petit Ruz'	Neuchâtel (NE)	Switzerland
21	Crissey 'Le Mont'	Saône-et-Loire	France
22	Crottet, Grièges, Replonges & Saint-André-de-Bâgé	Ain	France
23	Dracy-le-Fort 'Les Varennes'	Saône-et-Loire	France
24	Dun-les-Places 'Le Vieux Dun/Champs de la Barre'	Nièvre	France
25	Genas 'Sous Genas'	Rhône	France
26	Géovreissiat/Montréal-la-Cluse 'Derrière-le-Château'	Ain	France
27	Injoux-Génissiat 'La Bressane'	Ain	France
28	Kaiseraugst AG	Argovie/Aargau (AG)	Switzerland
29	Les Clées 'Sur les Crêts'	Vaud (VD)	Switzerland
30	Lux 'La Perrouze'	Saône-et-Loire	France
31	Lyon 'Boulevard périphérique Nord'	Rhône	France
32	Lyon '35 Rue Auguste-Isaac'	Rhône	France
33	Lyon-Vaise 'Gorge de Loup'	Rhône	France
34	Lyon 'Rue Elie Rochette/Rue du Père Chevrier'	Rhône	France
35	Lyon 'ZAC des Blanchisseries'	Rhône	France
36	Marcilly-Ogny 'Le Champ du Saule/ Les Champs d'Aniers'	Côte-d'Or	France
37	Montagnieu 'Roche Noire'	Isère	France
38	Montrond 'Grotte de la Margot'	Jura	France
39	Ouroux-sur-Saône 'Carrière des Boulets'	Saône-et-Loire	France
40	Ouroux-sur-Saône 'Le Grand Bois' & 'Le Taillis'	Saône-et-Loire	France
41	Ouroux-sur-Saône 'Le Petit Bois'	Saône-et-Loire	France
42	Plottes 'Beauvois'	Saône-et-Loire	France
43	Poncin 'Abri Gay'	Ain	France
44	Rances 'Champ-Vully'	Vaud (VD)	Switzerland
45	Ruffey-sur-Seille 'À Daupharde'	Jura	France
46	Saint-Aubin 'Les Prés-Allenot'	Jura	France
47	Saint-Georges-de-Reneins 'Boitrait'	Rhône	France
48	Saint-Marcel 'La Noue'	Saône-et-Loire	France
49	Saint-Marcel 'le Breuil'	Saône-et-Loire	France
50	Saint-Priest 'ZAC des Feuilly'	Rhône	France
51	Saint-Rémy 'Moulin-de-Droux'	Saône-et-Loire	France
52	Tournus 'La Croix Léonard'	Saône-et-Loire	France
53	Varennes-le-Grand 'La Maison Blanche'	Saône-et-Loire	France
54	Wetzikon 'Kempten, Tösstalstrasse 32–36'	Zurich (ZH)	Switzerland

Bevaix 'Treytel-A-Sugiez', 'Le Bataillard' and Concise 'Courbes-Pièces'.

Bell Beaker settlements

A thorough literature review demonstrates that the majority of sites have not provided sufficient data to allow for a full reconstruction of the habitat (Thevenot *et al.* 2015). This may be due to the state of preservation which was quite poor in most cases, or to the flimsiness of the structures themselves which is not conducive to their preservation in any conditions. It is therefore difficult to recognise any changes in the model of the Bell Beaker culture compared to that of the preceding cultural groups. Archaeological knowledge of Bell Beaker settlements in this region therefore remains partial so this study will only present the clearest examples of Bell Beaker architecture, and attempt to deduce general trends from the available data. In the following description, the site numbers refer to those used in Figure 8.2 and Table 8.1.

The site at Lux 'La Perrouze' (no. 30) is a dryland site located in the Saône valley. Structural remains include four cylindrical flat-based pits, a lenticular pit, and one post-hole (Fig. 8.3, ST 4). The first four pits can be interpreted as silos or stores, before being used for waste disposal (Ducreux 2013).

The site of Bevaix 'Le Bataillard' (no.8) is situated on the northern shore of Lake Neuchâtel but is a terrestrial site. The discovery of eight post-holes allowed the reconstruction of a rectangular structure (Fig. 8.4), measuring 3.7 m by *c.* 13 m (von Burg 2002; Leduq *et al.* 2008). The discoveries from Cortaillod 'Sur les Rochettes-Est' (no.19) (Fig. 8.5) permitted a more extensive reconstruction, from both an architectural and organisational point of view. This site is situated on a calcareous hill to the north of Lake Neuchâtel. The post-holes excavated represented the remains of seven structures, oriented NW–SE, and about 12–14 m apart. Erosion seems to have destroyed what would have been the centre of this settlement, which would have extended farther to the south-east. Five of the structures probably belong to the first phase of construction, with the last two, which overlapped the earlier structures, representing a later phase. These rectangular buildings consist of three rows of post-holes and vary between 3.8–4.6 m wide, and between 13.4–17 m long (von Burg 2002). Sieving the contents of the post-holes allowed for the identification of 70 taxa, in the form of seeds, fruits, and carbonised plant fragments, and over 4000 macroremains revealed an economy based on agriculture, especially the cultivation of spelt, and the gathering of wild food sources (von Burg 2002).

Despite being in the flood plain of the Saône River the site of Saint-Marcel 'La Noue' (no. 48) (Fig. 8.6) is a dryland site (Salanova *et al.* 2005). Hardly any post-holes have been found but the negative structures are well preserved and the hypothesis that the lack of post-holes is due to erosion must be dismissed. A four-post structure has been found and identified as a storage structure or linked to diverse activities such as flint knapping. The house structures are identifiable as floor areas with traces of walls measuring about 7 × 10 m. These wall traces form three parallel rows, oriented N–S. Two hypotheses have been proposed regarding the reconstruction of the building architecture. The first, that they are the remains of a temporary campsite, must be rejected due to the large number of archaeological artefacts found during the excavations, including over 370 pots. The second hypothesis is more acceptable, suggesting that they were constructed on sill-beams with mortises cut to hold the uprights and that they had a raised floor. This model, with some variation, has been proposed for the lacustrine Bronze Age site of Zurich 'Mozartstrasse' and of Rances 'Champ-Vully'.

The terrestrial site of Géovreissiat/Montréal-la-Cluse 'Derrière-le-Château' (no. 26) (Fig. 8.7) is situated in a steep valley between the Ain and the Rhône (Bailly *et al.*, 1998; Hénon et Vérot-Bourrély 1999; Besse 2003a). The large quantity of architectural remains seems to indicate a long-term occupation and a dozen buildings have been identified. These were built on three rows of post-holes, and often oriented E–W, perpendicular to the mountainside. The smallest structures measured 2 m^2 and were identified as grain stores, whilst a circular structure was interpreted as a possible enclosure (Fig. 8.7,2). The longest buildings measured 8 m and 14 m respectively, the larger having apsidal ends (Fig. 8.7,1) (Hénon & Vérot-Bourrély 1999). The other structures vary between 3.5–4.5 m × 6–11 m long however, the majority are between 6–8 m (Bailly *et al.* 1998).

The settlement of Lyon 'Boulevard péri-

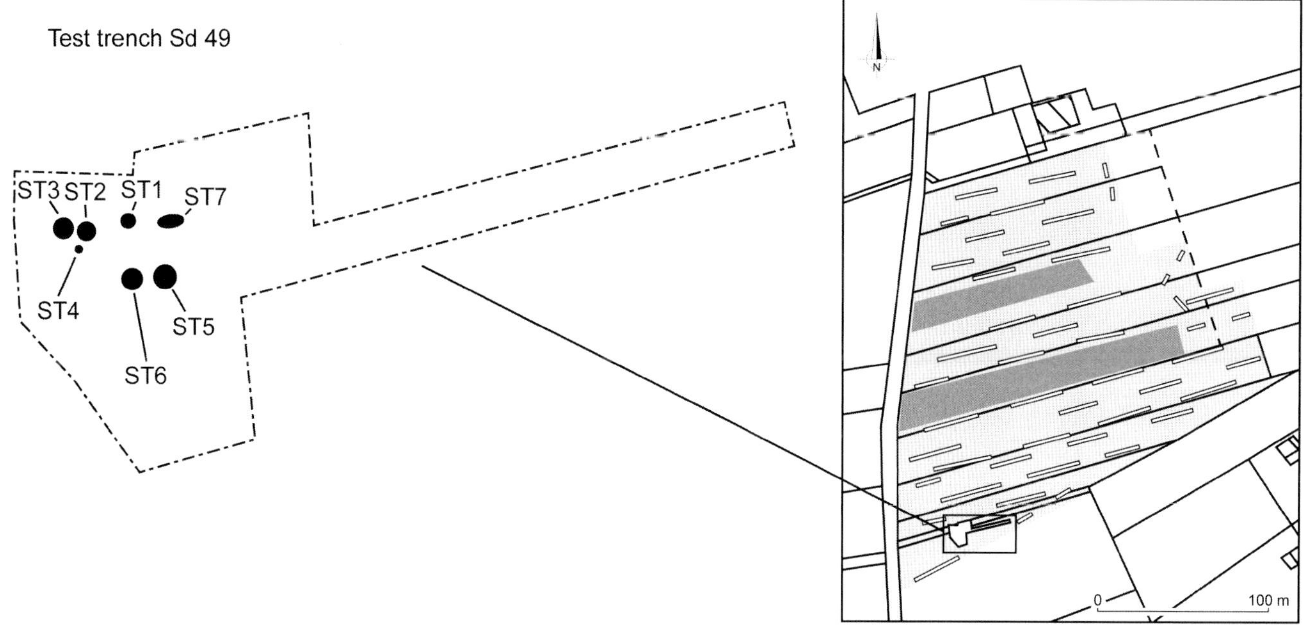

Figure 8.3: Plan of the Bell Beaker settlement at Lux 'La Perrouze' (Saône-et-Loire, F) (after Ducreux 2013, 398)

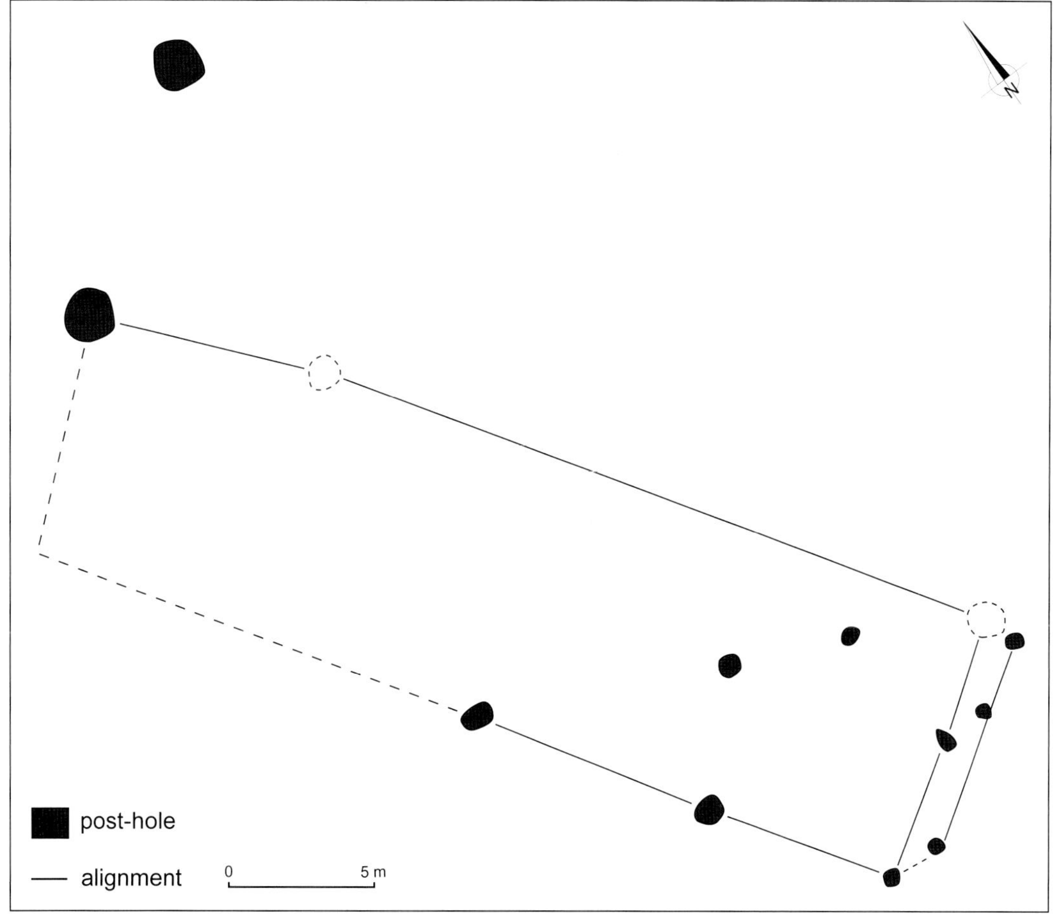

Figure 8.4: Plan of the Bell Beaker structure at Bevaix 'Le Bataillard' (Neuchâtel, CH) (after Leduq et al. *2008, 87)*

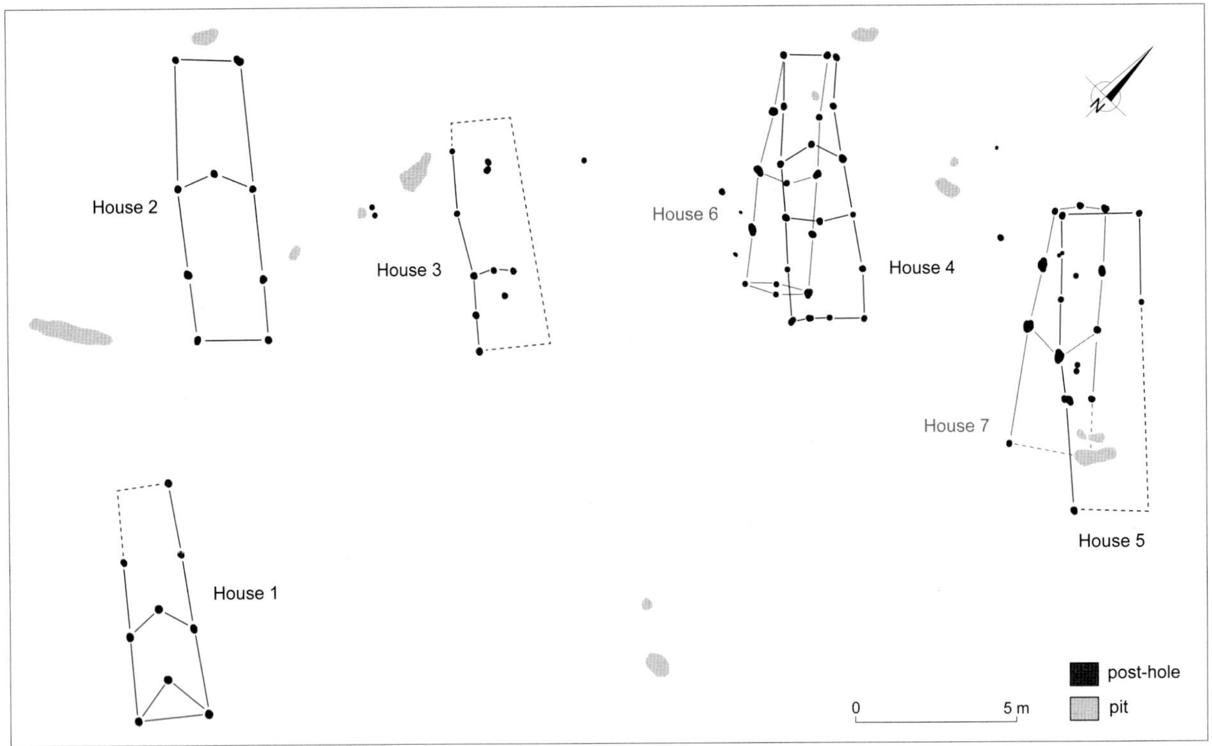

Figure 8.5: Plan of the seven Bell Beaker structures at Cortaillod 'Sur les Rochettes-Est' (Neuchâtel, CH) (after von Burg 2002, 52)

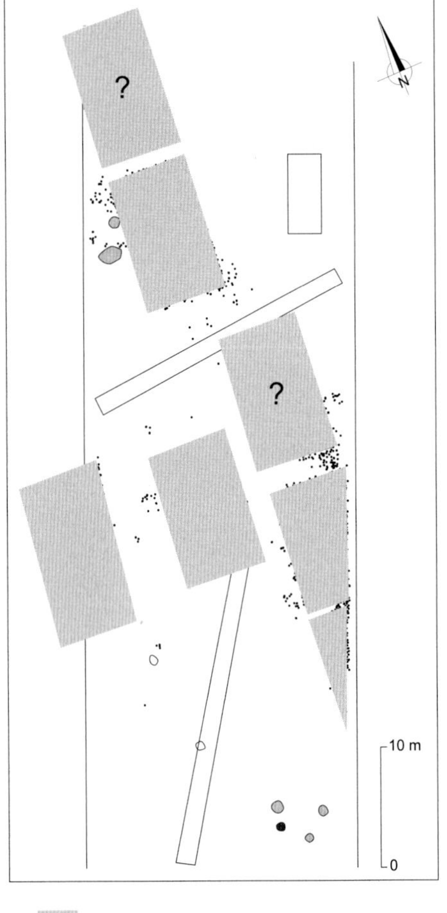

Post-hole Hearth Archaeological finds Potential buildings Effets de paroi

Figure 8.6: Saint-Marcel 'La Noue' (Saône-et-Loire, F). Wall effect and possible building outline (after Salanova et al. *2005, 47)*

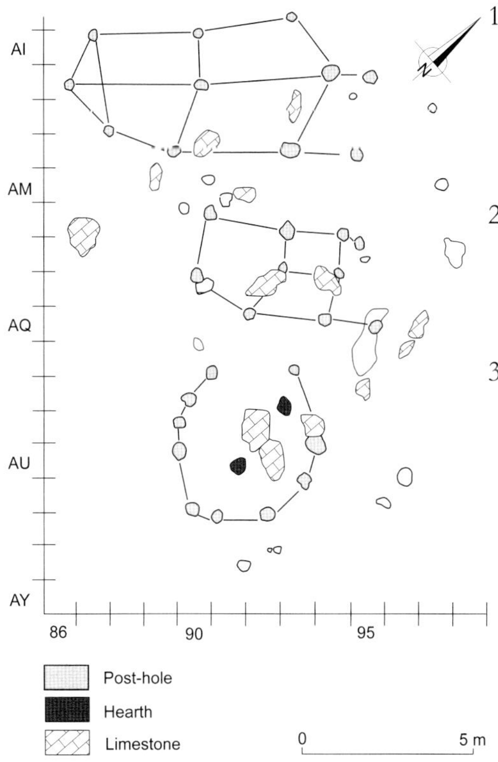

Figure 8.7: Géovreissiat/Montréal-la-Cluse 'Derrière-le-Château' (Ain, F). 1 – Apsidal ended building; 2 – Rectangular structure; 3 – Subcircular structure (after Bailly et al. *1998, 228)*

phérique Nord' (no. 31) (Fig. 8.8) is situated on a low terrace at the confluence of the Saône and the Rhône valleys and the Bell Beaker level yielded a single building plan. The posts of the structure were held in place through a support system of rocks and the overall plan measured 4 × 7 m. To the North lay activity areas involving heat or cooking, as well as waste disposal pits (Vital 2007).

The Bell Beaker settlement of Rances 'Champ-Vully' (no. 44) (Fig. 8.9) is situated on a moraine ledge between the Jura and the plain of Orbe (Gallay & Baudais 1985) and at this site five rectangular buildings belong to two successive phases (Besse 2003b). A post-built structure outlined an area of 3.5 × 6 m. The other buildings were probably built using a sill-beam technique combined with post supports, as presented above (Besse 2003b).

As well as open settlement sites, a few cave occupations attributed to the Bell Beaker culture are known in the study area. This is the case for example for the cave of Roche à Courchapon (Doubs), of Gigny (Jura), of

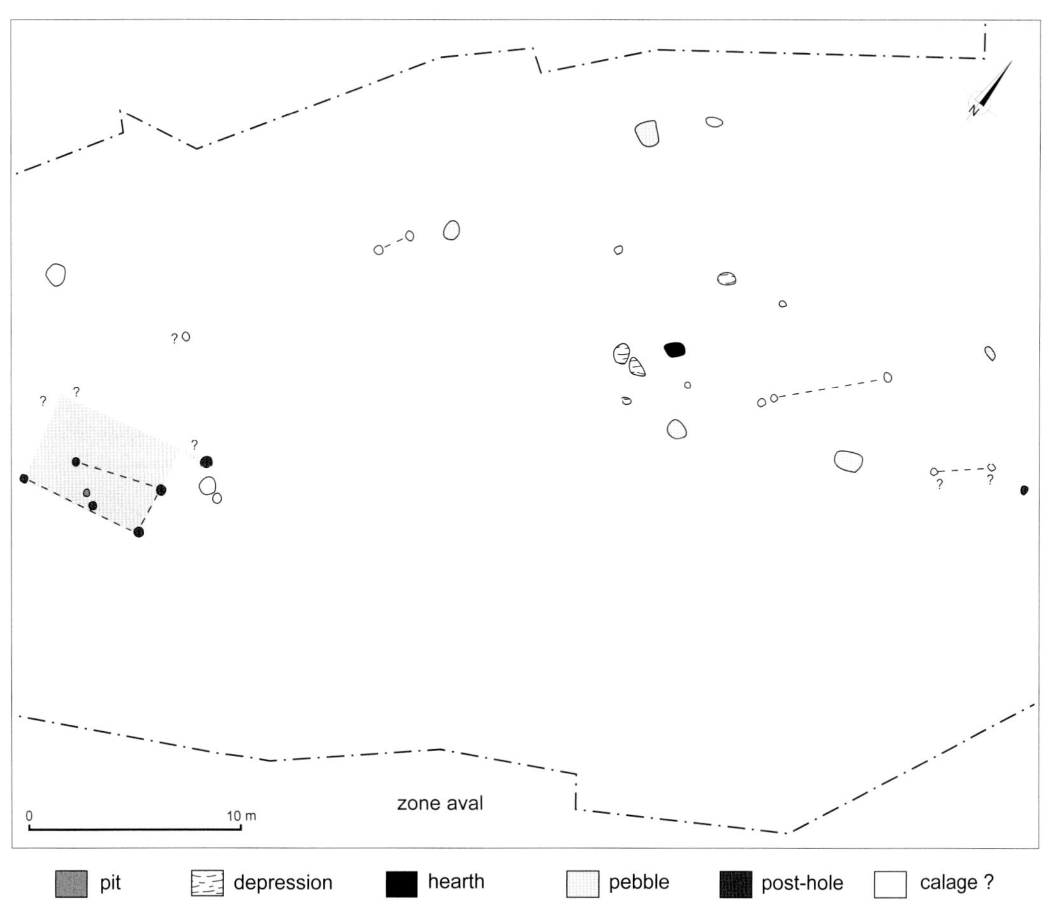

Figure 8.8: Plan of the Bell Beaker structures at Lyon 'Boulevard périphérique Nord' (F) (after Vital 2007, 73)

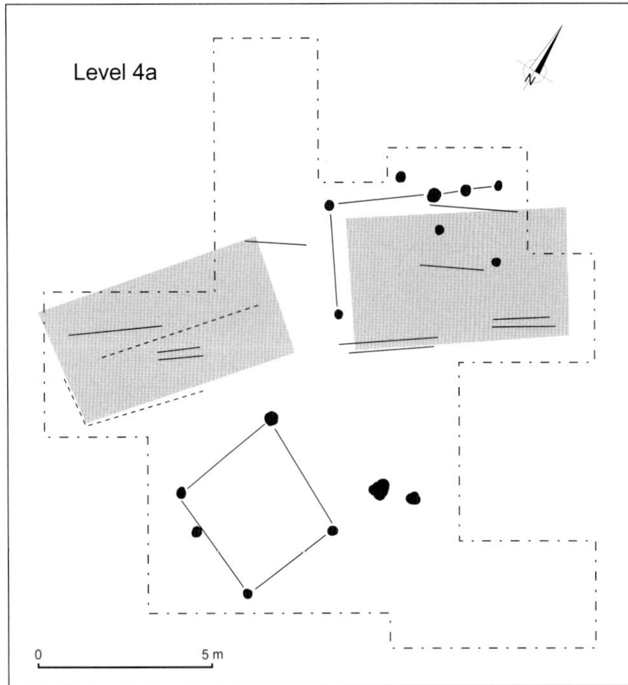

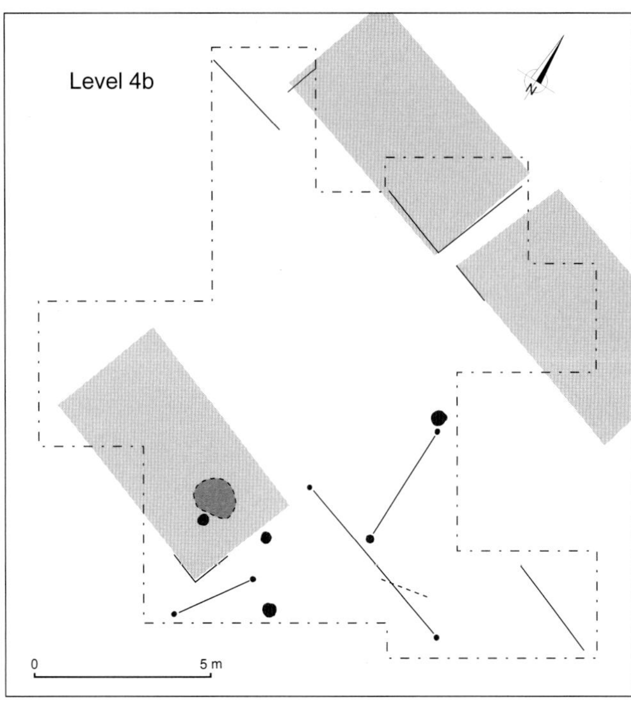

Figure 8.9: Schematic plan of the Bell Beaker levels at Rances 'Champ-Vully' (Vaud, CH) (after Gallay & Baudais 1985, 100)

Margot at Montrond (Jura) (Pétrequin & Pétrequin 1978), as well as Scey-en-Varais (Pétrequin & Piningre 1970) and at the Grotte du Gardon (Voruz *et al.* 2004).

Towards a synthesis of settlement models?

As previously stated, Bell Beaker settlements in central-eastern France and western Switzerland are not well understood. The data produced by the most informative sites show the extent to which architecture and orientation can vary. Some recurring features, however, deserve to be mentioned.

The first concerns the environment in which these settlements were established. All are located close to water, a river in most cases, or a lake for the sites of the Swiss Plateau, but they are not within wetland zones. The second concerns the type of architecture and in the majority of cases the structures are built on posts, without stone foundations. Two cases of mixed architecture, with both sill-beams and posts, have been observed on sites located within potential flood zones (Saint-Marcel 'La Noue' and Rances 'Champ-Vully'). The third observation concerns the size of the structures. Their width is particularly homogenous: between 3.5–4.5 m with the exception of Saint-Marcel 'La Noue'. It is worth noting, however, that this particular site had no post-holes, and that the architectural remains were defined using possible traces of sill-beams and the spatial distribution of archaeological material. The lengths of the buildings, on the other hand, varies between 6–17 m. The buildings at two sites located North of Lake Neuchâtel (Bevaix 'Le Bataillard' and Cortaillod 'Sur les Rochettes-Est') have produced the longest buildings measuring 13–17 m. The plans and dimensions of the buildings are therefore comparable to what we know of the pile dwelling settlements of the final Neolithic phases (see above).

Within the sites, there is often a unity of building forms in that the plans are rectangular with the only variations comprising a rectangular structure with apsidal ends, and a subcircular structure with dimensions varying from 6–14 m being those at Géovreissiat/Montréal-la-Cluse 'Derrière-le-Château'.

Breaks and continuity

This review of the pre-Bell Beaker and Bell Beaker culture settlements of central-eastern

France and western Switzerland allows us to make several statements. Firstly, the pile-dwelling villages known during the final Neolithic in the cultures of Chalain, Lüscherz, and Auvernier-Cordé are systematically abandoned shortly after 2450 BC (Mauvilly & Boisaubert 2005; Besse *et al.* 2011), and replaced by terrestrial sites during the Bell Beaker period. The arrival of this new culture is marked by a voluntary delocalisation towards terrestrial sites. There is therefore a distinct break between the final Neolithic and the Bell Beaker period. This phenomenon can be generalised to the entire region, and has also been observed in the French Alps (Billaud & Marguet 2005; 2007). It used to be believed that the lakes were abandoned due to rising water levels however the current climatic data show that the second half of the 3rd millennium BC corresponds to a climatic optimum, and therefore to improved conditions favourable to the establishment of on-shore settlements (Magny 2006).

It is worth mentioning that whilst this break is very marked, especially on the Swiss plateau, Bell Beaker settlements established north of Lake Neuchâtel tend to retain some characteristics of the Lüscherz and the Auvernier-Cordé type settlements namely that the buildings are always built using three rows of posts, and have similar dimensions. A width of around 4 m seems to have been the standard for several centuries, and the lengths of the buildings are comparable for the pre-Bell Beaker (10–20 m) and the Bell Beaker periods (13–17 m).

These parallels cannot be drawn for the other regions in our study area, since the settlements of pre-Bell Beaker cultures are not very well known. The few identified floor plans are similar to those of the Bell Beaker culture in that they are square to rectangular in shape. The locations of the sites, along the principal waterways, do not change.

Moreover, in western Switzerland, the analysis of data from funerary sites can be compared and contrasted to the data deduced from domestic structures. Whilst the settlements undergo a major change in the choice of location, continuity is observed in the cemetery of Sion 'Petit-Chasseur'. Indeed, this megalithic necropolis was constructed and used by both the final Neolithic ('Néolithique final Valaisan') and the Bell Beaker populations, with the latter not only re-using the structures built during the final Neolithic but adding their own funerary structures to the site (Desideri & Besse 2009).

An important break is also seen in the ceramic record, since it is the decorated Bell Beakers that define the Bell Beaker culture. It is worth noting, however, that the cultural groups of the final Neolithic each had their own pottery assemblages with their own characteristics. As for domestic ceramics in the Bell Beaker period, the assemblages were composed of styles that had already been present in the final Neolithic, such as vessels with horizontal cordons below the rim. New types of pottery also appear during the Bell Beaker period, such as vessels with perforations below the rim or with impressed fingernail decoration (Besse 2003a).

It must be stressed once more that it is not possible to identify breaks or continuums in the establishment of the Bell Beaker culture based on the domestic structures alone. They certainly constitute an important part of this process, but must be considered alongside other strands of data. Of particular importance in this regard is the diffusion of Grand-Pressigny flint daggers during the final Neolithic, yet they are absent during the Bell Beaker period. The lithic industry during the latter is characterised by semi-circular elements, arrowheads with concave bases and small thumbnail scrapers which are items that are not found in final Neolithic contexts. Copper artefacts, by contrast, are abundant during the final Neolithic in the Trois-Lacs region of the Swiss plateau, but rare during the Bell Beaker period and represented solely by awls found in funerary contexts.

Conclusion

Central-eastern France and western Switzerland is geographically located in the central part of the Bell Beaker distribution and the cultural groups that preceded the Bell Beakers occupy a small region, linked to the western half of this distribution. With the appearance of Bell Beakers, several other cultural components also appear such as some common ceramic types, the Palmela arrowhead, the archer's wrist guard, v-shaped perforated buttons, needle-shaped pendants, stelae and so on. The distribution of these Beaker-associated artefacts can, however, be quite varied. The Palmela points, for example, are found mostly in the Iberian peninsula and in south-west France, and have no connection with the northern part of the Bell Beaker extension. These artefact distributions can overlap, can be found in adjacent areas, or can be completely separated and each of these distributions represents a network. It is the combination and interaction of all these networks that constitute the Bell Beaker phenomenon which can therefore be defined as a mosaic of networks differing from one another but linked by the presence of Bell Beakers themselves.

Through artefacts studies we know that the majority of these objects are made and used locally and the same goes for the standard decorated Bell Beaker. It is therefore the 'concept' of the decorated Beaker that circulated, and not the pottery itself. This concept was transported by people, leading to the conclusion that the networks represent channels of diffusion.

The only point left to address is that of the mechanics of the transmission of this concept. The mobility of the population(s) must therefore be scrutinised and evaluated. The study of non-metric dental traits and aDNA on numerous populations, from the final Neolithic, Bell Beaker culture, and Bronze age, in several areas of Europe, demonstrates the various peopling scenarios possible (Desideri & Besse 2009; Desideri *et al.* 2012; Olalde *et al.* 2018). Ranging from a colonisation event and a process of gradual acculturation, the proposed models confirm the complexity of the establishment of the Bell Beaker culture. These results are corroborated by the timely isotopic analysis of strontium in Central Europe, in England (most famously on the Amesbury archer (Fitzpatrick 2011)) and in the Alps.

The transmission of the 'Bell beaker concept' to the generations responsible for its expansion should be understood in two ways, the first being a vertical transmission of knowledge between generations, or between people living in the same place but with a consequent age difference. The tradition was then maintained over time by repeated transmission to assure its permanence over one, two, or several centuries. Secondly, there must have been a horizontal transmission (multiple, rapid, and repeated) between people of the same or almost the same generation. The vertical and horizontal models can be combined.

This of course makes it difficult to identify schisms and continuums between the final Neolithic and the Bell Beaker period in central-eastern France and western Switzerland. The vectors are multiple, and complex, as is the case whenever and wherever the Bell Beaker phenomenon is studied. There is no centralised production of Bell Beakers. There is not one single economic network, and the phenomenon cannot be attributed to one population. The diversity of the cultural components of the Bell Beaker phenomenon and the mechanics of its transfer demonstrate the complexity of the network mosaic that governed the societies of the 3rd millennium BC. The region of central-eastern France and western Switzerland is at the very heart of these networks, with the establishment of settlements attesting political choices, including the settlement shift from lakesides dwellings to dryland locations. The architectural form of the domestic structures, on the other hand, remains the same from the final Neolithic to the Bell Beaker culture which demonstrates a similar social ordering in villages, based on the same house-centred unity, during these periods.

Acknowledgements

We wish to thank the members of 'Archéologie et Gobelets' for many years of discussion, conferences and publications which have allowed us to pursue research and further our understanding of the late Neolithic societies amongst which the Bell Beaker culture plays a major role. We also thank Claudine Abegg for her help in translating this text.

References

Arnold, B. 2012. Les Lacustres sur le littoral neuchâtelois: 150 années de recherches et un bilan. In Honegger, M. & Mordant, C. (eds), *L'Homme au bord de l'eau. Archéologie des zones littorales du Néolithique à la Protohistoire*, 175–83. Lausanne: Cahiers d'archéologie romande 132

Bailly, M., Besse, M., Gisclon, J.-L., Hénon, P. & Vérot-Bourrély, A. 1998. Le site d'habitat campaniforme de 'Derrière-le-Château' à Géovreissiat et Montréal-la-Cluse (Ain): premiers résultats. In D'Anna, A., Binder, D. & Blain, A. (eds), *Production et identité culturelle. Actualités de la recherche. Actes de La 2e session des Rencontres Méridionales de Préhistoire Récente, Arles, 8–9 Novembre 1996*, 225–39. Juan-les-Pins: Editions APDCA

Besse, M. 2003a. *L'Europe du 3e millénaire avant notre ère. Les céramiques communes du Campaniforme.* Lausanne : Cahiers d'archéologie romande 94

Besse, M. 2003b. Le Campaniforme de Champ-Vully à Rances (Vaud, Suisse). Genève: Unpubl. report

Besse, M. 2012. Prehistory of the Upper Rhône Valley: from Neanderthals to Modern Humans. *Archives des Sciences* 65, 229–36

Besse, M., Gallay, A., Mottet, M. & Piguet, M. 2011. La séquence culturelle du site du Petit-Chasseur (Sion, Valais). In *Autour du Petit-Chasseur. L'archéologie aux sources du Rhône (1941–2011)*, 79–88. Paris & Sion: Errance, Musée d'histoire du Valais

Billaud, Y. & Marguet, A. 2005. Habitats lacustres du Néolithique et de l'âge du Bronze dans les lacs alpins français. In Della Casa & Trachsel 2005, 169–79

Billaud, Y., Marguet, A. 2007. Les installations littorales de l'âge du Bronze dans les lacs alpins français. Etat des connaissances. In Richard, H., Magny, M. & Mordant, C. (eds), *Environnements et cultures à l'âge du Bronze en Europe occidentale. Actes du 129e Congrès national des Sociétés Historiques et Scientifiques (CTHS). Besançon, 19–21 avril 2004*, 211–25. Paris: Documents préhistoriques 21

Burg, A. von. 2002. Le Campaniforme sur le plateau de Bevaix. *Bulletin d'Archéologie Suisse* 25, 2, 48–57

Danérol, A., Orcel, A., Orcel, C. & Ramseyer, D. 1991. *Delley/Portalban II. Les villages néolithiques révélés par la dendrochronologie.* Fribourg: Archéologie Fribourgeoise 7

Della Casa, P. & Trachsel, M. (eds), 2005. *Wetland Economies and Societies. Proceedings of the International Conference in Zurich, 10–13 March 2004.* Zurich: Collectio Archæologica 3

Desideri, J. & Besse, M. 2009. Les rituels funéraires néolithiques de la Haute Vallée du Rhône (Valais, Suisse). In Boëtsch, G., Signoli, M. & Tzörtzis, S. (eds), *La mort en montagne: perceptions, représentations, rituels. Actes de l'Université européenne d'été 2007*, 23–38. Gap: Editions des Hautes-Alpes

Desideri, J., Piguet, M., Furestier, R., Cattin, F. & Besse, M. 2012. The end of Neolithic in Western Switzerland. Peopling dynamics through nonmetric dental study. In Fokkens, H. & Nicolis, F. (eds), *Background to Beakers. Inquiries in Regional Cultural Backgrounds of the Bell Beaker Complex,* 81–115. Leiden: Sidestone Press

Ducreux, F. 2013. Le site campaniforme de Lux La Perrouze (Saône et Loire). *Revue archéologique de l'Est* 62, 395–407

Fitzpatrick, A.P. 2011. *The Amesbury Archer and the Boscombe Bowmen. Bell Beaker Burials at Boscombe Down, Amesbury, Wiltshire.* Salisbury: Wessex Archaeology

Gallay, A. & Baudais, D. 1985. Rances, Champ-Vully Est (Vaud, Suisse). In *Première céramique, premier métal : du Néolithique à l'âge du Bronze dans le domaine circum-alpin (octobre 1985-Mars 1986)*, 99–108. Lons-le-Saunier: Musée municipal

Giligny, F. & Michel, R. 1995. L'évolution des céramiques de 2920 à 2440 av. J.-C. dans la région des Trois Lacs (Suisse occidentale). In Voruz 1995, 347–61

Giligny, F., Maréchal, D., Pétrequin, P., Pétrequin, A.-M. & Saintot, S. 1995. La séquence Néolithique final des lacs de Clairvaux et de Chalain (Jura). Essai sur l'évolution culturelle. In Voruz 1995, 313–46

Hénon, P. & Vérot-Bourrély, A., 1999. Le site de Derrière-le-Château, communes de Géovreissiat et Montréal-la-Cluse (Ain, France). Unpubl. report

Jeunesse, C., Pétrequin, P. & Piningre, J.-F. 1998. L'Est de la France. In Guilaine, J. (ed.), *Atlas du Néolithique européen. 2A: L'Europe occidentale*, 501–84. Liège: Etudes et recherches archéologiques de l'université de Liège 46

Leducq, A., Rordorf Duvaux, M. & Tréhoux, A. 2008. *Bevaix/Le Bataillard: occupations terrestres en bordure de marais.* Hauterive: Plateau de Bevaix 3

Lemercier, O., Martineau, R. & Duhamel, P. 2015. Bilan des datations radiocarbone et cadre chrono-culturel du Néolithique en Bourgogne. In Martineau, Pautrat & Lermercier 2015, 219–31

Magny, M. 2006. Le cadre climatique des habitats lacustres du Jura et des Alpes du Nord. In Dumont, A. (ed.), *Archéologie des lacs et des cours d'eau*, 70–85. Paris: Errance

Martineau, R., Pautrat, Y. & Lemercier, O. 2015, *La Préhistoire en Bourgogne. Etat des connaissances et bilan 1994–2005.* Dijon: Supplément à la Revue archéologique de l'Est 39

Mauvilly, M. & Boisaubert, J.-L. 2005. Entre terre et lacs dans les régions de Morat et d'Estavayer-le-lac (FR) – Quelle image après 30 ans de recherches assidues? In Della Casa & Trachsel 2005, 179–84

Mottet, M., Gentizon, A.-L., Haller, M. & Giozza, G. 2011. *Les bâtiments semi-enterrés de Bramois. Un habitat du Néolithique final en Valais (Suisse).* Lausanne: Cahiers d'archéologie romande 126

Olalde, I. *et al.* 2018. The Beaker phenomenon and the genomic transformation of Northwest Europe. *Nature*, 555, 7695, 190–6

Pétrequin, P. 1998. I. Les lacs de Chalain et de Clairvaux: dynamique évolutive des styles céramiques et transferts de population. *Gallia Préhistoire* 40 (1), 133–40

Pétrequin, A.-M. & Pétrequin, P. 1978. Le phénomène Campaniforme – Cordée en Franche-Comté. Chronologie et rapports avec les groupes régionaux. *Bulletin de la Société préhistorique française* 75 (10), 361–93

Pétrequin, P. & Piningre, J.-F. 1970. Mobilier du début de l'Age du Bronze, dans la Grotte de Scey-en-Varais (Doubs). *Bulletin de la Société Préhistorique Française* 67 (6), 180–81

Pugin, C. & Corboud, P. 2006. Un habitat littoral du Néolithique final en bordure de la rade de Genève. *Annuaire d'Archéologie Suisse* 89, 25–50

Salanova, L., Ducreux, F., Argant, A., Convertini, F., Gros, O., Gros, A.-C. & Saintot, S. 2005. L'habitat campaniforme de La Noue à Saint-Marcel (Saône-et-Loire): Eléments de définition du groupe bourguignon-jurassien. *Gallia Préhistoire* 47 (1), 33–146

Stöckli, W.E. 1995. L'évolution du Néolithique suisse. In W. E. Stöckli, U. Niffeler & E. Gross-Klee (eds), *SPM: La Suisse du Paléolithique à l'aube du Moyen-Âge*, 19–52. Bâle: Société Suisse de Préhistoire et d'Archéologi

Thevenot, J.-P. (ed.), 2005. *Le Camp de Chassey (Chassey-le-Camp, Saône-et-Loire): les niveaux néolithiques du camp de La Redoute.* Dijon: Supplément à la Revue archéologique de l'Est 22

Thevenot, J.-P., Martineau, R., Moreau, C., Lemercier, O., Bontemps, C., Ducreux, F., Prestreau, M., Duriaud, J. & Nicolardot, J.-P. 2015. Le Néolithique du bassin versant de la Saône (Saône-et-Loire, Côte-d'Or). In Martineau *et al.* 2015, 193–206

Vital, J. 2007. Un autre regard sur le gisement du boulevard périphérique nord de Lyon (Rhône) au Néolithique et à l'âge du Bronze. *Gallia Préhistoire* 49 (1), 1–126

Voruz, J.-L. (ed.), 1995. *Chronologies néolithiques. De 6000 à 2000 avant notre ère dans le Bassin rhodanien. Actes du colloque d'Ambérieu-en-Bugey, 19–20 septembre 1992.* Ambérieu-en-Bugey: Documents du département d'anthropologie et d'écologie de l'université de Genève 20

Voruz, J.-L., Perrin, T. & Sordoillet, D. 2004. La séquence néolithique de la grotte du Gardon (Ain). *Bulletin de la Société Préhistorique Française* 101 (4), 827–66

Winiger, A. 2008. La station lacustre de Concise. 1. Stratigraphie, datations et contexte environnemental. Lausanne: Cahiers d'archéologie romande 111

9

Bell Beaker settlements in southern Germany

Christian Strahm

The compilation of a corpus of Bell Beaker settlements corresponds to a holistic approach which attempts to understand the Bell Beaker Complex as an entity characterised by certain distinctive aspects and whose defining element is the Bell Beaker itself. Depending on the respective question, further components are assigned to it in order to understand the cultural structure as a whole. Some associated artefacts and practices have often been transferred from other groups (*ie* archaeological cultures) and are not exclusively Bell Beaker, which makes it problematic to describe the 'Bell Beaker Culture' as a holistic archaeological culture. The components are also regionally different or develop different interactions with other indigenous groups.

Procedure

It is therefore necessary to describe these components separately and to analyse their relationship to the artefacts that we perceive as Bell Beaker-specific. This approach will form the basis for the understanding of the whole Bell Beaker complex. Such an attempt has often been the subject of detailed investigations, whereby the affiliation of the components of the Bell Beaker Culture was often not even discussed; their characterisation as representing Bell Beaker-specific evidence was assumed (Strahm 2004a). This is especially true for the settlement evidence.

A consistent adherence to this approach would be entirely in line with the conventional holistic approach, the aim of which is to present the Bell Beaker complex as a coherent cultural phenomenon. However, we do not know whether this approach reflects historical reality. It is also possible to present the history of the late Neolithic from an anthropological point of view: the focus is not on the description of the sequence of holistic archaeological cultures such as the Corded Ware Culture, the Bell Beaker Culture or the numerous small-scale local groups, but rather on the interactions of the various aspects of the burial rites, the forms of settlement, the various intercultural interdependencies or the wide-ranging networks. Discussion of these combined phenomena may characterise the events better than the monolithic description of archaeological cultures and groups.

These preliminary remarks make it clear that the problem described also lies in the different use of some terms. It is therefore advantageous if the terms used in the following are clarified before our presentation of the settlements and settlement patterns.

Definitions

Bell Beaker Complex: All assemblages characterised by a Bell Beaker object (ceramic and non-ceramic objects) are summarised under this term. The Bell Beaker Complex is essentially composed of various elements in all regions: Bell Beaker Phenomenon, Complementary Ceramics and potentially also the Bell Beaker Culture.

Bell Beaker Phenomenon: The Bell Beaker phenomenon is the idea, ideology, or worldview, or metaphysical background behind this cultural expression. Archaeologically, the Bell Beaker phenomenon manifests itself through the Bell Beaker Set, which is defined by *Bell Beaker-specific* objects (Burgess & Shennan 1976; Strahm 2004b). It corresponds in content to the Bell Beaker Package.

Bell Beaker Package: See above.

Complementary Ware: Complementary Ware is a regional, indigenous ware that occurs in the Bell Beaker regions together with genuine Bell Beakers. It is identical with the ceramics of the local Final Neolithic and early Chalcolithic cultures, which becomes the Complementary Ceramic by assimilation of the Bell Beaker (for more about this taxonomy see Strahm 2004a).

Begleitkeramik: The *Begleitkeramik* is the Complementary Ware of the eastern group of Bell Beakers. The term *Begleitkeramik* was coined by Schránil (1928) and meant the pottery that accompanies the Bell Beaker in Bohemia. The term was then mistakenly applied to analogous phenomena in other regions, thus postulating a complete archaeological culture uniform throughout Europe. *Céramique d'accompagnement* means the same thing. According to the original definition, the term *Begleitkeramik* should only be used for the eastern group, it is the Complementary Ware of the eastern group (Besse & Strahm 2001; Strahm 2004a).

Bell Beaker Culture: The Bell Beaker Culture can be defined as a combination of finds containing Bell Beaker elements. It documents different cultural manifestations, so that an independently operating entity, a complete archaeological culture, can be reconstructed. It is formed when the Bell Beaker idea is fully integrated into an archaeological culture and this culture has developed further.

A decisive consequence of these definitions is the distinction between the 'Bell Beaker Phenomenon' and the 'Bell Beaker Culture'. While the former is only manifested in certain artefacts or finds combinations (the set), the Bell Beaker Culture can only be perceived if the Bell Beaker idea is integrated into an independently economic and settling entity (an archaeological culture). This also means that Bell Beaker settlements are always integrated into complexes connoted as belonging to the

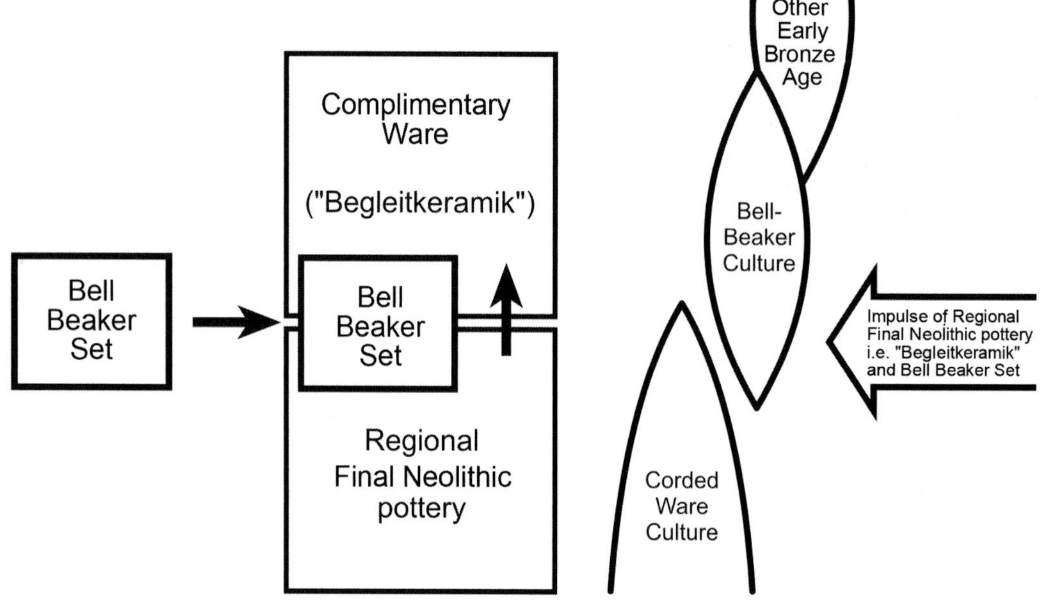

*Figure 9.1: The networking of the two Bell Beaker components: The Bell Beaker Set (Bell Beaker Phenomenon) is acculturated by the regional Final Neolithic groups and their ceramics become the Complementary Ceramics (*Begleitkeramik*) in eastern Central Europe. There local groups also integrated into the Bell Beaker Set and then spread as the Bell Beaker Culture to southern Germany, where it replaced the Corded Ware Culture around the middle of the 3rd millennium BC*

Bell Beaker culture, as shown schematically in Figure 9.1.

Bell Beaker Settlements

These considerations inevitably lead back to the starting point of the contribution. Settlements and settlement patterns are important in the characterisation of the Bell Beaker complex but, what constitutes an actual Bell Beaker Settlement? When can we speak of a Bell Beaker Settlement? Under this term, and apart from the contexts that can be clearly interpreted as graves, hoards, cult sites, production sites and so on, all assemblages that contain Bell Beaker artefacts can be subsumed but there are also problems of interpretation.

Many sites have produced pottery from different Final Neolithic cultures and rarely do they comprise Bell Beaker fragments alone. The fragmentary pottery can usually be assigned to Corded Ware or other local groups. In most cases we have sherd accumulations without any recognisable structural evidence. Similar sherd accumulations were also found in pits or ditch sections however, these too often lack structural associations.

In view of the poor evidence, it is often impossible to decide whether we are dealing with mixed and chronologically different assemblages or whether it is a uniform population that is continuing various traditions. These finds scatters or pit assemblages are not associated with any recognisable settlement structures, rather it is the topographical situation that identifies them as settlement sites. This circumstance is a characteristic feature of the late Neolithic and it is irrelevant to our question because it does not contain any statement about the settlement structure or the settlement pattern of the Bell Beaker Culture. These settlement sites are only of importance for the interpretation of the distribution pattern of the Bell Beaker Culture and are listed here only in summary form.

The Region of study

The region to be discussed in the following includes the western peripheral zone of the eastern group of the Bell Beaker Culture. In a geographical sense, these are the areas of southern Bavaria, south-western Germany (including Alsace) and eastern Switzerland, which is not yet a closed cultural area in this phase of development. It is characterised by the western distribution area of the *Begleitkeramik*, which, however, occurs mainly in eastern Central Europe. Only in the following phase did it develop into an independent cultural region comprising the various groups of the older North Alpine Early Bronze Age (Krause 2003 45ff; Merkl 2011, 151).

The settlement places of the Bell Beaker Culture

After all the difficulties described above, it is not surprising that the number of evaluable settlement structures is low in the Bavarian, Southern German and Eastern Swiss regions (Fig. 9.2).

Southern Bavaria

The northern foothills of the Alps, consisting of the region of southern Bavaria and eastern Switzerland, comprise the area south of the Danube and is bordered to the south by the northern limestone Alps and to the north by the Swabian and Franconian Alb and the Precambrian Bavarian Forest. It consists of the tertiary hilly country and the pleistocene hilly landscape of the Alpine foothills. The region of southern Bavaria exemplifies the problems that pertain to the study of settlement in the 3rd millennium BC. It is an excellent hunting region with fertile soils, it is surrounded by important mineral resources and crossed by important trade routes. The entire region has been well researched and there have been many large-scale excavations. Evidence of the Bell Beaker Complex such as graves, pottery spreads, cult sites and individual finds, is abundant. One might also expect good evidence for settlements but, as in other Bell Beaker provinces, the data are problematic. This is probably for two main reasons. Firstly, the settlement probably consisted of a loose, widely scattered land-take with small individual farms. Secondly the houses were probably built using a light construction method, requiring little in the way of dug foundations and therefore leaving little trace. Small houses are represented only by a few shallow post-holes.

Presumed settlement sites: Settlement pits and ditches

Apart from about 20 find sites with pottery spreads, on which no structures have been

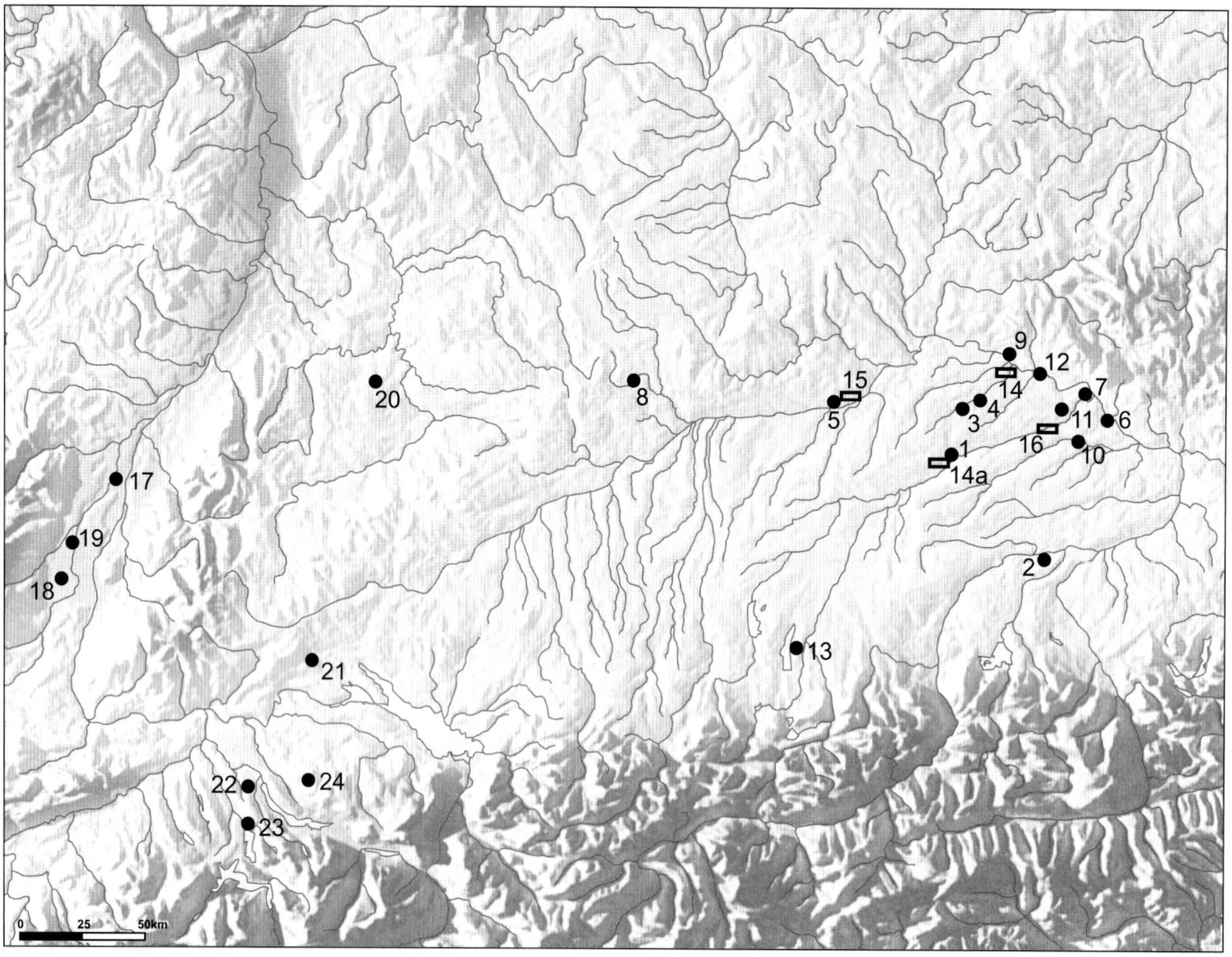

Figure 9.2: Distribution of settlement sites and presumed settlement sites of the Bell Beaker culture in southern Germany, eastern Switzerland and Alsace. Black spot – Presumed settlement sites (Pits, ditches and mounds). Black rectangle – House structures

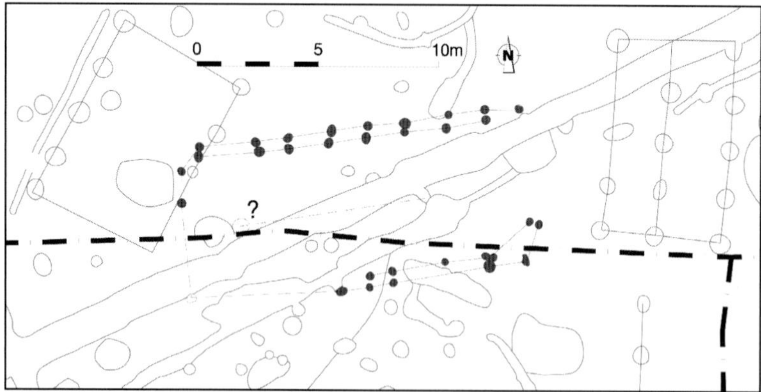

Figure 9.3: Atting, Aufeld. Detail of the overall plan with the post-holes of a Final Neolithic building hatched (after Zirngibl 2012, 55)

found, only 15 find sites with a total of 31 pits are known in southern Bavaria (Heyd 2004a, 10; Fig. 9.2). They may represent small, short-term settlements, but the evidence does not allow us to be proscriptive. These sites are given in Table 9.1.

House structures

The few house structures cannot be assigned to the Bell Beaker Culture with absolute certainty, since dating materials from the post-pits are missing. However, at all three sites Bell Beaker sherds were found in the immediate vicinity and there were also Bell Beaker graves close by.

At Atting, Aufeld (14) a house floor-plan, orientated E–W measured 14.5 × 5.2 m. It consisted of two rows of pairs of post-pits indicating double posts. Dating of the structure is not secure since there were no finds in the post-pits, but nearby lay a settlement pit with Bell Beaker pottery and three Bell Beaker grave groups (Fig. 9.3; Zirngibl 2012, 53–6).

At Ergolding (14a) the house ground-plan, was orientated NW–SE and measured >9 m long. It lay next to a small building measuring 3 × 3 m. Dating is not clear, but 10 m further

Table 9.1: Presumed settlements (without structural evidence) in Bavaria

Site	*No. on map*	*Features*
Altheim, Hochstrasse	1	Settlement pit
Altötting, Kapellplatz	2	6 settlement pits, 2 small ditches
Geiselhöring	3	Settlement Pit
Geiselhöring-Sallach	4	Settlement Pit
Ingolstadt, Audi Parking	5	Settlement Pit
Langenamming	6	Possible settlement pit
Mainkofen Neue Heilanstalt	7	Possible settlement pit
Nähermemmingen	8	6 settlement pits
Oberzeitldorn	9	Settlement pit
Prunn	10	2 large settlement pits
Wallersdorf	11	2 settlement pits
Sand	12	Settlement pit, overlying grave
Welpertshausen	13	Settlement pit

Figure 9.4: Großmehring, Baugebiet Ost I. Longhouse and smaller building with some double posts, (after report of the Bayerisches Landesamtfür Denkmalpflege)

to the south-east of the larger house was a pit containing Bell Beaker pottery (Piller & Richter 2012, 34 36).

Meanwhile, at Großmehring, Baugebiet Ost I (15), a longhouse was orientated NNW–SSE and measured at least 23 × 8 m. It was double-aisled and had some double posts. It lay next to a smaller building (8 × 5 m) and a few Bell Beaker sherds were found in the excavated area. Some 20 m to the east lay a rubbish pit with numerous Bell Beaker sherds (Fig. 9.4).

Finally, at Landau SüdOst (16), the ground-plan of a house was located. It was slightly oval, orientated N–S and measured 11 × 4.5 m. Adjacent to this were post-holes possibly representing a second, smaller structure (Fig. 9.5). Dating is again uncertain as there were no associated finds, but nearby lay 2 pits containing Bell Beaker pottery (Husty 2004a).

South-west Germany

Geographically, south-western Germany and Alsace, which belong to the same region in terms of cultural history, are a strongly structured region characterised by the Precambrian hills of the Black Forest and the Mesozoic Table Jurassic of the Swabian Alb. Three river systems, the Rhine with the Upper Rhine Plain, the Neckar and the upper course of the Danube, have shaped the settlement and the occupation of the land and they are also the most important cultural communication routes. This also determined the expansion and spread of the Bell Beaker Culture, which is concentrated in the Gunstregionen of the southern Upper Rhine area with the Kaiserstuhl, in the Neckar estuary, in the Stuttgart area and in the Hegau. The settlements and the places where the Bell Beaker Culture was found are focussed on important connecting routeways and at fording points, which affected settlement development. In this area, too, settlement evidence is scarce and once again there is a discrepancy between abundant graves and sparse settlement evidence. This does not afford a balanced analysis of the Bell Beaker Culture which is here documented only by graves, a few pits and individual finds. Pits, which represent evidence of a settlement, have been observed at the sites listed in Table 9.2.

In south-west Germany, single Bell Beaker fragments have also been found on a few hilltop sites, which do not prove settlement *per se*, but at least suggest some occupation in the uplands (Jeunesse & Denaire 2010, 191f.). These sites include Breisach, Münsterberg; Ebringen, Schönberg; Ehrenkirchen, Ölberg; Reusten,

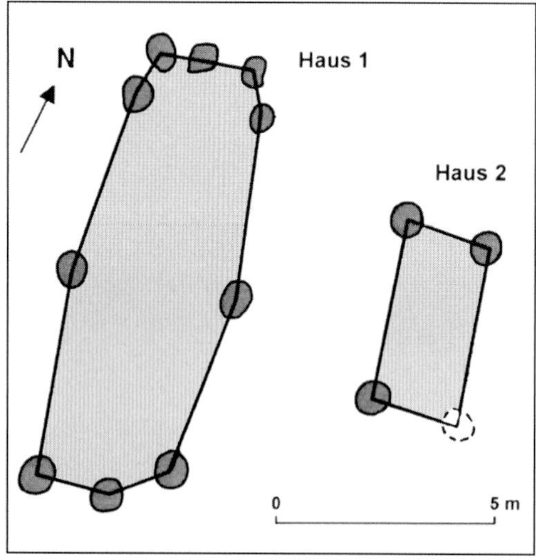

Figure 9.5: Landau SüdOst. Floor-plans of a residential house and an adjoining building; dashed lines = inferred post (after Husty 2004b, 152)

Figure 9.6: Erstein, Grassweg. Well 1152, situated 20 m beyond the settlement pits, and c. *2.5 m deep. The lining consists of planks from a hollowed oak trunk, which were dendrochronologically dated by Tegel (cf. Fig. 9.7). Late Bell Beaker pottery was found on the old land surface (after Croutsch* et al. *2010, Fig. 9.9)*

Table 9.2: Presumed settlement sites in south-west Germany: pits, ditches and wells

Site	*No. on map*	*Features*
Erstein, Grassweg/PAE	17	Several settlement pits were arranged in a NW–SE oriented row (Fig. 9.6). There was also a plank-lined well. The site produced numerous pottery fragments from the Late Bell Beaker Period and the well-lining was dated dendrochronologically to 2231 and 2215 BC (Fig. 9.7). Radiocarbon dates date the site to *c.* 2350–2150 cal BC (Croutsch *et al.* 2010)
Hattstatt 'Ziegelsheuer' (Haut-Rhin)	18	8 settlement pits containing Bell Beaker or Early Bronze Age pottery
Houssen (Haut-Rhin)	19	2 wells with Bell Beaker or Early Bronze Age pottery
Weil der Stadt, Eselsweg	20	A small pit with Bell Beaker shards (Fundber. Schwaben 18, 1967, 44)
Welschingen-Engen, Guuhaslen, Hegau	21	Irregular, curved trench, 30 m long and *c.* 1 m deep. Bell Beaker and settlement pottery of the Bell Beaker Culture were found in the lower part of the backfill (Fig. 9.8; Hald 2008)

Table 9.3: Settlement pits and cultural layers in eastern Switzerland

Site	*No. on map*	*Features*
Affoltern ZH – Zwillikon – Weid	22	Cultural layer without structures but with Bell Beaker ceramics and radiocarbon dated to *c.* 2500–2200 cal BC (Rigert 2002)
Cham ZG – Oberwil, Hof	23	Two large settlement pits with Bell Beaker period pottery. No structures observed. The pits were radiocarbon dated to *c.* 2500–2200 cal BC (Gnepf *et al.* 1997)
Wetzikon ZH Kempten	24	The site comprised a landscaped stream bed, on which lay a culture layer with rich finds of Bell Beaker, almost certainly from a settlement. The site was radiocarbon dated to *c.* 2400–2200 cal BC (Fig. 9.9; Rigert *et al.* 2005)

Kirchberg and Sasbach, Limberg. From more than 60 sites producing evidence of the Bell Beaker Culture, not a single unambiguous ground-plan of a house or structure has been preserved within the areas excavated.

Eastern Switzerland

Switzerland never appears as an archaeological unit in terms of Pre- and Early History. In western Switzerland, prehistoric cultures were oriented towards Western Europe, and Central European influences were effective in eastern Switzerland. This distinct cultural separation is evident throughout history and is also noticeable in Bell Beaker times. While in western Switzerland their remains, which consist both of settlements and graves, are seen as extensions of the eastern French Bell Beaker groups (Besse *et al.* this volume), the eastern Swiss artefacts are related to eastern Central European examples. The Bell Beaker presence in eastern Switzerland consists of the remains of settlement sites and a few individual finds but no graves have yet been found.

The settlement traces consist of pits and outcrops of cultural layers which contained Bell Beaker fragments and they attest an ephemeral type of settlement with no evidence for any

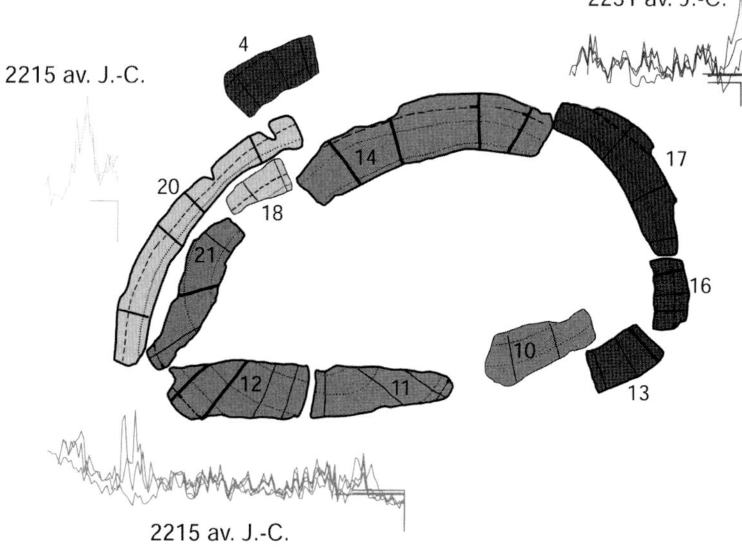

Figure 9.7: Erstein, Grassweg. The planks of the lower part of the Well 1152. The cross sections and the annual rings of the same trunk are characterised by different shades of grey (Drawing W. Tegel, after Croutsch et al. *2010, fig. 10)*

Figure 9.8: Engen-Welschingen, Guuhaslen. Irregular, curved trench, 30 m long, by c.*1 m deep. Bell Beaker sherds and settlement pottery of the Bell Beaker Culture were found in the lower fill, below the stone layer in the bottom of the ditch, (LRAKonstanz, Kreisarchäologie, Hald 2008)*

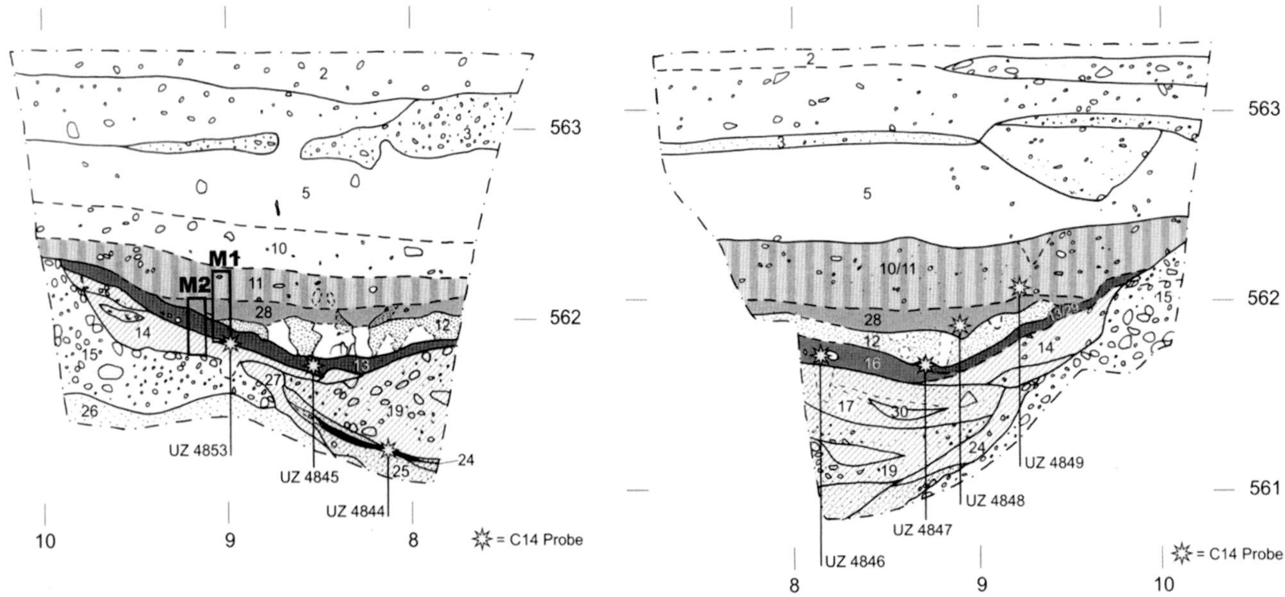

Figure 9.9: Wetzikon ZH Kempten. Landscaped stream bed, on which lay a cultural layer (black layer 13) with rich Bell Beaker domestic material (after Rigert et al. *2005)*

house structures. Other sparse finds comprise single Bell Beaker sherds (Rigert *et al.* 2005, 104). The settlement pits are listed in Table 9.3.

Conclusions

Only the detailed treatment of a topic reveals the gaps in our knowledge. While the presentation of new finds and assemblages usually causes great excitement with regard to the increase in knowledge, specific questions reveal the limits of a statement. This is particularly evident in the holistic description of the Bell Beaker Culture, which naturally depends on the current state of research which is very balanced in southern Germany, eastern Switzerland and Alsace. Our dataset is actually very good and our knowledge of the Bell Beaker Culture is extensive. There have also been numerous large-scale excavations here (and these are on-going), but they continue to paint the same picture of Bell Beaker settlement. Graves, mostly in widely scattered groups, are well documented, but there is hardly any evidence for settlement sites. Domestic activity is mostly represented by pits and spreads of cultural material. This argument has often been used to suggest small, perishable huts even though there is some rare evidence for structures of post construction (cf. the individual contributions in this volume, and: Lemercier & Strahm 2018). In this regional

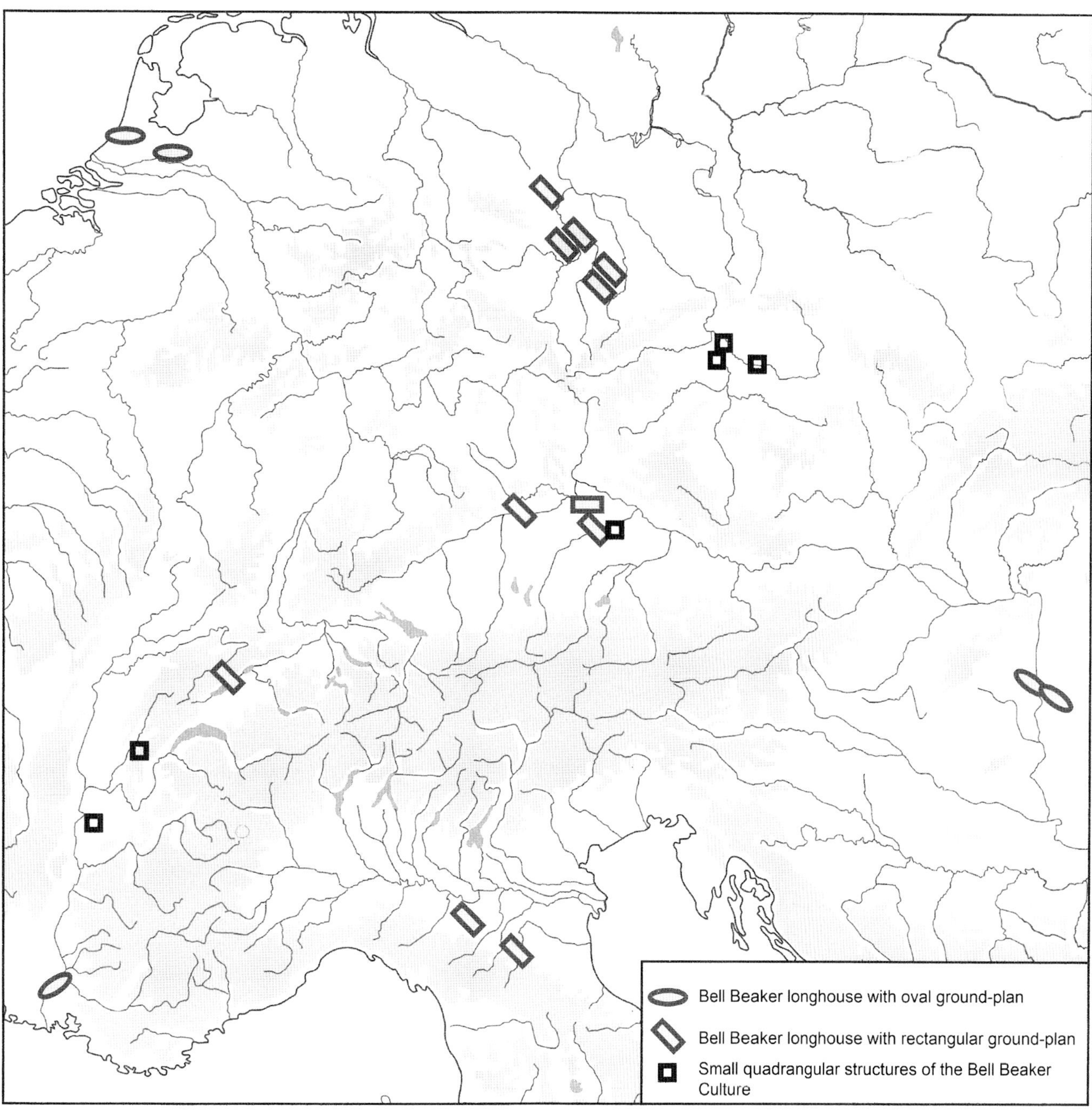

Figure 9.10: Distribution of the longhouses of the Bell Beaker Culture in Central Europe

study, the two ground-plans of Landau SüdOst should be mentioned (Husty 2004b) but the evidence is too scant to reconstruct the settlement. Consequently, we cannot attribute the lack of Beaker-associated house layouts and settlements to a gap in our research yet it remains a gap in our knowledge. It is also hard to imagine that the people responsible for the well documented Bell Beaker Culture, which developed a differentiated social network and which attached great importance to prestigious burial sites and in which semiotic expressions play a major role, could have lived only in flimsy huts. Consequently, we can only conclude that houses must have employed a special construction method, which left no traces in the ground, and which obviously did not require the digging of any negative features. The houses must have been built directly on the ground, presumably as post buildings utilising massive sleeper beams as we know from the end of the 4th millennium BC at, for example, sites from the Federsee. We may even postulate log buildings constructed directly on the old ground surface. Both construction methods are unlikely to leave much in the way of observable archaeological evidence.

Notwithstanding these hypotheses, large buildings or longhouses have been found in excavations in central Germany as a result of the recent large area excavations in response to developments (Spatzier & Schunke, this volume). Here, double-aisled ground-plans with double posts bear witness to great architectural skill. In addition, the large timber ceremonial enclosures, such as that at Pömmelte, clearly demonstrate the constructional abilities of these populations. Nevertheless, the type is not uniform and sometimes the narrow sides are rounded and sometimes the longitudinal walls are slightly bowed. It is likely, however, that the long-houses of this region had a special function. They do not appear to have been domestic buildings, as neither hearths nor indications of interior partitioning or ground discoloration have been observed. It is also striking that no typical domestic materials have ever been made in the interiors of these large houses. It seems to be a particularly important type of building but not always directly datable. The long house is common in central Germany and was first recognised as a Beaker type at Klobikau (Balfanz *et al.* 2015). In southern Germany, singularly in Switzerland and northern Italy its distribution coincides with that of the *Begleitkeramik*.

These long buildings belong to the group of large Bell Beaker buildings that we know from other regions and whose common characteristic is the unusually large size that distinguishes them from normal residential buildings. Ground-plans and construction techniques differ, but there are long distance similarities. Oval or boat-shaped layouts can be found in Spain, France, Britain and Hungary, though construction techniques differ according to local geology and topography (Fig 9.10).

Since the discovery of the first longhouse in Bopfingen (Krause 1997), which was originally dated to the Early Bronze Age, there has been much discussion about the tradition and function of this type (Nadler 2001). It is a Bell Beaker innovation that continued into the Early Bronze Age. The longhouse certainly has a certain social function and was a place for community action and social gathering. This architectural innovation and the socio-cultural manifestations documented with it point to the great changes that changed the world with the appearance of the Bell Beaker complex.

References

Balfanz, K., Frölich, M. & Schunke, T. 2015. Ein Siedlungsareal der Glockenbecherkultur mit Hausgrundrissen bei Klobikau, Sachsen-Anhalt, Deutschland. In Meller H., Arz, W. H., Jung, R. & Risch, R. (eds.), *2200 BC – Ein Klimasturz als Ursache für den Zerfall der Alten Welt? 7. Mitteldeutscher Archäologentag vom 23. bis 26. Oktober 2014 in Halle (Saale)*, Tagungen des Landesmuseums für Vorgeschichte Halle, Band 12/II, 747–3

Besse, M. & Strahm, C. 2001.The components of the Bell Beaker Complex. In: Nicolis (ed.), 2001, 103–10

Burgess, C. & Shennan, S. 1976. The Beaker phenomenon: some suggestions.In Burgess C., Miket R. (eds), *Settlement and Economy in the Third and Second Millenium B.C.*, 309–31. Oxford: British Archaeological Reports 33

Croutsch, C., Tegel, W. & Pascutto, E. 2010. Le site d'Erstein Grassweg/PAE: un habitat campaniforme dans le sud de la Plaine du Rhin supérieur. In Jeunesse C. & Denaire A. (eds), *Du Néolithique final au Bronze ancien dans le Nord-Est de la France. Actualité de la recherche, Actes de la table ronde de Strasbourg, 9 juin 2009*, 43–55. Association pour la Promotion de la Recherche Archéologique en Alsace

Gnepf, U., Hämmerle, S., Hochuli, St. & Schibler, J. 1997. Spuren einer glockenbecherzeitlichen Besiedlung in Cham ZG – Oberwil, Hof. *Jahrbuch der Schweizer Gesellschaft für Ur- und Frühgeschichte* 80, 95–110

Hald, J. 2008. Zum vorläufigen Abschluss der Ausgrabungen im vorgeschichtlichen Siedlungsareal 'Guuhaslen' bei Engen-Welschingen. *Archäologische Ausgrabungen in Baden-Württemberg 2008*, 100–5

Heyd, V. 2004a. Einleitung. In Heyd *et al.* 2004, 7–13

Heyd, V. 2004b. Die Siedlungsspuren der Glockenbecherkultur unter dem Kappellplatz von Altötting. In Heyd, *et al.* 2004, 121–46

Heyd, V., Husty, L. & Kreiner, L., 2004. *Siedlungen der Glockenbecherkultur in Süddeutschland und Mitteleuropa.* Arbeiten zur Archäologie Süddeutschlands 17. Büchenbach, Verlag Dr. Faustus

Husty, L. 2004a. Glockenbecherzeitliche Funde aus Landau a.d. Isar. In Heyd *et al.* 2004, 15–102

Husty, L. 2004b. Überlegungen zum Siedlungswesen der Glockenbecherkultur. In Heyd *et al.* 2004, 147–54

Jeunesse, C. & Denaire, A. 2010. Catalogue des sites du Néolithique final et du Bronze ancien dans le sud de la Plaine du Rhin supérieur. In Jeunesse & Denaire (eds), 2010, 187–202

Jeunesse, C. & Denaire, A. (eds), 2010. *Du Néolithique final au Bronze ancien dans le Nord-Est de la France.* Actualité de la recherche, Actes de la table ronde de Strasbourg, 9 Juin 2009, Association pour la Promotion de la Recherche Archéologique en Alsace

Krause, R. 1997. Frühbronzezeitliche Großbauten aus

Bopfingen (Ostalbkreis, Baden-Württemberg). Ein Beitrag zu Hausbau und Siedlungsweise der Bronzezeit.In Assendorp, J.J. (ed.), *Forschungen zur bronzezeitlichen Besiedlung in Nord- und Mitteleuropa. Internationales Symposium vom 9–11 Mai 1996 in Hitzacker*, 149–68. Espelkamp: Internationale Archäologie 38

Krause, R. 2003. *Studien zur kupfer- und frühbronzezeitlichen Metallurgie zwischen Karpatenbecken und Ostsee*. Vorgeschichtliche Forschungen 24, Rahden Westfalien.

Kreiner, L. 2004. Eine Siedlung (?) der Glockenbecherkultur in Prunn, Gde. Eichendorf. In Heyd *et al.* 2004, 103–20

Lemercier, O. & Strahm, C. 2018. Nids de coucous et grandes maisons. L'habitat campaniforme, épicampaniforme et péricampaniforme en France dans son contexte Européen. In Lemercier, O., Sénépart, I., Besse, M. & Mordant, C. (eds), 2018. *Habitations et habitat du Néolithique à l'âge du Bronze en France et régions voisines. Actes des Deuxièmes Rencontres Nord-Sud de Préhistoire Récente*. 459–79. Toulouse: Archives d'Écologie Préhistorique

Merkl, M. 2011. *Bell Beaker Copper Use in Central Europe: A Distinctive Tradition ?* Oxford: British Archaeological Reports International Series 2267

Nadler, M., 2001. Einzelhof oder Hauptlingshaus? – Gedanken zu den Langhäusern der Frühbronzezeit, 39–46. In: Eberschweiler, B., Köninger, J., Schlichtherle, H. & Strahm, C. (eds), 2001. *Aktuelles zur Frühbronzezeit im nördlichen Alpenvorland.* Hemmenhofener Skripte

Nicolis, F. (ed.), 2001. *Bell Beakers today. Pottery, people, culture, symbols in prehistoric Europe*, Proceedings of the International Colloquium, Riva del Garda, 11–16 May 1998, 103–110. Trento

Piller, C. & Richter, T. 2012. Eine Siedlungsgrube der Glockenbecherkultur aus Ergolding. *Das Archäologische Jahr in Bayern,* 2012, 34–6

Rigert, E., 2002. Glockenbecher im Knonauer Amt. *Jahrbuch des Schweizer Gesellschaft für Ur- und Frühgeschichte* 85, 55–66

Rigert, E., Jacomet, St. &Hosch, S. 2005. Eine Fundstelle der Glockenbecherzeit in Wetzikon ZH-Kempten. *Jahrbuch des Schweizer Gesellschaft für Ur- und Frühgeschichte* 88, 2005, 87–118

Schranil, J., 1928. *Vorgeschichte Böhmens und Mährens*. Berlin and Leipzig: Walter de Gruyter Co.

Strahm, C. 2004a. Das Glockenbecher-Phänomen aus der Sicht der Komplementär-Keramik, 101–26. In Czebreszuk J. (ed.), 2004, *Similar but Different. Bell Beakers in Europe*. Poznan: Adam Mickiewicz University

Strahm, C. 2004b. Le phénomène campaniforme et les composantes autochtones non campaniformes, *Bulletin de la Société Préhistorique Française* 101, 201–6

Zirngibl, B. 2012. 9 aus 49 – Eine Bilanzzum 'Aufeld' bei Atting. *Deggendorfer Vorträge,* 2012, 53–73

10

Late Neolithic and Bell Beaker settlements and houses in (eastern) Austria

Daniela Kern, Günter Morschhauser, Martin Penz and Oliver Schmitsberger

Settlements of the Final Neolithic, or to be more precise, settlements of the first three quarters of the 3rd millennium BC are not well known in Austria. In the last few decades only a small number of pits, sunken buildings and post-holes have been found but rarely do these form part of a complete house plan. Most of them are only known from preliminary reports and some of the buildings are only published in photographs with the result that not all the ground-plans of these buildings are available for study. That does not only hold true for the settlements of the time of the Bell Beaker Culture, but also for those of most of preceding and partly contemporary cultures in the territory of present-day Austria.

Native cultures before the arrival of Bell Beaker

These are, from the west to the east, the Cham-Culture with a distribution in southern Germany, Bohemia, Salzburg, Upper Austria and adjacent parts of Lower Austria and Styria. The Jevišovice-Culture (JC), distributed in southern Moravia, Lower Austria and north-west Slovakia. The Corded Ware Culture (CWC) which in Austria is mainly known from the Traisen Valley and from stray finds in Lower and Upper Austria. Finally, the Kosihy-Čaka/Makó-Culture (KČM) which is distributed in the eastern part of Lower Austria, Burgenland, South-eastern Moravia, western and southern Slovakia and in west and north Hungary.

The JC can be divided into an older (JC I – 'Facies Wachberg') and a younger phase (JC II). The younger phase can be further divided into three subphases IIa-IIc (IIa – middle Jevišovice, Spielberg; IIb – late Jevišovice also known as the Mödling-Zöbing-group after Ruttkay; IIc – the final Jevišovice-culture or more correctly the transition period to the following cultures). JC IIc is contemporary with an early stage of the local group of the CWC and the beginning of KČM (Schmitsberger 2006, 151). This mosaic of different cultural units in the same region is similar to the Strachotín-Mušov-type as defined by Šebela (1999, 227) or the mixed horizon of Strachotín-Držovice in Moravia as defined by Peška (2000, 267) that postulates a contemporaneity of the Jevišovice B, Bosáca, Globular Amphora Culture, KČM, the earliest Bell Beaker (BBC) and local groups of the CWC. We do not agree with the contemporaneity of Jevišovice B and the oldest Bell Beakers at least not for eastern Austria (Schmitsberger 2011, 119). Here contacts between JC IIa and the older CWC (unknown in Lower Austria) can be seen in the similarity and imitations of axes of the CWC (Schmitsberger 2003 with further literature) and in the cord decoration on ceramics. In Eastern Austria the KČM is younger than the JC with just a very short overlap if, indeed, there was an overlap at all (Ruttkay 1995, 178; 2002, 152; Medunová-Benešova 1977). This means that the KČM is definitely younger than the JC IIb (Mödling-Zöbing). The beginning of the KČM is contemporary with the CWC in Lower Austria (local group Herzogenburg) and the younger KČM with Bell Beakers (Schmitsberger 2011, 119). The youngest phase of the Herzogenburg CWC-group is also contemporary with the earliest BBC (Neugebauer-Maresch 1994, 76).

From the cultural units in Austria only JC settlements are moderately well known. Although about 100 (settlement) sites have been documented (Krenn-Leeb 2006) most of them are only represented by stray finds (Lantschner 1990) and only a few of them have been (partly) excavated like Krems-Hundssteig (Pieler 2002) and Meidling-Kleiner Anzingerberg (Krenn-Leeb 2010). Those settlements are small and most of them are situated on hilltops or mountain spurs (Krenn-Leeb 2006) although sometimes also on river terraces such as that at Aigen (Obenaus 2016, 184). On a mountain spur near Krems-Hundsteig lies a settlement that was fortified on one side by two ditches. Although a hearth, the remains of a loom (35 loomweights in a row), a floor, some vessels *in situ* and post-holes were excavated no ground-plan of a house could be reconstructed due to the small size of the trenches (Pieler 2002, 205, 209).

At present, KČM finds are known from about 30 sites. They again show up in the archaeological record mostly by stray find. Pits and post-holes of this cultural unit were recognised, for example, near Grub (Krenn-Leeb 1996, 190), Schleinbach (Schwammenhöfer 1989), Ziersdorf (Schmitsberger 2012) and Vienna 11, Csokorgasse 2–10 (Adler-Wölfl & Penz 2018; forthcoming). Remains of buildings such as those at Vienna 10, Oberlaa (Penz 2017; 2018a; 2018b; forthcoming) and Schwechat (Scholz & Müller 2011) are rare. As features are few in comparison to those from other periods excavated during substantial rescue excavations, they are mostly briefly mentioned in excavation reports. The settlement from Grub is described simply as a 'layer and some features' (Krenn-Leeb 1996, 190) and sometimes they can hide behind terms such as 'Neolithic features' in preliminary reports. This is particularly possible in areas such as Burgenland where the distribution of this group can be presumed because of the vicinity of the Hungarian find spots. Settlements of the CWC are so far unknown in Austria.

In the last few years several sunken houses have been found such as those at Haselbach (Trebsche & Fichtl 2018a, D2476-D2477; 2018b, 10–12), Hatzenbach (Drost & Lauermann 1999) and Laa an der Thaya (Stöckl 2016). They usually show up without or with just a few contemporary features but due to the scarcity of diagnostic finds (mostly small pieces of pottery) dating by archaeological comparison is difficult and it is only the radiocarbon dates from bones recovered from the sunken features of Haselbach and Hatzenbach that demonstrate that these buildings were in use from the first half to the middle of the 3rd millennium. A similar sunken house near Schrick was dated archaeologically to the JC (Artner 2006), but as almost no finds are published this cannot be verified. Some of these features are so small that it seems possible that they just represent the cellars of much larger buildings.

Final Neolithic houses of the Jevišovice Culture

The fortified settlement at Kleiner Anzingerberg in Lower Austria is the best-known JC settlement in Austria due to it being the focus of a long term research project. An area of 200 m^2 has been excavated and at least six layers of burned houses with hearths, oven plates, ceramic vessels, stone and bone tools, spindle whorls, loom weights and macroscopic plant remains have been found over the last 20 years. Results have been reported in several articles but nevertheless no complete ground-plan of a house has been published. What we can tell so far is that houses were erected on small artificial terraces and the clay floors had a foundation of stones and a screed floor of loess. The houses were of two-nave post constructions and in the earlier phases they were 6–8 m long whilst the more recent examples provided ground-plans of two room houses measuring 8–10 m long and 5–5.5 m wide. The walls were of wattle and daub construction and different activity zones (food processing, bone and stone tool production) could be recognised. Finds of spindle whorls and loom weights attest the manufacture of fabrics (Krenn-Leeb 2016 with further literature).

At Aigen (Lower Austria) several features were observed during a rescue excavation in 2015 on the edge of a terrace now used for growing vines (Obenaus 2016, 184–5). Parts of three sunken buildings were uncovered but their size could not be determined as just a small section along the edge of the terrace was investigated. A few pieces of diagnostic pottery dated the site to the JC.

Meanwhile during rescue excavations in 2004 at Furth bei Göttweig (Lower Austria) a sunken feature was discovered (Pieler & Hellerschmid 2005, 743; Schmitsberger 2006). As it measured just 3.9 × 3.5 m, it was interpreted as a workshop or a cellar. The pottery found in the fill can be dated to the Mödling-Zöbing-group of the JC. Amongst the assemblage were pots and amphorae with lugs or handles and rusticated lower bodies, bowls, jugs, one piece of a so-called casserole, a small stone axe, two flint tools and one worked bone. The sample of animal bone from this complex is small and the size of the fragments varies but nevertheless the remains of domestic cattle, sheep and pig were found as well as wild aurochs, red deer, wild boar, wild horse, beaver and tortoise (Kunst 2006).

In 2013 a sunken feature was excavated near Plaika (Lower Austria). It lay close to a fortified settlement of the JC and sherds from the fill of the house suggest that it dates to the same period. On its narrow side the presumed house had a post-hole but unfortunately the size of this building has not been published (Preinfalk & Preinfalk 2014, D1556).

In the JC pots, bowls, amphorae, jug-like cups, casseroles, terrine like vessels and interior decorated bowls with a cross shaped foot were in use. Characteristic is the so called 'Jevišovice-pot' with a plain burnished upper part and rusticated lower part below a cordon, a row of impressions or a flat incised line. Sometimes rims of storage- and cooking-pots are thickend and, especially in the older phases, have impressions. Cordons are very common in the earlier phases, but become more rare in the later phases when finally only short cordons are used. In the older phases carinated forms predominate whilst in the younger phases the bodies of the vessels are more rounded. From the JC IIa (rare) and more often from IIb onwards, pottery is decorated with cord impressions. 'Furchenstich' (furrowed decoration) is used throughout the whole of the JC (Ruttkay 1995; Medunová-Benešová1977; Schmitsberger 2006).

Final Neolithic houses of the Kosihy-Čaka/Makó Culture

In 2016 and 2017 parts of a KČM settlement were discovered in Vienna 10, Oberlaa, on the southern edge of Vienna (Penz 2017; 2018a; 2018b; forthcoming). The site was located on a smooth slope about 200–300 m away from a rivulet called the Liesingbach. The excavation campaign of 2016 located only two scattered round pits dating to the KČM and a partly preserved house plan of uncertain date. In the 2017 campaign seventeen domestic pits and three house plans (Fig. 10.1) were found. In the extensive excavation area (6750 m^2) only KČM occupation was detected. A cluster of round or oval pits (arranged like a 35 m long belt) was situated on the eastern edge and a group of three larger pits was located at the southern edge. Between these, three post-structured houses were recorded but it is possible that the ground-plans are incomplete because of top soil erosion resulting in the loss of the upper parts of the features. One short row of post-holes was found within the eastern group of pits. All of these structures are orientated approximately N–S.

House 1 measured 6.2 × 4.3 m and can be reconstructed from 9 post-holes (0.21–0.44 m in diameter with a maximum depth of 0.2 m) arranged in three rows. A single oval and funnel-shaped pit was found outside its eastern side (Fig. 10.1). House 2 was also a simple, almost rectangular structure with 6 (possibly 7) post-holes defining an area measuring 6 × 3.2 m (Fig. 10.1). House 3 seems to have been a small hut defined by 5 posts and measuring 5.3 × 4 m. The walls on the long side appear slightly concave (Fig. 10.1). The associated pits often yielded burnt debris such as clay and daub and fragments of oven plates. Other finds comprise

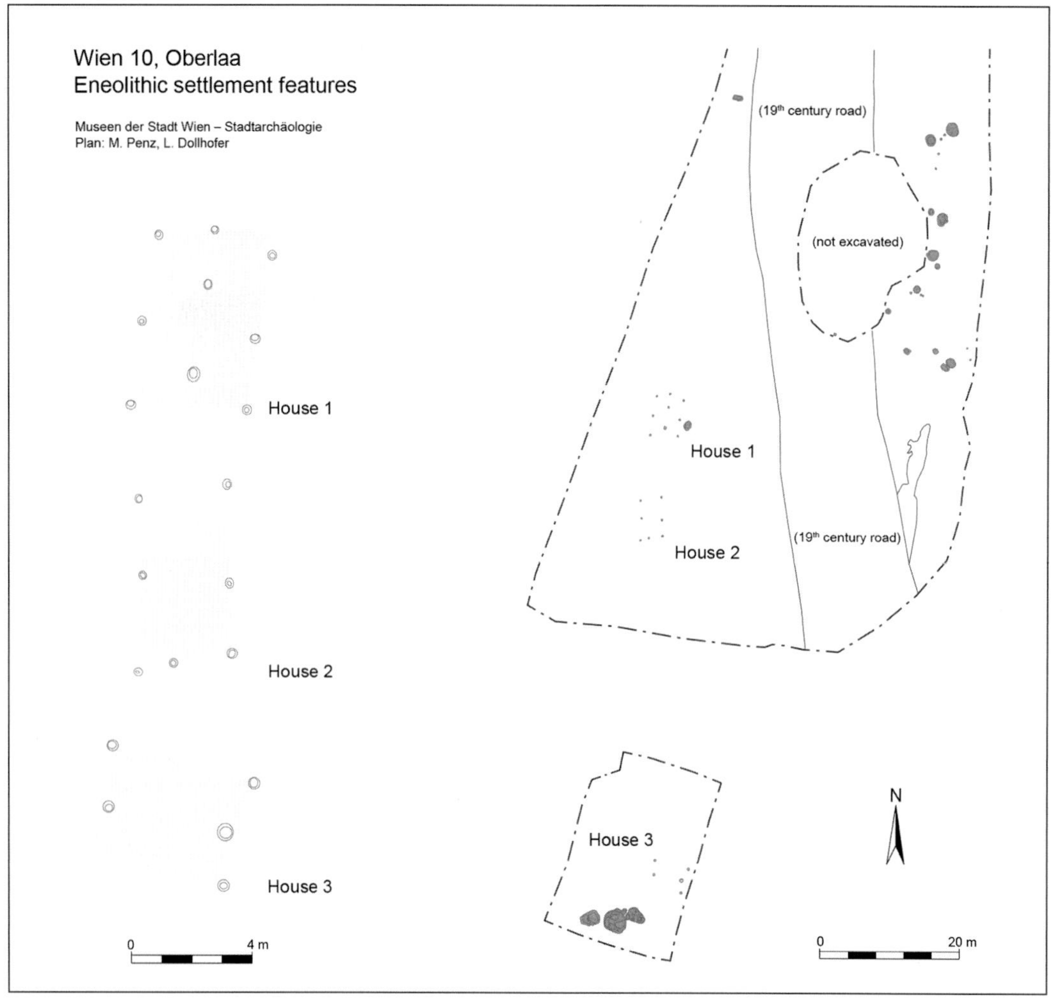

Figure 10.1: Kosihý-Čaka/Makó-settlement of Vienna 10, Oberlaa (M. Penz/ Stadtarchäologie Wien)

animal bones, fragments of cylindrical loom-weights, a spindle whorl, and the characteristic pottery of the KČM (Fig. 10.2).

At Schwechat (Lower Austria) part of a fortified settlement was excavated in 2009 and 2010. The 5 m wide ditch was investigated for a length of 10 m and proved to have been associated with a palisade, 26 post-holes of which were recorded. 'Some pits with pieces of pottery corresponding to those of the filling of the ditch' were uncovered near-by and a sunken feature measuring 3 × 2 m was interpreted as a house (Scholz & Müller 2011, 318).

The domestic assemblages of the KČM are characterised by dark, plain ware and vessel types comprise amphorae, jugs, mugs, bowls and pots. Amphorae have cylindrical necks, large handles and ribs whilst the pots, bowls and jugs have characteristic thickened rims, brushed and rusticated bodies and small knobs. Most pots have burnished upper parts and rusticated lower parts and thickened and rounded rims sometimes decorated with impressions. Fragments of internally decorated (footed) bowls are also present on most excavated KČM-sites (eg, Fig. 10.2,1).

Final Neolithic houses of the Corded Ware Culture

No CWC settlements have yet been discovered in Austria and most sites are represented by stray finds and graves. The dead were furnished with pottery, bone tools, shell ornaments, stone axes and tools and knives and ornaments of copper. Utilised stone is mostly local although Bavarian tabular chert is used for daggers and Baltic flint for both blades and daggers. Pottery types of the Herzogenburg-group of the CWC consist of bowls, jugs, cups, small and big amphorae, beakers and pots. The vessels are usually dark grey in colour, but some may be

Figure 10.2: Characteristic pottery from Kosihý-Čaka/Makó – settlement at Vienna 10, Oberlaa (M. Penz, L. Dollhofer/Stadtarchäologie Wien)

brown. Most of the vessels are undecorated, except for some cups and jugs that have filled triangles or bands under the rim and on the shoulder and the corded beakers. In one grave a corded beaker was accompanied with a footed bowl with internal decoration characteristic of the KČM (Kern 2011, Abb. 2). Bowls, pots and amphorae sometimes have ledge handles on the rim or close to the rim and bowls and amphorae have cordons

Figure 10.3: Sunken house at Laa an der Thaya – Südumfahrung (Ch. Stöckl/ASINOE)

with fingertip impressions. As all these types come from graves we do not know if they are representative of domestic pottery or whether there were any differences.

Final Neolithic houses of unknown cultural units

In Haselbach (Lower Austria) an almost rectangular sunken feature and a pit were discovered in 2016 (Trebsche & Fichtl 2018a). The diameter of the pit was 2.40 m and the size of the sunken house was 9.35 × 4.56 m with the impressions of planks recognisable on the floor. Just a few pieces of undiagnostic pottery were found. The radiocarbon date from the cranium of a *bos* places this complex in the first half of the 3rd millennium BC (Peter Trebsche pers. comm.).

In Hatzenbach (Lower Austria) a rectangular sunken feature measuring 7.8 × 4.2 m was discovered in 1998 (Drost & Lauermann 1999). The few pieces of pottery can be generally dated to the Final Neolithic and this was confirmed by the radiocarbon dating (Schmitsberger 2005, 193, Nr. 16). At Laa an der Thaya-Südumfahrung, Lower Austria a sunken house was uncovered during rescue excavations in 2015 (Stöckl 2016, 209 & Abb. 13) and at the base of the 9 × 5 m building (Fig. 10.3) an assemblage of pottery was found. Although three vessels – a pot, a bowl and an amphora – could be reconstructed the assignation to a cultural unit is problematic. The pot points towards the KČM and this feature dates definitely to after the JC IIb but probably before the BBC, most probably in the horizon of the JC IIc and early KČM and beginning of Somogyvár Culture.

In conclusion, the domestic assemblage associated with sunken houses mainly comprises small undiagnostic sherds and so the identification of this material is problematic. Nevertheless, it is possible to ascertain that fine ware such as bowls, cups and jugs as well as domestic ware such as pots and amphorae were present.

Bell Beaker settlements

Before 2005, only a few well documented Bell Beaker settlement features were known and most of them had been discovered during rescue excavations such as those at Lutzmannsburg (Ohrenberger 1971) and Vienna 11, Csokorgasse/Etrichstraße. In both these cases just local pottery was found. As most regional ware known in Austria from Bell Beaker graves is in poor condition, often missing the original surfaces and having a tendency to disintegrate when in contact with water, the good quality pottery found in the pits at Vienna 11, Csokorgasse/Etrichstraße was originally classified as belonging to the Urnfield Culture. It was not recognised as being BBC regional ware until 2006 even though the archaeozoologist had suggested an earlier date for the find assemblage based on the characteristics of the animal bones. This was later confirmed by radiocarbon dating (Czeika 2002, 23; Penz 2010). Other settlement sites such as Laa an der Thaya, Inneres Gerichtsfeld, Ruhof (both Toriser 1976) and Bisamberg (Hetzer 1949, 110–11) were only known from stray finds of Bell Beaker sherds that were presumed not to have derived from graves. In 2005 a sunken feature was unearthed in Vienna 3, Rennweg, containing a large number of regional ware sherds of unusually good quality and in 2008 pits with Bell Beaker and regional ware sherds were found near Maissau (Schmitsberger 2009, 468–80). In 2015 a settlement pit with regional ware was uncovered south of Laa an der Thaya (Stöckl 2016) and in 2014 ground-plans of four houses were identified during a rescue excavation in Walpersdorf in the Traisen valley (Morschhauser 2015). At least two of these houses were boat-shaped.

In 2015/2016 a well was excavated near Königsbrunn (Lower Austria) (Morschhauser 2018) and characteristic regional ware of the Bell Beaker Culture was found in the fill. Also in 2015, a rectangular wooden construction was recognised on an aerial photograph in the Attersee near Abtsdorf (Upper Austria) and underwater prospection indicated that the construction beams of a house survived. Radiocarbon dated this construction to *c.* 2400–2200 cal BC (Pohl 2016a, 295; 2016b, 32).

The Bell Beaker settlement pit that was found south of Laa an der Thaya lay close to the Final Neolithic sunken feature described above (Stöckl 2016). It contained several characteristic pieces of Bell Beaker pottery as well as bowls with thickened and T-sectioned rims, pots with round lugs on the shoulder or close to the rim and with scratched lower parts, amphorae with massive handles on the shoulder or the belly, and different kinds of cups and jugs. Amphorae with bow-shaped lugs are related to the KČM.

Near Maissau (Lower Austria) three pits were discovered in 2008 during rescue excavation. Two features (349 & 1091) had an oval shape and in the former pieces of regional ware, the fragment of a bow shaped pendant, bone tools and a lamella of a boar's tusk were found. Undiagnostic pottery, a V-perforated button and three bone points were found in the latter. In the associated pit complex (features 1108, 1116, 1144, 1199, 1237) several fragments of Bell Beakers and sherds of regional ware were found (Schmitsberger 2009, 468–80).

A settlement pit was excavated during rescue excavations in 1979 near Schwechat (Lower Austria). It was 1.60 m deep and had a diameter of 3.20 m. Cups, bowls with lugs under the rim, fragments of amphorae with cordons and with fingertip impressions, fragments with broad handles and the rusticated lower parts of vessels were found associated with charcoal and animal bones (Ruttkay & Stadler 1980). Also, in Vienna 3, Rennweg, a sunken feature was identified in the loess-like loam of a northward sloping terrace of the Danube about 0.5 m beneath the Roman occupation layer (Penz 2010). The pit (*c.* 1.5 m deep and 3.4–4.2 m across) had a flat bottom and was located in the north-eastern corner of the excavation area but unfortunately it could not be investigated entirely (Fig. 10.4).

Figure 10.4: Vienna 3, Rennweg, Bell Beaker pit or sunken house (interface), photo taken from the north-west (M. Mosser/ Stadtarchäologie Wien)

Due to erosion its almost vertical walls could not be detected exactly but some steps could be recorded and a larger one in the south-west corner may indicate an entrance. Other traces of construction such as post-holes or daub were absent and it is still unclear if we may interpret this pit as earth-cellar or even as a dwelling with a connected cellar. After use it was filled up with redeposited top soil containing animal bones and pottery.

As at other BBC sites the distinctive bowls with a sloping ledge on the inner rim are common, additionally those with double handles at the rim (small-sized strap handles as well as perforated lugs) can very likely be diagnosed as a distinctive BBC-types. Cups appear with handles, globular bellies and cylindrical or slightly arched necks. Stamped decoration occurred twice and in one case had a unique metope-like design (Fig. 10.5). But we also have vertically incised lines which shows that this assemblage does not represent a chronologically short phase.

Most of the bowls, cups, jugs and fine pots have a well-finished dark surface, very fine tempered and prepared clay. They are medium to well fired, and often have an exceptionally well-burnished or polished slip or engobe. Fragments of coarse ware like pots and storage vessels occasionally show slip or engobe-roughened surfaces, although a well-burnished surface (often with burnishing facets) may be found on the upper parts of the belly and shoulder. Handles and applications such as lugs

Figure 10.5: Stamp-decorated cup from the Bell Beaker pit or sunken house at Vienna 3, Rennweg (M. Penz/ Stadtarchäologie Wien)

or knobs are commonly attached to the rim or to just below it, but relief decoration such as ridges or ribs also appear at the transitional point between the neck and the belly of larger vessels or on the globular bellies of amphorae. Such plastic cordons often have fingerprints or other indentations and even some rims show impressed decoration. Also worth mentioning is the fact that a wheel-like spindle whorl and some rough utilised bone, resembling artefacts such as spatulae and awls, were also present but there were no stone artefacts. Like the ceramic finds the bones are highly fragmented and some pieces have cut marks. The remains of horses strongly dominate the assemblage of 786 assignable bones (82.30%; minimum number of individuals = 12). Domestic cattle (7.6%), sheep/goat (3.9%), pig (3.6%) and dog (0.4%) were also represented as was an element of wild species (2.2%) comprising deer, wild boar, aurochs and beaver. The bone material also afforded five radiocarbon dates that range from *c.* 2470–2140 cal BC (Penz 2010, 24).

In 1997 some dispersed irregular pits were found in the area Csokorgasse/Etrichstraße in Vienna 11. Three of them were definitely dated to the Final Neolithic (Penz 2014). Pit 3 produced a radiocarbon date of 2340–2140 cal BC (68.2%) (3810 ±50 BP, VERA-0814). The pottery assemblages confirm that they belong to the Final Neolithic and contain bowls with an inwardly thickened and stepped rim as well as cups and jugs with upright or slightly arched collars and with everted rims. We can also find handles or lugs attached to the rim. Animal bones appeared only in pit 3 and were not great in number. Of 71 identifiable bones there is a high percentage of horse (47.89%, minimum individuals = 4) associated with cattle (40.84%), pig (7.04%) and sheep/goat (4.23%) (Czeika 2002; 2013; Penz 2014).

In Walpersdorf (Lower Austria) ground-plans of four houses were uncovered (Morschhauser 2015). They stood parallel to each other close to an old arm of the river Traisen and were oriented NW–SE. It seems that they were erected with the narrow side of the buildings heading towards a trackway. Three of them were situated on one side, the fourth one on the opposite side of the track (Fig. 10.6).

It is possible that the settlement continues in the Southern direction as 'two prehistoric settlements' detected in 2006 were mentioned on the neighbouring plot in an excavation report (Blesl & Hermann 2007, 42), indicating that only undiagnostic finds were present in these features.

House 1 was defined by 22 post-holes, one more that might belong to it, and two or three post-holes of the northern long side seem to be missing. The building measured 16 × 6.5 m though the walls on the long sides were slightly convex giving the building a boat-shaped ground-plan. It was a twin nave construction and the south-eastern end was slightly wider than the north-western end which might be suggestive of an entrance (Fig. 10.7). House 2 is also boat-shaped (Fig. 10.8), of two nave construction, and defined by 25 post-holes. It measures 20 × 7 m and again the entrance can be assumed to have been on the south-eastern side of the building. This house produced the most finds. At house 3 (Fig 10.9), 16 post-holes were found but it seems that the south-eastern part of the building is missing. The surviving part measures 16 × 6 m. House 4 (Fig 10.10) is also probably partly preserved as only 9 post-holes were found, making the ground-plan look trapezoidal. It measured 10.5 × 5.80 m.

In some of the post-holes of the buildings, sherds of both coarse and fine wares were found (Fig. 10.11) and the diagnostic ceramics for Bell Beaker regional ware comprise cups, bowls with T-shaped rim and pots with lugs below the rim (Fig. 10.12). Many of the fragments showed signs of secondary burning (Fig. 10.13).

With regard to the domestic assemblages, most of the regional ware comprises dark or brown plain ware with few exceptions. Only cups and bowls are occasionally reddish brown like Bell Beakers. Surfaces are usually burnished or polished and the ceramic types present comprise cups, bowls, pots and amphorae like those that are known from the graves but preservation is better and most of the surfaces are still intact. Pots sometimes show rustication or roughened surface and have lugs close to the rim. Amphorae with cordons with fingertip impressions and lugs are common in settlement contexts. Bell Beakers are usually only represented in domestic contexts by small fragments with zoned decoration.

Houses – differences and similarities

From the few house-plans currently known it appears that there was a change from

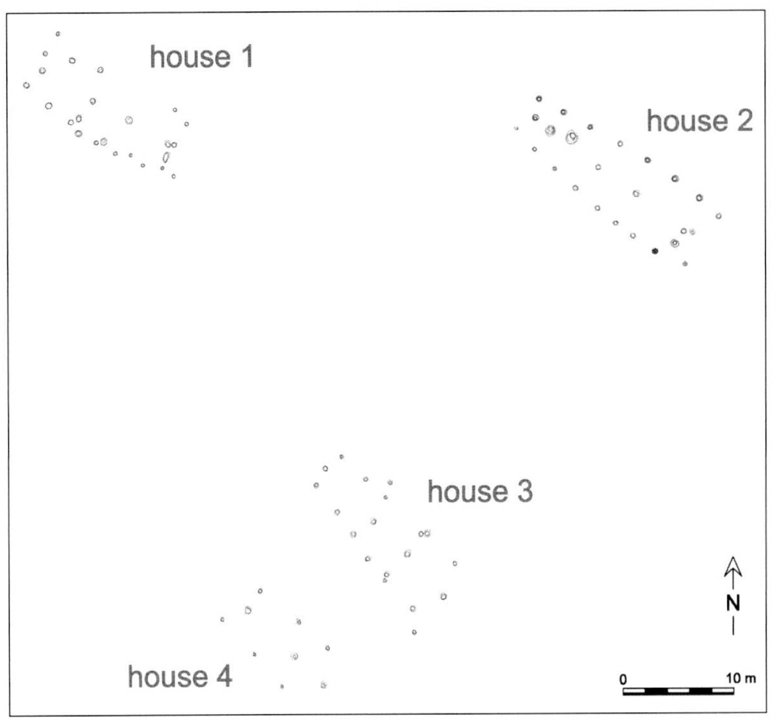

Figure 10.6: Lay-out of the Bell Beaker settlement of Walpersdorf (G. Morschhauser/ Ardig)

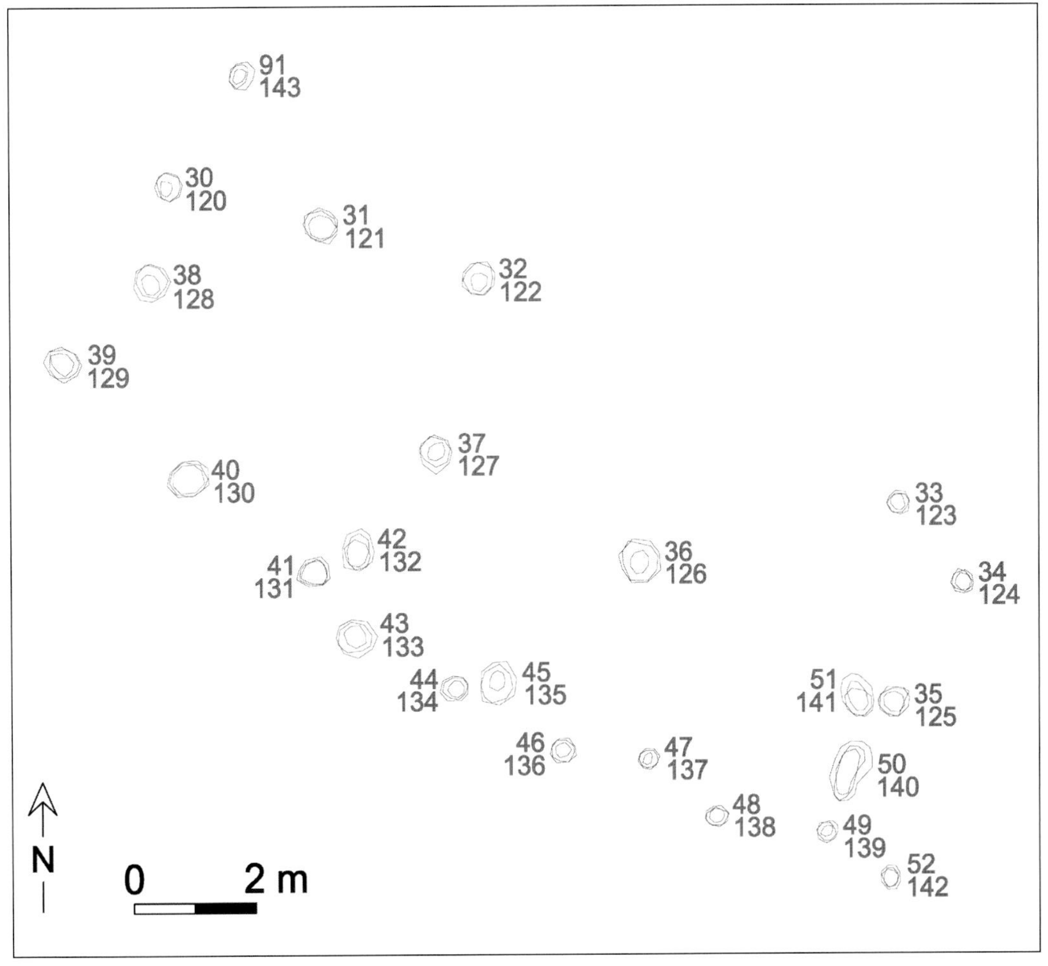

Figure 10.7: Walpersdorf, house 1 (G. Morschhauser/ Ardig)

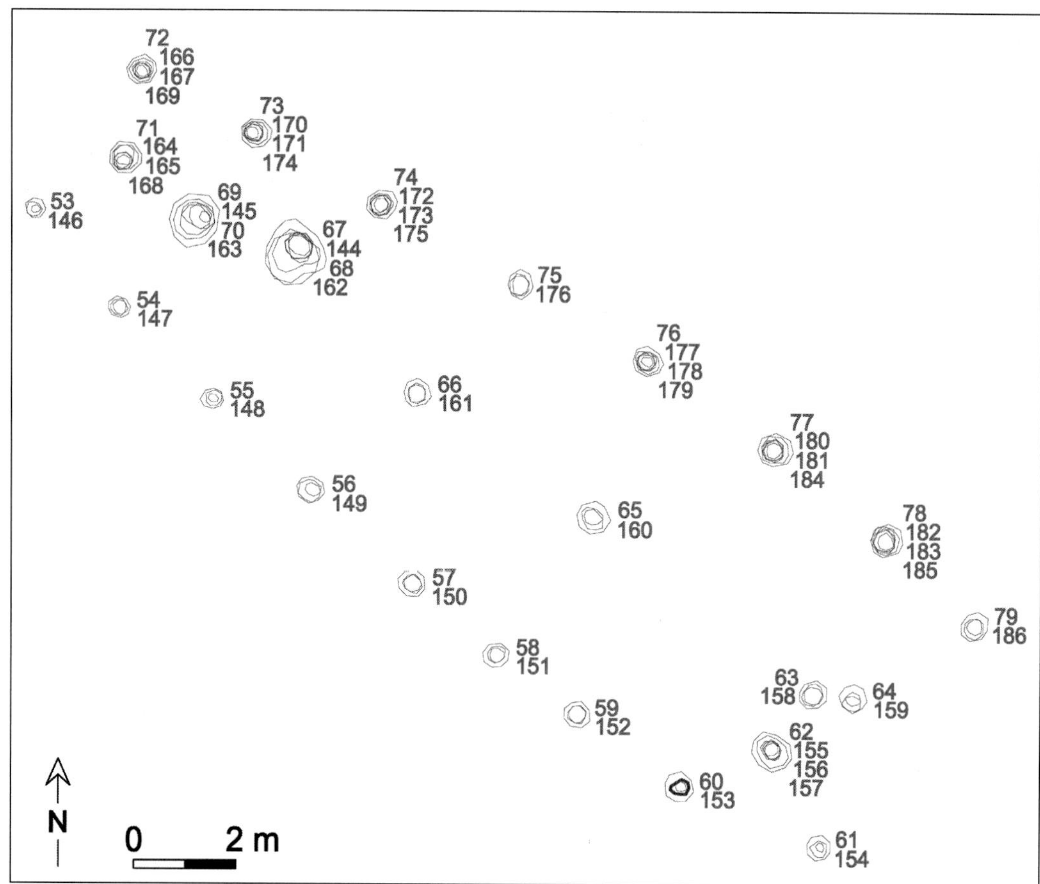

Figure 10.8: Walpersdorf, house 2 (G. Morschhauser/ Ardig)

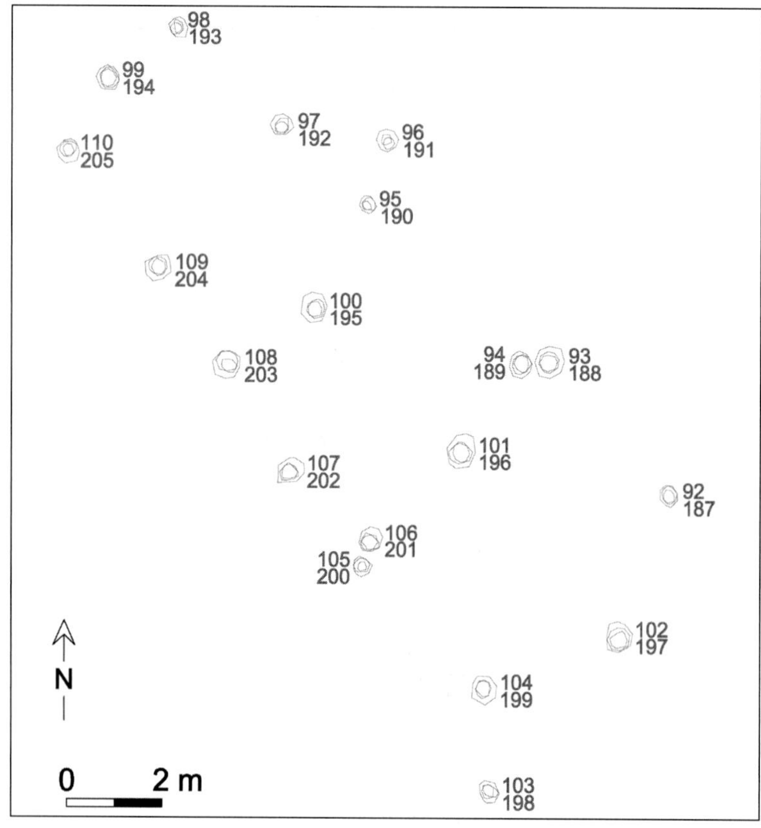

Figure 10.9: Walpersdorf, house 3 (G. Morschhauser/ Ardig)

smaller post construction and (partly) sunken buildings in the JC to boat-shaped longhouses constructed of posts in the BBC. The three buildings from Vienna 10, Oberlaa show that there were also post-built houses in Eastern Austria in KČM. From Hungarian KČM sites both sunken features and rectangular post constructions are also known (Kulcsár 2009, 62–4). In eastern Austria longhouses were built in the following Early Bronze Age, but they were not boat-shaped (Table 10.1).

The location of the Walpersdorf houses close to a rivulet is strikingly different to the settlements already known in the JC and that are mainly situated on small hilltops, mountain spurs or river terraces. KČM and BBC settlement seems to show a preference for lowland and low terraces in vicinity of rivers. This may just be a problem of visibility, as the known structures close to the waterways may be eroded on the one hand or covered by colluvium on the other and they are therefore not easy to detect. Nevertheless, the boat-shaped houses of Walpersdorf provide a connection to the similarly-shaped houses

Table 10.1: Final Neolithic houses in Austria

Cultural unit	*Site*	*Signature*	*Shape*	*Size*
Jevišovice	Kleiner Anzingerberg	Older phase	Post construction	6–8 × *c.* 4 m
	Kleiner Anzingerberg	Younger phase	Post construction	8–10 × 4.5–5.5 m
	Aigen	Obj. 1	sunken	Not known
	Aigen	Obj. 3	sunken	Not known
	Aigen	Obj. 4	sunken	Not known
	Furth	Obj. 10	sunken	3.9 × 3.5 m
	Plaika	Obj. 75	sunken	Not published
	Schrick	Obj. 630	sunken	6.2 × 4 m
Kosihy- Caka/Makó	Vienna-Oberlaa	House 1	9 posts?	6.2 × 4.3 m
	Vienna-Oberlaa	House 2	6 or 7 posts?	6 × 3.2 m
	Vienna 10-Oberlaa	House 3	5 posts?	5.3 × 4 m
	Schwechat		sunken	3 × 2 m
unknown	Haselbach	Obj. 24-21	sunken	9.35 × 4.56 m
	Hatzenbach	V5	sunkel	7.8 × 4.2 m
	Laa an der Thaya	SE 426	sunken	9 × 5 m
Bell Beaker	Walpersdorf	House 1	22 posts	16 × 6.5 m
	Walpersdorf	House 2	25	20 × 7 m
	Walpersdorf	House 3	16?	16 × 6 m
	Walpersdorf	House 4	9?	10.5 × 5.8 m
	Vienna 3, Rennweg	Pit 236	sunken	4.2 × 3.4 m

along the Danube from Bavaria, for example at Landau SüdOst (Husty 2004, Abb. 2 + 3) via the Traisen valley in Lower Austria to Hungary, at settlements such as Albertfalva (Endrödy & Remenyi 2016) and other sites of the Bell Beaker Csepel-group (Endrödy & Remenyi 2016, fig 69.1; Endrödy *et al.* this volume). They seem to be of a form common in the late BBC (Endrödy & Remenyi 2016, fig 69.2).

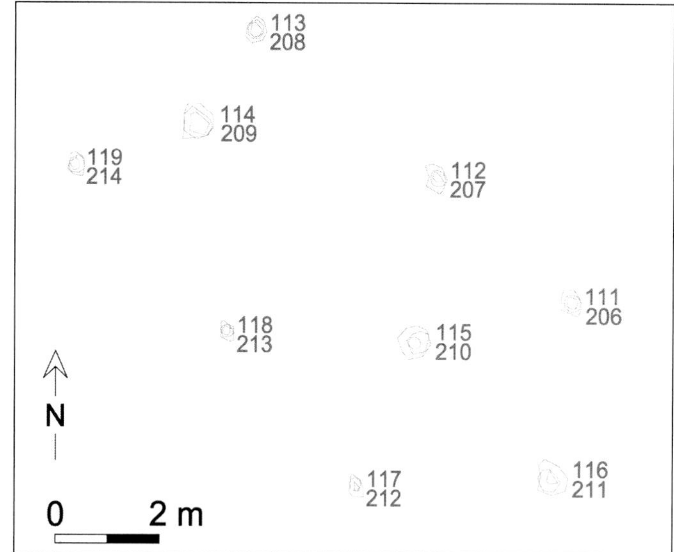

Figure 10.10: Walpersdorf, house 4 (G. Morschhauser/ Ardig)

Pottery and stone tools – differences and similarities

The scarcity of archaeological finds in some contexts and the differences in the archaeological record concerning the different cultural units makes it hard to detect changes in the material culture. Luckily our knowledge of domestic pottery of the BBC has increased significantly in the last decade due to the sites of Maissau, Vienna 11, Csokorgasse/ Etrichstraße, Vienna 3, Rennweg and Laa an der Thaya-Südumfahrung.

The comparisons of the vessels and thin sections of the vessels found in the CWC graves and the regional ware of the BBC graves in Franzhausen show that they are similar in form, matrix and production and there are only a few differences proving that there was not a clear division between CWC and BBC regional ware. The undecorated fine ware such

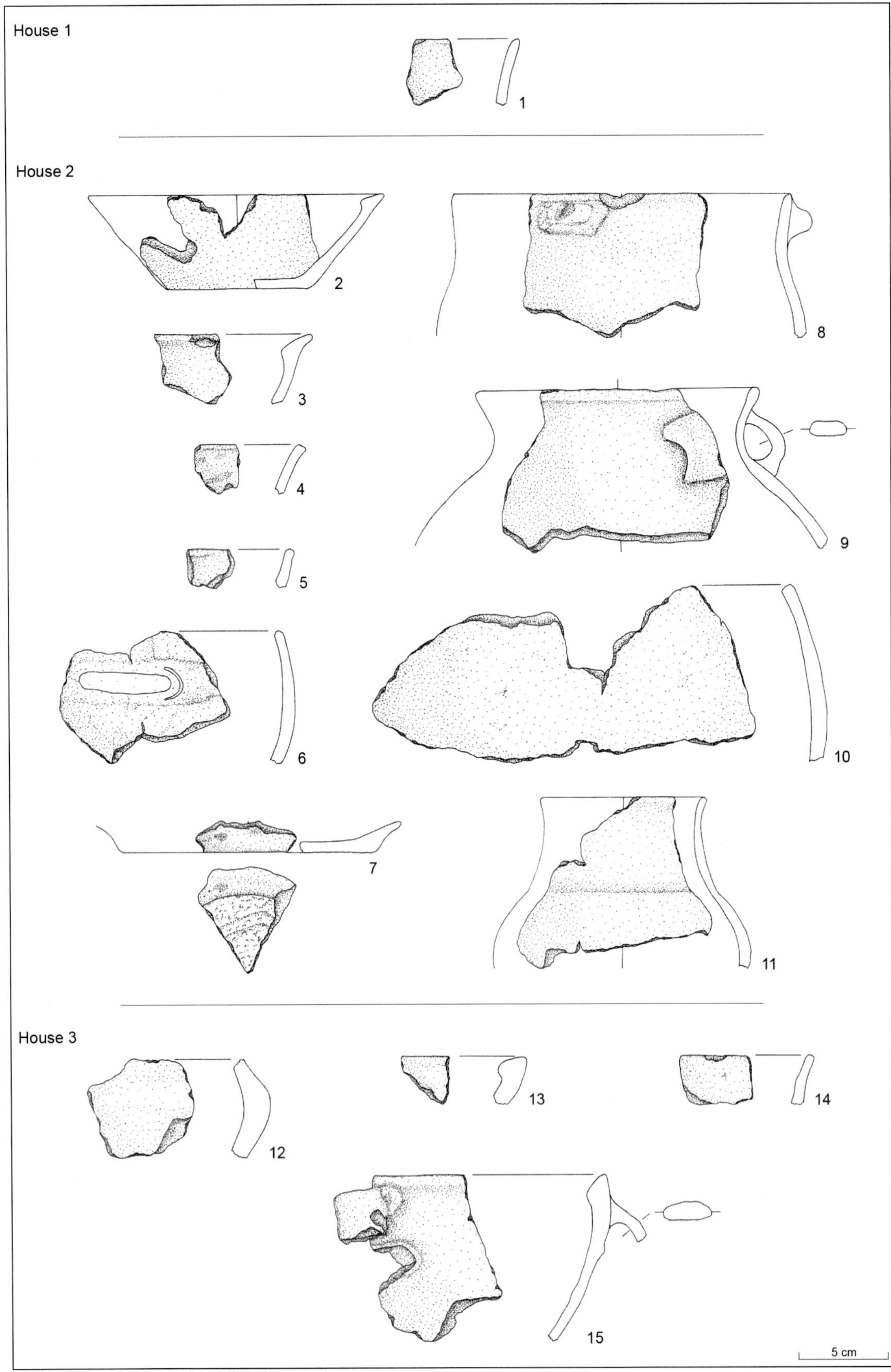

Figure 10.11: Walpersdorf, pottery from houses 1, 2 and 3 (A. Preinfalk/ARDIG)

Figure 10.12: Walpersdorf, pottery from post-hole SE 70 of house 2 (G. Morschhauser/ ARDIG)

as cups and jugs show few changes from late JC via KČM and CWC to BBC regional ware. Bowls change significantly in terms of the shape of the rim. In the domestic ware, types or at least frequency of types, seem to differ from one culture to the other. In KČM and CWC contexts amphorae are common. As far as we know there are no complete BBC amphorae from settlement sites in present-day Austria, but several fragments show that those types that accompanied cremations were also used in settlement context. The eponymous Bell Beaker quickly disappeared from eastern Austria and just a few vessels of the regional ware show stamped decoration like the mug from Rennweg (Fig. 10.5). The regional ware not only of BBC but also of KČM develops into the ceramics of the Early Bronze Age, but already shows three regional differences or at least different influences. In Northern Lower Austria it changed slowly to Protoaunjetitz/ Aunjetitz Culture, in the south-eastern part of Lower Austria and Burgenland via Leitha-Group to Wieselburg Culture and in the Southwestern part of Lower Austria and the western part of Upper Austria via Leitha-Group/Unterwölbling I to Unterwölbling Culture. Bearing in mind that domestic ware is the most traditional part of pottery, this shows clearly the different 'origin' or traditions of these different archaeological groups, not only in producing pottery but also in the way of cooking or in the way that products were processed.

Since settlements of the Corded Ware Culture are not known or cannot yet be recognised, stone and flint artefacts are mostly known from graves and as stray finds. As mentioned before in the CWC graves in the Traisen Valley axes, blades and daggers were found. Most of the raw material is local, but Baltic flint for blades and Bavarian tabular chert was used for daggers. As there are very few 'stone' artefacts other than wrist-guards published from Bell Beaker contexts comparison is not yet possible.

Environmental data

Environmental data for the Final Neolithic are limited with exception of preliminary reports and results of the investigations concerning the JC settlements from Kleiner Anzingerberg and Furth. A high number of fish was recorded

Table 10.2: Bell Beaker settlement sites in Austria

Cultural Unit	*Site*	*Features*	*Literature*
Bell Beaker with Bell Beaker	Bisamberg	Stray finds	Hetzer 1949, 110–11, Abb. 19
	Großhöflein/Föllik	Stray finds	Hetzer 1949, 90–2, Abb. 3 & 4
	Hafnerbach	dislocated	Preinfalk 2004, 16
	Hellbrunnerberg	Settlement layer?	Hell 1974, 3–4 Moosleitner 1989, 269–70
	Laa/Thaya, inneres Gerichtsfeld	Stray finds	Toriser 1976, 35–6; Neugebauer 1981, 57, Abb. 2/6–15, Abb. 3/1–5
	Maissau	Pits	Schmitsberger 2009
	Ruhhof	Stray finds	Neugebauer 1981, 57–60, Abb. 3/11–16, Abb. 4, Abb. 5–7
	Vienna 22, Aspern	Stray finds	Kastner 1939, 128–31; Penz 2013, 89–90
Bell Beaker just regional ware	Laa an der Thaya-Südumfahrung	Pit	Stöckl 2016
	Lutzmannsburg	2 pits	Ohrenberger 1971
	Oberbierbaum	Postholes	Neugebauer &Neugebauer 1994, Abb. 15 & 16
	Schwechat	Pit	Ruttkay & Stadler 1980
	Vienna 3, Rennweg	Pit or sunken house	Penz 2010; Czeika 2010
	Vienna 11, Csokorgasse/Etrichstraße	3 pits	Penz 2014
	Walpersdorf	4 houses	Morschhauser 2015
	Königsbrunn bei Enzersfeld	Well	Morschhauser 2018

Figure 10.13: Walpersdorf, pottery from post-hole SE 107 of house 3 (G. Morschhauser/ARDIG)

from the JC settlements of Krems, Hundssteig (Pieler 2002, 505) and Kleiner Anzingerberg (Krenn-Leeb 2002, 173) as well as the KČM settlement of Grub (Krenn-Leeb 1996, 190) that was situated very close to the river March.

The BBC pits from Vienna 3, Rennweg and 11, Csokorgasse/Etrichstraße stand out for their high percentage of horse bones (Fig. 10.14) the detailed analysis of which gives greater insight into early horse domestication (Czeika 2013). The bones are small and robust like those of wild horses whereas the wide variance of their dimensions indicates a tendency towards an archaic form of domestic horses. We cannot yet find much evidence for the emergence of horses within the distribution area of the BBC anywhere in Middle Europe except in the Csepel group of the Budapest region. Elsewhere the high importance of horses or even horse-breeding at this time can only be ascertained in the more distant steppe areas of Eastern Europe. With a copper blade of steppe nomadic shape from Vienna 22-Essling (Zimmermann 2003) we have further proof of a connection to the Pontic-Caucasian region which is commonly considered to be one of the locations for the origin of horse-breeding. Having made this point, the Viennese horse bones do not appear to compare closely to the Csepel horses in terms of archaeozoological detail, but reference data are scarce. As a matter of fact, this evidence

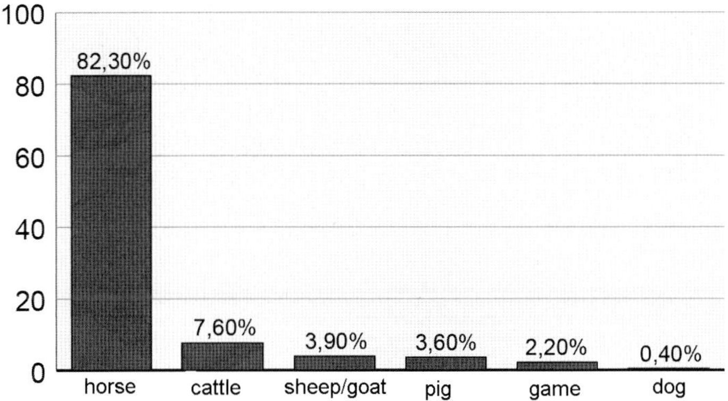

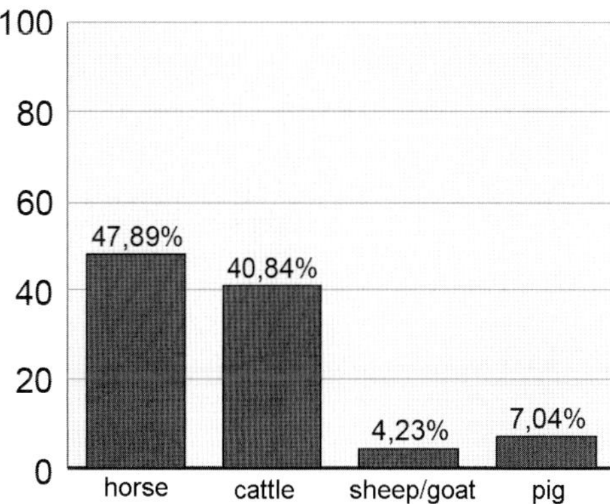

Figure 10.14: Archaeozoology of Vienna 3, Rennweg and Vienna 11, Csokorgasse / Etrichstraße

may indicate a specialised mode of life and an economic focus on the part of certain societies in the eneolithic Danube region.

Acknowledgement

We want to thank Peter Trebsche for making the unpublished radiocarbon date from Haselbach available for this article.

References

Adler-Wölfl, K. & Penz, M. 2018. Wien 11, Csokorgasse 2–10, *Fundort Wien* 21, 210–17

Adler-Wölfl, K. & Penz. M. forthcoming. Bericht zur Grabung Wien 11, Csokorgasse 2–10, Mnr. 001103.17.02, *Fundberichte aus Österreich* 56/2017

Artner, G. 2006. Die endneolithische Siedlung von Schrick. In Hofer, N. (ed.), Trassenarchäologie. Neue Straßen im Weinviertel. *Fundberichte aus Österreich Materialhefte, Reihe A, Sonderheft,* 4, 15–17

Blesl, C. & Hermann, L. 2007, Walpersdorf, *Fundberichte aus Österreich,* 45/2006, 42

Czeika, S. 2002. Über die Datierbarkeit archäozoologischer Funde – Fallbeispiel Csokorgasse. *Fundort Wien,* 5, 18–29

Czeika, S. 2010. Pferde aus der Jungsteinzeit. Endneolithische Tierreste vom Rennweg 16, Wien 3. *Fundort Wien,* 13, 32–49

Czeika, S. 2013. Glockenbecherzeitliche Pferdereste aus Wien – ein Diskussionsbeitrag. *Beiträge zur Archäozoologie und Prähistorischen Anthropologie,* 9, 2013, 51–8

Drost, F. & Lauermann, E. 1999. Hatzenbach, *Fundberichte aus Österreich* 37/1998, 697–8

Endrödi, A. & Reményi, L. (eds), 2016. *A Bell Beaker Settlement in Albertfalva, Hungary (2470–1950 BC),* Budapest: Budapest History Museum and Kódex Könyvgyártó Ltd

Hell, M. 1974. Die Halbhöhle am Hellbrunnerberg bei Salzburg als urzeitliche Wohnstelle, *Archaeologia Austriaca,* 56, 1–12

Hetzer, K. 1949. Beiträge zur Kenntnis der Glockenbecherkultur in Österreich, *Archaeologia Austriaca,* 4, 87–115

Husty, L. 2004. Überlegungen zum Siedlungswesen der Glockenbecherkultur. In Heyd V., Husty L. & Kreiner, L. (eds), *Siedlungen der Glockenbecherkultur in Süddeutschland und Mitteleuropa, Arbeiten zur Archäologie Süddeutschlands* 17, 147–54

Kastner, F. 1939. Funde der Vučedol (Laibacher-) *Kultur und der Glockenbecher Kultur von Aspern (Wien 22.Bezirk),* Wiener Prähistorische Zeitschrift 26, 117–34

Kern, D. 2011, Ostösterreich im Endneolithikum – Am Ende der Welt? In Doppler, Th., Ramminger, B. & Schimmelpfennig, D. (eds), *Grenzen und Grenzräume? Beispiele aus Neolithikum und Bronzezeit.* Fokus Jungsteinzeit 2. Kerpen-Loogh 2011, 25–35

Krenn-Leeb, A. 1996. *Grabungsbericht über Neolithische Siedlungsreste und Bronzezeitliche Gräber in der Flur Unterhaspel, KG Grub an der March, NÖ.,* Forschungen in Stillfried 9/10, 189–90

Krenn-Leeb, A. 1998. Die jung- und endneolithische Besiedlung von Spielberg-Pielamünd (VB Melk, Niederösterreich). Unpubl. Dissertation, University of Vienna

Krenn-Leeb, A. 1999. Die Fazies Spielberg als Mittler zwischen der älteren und jüngeren Jevišovice-Kultur in Niederösterreich? Neue Erkenntnisse zum älteren Abschnitt des Endneolithikums. *Mitteilungen der Anthropologischen Gesellschaft in Wien,* 128, 45–67

Krenn-Leeb, A. 2002, *Neue Forschungen zum Siedlungswesen der Jevišovice-Jultur in Niederösterreich.* Nitra: Otázky neolitu a eneolithu našich krajín-2001, 167–86

Krenn-Leeb, A. 2006. Höhensiedlungen der Jevišovice-Kultur in Niederösterreich: Stereotypes Siedlungsverhalten und historische Topographie – Eine Bestandsaufnahme. In Krenn-Leeb, A. (ed.), 2006, *Wirtschaft, Macht und Strategie. Höhensiedlungen und ihre Funktionen in der Ur- und Frühgeschichte.* Wien: Archäologie Österreichs Spezial 1, 23–40

Krenn-Leeb, A. 2009. KG Meidling. *Fundberichte aus Österreich,* 47/2008, 523

Krenn-Leeb, A. 2010. *Humanökologie der Kupferzeit – Interaktionen und Wirkungszusammenhänge zwischen Mensch, Gesellschaft und Umwelt am Beispiel der Jevišovice-Kultur: Zwischenbilanz des Forschungsprogramms.* Wien:

Archäologische Forschungen in Niederösterreich, 4, 28–47

Krenn-Leeb, A. 2016. Hausarchitektur und Raumnutzung am Kleinen Anzingerberg, Niederösterreich. Das Haus und seine Wohn-, Arbeits- sowie Kommunikationssphären in der Kupferzeit. *Mitteilungen der Anthropologischen Gesellschaft in Wien*, 146, 11–46

Kulcsár, G. 2009. *The Beginnings of the Bronze Age in the Carpathian Basin. The Makó-Kosihy-Čaka and the Somogyvár-Vinkovci Cultures in Hungary*. Budapest: Varia Archaeologica Hungarica, 23

Kunst, G. K. 2006. Tierreste aus der endneolithischen Grubenhütte von Furth bei Göttweig. In Krenn-Leeb, A., Grömer K. & Stadler P. (eds), Ein Lächeln für die Jungsteinzeit. Festschrift für Elisabeth Ruttkay, *Archäologie Österreichs* 17 (2), 153–63

Lantschner, M. 1990. Spätneolithische Siedlungsfunde aus Oberthürnau, Gem. Drosendorf-Zissersdorf, VB Horn, Niederösterreich. *Archaeologia Austriaca*, 74, 1–32

Medunová-Benešová, A. 1977. *Jevišovická kultura na jihozápadní Moravě (Jevišovice-Kultur in Südmähren)*. Brno: Studie archeologického ústavu Československé akademie věd v Brně 5/3

Moosleitner, F. 1989. Hellbrunnerberg. *Fundberichte aus Österreich,* 27/1988, 269–70

Morschhauser, G. 2015. Bericht zur archäologischen Maßnahme ‚Kiesgrube Walpersdorf'. *Fundberichte aus Österreich* 53/2014, Digitaler Teil D3775-D3784

Morschhauser, G. 2018. Königsbrunn. *Fundberichte aus Österreich,* 55/2016, 217–18 and Digitaler Teil D2832-D2838

Neugebauer, J.-W. 1981. Glockenbecherfunde im Raum Laa a. d. Taya, Niederösterreich. *Archaeologia Austriaca*, 65, 53–61

Neugebauer, C. & Neugebauer, J.-W. 1994. (Glocken-) Becherzeitliche Gräber in Gemeinlebarn und Oberbierbaum, NÖ., *Mitteilungen der Anthropologischen Gesellschaft in Wien*, 123/124, 193–219

Neugebauer-Maresch, C. 1994, Überblick über das Endneolithikum im Unteren Traisental. In: Die Fragen der Bronzezeit. Archäologische Konferenz des Komitates Zala und Niederösterreichs III. Keszthely, 5–7.10.1992, Zalai Múzeum 5, 1994, 73–83

Obenaus, M. 2016. Aigen. *Fundberichte aus Österreich,* 54 /2015, 184–5

Ohrenberger, A. 1971. Lutzmannsburg. *Fundberichte aus Österreich,* 9/1970, 248

Penz, M. 2010. *Eine Siedlungsgrube der späten Glockenbecherkultur aus Wien 3, Rennweg 16 (Vorbericht). Fundort Wien,* 13, 20–31

Penz, M. 2013. Die ur- und frühgeschichtliche Besiedlung in Aspern, Wien 22 – ein Überblick. *Fundort Wien*, 16, 84–95

Penz, M. 2014. Spätneolithische Funde aus dem Bereich Wien 11, Csokorgasse. *Fundort Wien*, 17, 192–210

Penz, M. 2017. Wien 10, Grundäckergasse 14–20/ Bauplatz 5. *Fundort Wien*, 20, 194–6

Penz, M. 2018a. Oberlaa-Land, *Fundberichte aus Österreich,* 55/2016, 581–2 and Digitaler Teil D 8896-D8900

Penz, M. 2018b. Wien 10, Laaer-Berg-Straße 316, *Fundort Wien*, 21, 217–22

Penz, M. forthcoming. Oberlaa, *Fundberichte aus Österreich,* 56/2017

Peška, J. 2000. K vybraným problémům relativní chronologie v období mladého a pozdního Eneolitu na Moravě (Zu einigen ausgewählten Problemen der relativen Chronologie in der Periode des Jung- und Spätneolithikums Mährens). *Pravěk* 9, 243–68

Pieler, F. 2002. Die archäologischen Untersuchungen der spätneolithischen Befestigungsanlage von Krems-Hundssteig. In: Wewerka B., Bericht zu den Ausgrabungen des Vereins ASINOE im Projektjahr 2001, *Fundberichte aus Österreich,* 40/2001, 503–13

Pieler, F. & Hellerschmid I. 2005. Ein urnenfelderzeitliches Gräberfeld in Furth bei Göttweig. In B. Wewerka, Bericht über die die Ausgrabungen des Vereins ASINOE im Projektjahr 2004, *Fundberichte aus Österreich,* 43/2004, 742

Pohl, H. 2016a. Abtsdorf. *Fundberichte aus Österreich,* 54/2015, 294–6

Pohl, H. 2016b. Drei Jahre unterwasserarchäologisches Monitoring an den österreichischen UNESCO-Welterbestätten Prähistorische Pfahlbauten um die Alpen, *Archäologie Österreichs*, 27 (1), 29–35

Preinfalk, F. 2004. Hafnerbach. *Fundberichte aus Österreich,* 42/2003, 16

Preinfalk, A. & F. 2014. Plaika. *Fundberichte aus Österreich,* 52/2013, Digitaler Teil, D1525-D1561

Ruttkay, E. 1995. Spätneolithikum. In Lenneis, E., Neugebauer-Maresch, Ch. & Ruttkay, E., Jungsteinzeit im Osten Österreichs, Wissenschaftliche Schriftenreihe Niederösterreich 102/103/104/105. *Forschungen zur Ur- und Frühgeschichte*, 17, 108–209

Ruttkay, E. 2002. Das endneolithische Hügelgrab von Neusiedl am See, Burgenland. *Budapest Régiségei*, 36, 145–70

Ruttkay, E. & Stadler, P. 1980. Schwechat. *Fundberichte aus Österreich,* 18/1979, 308–10

Schmitsberger, O. 2003. Neufunde endneolithischer Streitäxte aus Oberösterreich und dem angrenzenden Niederösterreich. *Jahrbuch des Oberösterreichischen Musealvereines*, 148 (1), 9–18

Schmitsberger, O. 2005. Eine Siedlung der klassischen Badener Kultur in Stoitzendorf im Weinviertel. *Fundberichte aus Österreich*, 43/2004, 135–96

Schmitsberger, O. 2006. Die Siedlung zum 'Doppelgrab von Palt' der Jevišovicekultur. In Krenn-Leeb, A., Grömer, K. & Stadler P. (eds), Ein Lächeln für die Jungsteinzeit. Festschrift für Elisabeth Ruttkay, *Archäologie Österreichs* 17 (2), 141–54

Schmitsberger, O. 2009. Ausgrabungen auf der Trasse der Ortsumfahrung Maissau 2008/Fläche '1-Süd': Befunde vom Altneolithikum bis zum Frühmittelalter, Niederösterreich. *Fundberichte aus Österreich,* 47/2008, 438–500

Schmitsberger, O. 2011. Ausgewählte Befunde und Funde der Kupferzeit sowie der Bronzezeit von der Trasse der Ortsumfahrung Maissau, Niederösterreich. *Fundberichte aus Österreich,* 49/2010, 101–144

Schmitsberger, O. 2012. 20 Jahre ASINOE 1991–2011. Ein archäologisches Resümee. *Fundberichte aus Österreich*, 50/2011, 113–37

Scholz, U. & Müller, S. 2011. Schwechat. *Fundberichte aus Österreich*, 48/2010, 317–19

Schwammenhöfer, H. 1989. Endneolithisch Keramik aus Obersulz und Schleinbach im Weinviertel, Niederösterreich. *Fundberichte aus Österreich*, 27/1988, 99–120

Šebela, L. 1999. Die Entwicklung der äneolithischen Besiedlung am Nordhang der Pollauerberge. In Kuzma I. (ed.), *Otázky neolitu a eneolitu našich krajín – 1998. Zborník referátov zo 17. Pracovného stretnutia bádatelov pre výskum neolitu a eneolitu Čiech, Moravy a Slovenska, Dudince 22–24.9, 1998*, 223–39. Nitra: Materialia Archaeologica Slovaca 2

Stöckl, Ch. 2016. Laa/Thaya Südumfahrung 1/2015. *Fundberichte aus Österreich*, 54/2015, 209–10

Toriser, A. 1976. Funde der älteren Glockenbecherkultur aus Laa a.d.Thaya, p.B. Mistelbach, NÖ. *Archaeologia Austriaca*, 59/60, 29–41

Trebsche, P. & Fichtl, S. 2018a. Projekt 'Keltische Siedlungszentren in Ostösterreich' – Bericht der Ausgrabung 2016 in Haselbach, *Fundberichte aus Österreich*, 55/2016, 211–13 and Digitaler Teil D2467-D2486

Trebsche, P. & Fichtl S. 2018b. Das keltische Siedlungszentrum von Haselbach. Die französisch-österreichischen Ausgrabungen 2015–2016, *Archäologie Österreichs*, 27 (2), 2016, 2–19

Zimmermann, T. 2003. Zwischen Karpaten und Kaukasus – Anmerkungen zu einer ungewöhnlichen Kupferklinge aus Wien-Essling. *Archäologisches Korrespondenzblatt*, 33, 469–77

11

Bohemia and Moravia – local and Beaker: Bell Beaker domestic sites in the context of the Late Eneolithic/Early Bronze Age cultural sequence

Jan Turek

When discussing Beaker settlements in Bohemia and Moravia, we need to clarify what exactly we are looking for. If we are seeking for continuity, we can find it in the ongoing tradition of the Eneolithic-Bronze Age Pottery Complex as it was introduced by Neustupný (1995). If we are looking for change, we can observe severe restrictions in the settlement pattern that had already started in the preceding Corded Ware period.

The Bell Beaker phenomenon was traditionally considered to be an alien cultural entity interrupting the local settlement continuity (eg, Neustupný, J. 1962), but is this really the case? It is perhaps the specific decorated pottery coming from Western Europe, the emphasis on single burials coming from the East and, more generally, the European spread of a certain degree of cultural uniformity that resulted in such views. However, looking at the evidence from domestic sites we can see much more in terms of local traditions, ties to the natural properties of the landscape and the traditions of Central European farming communities. In studying the less visible and less obvious evidence of Beaker domestic sites, it is hoped that perhaps we may better understand the seemingly enigmatic phenomenon of the Beaker World.

Moravia and Bohemia are currently amongst the richest European regions for Bell Beaker domestic sites and despite the fact that most of the sites were excavated last century, they are well published (Ondráček *et al.* 2005; Turek *et al.* 2003; Turek 2008a). Also, in recent years, some new sites (Pavlů 2000; Stolz & Stolzová 2002; Limburský 2013) and new types of evidence such as Beaker longhouses (formerly only known in Bohemia) have come to light in Bohemia (Turek 2011; Zápotocký 2014) and Moravia (Peška 2013 with further references). The following text will focus on individual issues of Bell Beaker settlements in Bohemia and Moravia in their environmental and social setting.

Environment and economy

The perceived lack of Corded Ware and Bell Beaker domestic sites started the debate on the economic basis of populations of the 3rd millennium BC. Some scholars even presumed that cereal farming played only an insignificant role in the subsistence strategies of Bell Beaker users (Sangmeister 1974) and the same assumption was made for the preceding Corded Ware period (Buchvaldek 1967, 121–2). This circular argument continued almost until the end of last century. Vencl (1994) adhered to the nomadic model for Corded Ware communities and even suggested a mobile life based on chariots.

Havel and Pavelková (1989, 32) observed the increased incidence of dental decay in the Czech Bell Beaker population which they considered as evidence for the increased consumption of heat-treated meat foods. This is again an example of the effects of the circular argument as this assumption is in stark contrast to the generally established beneficial effect of protein consumption on dental health and its deterioration with the onset of Neolithic carbohydrate (cereal) consumption (Cohen & Arnelagos 1984). The increased incidence of tooth decay observed by Havel and Pavelková can, instead, be taken to infer well-established grain farming as the foundation of Bell Beaker subsistence (Turek 1996).

Contrary to these assumptions, Neustupný (1969; 1997) had no doubts about the continuity of Neolithic grain farming even for 3rd millennium BC populations (for the same conclusions see Turek 1995; 1996). Generally speaking, the Late Eneolithic was characterised by farming using a field rotation system, the utilisation of a plough and probably the use of draught animals. However, palynological and archaeobotanical data that would enable a more precise reconstruction of the agricultural use of the land and cultivated crops are still missing.

Domestic plants

The lack of settlements and systematic environmental sampling is currently preventing any conclusions regarding the use of domestic plants in Bell Beaker domestic contexts. In the 1980's, Tempír carried out an analysis of archaeobotanical remains from the South Moravian sites of Bořitov VII, Brno – Obřany I, Holubice II and Žádovice (Turek *et al.* 2003).

Amongst the wild and domestic plants we can identify eincorn, emmer, spelt wheat, common wheat, barley, vetch/horsebean and cannabis. Peška (2013, 207) also mentioned millet from the settlement at Hulín 1 and flax from Hulín-Pravčice 2.

Livestock

If we try to evaluate subsistence economies during the Bell Beaker period in Bohemia and Moravia, we are struggling with the lack of well-studied domestic contexts but the currently available assemblages of animal bones from domestic environments do not indicate a deflection from the Neolithic model of domestic livestock.

An important contribution towards such discussion is the synthesis published by Kyselý (2012, 431–52) in which he compared all finds of animal bones from the Bell Beaker domestic and funerary contexts in Czech Republic and reached the conclusion that there is no major difference between the Bell Beaker livestock and other Neolithic and Early Bronze Age periods. Certainly there are some minor differences, such as higher representation of cattle in the Beaker period than in the Middle Eneolithic Řivnáč Culture contexts.

Domestic cattle represent the most abundant species found in Bell Beaker settlements (over 70%) while pig and sheep/goat were represented by about 15% each. Other domestic mammals are only marginal (dog 1.8% and horse 0.4%). Horses are generally underrepresented in Czech Beaker contexts, especially if compared to Hungary, where the horse is much better represented on sites such as Csepel Háros (45%, Bökönyi 1974), Csepel Hollandi ut. (60%, Bökönyi 1978) and most recently Albertfalva (44%, Lyublyanovics 2016, 214). This real difference in livestock most likely reflects the difference in landscape morphology and land use between Bohemia and Moravia and the open plain of Hungary.

A remarkable difference in fauna can be seen when the evidence from Beaker domestic sites is compared to that from funerary contexts. Cattle was represented in graves only by 9%, sheep/goat by 32% and the most favourite meat offering was pork (over 60%). This is perhaps reflecting the practice of smaller species (pig, goat, sheep) being used as offerings during the funerary ceremonies while cattle were rarely slaughtered and used more for diary production within settlements. Dishes included in Beaker burial assemblages represented a cultural and perhaps even regional identity. The most common cuts of meat come from the saddle and legs (sacrum and pelvis, less frequently radius and ulna) of pork or mutton. The reason for the choice of pork is very probably a reflection of a certain identity as the symbolism of food prepared for the funerary feasting is an important cultural issue (Turek 2008a, 154).

A total of 89% of ox bones found in a settlement context at Praha-Hostivař came from adult individuals; only one bone was from an animal around two years of age. This is at variance with the model of seasonal culling prior to the arrival of winter and could suggest special care for cattle in the winter months; it also suggests the possibility of exploiting alternative sources such as forest grazing (Turek 2008a, 154).

Domestic cattle also played an important role in traction. From the settlement at Holubice II (Vyškov District) in South Moravia traces of a yoke binding were discovered due to the rotational deformation of the basal portion of a horn (Peške 1985).

Notably absent are the bones from wild game both in the settlements, as well as funerary contexts. Some 98.7% of all animal remains are of domestic species (Kyselý 2012). Hunting, which, due to the emphasis of archery in burial rites, was considered to be an important part of Bell Beaker subsistence (Neustupný, J. 1962, 184) was obviously an economically marginal activity and archery must have been predominantly connected to warfare prestige.

The local Cultural Sequence before and after Bell Beakers

During the 3rd millennium BC, rather than discontinuity, we can see change in the archaeological record suggesting that there was a distinctive pattern of highly visible funerary activity of single inhumations and highly invisible evidence of settlement activity. This trend had already started in the preceding Corded Ware period (about 2900/2800 BC). Archaeological evidence for the Bell Beaker domestic sites in Bohemia needs to be considered as a part of the Late Neolithic/ Early Bronze Age Cultural Sequence.

In Central Europe, this mostly concerns the significant, uninterrupted continuity of the Eneolithic-Bronze Age Bell Beaker Complex (Neustupný 1995), characterised by accompanying pottery arising from the Somogyvár-Vinkovci cultural tradition, which survived Bell Beakers and evolved into the pottery style of the early Únětice culture. As regards the motivation for abandoning or partly diverting from the local cultural tradition by the local population by accepting a new Beaker cultural element, there are several possible explanations. The present writer is of the opinion that the spreading of Bell Beaker material culture may not necessarily have been related to any major population movements. The process could be explained in terms of increased regional communications in the form of marriages and the migration of individuals, as described for example by Brodie (1997) in his model of contacts through the 'Chalcolithic frontier'. Brodie combines the desire of people in non-Chalcolithic North-western Europe to establish economic and social links with communities possessing knowledge of copper production technology. This is likely to be merely a part of the explanation. A new ideology or, more precisely, a new cult also seems to have been a major accelerator for this cultural exchange.

The phenomenon that in Central Europe is called the Bell Beaker Culture can be categorised as a strict or fundamentalist culture (Neustupný 2011, 177). Arbitrary symbolic and expressive systems are changing rapidly with the rise of strict cultures. The changes may affect the form of artefacts, burial rites, settlement forms, and perhaps of some aspects of social relations and cosmology. The introduction of the Bell Beaker package did not cause discontinuity of the previous cultural development, rather, in many ways, we can recognise a notable continuity with the previous Corded Ware period. It is these strict cultures that are characterised by a sudden onset and at least at the initial stage by a very uniform expression spreading rapidly over large territories. The symbolic content of the Bell Beaker Package may have been locally modified in different regional contexts as well as in the peripheral areas. Beyond the periphery, in neighbouring cultural areas, only some cultural elements were adopted and possibly even without their original symbolic meaning.

We should bear in mind that the cultural and symbolic importance of the package of culturally specific artefacts ('Bell Beaker Package') spread in Europe together with an ideology or religion of some kind, but in some local and peripheral areas the artefacts could acquire new social importance. The motivation for the adoption of certain cultural elements could be associated with the prestige of exotica rather than with the original symbolic content. We cannot assume that the spread of Bell Beaker material culture into peripheral and neighbouring areas was also associated with the spread of the original Beaker ideology. In some regions of western and northern Europe the Bell Beaker spread was associated with the transmission of copper metallurgy. It is believed that somewhere in the Lower Rhine region there existed some kind of boundary between communities possessing copper metallurgical know-how and west Europeans without the knowledge of copper production (Brodie 1997, 307–11 'Chalcolithic frontier'). Knowledge of technology and the use of copper objects played a particularly prestigious role that may have shaped the status of individuals and perhaps also the identity of entire communities.

Beaker domestic pottery

The range of pottery types represented in the burial context is rather limited and it represents a certain symbolic package of pots. The lack of settlement finds meant that most of the chronological models were based on the pottery from graves, but it is now obvious that the choice of pottery for funerary contexts is a kind of identity manifestation and as such is sending us an intentionally set message that is schematic and in some respect misleading for our understanding of the continuity and nature of the cultural processes of the 3rd millennium BC. By the analysis of funerary and domestic ceramics, we can obtain a fuller picture.

Continuity and change in pottery production

The analysis of Central European Copper Age ceramics (Rehman *et al.* 1992) has demonstrated the Bell Beaker domestic production of both main lines of ceramic styles, namely decorated beakers and accompanying ceramics, with some local shifts at short distances. The spread of technology and ceramic style could occur due to marriage relations between more or less remote regions. Such communications between prehistoric communities was often motivated by a desire to secure the access to strategic raw materials and technologies (Brodie 1997).

Traditionally it was assumed that the Beaker domestic pottery production differed from the funerary and 'prestigious' or 'ceremonial' pottery (mainly decorated Beakers). Whilst there are certainly differences or restrictions in the choice of certain pottery types for use in burial assemblages, we cannot simply label this pottery as purely funerary. Nevertheless, there are certain types of pottery represented in the domestic context and almost systematically excluded from the burial assemblages, such as storage jars, large coarse ware pots and most amphorae.

There are domestic sites, where decorated Bell Beakers occurred together with varying amounts of coarse wear, such as Olomouc Slavonín (Fig. 11.1) and Žádovice (Fig. 11.2) in Moravia or Radovesice (Fig. 11.3) in North Bohemia and sites with domestic wear following purely the local pottery tradition with no Bell Beakers, such as Brno-Obřany (Fig. 11.4) or Liptice (Figs 11.5 & 6) in Bohemia. This could be simply interpreted as a chronological development but is this really the case?

A new phenomenon in pottery production is a distinctive Moravian Corded Ware and Bell Beaker Culture interaction. The majority of pottery forms from Slavonín seem to have a connection to the Kosihy-Čaka/Makó and to the Somogyvár-Vinkovci cultures even though it is not identical. It seems that the strict 'rule' against sinking the Corded Ware settlement features was weakening during the late phase in Moravia (so-called Moravina local Corded Ware) and some new secure settlement contexts occurred in Central Moravia (such as Hulín-Pravčice 1, see Fig. 11.7, Peška 2013, fig. 65). For very first time this gives us the opportunity to follow some kind of transition between the late Corded Ware domestic pottery and *Begleitkeramik* pottery associated with decorated Bell Beakers. This development is invisible in the burial assemblages as their composition is 'ideologically' set. In other words, while the old and new tradition in pottery production was in common use within settlement sites, in funerary contexts a symbolic choice of pottery style was made and either Corded Ware or Bell Beaker was present: the blending of old and new

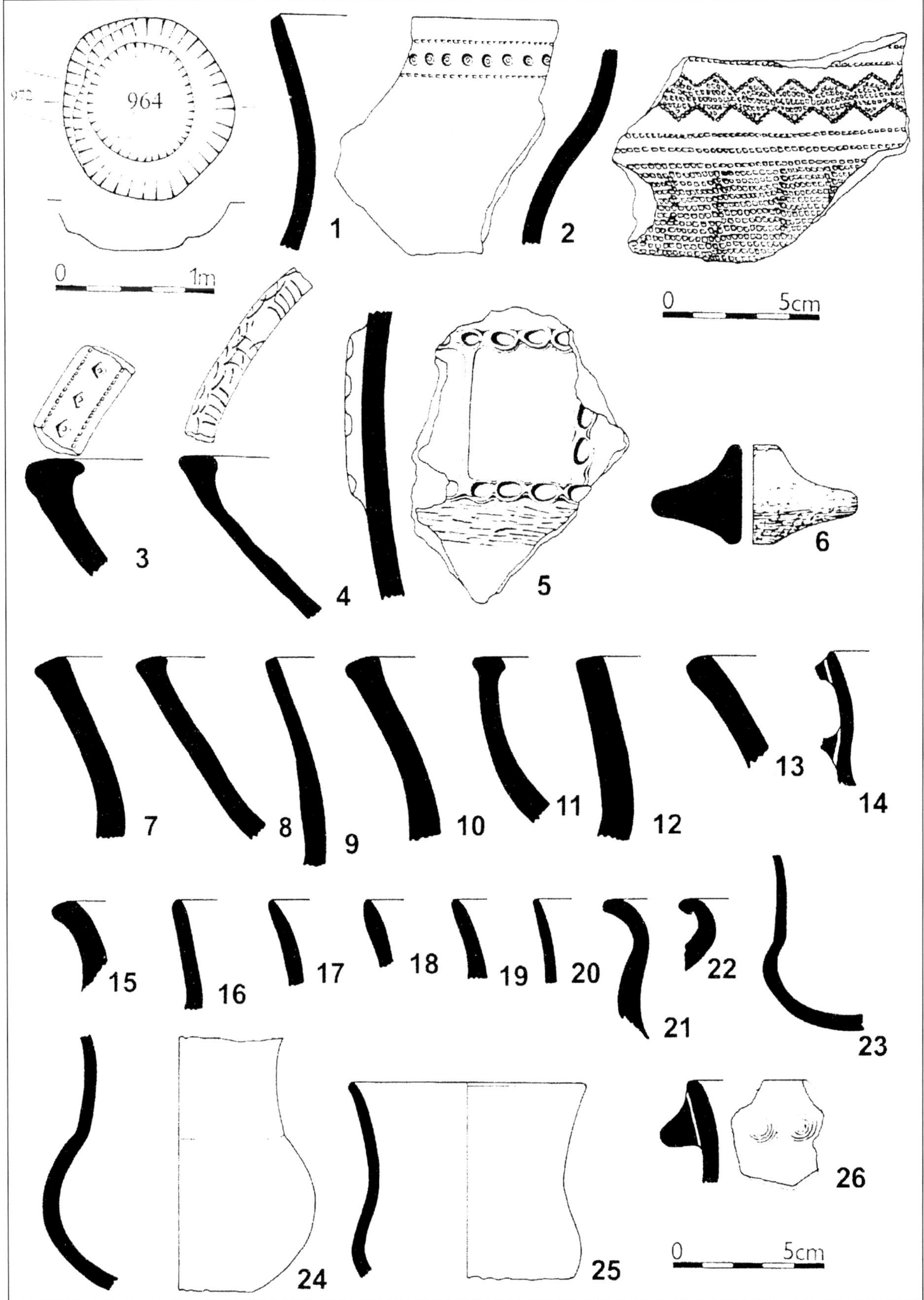

Figure 11.1: Feature 964 and associated pottery from Olomouc-Slavonín (district Olomouc), (after Peška 2013)

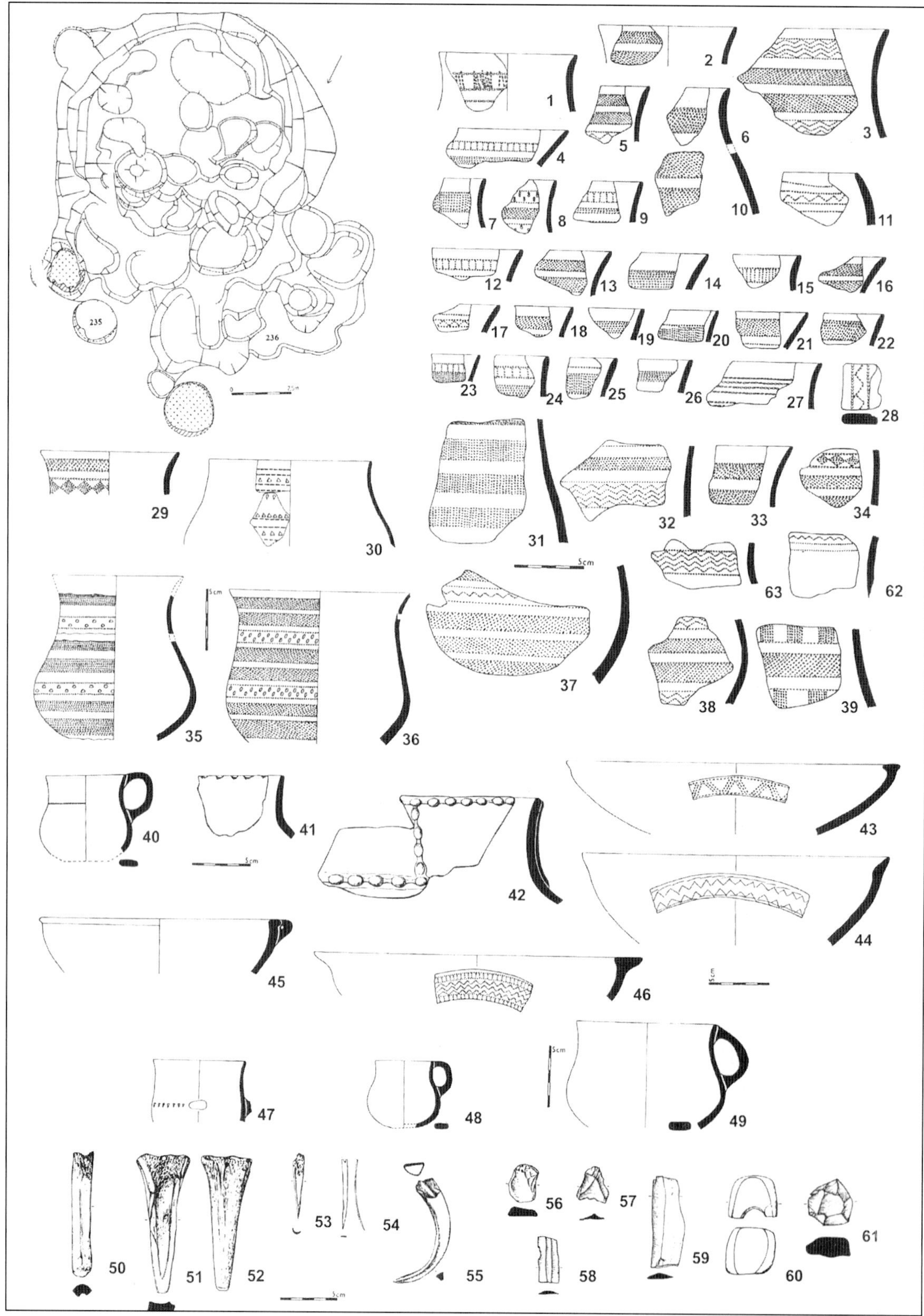

Figure 11.2: Feature 168/86–87 and associated assemblage Žádovice (Hodonín district), (after Matějíčková 1999)

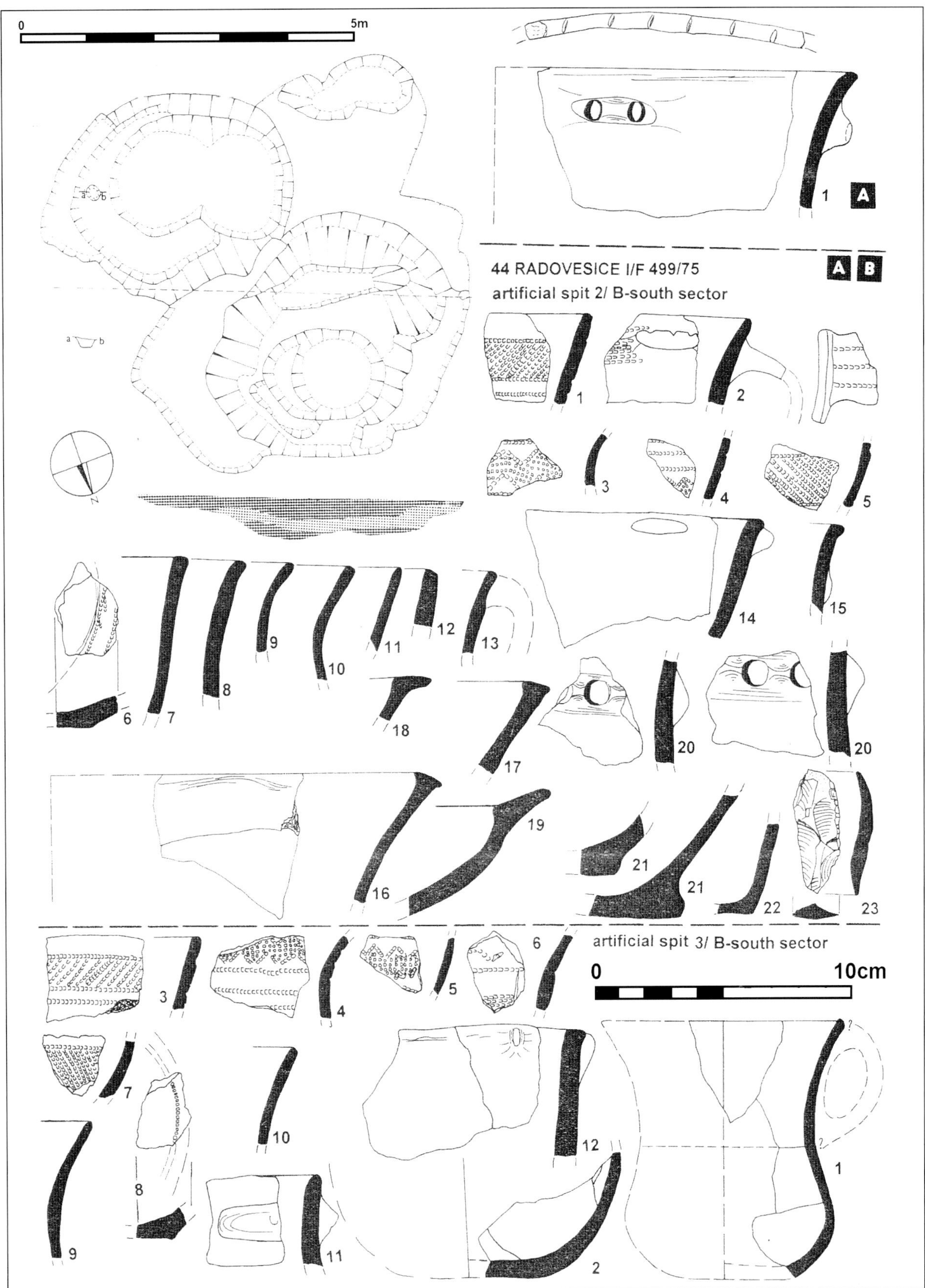

Figure 11.3: Feature 499/75 and associated assemblage from Radovesice (Teplice district) (after Turek 1993)

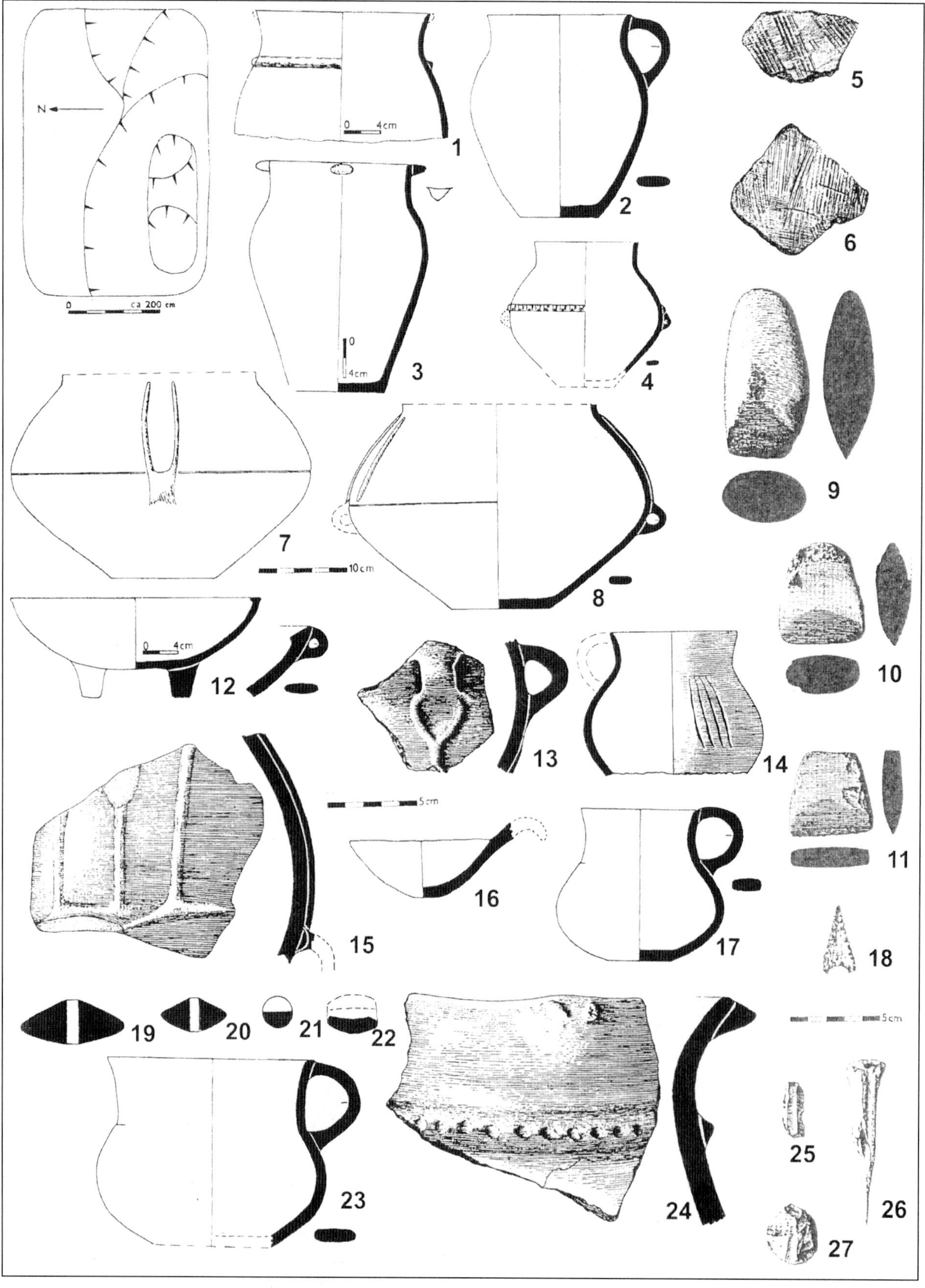

Figure 11.4: Domestic assemblage from Brno-Obřany (district Brno-město, after Ondráček et al. *2005)*

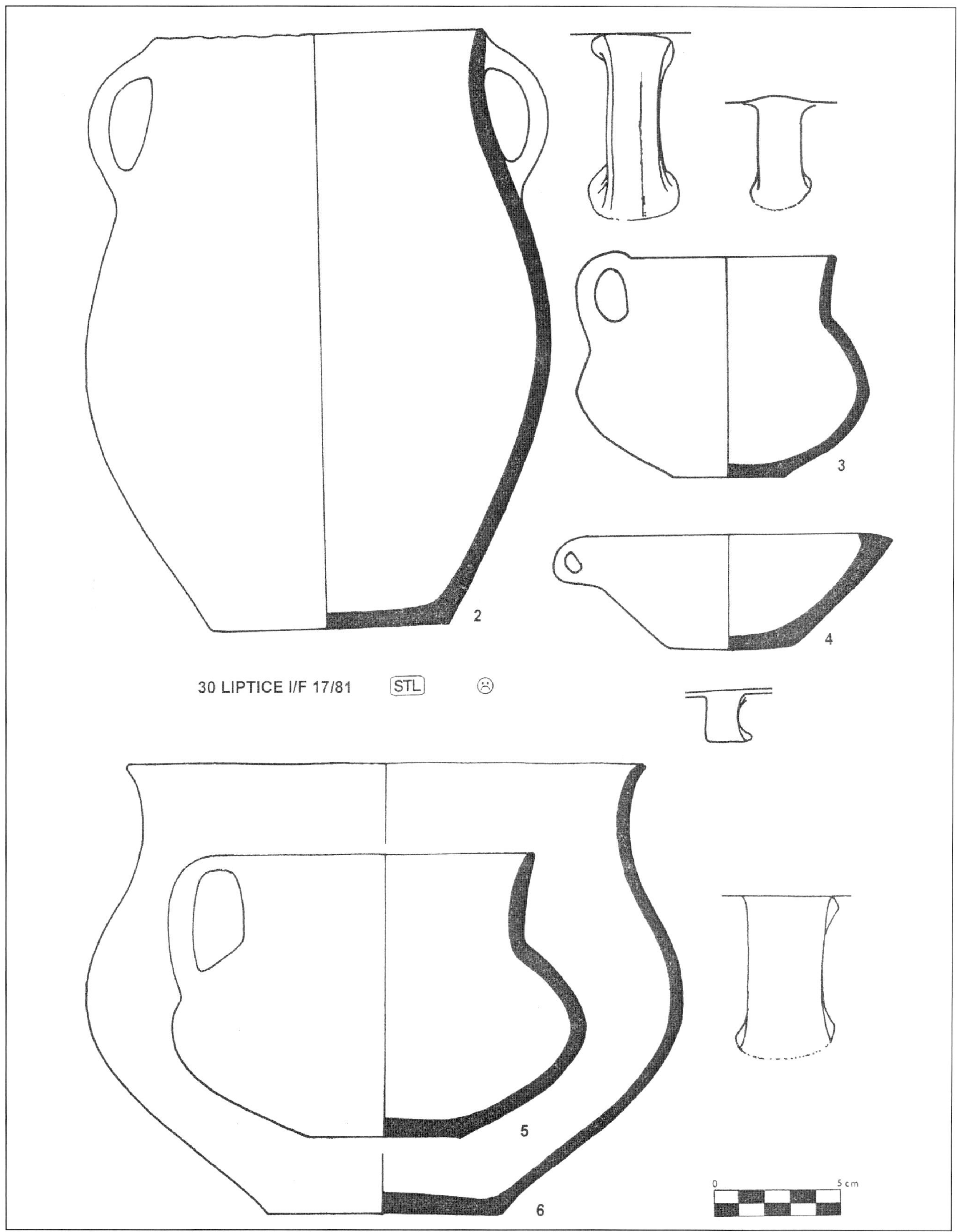

Figure 11.5: Feature 17/81 and associated assemblage from Liptice I, (Teplice district) (after Turek 1993)

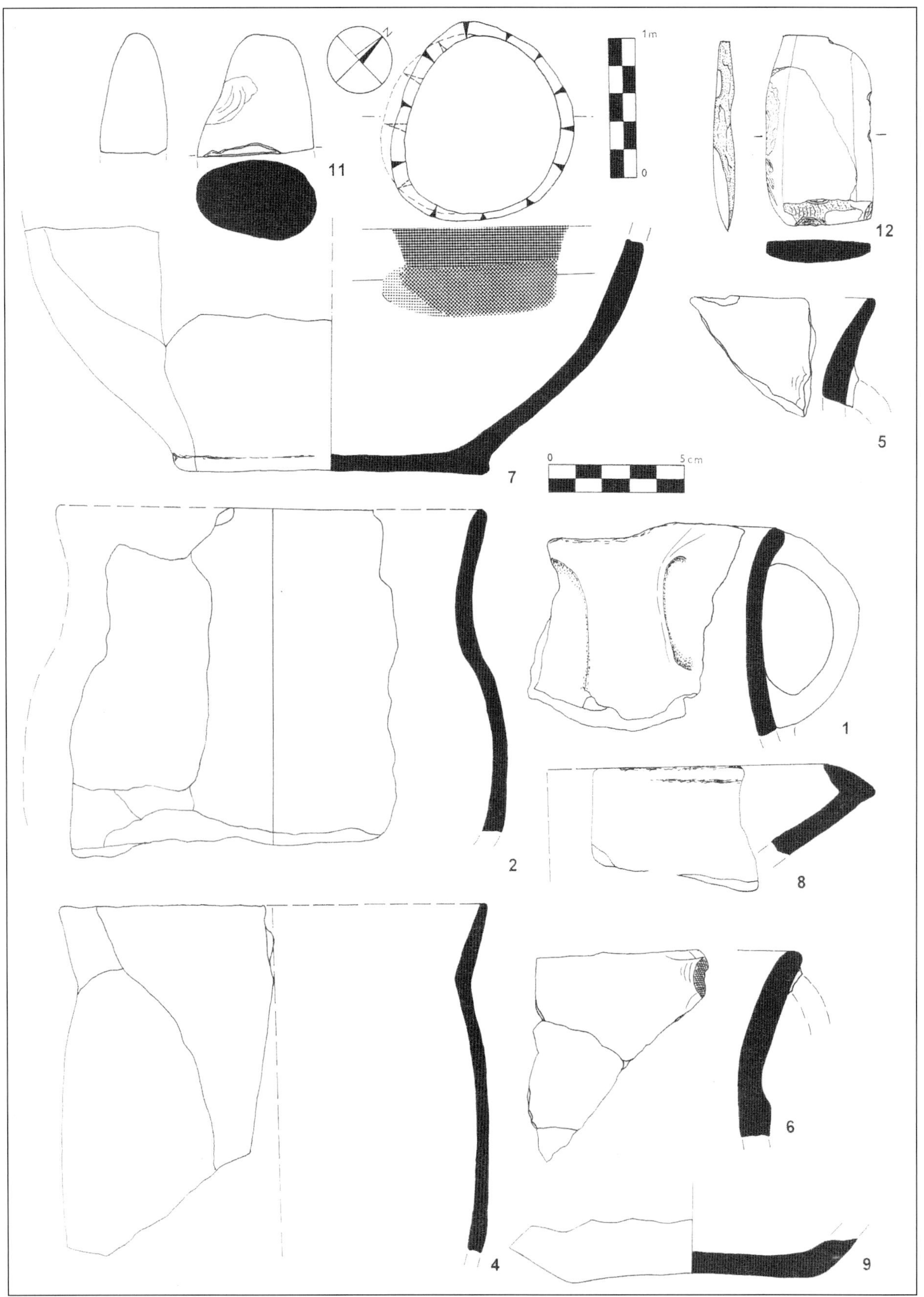

Figure 11.6: Feature 12/82 and associated assemblage from Liptice II, (Teplice district) (after Turek 1993)

pottery styles was symbolically unacceptable. Central Moravia seems to be a key region for the reconstruction of the development sequence of the domestic pottery as in other regions, such as Bohemia we are missing this kind of link.

It has already been observed that there were perhaps two technological types occurring in the *Begleitkeramik* at the settlement of Olomouc-Slavonín (Turek *et al.* 2003, 200). Group A comprised coarse pottery made of sandy clay, no surface polishing and a lower degree of firing. Sometimes the surfaces were rusticated by straw impressions. This appears in the context of Moravian Corded Ware settlement features, in Moravian Corded Ware graves and in Bell Beaker Culture features where it is associated with decorated Bell Beakers and bowls. Group B (Fig. 11.1) vessels are represented by a higher quality ware, well-fired polished surfaces and use of slip. This pottery is commonly found together with decorated Beakers. It appears only in purely Bell Beaker Culture contexts without any traces of Corded Ware. In archaeological features, Group A predominates over Group B by a ratio of about 30:6.

Local ceramic production before and after Beakers

While the accompanying pottery (*Begleitkeramik*) had a crucial influence on the style and morphology of the Únětice and even later Věteřov pottery production in Bohemia and Moravia, the decorated Bell Beakers entirely disappeared from the material culture of Central Europe (Turek 2013). For a better understanding of the degree of acceptance of the Bell Beaker cultural uniformity it is very important to compare the subsequent development in different European regions after the decline of the Phenomenon. While most of the Eastern Province continued in the local common ware (*Begleitkeramik*) tradition after 2300/2000 cal BC (Únětice, Nagyrév) the Bell Beaker decorated ware disappeared with no visible impact on the local pottery sequence. A different development of the Bell Beaker tradition may be observed for example in the British Isles, where the Early Bronze Age Food Vessels and Collared Urns continue some Bell Beaker influence. Furthermore, the Early Bronze Age pottery in the Low Countries and the barbed wire decoration motif originated in the style of the local late Veluwe style Bell Beakers.

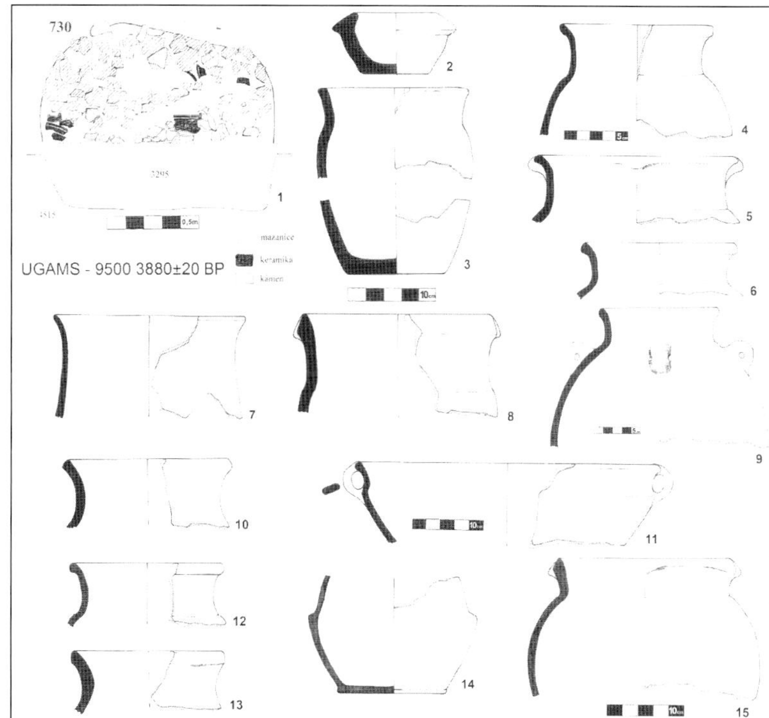

Figure 11.7: Feature 730 and associated pottery from Hulín-Pravčice, U obrázku (okr. Kroměříž), (after Peška 2013).

Within the Beaker *Begleitkeramik* some characteristic features of the decorated ware survived, namely those of bowls. The T-shape widened rim of the Beaker '*Begleitkeramik*' bowls has a very distant pedigree in the Palmela bowls of the western Iberian Peninsula. This style spread together with the Bell Beaker decorated ware as a part of the Beaker Package over vast territories and became part of the stylistic composition of the Central European Bell Beaker common ware. This specific type of bowl, together with the polypod bowls (perhaps a Corded Ware tradition) survived in the pottery production of some Early Bronze Age cultures, such as in Věteřov (Reinecke A2/A3).

The structure and size of settlement areas and units

Despite the growing number of newly discovered settlement sites, the overall image of Late Eneolithic settlement areas remains quite indecipherable. The settlement structure in the Bell Beaker period was apparently made up of a network of small settlements (Shennan 1993; Turek & Peška 2001) with close spatial relationships to burial areas

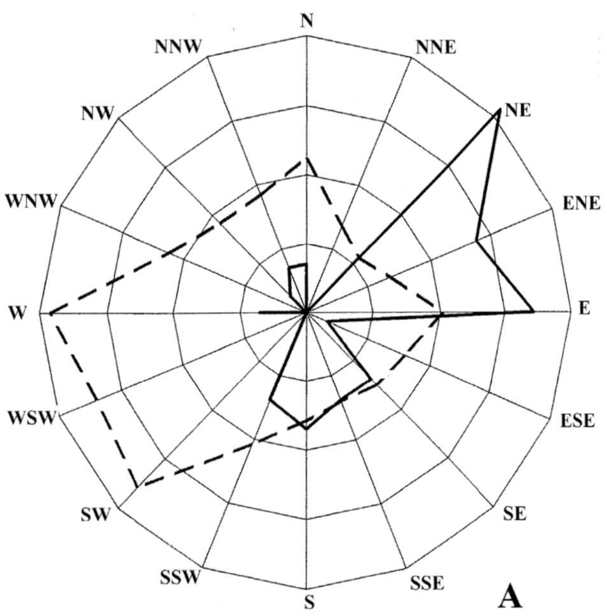

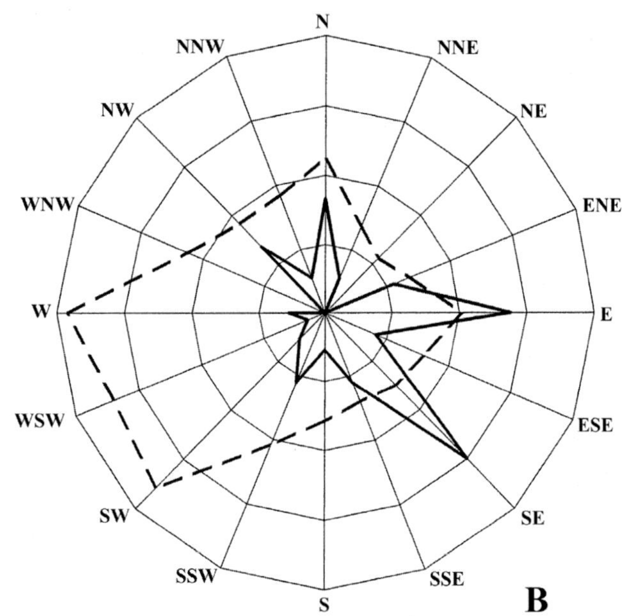

Figure 11.8: A – representation of slope aspect of Corded Ware sites in the Prague region (continuous line) in relation to wind directions (broken line) as recorded by Prague-Ruzyně meteorological station (1946–1965). Each gradation = 5%; Windless = 11.3 %; Sites in flat landscape = 5.2%; (after Turek 1996). B – Representation of slope aspect of Bell Beaker sites in the Prague region (continuous line) in relation to wind directions (broken line) as recorded by Prague-Ruzyně meteorological station (1946–1965). Each gradation = 5%; Windless = 11.3 %; Sites in flat landscape = 19.7%

(Turek 1996). The small settlement units could have shifted relatively frequently within restricted areas, probably along watercourses as the main communication corridors. The typical Eneolithic community was composed of two to six families, each with an average of four members (Neustupný 1983; 2001; 121–2). The size of the resulting settlement units (10 to 25 individuals) would almost precisely match the size of burial groups, which would then represent an image of a relatively short-term settlement phase. Bell Beaker Culture cemeteries were typically built on gentle slopes and terraces, and it is therefore possible that settlement areas were situated lower, in the vicinity of the river or stream.

Unfortunately, the structure of Bell Beaker Culture settlement has not been a traditional research topic of archaeological excavations in Bohemia. Finds from cemeteries were regarded as more important sources for chrono-typological studies. Of the nearly 500 sites (including isolated finds) that Hájek recorded up until the beginning of the 1980s (Hájek 1968 and an unpublished card index, completed around 1980), only 20 were certain settlement locations. The low number of known settlements could be caused by several factors and especially the character and small number of negative features that typically make up the archaeologically visible remains of a settlement. The low number of recognised settlements is also often due to settlement pottery that is difficult to identify, as well as the fact that the distinguishable remains of settlements very often fall into the late phase of the Bell Beaker Culture, which is lacking the characteristic and easily identifiable decorated pottery of the early phase. While Hájek could record only a single settlement site in north-west Bohemia in 1968, a review of the finds inventory along with the results of new excavations (Turek 1993; 1995; 1998) has increased this figure to 14.

An analysis of the preference in the orientation of sloped locations with predominantly burial finds in the region of Prague produced noteworthy results, suggesting a distinct bias towards an eastern exposure for both Corded Ware and Bell Beaker sites (see Fig. 11.8,a–b; Turek 1996, figs 15–16; Turek & Peška 2001, fig. 4b). This may be an attempt to shelter from the prevailing westerly winds but as the data mainly relate to burial sites, the choice of leeward slopes may be less significant. The preference might indicate either a possible close spatial relationship between residential and burial components or that the symbolism of the eastern sun was important in funerary rites. Possible evidence of the sun cult can be observed not only in the emphasis placed on the orientation of grave pits and the body of the deceased toward the cardinal directions,

Figure 11.9: Simplification of the Pedological map ČR 12–24 Praha (ÚÚG 1988) of the Prague region. Circles represent Corded Ware sites, triangles represent Bell beaker sites. Dotted areas: loess soil with Brown-soil cover. Hatched (oblique) areas: loess substances with sandstone, arenaceous marl and slate 'islands' with chernozem cover. Hatched (vertically): floodplain soils. Black (shaded): anthropogeneous sediments. White areas: nonloessic subsoils (after Turek 1996)

but also in artefacts interpreted as solar discs (shells with the motif of concentric circles and a cross) in the period of the Corded Ware Culture and in similar solar motifs occurring on V-perforated buttons from the Bell Beaker Culture (see Radovesice, grave no. 53/80-I, Turek & Černý 2001, fig. 3).

Sites in the Prague region were most commonly distributed along smaller tributaries of the Vltava River but only a few were situated directly on the main watercourse itself. Despite the fact that a majority of the sites were of a burial nature, their distinct link to the proximity of a watercourse was clearly demonstrated in that nearly half of the sites were located within 250 m of the nearest stream. The majority of analysed sites were situated on loess subsoils or in their immediate vicinity (see Fig. 11.9; Turek 1996, 22, map 2; Turek & Peška 2001, fig. 6). Locations of this kind were preferred over others even in the case of highly restricted loess zones (eg, Holešovice-brewery), which could be proof of close links to a type of soil favourable for farming. This situation had already been observed at a Corded Ware Culture site in the Ohře River basin (Neustupný, E. 1956, 413). Nevertheless, it should be kept in mind that Rulf (1983, 61–6, 76–7) characterised the Corded Ware and Bell Beaker sites of the Český Brod Plateau as locations concentrated primarily on non-loess soil therefore links to a specific type of soil may be regionally variable.

Settlement areas

Archaeologically identifiable traces of settlement areas from the Bell Beaker period are relatively limited. The average number of sunken features within a single settlement unit is between 1 and 3 and there seems to be little regularity in the arrangement of houses and other economic structures within individual Eneolithic villages (Neustupný, E. 2001, 121).

Large-scale excavations such as at Liptice in the Teplice district (see Fig. 11.10; Turek 1995; 1998) or in Olomouc-Slavonín (7.7

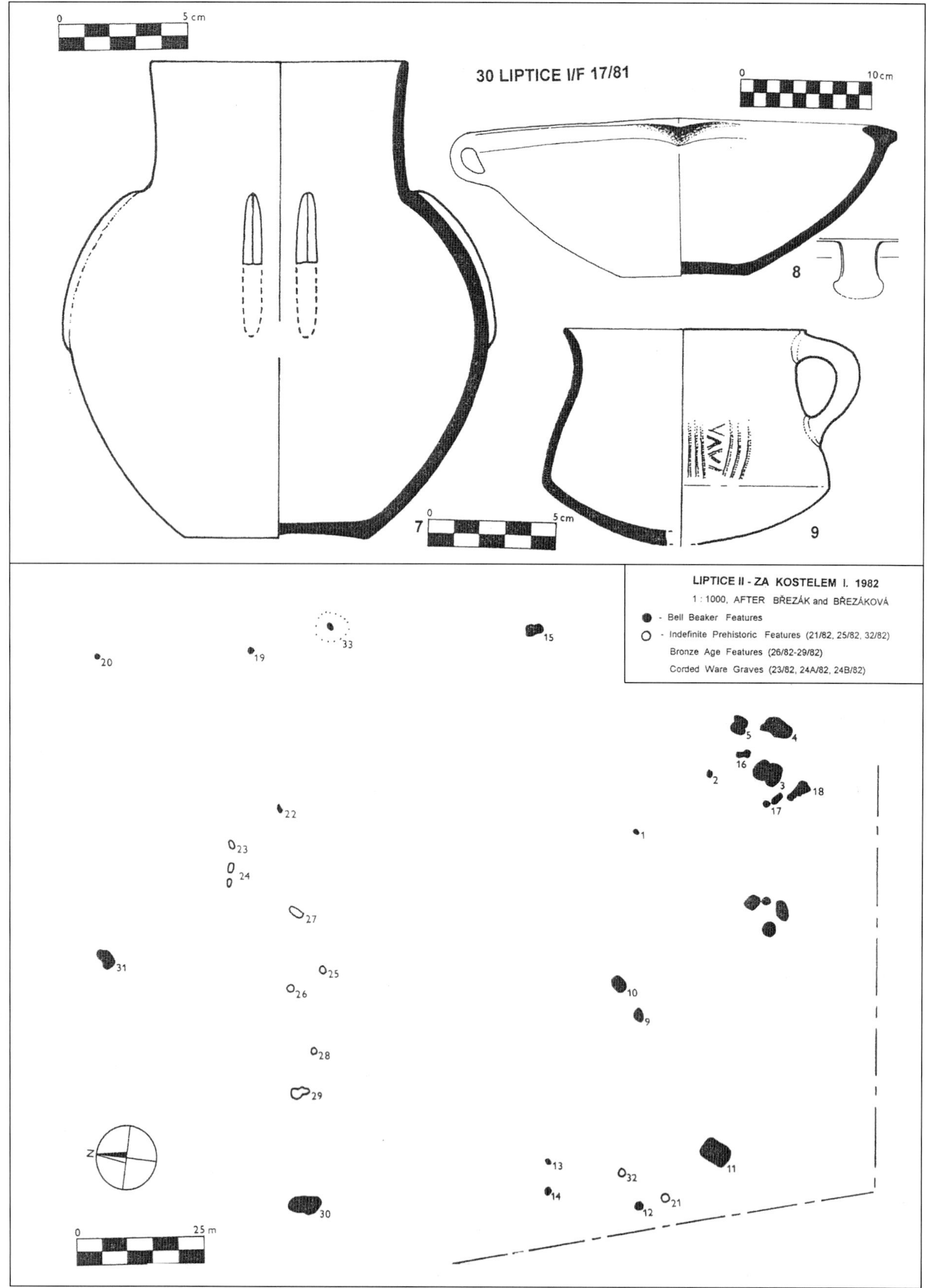

Figure 11.10: Settlement plan and associated pottery from Liptice II, (Teplice district) Bell Beaker features in black (after Turek 1993)

hectares; Turek *et al.* 2003) suggest a structure of smaller clusters of sunken features spaced at a distance of 50–250 m. Also nine features investigated in Žádovice (Hodonín district, see Fig. 11.11) were scattered along the 100 m long excavated strip (Matějíčková 1999). Six of these pits partially enclosed a space of *c.* 30 × 50 m that contained no other contemporary features. A dwelling could originally have stood in this space. A similar arrangement of sunken features can likewise be seen at the settlement in Liptice. Liptice II (Muška 1981) remains the largest investigated settlement from the Bell Beaker period in Bohemia. Excavations uncovered 24 sunken features spread over an area of approximately 1.5 hectares (Fig. 11.10). Two settlement features discovered by Moucha during the construction of bus garages in Lovosice (North Bohemia) also stood alone within a large excavated area (Hájek 1968, 60–2).

This pattern of 'invisible' houses associated with one small and shallow circular or semi-circular pit (base of a silo?) and perhaps another large amorphous construction pit (for exploitation of clay for wall plastering) is perhaps the most common model of a Bell Beaker hamlet. This may also be why sites with seemingly rich surface scatters of artefacts, for example at Tuchoměřice Kněžívka (Turek & Daněček 1997) where numerous pottery fragments, stone wristguards (Fig. 11.12,a), and flint arrowheads (Fig. 11.12,b) were found, are represented by only two or three sunken features with the majority of the occupation level destroyed by ploughing. This general paucity of negative domestic features is very probably part of the continuity of the Corded Ware settlement pattern.

Sunken settlement features can be categorised into two basic groups: large amorphous pits composed of a greater number of smaller pits of varying depth with a bowl-shaped and rugged base such as feature 499/75 from Radovesice: (Turek & Peška 2001, 423, Fig. 11.10). The second type of feature comprises smaller round pits with a flat base as at Liptice, feature 2/82). Probably serving different purposes, the two types of features appear in both Bohemian and Moravian Bell Beaker groups such as at Olomouc-Slavonín, feature 964, (Turek & Peška 2001, 424, Fig. 11.11) and in Bavaria.

A positive reconstruction of the residential structure of Bell Beaker Culture in Bohemia is still not possible. The sunken features with a right-angled shape discovered earlier and interpreted as pit houses such as Praha-Lysolaje, Jenštejn (Hájek 1936–38, 119–22,

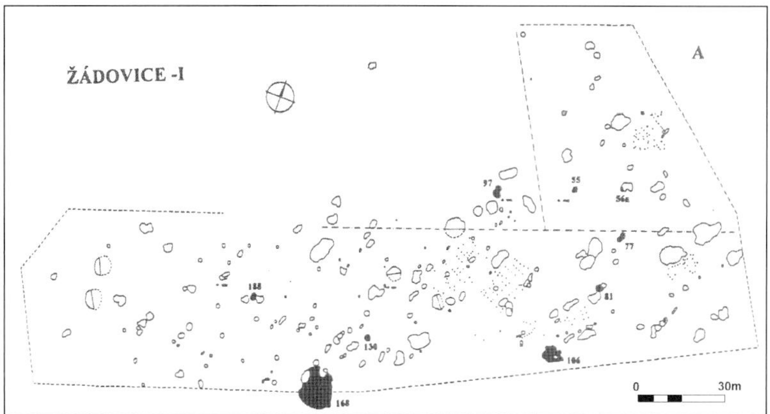

Figure 11.11: Settlement plan of Žádovice (Hodonín district). Bell Beaker features in black (after Matějíčková 1999)

Figure 11.12: A – stone wristguard from the surface scatter on the Bell Beaker settlement site at Tuchoměřice-Kněžívka (Prague-West district). B – flint arrowhead from the surface scatter on the Bell Beaker settlement site at Tuchoměřice-Kněžívka (Prague-West district) (photographs by Vladimír Daněček)

Abb. 1–2) and Praha-Hostivař (Mašek 1976) are not standard types of dwellings. While the most recent large-scale excavation in central Moravia at Olomouc-Slavonín (Turek *et al.* 2003) produced evidence of simple lines of post-holes, none of them could be interpreted as part of the ground-plan of a dwelling.

Currently the most updated account for Bell Beaker settlements in Moravia is the catalogue of domestic sites compiled in the early 1990s and later updated by Ondráček and Dvořák (Ondráček *et al.* 2005). The list of Moravian settlements includes 225 sites from 145 parishes. There are 68 sites listed with evidence of sunken features, 18 sites with evidence of an occupation layer, 29 sites recorded by field-walking and many other settlement sites may be suggested from isolated finds and residual intrusive Beaker pottery in sunken features of other periods (Turek *et al.* 2003).

The blending of domestic and funerary activities

The close spatial relationship between the settlement and funerary areas on Bell Beaker sites has been repeatedly stated (Turek 1996) but the question remains as to what was the degree of spatial overlapping and blending of activities. In several cases Beaker funerary groups are in close proximity to settlement sites. This is based on direct evidence from excavated sites and indirectly suggested by geomorphological, soil substrata and slope exposition analysis (Turek 1996). There are only rare cases in which settlement features were directly re-used for funerary purposes. At Velké Přílepy (Prague-West District) an extraction pit was re-used for the setting of a cremation pyre and human remains and burial assemblages were found *in situ* (Turek 2008b). Despite the close proximity of funerary and residential areas we can see certain limits in the blending of functions. The common secondary use of settlement pits for regular funerary purposes and burial zones directly overlapping settlements found in the Early Bronze Age Únětice Culture is unknown in a Bell Beaker context (Kruťová & Turek 2004).

Beaker houses: a puzzle

Until recently there was no evidence of Bell Beaker associated dwellings in Bohemia and Moravia. The currently available evidence is still very limited and imperfectly understood (Turek 2011). The reconstruction of the shapes of Beaker dwellings needs to be done in the overall context of the Neolithic/Eneolithic traditions of domestic architecture. Since the beginning of the Neolithic period and first LBK settlements there is evidence for post constructed longhouses and these continued throughout the Stroke pottery and Lengyel Cultures as well as the TRB.

Up to ten longhouse post structures of the late TRB (Salzmünde) period were uncovered during road bypass construction at Líbeznice in Central Bohemia (Turek 2010). The roof ridges were mainly oriented in an east–west direction. Two complete ground-plans were found with dimensions of 23 × 6 m (House 1) (Turek 2014, fig. 2) and 21 × 7 m (House 2) (Turek 2014, fig. 3). House 1 is characterised by a simple sill-beam line of posts. House 2 had a different internal structure with cross-lines of posts, perhaps creating three compartments.

Direct analogies for the Líbeznice long-houses were discovered during the 1971–1972 and 1977 excavations at Březno (Louny district, North-west Bohemia). Two houses probably dated to the earlier TRB period measured 24 × 7 m (House 88) and 33 × 6 m (House 96). In both cases there was a row of roof ridge post-holes along the main axis of the house. Both houses were orientated NW–SE (Pleinerová 1990). Another example of a TRB longhouse comes from Kozly-Čihadla (Mělník District) excavated in 1950s near to a Bell Beaker house (Zápotocký 2014).

The Baden Culture and Middle Eneolithic (Řivnáč – Cham – Jevišovice B) settlements in Bohemia and Moravia are mainly represented by hill top sites and rather small houses with sunken floors (Podborský 1993; Neustupný 2008) but it is uncertain whether these features really represent the main type of dwelling.

For the following Corded Ware period we have almost no evidence of settlements either in Bohemia (Turek 1995) or Moravia (Turek & Peška 2001). All of the presumed settlement sites are represented only by fragments of pottery and occasionally in Moravia by late Corded Ware settlement pits with pottery finds perhaps suggesting a transition to the Bell Beaker period (Turek & Peška 2001; Turek *et al.* 2003). There are no traces of any kind of houseplan on these Corded Ware sites.

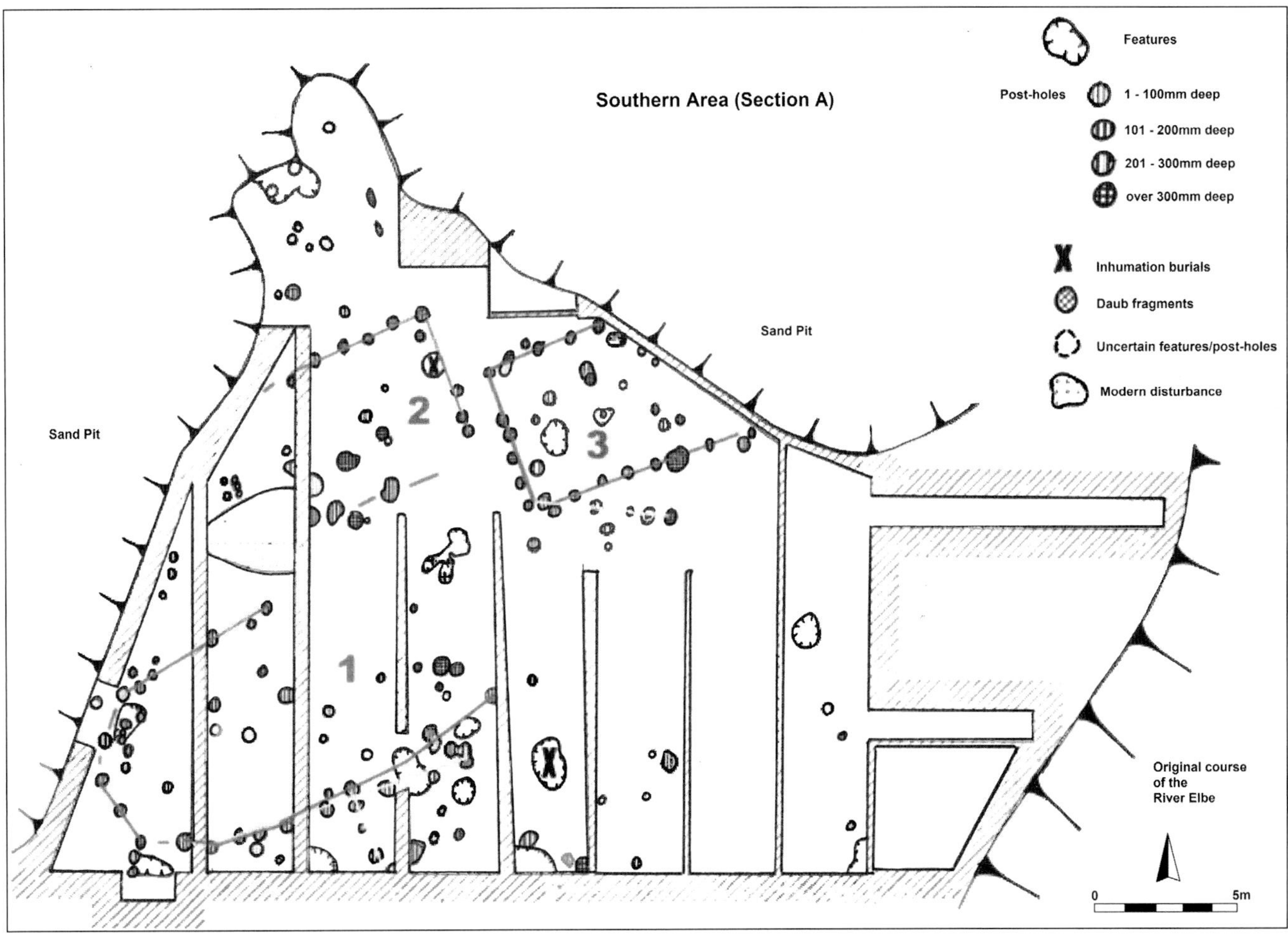

Figure 11.13: Ground-plan of Eneolithic and Early Bronze Age houses at Kozly (Mělník district) Ground-plan No. 1 – Bell Beaker Period (after Zápotocký 2014)

The lack of solid evidence for house constructions at the end of the Eneolithic period resulted in a quest for alternative interpretations regarding the habitation strategies at this time. Log cabin surface constructions were considered as an alternative to the longhouse tradition of the preceding Neolithic period (Turek 2008a; Strahm this volume). In the case of the Corded Ware period, most regions of Central and Eastern Europe lack traces of house sites and mobile or semi mobile settlement patterns were considered including the use of mobile structures (Vencl 1994). This hypothesis was, however, soon rejected (Turek 1995; Neustupný 1997).

Some 20th century excavations in Bohemia uncovered evidence of rectangular, square or oblong features interpreted as dwellings with sunken floors such as Prague-Lysolaje and Jenštejn (Hájek 1936–38, 119–22, Abb. 1–2) and Prague-Hostivař (Mašek 1976) and in Moravia at Mušov, Klobuky, and Těšetice (Peška 2013, 165; Ondráček *at al.* 2005). These features probably do not represent a common type of dwelling as they lack any traces of hearths and if they were a common Bell Beaker dwelling, one might expect them to have been found more frequently.

Currently it seems most probable that the common dwelling construction in Bohemia and perhaps Moravia were post structures in the form of longhouses as are known from some neighbouring regions, such as the area of present day Budapest (Endrődi & Reményi 2016 with further references and this volume) and recently also from Saale-Gebiet (Conrad *et al.* 2018).

The first evidence for a post structure related to the Bell Beaker period comes from Kozly (Zápotocký 1960) in Central Bohemia (Fig. 11.13), where the remains of at least one were uncovered (Zápotocký 2014, fig. 12:1). The Beaker house was oriented E–W with the southern wall characteristically curved. The preserved length of the incomplete structure was 14 × 7–7.5 m. Zápotocký excavated several

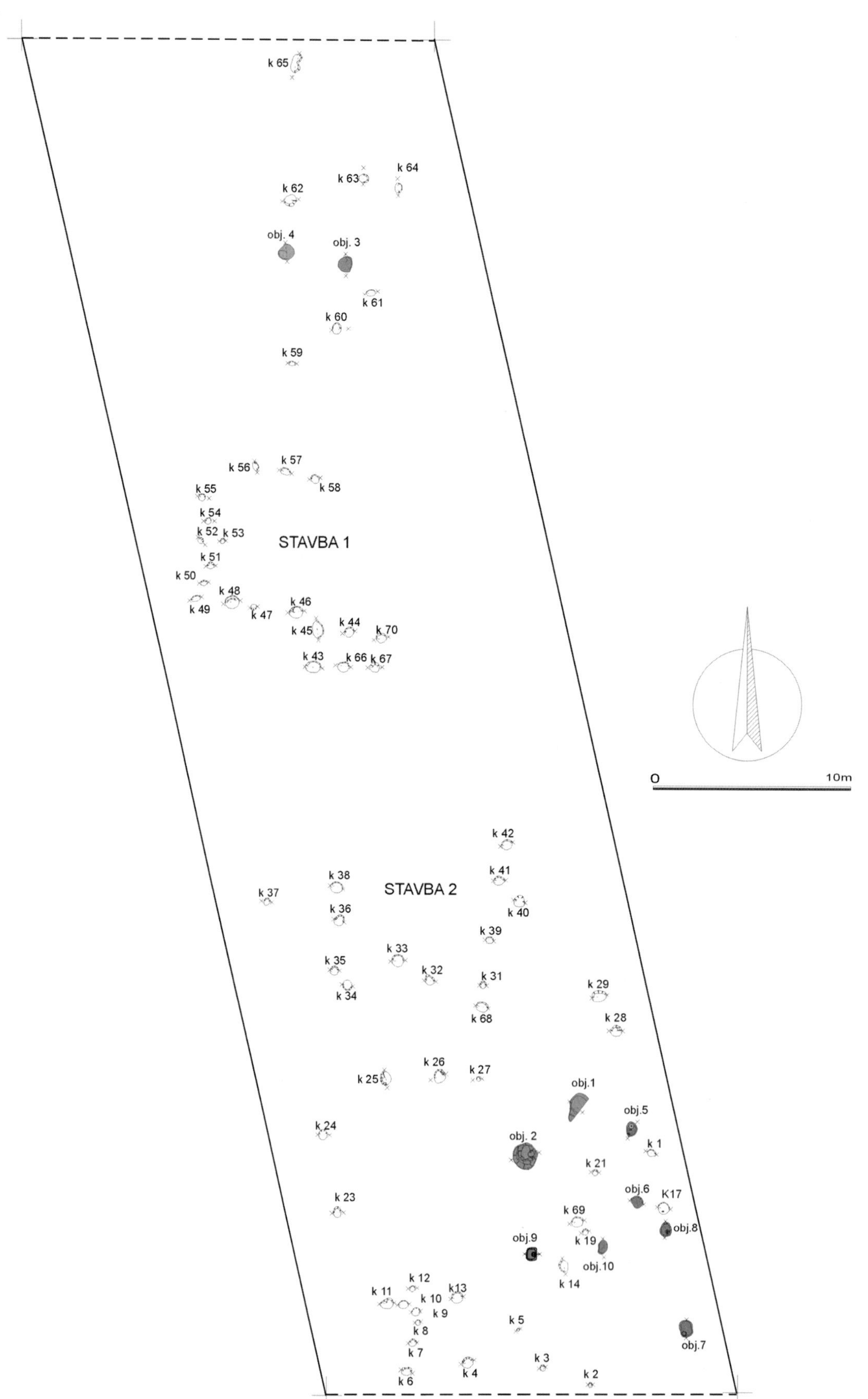

Figure 11.14: Two post-hole structures (houses) and Bell Beaker cemetery at Hostivice (Prague-West district) (after Hložek & Turek 2007)

post-hole defined longhouses with a timespan of at least 2000 years, starting with the Michelsberg Culture, TRB Culture, Bell Beaker Culture and Únětice Culture. An important factor was the location of the settlement site on the bank of the then active River Elbe, one of the most important long-distance routes in prehistoric Bohemia. Termination of over 2000 years of the settlement continuity might have been caused by the river shift towards the south, which turned the nearby meander into the blind shoulder of the river (Zápotocký 2014).

A group of predominantly child burials was excavated in close proximity to two post-hole structures, perhaps longhouses in Hostivice near Prague (Hložek and Turek 2007). In particular, building 2 (Fig. 11.14) is by its orientation, dimensions, shape and number and spacing of post-holes almost identical to the structure from Líbeznice (see below). The dating of these structures to the Bell Beaker period is not entirely secure, as there were almost no finds in the post-holes though there was a rim of a Beaker *Begleitkeramik* bowl in the fill of post-hole No. K69. Further fragments of pottery with rusticated surfaces were found in post-hole No. K31. This pottery is similar to the large storage vessels known from Beaker settlements but they can easily be of later Early or Middle Bronze Age origin.

If both the funerary and domestic component in Hostivice belong to the Bell Beaker period (and finds of other periods were not identified on this site), then it is certainly a remarkable spatial blending of both components. The proximity of the residential area and cemeteries has already been observed on Bell Beaker sites such as in Prague Kobylisy, Prague Hostivař and elsewhere (Turek 1996), however the fact that only child burials accumulate near residential buildings is also significant. Burying children indoors or in the immediate vicinity of homes is a well-documented phenomenon in some prehistoric periods, as well in some ethnological observations (Turek 2005 with further references).

About 250 m north-west of the TRB settlement at Líbeznice (mentioned above), a Bell Beaker settlement pit and at least 17 post-holes were uncovered during excavations in 2009. The group of post-holes created an incomplete oblong/oval ground-plan measuring 15 × 7.5 m and along a N–S axis

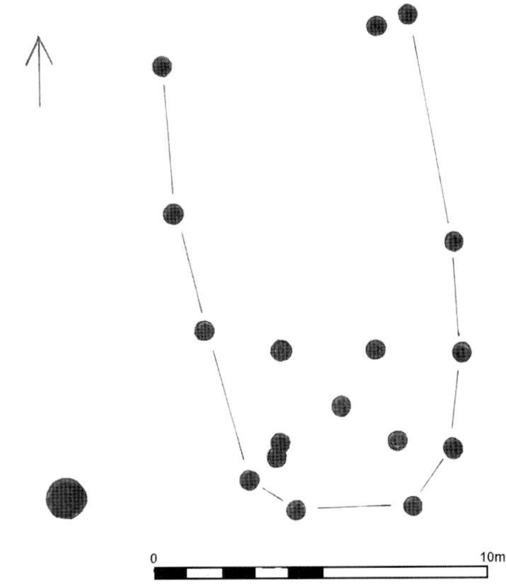

Figure 11.15: Round-plan of a Bell Beaker house and small settlement feature at Líbeznice G (Prague-East district) (after Turek 2011)

(Fig. 11.15) Unfortunately, there were no directly associated finds and the assigning of this house to the Bell Beaker period is based on indirect data such as the immediate proximity of a pit containing a large number of *Begleitkeramik* fragments and daub with wattle impressions and which may be related to the destruction of the nearby house. Furthermore, the isolation of this group of features does not suggest a link with any other chronological unit (Turek 2010; 2011).

Conclusions

Based on the current state of knowledge it is possible to assume that the Beaker dwellings in Bohemia were longhouses presumably with shallow-anchored posts possibly utilising sill-beams. Such structures have not yet been discovered in Moravia, but it is probably only a matter of time until such evidence will be identified. Recent discoveries of five ground-plans of Bell Beaker houses come from Vereinigte Schleenhein (Leipzig) in Saale-Gebiet (Conrad *et al.* 2018; Spatzier & Schunke this volume). The houses of trapezoid ground-plan are orientated SE–NW and ranging between 12–18 m long by 4–7 m wide. The post-holes were relatively shallow as was the case of the sites from Bohemia (see above). There was only a very limited number of other settlement sunken features (including a well and individual burials) located near to the houses. Other nearby and well-preserved analogies come from the territory of present-day Budapest and are discussed by Endrődi and Reményi (this volume).

Similar more or less boat shaped longhouses of the Bell Beaker period are known from very distant regions of Europe as described elsewhere in this volume. It may well be possible that this type of construction was a part of the Beaker Package in a broad sense and as such yet another uniform element uniting European regions with different cultural and economic backgrounds.

References

Bökönyi, S. 1974. *History of domestic mammals in Central and Eastern Europe*, Budapest, Akadémiai Kiadó

Bökönyi, S. 1978. The earliest waves of domestic horses in East Europe. *The Journal of Indo-European Studies 6,* 17–6

Brodie, N. 1997. New perspectives on the Bell Beaker Culture. *Oxford Journal of Archaeology* 16 (3), 297–314

Buchvaldek, M. 1967. *Die Schnurkeramik in Böhmen.* Acta Universitatis Carolinae. Philosophica et Historica Monographia 19, Praha

Cohen, M. N. & Armelagos, G. J. (eds), 1984. *Palaeopathology at the Origins of Agriculture.* Gainsville: University Press of Florida

Conrad, M., Schmalfuss, G. & Richter, K.-H. 2018. Vorbericht über ein endneolithisches Siedlungsareal im Tagebau Vereinigtes Schleenhain (SH-22). *Archaeo* 14, 42–8

Endrődi, A. & Remenyi, L. 2016. *A Bell Beaker settlement in Albertfalva, Hungary (2470–1950 BC).* Budapest: Budapest History Museum

Hájek, L. 1936–38. Kulturní jámy s keramikou zvoncovitých pohárů, *Památky archeologické* 31, 119–122

Hájek, L. 1968. Kultura zvoncovitých pohárů v Čechách. *Archeologické studijní materiály 5.* Praha: Archeologický ústav ČSAV

Havel, J. & Pavelková, J. 1989. Pohřební ritus a antropologické zhodnocení populační skupiny kultury zvoncovitých pohárů z území Čech, *Archaeologica Pragensia* 10, 5–55

Hložek, J. & Turek, J. 2007. Sídliště a pohřebiště z období zvoncovitých pohárů na katastru obce Hostivice, okr. Praha-západ – Bell Beaker settlement and funerary site at Hostivice (district Prague-west), *Archeologie ve středních Čechách* 11, 177–194

Kruťová, M. & Turek, J. 2004. Some spatial aspects of the ritual behavioural at the beginning of Bronze Age. In Šmejda, L. & Turek, J. (eds), 2004: *Spatial Analysis of Funerary areas*, 48–56. Plzeň: Nakladatelství Čeněk

Kyselý, R. 2012. Souhrnná analýza osteozoologických nálezů z období kultury zvoncovitých pohárů v Čechách a na Moravě, Pravěk (NŘ) Supplementum 24, Sv. I, 431–52

Limburský, P. 2013. Sídlištní nálezy kultury se zvoncovitými poháry ve Vlíněvsi, okr. Mělník. *Archeologické rozhledy* 65 (1), 175–92

Lyublyanovics, K. 2016. 10.5. Animal Bones from the Bell Beaker Settlement of Albertfalva, Budapest. In Endrődi, A. & Remenyi, L. 2016. *A Bell Beaker settlement in Albertfalva, Hungary (2470–1950 BC),* 204–16. Budapest: Budapest History Museum

Mašek, N. 1976. Sídlištní objekt kultury zvoncovitých pohárů v Hostivaři-Praha 10, *Archeologické rozhledy* 28, 18–30

Matějíčková, A. 1999. Sídliště kultury zvoncovitých pohárů v Žádovicích (okr. Hodonín) – Siedlung der Glockenbecherkultur in Žádovice (Bez. Hodonín). *Pravěk NŘ*, Supplementum 5, Brno: Ústav Archeologické Památkové Péče Brno, V.V.I.

Muška, J. 1981. The settlement and cemetery sites of the Bell Beaker culture at Radovesice by Bílina. *Archaeological news in the Czech Socialist Republic,* 51. Prague – Brno: Xe Congrès International des sciences préhistoriques et protohistoriques Mexico 1981

Neustupný, E. 1956. Hrob z Tušimic a některé problémy kultur se šňůrovou keramikou, *Památky archeologické* 56, 392–452

Neustupný, E. 1969. Economy of Corded Ware Cultures. *Archeologické rozhledy* 21, 43–68

Neustupný, E. 1983. The demography of prehistoric cemeteries, *Památky archeologické* 74, 7–34

Neustupný, E. 1995. The significance of facts, *Journal of European Archaeology* 3 (1), 189–212

Neustupný, E. 1997. Šňůrová sídliště, kulturní normy a symboly, *Archeologické rozhledy* 49, 304–322

Neustupný, E. 2001. Grundzüge der Bevölkerungsgeschichte Böhmens im Äneolithikum. In Lippert, A., Schultz, M., Shennan, S. & Teschler-Nicola, M. (eds), *Mensch und Umwelt während des Neolithikums und der Frühbronzezeit in Mitteleuropa,* 119–125. Rahden/ West: Verlag Marie Leidorf

Neustupný, E. (ed.), 2008. *Eneolit. Archeologie pravěkých Čech 4.* Praha: Archeologický ústav AV ČR

Neustupný, E. 2011. Pulzování archeologických kultur. In Bárta, M. & Kovař, M. (eds), *Kolaps a regenerace: cesty civilizací a kultur. Minulost, současnost a budoucnost komplexních společností,*173–83. Praha: Academia

Neustupný, J. 1962. Na sklonku doby kamenné. Lid kultury se zvoncovitými poháry v Čechách a na Moravě, Časopis Národního musea 131, 180–195

Nicolis, F. (ed.), 2001. *Bell Beakers today, Pottery, people, culture, symbols in prehistoric Europe. Proceedings of the International Colloquium Riva del Garda (Trento, Italy) 11–16 May 1998.* Trento: Provincia Autonoma di Trento, Servizio Beni Culturali Ufficio Beni Archeologici

Ondráček, J., Dvořák, P. & Matějíčková, A. 2005. Siedlungen der Glockenbecherkultur in Mähren. Katalog der Funde. *Pravěk (NŘ) Suplementum* 15. Brno: Ústav Archeologické Památkové Péče Brno, V.V.I.

Pavlů, I. 2000. První sídliště kultury zvoncovitých pohárů na Čáslavsku, In Čech, P. and Dobeš, M. (eds), *Sborník Miroslavu Buchvaldkovi*, 195–9. Most: UAPP Most

Peška, J. 2013. *Morava na Konci Eneolitu.* Olomouc: AN CERM

Peške, L. 1985. Osteologické nálezy kultury zvoncovitých pohárů z Holubic a poznámky k zápřahu skotu v eneolitu, *Archeologické rozhledy* 37, 428 – 440

Pleinerová, I. 1990. Dva eneolitické dlouhé domy z Března. *Památky Archeologické* 81, 255–274

Podborský, V. (ed.), 1993. Pravěké dějiny Moravy, Vlastivěda Moravská, Země a lid. *Nová řada*, sv. 3. Brno: Matice Moravská

Rehman, F., Robinson, V. J. & Shennan, S. J. 1992. A neutron activation study of Bell Beakers and associated pottery from Czechoslovakia and Hungary, *Památky archeologické* 83, 197–211

Rulf, J. 1983. Přírodní prostředí a kultury českého neolitu a eneolitu, Památky archeologické 74, 35–95

Sangmeister, E. 1974. Zwei Neufunde der Glockenbecherkultur in Baden-Württemberg. Ein Beitrag zur Klassifizierung der Armschutzplatten in Mitteleuropa, *Fundberichte aus Baden-Würtemberg* 1, 103–156

Shennan, S. J. 1993. Settlement and Social Change in Central Europe, 3500–1500 BC, *Journal of World Prehistory* 7 (2), 121–161

Stolz, D. & Stolzová, D. 2002. Nové sídliště kultury zvoncovitých pohárů a další pravěké nálezy na území Králova Dvora, *Archeologie ve středních Čechách* 6, 163–177

Turek, J. 1993. Osídlení z období zvoncovitých pohárů v povodí řeky Bíliny v severozápadních Čechách. Unpubl. MA thesis manuscript. Praha: Philosophical Faculty, Charles University

Turek, J. 1995. Sídlištní nálezy kultuy se šňůrovou keramikou v Čechách. Otázka charakteru hospodářství v závěru eneolitu. The first evidence of Bohemian Corded Ware Settlements and the question of their economy, *Archeologické rozhledy* 47, 91–101

Turek, J. 1996. Osídlení Pražské, kotliny v závěru eneolitu. Nástin problematiky období zvoncovitých pohárů. The Prague region in the Late Eneolithic period. *Archeologica Pragensia* 12, 5–58

Turek, J. 1998. The Bell Beaker Period in north-west Bohemia. In Benz, M. & Willigen, S. Van (eds), *Some New Approaches to The Bell Beaker 'Phenomenon' Lost Paradise.?,* 107–19. Oxford: British Archaeological Reports International Series 690

Turek, J. 2005. Praha kamenná. Neolit – mladší doba kamenná; Eneolit – pozdní doba kamenná. In Lutovský, M. and Smejtek, L. (eds), *Pravěká Praha*, 157–348. Praha: Libri

Turek, J. 2008a. 5.3 Kultura zvoncovitých pohárů. In Neustupný, E. (ed.), Čechy v Pravěku 4 – Eneolit, 98–111, Tab. 50. Archeologický Ústav v.v.i.

Turek, J. 2008b. Significance of cremation in the funerary practices of the Bell Beaker Eastern Province. In Baioni, M., Leonini, V., Lo Vetro, D., Martini, F., Poggiani Keller, R. & Sarti, L. (eds), *Bell Beaker in everyday life, Proceedings of the 10th Meeting 'Archéologie et Gobelets', Florence – Siena – Villanova sul Clisi, May 12–15, 2006*, 271–9. Firenze: Museo Fiorentino Di Preistoria 'Paolo Graziosi'

Turek, J. 2010. Doklady obytných staveb z období nálevkovitých a zvoncovitých pohárů v Líbeznicích u Prahy – New evidence of the TRB and Bell Beaker dwelling constructions from Líbeznice (District Prague-east), Praehistorica 19, 415–30. Praha: Univerzita Karlova

Turek, J. 2011. Pravěké osídlení na trase silničního obchvatu Líbeznic a otázka forem obydlí v období zvoncovitých pohárů, Prehistoric sites along the motorway bypass of Líbeznice. Question on interpretation of Bell Beaker dwelling structures, Archeologie ve středních Čechách 15, 785–796, fototab. 19

Turek, J. 2013. Echoes and Traditions of the Bell Beaker Phenomenon, In Bartelheim, M., Peška, J. & Turek, J. (eds), From Copper to Bronze. Cultural and Social Transformations at the Turn of the 3rd/2nd Millennia BC in Central Europe, Gewidmet PhDr. Václav Moucha, CSc. anlässlich seines 80. Geburtstages, 9–23. Langenweissbach: Beitrage zur Ur- und Frühgeschichte Mitteleuropas 74

Turek, J. 2014. New evidence of FBC longhouses in Central Bohemia, In Furholt, M., Hinz, M., Mischka, D., Noble, G. & Olausson, D. (eds), *Landscapes, Histories and Societies in the Northern European Neolithic*, 219–25. Bonn: Rudolf Habelt GmbH

Turek, J. & Černý, V. 2001. Society, gender and sexual dimorphism of the Corded Ware and Bell Beaker populations. In Nicolis, F. (ed.), 2001, 601–12

Turek, J. & Daněček, V. 1997. Nově objevená eneolitická naleziště na Kladensku a Slánsku. Poznámky ke studiu kamenné broušené industrie českého eneolitu. Some recently discovered Eneolithic sites in the Kladno – Slaný region. Thoughts on Stone axe production in the Bohemian Eneolithic Period. *Archeologie ve středních Čechách* 1, 127–41

Turek, J. & Peška, J. 2001. Bell Beaker settlement pattern in Bohemia and Moravia. In Nicolis, F. (ed.), 2001, 411–28

Turek, J., Dvořák, P. & Peška, J. 2003. Archaeology of Beaker settlements in Bohemia and Moravia. An Outline of the Current State of Knowledge, 183–207. In Czebreszuk, J. & Szmyt, M. (eds), 2003, *The Northeast Frontier of Bell Beakers*, 265–76. Oxford: British Archaeological Reports International Series 1155

Vencl, S. 1994. K problému sídlišť kultur s keramikou šňůrovou – Some comments on the problem of Corded-Ware culture settlement sites. *Archeologické Rozhledy* 46, 3–24

Zápotocký, M. 1960. Sídliště kultury zvoncovitých pohárů u Kozel na Neratovicku. *Památky Archeologické* 51, 5–26

Zápotocký, M. 2014. K osídlení labské nivy v eneolitu a době bronzové: sídlištní areál s půdorysy kůlových domů u Kozel (okr. Mělník), *Archeologické Rozhledy* 66, 651–94

12

Houses and settlements of the Bell Beaker groups in the Carpathian Basin: cultural and economical contexts

László Reményi, Anna Endrődi, Ferenc Gyulai and Katalin T. Biró

Pre-Bell Beaker native cultures in the Carpathian Basin

Cultural questions

Bell Beaker groups appeared in the Carpathian Basin at the end of the transitional period between the Copper Age and the Bronze Age, around 2500 BC in two distinct geographical regions: the Alpokalja ('Alpenostrand') (the south-western margin of the distribution zone of the Moravian Beaker group: the Oggau-Wipfing-Ragelsdorf-Oberbierbaum Group) and the narrow riparian strip of the Danube around Budapest (Bell Beaker-Csepel group). The end of the Late Copper Age (Table 12.1) can be seen to mark the decline and disappearance of the Baden Culture which comprised regional groups with similar cultural features spread over a large geographical area. The demise of the Late Copper Age cannot be interpreted as a sudden and drastic change, much more as process already started after the turn of the 4th and 3rd millennia BC. At this time new local cultural networks appeared within the territory of the Baden complex. Along the Croatian and Hungarian Danube, as far as Budapest, sites of the Kostolac circle formed a communication network (Bondár 1984; Endrődi 1992a) while more to the South, along the Danube, sites of the Vučedol Culture emerged (Durman 1988). In other areas of the Carpathian Basin we still have sites of the latest Baden cultural complex. On the eastern parts of the Great Hungarian Plain (the westernmost extension of the Eurasian steppe) the cultural landscape was further coloured by the infiltration of eastern European (Yamnaja) kurgan cultures (Ecsedy 1979b; Dani & Horváth 2012).

The latest Baden settlements can be dated to 2600–2500 cal BC (Horváth *et al.* 2008; Dani & Horváth 2012, 97; Horváth 2014, 649–53) as can the earliest sites of the Hungarian Early Bronze Age. Radiocarbon dates for the Somogyvár-Vinkovci sites date this cultural unit from 2600–2300/2250 cal BC. Most of the ^{14}C dates obtained from the Makó-Kosihy-Čaka Culture sites are spread between 2560–2100 cal BC (Durman & Obelić 1989;

Table 12.1: Chronological system of the Early Bronze Age in Hungary and Central Europe

Absolute chronology BC	*Hungarian chronology*	*Cultures*	*Central Europe*
2600/2500–2500	EBA1	Vučedol Makó-Kosihy-Čaka, Somogyvár-Vinkovci, Yamnaja	Late/Final Neolithic, Chalcolitic
2500–2300/2200	EBA2a	Bell Beakers, Makó-Kosihy-Čaka, Somogyvár-Vinkovci, Yamnaja	
2300/2200–2200/2100	EBA2b	Bell Beakers, Makó-Kosihy-Čaka, Somogyvár-Vinkovci, Nagyrév, Nyírség, Pitvaros, Yamnaja	EBA
2200/2100–2000/1900	EBA3	Bell Beakers, Makó-Kosihy-Čaka, Somogyvár-Vinkovci, Nagyrév, Nyírség, Hatvan, Perjámos	

Raczky *et al.* 1992; Forenbaher 1993, 242, fig. 3, fig 8; Primas 1996, 165–9; Kulcsár 2011, 15; Kulcsár & Szeverényi 2013).

In parallel to the decline of the Baden and Kostolac sites is an expansion of the Vučedol network (Durman 1988) that appeared in the north-western Balkans from the Adriatic to the south-western margin of the Carpathian Basin, reaching the southern parts of Baranya county and the Danube. The cultural unity was also marked by multi-layered (tell) settlements in the Carpathian Basin (Ecsedy 1983) suggesting a stable cultural and economic network producing sufficient surplus to maintain and defend a large community.

The Vučedol network did not survive for long after the disappearance of the Baden sites. The latest Vučedol sites also date from 2600–2500 cal BC (Durman & Obelić 1989; Della Casa 1995; Forenbaher 1993) and the tells were replaced by settlements of the Somogyvár-Vinkovci with a much looser structure and variable size (Dimitrievič 1982; Tasić 1984; Ecsedy 1979a; 1983; Bondár 1995; Kulcsár 2009, 225–354). This cultural unit spread over Croatia, the south-western Carpathian Basin and to the east of the Alps and played an important connecting role between the north-western Balkans, the Adriatic, the eastern Alps and the Moravian and Bohemian Basins by exploiting communication channels that had been in use since the Neolithic.

As a result of large rescue excavations and post-excavation analysis the transitional period between the Copper and Bronze Ages can be narrowed down to about a hundred years from 2600–2500 cal BC. This period is represented in S and W Transdanubia by the latest Vučedol and the formative Somogyvár–Vinkovci Cultures, which overlap chronologically. In the other regions of the Carpathian Basin are the latest Baden communities and the small units of the Makó–Kosihy–Čaka Culture. In eastern Hungary, the Pit Grave (Yamnaja) population arrived (Fig 12.1).

Ceramics and lithics of the native cultures (Somogyvár–Vinkovci, Makó–Kosihy–Čaka)

Due to the common roots, system of contacts and similar economies, the pottery of the Somogyvár–Vinkovci, Makó–Kosihy–Čaka Cultures share several similarities in forms and decoration. The tempering of the clay in both cultures used sand or small pebbles and the vessels are typically brown, grey or black. The surface is often rusticated, decorated by polishing (mainly on the shoulders and necks) and have plastic ribs and more rarely, incised motifs and dots (Kalicz 1968; 1984; Ecsedy 1979a; Bondár 1995; Kulcsár 2009, 90–1, 276).

Apart from simple household vessels, *Askoi* are known from certain sites of the Makó–Kosihy–Čaka group, and internally decorated pedestal bowls are known from both the Somogyvár–Vinkovci and the Makó–Kosihy–Čaka Cultures. They may be more symbolic vessels and have their roots in the Vučedol Culture (Kulcsár 2009, 121–41, 308–19). Asymmetrical jugs, known from the Makó–Kosihy–Čaka find assemblages may also be Vučedol in origin though they are also known other central European Early Bronze Age cultures (Kulcsár 2009, 98–101). A decorated specimen was found at the site of

Figure 12.1: Map of the Carpathian Basin 2600/2500 BC). 1 – Makó-Kosihy-Čaka; 2 – Late Vučedol / Early Somogyvár-Vinkovci; 3 – Yamnaja, 4 – Corded Ware

Szigetszentmiklós of the Bell Beaker-Csepel group (Endrődi 1992b, 93–4, figs 15–16).

The most typical domestic vessels comprise a variety of handled jugs (Ecsedy 1978; 1979a; Kalicz 1968;1984; Kulcsár 2009, 91–102; 284–95) also found on Bell Beaker sites as are cups, and smaller handle-less drinking vessels ('glasses'). Flasks are also present and the variability and the wide distribution of vessels used for the storage and consumption of liquids are probably related to an increase in dairy products and alcoholic beverages. Bowls were also produced in a variety of forms and all types are generally distributed in the regional Beaker groups as well as in later Early Bronze Age cultures (Bondár 1995; Kulcsár 2009, 105–21, 298–306). There were also various storage and cooking vessels.

Bronze Age lithics are still poorly understood in Hungary, especially in terms of large assemblages (T. Biró 2000, Farkas-Pető & Horváth 2014 etc.). Copper Age, especially Late Copper Age lithic assemblages, are better understood (eg, Balatonőszöd: Horváth 2014; Budakalász: Cs. Balogh 2010) and we can see that several of the Beaker lithic industry features were already present in Baden Culture assemblages, such as the use of Buda hornstone in the area of Budapest (T. Biró 1998). We can also assume that the Characteristic bifacial knifes and some projectile points also appear in Late Copper Age contexts but as yet there are no contemporary Early Bronze Age lithic assemblages.

Settlements and houses in the Late Copper Age and Early Bronze Age Carpathian Basin

The large number of sites from the Neolithic (3600/3500–2500/2500 BC) Baden Culture that have been excavated in Hungary indicate a dense network of settlements marked by hearths, ovens and pits but the remains of houses are represented only by daub fragments. In the Late Copper Age, in the area of Budapest, sites of the Baden Culture were basically concentrated in a narrow strip along the right bank of the Danube where they formed an almost continuous chain of settlements from Békásmegyer to the southern parts of Buda. In spite of the fact that the sites of both the Baden Culture and the Beaker-Csepel Group were distributed in the same area, more detailed analysis identified differences in the settlement network of the two periods. The different settlements were clearly separated from each other and the Late Copper Age sites were further from the river. About 0.20 m higher than the Late Copper Age settlement, graves of the Early Bronze Age were found and we might suppose that this was due to significant changes in water level and the floodplain of

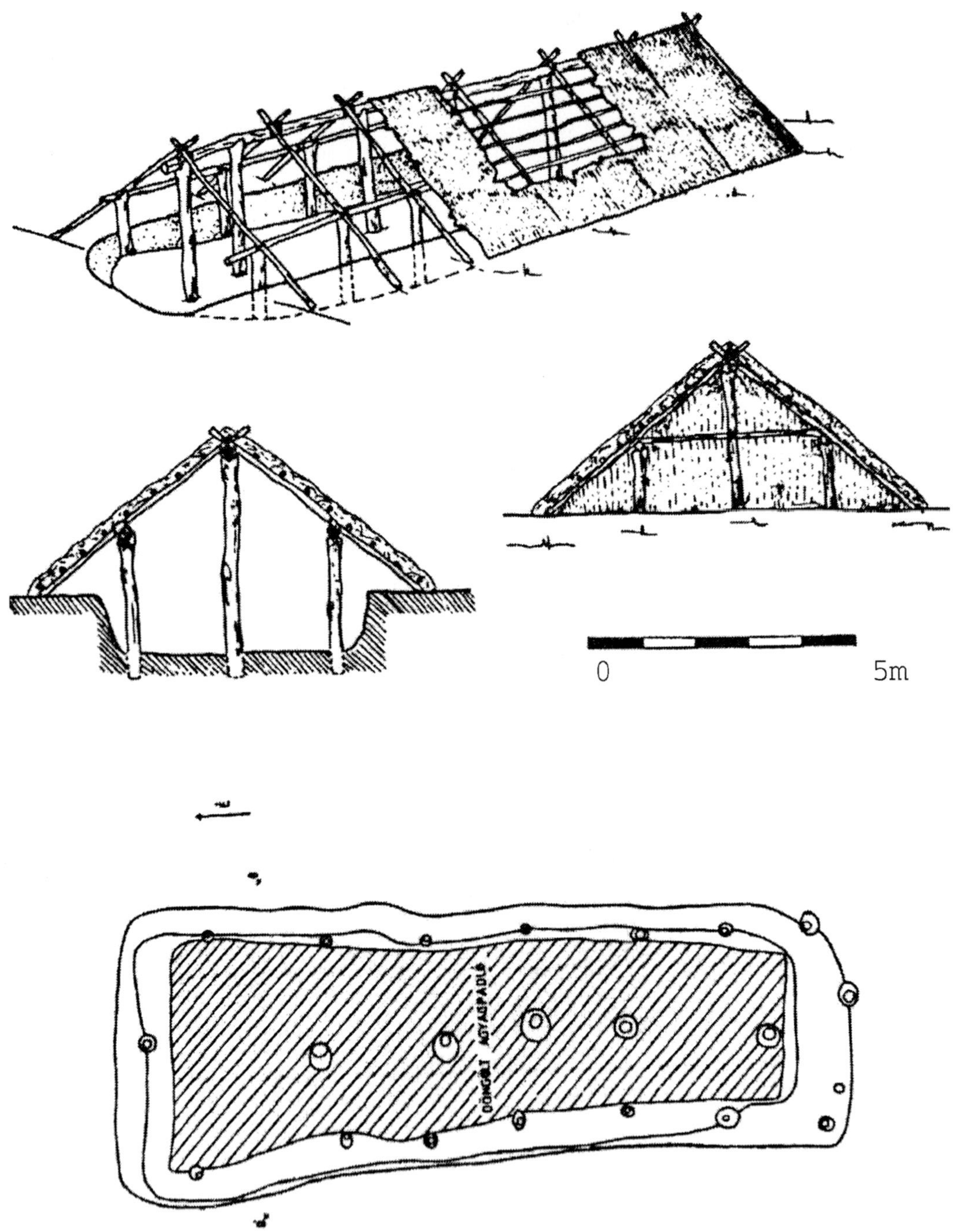

Figure 12.2: House of the Makó–Kosihy–Čaka Culture in Abda-Hármasok (after Figler 1996, fig. 1)

the Danube. In the Late Copper Age, the flood-free river terrace was 200–300 m further from the river than in the second period of the Early Bronze Age and this fluctuation might be another explanation for this phenomenon and may be connected with climatic changes (Endrődi & Reményi 2016, 28).

The Makó-Kosihy-Čaka Culture partly preceded and overlapped the Bell Beaker-Csepel group. The absolute chronological range of the Makó-Kosihy-Čaka Culture extends from 2800/2700–2500/2300 cal BC (Kulcsár 2009) and the settlements in the region of Budapest (Kulcsár 2009, IIIrd region) were mainly located to the west of the Danube as were the Bell Beaker-Csepel group settlements. This may be geomorphological as the left side of the Danube was swampy during the Early

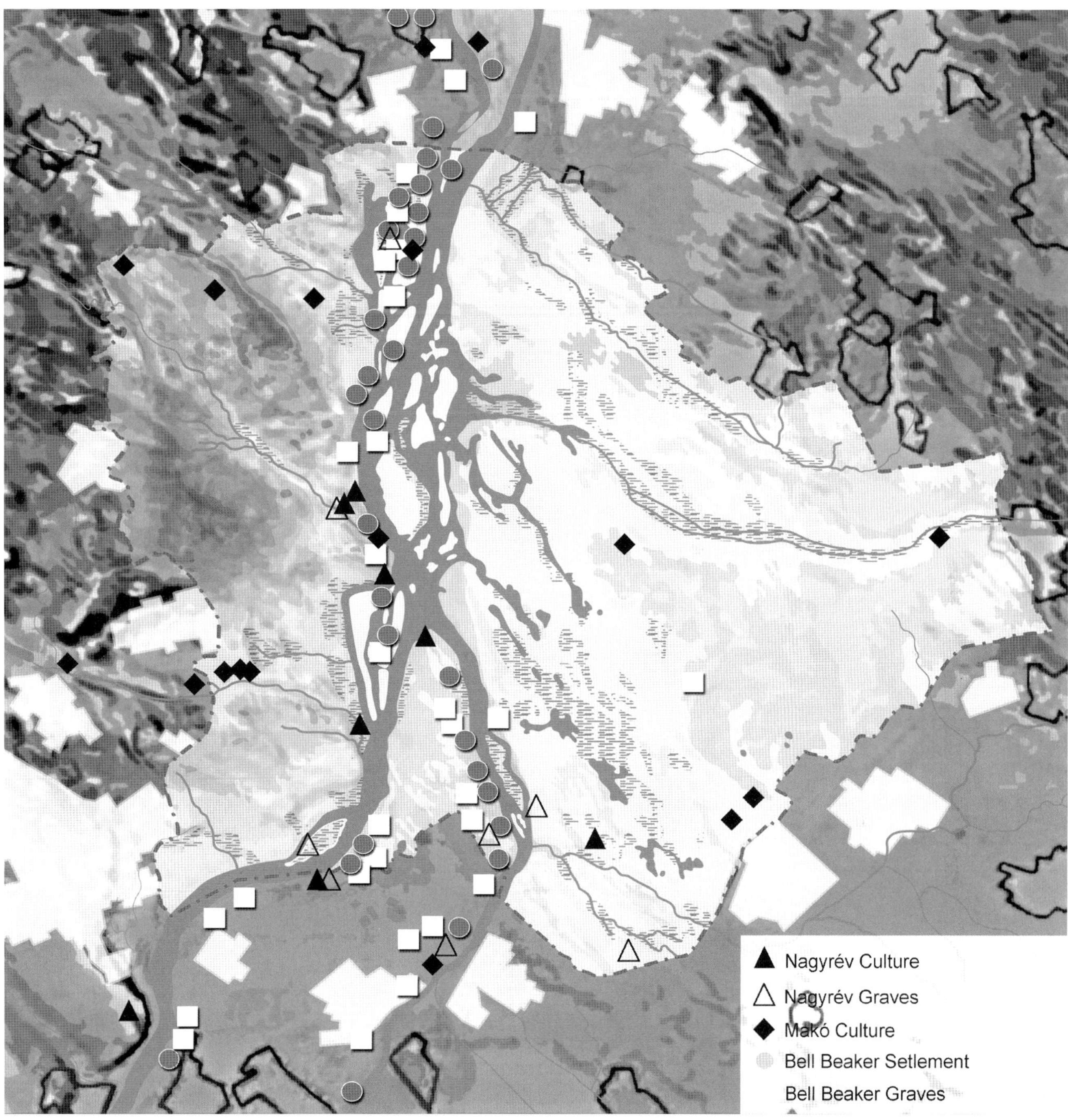

Figure 12.3: Archaeological sites of Bell Beaker-Csepel Group and the contemporary archaeological cultures

Bronze Age in this area. The settlements were located near the natural crossing points (fords) of the Danube; however, the Makó-Kosihy-Čaka and the Bell Beaker-Csepel group settlements were regionally separated.

Traces of large post-built rectangular houses were found on five settlements of the Makó-Kosihy-Čaka Culture (Kulcsár 2009, IIIrd region). Their size (eg, Csongrád, Vidresziget – 259 m^2, Salgótarján, Pécskő-puszta – 247 m^2) suggested that they were communal houses (Kulcsár 2009, 62, 63). Several other rectangular buildings were found and in one case (Nyergesújfalu, József-puszta) had a sunken floor surrounded by posts and had several hearths. So-called pit-houses are also known from SW Slovakia (Nitrianský-Hrádok, Zameček – Kulcsár 2009, 63, 6) and a similar house (Fig. 12.2) was found on the Abda settlement of the Makó-Kosihy-Čaka Culture

Figure 12.4: Map of the Carpathian Basin 2500–2300/2200). 1 – Early Nagyrév (Proto-Nagyrév); 2 – Makó-Kosihy-Čaka; 3 – Somogyvár-Vinkovci Culture; 4 – Bell Beaker Groups; 5 – Corded Ware; 6 – Nyírség; 7 – Pitvaros; 8 – Gyula-Roşia; 9 – Ljubjana

(Figler 1996, 1. ábra). These settlements were typically founded on lowland areas and in river valleys and, in the case of the smaller settlements, the population was involved in cereal cultivation and shepherding livestock. Two types of settlement were differentiated: (1) 'campsite-like' settlements producing a few pits and inhabited for a short time and (2) larger, longer occupied settlements with pits, houses, ditches, trenches and open-air hearths. Kulcsár emphasised the functional differences between the two settlement types (2009, 69–70) and in her opinion, this cannot be interpreted as a result of differences in social hierarchy. In the region of Budapest the Makó-Kosihy-Čaka settlements are located at a greater distance from the Danube, on higher flood-plain levels, than the settlements of the Bell Beaker-Csepel group (Fig. 12.3).

Settlements of the Somogyvár-Vinkovci Culture (2600/2500–2300 cal BC (Kulcsár 2009, 232–5, fig. 39)) can be found within three larger territorial units. Relevant to the Bell Beaker-Csepel group for trade and cultural contacts are the sites in southern, western and northern Transdanubia, the closest being Dunaföldvár, and more to the south, Bölcske. The settlements typically comprise a few round and shallow pits and some clay extraction pits (Kulcsár 2009, 263). Higher and fortified settlements surrounded by protective ditches, for example Kaposújlak-Várdomb, are characteristic of this culture and replaced the earlier Vučedol settlement. On the fortified settlement of Pécs-Nagyárpád there were some rectangular buildings with sunken floors measuring 10–15 m^2 associated with refuse pits, hearths and clay extraction pits. Two houses measured 30–40 m^2 and were interpreted by the excavator as 'community structures' (Kulcsár 2009, 265–6).

Börzönce, Temető-dűlő, was considered an open, short-term settlement comprising 30 pits (Kulcsár 2009, 269). Further houses are known from Vörs, Battyáni disznólegelő (Hog pasture) measuring 2 × 4 m and with a plastered clay floor. At Csepreg were partially sunken houses measuring 7 × 7.5 m. From this settlement evidence, Kulcsár concluded that there was a more mobile and less formal society than in the preceding Vučedol period (2009, 268).

Changes after the appearance of Bell Beaker groups in the Carpathian Basin

Cultural and social changes

The Bell Beaker sites in the Carpathian Basin were concentrated in two narrow geographical zones (Fig. 12.4). The sites in western Transdanubia on the eastern fringes of the Alps (the Oggau-Wipfing-Ragelsdorf-Oberbierbaum Group) can be interpreted as the south-eastern margin of the Moravian

Bell Beaker complex (Reményi & Dobozi 2012). Approximately 60 Bell Beaker sites are known along the Budapest area of the Danube (Bell Beaker-Csepel Group). With the 'Beaker phenomenon' interpretation of the 'New Archaeology' (Shennan 1976), Rózsa Kalicz-Schreiber and Nándor Kalicz emphasised the importance of the native cultures of the Carpathian Basin in the formation process (Somogyvár–Vinkovci, Makó–Kosihy–Čaka). They assigned to the Bell Beaker sphere only the elements of the Beaker package and inhumation burials. The associated pottery, or *Begleitkeramik*, was native in origin and the cremation burials were interpreted as those of the Makó–Kosihy–Čaka population.

The data from large and recently excavated cemeteries, as well as the latest genetic data, do not favour the influence of native cultures over the migration. In these Danubian Beaker cemeteries, the ratio of inhumations and cremations with scattered ashes or urns corresponds to the ratio known from Moravian and Bohemian cemeteries (Turek 2006). In the case of the central European groups and those of the Carpathian Basin we have to consider similar cultural antecedents and parallel phenomena: the Somogyvár–Vinkovci and Makó–Kosihy–Čaka Cultures respectively. The basic difference lay in the closer contact of the Moravian and Bohemian groups with the Corded Ware network though the Makó–Kosihy–Čaka Culture was also in connection with this large eastern complex. Radiocarbon data (Albertfalva: 2470–1950 BC) and settlement historical evidence indicates that in the region of Budapest, the sites of the Nagyrév Culture existed in parallel with the sites of the Bell Beaker-Csepel group. Early Nagyrév cemeteries comprising smaller groups of graves were found close to the Bell Beaker cemeteries but always separate and never mixed. On the sites of the Bell Beaker-Csepel group, finds belonging to the Nagyrév Culture are rare so the sites of the two cultural units operated in parallel in the same region.

The local origin of the cremation graves and the associated pottery and the connection of the Bell Beaker-Csepel Group to the Nagyrév culture can be questioned. As a result of the recently published DNA study (Olalde *et al.* 2018), the Bell Beaker-Csepel group population can be related to the European Bell Beaker circle and can be interpreted as an independent group of the European network, closely connected to the Moravian and Bohemian groups influenced by local factors (Turek 2006).

The European Bell Beaker network (Shennan 1976; Sherratt 1987; 1997, 219; Turek 2006) was a complex economical network where individual regional groups shared their resources. Apart from the elements of the Beaker package, special resources like copper and stone artefacts were exchanged within the network. In the case of the Bell Beaker-Csepel group we cannot assume significant copper metallurgy (Endrődi *et al.* 2003; Reményi *et al.* 2006; Endrődi & Reményi 2016, 142–52) and compared to Alpine areas, there are no significant ore deposits along the middle reaches of the Danube. The lithic industry, based mainly on local resources, was fairly well developed (see below) and the Beaker groups of the Central European territories also had access to such local raw materials. The complex agricultural system of the Bell Beaker-Csepel group most probably produced a surplus and horses seem to have been an important contribution to the European Bell Beaker network (see below) and was perhaps the resource that specifically connected the Middle Danube Basin to the European Bell Beaker economic system (Endrődi *et al.* 2008).

As with the Central European group, the formation of the Bell Beaker groups in the Carpathian Basin resulted in the emergence of a more differentiated society when compared to the native cultures. The Somogyvár–Vinkovci sites and the smaller habitation sites of the Makó–Kosihy–Čaka Culture suggest a more segmented social system in the period preceding the Bell Beaker groups. Social differentiation cannot be attested for the Makó–Kosihy–Čaka Culture, but in the Somogyvár–Vinkovci Culture, burial mounds associated with high status individuals did occur and fortified settlements indicating settlement hierarchy were common.

Though the settlements of the Bell Beaker groups were more concentrated, we have little evidence for settlement hierarchy. Houses and the strontium isotope study of skeletal material suggest that society was basically built on nuclear families. The almost completely excavated settlement at Albertfalva and the Budakalász cemetery allow the estimation of the size of these communities. At Albertfalva

15–16 houses dating to different phases have been identified (Endrődi & Reményi 2016, 29) whilst at Budakalász about 1000 graves were located and radiocarbon dates demonstrated continuous use of the cemetery over some 500 years (Czene & Ottományi 2007).

Unlike in the settlements, in the cemeteries we can observe spectacularly opulent graves for high status persons of both genders (Kalicz-Schreiber & Kalicz 2000; 2001). Copper daggers belonging to the Beaker package were probably more of symbolic than practical significance and chipped stone projectile points and wristguards indicate a hunter and/or warrior elite and a more differentiated society representing a transition to the ranked and the stratified societies leading to simple chiefdoms. The Beaker settlements in the Carpathian Basin were partly contemporary with the beginnings of Bronze Age tell cultures usually interpreted as representing hierarchical societies (Reményi 2005; Heyd 2013).

The pottery of the Beaker communities of the Carpathian Basin

In Beaker pottery assemblages the most spectacular items are the comb-zoned Bell Beakers themselves and pedestal vessels that separate them from native cultural ceramics (Strahm 2004, Abb. 3). Most of the pottery, however, belongs to the *Begleitkeramik* that is also found in the local native cultures such as bowls, jugs, cups, glasses, pots and amphorae (Besse & Strahm 2001; Besse 2003), the best parallels being found in the Bohemian and Moravian Beaker groups. The bowls with obliquely and horizontally incised (T-profile) rims represent the most common type of ceramic in the eastern domain but is unknown in local native assemblages and Besse hypothetically assigned these bowls to regional types (2003, fig 125). The formal parallels for the S-profile jugs and cups found on the settlements are mainly known from the central European Beaker groups and Besse (2003, fig. 125) thought that Type 34 and Type 35 cups originated in the Corded Ware/Vučedol and Corded Ware respectively. Meanwhile, research on several elements of the *Begleitkeramik* located other connections such as various types of handled jugs with the Vučedol circle of the northern Balkans or the Makó-Kosihy-Čaka and Somogyvár-Vinkovci Cultures in the Carpathian Basin (eg, Buchvaldek 1978, 61; Kalicz-Schreiber & Kalicz 1999; Gallay 2001, figs 6 & 12; Strahm 2004).

Lithic industries of the Early Bronze Age in Hungary with special regard to the Beaker communities

For a long time, the study of Bronze Age assemblages was neglected in comparison to earlier periods (T. Biró 2000). With the growing interest in mobility and technology, as well as studies of settlements and cemeteries, more and more Bronze Age sites became involved in lithic analysis and the map (Fig. 12.5) shows Bronze Age sites with a published lithic industry supplemented by personally-held data. Many of these sites can be associated with the Beaker Culture.

The raw material found on Beaker sites is dominated by local Buda hornstone and Triassic chert (Károly 1936) but the quality of the raw material is quite poor. The qualities of the material seem to influence the basic character of the lithic industry which is dominated by flakes. The obsidian found on Beaker sites so far is exclusively of C1 (Slovakian) type (T. Biró 2014). Among the occasional 'long distance' raw materials, we can observe Trans-Carpathian flint (Jurassic Krakow flint and Prut flint) in very small quantities. With regard to the polished stone tools, local basalt and andesite were used as well as more distant raw materials (Szakmány 2009). The ground stone implements, including wristguards were mainly made of sandstone and quartzite.

The high number of flakes and flake tools on Beaker sites is striking. Characteristic special forms include projectile points and bifacially retouched knives. Borers, burins and retouched blanks (flakes/blades) occur in average quantities and truncated implements and both end- and side-scrapers are relatively rare. A selection of typical Beaker stone tools is presented on Fig. 12.6.

The Bell Beaker sites in the region of Budapest therefore based their chipped stone tool production on locally available materials supplemented by more distant and better quality material for the production of chipped stone artefacts as well as high quality imports such as obsidian and Transcarpathian flint. The study of the Bell Beaker ground stone industry is less advanced but both local raw materials and

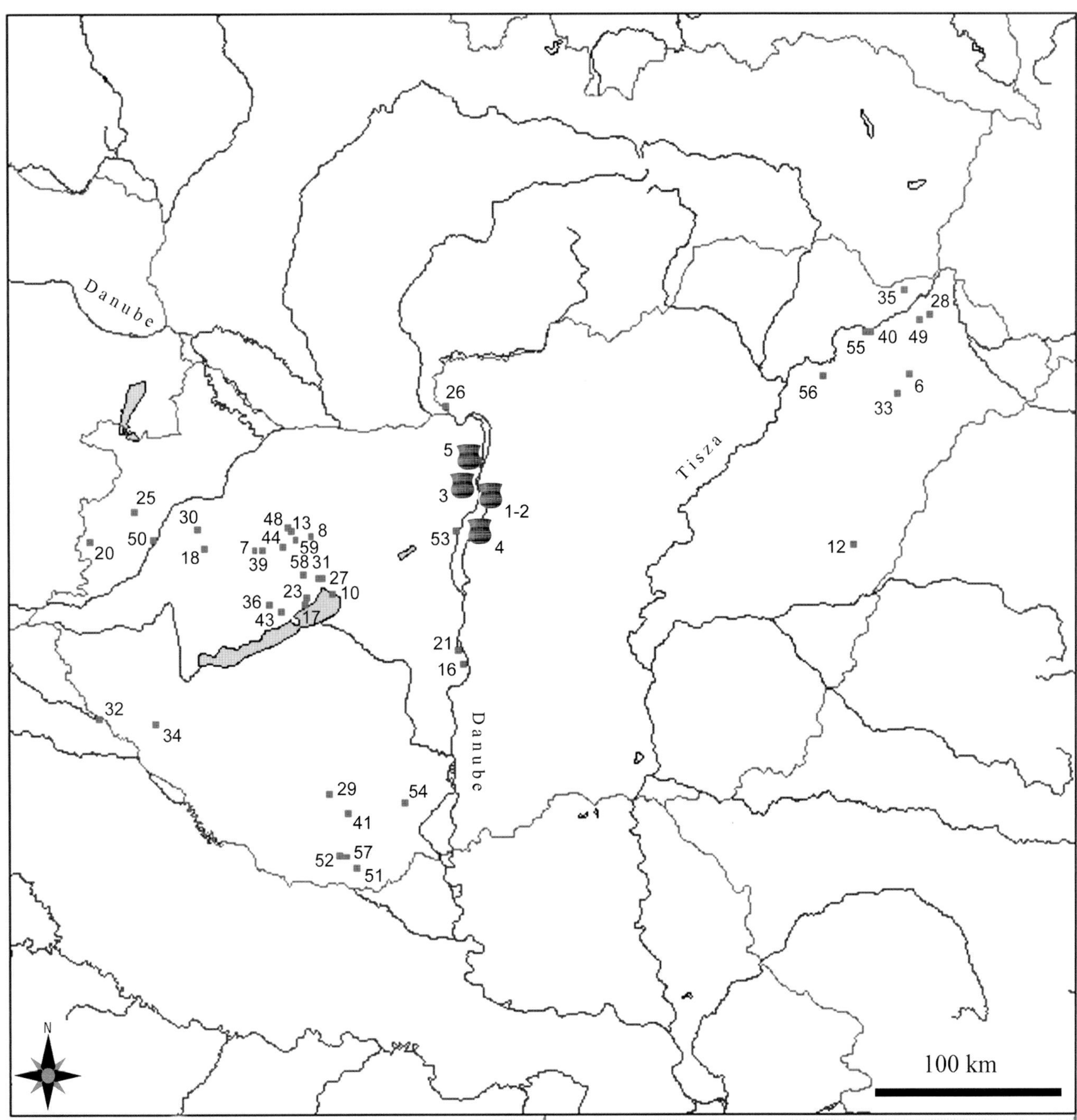

Figure 12.5: Bronze Age sites with lithic materials from Hungary. Key: 1. Budapest, Csepel, Hollandi út; 2. Budapest, Csepel, Rákóczi F. u. 311; 3. Budapest, Albertfalva; 4. Szigetszentmiklós, Üdülősor; 5. Budakalász M0/12; 6. Apagy, Nagyharaszti tanya; 7. Bakonyjákó, Malomoldal; 8. Bakonynána, Irtásföld; 9. Balatonkenese-Akarattya, alagut; 10. Balatonkenese-Akarattya; 11. Békásmegyer, Királyok útja / Vöröshadsereg u; 12. Berettyóújfalu, Herpály; 13. Borzavár, Alsótündérmajor I; 14. Borzavár, Bocskorhegy; 15–16. Bölcske-Vörösgyír; 17. Csopak, Öreghegy; 18. Csögle; 19. Dozmat Csompatka; 20. Dozmat, Másfeles földek; 21. Dunaföldvár; 22. Felsőörs, Föszöllök; 23. Felsőörs, Cser; 24. Felsőörs. Bárókert; 25. Gór, Kápolnadomb; 26. Ipolydamásd, Sziget; 27. Királyszentistván, Disznó domb; 28. Kisvárda; 29. Kovácsszénája, Füstöslik; 30. Külsővat; 31. Litér, Papvásárhegy; 32. Muraszemenye, Aligvári mező; 33. Nagykálló, Telekoldal; 34. Nagykanizsa, Inkey kápolna; 35. Nagyrozvágy, Papdomb; 36. Nagyvázsony, Baráti dűlő; 37–39. Németbánya, Felsőerdei dűlő; 40. Paszab Hordozódűlő; 41. Pécs; Nagyárpád; 42. Pécsely; Homokbánya, Ebhegy; 43. Pécsely, Vekenye; 44. Pénzesgyőr, Halastóárki dűlő I; 45. Porva, Ménesjárás II; 46. Porva, Ménesjárás III; 47. Porva, Pálinkaházpuszta; 48. Porva, Győri úti rétek; 49. Rétközberencs, Paradomb; 50. Sárvár, Faképi dűlő; 51. Siklós; 52. Szava; 53. Százhalombatta, Földvár; 54. Szebény, Paperdö; 55. Tiszabercel, Ráctemető; 56. Tiszavasvári, Józsefháza; 57. Túrony. 58; Veszprém, Vár, Ifjusági park; 59. Zirc, Aklipuszta III

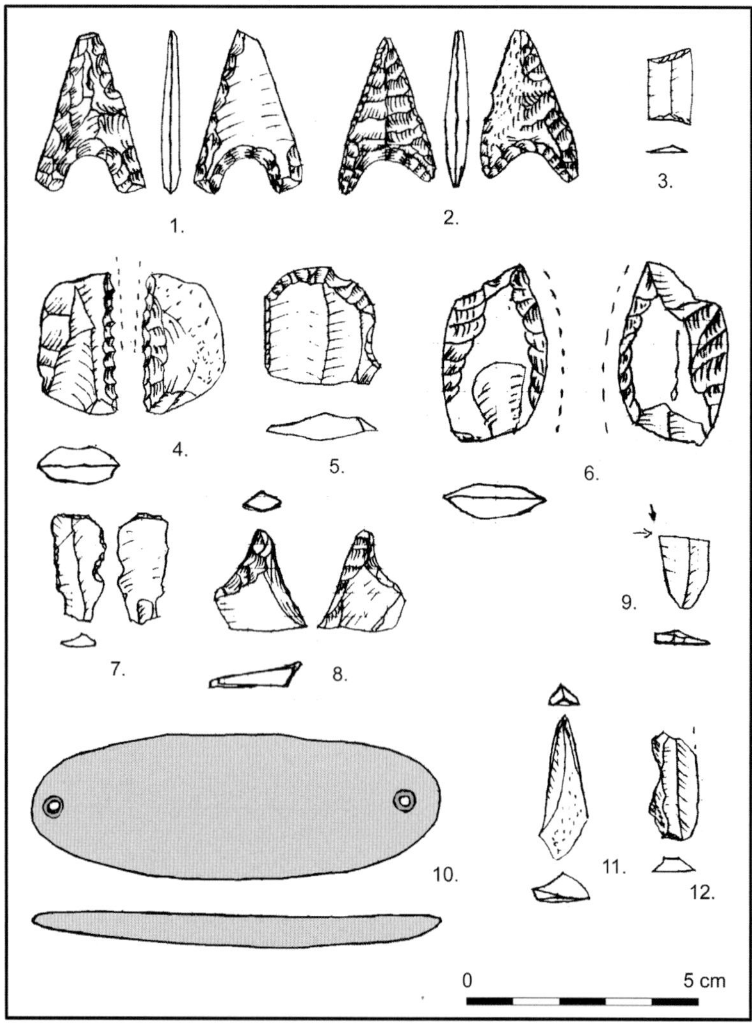

Figure 12.6: Selection of characteristic tool types of the Beaker communities from Hungary (Budapest, Albertfalva)

long-distance imports (basalt, andesite, contact metabasite and serpentinite) can be identified.

Houses of the Bell Beaker-Csepel group

The sites of the Bell Beaker-Csepel group are connected with the strategically important Danube bank, the former flood-plain islands and Csepel Island (Fig. 12.3). Among the 22 settlements known so far there are seven sites where we can partly or completely reconstruct house-plans. Five of these Early Bronze Age houses are near the Danube in the region of Budapest or Csepel Island and two are in western Transdanubia.

An area of 11640 m² at Budapest-Albertfalva was excavated by the authors and lay at the northern end of a former flood-plain island. Eleven post-built houses could be reconstructed, each having bowed sides and the settlement might have comprised 15–16 houses (Fig. 12.7). Not all the archaeological features are contemporary and the settlement was occupied for *c.* 500 years between 2470–1950 cal BC. The houses average 12 × 5.4 m. The mean number of the uprights is around 5 or 6 and the total number of post-pits averages around 29–30. The diameters of the central post-holes supporting the ridged roof exceed 0.5 m while the post-holes for the side walls measure only 0.2–0.38 m. The floor areas of the houses vary between 45–72 m² (Figs 12.7–10). One or two entrances have been observed and, in some cases, the entrance was protected by a windbreak (Fig. 12.8). In most of the houses an internal division of the space could be observed and this typically suggested that the south-eastern part of the house was separate, probably living quarters, while the rest of the building must have served another purpose such as for daily tasks, storage or sheltering livestock. The clay extraction pits along the sides of the houses could later serve as work areas and household units may have specialised in different activities (Endrődi & Reményi 2016, 87–93). The clay-plastered wattle walls were roofed with reed or, as seems likely from the archaeobotanical studies, bulrushes whilst the posts were obtained from the hard-woods of the riparian forests (Bodor 2016, 200–4). The roughly identical orientation and identical structure of the houses indicates conscious planning.

A special feature of the buildings is the bowed side walls and it was noted that the bows formed arcs of circles with an identical radius meaning that the post-holes marking the walls of the individual houses were set along two intersecting circles of identical radius (Fig. 12.7) and this suggests that the walls were laid out using a specific measure (Endrődi & Reményi 2007). The houses were oriented on the winter solstice so that ritual and environmental considerations (prevailing wind direction, maximising sunshine absorption, geological conditions, soil fertility) were also involved in their construction (Endrődi & Pásztor 2006).

Budapest-Sopron út is located 1 km to the east of the Danube, at a distance of 2.8 km from Albertfalva. The settlement was probably established on a smaller flood-plain island or a wide, elongated hill (Szilas *et al.* 2014). A post-built house with bowed sidewalls and a few refuse pits were found in the excavated area. The house measured 13.4 × 5 m (Fig. 12.11) and was orientated WNW–ESE, a little different from those at Albertfalva, though the structure of the house was very similar.

In the vicinity of the Soroksár branch of the Danube at Csepel-Hollandi út (in the area of southern Budapest), intensive occupation was observed in an area of 300 m², comprising some 100 post-holes and 25 pits (Kalicz-Schreiber 1976, fig. 6). The post-holes were concentrated in the northern and southern part of the excavation area and, using Albertfalva as a model, two houses with post-built curved walls can be identified (Fig. 12.12).

Szigetszentmiklós-Üdülősor has one of the longest EBA settlement sequences on Csepel Island. It is located on a wide, flood-free row of undulations and some 1232 archaeological features of the Bell Beaker-Csepel group were found here in an area of 8300 m². Amongst these were ten post-built houses with curved walls and oriented WNW–ESE. The houses measured 10–16 × 4–6 m (Fig. 12.13; Endrődi & Horváth 2009) and their structure is identical to those at Albertfalva and Sopron út. The settlement of Szigetszentmiklós-Üdülősor, however, has a different arrangement to that observed at Albertfalva. The large clay extraction pits and most of the refuse pits were sited near the Danube while the houses were further from the bank. About 100m from the houses, over a former side-branch of the Danube, lay the associated cemetery.

At Szigetcsép, Tangazdaság, south of Szigetszentmiklós-Üdülősor, lay another Bell Beaker settlement. Some 20 pits and 17 post-holes were found in two small trenches (400 m² and 210 m²) (Korek 1984, 2. kép; Ecsedy 1988). Due to a lack of analogy, houses were not recognised at the time of excavation but the two groups of post-holes can now be seen to represent a house or houses. Szigetcsép might represent one element of a chain of settlements along the river bank on Csepel Island (Endrődi & Reményi 2016, 74).

One of the Early Bronze Age settlements in western Transdanubia is Bucsu, Hosszú Aszú-dűlő (Vas county) where, 5 'boat-shaped' houses of the Bell Beaker Culture and a few refuse pits were excavated (Ilon 2005, 197). The houses occurred in two groups, separated by 180 m and with an E–W orientation. In the first group House 1 measured 6.3 × 4.25 m,

Figure 12.7: Beaker Settlement at Budapest, Albertfalva, Layout. After Endrődi & Reményi 2016. (Bell Beaker-Csepel Group)

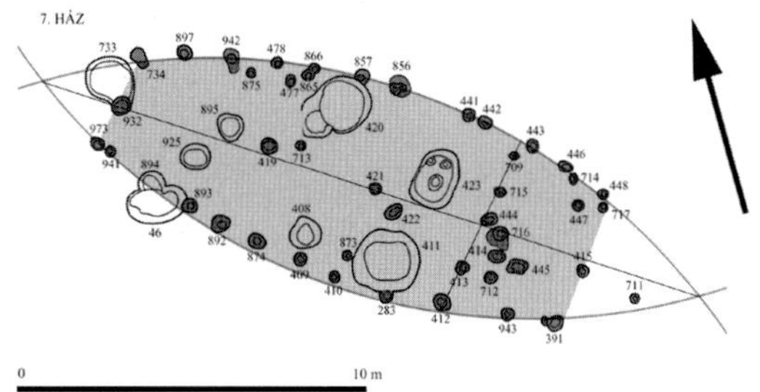

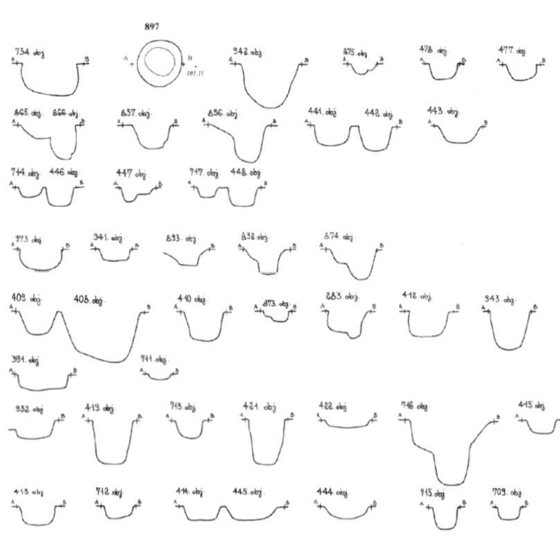

Figure 12.8: Post-structured house with arched sidewalls at Albertfalva settlement. After Endrődi & Reményi 2016 (Bell Beaker-Csepel Group)

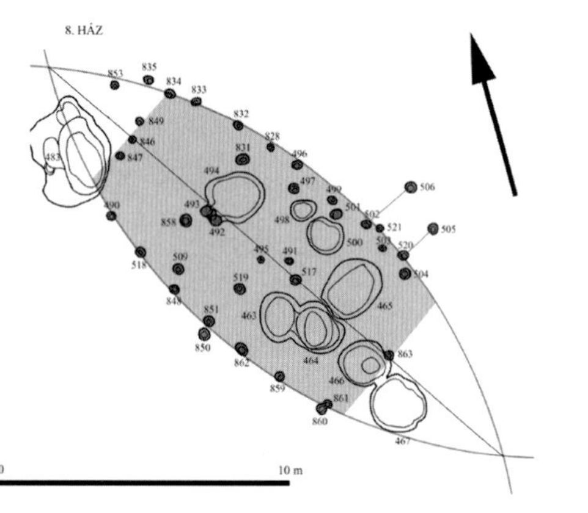

Figure 12.9: Post-structured house with arched sidewalls at Albertfalva settlement. After Endrődi & Reményi 2016 (Bell Beaker-Csepel Group)

House 2 measured 7.9 × 6.25 m, and House 4 measured 13.3 × 9.7 m. In the second group House 6 proved to be 9.75 × 7.25 m and House 7, 12.5 × 8.75 m (Ilon 2011, 98). The settlement plan of the site and the finds remain unpublished.

At Vát in Vas county, rescue excavations over an area of 12324 m^2 located 1350 archaeological features (Reményi & Dobozi 2012). The majority (1300) were post-holes, and although difficult to date, most features could be assigned to the Early Bronze Age. Some of the post-holes were associated with houses and other buildings (Reményi & Dobozi 2012, 2. ábra) and arranged in four basic types. The first is represented by two large rectangular houses around 10 × 7 m. and orientated NE–SW. There were traces of central roof supports but the post holes from the NE walls were missing. The other main type was a post-built house with curved walls, oriented NW–SE, and approximately 14–15 m long. The third building type comprised smaller rectangular post-built structures with various orientations (Fig. 12.14). The fourth type is represented by only one post-built house with a sunken floor. The orientation and the dimensions of this house are almost identical to another building close by but built directly on the ground surface.

Of these buildings, the large rectangular examples, the curved wall structures and the sunken floored example were interpreted as houses. The smaller ones were interpreted mainly as ancillary agricultural buildings (Reményi & Dobozi 2012). The larger houses are basically oriented NE–SW, the smaller ones to ENE–WSW and the bowed wall house is more similar to the Albertfalva houses being oriented NW–SE.

Along the Danube, NW–SW oriented post-built houses with curved side-walls have been identified at Budapest-Albertfalva; Szigetszentmiklós, Üdülősor; Csepel, Hollandi út; Budapest XIth district, Sopron u. and can be assigned to the Bell Beaker-Csepel group while the two sites in western Hungary (Vas county: Bucsu, Hosszú Aszú-dűlő and Vát) are more associated and/or contemporary with the Moravian Oggau-Wipfing-Ragelsdorf-Oberbierbaum-group. This period is coeval with the 2b phase of the Hungarian Early Bronze Age (late Bell Beaker-Csepel group, early phase of the Nagyrév Culture – Kalicz-Schreiber 1984; Reményi & Dobozi 2012). In the case of the larger post-supported houses

Figure 12.10: Post-structured house with arched sidewalls at the Albertfalva settlement. After Endrődi & Reményi 2016 (Bell Beaker-Csepel Group)

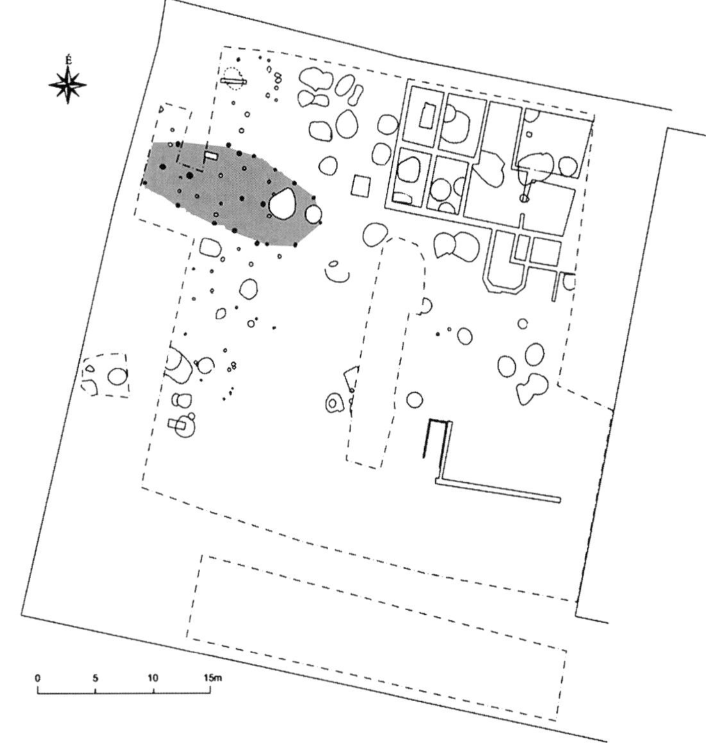

Figure 12.11: Post-structured house with arched sidewalls at Budapest, Sopron út. After Szilas et al. *2014 (Bell Beaker-Csepel Group)*

in western Transdanubia, the influence of the Makó Culture is also evident (Endrődi & Reményi 2016).

Changes in farming and land use in the Beaker period

As a result of the archaeobotanical evidence amassed over the last 20 years, more information is available for the economic changes that took place in this transitional period. Macro-botanical remains from 13 sites of the Late Copper Age Baden Culture, 2 sites of the Early Bronze Age Makó-Kosihy-Čaka Culture and 6 sites of the Bell Beaker-Csepel group have been investigated, mainly from the area around Budapest. Samples of the Baden Culture were mainly collected from pits, hearths, wells and complete vessels, in one case, from a ritual animal burial (Gyulai 2004). About half of the samples from Bell Beaker contexts were collected from pits, hearths, houses and vessels, and the rest were collected from graves, both inhumations and cremations (Gyulai 2013) and at Budakalász M0 a complete

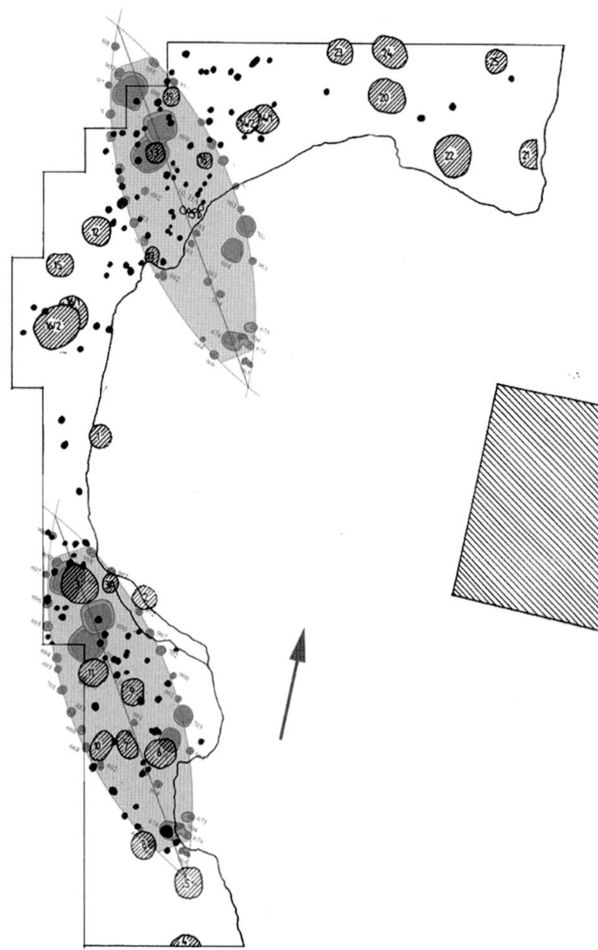

Figure 12.12: Csepel Island, Hollandi út. Possible Post-structured houses. After Kalicz-Schreiber 1976 (Bell Beaker-Csepel Group)

Figure 12.13: Post-structured house with arched sidewalls at Szigetszentmiklós-Üdülősor (Csepel-Island) after Endrődi-Horváth 2009, 154, fig. 4 (Bell Beaker-Csepel Group)

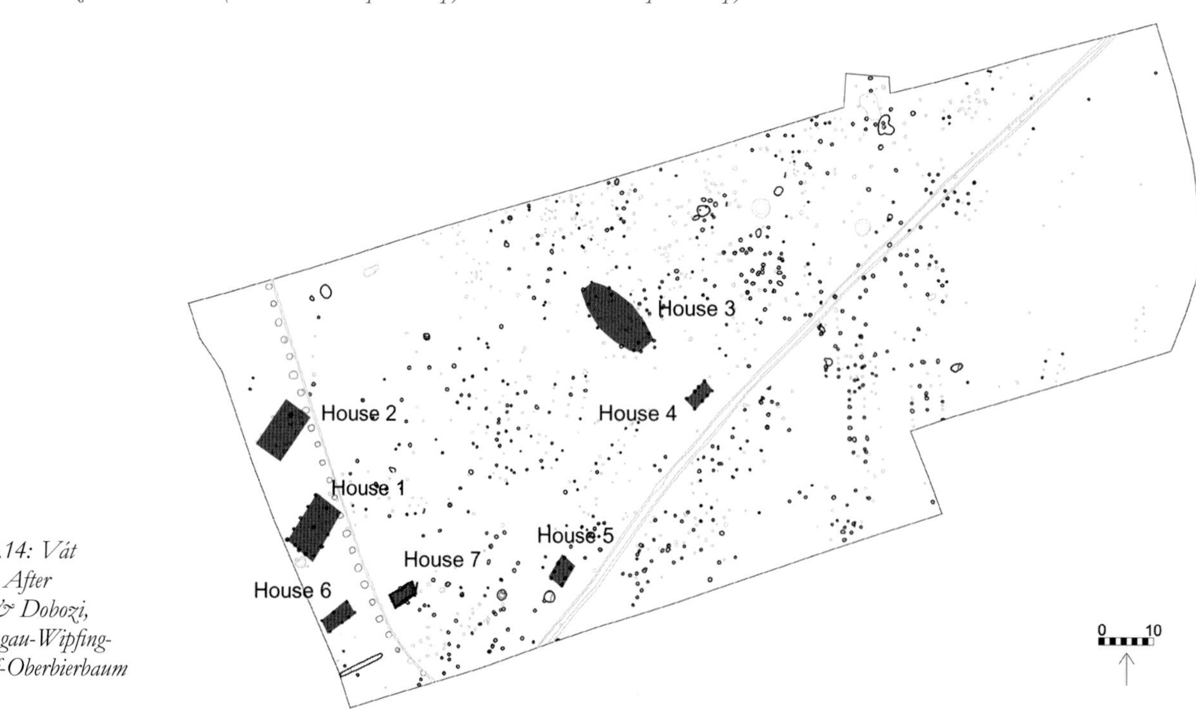

Figure 12.14: Vát settlement. After Reményi & Dobozi, 2009 (Oggau-Wipfing-Ragelsdorf-Oberbierbaum Group)

cemetery was investigated (Gyulai 2014). On the Baden Culture sites mainly cereal pulp was found in the limited samples whilst from the more extensively sampled Beaker contexts we have a large number of food remains from approximately 1000 samples representing leavened bread, semolina residues of different grain sizes, meat residues and bakery products. Compared to the Late Copper Age, we see an increase in plant diversity whilst on Baden Culture sites only the fruit / seeds of 56 plant species were identified, 82 different taxa were identified in the Bell Beaker-Csepel group. The sites of the Makó-Kosihy-Čaka Culture produced seeds from only seven identified plant species.

There are interesting differences in plant species found at the above two cultures. In the Bell Beaker contexts, the number of species and their distribution increases. On all Beaker sites there were cultivated plants, their associated weed species and local wild taxa suggesting that by the Bell Beaker period, agricultural activity had become more intensive. The Baden samples comprised 13 cultivated plant species, exactly the same as that of the Beaker sites and though the similarity appears strong, there are certain differences. The cultivation of hulled multi-row barley was of great importance however, hull-less two-row barley was also present. The second most important cereal for both cultures was hulled wheat with the most popular variety being einkorn and the second emmer. Grains of hull-less wheat (sowing wheat and dwarf wheat) were very rare but that is typical for prehistory in general. Millet and rye were found more on the Baden sites. This suggests that in the Beaker period, the production of cereals was more targeted. Finally, in the Baden Culture, leguminous plants consisted of small-seeded lentils and field peas whilst on the Beaker sites, small-seeded horsebeans were also present. The Beaker communities no longer experimented with several cereal types but used the species that were the safest to cultivate (barley, einkorn and emmer). The increase in leguminous plants shows the development of horticulture and the increasing permanence of settlement.

The increase of the number of weed species in the Early Bronze Age is also consistent with the development of cereal farming and horticulture and their number was one and half times higher than in the Late Copper Age. The increase is especially significant for the weeds relating to autumn cereals though those relating to spring cereals and so-called root crops are also higher. All these denote the separation of weed species, the existence of plough and hoe cultivation, and especially the increase in the cultivation of autumn cereals. The large number of cereal-associated weeds also indicates local production and processing. On the Beaker sites, there is also a considerable increase in the number of settlement weeds. Ruderalia are doubled, showing the increase in human activity and the quantity of these species is proportional to the size of the settlements as they grow around houses and barns, along pathways, and anywhere with constant treading and high soil nitrogen content. Species of meadow and pasture origin were also more frequent in the Bell Beaker samples and the increase in the number of species is probably proportional to the expansion of livestock. At Albertfalva, one of the large pits contained threshing waste (chaff fragments, ears, spikes, weed seeds and straw fragments) suggesting a certain degree of spatial organisation (Endrődi & Reményi 2016, 29–68). In the number and ratio of woodland species we find considerable differences. Arboreal species are more typical of the Late Copper Age whilst species from clearings were encountered only in the Early Bronze Age, probably due to the increase in cereal cultivation.

On the basis of the archaeobotanical remains it seems that the Baden communities avoided the wet places close to the water while Beaker communities typically preferred them. These areas may have been too wet for Baden Culture agriculture. For example, on the Baden settlement at Szigetszentmiklós-Üdülősor, no archaeobotanical remains were found whilst at the same locality, on the Bell Beaker settlement, more than 500 remains of 127 plant species were identified (Gyulai 2003). The biggest difference between the Late Copper Age and Early Bronze Age plant species was the amount of riparian and limnic species. While on the Baden sites only one of these taxa was found, in the Beaker samples there were seven. These observations are also supported by settlement historical arguments and most probably, the shift to the proximity of water in the Bronze Age resulted from climatic factors. When compared to the Baden period, the number of species with higher relative demands on temperature and light increased in the Beaker period suggesting that the Beaker period was one of climatic amelioration.

The palynology at Albertfalva supports the observations made from the plant macro-remains (Bodor 2016). The pollen spectrum was dominated by non-arboreal species and arboreal vegetation was rarely seen, comprising only elements of the riparian hard-wood forest (hazel, pedunculate oak, small-leaved lime). The scarcity of arboreal vegetation could be the result of clearings and we can suppose that the trees were needed as construction timber as well as for fuel. The rich non-arboreal vegetation pictures a settlement with well-trodden path-ways, with middens, and with cultivated gardens producing herbs and root crops. The agrarian activity was dominated by pastures and cultivated grasslands and meadows, probably with intensive animal farming.

Animal husbandry underwent significant changes from the Late Copper Age to the Beaker period. In the Baden communities, cattle played a major role along with small ruminants (Horváth 2007) that formed the main livestock of the Somogyvár-Vinkovci and the Makó-Kosihy-Čaka Cultures. The stock-raising of the Beaker communities is completely different with about half of the total animal bone representing horses (Lyublyanovics 2016) with a significant presence of cattle (*c.* 30%) and the ratio of small ruminants is relatively low (Lyublyanovics 2016). Horses were known in considerable numbers in the Baden Culture period probably associated with the appearance of the pit-grave kurgan burials (Ecsedy 1979b; Sherratt 1997, 218; Endrődi *et al.* 2008). On the settlements of the Bell Beaker-Csepel group, however, the number of horses is so high that the distribution area of the Beaker population may have served as a secondary domestication centre (Piggott 1983, 89). The appearance of the Bell Beaker communities within the Carpathian Basin can not only be characterised by cultural changes. Apart from the appearance of the elements of the 'Beaker package', similarly spectacular changes took place in land-use and farming. The complex system, based on horse keeping, advanced cereal cultivation and complementary horticulture illustrates a more intensive economic model than that of the Late Copper Age.

References

Balogh, É. Cs. 2010. The lithic finds from Budakalász. In Bondár, M. and Raczky, P. (eds), *The Copper Age cemetery of Budakalász*, 380–407. Budapest: Pytheas

Besse, M. 2003. *L'Europe du 3e millénaire avant notre ère: les ceramiques communes au Campaniforme.*Lausanne: Cahiers d'achéologie romande, 94

Besse, M. & Strahm, Ch. 2001. The components of the Bell Beaker Complex. In Nicolis (ed.), 2001, 103–10

Bodor, E. 2016. Palynological results from Albertfalva. In Endrődi, A. & Reményi L. (eds), 2016, 200–3

Bondár, M 1984. Neuere Funde der Kostolac- und der Spätbadener Kultur in Ungarn. *Acta Archaeologica Academiae Scientiarum Hungaricae* 36, 59–83

Bondár, M.1995. Early Bronze Age Settlement patterns in south-west Transdanubia. *Antaeus* 22, 197–268

Buchvaldek, M.1978. Otáza kontinuity v českomoravském mladšim eneolitu. Zur Frage der Kontinuität im Äneolothikum in Bohmen und Mähren. *Praehistorica*, 7, 35–64

Czene, A. & Ottományi, K. 2007. Budakeszi–Szőlőskert, Tangazdaság (MRT 7, 4/8. lh.). In Kisfaludy, J. (ed.), *Régészeti Kutatások Magyarországon 2006,* 162 *(Archaeological investigation in Hungary 2006.)* Budapest: Kulturális Örökségvédelmi Hivatal & Magyar Nemzeti Múzeum

Dani, J. & Horváth, T. 2012. Őskori kurgánok a magyar Alföldön. A Gödörsíros (Jamnaja) entitás magyarországi kutatása az elmúlt 30 év során. Áttekintés és revízió. Budapest: Archaeolingua

Della Cassa, P. 1995. The Cetina group and the transition from Copper to Bronze Age in Dalmatia. *Antiquity* 69, 565–76

Dimitrijević, S. 1982. Die frühe Vinkovci-Kultur und ihre Beziehungen zu Vučedoler Substrat im Lichte der Ausgrabungen in Vinkovci (1977/78). *Opuscula Archaeologica* 7, 7–36

Durman, A. (ed.), 1988. *Vučedol – treće tisućljeće p.n.e. Vučedol – three thousand years BC* Zagreb: Muzejsko-galerijski centar, Zagreb

Durman, A. & Obelić, B. 1989. Radiocarbon dating of the Vučedol Culture Complex. *Radiocarbon* 31 (3), 1003–9

Ecsedy, I. 1978. Excavations at Lánycsók in 1976. Preliminary report. *Janus Pannonius Múzeum Évkönyve* 22 (1977), 119–35

Ecsedy, I. 1979a. Die Siedlung der Somogyvár–Vinkovci Kultur bei Szava und einige Fragen der Frühbronzezeit in Südpannonien. *Janus Pannonius Múzeum Évkönyve* 23 (1978), 97–136

Ecsedy, I. 1979b. *The People of the Pit-Grave Kurgans in Eastern Hungary.* Budapest: Fontes Archaeologici Hungariae

Ecsedy, I. 1983. Ásatások Zók-Várhegyen (1977–1982). Előzetes jelentés. (Excavations at Zók-Várhegy. (1977–1982) Preliminary report). *Janus Pannonius Múzeum Évkönyve* 27 (1982), 59–106

Ecsedy, I. 1988. Ásatások Szigetcsép–Tangazdaság lelőhelyen II. A korabronzkori település leletei. (Excavations at Szigetcsép–Tangazdaság II. The Early Bronze Age settlement). *Communicationes Archaeologicae Hungariae,* 1988, 5–18

Endrődi, A. 1992a. Késő rézkori leletek Szigetszentmiklós-Üdülősoron. Late Copper Age Assemblages at Szigetszentmiklós-Üdülősor. In Havassy P. & Selmeczi, L. (eds), 63–82

Endrődi, A. 1992b. A korabronzkori Harangedény kultúra telepe és temetője Szigetszentmiklós határában. (The settlement and cemetery of the Bell Beaker Culture in the district of Szigetszentmiklós.) In Havassy P. & Selmeczi, L. (eds), 1992. 83–201

Endrődi, A. & Horváth, A. 2009. Régészeti kutatások Szigetszentmiklós-Üdülősoron az M0 autóút nyomvonalán. (Archaeological investigations at Szigetszentmiklós-Üdülősor in the path of the M0 motorway.). *Aquincumi füzetek* 15, 150–66

Endrődi, A. & Pásztor, E. 2006. Symbolism and Traditions in the Society of Bell Beaker–Csepel Group. *Archaeologiai Értesítő* 131, 7–25

Endrődi, A. & Reményi, L. 2007. Kora bronzkori ház és településrekonstrukció a Harangedény–Csepel csoport Budapest (XI. kerület), Albertfalva lelőhelyén. (Reconstruction of and Early Bronze Age house and settlement at the Budapest–Albertfalva site of the Bell–Beaker–Csepel group) Ősrégészeti Levelek 7 (2005), 128–34

Endrődi, A. & Reményi, L. (eds), 2016. *A Bell Beaker Settlement in Albertfalva, Hungary (2470–1950 BC)*. Budapest: Budapest History Museum & Kódex Könyvgyártó Ltd

Endrődi, A., Reményi, L., Baradács, E., Kiss, Á. Z., Uzonyi, I., Montero, I. & Rovira, S. 2003. Technological study of Beaker metallurgy in Hungary. In *Archaeometallurgy in Europe, Proceedings* 2, 29–38

Endrődi, A., Gyulai, F. & Reményi, L. 2008. The roles of the enviromental and culturalfactors in the everyday life of Bell Beaker Csepel Group. *Millenni. Studi di Archeologia Preistorica,* 6, 235–56

Farkas-Pető, A. & Horváth, T. 2014. Archaeometric database of archaeological stone tools (a suggestion for new data processing method). *Archeometriai Műhely / Archaeometry Workshop* 11(2), 103–14. http://www.ace.hu/am/2014_2/AM-14-02-FPA.pdf.

Figler, A. 1996. Adatok Győr környékének bronzkorához. (Angaben zu Bronzezeit in der Umgebung von Győr.) *Pápai Múzeumi Értesítő* 6. (1996), 7–29

Forenbaher, S. 1993. Radiocarbon dates and absolute chronology of the Central European Early Bronze Age. *Antiquity* 67, 218–20 & 235–56

Gallay, A. 2001. L'énigme campaniforme. In Nicolis (ed.) 2001, 41–58

Gyulai, F. 2003. Archaeobotanical remains and environment of Bell Beaker Csepel-Group. In Czebreszuk, J. & Szmyt, M. (eds.) 2003. *The Northeast Frontier of Bell Beakers. Proceedings of the symposium held at the Adam Mickiewicz University, Poznań (Poland), May 26–29 2002,* 277–82. Oxford: British Archaeological Reports International Series 1155

Gyulai, F. 2004. A rézkori Baden-kultúra növényvilága. (Plants of the Baden Culture.) In Endrődi (ed.), 2004. *Hétköznapok és vallásos élet a rézkor végén. A Baden-kultúra 5000 éves emlékei Budapesten. (Everyday life and spirituality at the end of the Copper Age. 5000 years old remains of the Baden Culture in Budapest.)*,2 1–6. Budapest: Budapest History Museum

Gyulai, F. 2013. New archaeobotanical Data of the Bell Beaker Csepel Group. In Martínez, M.P. & Salanova, L. (eds), 2013. *Current researches on Bell Beakers Proceedings of the 15th International Bell Beaker Conference: From Atlantic to Ural. 5th–9th May 2011 Poio,Pontevedra, Galicia, Spain,* 89–96. Santiago de Compostela: Galician ArchaeoPots

Gyulai, F. 2014. The archaeobotanical evidence of burial rites of Bell Beaker-Csepel Group. In Besse, M. (ed.), 2014. *Around the Petit-Chasseur Site in Sion Switzerland) and new approaches to the Bell Beaker Culture. Proceedings of the International Conference held at Sion (Switzerland) October 27th–30th, 2011,* 277–84. Oxford: Archaeopress Archaeology

Havassy, P. & Selmeczi, L. (eds.), 1992. *Régészeti kutatások az M0 autópálya nyomvonalán I. (Archaeological researches on the line of Motorway M0 I.)*. Budapest: Budapest History Museum

Heyd, V. 2013. Europe 2500 to 2200 BC: Between Expiring Ideologies and Emerging Complexity. In Fokkens, H. & Harding, A. (eds), *The Oxford Handbook of the European Bronze Age,* 47–67. Oxford: Oxford University Press

Horváth, T. 2007. Állattemetkezések Balatonöszöd-Temetői dűlő Bádeni lelőhelyen. (Animal Burials in the Late Copper Age Baden Site: Balatonöszöd-Temetői dűlő.) *Somogyi Múzeumok Közleményei* 17, 107–51

Horváth, T. 2014. *The prehistoric settlement at Balatonőszöd-Temetői –dűlő.* Budapest:Varia Archaeologica Hungarica 29

Horváth, T., S. Svingor, É. & Molnár, M. 2008. New Radiocarbon Dates for the Baden Culture. *Radiocarbon* 50 (3), 447–58

Ilon, G. 2005. Bucsu, Hosszú–Aszú dűlő. In Kisfaludy, J. (ed.), 2005. *Régészeti Kutatások Magyarországon 2004. (Archaeological investigation in Hungary 2004),* 179. Budapest: Kulturális Örökségvédelmi Hivatal & Magyar Nemzeti Múzeum

Ilon, G. 2011. Szombathely–Zanat Bogácai–értől keletre Bucsu, Hosszú – Aszú dűlő In *Időcsiga. Újabb eredmények Vas Megye őskorának kutatásában (Zeitschnecke. Neue Forschungsergebnisse zur Vorgeschichte vom Komitat Vas.)* Szombathely, 96–102

Kalicz, N. 1968. *Die Frühbronzezeit in Nordostungarn.* Archaeologia Hungarica 45. Budapest: Akadémiai Kiadó

Kalicz, N. 1984. Die Makó-Kultur. In Tasić (ed.), 1984, 93–108

Kalicz-Schreiber, R. 1976. Die Probleme der Glockenbecherkultur in Ungarn, 183–215. In Lanting, J.N. & Van der Waals, J.D. (eds), 1976, *Glockenbecher Symposion Oberried 1974.* Bossum/Haarlem: Fibula-van Dishoeck

Kalicz-Schreiber, R. 1984. Komplex der Nagyrév–Kultur. In Tasić (ed.), 1984, 133–91

Kalicz-Schreiber, R. & Kalicz, N. 1999. A Somogyvár-Vinkovci kultúra és a Harangedény-Csepel-csoport Budapest kora bronzkorában. (Die Somogyvár-Vinkovci-kultur und die Glockenbecher in der Frühbronzezeit von Budapest.) *Savaria* 24/3 (1998–1999), 83–114

Kalicz-Schreiber, R. & Kalicz, N. 2000. A harangedények szerepe a Budapest környéki kora bronzkor társadalmi viszonyainak megjelenítésében. (The role of Bell Beakers in reflecting social relations in trhe Early Bronze Age of Budapest.) *Archaeologiai Értesítő* 125 (1998–2000), 45–78

Kalicz-Schreiber, R. & Kalicz, N. 2001. Were the Bell

Beaker as Social Indicators of the Early Bronze Age in Budapest? In Nicolis (ed.), 439–58

Károly, E. 1936. Szarukövek a Budai hegységben. (Hornstone in the Buda Mts.). *Földtani Közlöny* 66, 254–77

Korek, J. 1984. Ásatások Szigetcsép–Tangazdaság lelőhelyen I. A későrézkori település leletei (Ausgrabungen auf dem Fundort Szigetcsép–Tangazdaság I. Funde der Spätkupferzeitlichen Siedlung.) *Communicationes Archaeologicae Hungariae* 1984, 5–29

Kulcsár, G. 2009. *The Beginnings of the Bronze Age in the Carpathian Basin. The Makó–Kosihy–Čaka and the Somogyvár–Vinkovci Cultures in Hungary.* Budapest: Varia Archaeologica Hungarica 23

Kulcsár, G. 2011. Untangling the Early Bronze Age in the Middle Danubian Valley. In Kovács, Gy. &, Kulcsár, G. (eds), *Ten thousand years along the middle Danube.* Varia Archaeologica Hungarica 21. Budapest, 179–210

Kulcsár, G. & Szeverényi, V. 2013. Transition to the Third Millennium BC in the Carpathian Basin, 67–92. In Heyd, V., Kulcsár, G. & Szeverényi, V. (eds), 2013, *Transition to the Bronze Age.* Budapest: Archaeolingua

Lanting, J.N. & Van der Waals, J.D. (eds), 1976, *Glockenbecher Symposion Oberried 1974.* Bossum/ Haarlem: Fibula-van Dishoeck

Lyublyanovics, K. 2016. Animal bones from the Bell Beaker settlement of Albertfalva, Budapest. In Endrődi, A. & Reményi, L. (eds.) 2016, 204–16

Nicolis, F. (ed.), 2001. *Bell Beakers today, Pottery, people, culture, symbols in prehistoric Europe. Proceedings of the International Colloquium Riva del Garda (Trento, Italy) 11–16 May 1998.* Trento: Provincia Autonoma di Trento, Servizio Beni Culturali Ufficio Beni Archeologici

Olalde, I. *et al.* 2018. The Beaker Phenomenon and the Genomic Transformation of Northwest Europe. *Nature,* 555, No. 7695, 190–6

Piggott, S. 1983. *The Earliest Wheeled–transport from the Atlantic Coast to the Caspian Sea.* London: Thames and Hudson

Primas, M. 1996. *Velika Gruda I. Hügelgräber des frühenJahrtausends v. Chr. im Adriagebiet – Velika Gruda, Mala Gruda und ihr Kontext. Tumulus burials of the early third Millennium BC in the Adriatic – Velika Gruda, Mala Gruda and their context.* Bonn: Dr. Rudolf Habelt GmbH

Raczky, P., Hetrelendi, E.& Horváth, F. 1992. Zur absoluten Datierung der bronzezeitlichen Tell-kulturen in Ungarn. In Meier-Arendt, W. (Hrsg.) *Bronzezeit in Ungarn. Forschungen in Tell-Siedlungen an Donau und Theiss* 42–7. Frankfurt am Main: Stadt Frankfurt Dez. Kultur u. Wissenschaft

Reményi, L. 2005. The Golden Age of the Carpathian Basin and the Beatiful Warrior. In Hjørungdal, T. (ed.), 2005. *Gender Locales and Local Genders in Archaeology,* 1–11. Oxford: British Archaeological Reports International Series 1425

Reményi, L. & Dobozi, Á. 2012. Harangedényes településrészlet Vát (Vas megye) határában, Vát – Rátka–patak keleti oldala, 86–os sz. főút, Vát – Szombathely elkerülő 1. lelőhely. (Bell Beaker Culture settlement section in the vicinity of Vát (Vas County). Eastern side of Vát – Rátka Stream, Site No. 1 at Main Road No. 86, Vát – Szombathely bypass). Évkönyv és jelentés a *Kulturális Örökségvédelmi Szakszolgálat 2009. évi feltárásairól. (Field Service for Cultural Heritage 2009 Yearbook and Review of Archaeological Investigations.),* 119–35. Budapest: Hungarian National Museum Centre for National Cultural Heritage

Reményi, L., Endrődi, A., Baradács, E., Kiss, Á.Z., Uzonyi, I., Montero, I. & Rovira, S. 2006. Possible links between Hungarian and Spanish Beaker Metallurgy. In Denker, A., Adriaens, A., Dowsett, M. & Giumlia-Mair, A. (eds), *Cost Action G8: Non–destructive testing and analysis of museum objects,* 17–24. Stuttgart: Fraunhofer IRB Verlag

Shennan, S., 1976. Bell Beakers and their context in central Europa, 231–9. In Lanting, J.N. & Van der Waals, J.D. (eds), 1976, *Glockenbecher Symposion Oberried 1974.* Bossum/Haarlem: Fibula-van Dishoeck

Sherratt, A. 1987. 'Cups that cheered'. In Waldren, W.H. & Kennard, R.C. (eds), 1987. *Bell Beakers of the Western Mediterranean, The Oxford International Conference 1986,* 81–114. Oxford: British Archaeological Reports International Series 331

Sherratt, A. 1997. *Economy and Society in Prehistoric Europe.* Edinburgh: Edinburgh University Press

Strahm, Ch. 2004. Das Glockenbecher-Phänomen aus der Sicht der Komplementär-Keramik. In Czebreszuk, J. (ed.) 2004. *Similar bur different. Bell Beakers in Europe,* 101–26. Poznań: Adam Mickiewicz University

Szakmány, Gy. 2009. Magyarországi csiszolt kőeszközök nyersanyagtípusai az eddigi archeometriai kutatások eredményei alapján. (Types of polished stone tool raw materials in Hungary.) *Archeometriai Műhely/ Archaeometry Workshop* 6, 1, 11–30

Szilas, G., Tóth–Farkas, M. & Biller, A.Zs. 2014. Újabb régészeti kutatások a lágymányosi dombsororon (Recent archaeological research in the Lágymányos Hills.) *Aquincumi Füzetek* 20, 113–17

T. Biró, K. 1998. Limits and Connections. In Németh, M. (ed.), 1998. *Aquincum Nostrum. The Roman town in the modern cit,* 2, 152–57. Budapest: Budapest History Museum

T. Biró, K. 2000. Kőeszközök a bronzkorban. (Stone tools in the Bronze Age). *Komárom–Esztergom Megyei Múzeumok Közleményei* 7, 237–52

T. Biró, K. 2014. Carpathian Obsidians: State of Art. In Yamada, M. & Ono, A.(eds), *Lithic raw material exploitation and circulation in Préhistory. Études et Recherches Archéologiques de L'Université de Liège,* 138, 47–69

Tasić, N. 1984 Die Vinkovci Kultur. In Tasić (ed.), 1984. 15–32

Tasić, N. (ed.), 1984. *Kulturen der Frühbronzezeit des Karpatenbeckens und Nordbalkans.* Beograd, Balkanološki institut SANU

Turek, J. 2006. Obodní Zvoncovitých Poharu v Europě. (The Bell Beaker period in Europe.) *Archeologie ve středních Čechách* 10, 275–368

13

Settlements and social development of the 3rd millennium BC in central Germany

André Spatzier and Torsten Schunke

Central Germany is generally defined as being the Middle Elbe-Saale region, located North, East and South of the Harz Mountains and within the federal states of Saxony, Thuringia and Saxony-Anhalt. In the north it is limited by the lowlands of northern Germany with mostly poor-quality soils and in the south by the Thuringian Forest and the Ore Mountains. The areas south-east to north-east of the Harz mountains were key settlement regions during the Neolithic, due to the excellent soils and the balanced climate. In addition, natural deposits of salt and copper are important, although the use of local copper sources in the Neolithic remains to be confirmed. This paper starts with a brief regional overview of the cultural development during the 3rd millennium BC and outlines the general character of the settlement and economic strategies of the different archaeological cultures.

The aim of this paper is to present new insights into settlements and house structures of the Final Neolithic, namely the Schönfeld culture, the Corded Ware culture and the Bell Beaker culture, in Central Germany (Fig. 13.1) and to relate them to those of the subsequent Early Bronze Age Únětice culture. Mainly based on the evidence discovered within the last 15 years, the settlement history of the period between approximately 2800–2000 BC will be re-evaluated.

Cultural chronology of the Neolithic in central Germany

There has been no consistent approach to the periodisation of the Neolithic in the region and in this paper the widely accepted terminology proposed by Lüning (1996) will be used. The late 4th and the 3rd millennium BC are therefore referred to as the Late Neolithic and Final Neolithic (Fig. 13.2).

To date, only a very few floor plans of comparatively small buildings dating to the 4th millennium BC are known meaning that we know little about settlement structures for the Later Neolithic over a period of almost 1000 years. During this time LBK-type longhouses were no longer built but smaller buildings that barely leave any archaeological trace, such as blockhouses with beam constructions, were in use. This may also reflect changes in the social and economic regimes. There are only four unambiguous house plans dating to the later 4th millennium BC and they belong to the Salzmünde culture (von Rauchhaupt &

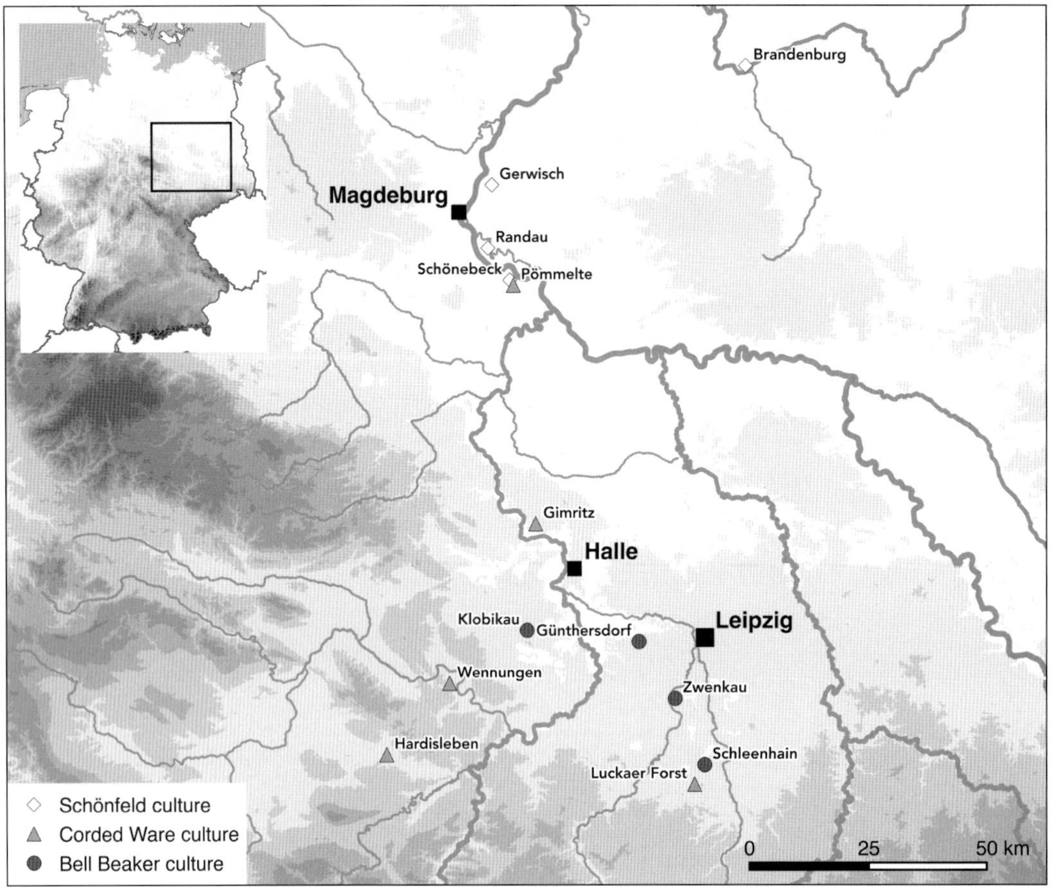

Figure 13.1: Map of the Final Neolithic settlement sites with buildings in Central Germany mentioned in this paper. Basemap: GTOPO30 and SRTM 1, courtesy of USGS

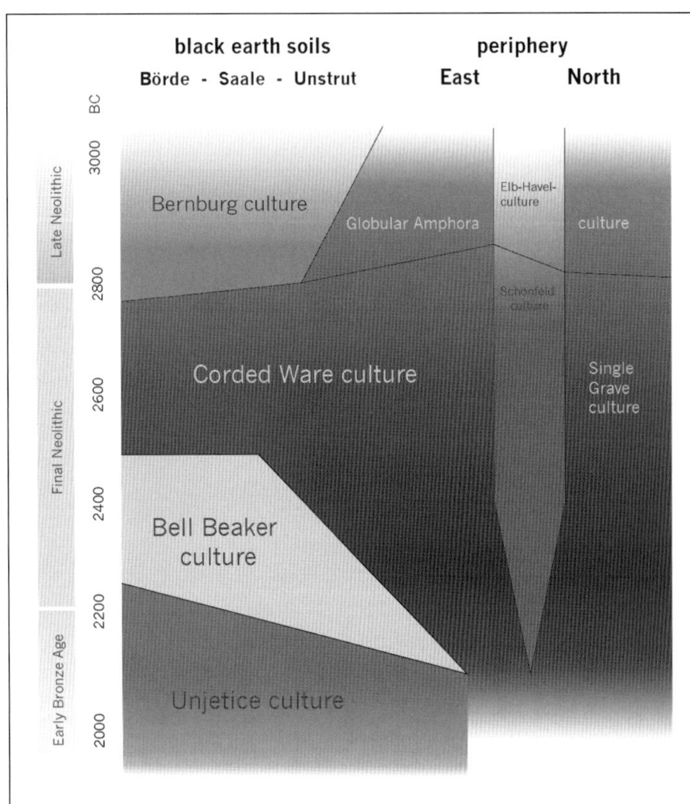

Figure 13.2: Schematic chronology of the 3rd millennium BC in Central Germany highlighting the interrelation of the cultural development and high-quality soils. Drawing: T. Schunke

Viol 2014). Post-built structures described in some of the older publications (Dirks 2000, 103–6) do not withstand critical review. With the Bernburg culture in the Late Neolithic, the very late 4th millennium BC, there is evidence for the first pit houses with sunken floors (Behrens & Schröter 1980, 35 fig 14; Lüning 1999; Wehmer 2016), for open village-like settlements and for the last Neolithic fortified hill-top settlements (Müller 1990).

Shortly before 3000 BC, the Globular Amphora culture appears for this first time in Central Germany. This had a settlement system that seems to have reflected a much more mobile way of life that relied on intensive livestock farming (transhumance) (Beier 1988, 47). Coming from the east, those people initially only settled in areas that were not already occupied by the more agrarian Bernburg culture (Schwarz 2013, 234–37 fig. 6; Woidich 2014, 229). Nevertheless, the mix of ceramics on the settlements shows that these two cultures interacted (Beier 1988, 43 Karte 2). The Globular Amphorae users were the first to settle in areas with poor-quality soils and

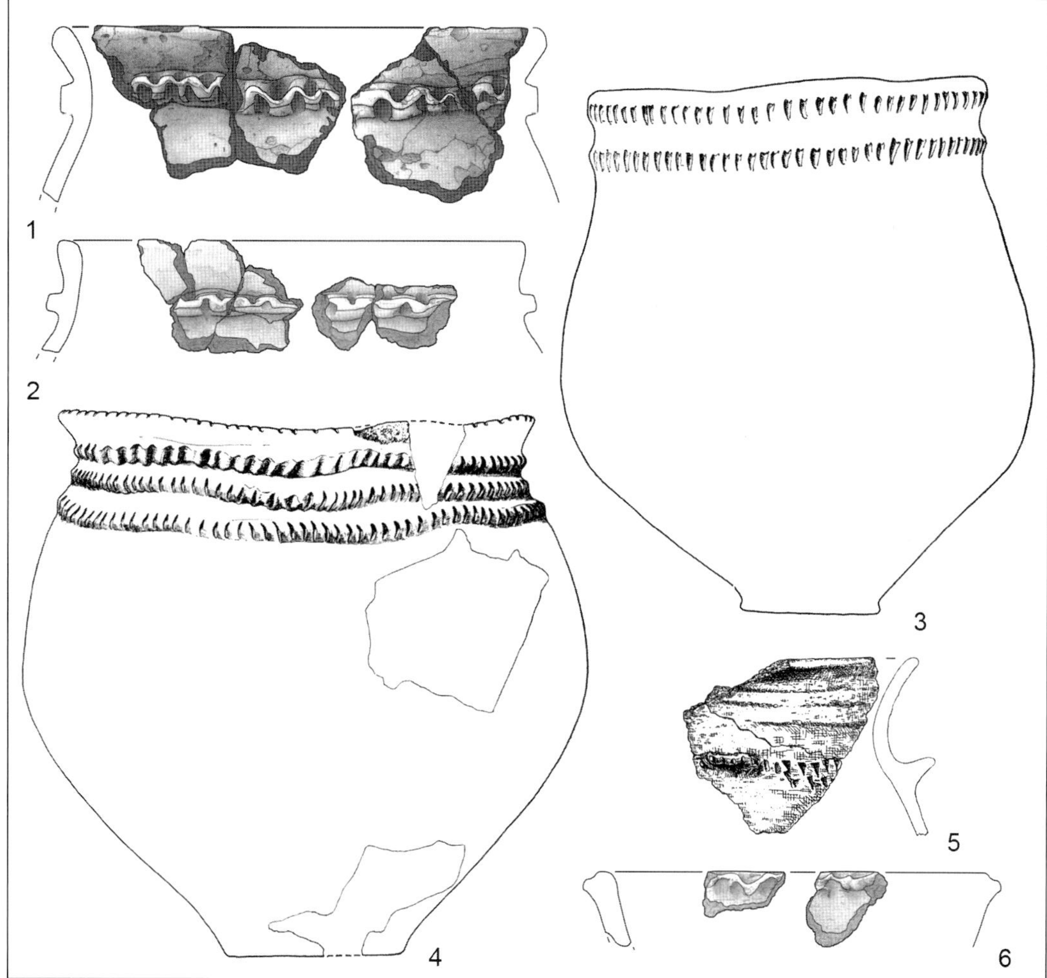

Figure 13.3: Settlement ceramics of the Corded Ware Culture in Central Germany. 1, 2, 7 – fragments of storage vessels with short wave cordons, Pömmelte (Salzland district) (Spatzier 2017, Taf. 50); storage vessels with decorated fillets; 3 – Halle-Lettin (city of Halle) (Matthias 1982, Taf. 46/2); 4 – Großlehna (Leipzig) (Matthias 1987, Taf. 9/7); 5 – vessel fragment, Gutenberg (Saale district) (Hoffmann & Schmidt 1961, Abb. 1). Scale: 1:4

their supposedly mobile economy is reflected in the settlement evidence where houses have not been clearly identified. Furthermore, the cylindrical or frustoconical storage pits, typical for most Neolithic cultures and the Bernburg culture are almost completely absent (Beier 1988, 45–7; Woidich 2014, 99; Hubensack 2016, 82) and for this reason these settlements were often called 'camps' (Woidich 2014, 97).

Around 2800 BC, a clear break can be detected when the Late Neolithic traditions almost completely disappeared and which coincided, on a supra-regional level, with the appearance of the Corded Ware complex (Corded Ware culture and Single Grave culture) in Eastern, Central and Northern Europe. The mobile settlement and economic practices of the Globular Amphora culture now became widely accepted. Only in a few small areas did cultural groups emerge that continued to practice some Late Neolithic traditions, such as the extraordinary Schönfeld culture. Around 2500 BC the Bell Beaker culture appeared in Corded Ware areas but it is still unclear how they coexisted or whether the two cultures excluded each other on a microregional level. Their cultural expressions suggest that they distanced themselves. In addition, the re-appearance of longhouses and the almost exclusive colonisation of high-quality soil by the Bell Beaker people indicate that they re-introduced an economy focused on arable agriculture which was also the basis of the Únětice culture that spread all over Central Germany in the 23rd/22nd century BC. Although it was the first Bronze Age culture, it remained rooted in Neolithic traditions until the end of the 3rd millennium.

Settlement ceramics of the Corded Ware culture

In contrast to more than 2000 graves with standardised vessels comprising beakers, bowls

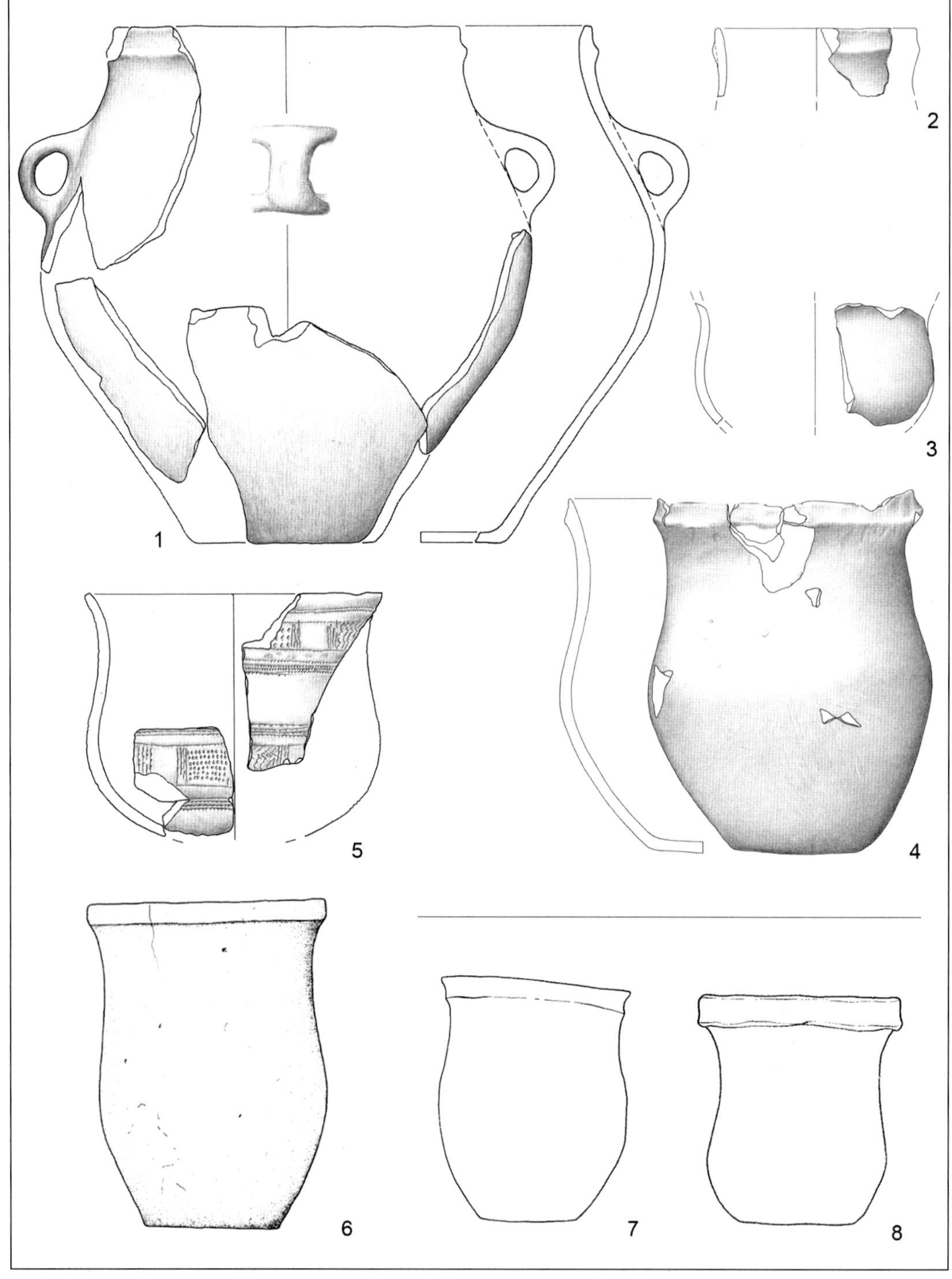

Figure 13.4: Settlement ceramics of the Bell Beaker Culture in Central Germany. 1–5 Vessel fragments found in a settlement pit at Bad Lauchstädt (Saale district)(Schunke 2017b, Abb. 14); 6–9 Beakers with cordon below the rim from Esperstedt and Schraplau (Saale district) (6, 7 – Leinthaler et al. *2006, Abb. 4/1; 7: Matthias 1974, Taf. 115/9) and Besedau (Salzland district) (8 – Matthias 1987, Taf. 53/1). Scale: 1:3*

and amphorae, only a few settlement sites are known for the Corded Ware culture. One settlement feature, wells, that usually contained typical amphorae, suggesting that these may have been used to draw water (Dalidowski *et al.* 2016, 91 Abb. 6; Kretschmer *et al.* 2016, 55 Abb. 35; Schunke 2009, 280 Abb. 2/3–4). Exceptional finds comprise organic vessels with three birch bark beakers from two wells excavated near Zwenkau (Leipzig, Saxony) (Campen 1999), and two wooden bowls found in a grave near Stedten (Mansfeld, Saxony-Anhalt) (Matthias 1974, Taf. 122/2–3).

Large storage vessels have only occasionally been found in settlements and the only type representing a distinct Corded Ware settlement ware are large pots with wavy cordons (Fig. 13.3,1,2,6; Beran 1995; Krautwurst 2002).

Apart from the eponymous moulding around the neck, the poor quality of manufacture is conspicuous. Radiocarbon dates place them in the earlier 3rd millennium BC (Spatzier 2017, 246) associated with the so-called 'Einheitshorizont'. Beran (1995, 84) assigned them to the 'Gerwisch horizon' representing the oldest phase of the Central German Corded Ware complex, whereas he assigned large vessels with notched cordons and punctures to the younger 'Biederitz horizon' (Fig. 13.3,3–4). The most important discovery of the latter form was at Großlehna (Leipzig) and, in addition to the large pot with three notched cordons (Fig. 13.3,4), many fragments of beakers and amphorae and several stone axes were found. A similar specimen with a cordon decorated with cuneiform punctures and with a small pedestalled base, the latter typical of the Final Neolithic, was found at Halle-Lettin (Fig. 13.3,3). One sherd from a large pot without a cordon but decorated with cuneiform 'stitching' and a handle (Fig. 13.3,5) was found in a settlement pit at Gutenberg (Saale district, Saxony-Anhalt) and was associated with, among other finds, a very rare spindle whorl for this period.

Settlement ceramics of the Bell Beaker culture

While Bell Beakers or so-called *Begleitkeramik*, are known from about 600 graves in the Middle Elbe-Saale region (Hille 2012), settlement ceramics of the Bell Beaker culture were almost unknown in Central Germany until the end of 20th century. The only assemblage of a plausible domestic character was discovered near Streckau (Burgenland district, Saxony-Anhalt) and published only as a note (Neumann 1929, 61–2).

With recent large-scale excavations this situation has changed slightly. One very important discovery that defines typical Bell Beaker settlement pottery was excavated in 2008 near Bad Lauchstädt (Saale district, Saxony-Anhalt) (Schunke 2017b) where, at the bottom of a pit, the sherds of one decorated 'Metopenbecher' and one large handled biconical vessel with a horizontal cordon below the rim were found (Fig. 13.4,1–5). As a result, relatively slender beakers with horizontal cordons around the rim (Fig. 13.4,6–8) that had been found in graves and that had hitherto mostly been assigned to the Corded Ware culture, can now be seen to be Bell Beaker (Schunke 2017b, 59–63). Beaker sherds with these characteristics were recently found in a multi-period settlement near Göttwitz (Leipzig) (Conrad *et al.* 2016, 185 Abb. 4/1), in a ceramic deposit found near Gatersleben (Salzland district, Saxony-Anhalt) (Kleinecke 2018, 133 Abb. 12/4a) and in a grave excavated near Esperstedt (Saale district Saxony-Anhalt) (J. Eichentopf pers. comm.).

Several new settlement sites have been investigated particularly in the area south of Leipzig. The features did not contain large assemblages and the sparseness of the finds may be one reason that Bell Beaker habitation sites are generally difficult to identify. Characteristic Bell Beaker pottery is still very rare. However, due to our increased knowledge of associated undecorated vessels, more domestic features and habitation sites can now be assigned to the Bell Beaker culture (Queck 2013; Balfanz *et al.* 2015; Conrad *et al.* 2017, 42 Abb. 1). Undecorated cups and jugs with a handle originating at or slightly below the rim (Fig. 13.5,3 & 7), various round-bellied to biconical vessels with simple horizontal cordons around the upper part of the vessel or below the rim (Fig. 13.5,1 & 4) can now be seen to have Beaker associations. It is still not yet possible to define precisely the vessel types within Bell Beaker domestic assemblages. For example, S-profiled bowls and large, similarly profiled, jug-like vessels (Fig. 13.5,5) seem to be relatively common. Large vessels with a horizontal cordon below the rim, such as the one represented by fragments from Paschkowitz (Leipzig, Saxony) (Conrad *et al.* 2014a, 108 Abb. 8/3), are rare. Occasionally round and elongated knobs (Fig. 13.5,11) are also applied to the vessels.

A group comprising biconical, beaker-like vessels with cordons around the neck and baggy biconical vessels with handles on the upper part of the shoulder (Fig. 13.6) can be identified as the 'Zwenkau *facies*', first discovered at the Early Bronze Age settlement of Zwenkau (Leipzig, Saxony). Originally assigned to the Proto-Únětice (Schunke 2009, 282–89), these assemblages may be a regional manifestation of the late or final Bell Beaker culture along its eastern and northern periphery (Schunke 2017b, 66–72). The 'Zwenkau *facies*' was also found at the circular enclosure of Pömmelte (Salzland district, Saxony-Anhalt),

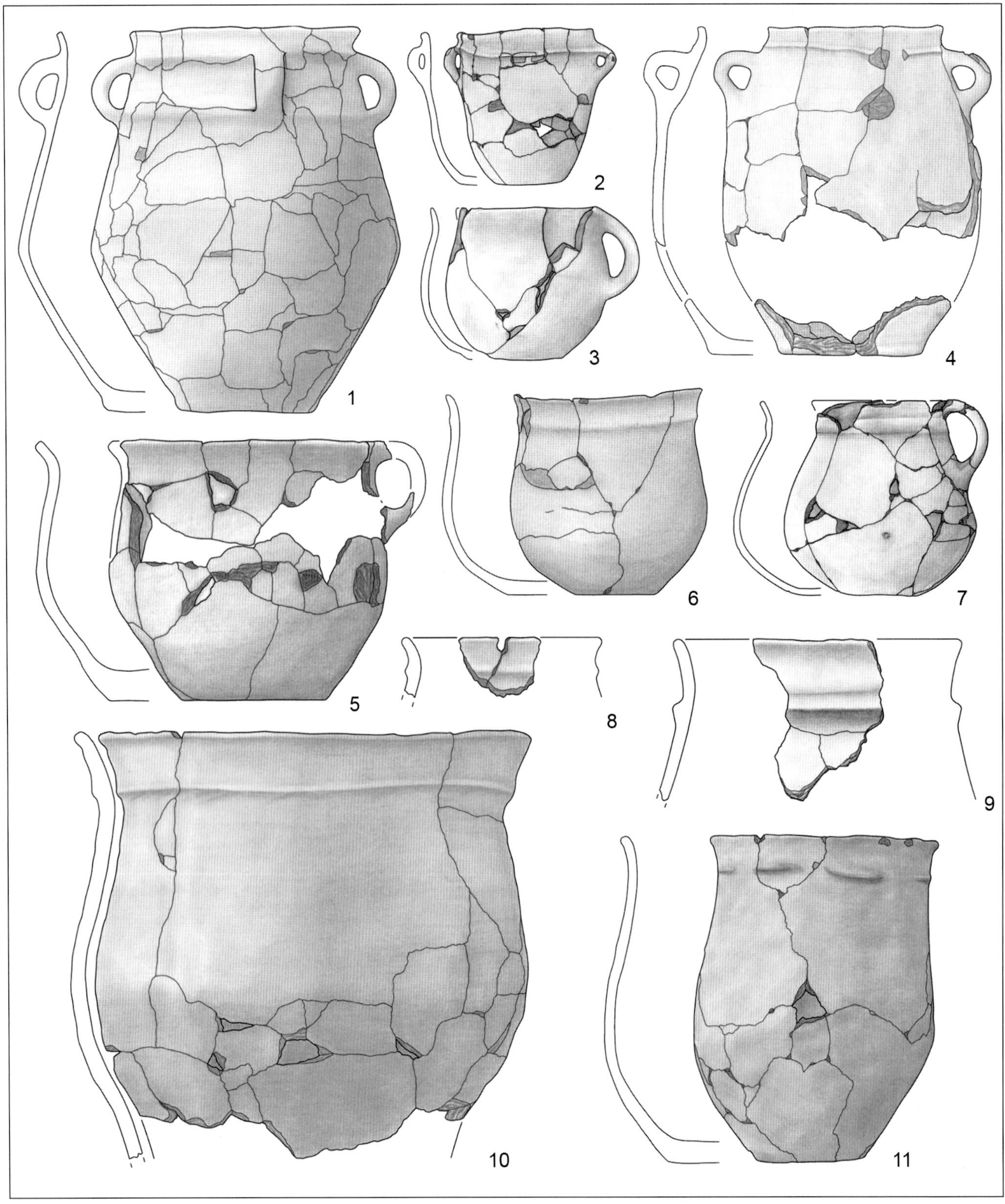

Figure 13.5: Vessels found at the circular enclosure of Pömmelte (Salzland district). Such vessels date to the 23rd to 21st century BC and are almost unknown in burial contexts. Scale: 1:4. After Spatzier 2017, Taf. 5/1, 12/13, 27/3, 31/5, 32/2, 32/3, 33/1, 42/1, 45/1, 46/6, 47/1

Figure 13.6: Vessels of the 'Zwenkau facies*' – 'giant beaker-like' vessels and biconical vessels with cordons around the neck – found in a well-like feature at Zwenkau (Leipzig). After Schunke 2017a, Abb. 18*

initially built around 2300 BC by Bell Beaker users and in continuous use until 2050 BC after the transition to Únětice (Spatzier 2017). The Pömmelte enclosure strongly suggests that at the end of its development the 'Zwenkau *facies*' probably existed parallel to the Early Bronze Age Únětice culture that had already been established west of the Saale-Unstrut region.

A special type of pot belonging to the 'Zwenkau *facies*' are beakers with a horizontal cordon around the neck (Fig. 13.5,8,9 & 6). They are smaller than but comparable to the giant beakers of the North European Final Neolithic, can be described as 'giant beaker-like' vessels (Schunke 2009, 283; Spatzier 2017, 86–91)and possibly were the starting point of the giant beaker development (Schunke 2017b, 70). The absence of cordons below the rim at Zwenkau and, with one exception, at Pömmelte, both sites representing the largest assemblages of this date so far, may suggest a chronological development from rim-cordoned vessels of the Bell Beaker culture to the neck-cordoned vessels of the 'Zwenkau *facies*'.

Building and settlement structures

Schönfeld culture

The houses from Gerwisch, Brandenburg and Randau are the oldest definite settlements with houses of the Final Neolithic in Central Germany, and in particular of the Schönfeld culture (see Schlette 1958, 135; Schlette 1969, 157). The house discovered near Gerwisch (Jerichower Land, Saxony-Anhalt) (Engel 1930, 181–2, Abb. 119A; Fig. 13.1,3) had a rectangular floor plan measuring about 13.5 × 5.6 m. It was oriented E–W and is the only one that was built using bedding trench construction. The walls comprised rows of closely-spaced posts of 0.1 m diameter sunk into 0.2 m wide and 0.5 m deep foundation trenches. The house was divided into an eastern vestibule, perhaps open towards the E, and a western room with one hearth and three entrances, both separated by a wall with a connecting entrance. The floor consisted of rammed earth and sand.

Although located in Brandenburg, the site of Brandenburg-Neuendorf will be mentioned. Here, a one-aisled post-built house of 8 × 4.2 m and oriented NE–SW was excavated (Krause & Gahrau-Rothert 1941). The outer walls comprised posts of about 0.15 m diameter that were arranged at regular distances of up to 0.6 m and sunk into 0.3 m wide and 0.4–0.5 m deep post-pits. Due to preservation, entrances are uncertain. Near to the southern wall there was a hearth, and a refuse pit located in the interior contained about 30 kg of sherds, many of them deriving from decorated vessels of the Schönfeld culture, associated with a few flint artefacts.

The site of Randau (Salzland district, Saxony-

Figure 13.7: Plan of the Schönfeld Culture settlement at Schönebeck-Felgeleben (Salzland district). Plan After Spatzier forthcoming, fig. 1

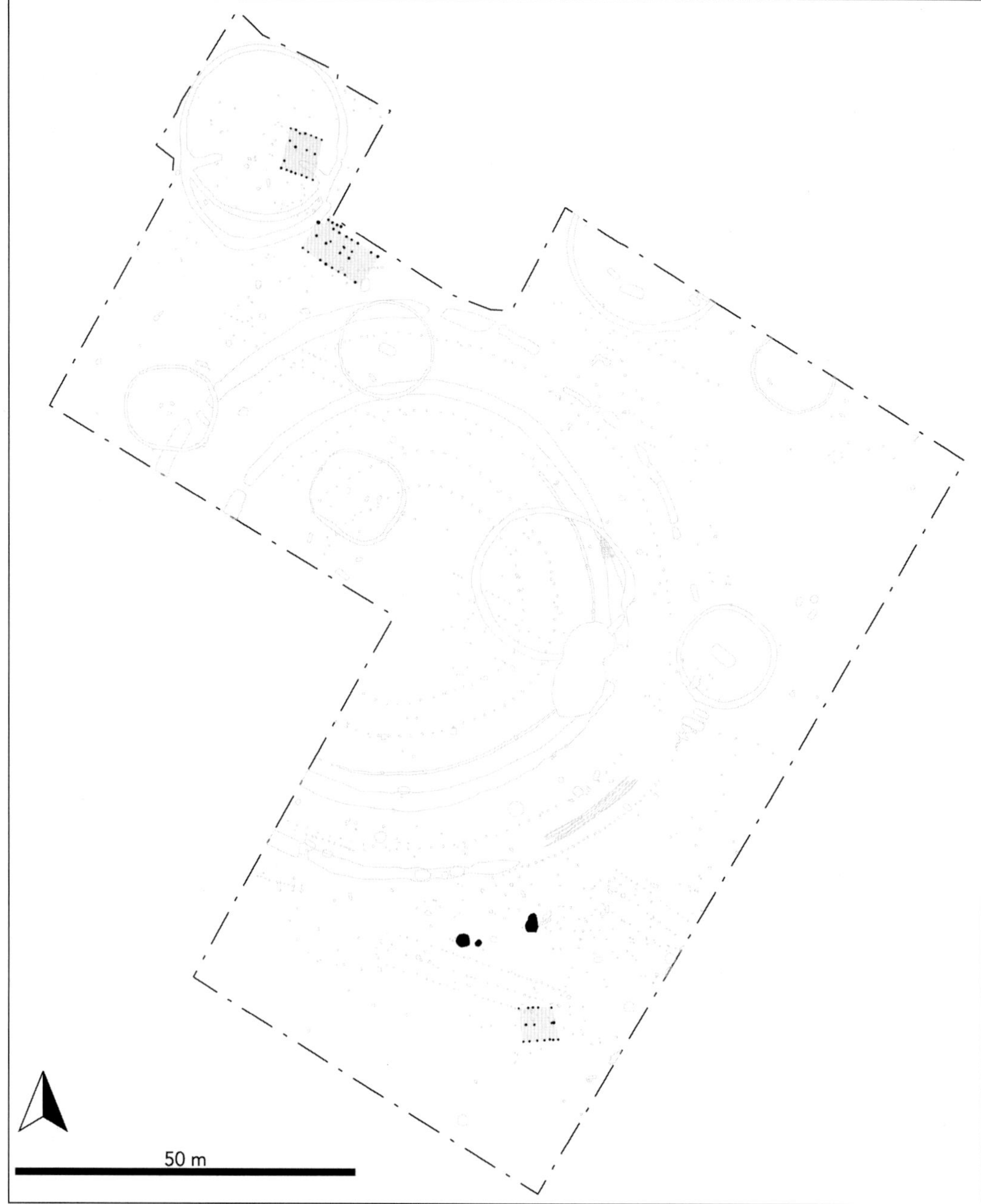

Anhalt) provides insight into the inner structure of a Schönfeld culture house (Lies 1942; Lies 1947). A clearly distinguishable occupation layer was preserved following the collapse of the building. The floor plan (Fig. 13.10,1) revealed two equal connected sections. The first section is one-aisled with two central hearths in the West whilst the second is two-aisled and slightly less wide. Together they constitute a building measuring 19.75 × 5.5 m orientated W–E. According to Lies, the pine wall posts were 0.18–0.2 m in diameter and sunk into 0.6–0.7m deep post-holes set 0.7 m apart. Most of the Schönfelder bowls and stone axes were found within the western section and supposedly represent the 'complete house assemblage'. With respect to the distribution of the finds, Lies suggested the house's western section comprised a living room and a workroom. Both areas were separated by a post-built inner wall. High phosphate concentrations and almost no finds in the northern part of the two-aisled eastern section suggested that it was used as a stable for livestock, though this idea was later rejected (Schlette 1958, 135; Schlette 1969, 157).

Discovered quite recently, the site of

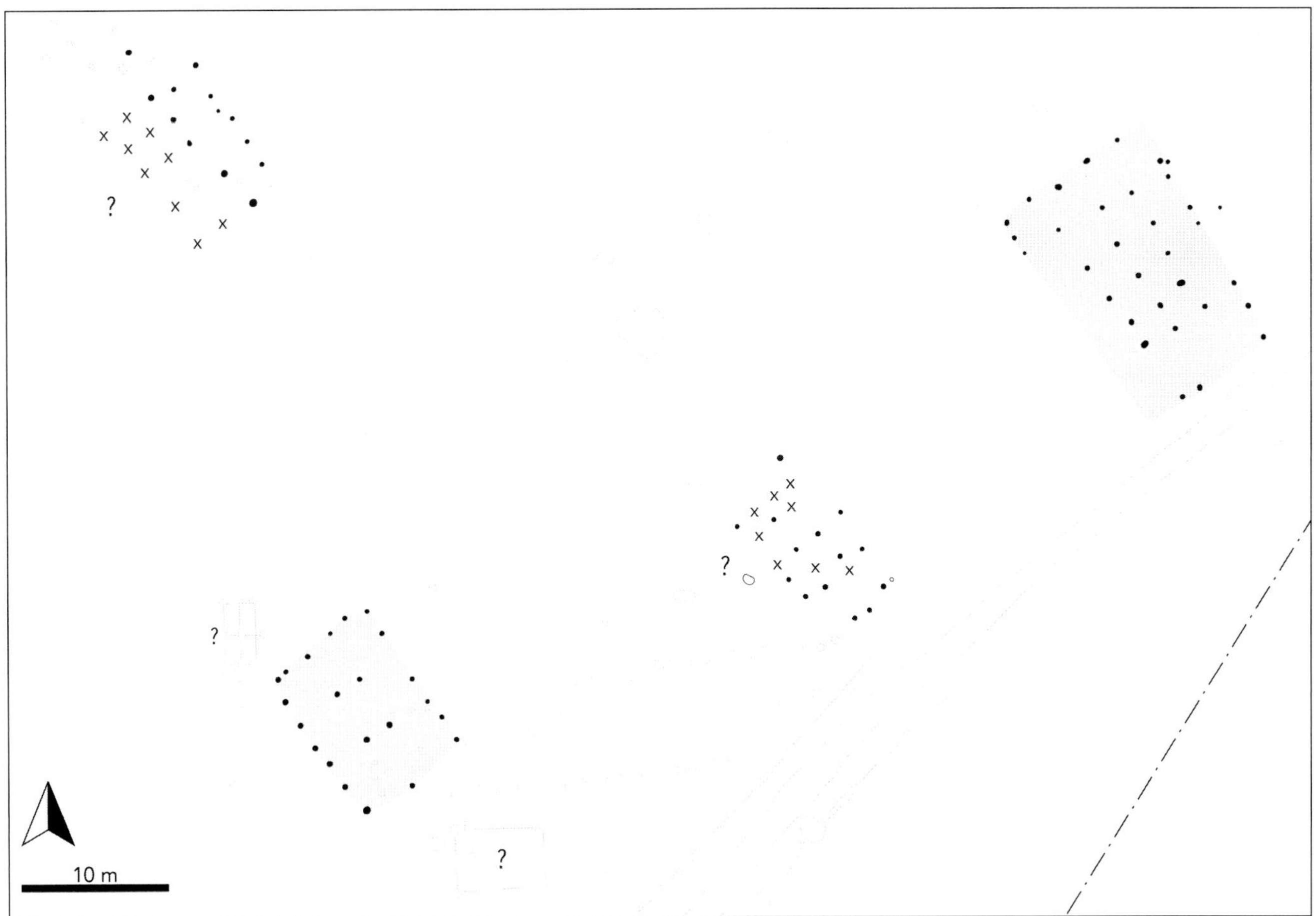

Figure 13.8: Plan of the Corded Ware settlement at Wennungen (Burgenland district, Saxony-Anhalt). After Kegler 2012, Abb. 3

Schönebeck-Felgeleben (Salzland district, Saxony-Anhalt) may shed light into the organisation of a Schönfeld settlement. During the excavation of the Early Bronze Age circular enclosure (Spatzier 2017, 277–9; forthcoming), three post-built houses and some settlement pits were found (Fig. 13.7). While several post-pits of the rectangular house 1 contained sherds with Schönfeld culture decoration, the affinity of the other two smaller and squared-shaped houses is less secure and all three houses remain to be radiocarbon dated. About 5m to the north of house 1 there was house 2 and about 100 m to the south there were three settlement pits and, only 10 m further southwards, house 3. Apart from typical Schönfeld sherds, the pits contained some flint artefacts and querns.

The floor plan of house 1 (Fig. 13.10,2) measured 10.3 × 5.15 m and consisted of 27 posts with the north-western third being slightly trapezoidal with a 4.65 m wide gable wall. It was oriented SE–NW and there was a small annex to the north. Gaps in the regular post settings of the outer walls suggest up to three entrances. The outer wall posts were regularly spaced and the post-pits were 0.17–0.33 m wide and 0.06–0.15 m deep. The pits of the roof supports were set 1.6–2.4 m apart and were slightly wider and deeper than the wall posts. That this middle row did not extend into the house's south-eastern third indicates a division of the interior into a two-aisled western and a one-aisled eastern section, the latter perhaps an ancillary structure as gaps along the outer wall suggest. Fragments of Schönfeld vessels come from the internal post-pits. Differing from house 1, houses 2 and 3 have similar floor plans and sizes. Measuring 5 × 6 m and 5.3 × 5 m, they are almost square, two-aisled, and oriented ESE–WNW and E–W respectively. The roof supports of house 2 are not located centrally, but shifted northward, thereby creating two asymmetric aisles.

Apart from the E–W orientation, a common feature of Schönfeld buildings is their bipartite nature. While in Randau it is a one-aisled section in the west, putatively for living/working, and a

Figure 13.9: Plan of the Bell Beaker settlement at Klobikau (Saale district). In the settlement (upper left) nine clusters of post-pits, including three houses and one linear post structure, are highlighted dark grey, the detail (lower left) is highlighted light grey. After Balfanz et al. *2015, Abb. 2*

two-aisled section in the east, Schönebeck and Gerwisch supposedly share the same general structure of a western 'occupation' section and an eastern one-aisled anteroom open towards the east. In general, the sizes of all Schönfeld culture houses (or the sections of the Randau house) are approximately 10 × 5 m, only the smaller Schönebeck houses 2 and 3 measure half of this length, approximately 5 × 5 m. Therefore Randau perhaps represents two adjacent common type dwelling structures of the Schönfeld culture measuring 10 × 5 m and the two small Schönebeck houses perhaps representing ancillary buildings.

Corded Ware culture

Settlement evidence for the Corded Ware culture remained scarce until the early 2000s with the discovery of wells and structures at Droßdorf (Kretschmer *et al.* 2016, 55), Espenhain and Hain (all Leipzig, Saxony) (Dalidowski *et al.* 2016, 91, 93), Löbnitz-Roitzschjora (Nordsachsen, Saxony) (Schmalfuß & Tolksdorf 2016, 132–5, 139–41) and Quedlingburg (Harz, Saxony-Anhalt) (Peters 2006). However, the oldest evidence comes from excavations in 1953–1955 where several settlement structures were discovered in the Luckaer Forst (Altenburger Land, Saxony) (Höckner 1957, 126–70, 175–81). The excavator mentioned 11 so-called 'Siedelplätze' that can be interpreted as the remains of rectangular houses of 6–9 × 4–6 m, their narrow sides mostly facing from east to south. In one case the platform floor was delimited by a small earthen bank, supposedly the remnants of collapsed walls. Since the remains of those houses were shallow and no traces of posts were found,

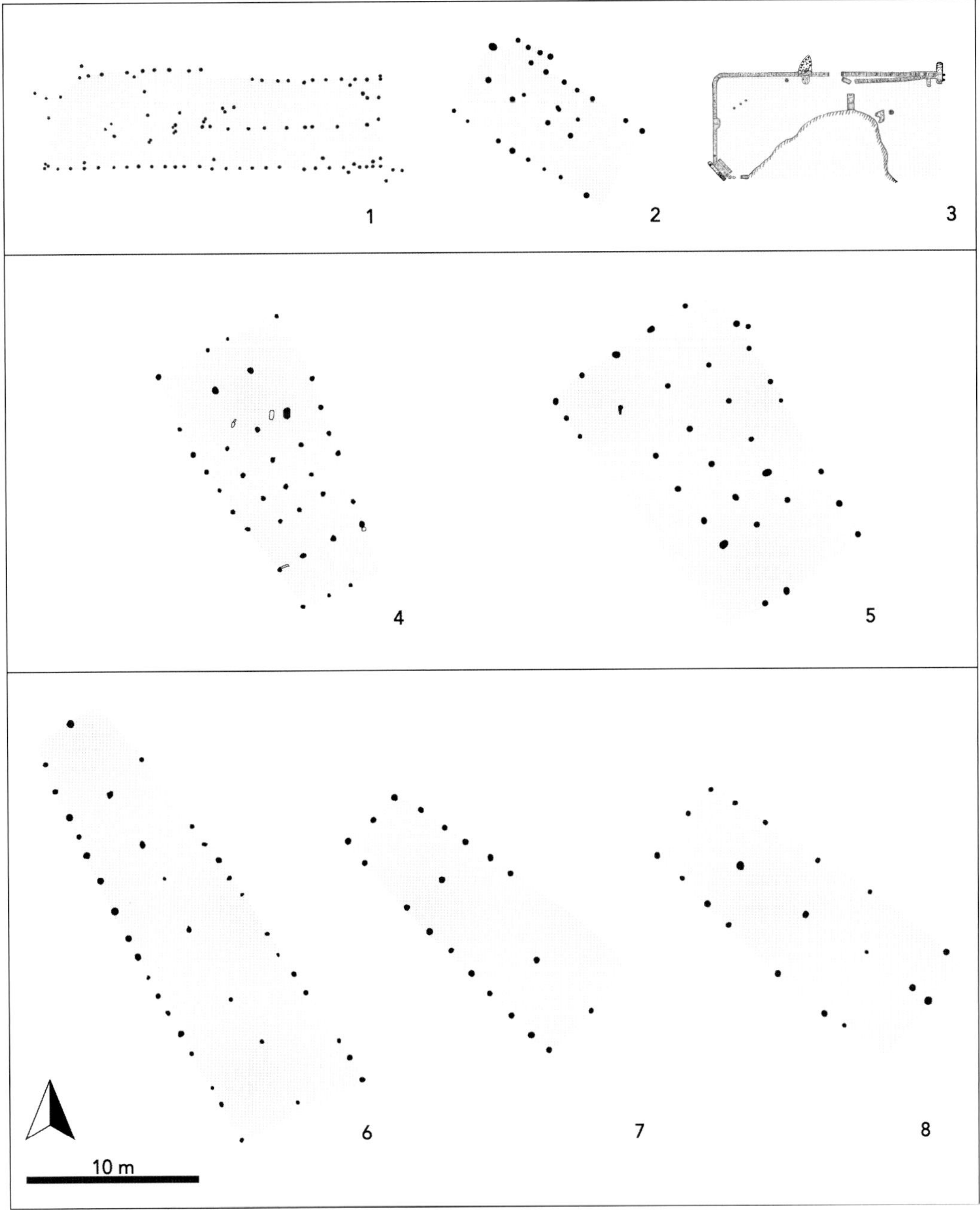

Figure 13.10: Floor plans of houses of the Final Neolithic. 1–3 Schönfeld Culture; 4–5 Corded Ware Culture; 6–8 Bell Beaker Culture: 1 – Randau (Salzland district) after Lies 1947, 47; 2 – Schönebeck-Felgeleben (Salzland district); 3 – Gerwisch (Jerichower Land) after Engel 1930, Abb. 119A; 4 – Gimritz (Saale district) after Muhl et al. *2010, 48; 5 – Wennungen (Burgenland) cf. Kegler 2012, Abb. 3; 6 & 7 – Klobikau (Saale district) after Balfanz* et al. *2015, Abb. 4; 8 – Schleenhain (Leipzig) after Conrad* et al. *2017, Abb. 3.*

Höckner concluded that their foundations must have been beam constructions; debris from wattle-and-daub comes from one of the barrows of the site. Within several of the houses there were dome-shaped ovens or other hearths evident from concentrations of burnt clay and charcoal.

The discoveries at Luckauer Forst resemble those from regions in adjacent Brandenburg. Dense scatters of Corded Ware finds are 0.5 m deep, cover areas of 5–10 × 10–20 m, are mostly oriented E–W and are interpreted as the sunken floors of rectangular houses (Beran 2008; 2012; 2016). They resemble Danish sites and may have been post-and-beam buildings with turf walls. At sites with multiple houses, such as Heinersbrück 31 and 35, it is likely that only one house existed at a time (Beran 2008, 202). With respect to the settlement landscape, in the regions of Lower Lusitia and around Potsdam (near Berlin) small single-house farmsteads or hamlets probably co-existed at distances of 300–500 m along the rivers. In the case of the Potsdam area there is 'increasing evidence for a long-lasting Scandinavian-type single hamlet settlement structure during the entire Late and Final Neolithic and also during the Early Bronze Age' (Beran 2016, 102).

The first unambiguous remains of post-built houses of the local Corded Ware were excavated near Gimritz (Saale district, Saxony-Anhalt) close to Corded Ware graves (Jarecki 2008; Muhl *et al.* 2010, 48). This site yielded pits and at least two, perhaps several, houses separated by larger open areas, and possibly amorphous concentrations of post-pits. While the floor plans of some of the post-built houses were only partly preserved, one smaller and one larger building, were almost complete. The larger house (Fig. 13.10,4) was oriented NNW–SSE and had a trapezoidal layout about 15.5 m long and gable walls of about 9 m (NNW) and 5 m (SSE) wide (cf. Muhl *et al.* 2010, 48). The outer walls' posts were uniformly spaced about 1.5 m apart and enclosed an area of roughly 100 m^2. The posts in the interior attest internal division into three parts of equal length: the middle section with a trapezoidal setting of 12 posts making it four-aisled, the front and back sections with pairs of posts located perpendicular to the houses' axis. Deposits of ceramics in some of the post-pits suggest that the upright timber logs had been extracted after abandonment (cf. Muhl *et al.* 2010, 49).

Possible Corded Ware houses were excavated at two sites near Wennungen (Burgenland district, Saxony-Anhalt) again close to Corded Ware graves (Kegler 2012). At the first site, there were traces of at least two, perhaps four post-built houses, all oriented along a NW–SE–axis (Fig. 13.8). The two houses with almost complete floor plans have an internal structure very similar to the house from Grimritz although they do not have the obvious tripartite divisions. Nevertheless, despite the absence of finds, they can be assigned to the Corded Ware culture by analogy. Like the Gimritz house, the larger house No. 4 has a (slightly) trapezoidal layout (Fig. 13.10,5) and the floor plan suggests a four-aisled construction. House 2, with complete floor plan, was rather more rectangular but had a comparable inner setting of four posts. According to the original excavation plan, house 4 measured 16.6 × 11.7/8.9 m and house 2 about 10.9 × 8.50 m. Based on this evidence, Houses 1 and 3 were reconstructed by the excavator from post concentrations located nearby but this is very contentious.

At the second site near Wennungen two post-built houses of equal size and layout were recorded next to a group of Corded Ware burials. Being composed of 12 post-pits evenly arranged 2.8 m apart and in three rows orientated NNW–SSE, these rectangular settings (about 8.6 × 5.7 m according to Kegler 2012, 102) resemble the settings of the houses described above and they were tentatively attributed to the Corded Ware culture (Kegler 2012, 102). However, this is unlikely as the post-holes are exceptionally large compared to those of other houses dating to the Late Neolithic, Final Neolithic, and Early Bronze Age (cf. Duchnewski *et al.* forthcoming; Spatzier 2017, 52–8, esp. 38 and 58).

The latest evidence was discovered near Hardisleben (Sömmerda, Thuringia), where the floor plans of at least two trapezoidal buildings were excavated (M. Küßner pers. comm.). They were aligned along a NNW–SSE axis with the wider gable walls facing to the north-north-west. One building, measuring approximately 16.3 × 9/6 m, is strikingly similar to the Gimritz house. A recent discovery from near Pömmelte (Salzland district, Saxony-Anhalt) can possibly be added. Here traces of a post-built house were recorded suggesting a three-aisled slightly trapezoidal structure oriented SE–NW. The house measures about 10.1 m long, the gable wall in the south-east about 10.3 m wide and that in the north-west about 8.8 m. Hopefully radiocarbon dating will clarify the chronology and the affiliation of this building.

Finally, only some 100 m away from the famous Corded Ware burials of Eula (city of Naumburg, Burgenland district, Saxony-Anhalt) (Meyer *et al.* 2009), the scant remains of a settlement of that period were discovered (Muhl *et al.* 2010, 78–83). Some post-pits have been interpreted as the incomplete floor plans of two houses of about 13 × 5 m and 9 × 5 m but this is contentious and unconvincing at least in the case of the smaller unit. The other structure was oriented roughly NW–SE, one-aisled, and may have had two inner sections.

Summarising the evidence from Central Germany, the only houses of certain Corded Ware affiliation are those from Luckauer Forst and Gimritz, both associated with typical Corded Ware finds, though the houses at

Wennungen (houses 2 and 4) and Hardisleben have to be added by layout analogy. The sill beam houses at Luckauer Forst are unique in Central Germany, but find comparison in Brandenburg. The new discoveries shift the evidence from beam constructions to post-built constructions in the region and suggest some degree of standardisation. The buildings from Gimritz, Wennungen and Hardisleben share a trapezoidal layout with straight side walls and an orientation along the NNW–SSE-axis and NW–SE-axis with the wider gable walls facing to the NNW and NW respectively. These 'Gimritz' type houses (Fig. 13.10.4–5) have a distinct setting of three post rows in the interior that, at least in Gimritz, separates the five-aisled middle section from the north-western and the south-eastern sections. In addition, buildings from Wennungen and Hardisleben suggest that a version of this house type was three-aisled through its entire length. Still, it remains to be seen if trapezoidal, multi-aisled post buildings of the 'Gimritz type' are the 'typical' houses of the Corded Ware groups of Central Germany.

Bell Beaker culture

Until quite recently, except for very few possible 'settlement pits' of certain Bell Beaker affiliation, like those from Seehausen (Börde district, Saxony-Anhalt) and Porst (Bitterfeld-Anhalt, Saxony-Anhalt) and small collections of stray finds from field walking, there was no evidence for settlement sites. The first real traces of Bell Beaker settlements were excavated about a decade ago near Bad Lauchstädt (Saale district, Saxony-Anhalt) (Schunke 2017b, 55–66).

In the early 2000s a simple rectangular arrangement of posts measuring about 20 × 6 m and aligned W–E was found near Rothenschirmbach (Mansfeld-Südharz, Saxony-Anhalt). It was interpreted as Bell Beaker in date because of the small Bell Beaker cemetery located only about 120 m to the east and the fact that no features of any other date were recorded in the excavation (Müller 2006, 98–9). A similar assumption was proposed for the rather amorphous post settings discovered near Auterwitz (Mittelsachsen, Saxony) (Conrad 2010, 71; Umweltzentrum-Ökohof-Auterwitz-e.V. 2014, 12–14) again based on the fact that some nearby pits contained Bell Beaker ceramics or culturally unspecific sherds and there were no finds from other periods. These structures are ambiguous in date, affinity and layout.

The first proven Bell Beaker buildings were discovered only a few years ago near Klobikau (Saale district, Saxony-Anhalt) (Balfanz *et al.* 2015). Besides the information about the houses themselves, the excavation provides valuable insights into the organisation of Bell Beaker settlements, although only a narrow strip, less than 100 m wide, was investigated. Nine separate clusters of post-pits extended over a length of about 1km and three of them represent floor plans of two-aisled trapezoidal longhouses orientated SE–NW, with the wider gable walls facing towards the south-east (Fig. 13.9).

House 1 (Fig. 13.10,6) is the largest measuring about 26 m long. The south-east gable wall was 7.5 m wide and the north-western gable wall was considerably narrower, supposedly about 4 m. The side walls were slightly convex with posts set medium distances apart, the middle row posts aligned straight and with wider distances. House 2 (Fig. 13.10,7), located 140 m towards the NE, is similar but only 16.5 m long and supposedly about 6.7 m wide near the wider gable wall. Its floor plan was slightly trapezoidal with slightly convex side walls. The floor plan of house 3 is a little irregular towards the south-east end but reflects the same general layout and has the same orientation measuring 13 m × *c.* 6 m. In addition, 46 pits (some forming pit clusters) contained Bell Beaker sherds or were radiocarbon dated to this period, and three Bell Beaker graves were found in the same area.

A stretch of about 440 m lacking structural evidence suggests either a division of the settlement into a north-eastern and south-western area, or that there was more than one settlement. Furthermore, radiocarbon dates prove that the settlement existed between the 25th and the 21st centuries cal BC and suggest a multi-phased occupation (Balfanz *et al.* 2015, 757–8, Abb. 7).

The site of Klobikau suggests that local Bell Beaker people lived in farmsteads or hamlets that consisted of one single house or very few houses perhaps, if contemporary, located several hundreds of meters apart. This is confirmed by recent discoveries at the open coal mine at Schleenhain, Groitzsch (Leipzig, Saxony) (Conrad *et al.* 2017) and about 45 km to the south-east of Klobikau where an area covering many hectares was investigated. Four, perhaps five post-built houses were recorded at three or four locations over 1 km apart. Although none of the houses is dated, the similarity of the floor plans to those described above strongly suggests that they belong to the Bell Beaker period. In addition, settlement pits and possible water supply features, perhaps wells, dating to the late 3rd millennium BC were located in the vicinity.

The arrangements of the post-pits at Schleenhain are not as regular as at Klobikau but share the same layout. Three houses were two-aisled and trapezoidal aligned ESE–WNW and SE–NW, the wider gable walls facing ESE and SE respectively. The wall posts were set in medium distances, the middle row posts widely spaced. House 1 (Fig. 13.10,8) measured 18 × 7 m (SE) / 5 m (NW) and is the only one with slightly convex side walls. House 2 was located about 40 m to the south and appears to be shorter, perhaps due to preservation. Two other buildings, houses 3 and 13, were spatially separated and discovered more than 200 m and another 800 m westwards. The approximate dimensions of the floor areas are 18 × 6.5 m (ESE) / 4.5 m (WNW) and 12.5 × 6 m (ESE) / 4 m (WNW) respectively. The possible remains of a fifth house were excavated a little southward between the latter two but the floor plan and its alignment are uncertain.

Based on Klobikau and Schleenhain, a house excavated at Zwenkau (Leipzig, Saxony) can be added to the corpus. It was found within a large Early Bronze Age settlement (Stäuble 1997), partly overlain by a typical Early Bronze Age house. The two-aisled floor plan, oriented SE–NW, has a trapezoidal layout with slightly convex side walls. It measured 15.35m × 5.2m in the SSE (Hansen 2010, 72–4, Taf. 22 left). The shape of the NW end of the house is not entirely clear. At Günthersdorf (Saale district, Saxony-Anhalt) a site located more or less midway between Klobikau and Schleenhain (M. Fröhlich pers. comm.) a trapezoidal house, 17.5 × 6.7/5.5 m, with slightly convex long sides, was oriented SE–NW with the wider gable wall facing SE. A second, poorly preserved floor plan with similar dimensions was oriented ESE–WNW.

While our knowledge of Bell Beaker settlement pottery increases, evidence for domestic buildings remains extremely rare. The only buildings undeniably dating to the younger Final Neolithic and associated with Beakers are those from Klobikau. Comparable floor plans were discovered at Schleenhain, seemingly represent the same type of construction. There is an undeniable affinity between the Corded Ware 'Gimritz type' houses (Fig. 13.10,4 & 5) and those of the Bell Beaker 'Klobikau type' (Fig. 13.10, 6 & 8) – the generally trapezoidal layout. The 'Klobikau' houses, however, represent a remarkably different kind of building. Apart from their opposite alignment along the SE–NW axis with the wider gable wall facing SE, the constructions had a smaller length:width ratio, were two-aisled throughout their entire length with widely space middle post rows, and at least in several cases had slightly convex side walls. In addition, the buildings were scattered and suggest that Bell Beaker users lived either in small single units like farmsteads or in small hamlet-like residential groups. As with the Corded Ware it remains to be seen if future discoveries will confirm a consistent mode of house construction and settlement organisation.

Únětice culture

To understand the chronological development of house building and settlement structure in the 3rd millennium BC, it is necessary to turn to the Early Bronze Age that first appears in Central Germany during the 23rd century BC. With recent large-scale excavations, domestic structures have been frequently discovered making it impossible to present all sites here, not to mention all houses. Today we are able to detect standard Únětice house types plus regional variations with possible influences from neighbouring regions (Duchnewski *et al.* forthcoming). Most common, and therefore the standard Early Bronze Age house type in Central Germany, are those of the 'Zwenkau' type (Fig. 13.11,2) named after the site where they were first excavated. The type comprises two-aisled, post-built longhouses aligned along an E–W axis (ranging from to NE–SW to SE–NW) and typically 20–35 m long and 5–7 m wide. They have 'closed' apsidal or 'bevelled' western gable walls defined by a straight line of posts with missing posts at the corners, and apparently 'open' eastern gable walls. The central row consists of widely spaced posts and bifurcates at the apsidal end to form a 'yoke'

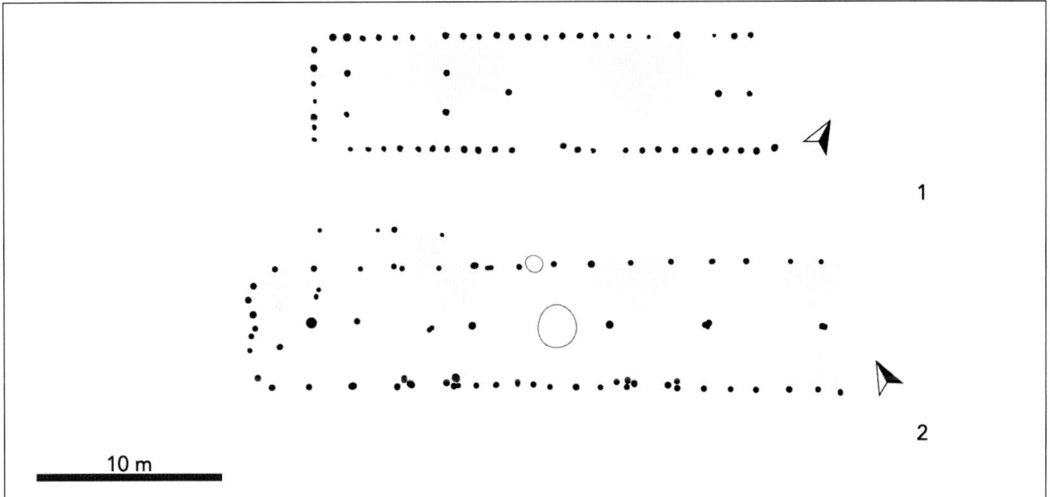

Figure 13.11: Floor plans of houses of the Early Bronze Age Únětice Culture. 1 – Salzmünde (Saale district) after Duchnewski et al. *forthcoming, Abb 3; 2 – Pömmelte (Salzland district) after Spatzier 2017, Abb. 16 bottom*

arrangement of roof supports. One or two entrances (depending on the house length) are located in the southward facing walls and are represented by simple gaps and gaps with internal flanking posts or with triangular post arrangements.

Variations in the typical design can often be observed (Duchnewski *et al.* forthcoming). The first (Fig. 13.11,1) is defined by two of the 'yoke' post-holes standing relatively close to each other in the W part of the house as at Salzmünde-Schiepzig (Saale district, Saxony-Anhalt). The second is defined by two 'yoke' post-holes standing at a fair distance from each other and with one roof ridge post set centrally between them as defined at Schloßvippach (Sömmerda, Thuringia). Such houses are also found at Salzmünde (Saale district, Saxony-Anhalt) and possibly at Zwenkau (Leipzig, Saxony) thereby suggesting that they represent a 'traditional' and functional construction, not a locally restricted mode of house building.

The inner structure is even more emphasised in some buildings with multiple 'yokes' in the west, where a two-aisled eastern part and a three-aisled western part can be clearly distinguished. These houses represent a third version so far only known from Thuringia at sites like Schloßvippach. Furthermore, a very few houses are three-aisled throughout their entire length such as Dermsdorf (Sömmerda, Thuringia) (Küßner 2015, 196), Schweta, (Mittelsachsen, Saxony) (Conrad *et al.* 2014b, 126 Abb. 9), Zwenkau (Leipzig, Saxony) (Stäuble 1997, 134; Schunke 2009, 304–9) and these can be identified as a fourth version that shares the other characteristics of the 'Zwenkau' type houses, if it is not a house type on its own. The three-aisled houses probably represent a constructional necessity as they were considerably larger and, particularly, wider than the 'standard' buildings. The dimensions of the largest houses are 57 × 9 m (Zwenkau) and 44 × 11 m (Dermsdorf).

Further variations, but not yet defined 'types', are indicated by the form of the gable walls. A few houses have completely rounded apses, whilst in other cases the western gable walls were straight with angular corners. Sometimes, the eastern gable walls have an antae-like appearance with the side walls protruding beyond the middle post row, or alternatively the middle post row protrudes, the eastern wall posts are shifted towards the middle axis, and the houses' E end takes on a rounded or 'bevelled' appearance. There are also houses without a yoke-like arrangement found only in the northern periphery of the Únětice culture such as at Benzingerode (Harz, Saxony-Anhalt) (Brauer 2005, 96 Abb. 5), Pömmelte (Salzland district, Saxony-Anhalt) (A. Spatzier pers. comm.) and they perhaps reflect Northern European influences.

The settlement organisation comprising single units forming small residential groups that slowly evolves in the Final Neolithic is well known for the Únětice culture. One illustrative example is the site of Bad Lauchstädt (Saale district, Saxony-Anhalt) (Schunke 2017a), which represents a farmstead, the most common Únětice settlement type. In an area of about 1ha two houses and domestic pits surrounded a featureless area in the west, north and east, possibly a court- or farmyard that in the south was delimited by a group of flat graves. Near Salzmünde (Saale district, Saxony-Anhalt) a larger settlement comprised three separated house locations representing farmsteads (Duchnewski *et al.* forthcoming). The first location, with three longhouses representing three consecutive phases, was located near a depression that can be interpreted as a working area for the slaughtering of animals, and to which a walkway lead, by-passing six graves, from one of the houses. The second area is marked by one house, some pits and a group of five graves discovered about 100 m to the north. The third was located about 400 m to the east of the first and is represented by five longhouses whose exact chronology remains unclear and of which at least two must have been successive. There are also some pits and four flat graves. These three farmsteads, possibly consisting of only one house at a time, represent individual economic units that together constituted a larger settlement entity or hamlet. According to typology and radiocarbon dating, the farmsteads, and the hamlet, existed in the 22nd to the 20th century cal BC (Duchnewski *et al.* forthcoming, 103–4, 110–2).

While the situation discovered at Salzmünde is reminiscent of the structure of the Bell Beaker settlement site at Schleenhain, with the Early Bronze Age something unknown before (apart from the Early and Middle Neolithic) can be observed: the agglomeration of more than only a few buildings at one place. The largest settlement site of this kind was excavated near Zwenkau (Leipzig, Saxony), where 38 long houses, some pits and a minimum of four wells were found within an area of about 50 hectares (Stäuble 1997; Huth & Stäuble 1998, 188–97). While in the southern sectors five farmstead-like venues comprising one to four longhouses, some of them superimposed, were detected *c.* 200–400 m from each other (a situation comparable to Salzmünde), in the north there was an agglomeration of about 25 long houses, again some overlapping. At least three main settlement phases can be differentiated based on the overlapping floor plans and the chronology of the finds (Stäuble 1997, 134; Schunke 2009, 276) and we might assume that several buildings are contemporary and perhaps constituted a village-like settlement.

The village-like hypothesis is also plausible for an Early Bronze Age settlement adjacent to circular sanctuary of Pömmelte (Salzland district, Saxony-Anhalt) (Spatzier 2017). About 20 longhouses and several pits were discovered and distributed along a *c.* 300 m long stretch extending from south to west of the enclosure (Spatzier 2017, 52–58; D. Jurkenas & A. Spatzier pers. comm.). Excavations have not yet reached the limits of this settlement. Radiocarbon dates for three houses indicate a range of 2330–1960 cal BC (95% probability; Spatzier 2017, 246, table A69), but their exact chronology still has to be established and overlapping or almost contiguous houses indicate successive building phases.

Summary and conclusion

The profound social changes that began around 3000 BC are reflected in a radical transformation of the character of the settlement system in Central Germany. With the appearance of the Globular Amphora culture, a nomadic or semi-nomadic economy was introduced that left almost no traces of domestic structures. The traditional view that this mobile lifestyle became widespread in the Corded Ware culture is challenged by the evidence of permanent settlement sites with large post-built houses discovered over the last 15 years. It now seems likely either that groups with a more sedentary lifestyle coexisted alongside the mobile groups, or that after an initial phase that began with or was triggered by migration into Central Europe in the early 3rd millennium BC (Haak *et al.* 2015; Allentoft *et al.* 2015), a lifestyle with permanent settlements was adopted by at least some social groups. That the so-called *Ofengruben* (oven pits) – commonly regarded as Corded Ware settlement features – occur without other settlement structures and are radiocarbon dated to between 3000–2550 BC (Becker *et al.* 2015) may support the latter hypothesis. Alternatively, the outstanding structure and size of the 'Gimritz' type houses may suggest that they did not serve domestic but rather communal or even ceremonial purposes and is not settlement evidence *sensu stricto*. Future research and increased absolute dating will hopefully clarify this situation.

The social changes in the 3rd millennium BC are also reflected by the construction and, particularly, the size of the buildings. The Schönfeld culture houses are rather small (Fig. 13.10.2 & 3) and may confirm that this extraordinary regional group continued some Late Neolithic traditions from the preceding Bernburg culture. The building from Randau (Fig. 13.10,1) appears exceptionally large but may be a composite of two Schönfeld 'standard-size' houses of about 10 × 5 m (see above). Constructions of the Corded Ware culture are dramatically different with considerably larger floor areas covering roughly about 90–170m^2. The common Corded Ware building was the 'Gimritz' type house (trapezoidal, aligned NW–SE, four-aisled middle section, a version perhaps completely three-aisled; Fig. 13.10,4&5). This trend continues with the Bell Beaker culture 'Klobikau' type houses (trapezoidal, aligned SE–NW, two-aisled; Fig. 13.10,6–8) with floor spaces of roughly 60–150 m^2, but again with a different construction technique. The Bell Beaker houses are more slender and have opposing alignments compared to Corded Ware houses, reflecting the same duality in the funerary customs of these two cultures. Being generally slender, it might be no coincidence that Klobikau house 1 is the first example of a longhouse to be found after the Middle Neolithic in Central Germany.

Regarding the approximate layout and the orientation, the Bell Beaker buildings ('Klobikau' type; Fig. 13.10,6–8) are generally similar to those of the Únětice culture ('Zwenkau' type; Fig. 13.11): two-aisled, aligned E–W to SE–NW, seemingly 'open' gable walls facing eastwards. This suggests that the Early Bronze Age building tradition was based on its Bell Beaker predecessor. A certain continuity can also be supposed regarding the structure of the settlements. After the reappearance of a settlement system with isolated houses in the Corded Ware culture, there are possible indications of small residential groups, or hamlets, alongside farmsteads in the Bell Beaker culture. With the Early Bronze Age this trend perhaps led to the emergence of larger, village-like settlement structures with several houses existing at the same time. This pattern of growing settlements is paralleled with the increased size of the Únětice buildings that normally covered 80–250 m^2 and even up to 500 m^2. This continuity can also be seen in other cultural elements such as ceramic production, general burial customs or the significance of golden hair rings as status symbols. The Bell Beaker – Únětice transition is, so far, best reflected at the sites of Zwenkau and Pömmelte.

In conclusion, the changes in settlement structure correlate with the profound social changes characterising the transition from the Late Neolithic to the Final Neolithic and to the Early Bronze Age. Large communal structures typical for the Late Neolithic, such as earthworks or megalithic and sub-megalithic funerary monuments, disappeared in the early 3rd millennium. With the beginning of the Final Neolithic, and the appearance of Corded Ware, there was a change from a society focussed on community towards one that emphasised the individual. This heralded the emergence of early elites, namely warrior heroes, within the flat hierarchy of the segmentary societies of the Final Neolithic. Despite the growing number of houses, this social stratification is not (yet?) evident in settlement contexts. However, the Bell Beaker – Únětice continuity regarding house construction, the increasing size of the houses and perhaps of the settlements is one more piece of evidence that suggests that the Final Neolithic and particularly the Bell Beaker culture was the foundation for the development of the marked hierarchies and princely graves of the Únětice culture at the beginning of the 2nd millennium BC.

References

Allentoft, M.E., Sikora, M., Sjogren, K.-G., Rasmussen, S., Rasmussen, M., Stenderup, J., Damgaard, P.B., Schroeder, H., Ahlstrom, T., Vinner, L., Malaspinas, A.-S., Margaryan, A., Higham, T., Chivall, D., Lynnerup, N., Harvig, L., Baron, J., Casa, P.D., Dabrowski, P., Duffy, P.R., Ebel, A.V., Epimakhov, A., Frei, K., Furmanek, M., Gralak, T., Gromov, A., Gronkiewicz, S., Grupe, G., Hajdu, T., Jarysz, R., Khartanovich, V., Khokhlov, A., Kiss, V., Kolar, J., Kriiska, A., Lasak, I., Longhi, C., McGlynn, G., Merkevicius, A., Merkyte, I., Metspalu, M., Mkrtchyan, R., Moiseyev, V., Paja, L., Palfi, G., Pokutta, D., Pospieszny, L., Price, T.D., Saag, L., Sablin, M., Shishlina, N., Smrcka, V., Soenov, V.I., Szeverenyi, V., Toth, G., Trifanova, S.V., Varul, L., Vicze, M., Yepiskoposyan, L., Zhitenev, V., Orlando, L., Sicheritz-Ponten, T., Brunak, S., Nielsen, R., Kristiansen, K. & Willerslev, E. 2015. Population genomics of Bronze Age Eurasia. *Nature* 522, 167–72

Balfanz, K., Fröhlich, M. & Schunke, T. 2015. Ein Siedlungsareal der Glockenbecherkultur mit Hausgrundrissen bei Klobikau, Sachsen-Anhalt, Deutschland. In Meller *et al.* (eds), 2015, 747–64

Becker, M., Fröhlich, M., Balfanz, K., Kromer, B. & Friedrich, R. 2015. Das 3. Jt. v.Chr. zwischen Saale und Unstrut – Kulturelle Veränderungen im Spiegel der Radiokohlenstoffdatierung. In Meller *et al.* (eds), 2015, 715–46

Behrens, H. & Schröter, E. 1980. *Siedlungen und Gräber der Trichterbecherkultur und Schnurkeramik bei Halle (Saale).* Berlin: Verlag der Wissenschaften (Veröffentlichungen des Landesmuseum für Vorgeschichte Halle 34)

Beier, H.-J. 1988. *Die Kugelamphorenkultur im Mittelelbe-Saale-Gebiet und in der Altmark.* Berlin: Verlag der Wissenschaften (Veröffentlichungen des Landesmuseums für Vorgeschichte Halle 41)

Beran, J. 1995. Zur chronologischen Gliederung schnurkeramischer Siedlungsfunde. In Beier, H.-J. & Beran, J. (eds), *Selecta Praehistorica. Festschrift J. Preuss*, 83–96. Wilkau-Haßlau: Beier & Beran (Beiträge zur Ur- und Frühgeschichte Mitteleuropa 7)

Beran, J. 2008. Untersuchungen zur spät- und endneolithischen Besiedlungsstruktur in der Niederlausitz. Ausgrabungen im Braunkohlentagebau Jänschwalde. In Dörfler, W. & Müller, J. (eds), *Umwelt-Wirtschaft-Siedlungen im dritten vorchristlichen Jahrtausend Mitteleuropas und Südskandinaviens. Internationale Tagung Kiel 4–6 November 2005*, 183–209. Neumünster: Wachholtz (Offa-Bücher 84)

Beran, J. 2012. Siedlungen in der Jungsteinzeit. In Schopper, F. & Dähnert, D. (eds), *Archäologie in der Niederlausitz*, 94–97. Cottbus: Branderburgisches Landesamt für Denkmalpflege und Archäologisches Landesmuseum

Beran, J. 2016. Empires and Revolutions in the 3rd Millennium: Supra-Regional Rule and Extra Economic Compulsion as a Causative Background of Widespread Cultural Phenomena. In Furholt, M, Großmann, R. & Szmyt, M. (eds), *Transitional Landscapes? The 3rd Millennium BC in Europe. Proceedings of the International Workshop 'Socio-Environmental Dynamics over the Last 12,000 Years: The Creation of Landscapes III (15th–18th April 2013)' in Kiel. Human Development in Landscapes 9*, 101–10. Rahden/Westfalen: Marie Leidorf (Universitätsforschungen zur Prähistorischen Archäologie)

Brauer, J. 2005. Ein Hausgrundriss der frühbronzezeitlichen Aunjetitzer Kultur. In Meller, H. (ed.), *QuerSchnitt. Ausgrabungen an der B 6n, Benzingerode-Heimburg*, 94–100. Halle/Saale: Landesamt für Denkmalpflege und Archäologie Sachsen-Anhalt (Archäologie in Sachsen-Anhalt, Sonderband 2)

Campen, I. 1999. Noch ein Brunnen. Der erste schnurkeramische Siedlungsnachweis. *Archäologie aktuell im Freistaat Sachsen* 5/1997, 112–115

Conrad, M. 2010. Glockenbecherkultur. In Heynowski, R. & Reiß, R. (eds), *Atlas zur Geschichte und Landeskunde Sachsen. Beiheft zur Karte B I 1.1.–1.5. Ur- und Frühgeschichte Sachsens*, 69–73. Leipzig-Dresden: Sächsische Akademie der Wissenschaften zu Leipzig und Staatsbetrieb Geobasisinformation und Vermessung Sachsen

Conrad, M., Tinapp, C. & Schneider, B. 2014a. Siedlungsarchäologische Befunde im Haselbachtal. Die Grabungen an der S 31 bei Mügeln: PAK-01, MUE-08, MUE-09. *Ausgrabungen in Sachsen* 4, 103–14

Conrad, S., Conrad, M. & Ender, W. 2014b. Das polykulturelle Siedlungs- und Bestattungsareal östlich der Döllnitz bei Schweta. *Ausgrabungen in Sachsen* 4, 121–31

Conrad, S., Conrad, M., Ender, W., Tinapp, C. & Herbig, C. 2016. Die vor- und frühgeschichtliche Besiedlung im Döllnitztal bei Göttwitz (Stadt Grimma, Lkr. Leipzig). *Ausgrabungen in Sachsen* 5, 182–200

Conrad, M., Schmalfuß, G. & Richter, K.-H. 2017. Vorbericht über ein endneolithisches Siedlungsareal im Tagebau Vereinigtes Schleenhain (SH 22). *Archæo* 14, 42–48

Dalidowski, M., Heine, Y. & Homann, A. 2016. Siedlungsspuren endneolithischer Kulturen. *Ausgrabungen in Sachsen* 5, 87–94

Dirks, U. 2000. *Die Bernburger Kultur in Niedersachsen.* Rahden/Westfalen: Marie Leidorf (Beiträge zur Archäologie in Niedersachsen 1)

Duchnewski, B., Moser, A., Schunke, T. & Viol, P. forthcoming. Frühbronzezeitliche Hausgrundrisse und Siedlungsnachweise bei Schiepzig und Salzmünde, Lkr. Saalekreis. In Meller, H. & Friederich, S. (eds), *Ein Ort – zwei Kulturen. Die Ausgrabungen im Vorfeld des Baus der A 143 bei Salzmünde, Saalekreis.* Halle/Saale: Landesamt für Denkmalpflege und Archäologie Sachsen-Anhalt (Archäologie in Sachsen-Anhalt, Sonderband 21/II)

Engel, C. 1930. *Bilder aus der Vorzeit an der mittleren Elbe.* Burg: Hopfer

Evers, M. 2013. *Die frühbronzezeitliche Besiedlung der Makroregion um Nebra.* Dissertation, Martin-Luther-Universität Halle-Wittenberg

Haak, W., Lazaridis, I., Patterson, N., Rohland, N., Mallick, S., Llamas, B., Brandt, G., Nordenfelt, S., Harney, E., Stewardson, K., Fu, Q., Mittnik, A., Banffy, E., Economou, C., Francken, M., Friederich, S., Pena, R.G., Hallgren, F., Khartanovich, V., Khokhlov, A., Kunst, M., Kuznetsov, P., Meller, H., Mochalov, O., Moiseyev, V., Nicklisch, N., Pichler, S.L., Risch, R., Rojo Guerra, M.A., Roth, C., Szecsenyi-Nagy, A., Wahl, J., Meyer, M., Krause, J., Brown, D., Anthony, D., Cooper, A., Alt, K.W. & Reich, D. 2015. Massive migration from the steppe was a source for Indo-European languages in Europe. *Nature*, advance online publication. doi: 10.1038/nature14317. http://www.nature.com/nature/journal/vaop/ncurrent/abs/nature14317.html#supplementary-information

Hansen, D. 2010. *Die frühbronzezeitlichen Haus- und Brunnenbefunde von Zwenkau-West im regionalen und überregionalen Vergleich.* Magisterarbeit, Friedrich-Schiller-Univeristät Jena

Hille, A. 2012. *Die Glockenbecherkultur in Mitteldeutschland.* Halle/Saale: Veröffentlichungen des Landesamtes für Denkmalpflege und Archäologie Sachsen-Anhalt 66

Höckner, H. 1957. Ausgrabung von schnurkeramischen Grabhügeln und Siedelplätzen im Luckaer Forst, Kreis Altenburg. *Arbeits- und Forschberichte zur sächsischen Bodendenkmalpflege* 6, 58–181

Hoffmann, W. & Schmidt, B. 1961. Wichtige Fundmeldungen und Neuerwerbungen des Jahres 1958. *Jahresschrift für mitteldeutsche Vorgeschichte* 45, 278–98

Hubensack, V. 2016. Die Kugelamphorenkultur in Eula. *Ausgrabungen in Sachsen* 5, 78–86

Huth, C. & Stäuble, H. 1998. Ländliche Siedlungen der Bronzezeit und älteren Eisenzeit. Ein Zwischenbericht aus Zwenkau. In Küster, H., Lang, A. & Schauer, P. (eds), *Archäologische Forschungen in urgeschichtlichen Siedlungslandschaften. Festschrift G. Kossack*, 185–230. Bonn: Habelt.

Jarecki, H. 2008. Endlich: eine schnurkeramische Siedlung. *Archäologie in Deutschland,* 2008, 51

Kegler, J.F. 2012. Haus und Hof – Schnurkeramische und bronzezeitliche Häuser oberhalb der Unstrut. In Meller, H. (ed.), *Neue Gleise auf alten Wegen I. Wennungen und Kalzendorf*, 99–105. Halle/Saale: Landesamt für Denkmalpflege und Archäologie Sachsen-Anhalt (Archäologie in Sachsen-Anhalt, Sonderband 19)

Kleinecke, J. 2018. Nachweise der Glockenbecherkultur in der vorgeschichtlichen Siedlungslandschaft bei Gatersleben. In Meller, H., Friederich, S. & Weber, T. (eds), *Archäologie in Gatersleben. Ackerbau über Jahrtausende hinweg* 30, 125–33. Halle/Saale: Landesamt für Denkmalpflege und Archäologie Sachsen-Anhalt (Archäologie in Sachsen-Anhalt, Sonderband 30)

Krause, P. & Gahrau-Rothert, L. 1941. Ein jungsteinzeitliches Haus der Schönfelder Gruppe von Brandenburg (Havel)-Neuendorf. *Nachrichtenblatt für Deutsche Vorzeit* 17, 193–7

Krautwurst, R. 2002. Zur Bedeutung der schnurkeramischen Wellenleistenkeramik. In Müller, J. (ed.) *Vom Endneolithikum zur Frühbronzezeit: Muster sozialen Wandels? (Tagung Bamberg 14–16 Juni 2001)*, 89–96. Bonn: Habelt Universitätsforschungen zur Prähistorsichen Archäologie 90

Kretschmer, S., Viol, P., Stäuble, H., Herbig, C., Muigg, B., Tegel, W. & Tinapp, C. 2016. Der Fundplatz Droßdorf im Tagebaufeld Peres (Lkr. Leipzig). *Ausgrabungen in Sachsen* 5, 30–57

Küßner, M. 2015. Leubingen und Dermsdorf, Lkr. Sömerda – 'Fürstengrab', Großbau und Schatzdepot der frühen Bronzezeit. In Spazier, I. & Grasselt, T. (eds), *Erfurt und Umgebung*, 194–7. Langenweißbach: Beier & Beran (Archäologische Denkmale in Thüringen 3)

Leinthaler, B., Bogen, C. & Döhle, H.-J. 2006. Spätneolithische Befunde von Alberstedt. In H. Meller (ed.), *Archäologie auf der Überholspur: Ausgrabungen an der A 38*, 83–97. Halle/Saale: Landesamt für Denkmalpflege und Archäologie Sachsen-Anhalt (Archäologie in Sachsen-Anhalt, Sonderband 5)

Lies, H. 1942. Ausgrabung eines Wohnhauses der jungsteinzeitlichen Schönfelder Gruppe in Randau bei Magdeburg. *Nachrichtenblatt für Deutsche Vorzeit* 18, 12–15

Lies, H. 1947. Beiträge zu jungsteinzeitlichen Besiedlungsgeschichte der Binnendünen im Elbgebiet bei Magdeburg. *Mitteilungen aus dem Museum für Naturkunde und Vorgeschichte Magdeburg*, 1947, 41–7

Lüning, J. 1996. Erneute Gedanken zur Benennung der neolithischen Perioden. *Germania* 74, 233–7

Lüning, J. 1999. Ein Grubenhaus der Bernburger Kultur aus Schweinfeld, Landkreis Schweinfurt. In Herrmann, F.-R. (ed), *Festschrift für Günter Smolla II*, 415–69. Wiesbaden: Landesamt für Denkmalpflege Hessen (Materialien zur Vor- und Frühgeschichte von Hessen 8).

Matthias, W. 1974. *Kataloge zur mitteldeutschen Schnurkeramik. Teil IV: Südharz-Unstrut-Gebiet*. Berlin Verlag der Wissenschaften (Veröffentlichungen des Landesmuseums für Vorgeschichte Halle 28).

Matthias, W. 1982. *Kataloge zur mitteldeutschen Schnurkeramik. Teil V: Mittleres Saalegebiet*. Berlin Verlag der Wissenschaften (Veröffentlichungen des Landesmuseums für Vorgeschichte Halle 35).

Matthias, W. 1987. *Kataloge zur mitteldeutschen Schnurkeramik. Teil VI: Restgebiete und Nachträge*. Berlin Verlag der Wissenschaften (Veröffentlichungen des Landesmuseums für Vorgeschichte Halle 40).

Meller, H., Arz, H. W., Jung, R. & Risch, R. (eds), 2015. *2200 BC – Ein Klimasturz als Ursache für den Zerfall der Alten Welt? /. Mitteldeutscher Archäologentag vom 23. bis 26. Oktober 2014 in Halle (Saale)*. Tagungen des Landesmuseum für Vorgeschichte 12/II. Halle/Saale: Landesamt für Denkmalpflege und Archäologie Sachsen-Anhalt

Meyer, C., Brandt, G., Haak, W., Ganslmeier, R.A., Meller, H. & Alt, K.W. 2009. The Eulau eulogy: Bioarchaeological interpretation of lethal violence in Corded Ware multiple burials from Saxony-Anhalt, Germany. *Journal of Anthropological Archaeology* 28, 412–23

Muhl, A., Meller, H. & Heckenhahn, K. 2010. *Tatort Eulau. Ein 4500 Jahre altes Verbrechen*. Stuttgart: Theiss

Müller, D.W. 1990. Befestigte Siedlungen der Bernburger Kultur – Typen und Verbreitung. *Jahresschrift für mitteldeutsche Vorgeschichte* 73, 271–86

Müller, U. 2006. Die Kinder von Rotenschirmbach. In Meller, H. (ed.), *Archäologie auf der Überholspur: Ausgrabungen an der A 38*, 98–107. Halle/Saale: Landesamt für Denkmalpflege und Archäologie Sachsen-Anhalt (Archäologie in Sachsen-Anhalt, Sonderband 5)

Neumann, G. 1929. Die Gliederung der Glockenbecherkultur in Mitteldeutschland. *Prähistorische Zeitschrift* 20, 3–69

Peters, E. 2006. Ein Brunnen der Schnurkeramik mit Holzeinbau. In Meller. H. (ed.), *Archäologie XXL. Archäologie an der B6n im Landkreis Quedlinburg*, 89–92. Halle/Saale: Landesamt für Denkmalpflege und Archäologie Sachsen-Anhalt (Archäologie in Sachsen-Anhalt, Sonderband 4)

Queck, T. 2013. Großlöbichau, Saale-Holzland-Kreis – ein mehrperiodiger Fundplatz. *Neue Ausgrabungen und Funde in Thüringen* 7, 83–96

Schlette, F. 1958. *Die ältesten Haus- und Siedlungsformen des Menschen auf Grund des steinzeitlichen Fundmaterials Europas und ethnologischer Vergleiche*. Berlin Verlag der Wissenschaften (Ethnografisch-archäologische Forschungen 5)

Schlette, F. 1969. Das Siedlungswesen der Becherkulturen. In Behrens, H. & Schlette, F. (eds), *Die neolithischen Becherkulturen im Gebiet der DDR und ihre europäischen Beziehungen*, 155–68. Berlin Verlag der Wissenschaften (Veröffentlichungen des Landesmuseum für Vorgeschichte Halle 24)

Schmalfuß, G. & Tolksdorf, J.F. 2016. Ein mehrphasiges Siedlungsareal mit einem Hausgrundriss und Brunnenkonstruktionen vom Endneolithikum bis zum Mittelalter bei Löbnitz-Roitzschjora, Lkr. Nordsachsen. *Ausgrabungen in Sachsen* 5, 126–49

Schunke, T. 2009. Die frühbronzezeitliche Siedlung Zwenkau und ihre wirtschaftliche Basis. In Bartelheim, M. & Stäuble, H. (eds), *Die wirtschaftlichen Grundlagen der Bronzezeit Europas. The Economic Foundations of the European Bronze Age*, 273–319. Rahden/Westfalen: Marie Leidorf (Forschungen zur Archäometrie und Altertumswissenschaft 4)

Schunke, T. 2017a. Der Alltag in der frühen Bronzezeit – Ein Gehöft mit Gräbergruppe und Siedlungsbestattungen bei Bad Lauchstädt, Saalekreis. In Meller, H. & Becker, M. (eds), *Neue Gleise auf alten Wegen II – Jüdendorf bis Gröbers,* 146--9. Halle/Saale: Landesamt für Denkmalpflege und Archäologie Sachsen-Anhalt (Archäologie in Sachsen-Anhalt, Sonderband 26/I)

Schunke, T. 2017b. Eine Siedlungsgrube der Glockenbecherkultur und endneolithische Gräber bei Bad Lauchstädt, Saalekreis. *Jahresschrift für mitteldeutsche Vorgeschichte* 96, 43–76

Schwarz, R. 2013. Das Mittelneolithikum in Sachsen-Anhalt – Die Kulturen und ihre Erdwerke. In Meller, H. (ed.), *3300 BC. Mysteriöse Steinzeittote und ihre Welt. Sonderausstellung vom 14.11.2013 bis 18.05.2014 im Landesmuseum für Vorgeschichte Halle*, 231–8. Halle/Saale: Nünnerich-Asmus Verlag

Spatzier, A. 2017. *Das endneolithisch-frühbronzezeitliche Rondell von Pömmelte-Zackmünde, Salzlandkreis, und das Rondell-Phänomen des 4.–1. Jt. v. Chr. in Mitteleuropa.* Halle/Saale: Landesamt für Denkmalpflege und Archäologie Sachsen-Anhalt (Forschungsberichte des Landesmuseums für Vorgeschichte Halle 10)

Spatzier, A. forthcoming. The enclosure complex Pömmelte-Schönebeck. In Meller, H. & Bertemes, F. (eds), *Der Aufbruch zu neuen Horizonten. Neue Sichtweisen über die Europäische Frühbronzezeit.* Halle/Saale: Landesamt für Denkmalpflege und Archäologie Sachsen-Anhalt (Tagungen des Landesmuseum für Vorgeschichte 19)

Stäuble, H. 1997. Die frühbronzezeitliche Siedlung in Zwenkau, Landkreis Leipziger Land. In J. J. Assendorp (ed.), *Forschungen zur bronzezeitlichen Besiedlung in Nord- und Mitteleuropa. Internationales Symposium vom 09–11. Mai 1996 in Hitzacker*, 129–48. Espelkamp: Marie Leidorf (Internationale Archäologie 38)

Umweltzentrum-Ökohof-Auterwitz-e.V. 2014. Glockenbecherzeitliche Siedlung bei Auterwitz. In Umweltzentrum Ökohof Auterwitz e. V. (ed.), *Anlage 9. Ausführliche flächenspezifische Ergebnisse der archäologischen Schadenserhebung*, 12–14. Auterwitz

von Rauchhaupt, R. & Viol, P. 2014. Hausgrundrisse der Salzmünder Kultur. In Meller, H. & Friederich, S. (eds), *Salzmünde-Schiepzig – ein Ort, zwei Kulturen. Ausgrabungen an der Westumfahrung Halle (A 143), Teil I*, 294–301. Halle/Saale: Landesamt für Denkmalpflege und Archäologie Sachsen-Anhalt (Archäologie in Sachsen-Anhalt, Sonderband 21/I)

Wehmer, M. 2016. Ein spätneolithisches Grubenhaus aus Windehausen, Lkr. Nordhausen. In Beran, J., Einicke, R., Schimpff, V., Wagner, K. & Weber, T. (eds), *Lehren – Sammeln – Publizieren. Festschrift Hans-Jürgen Beier*, 18–97. Leipzig: Universitätsverlag

Woidich, M. 2014. *Die Westliche Kugelamphorenkultur. Untersuchungen zu ihrer raum-zeitlichen Differenzierung, kulturellen und anthropologischen Identität.* Berlin Topoi – Berlin Studies of the Ancient World / Berliner Studien der Alten Welt 24

14

Bell Beaker domestic sites and houses in the Polish lands: Odra and Vistula Catchments

Janusz Czebreszuk and Marzena Szmyt

Bell Beakers on the Odra and Vistula rivers

Since the beginning of research into Bell Beakers, the Polish lands have been considered as part of their larger world. Lower Silesia was already included in the classic early work by Bosch-Gimpera (1926) and in the inter-war period, the first signs of Bell Beaker presence were recorded in Lesser Poland (Żurowski 1932). In both cases grave finds provided the evidence.

The most debated question was that of the Bell Beaker presence in the Polish Lowlands (west of the lower Vistula). Already in the 1920s and '30s, Kozłowski (1920) and Kostrzewski (1935) pointed to the presence of Bell Beakers in Kujawy and this was most strongly championed by Jażdżewski (1937). This, however, was contested by other researchers (Machnik 1979; Kamieńska & Kulczycka-Leciejewiczowa 1970) and was only revisited in the 1970s by Kośko (1979) and in the 1980s, following new discoveries of settlements with Bell Beaker traits (Kośko 1988: 161–2; Czebreszuk & Szmyt 1992; Makarowicz 1993; Czebreszuk & Makarowicz 1995; Makarowicz & Czebreszuk 1995; Czebreszuk 1996).

As far as we can tell today, the Bell Beakers appeared in the Polish lands soon after 2400 BC in two different versions and from two separate directions (Czebreszuk & Makarowicz 1995; Makarowicz 2003; Czebreszuk & Szmyt 2012; Włodarczak 2017a): they came to the uplands from the south and south-west (Moravia, Bohemia) and migrated into the lowlands from the west (Jutland, Mecklenburg).

In the uplands (western part of Lesser Poland, Upper and Lower Silesia), the migration from the south resulted in the formation of a local branch of the Bell Beaker eastern group. Its remains include small cemeteries and single graves with typical grave goods (Budziszewski & Włodarczak 2010). The Bell Beakers were a major accelerator of cultural changes, leading about 2200 BC to the rise of the first upland signs of the Early Bronze Age (Kadrow 1995; 2001; Włodarczak 2017b).

In the lowlands (western Pomerania and Kujawy, Mazurian Lakeland), Bell Beakers emerged in the milieu of the late Corded Ware Culture and their presence is documented chiefly from settlement sites (Fig. 14.1). They served to distinguish a Bell Beaker northern group (Czebreszuk 2002) in which the so-called Iwno Culture formed – the principal

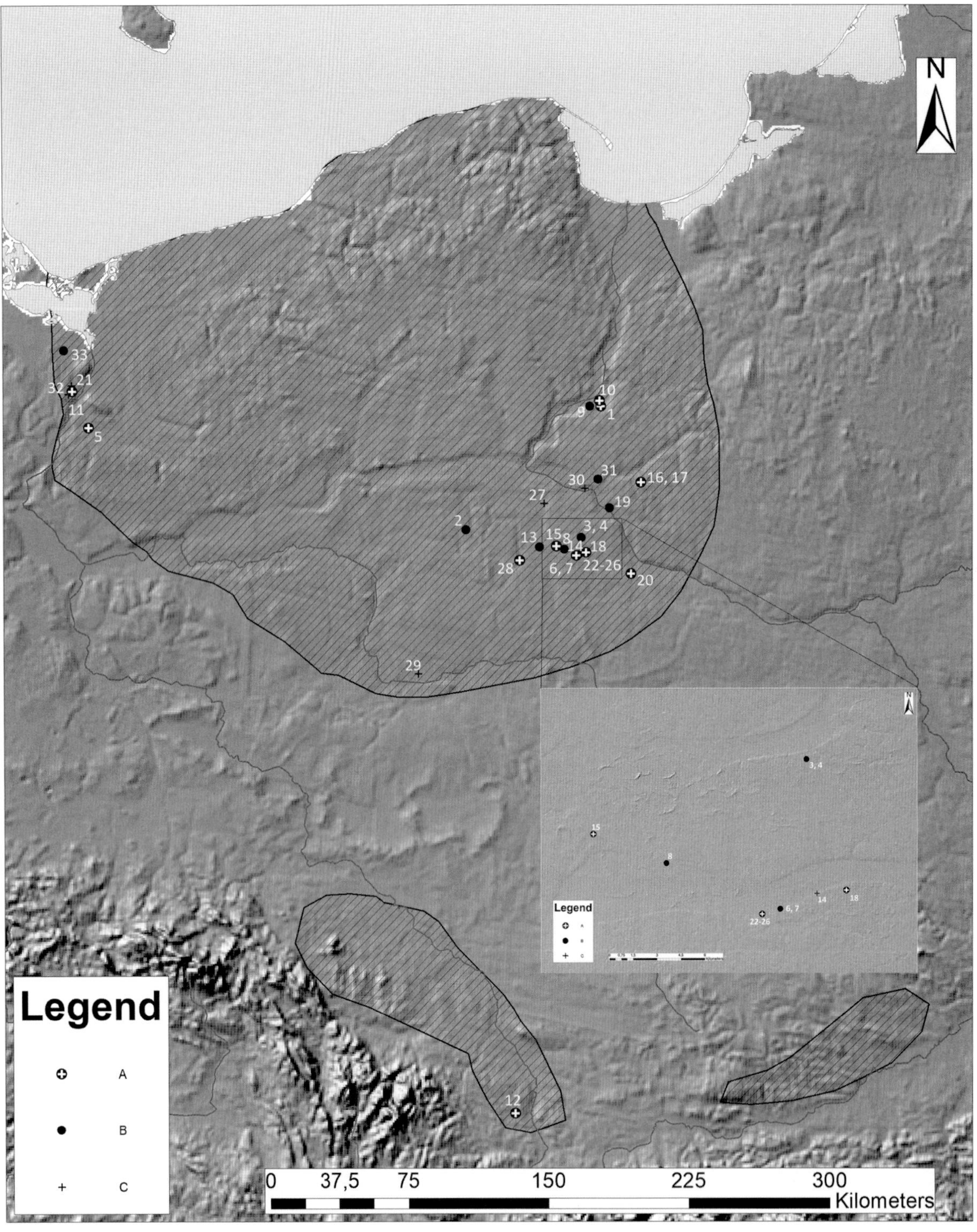

Figure 14.1: Location of Bell Beakers settlement sites in Polish lands. Prep. by J. Czebreszuk, M. Ławniczak. Key: A – sites excavated, ground features revealed; B – sites excavated, ground features not revealed; C – sites investigated without excavation; 1 – Biały Bór 17; 2 – Bożejewice 22; 3 – Chlewiska 56; 4 – Chlewiska 70; 5 – Chwarstnica 3; 6 – Dęby 29; 7 – Dęby 29A; 8 – Dziewa 14; 9 – Gogolin 7; 10 – Grudziądz-Mniszek 3; 11 – Karwowo 25; 12 – Kornice 33; 13 – Krusza Zamkowa 3; 14 – Krzywosądz 3; 15 – Łąkocin 1; 16 – Macikowo 3; 17 – Macikowo 9; 18 – Narkowo 16; 19 – Osiek nad Wisłą 8; 20 – Potok 1; 21 – Przylep 5; 22 – Smarglin 22; 23 – Smarglin 39; 24 – Smarglin 49; 25 – Smarglin 51; 26 – Smarglin 53; 27 – Stara Wieś 9A; 28 – Strzelce-Krzyżanna 40; 29 – Sulęcinek; 30 – Toruń 243; 31 – Toruń-Grębocin III; 32 – Warzymice 2; 33 – Zalesie 2; administration units: 1–4, 6–10, 13–20, 22–28, 30–31 – Kujawy-Pomerania voivodeship; 5, 11, 21, 32–33 – West Pomerania voivodeship; 12 – Silesia voivodeship; 29 – Greater Poland voivodeship

expression of the Early Bronze Age in the Polish lowlands (Czebreszuk 2001). Recent field research has witnessed the emergence of spectacular pieces of evidence, suggesting the existence of a vast zone of Bell Beaker cultural impact, covering north-eastern Poland (Manasterski 2009; Wawrusiewicz, *et al.* 2015) and Belarus (Czebreszuk & Krywaltsewitsch 2003).

The major difference between the Bell Beakers in the south and north of Poland concerns the duration of the tradition. In Silesia and Lesser Poland, Bell Beakers are known chiefly from graves and the phenomenon is characterised by its brevity (Lesser Poland: *c.* 2400–2250 BC; Budziszewski & Włodarczak 2010), soon to be replaced by the Únětice Culture in Silesia and the Mierzanowice Culture in Małopolska. In contrast, in the lowlands, Bell Beakers are part of a long sequence of cultural transformations, encompassing the Corded Ware Culture, Bell Beakers/Iwno Culture and Trzciniec Culture (Czebreszuk 1996; 2001; Makarowicz 1998; 2010) and their chronology is different covering the period 2400–1900 BC (Czebreszuk 2001). When describing the transformation sequence, use was made of the concepts of Corded Ware and Bell Beaker 'cultural packages' (Czebreszuk 2001).

The 'Corded Ware' package is known chiefly from graves although its individual elements are also sporadically found in ephemeral settlements (campsites). It is composed of a clay vessel (beaker or a functionally corresponding form), flint shaft-hole axe, flint knife and archer's flint equipment (such as projectile points). Hence, these are objects to drink from (beakers) and implements needed in fighting or hunting (shaft-hole axe, knife, bow). Importantly, not all graves featured the full set of artefacts and discoveries have been made of incomplete versions containing a vessel only, a vessel and a shaft-hole axe, a vessel and a knife, or a vessel and archery equipment.

The elements of the 'Bell Beaker' package, in turn, are recorded mainly in settlement material, less often in grave assemblages. These are above all ceramic vessels, indicating connections, in terms of form and ornaments, to Bell Beaker patterns. Among them, the primary position is held by the Bell Beaker with zone and zone-metopic decoration made using toothed combs (Smarglin 53, Fig. 14.2 & 3; Narkowo 16, Fig. 14.4) or incision (Dęby 29A, Fig. 14.5). Less frequent artefacts include stone wristguards (Czebreszuk 2000) and flint daggers (Czebreszuk & Kozłowska-Skoczka 2008). On the south-western Baltic coast, such objects are particularly strongly connected to the Bell Beaker tradition.

Importantly, both packages supplemented their respective substrata. The Bell Beakers did not supplant older Corded Ware Culture elements but appeared against this background (Czebreszuk 2003). In turn, Trzciniec cultural groups, later settling in Kujawy, are a techno-stylistic continuation of the Bell Beaker group known as the Iwno Culture. A detailed periodisation and chronological scheme was developed for Kujawy, where Bell Beaker traits are identified between 2400–1900 BC and fit into the sequence of regional changes of pottery technology and style (Czebreszuk 1996; Czebreszuk *et al.* 2000) namely, Corded Ware culture 4 – Bell Beakers/Iwno 1 – Bell Beakers/Iwno 2 – Bell Beakers/Iwno 3/ Trzciniec 1 – Trzciniec 2.

These phases can be described as follows (Czebreszuk 1996):

- *Bell Beakers/Iwno 1*: in the context of traits known from CWC 4, there appeared pottery decorated with zone motifs made with cord impressions or using toothed comb. There is also relief decoration such as cordons most often notched or bearing finger impressions, as well as appliqué bosses.
- *Bell Beakers/Iwno 2*: absence of cord ornaments, but toothed comb continued to be used, although incision later came to the fore. Zoned decoration continued to dominate and only in this phase did metopic motifs occur. Vessel morphology saw, for the first time, tulip-shaped flared lips.
- *Bell Beakers/Iwno 3*: ornaments were limited to incised motifs (several lines on the upper portion of the belly) and cordons. Vase-like vessels with an S-shaped profile dominated followed by slimmer pots also with an S-shaped profile and cordons on the shoulder.

Native cultures before the arrival of Bell Beakers

When the Bell Beakers were arriving in the early second half of the 3rd millennium BC, native

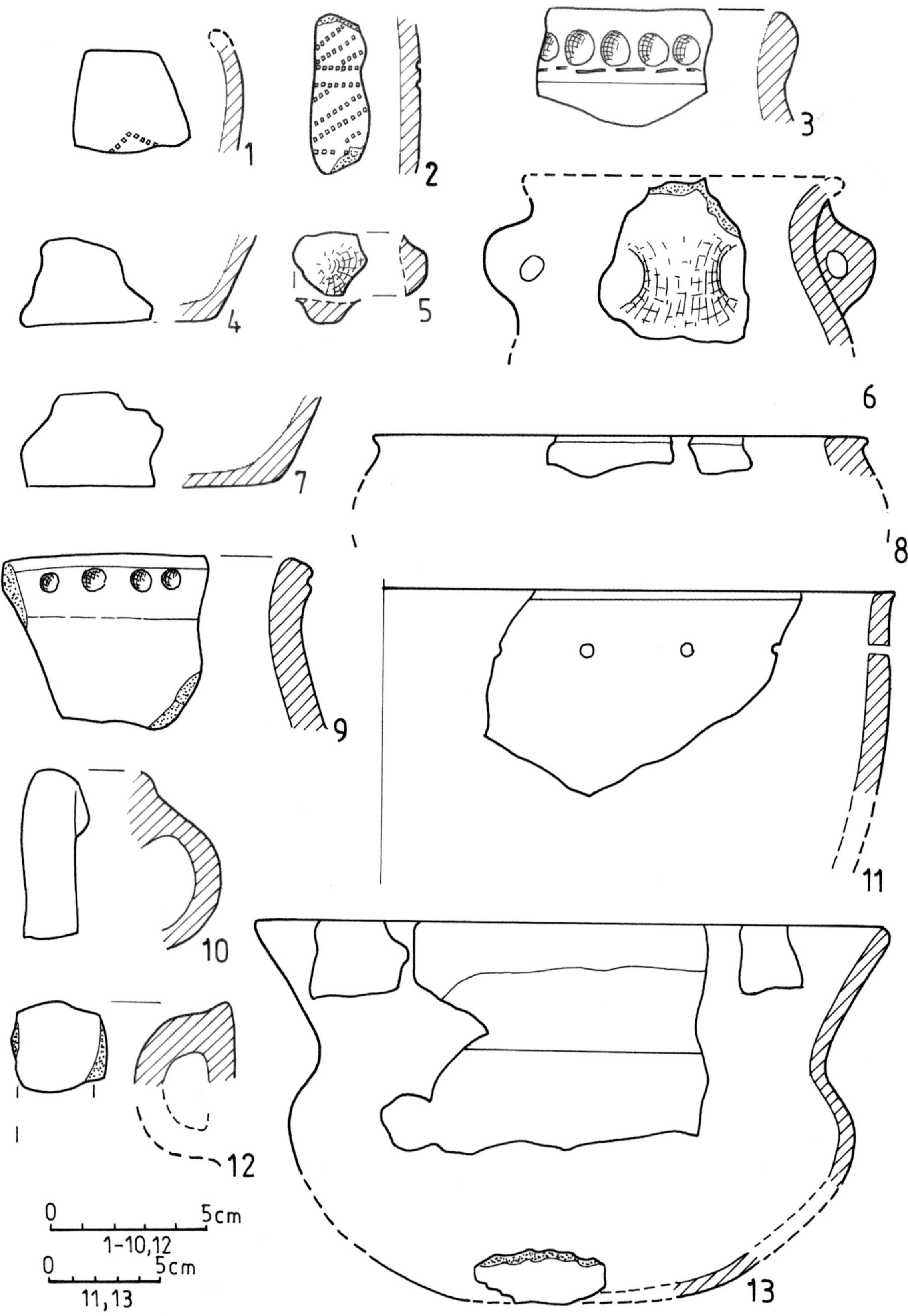

Figure 14.2: Smarglin, site 53, Kujawy-Pomerania voivodeship. Selected pottery (after Makarowicz 1993)

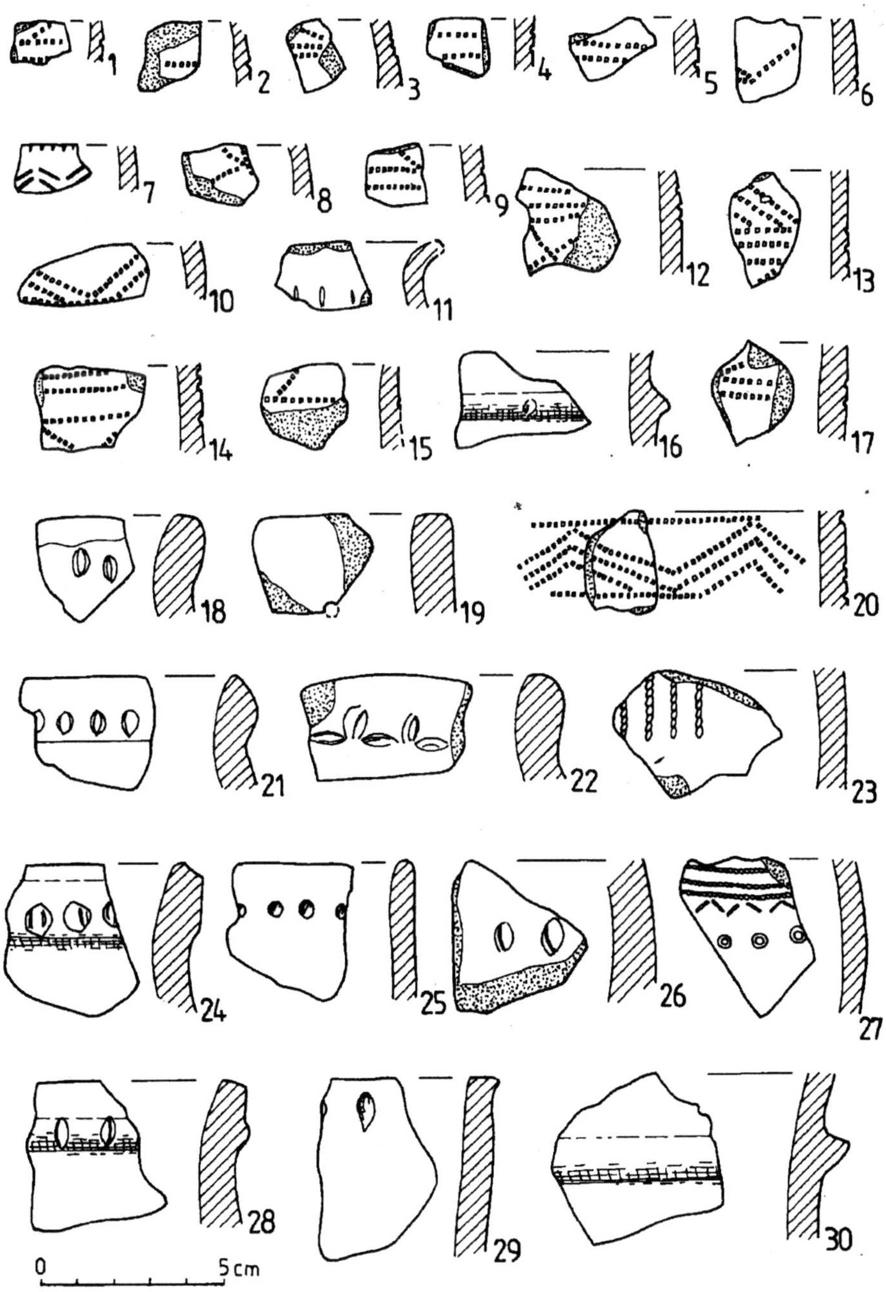

Figure 14.3: Smarglin, site 53, Kujawy-Pomerania voivodeship. Selected pottery (after Makarowicz 1993)

communities represented various Late and Final Neolithic traditions (Włodarczak 2017a). The most important were the Corded Ware Culture (classic and late phases), the Globular Amphora Culture (decline of the classic horizon and the late horizon) and Subneolithic groups such as the Neman Culture. In some regions, the youngest Funnel Beaker Culture communities could have still survived. Out of the named communities, most subsisted on various types of agriculture, involving either a balance between crop cultivation and animal raising (Funnel Beaker Culture), predominance of animal raising (Globular Amphora Culture) or the overwhelming reliance on animal husbandry (Corded Ware Culture). A different view is taken of the Subneolithic and the name refers to groups of hunter-gatherers, existing on the fringes of the agricultural world.

The Corded Ware Culture spread across the entire area under discussion on both uplands and lowlands from *c.* 2900–2800

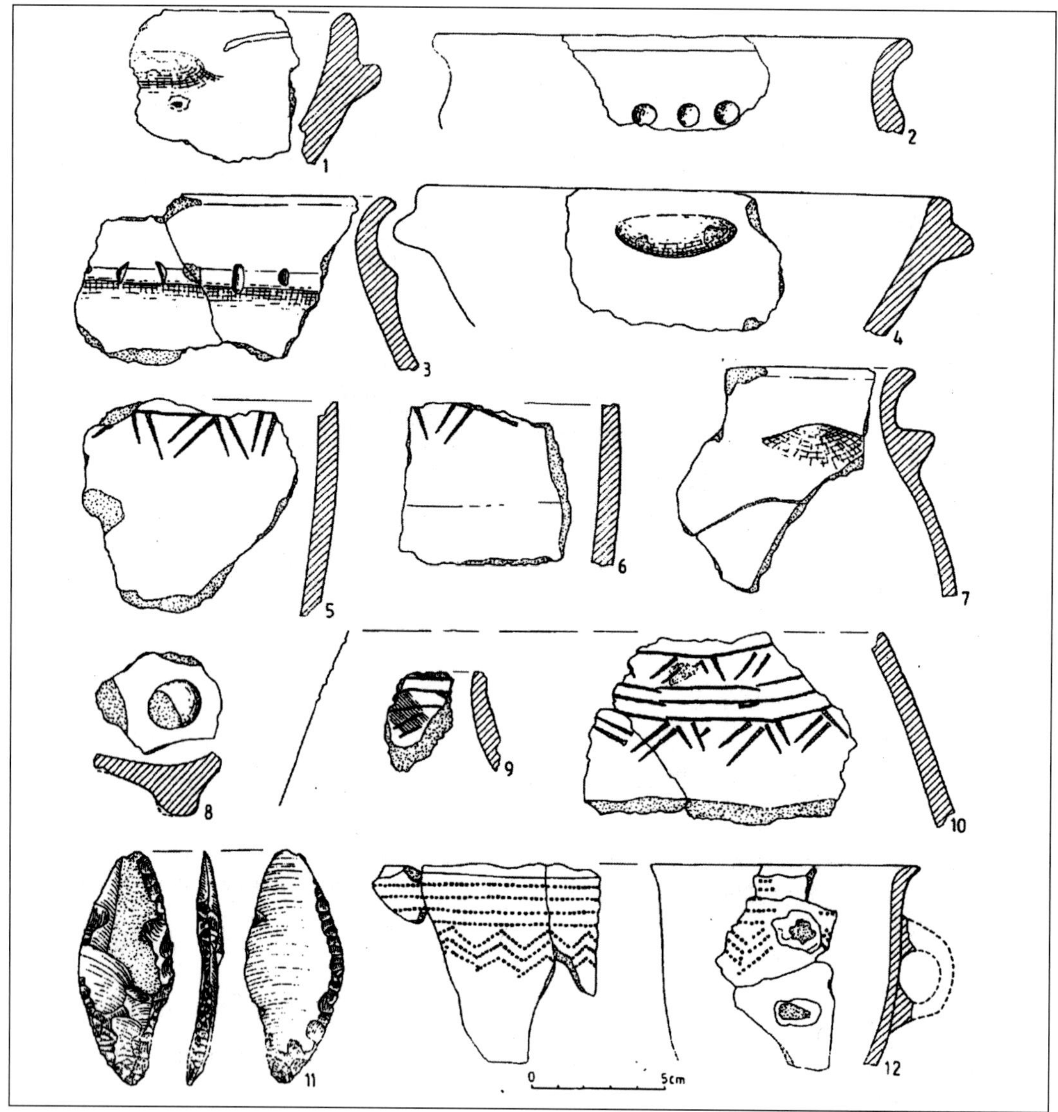

Figure 14.4: Narkowo, site 16, Kujawy-Pomerania voivodeship. Selected artefacts (after Czebreszuk & Przybytek 1997; Czebreszuk & Szmyt 2008a)

BC (Włodarczak 2017a). Its relics include mainly graves, often covered by a barrow and holding the remains of a single individual associated with an accompanying set of objects: a clay vessel (a beaker, amphora or pot), stone shaft-hole axe and flint weapons (a knife or arrowheads). Corded Ware dwelling structures are less well known but appear small and were used for only short periods of time. Usually, all that is left of them is a pottery concentration and several small pits at the most (Czebreszuk & Szmyt 2008a; 2011; Włodarczak 2017a).

The second cultural tradition that was present in the Polish lands when the Bell Beakers arrived was the Globular Amphora Culture that had developed in the 4th millennium BC (Szmyt 2017). The early second half of the 2nd millennium saw the decline of its classic horizon and coincided with its late horizon. Globular Amphora remains are known, albeit with varying intensity, from the lowlands and some portions of the uplands. These are both graves with one or several burials (in an extreme case, up to 30 individuals) as well as medium-sized and small settlements (with several or just one house) or campsites with no structural traces at all (Czebreszuk & Szmyt 2008a; 2011).

The latest traces of the Funnel Beaker Culture presence, in existence already since the 5th millennium BC (Rzepecki 2011; Nowak 2009), are dated to the middle of the 3rd millennium BC. They were recorded in Kujawy (Kośko & Szmyt 2007) and central Pomerania (Wierzbicki 1999). These are domestic sites

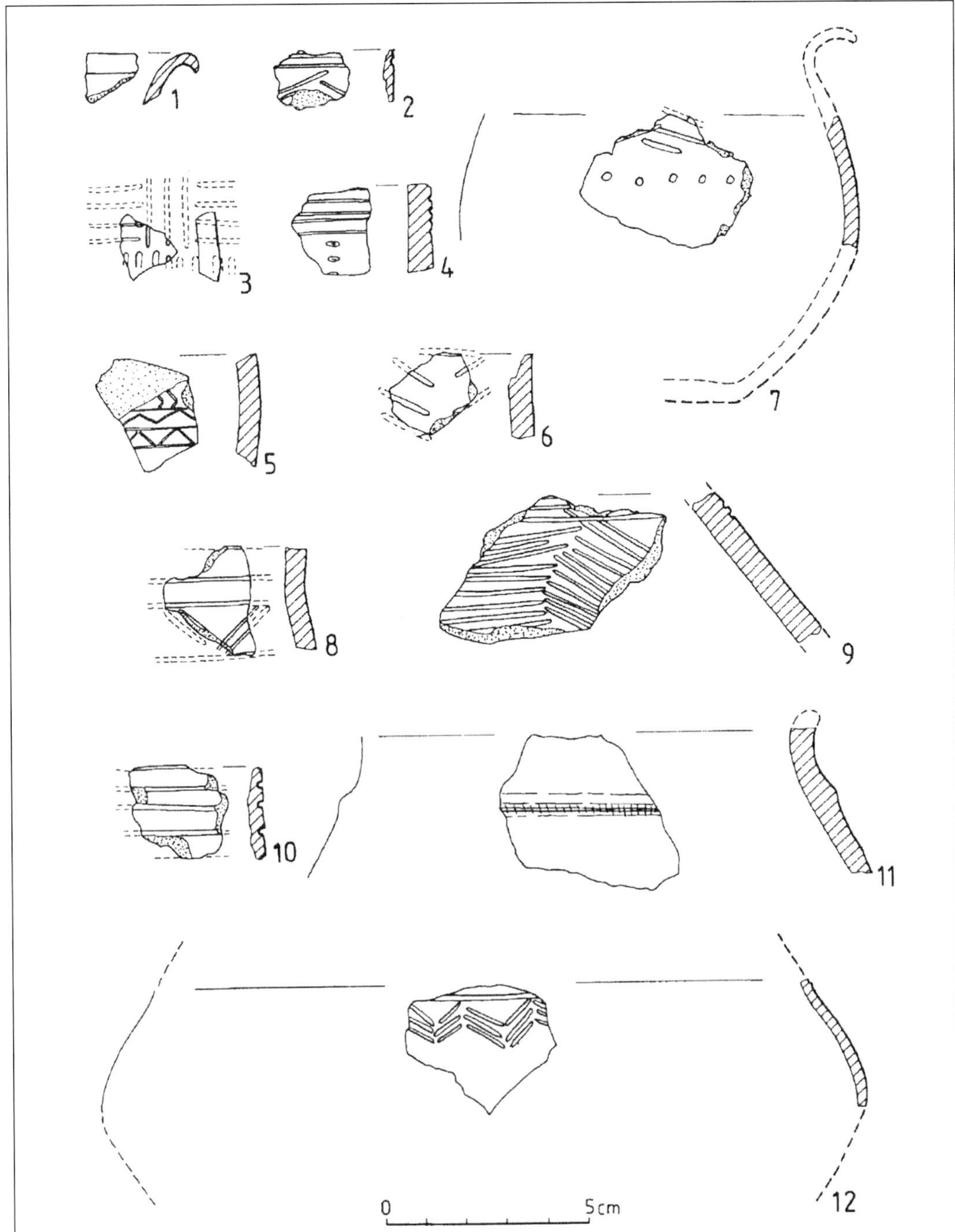

Figure 14.5: Dęby, site 29A, Kujawy-Pomerania voivodeship. Selected pottery (after Czebreszuk 1996)

with relatively well-preserved pits but without traces of houses or structures.

The Subneolithic groups formed various communities from the forest zone of eastern Europe (Piezonka 2012). In the course of their long life-time, the origins of which go back to the 5th millennium BC, they adapted many innovations from agricultural communities but hardly changed their lifestyle (Sobieraj 2017). Around the middle of the 3rd millennium, Subneolithic settlement traces are known mainly from the lowlands (Józwiak 2003) with their greatest concentration being located in north-eastern Poland (Sobieraj 2017). They represent the so-called Neman Culture and its mutation, known as the Linin horizon (Józwiak 2003). Archaeological evidence highlights their close connections to the Corded Ware Culture and in part to Bell Beakers (Józwiak 2003; Wawrusiewicz *et al.* 2015).

Domestic pottery before Bell Beakers

Each of the cultures mentioned earlier used a characteristic ceramic assemblage differentiated by their fabric, form and ornamentation.

The typology of Corded Ware Culture vessels has many regional varieties, but an assemblage characteristic of its developed and late phases includes beakers and amphorae ornamented with various patterns of cord impressions. They are accompanied by pots of '*Wellenleisten*' type and bowls. Unlike in the older phase, when the fabric was usually tempered with grog, the younger phases saw considerable differences in technological recipes. The most popular ones used crushed stone with a small and medium particle size (Czebreszuk 1996).

Throughout the currency of the Globular Amphora Culture, pottery was made of mineral-tempered clay and specifically coarse and medium grains of crushed stone. It could be accompanied by other admixtures as, for instance, sand, mica or organic materials, but the major role was always played by crushed stone (Szmyt 1996; 2013). Vessel forms, decorative motifs and techniques were rich and varied. The most frequently found forms included amphorae, vases, bowls, pots, mugs and jugs. Clay was also used to make the so-called drums. In the classic horizon, pottery was ornamented with stamped, cord or finger impressions and straight or wavy cordons and bosses. In the late horizon, cord impressions ceased to be used, with the decoration being greatly simplified. It was limited to stamp or finger impressions, relief strips and appliqué bosses. The range of vessel forms also narrowed to include pots, beakers, vases and possibly amphorae.

The Funnel Beaker pottery fabric varied depending on the macro-region. With respect to the regions from which the latest Funnel Beaker pottery assemblages come (Wierzbicki 1999; Kośko & Szmyt 2007; Szmyt 2013), the principal difference was in the temper used. Specifically, in Kujawy, it was in principle grog, with large grains being used in late phases. In Pomerania, crushed stone was mostly used, with grog being used less often. From the rich range of vessel forms, the youngest phases saw funnel beakers, vases and pots and decoration was limited to vertical, incised lines (Pomerania), stamp motifs and finger impressions (Kujawy).

The pottery of the Neman Culture (Jóźwiak 2003) was made with a temper of plants, medium- and coarse-grained crushed stone (often of a white colour) and sometimes sand. The range of forms was rather modest, with S-profile pots, very frequently with a pointed base. Vessel surfaces were burnished with strands of grass and the pottery was ornamented with dense, multiple geometric motifs.

Stone and flint tools used before Bell Beakers

All-over ground stone shaft-hole axes were a special characteristic of the Corded Ware Culture. As regards flint artefacts, the most characteristic were projectile points and retouched blade-knives. In turn, the most typical Globular Amphora culture tools were ground axes made of banded flint extracted from a mine in Krzemionki Opatowskie in the Holy Cross Mountains. Known from settlement sites, flint assemblages include chiefly fine artefacts produced by the bipolar technique. There are few classic forms of retouched tools (Szmyt 2013; 2017). The most typical flint tools are small polishing plates (Chachlikowski 2013). In the final phase of the Funnel Beaker Culture, flint processing relied on local raw materials of various quality, with imported excellent flint types being used only marginally. Blades and flakes of which only a small number was retouched, are common and most of the tools were *ad hoc* forms used without any preparation (Domańska 2013). Neman Culture populations worked only local raw materials, employing both classic and bipolar techniques (Wawrusiewicz, *et al.* 2015).

Houses before Bell Beakers

Nothing is known of Corded Ware Culture dwellings, whereas diverse house forms have been identified at Globular Amphora and very late Funnel Beaker sites, as well as at Subneolithic sites. In all three cultural units, these were either above-ground post-built houses or shallow pit-houses. In the Globular Amphora settlements, they came in various shapes (rectangular, trapezoid, polygonal and irregular), while their size varied between 15 and 60 m² (Szmyt 1996). The design of Funnel Beaker houses was similar but they had more regular forms and their size range was greater (features of about 90 m² have been encountered, *see* Kulczycka-Leciejewiczowa 1993). In turn, on Subneolithic sites, small features are usually found, often being around 20 m² in area and being of various shapes such as round, rectangular and polygonal (Jóźwiak 2003).

Importantly, the vast majority of houses (including all Funnel Beaker Culture features) are dated to the period before the middle of the 3rd millennium with very few being encountered later. Their decrease is related to a change in settlement forms and in the course of the 3rd millennium BC, settlements were subject to several coupled reduction trends observable in all cultural units. These trends involved the contraction of the area covered by a settlement, simplification of the settlement infrastructure and a drop in the number of artefacts left within a settlement. As a result, in the middle of the 3rd millennium, the form that came to dominate was a small settlement, without any relatively permanent structures (including houses) and with, at best, only several pits (sometimes none) and very few artefacts. Such settlement traces are interpreted as an ephemeral place of residence, used for a short time by a small group of people who were leading a mobile lifestyle. Archaeometrically, such traces are hard to identify, not to say almost undetectable (Czebreszuk & Szmyt 2008a; 2008b). This form of ephemeral settlement or campsite was especially typical of the Corded Ware Culture, but also dominated other contemporary cultural units around the middle of the 3rd millennium BC. The situation began to change slowly around 2400 BC, coinciding with the first Bell Beaker stimuli, but only in the lowlands.

Bell Beaker houses

The arrival of Bell Beakers in the lowlands triggered changes in settlement patterns, involving a slow departure from the model described above. From 2400 BC, settlement networks seem to have stabilised again, leading to the remodelling of the existing social organisation. Settlements gradually grew in size and were occupied for increasingly longer periods, turning into places used on a slightly more permanent basis. Within them, traces of domestic structures are recorded that are followed in time by houses (Czebreszuk & Szmyt 2008b). Next to isolated graves, grave clusters also appear soon leading to cemeteries. This process, culminating in the Early Bronze Age, has been particularly well traced in Kujawy (Czebreszuk 2001).

So far, about 30 Bell Beaker settlement sites have been found in the Polish lands (Fig. 14.1): 18 in Kujawy, eight in the Chełmno Land and single ones in other regions: five on the Lower Odra and one each in Silesia and Greater Poland (Czebreszuk 2001; Furmanek *et al.* 2015; Furmanek 2017). Not all bear traces of stability or relative permanence. On the contrary, they are very varied but always more tangible than the ephemeral settlements of the Corded Ware Culture (*see* section 7 below). What matters, however, is the fact that between 2400–2200 BC, the settlement decline mentioned earlier was reversed.

Around the same time, a new type of dwelling structure emerged in the form of rectangular houses with post walls and a floor partially sunk into the ground. They reached 6–5 × 4–3 m at sites such as Smarglin 22, Grudziądz-Mniszek 3, and Biały Bór 17 and huts with a partially sunken floor became the principal dwelling model in Kujawy and the Chełmno Land in the Bell Beaker period. They find the closest analogies in northern Jutland, where the Myrhøj group existed at that time (Simonsen 2017; Sarauw this volume). These were structures that were far more robust than all other houses of the immediately preceding period and, in comparison with Globular Amphora and Funnel Beaker huts, were more uniform in terms of design.

In all locations where excavation was large enough, two situations were identified whereby either several structures existed at the same time, making up one settlement of several houses, or else structures were erected in a sequence, covering two or more chronological phases. In Silesia, however, at the site of Kornice 33, another type of house was identified comprising a rectangular post structure, measuring 14 × 5.3 m with one shorter wall creating an apsidal shape. Similar features are known from the Bell Beaker eastern group in Bohemia, Moravia and

Hungary (Furmanek *et al.* 2015; 532; Turek & Reményi *et al.* this volume).

There are also many examples of completely destroyed settlements, situated in sandy areas or on eolian cover sands. Currently, they are recorded as clusters of movable finds (pottery, flints and lithics), occupying areas between 10 and 20 m in diameter. They may be traces left by sunken-floor houses such as at Dęby 29, Dęby 29A and many others.

Overview of Bell Beaker settlement sites

Below, concise descriptions of sites that are interpreted as the remains of Bell Beaker settlements are provided (Fig. 14.1).

Biały Bór 17, Chełmno Land (Bokiniec 1987)

Excavations revealed one feature of 4 m^2, around which pottery was concentrated. The pottery was decorated with horizontal cord impressions, incised lines, horizontal cordons and an exceptional motif of horizontal cord impressions alternating with horizontal incised lines. The feature probably represents the remains of a shallow pit-house and corresponds to phase 1 of the Bell Beaker period in Kujawy.

Bożejewice 22, Kujawy (Makarowicz 2000)

Excavations revealed no features but a concentration of pottery ornamented with motifs of several horizontal incised lines and cordons. These finds probably represent the remains of a small settlement dated to phase 3 of the Bell Beaker period according to Makarowicz (2000, 458: Iwno phases II–III).

Chlewiska 56, Kujawy (Czebreszuk 1996)

Excavations found no features in an area of about 35–40 m in diameter, but a small assemblage of pottery with zone incised ornament, cordons and appliqué bosses was found as well as vessels with a tulip-shaped flared lip. These are probably the remains of a settlement (with a single structure?) of phase 2 of the Bell Beaker period.

Chlewiska 70, Kujawy (Czebreszuk 1996)

Excavation revealed no features but a small assemblage of pottery with incised zonal decoration and cordons (straight, with notches and dents) as well as appliqué bosses, This dates to Bell Beakers 1–2.

Chwarstnica 3, Lower Odra

Investigations comprising test pits revealed surface and stratified finds and features. Numerous potsherds bearing combed zone motifs incision and cord techniques, were located as were even more numerous flints connected with the manufacture of large bifacial tools and especially daggers suggesting that it must have been a vast and long-term settlement. The limited range of the excavations prevents the reconstruction of the nature of the dwellings and the chronology has yet to be resolved.

Dęby 29, Kujawy (Czebreszuk & Szmyt 1992; 2008b)

No features were revealed in the excavations but there was a rich ceramic assemblage including pots with incised and cord-impressed zone-metopic and zone decoration. The flint assemblage comprised dagger fragments and projectile points. The settlement lay on the undamaged part of a dune on which at least three finds scatters have survived, each about 10 m in diameter. These are probably the remains of three light dwelling structures dating to phase 2 Bell Beakers.

Dęby 29A, Kujawy (Czebreszuk 1996)

No features were excavated but rather a concentration of pottery ornamented with combed and incised zone and metopic motifs (Fig. 14.5). This was the same dune as Dęby 29 and represented further remains of a light dwelling. This dates to phase 1–2 Bell Beakers.

Dziewa 14, Kujawy (Makarowicz 2000)

Once again there were no features but a small assemblage of pottery was recovered (43 fragments) comprising motifs of incised lines accompanied by appliqué bosses, and cordons. This possibly represents the remains of a small settlement dated to phase 3 Bell Beakers according to Makarowicz (2000: 458: Iwno phase II).

Gogolin 7, Chełmno Land (Bokiniec 1987)

A small assemblage of pottery was found with comb and incised zone decoration and horizontal cordons. This possibly represents the remains of a small settlement dated to phase 2 Bell Beakers.

Grudziądz-Mniszek 3, Chełmno Land (Bokiniec & Marciniak 1987)
Many features were found in the excavations at this site including post-holes and over a dozen pits. It lay on a dune that had already been settled by Corded Ware communities and discoveries included many concentrations of pottery bearing incised zone decoration, and vessels with a tulip-shaped lip and sharp shoulder with clear links to the Únětice Culture. The remains of a loom were also found comprising the fragments of over a dozen cylindrical loom weights (Bokiniec & Marciniak 1987: 225). In all likelihood, this was a sequence of several homesteads from the transition period between the Neolithic and Bronze Ages, and also dated to Bell Beaker 3. The excavators suggested that the occupation of the area by a Bell Beaker population left behind the remains of at least five rectangular post structures, measuring about 5 × 4 m and arranged almost in a star with respect to one another (Bokiniec & Marciniak 1987: 226). In at least three, there were the remains of sunken floors, measuring about 2.5 × 2.5 m, 3 × 2.5 m and 5 × 2 m (Fig. 14.6). The presence of a loom may suggest a greater permanence of settlement.

Karwowo 25, Lower Odra
Surface survey by M. Dziewanowski found a large potsherd, with comb-zoned decoration. It is not certain if these are the remains of a settlement.

Kornice 33, Silesia (Furmanek* et al. *2015; Furmanek 2017)
Excavations revealed two pits set 66 m apart, containing a rich ceramic assemblage (Fig. 14.7), and a post structure, which may be connected to the settlement stage under discussion. The outline of the structure is rectangular measuring 14 × 5.3 m, with one shorter wall being apsidal in shape (Figs 14.8 & 9). The features of this settlement have connections to Bell Beakers in Bohemia, Moravia and the vicinity of Budapest. A neighbouring Bell Beaker cemetery (250 m away from the settlement) yielded four radiocarbon dates, which indirectly date the settlement to *c.* 2200 BC.

Krusza Zamkowa 3 ('west campsite'), Kujawy (Makarowicz & Czebreszuk 1995)
No features were found in the excavations but there was a small assemblage of pottery with zoned decoration made using cord, comb and incision. A flint dagger was also found and the remains probably represent a small settlement dated to Bell Beaker 1–2.

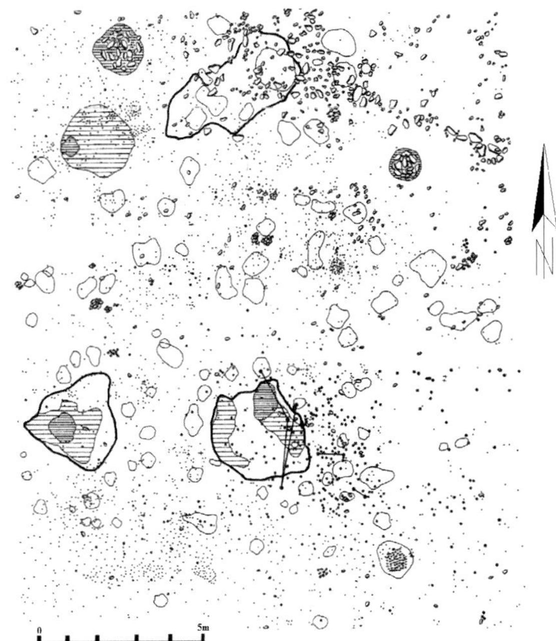

Figure 14.6: Grudziądz-Mniszek, site 3, Kujawy-Pomerania voivodeship. Location of features. The traces of Bell Beaker houses with sunken floors are marked with bold lines (after Bokiniec & Marciniak 1987, with alterations)

Krzywosądz 3, Kujawy (Makarowicz & Czebreszuk 1995)
Surface survey produced a small assemblage of pottery with comb-zoned decoration, possibly representing the remains of a small settlement dated to phase 1 Bell Beakers.

Łąkocin 1, Kujawy (Makarowicz 2000)
Excavation located three pits and three post-holes associated with a large assemblage of pottery (878 potsherds), decorated mainly with horizontal cordons, rows of finger impressions and horizontal incised lines. In all likelihood these are remains of a settlement dating to phase 3 Bell Beakers according to Makarowicz (2000: 458: Iwno phase II–III).

Macikowo 3, Chełmno Land (Bokiniec 1995)
Surface survey located a small assemblage of pottery, resembling that from Macikowo 9, but less varied in style. These may represent the remains of a small settlement (up to 30 m in diameter), possibly dated to phase 3 Bell Beakers.

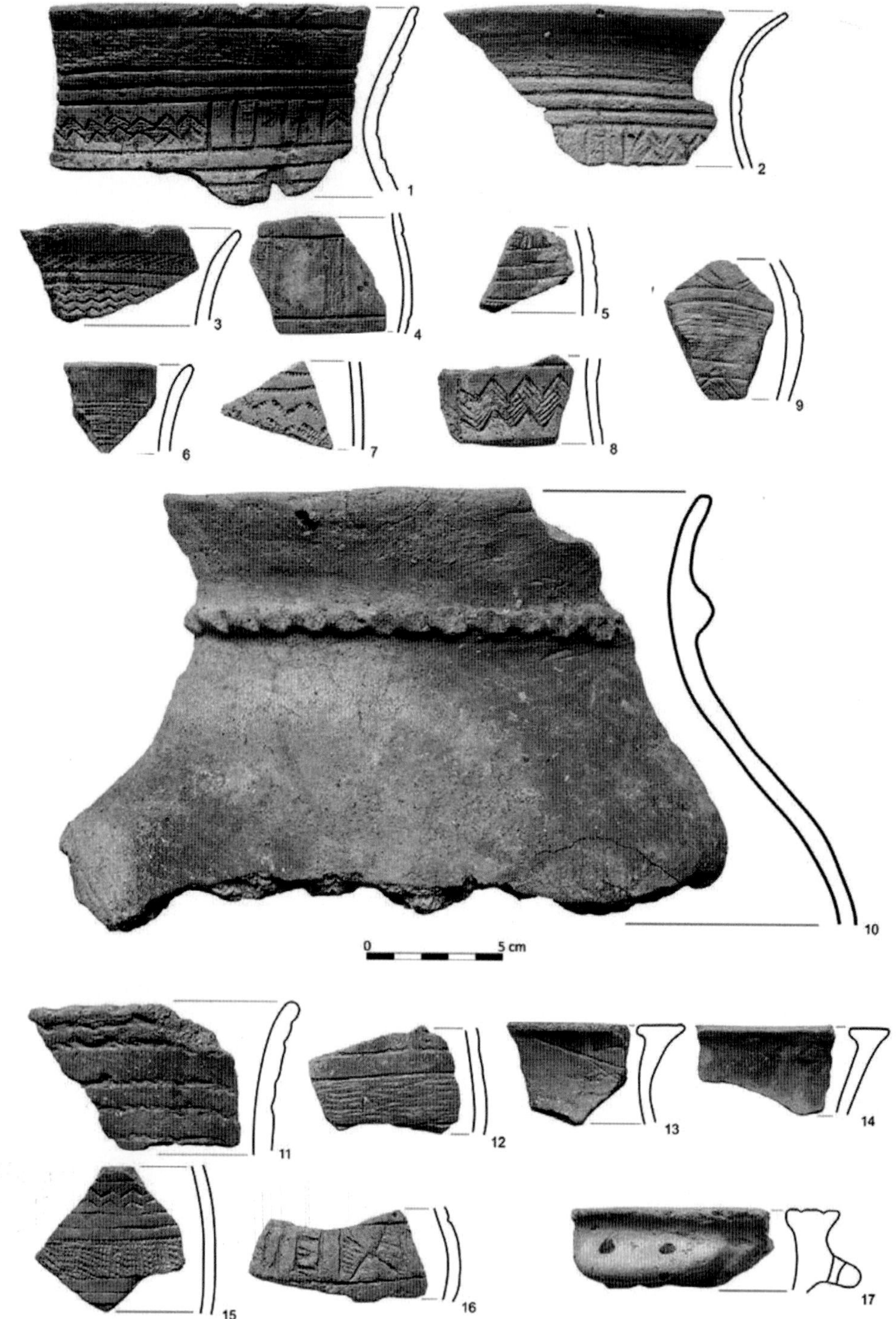

Figure 14.7: Kornice, site 33, Silesia voivodeship. Selected Bell Beaker pottery from settlement features (after Furmanek 2017)

Macikowo 9, Chełmno Land (Bokiniec 1995)

Test excavations revealed a few features and a pottery assemblage showing long-term settlement from the Late Neolithic to the Early Bronze Age. Motifs on the pottery comprise multiple horizontal cord impressions (Corded Ware Culture), horizontal incised lines, single cordons and appliqué bosses. The settlement remains probably date to phase 3 Bell Beakers.

Narkowo 16, Kujawy (Czebreszuk & Przybytek 1997; Czebreszuk & Szmyt 2008b)

Excavations (Fig. 14.10) revealed a few features including settlement pits and a rich

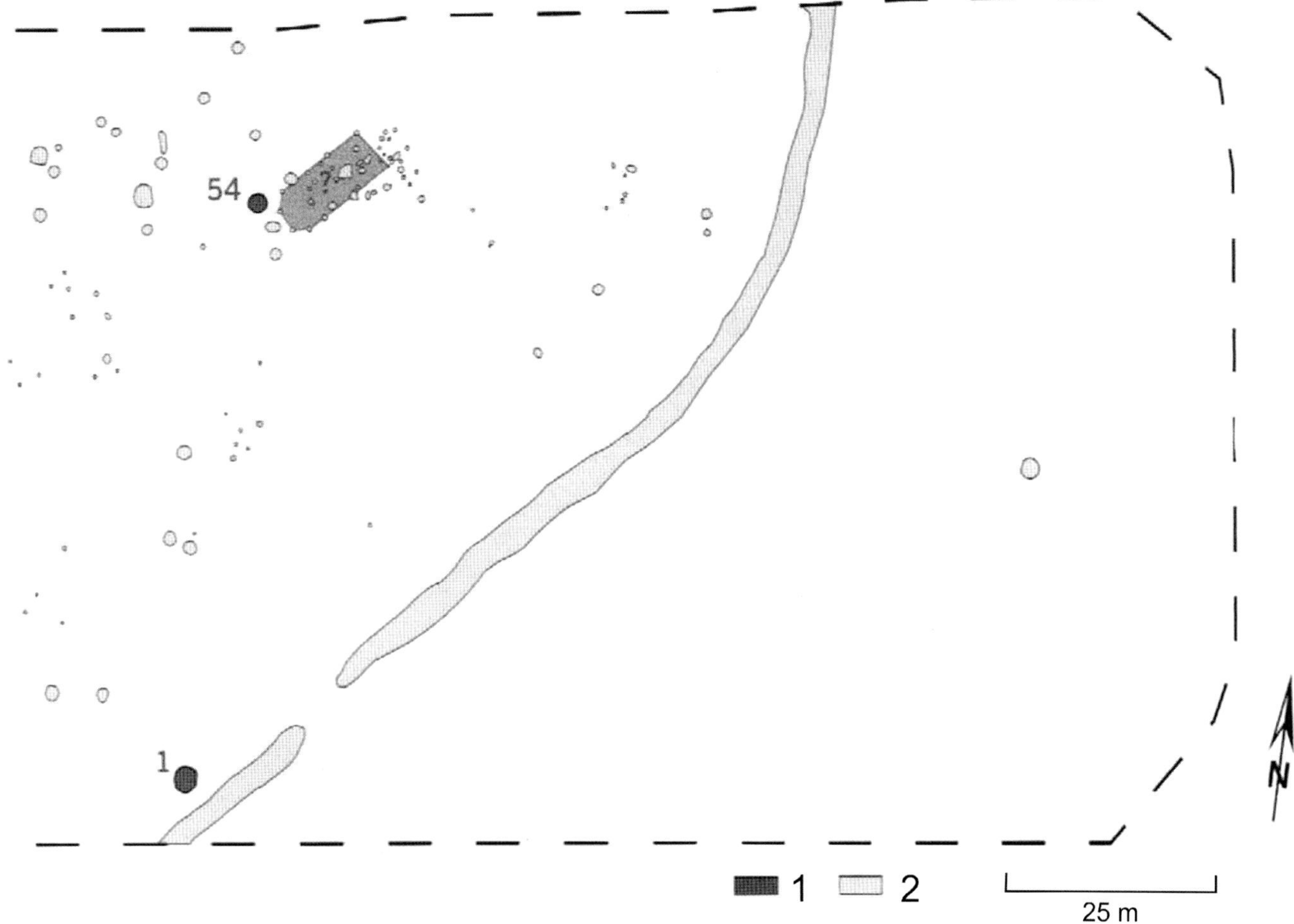

Figure 14.8: Kornice, site 33, Silesia voivodeship. Location of features (after Furmanek et al. *2015) Key: 1 – Bell Beaker pits (no. 1 and 54) and a post-structure; 2 – other features*

pottery assemblage consisting of comb-zoned sherds and vessels with notched/dented cordons (Fig. 14.4). Several post structures are superimposed upon one another, making them difficult to reconstruct and this suggests that this must have been a long-term settlement dated to phase 1 Bell Beakers.

Osiek nad Wisłą 8, Chełmno Land (Bokiniec 1995)

Test excavations located many concentrations of Neolithic and Early Bronze material located on a dune. Two concentrations of ceramic material were referred to as 'campsite S' (10 × 16 m) and 'campsite N' (about 12 m diameter). The pottery was only decorated with single cordons and motifs of horizontal incised lines. Vessels with tulip-shaped flared lips were found in two concentrations, possibly representing the remains of two houses, are dated to phase 3 Bell Beakers.

Potok 1, Kuiavia (Bokiniec 1989)

Excavations (1,372 m^2) on a sandy hill surrounded by waterlogged terrain located several pottery concentrations producing a total of about 2500 potsherds as well as associated features. The artefacts date to all phases of the Late Neolithic and Early Bronze Age and the sequence commences with simple cord-decorated pottery (Corded Ware culture, phases 2 and 3). An exceptional Maritime Beaker sherd appears to have been associated with this material and is so far unique in the Polish Lowland. In addition, pottery bearing comb-zoned motifs (phase 1 Bell Beakers) and zone and metopic incised motifs (Bell Beaker 2) was also identified. Other decoration includes cordons (usually single ones) and slender S-shaped vessels decorated with multiple incised lines (Bell Beaker 3). The site was intensively used throughout the second half of the 3rd and the early 2nd millennia BC but the small number of features recorded is a result of modern damage.

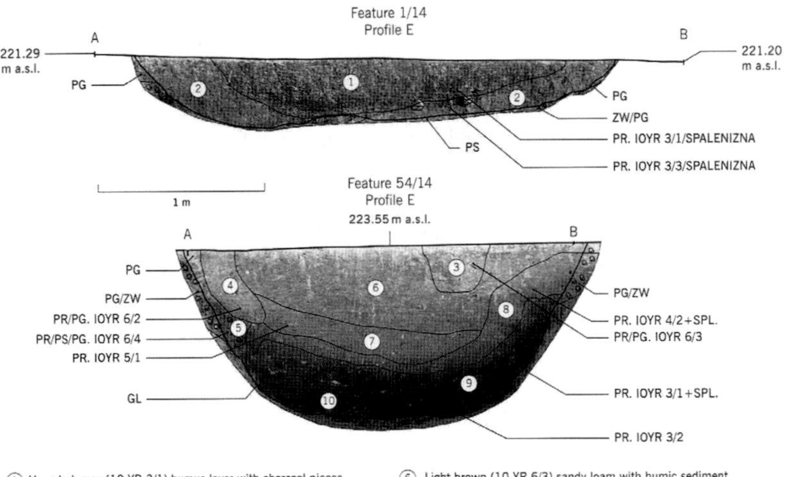

Figure 14.9: Kornice, site 33, Silesia voivodeship. Cross-sections of the Bell Beaker pits (after Furmanek et al. *2015)*

Przylep 5, Lower Oder
Investigations by M. Dziewanowski located a concentration of comb-zoned pottery possibly representing the remains of a small settlement dated to Bell Beaker 1.

Smarglin 22, Kujawy (Czebreszuk & Przybył 2002; Czebreszuk & Szmyt 2008a)
Excavations revealed a house with a partially sunken floor measuring about 5 × 3.5 m (Figs 14.11–13). This structure has obvious connections to the Myrhøj group in northern Jutland. accompanying features include a storage pit. The rich ceramic assemblage comprised sherds decorated most often with zones of twisted cord and rows of finger impressions. Reconstructable vessel forms included mugs (with complex cord and impressed decoration) and undecorated Beakers. The settlement is dated to Bell Beaker 1.

Smarglin 39, Kujawy (Czebreszuk 1996)
Surface survey located a concentration of sherds spread over an area of around 12 m in diameter. The potsherds were comb-zoned and may be the relics of a small settlement, perhaps even with a house, dated to Bell Beaker 1.

Smarglin 49, Kujawy (Makarowicz & Czebreszuk 1995; Czebreszuk 1996)
Surface survey located a concentration of sherds spread over an area of around 12 m in diameter similar to Smarglin 39 above. The sherds were comb-zoned and cordoned and may have been the remains of a small settlement (with a single house?) dated to Bell Beaker 1.

Smarglin 51, Kujawy (Makarowicz & Czebreszuk 1995)
Excavation failed to locate features but recovered a few pottery sherds with combed and incised zoned decoration. This may have been an extensive settlement, dated to Bell Beaker 2.

Smarglin 53, Kujawy (Makarowicz 1993)
An excavation area of 480 m^2 uncovered thirty features of which three belonged to Bell Beakers (Figs 14.14–15). No outlines of any structures could be traced but sherds (often highly comminuted) were scattered over the entire excavated area. Comb-zoned decoration and finger impressed cordons (Bell Beaker 1; Figs 14.2 & 3) were found in the assemblage. The excavated area is part of a larger site intensively occupied through many settlement phases during the currency of Bell Beakers.

Stara Wieś 9A, Kujawy (Makarowicz & Czebreszuk 1995)
Rescue excavations produced a few comb-zoned sherds possibly representing the remains of a small settlement dated to Bell Beaker 1.

Strzelce-Krzyżanna 40, Kujawy (Makarowicz 2000)
Excavations revealed a single pit and about

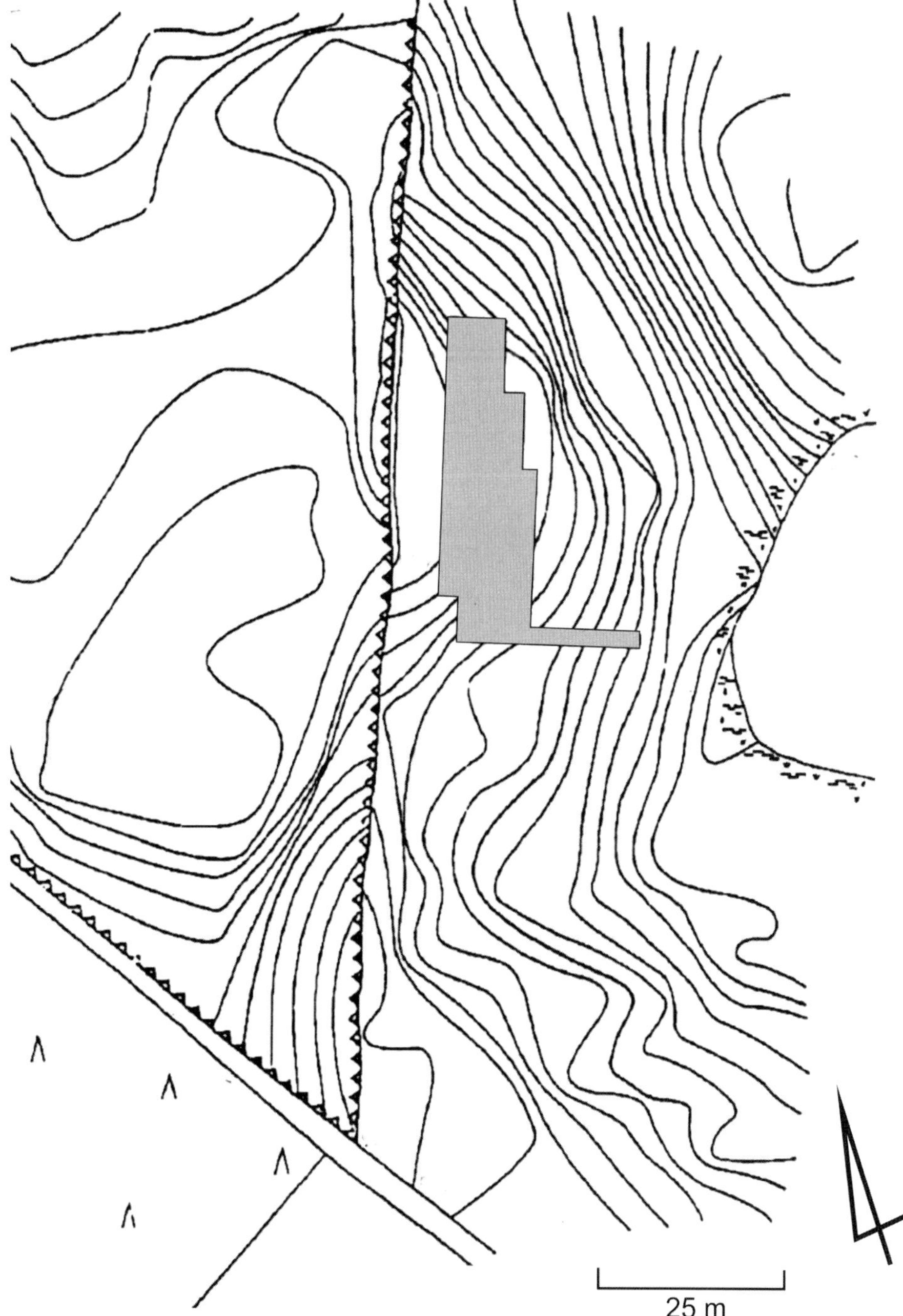

Figure 14.10: Narkowo, site 16, Kujawy-Pomerania voivodeship. Site plan. Key: excavated area marked in grey (after Czebreszuk & Przybytek 1997; Czebreszuk & Szmyt 2008a)

60 sherds of pottery on a surface 50–60 m long. The pottery was decorated with cordons and incised lines and possibly represents a settlement dated to Bell Beaker 3.

Sulęcinek, Greater Poland (Makarowicz & Czebreszuk 1995)

Old materials in the collections of the Archaeological Museum in Poznań were collected over a large area of a dune and comprises an assemblage of incised zoned and metopic pottery. There are also forms with a tulip-shaped flared lip. These possibly represent the remains of a settlement dated to Bell Beaker 2 and 3.

Toruń 243, Siedlisko' 1 and Siedlisko' 2, Chełmno Land (Bokiniec 1995)

Ceramics decorated with incised zones and horizontal cordons (single and double) have

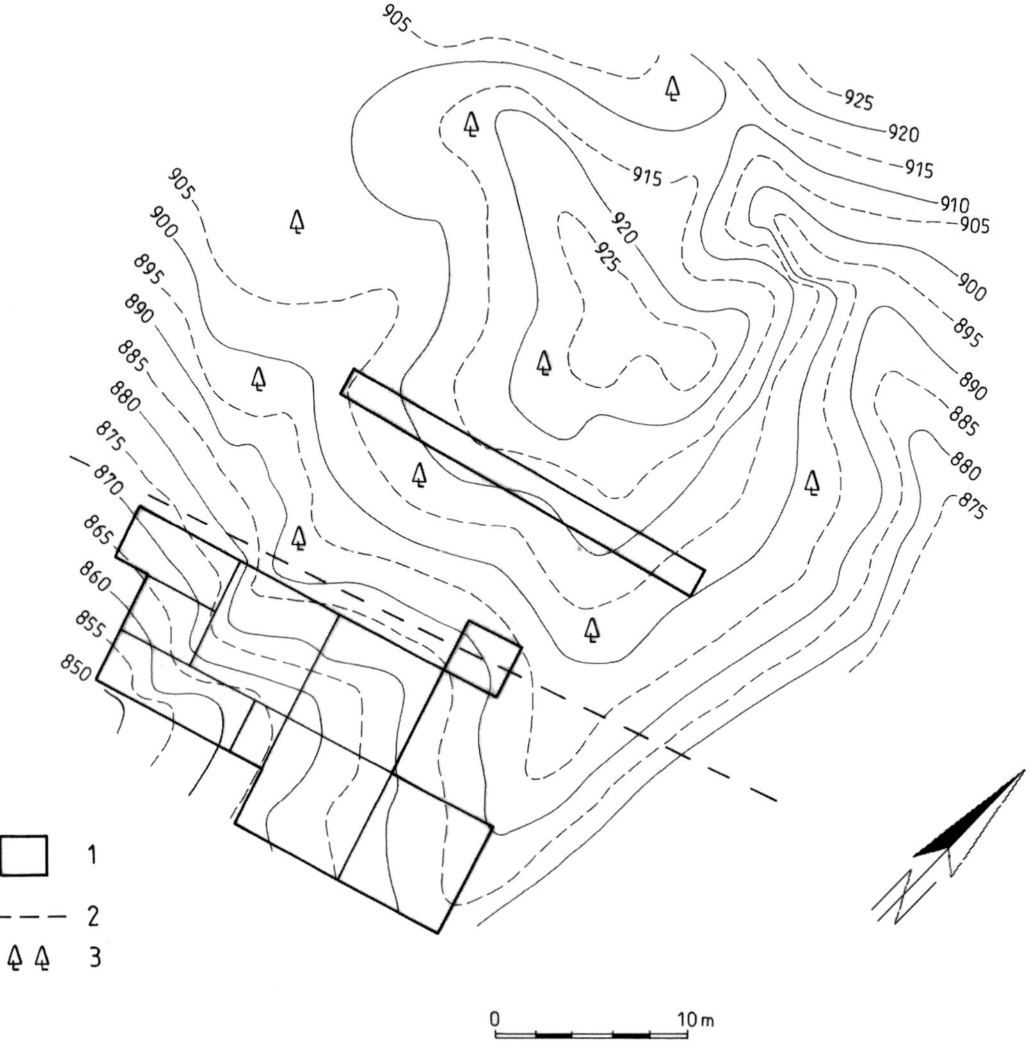

Figure 14.11: Smarglin, site 22, Kujawy-Pomerania voivodeship. Site plan. Key: 1 – excavated area; 2 – contour lines; 3 – forested area (after Czebreszuk & Przybył 2002; Czebreszuk & Szmyt 2008a)

been found as well as slender S-profile pots and vessels with a tulip-shaped flared lip. At least two concentrations, possibly representing two structures, were dated to Bell Beaker 2 and 3.

Toruń-Grębocin III, Chełmno Land (Bokiniec 1987)
Excavations produced no features but rather a large assemblage of pottery decorated with comb-zoned motifs as well as with incision and twisted cord. An equally rich assemblage of flints, including cordate projectile point was also recovered. This site possibly represents the remains of a sequence of campsites from Bell Beaker 1 and 2.

Warzymice 2, Lower Odra
Excavations by M. Dziewanowski and M. Pawłowski located some features and an assemblage of pottery decorated with comb-zoned motifs. They probably represent the remains of a settlement dated to Bell Beaker 1.

Zalesie 2, Lower Odra (Papis 2013)
Excavations produced no features but a small assemblage of comb-zoned pottery and sherds with notched cordons possibly representing the remains of a settlement dated to Bell Beaker 1.

Environmental data and the question of economic change

Bioarchaeological sources are meagre for Bell Beaker settlements as a result of most relevant sites being located on sands with poor preservation. The Kornice 33 settlement yielded evidence for cereals (einkorn or emmer wheat and unspecified cereals) and animals. In turn, the analysis of collagen from human remains collected at a cemetery accompanying the settlement has revealed a substantial component of plant food in the diet (Furmanek *et al.* 2015; Furmanek 2017). In a ritual feature at the site of Supraśl 6 (north-east Poland), a deposit of burnt bones was exposed amongst which were domestic pigs, cattle and sheep/goat (Wawrusiewicz *et al.* 2015, 99). Organic remains of plant origin were also found adhering to the vessel walls from another ritual feature at Supraśl (Rosiak & Kałużna-Czaplińska 2015, 280). Analysis of settlement locations shows a preference for areas with a long occupational history as well as a tendency to locate settlements on sandy terrain.

As already outlined above, the changes in settlement patterns must have correlated to social and economic transformations. The latter, however, are not easy to describe as source data are scarce. It can only be assumed that the point of departure was an economic system dominated by nomadic or possibly semi-nomadic stock raising. Slow and gradual changes limited the role of this agricultural regime or modified it considerably for example from nomadic to semi-nomadic and then to semi-sedentary. The changes also involved agriculture becoming more focused on crop cultivation perhaps as a result, to varying degrees, of local natural and 'political' conditions. This was confirmed by palynological analyses in the vicinity of the sites at Supraśl (Kupryjanowicz & Szal 2015).

It must be acknowledged that these changes may have occurred at different rates and in different ways in different areas, even if those areas were neighbours. Such a diversity is evidenced by palynological profiles from, for example, Kujawy, which document human pressures on the landscape (Makohonienko 2008).

Final remarks

Bell Beakers appeared in the Polish lands soon after 2400 BC in two different versions and from two separate directions. From the south and south-west (Moravia, Bohemia) they came to the Polish uplands (Lesser Poland, Silesia), while from the west (Jutland, Mecklenburg) they migrated to the lowlands (Pomerania, Kujawy, Chełmno Land). Recent field research suggests the existence of a vast zone of Bell Beaker cultural impact, also extending to north-eastern Poland. When the Bell Beakers were arriving in the early second half of the 3rd millennium BC, native communities represented various Late and Final Neolithic traditions, but were mostly connected to the Corded Ware Culture.

From the turn of the 4th millennium BC several common trends regarding the reduction of settlement sites can be observed. Firstly, the area of a settlement contracts. Secondly the settlement infrastructure becomes more simplified and thirdly there is a fall in the number of artefacts left within a settlement. As a result, in the middle of the 3rd millennium, the dominant form of settlement became somewhat ephemeral and as a result they have been described as campsites for mobile populations

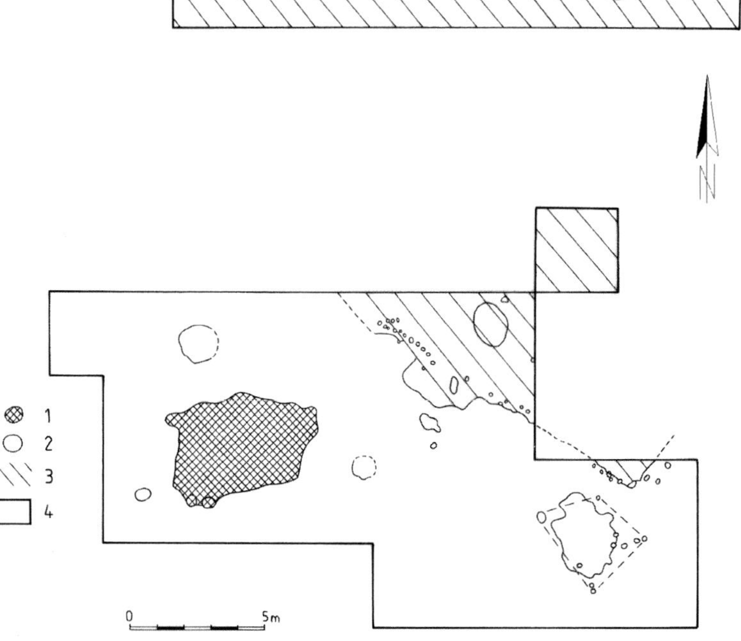

Figure 14.12: Smarglin, site 22, Kujawy-Pomerania voivodeship. Location of features. Key: 1 – Bell Beaker house with sunken floor; 2 – other features; 3 – Neolithic structure; 4 – trenches (after Czebreszuk & Przybył 2002; Czebreszuk & Szmyt 2008a)

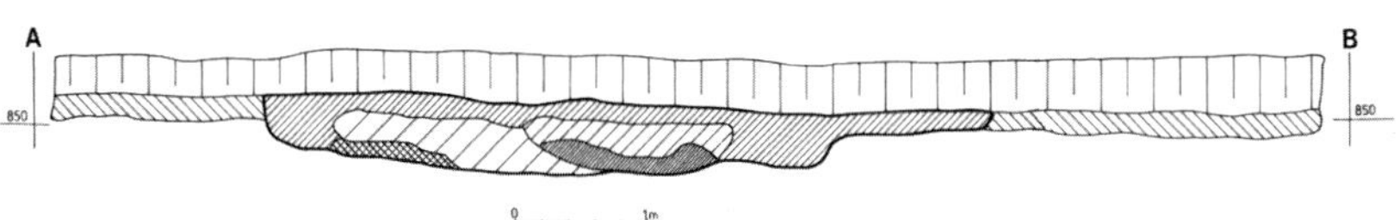

Figure 14.13: Smarglin, site 22, Kujawy-Pomerania voivodeship. Cross-section of the Bell Beaker house (after Czebreszuk & Przybył 2002; Czebreszuk & Szmyt 2008a)

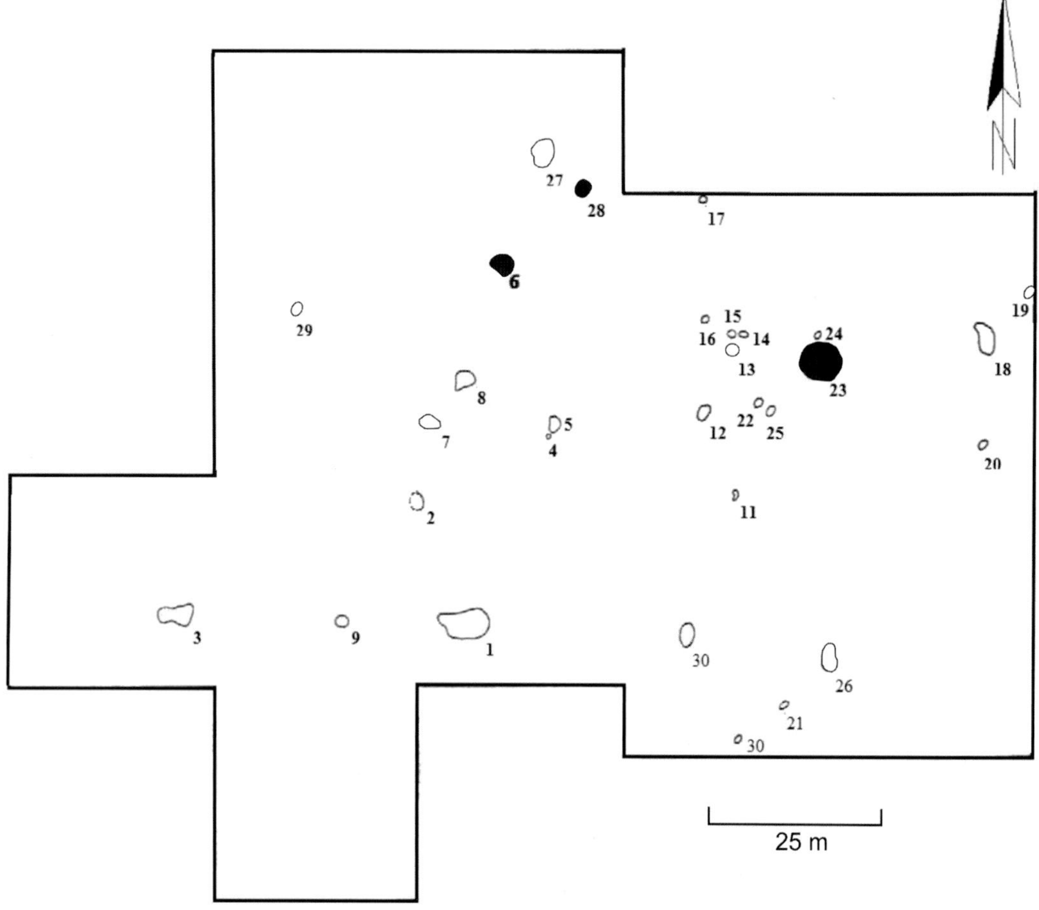

Figure 14.14: Smarglin, site 53, Kujawy-Pomerania voivodeship. Location of features. Key: Bell Beaker features marked in black (after Makarowicz 1993)

who left no permanent structures, few, if any, domestic features and very few artefacts.

The situation began to change slowly around 2400 BC with the first stimuli from Bell Beakers. A tendency can be seen to stabilize the settlement network again leading to the remodelling of the existing social organisation. This process will ultimately culminate in the Early Bronze Age fortified settlements of the Unětice Culture.

So far, just over 30 Bell Beaker settlement sites have been exposed in the Polish lands with 18 having been found in Kujawy, eight in the Chełmno Land, five on the Lower Odra and one each in Silesia and Greater Poland. There are still no examples from Lesser Poland. Initially, in the northern part of the Polish lands, the settlements were very similar to those 'campsites' of the Corded Ware Culture but the influence from Jutland (Myrhøj group) became stronger and this is reflected in the new forms of house constructions that appeared in the Lowlands. These were timber post-constructed buildings with a partially sunken floor. They constitute a specific form of building in the Polish Lowland that was specifically associated with Bell Beakers. Gradually, the accompanying infrastructure represented by pits, hearths and domestic debris increases suggesting a greater permanency of occupation. These patterns, introduced by the users of Bell Beakers, became the basis for the development of more permanent and even defensive settlement in the subsequent stages of the Bronze Age.

Acknowledgements

The authors would like to thank M. Dziewanowski, K. Kowalski and M. Urbanowski for information regarding Chwarstnica 3 (Lower Odra), M. Dziewanowski for information regarding Karwowo 25 and Przylep 5 (Lower Odra), and M. Dziewanowski and M. Pawłowski for information regarding Warzymice 2 (Lower Odra). This chapter was created as part of the

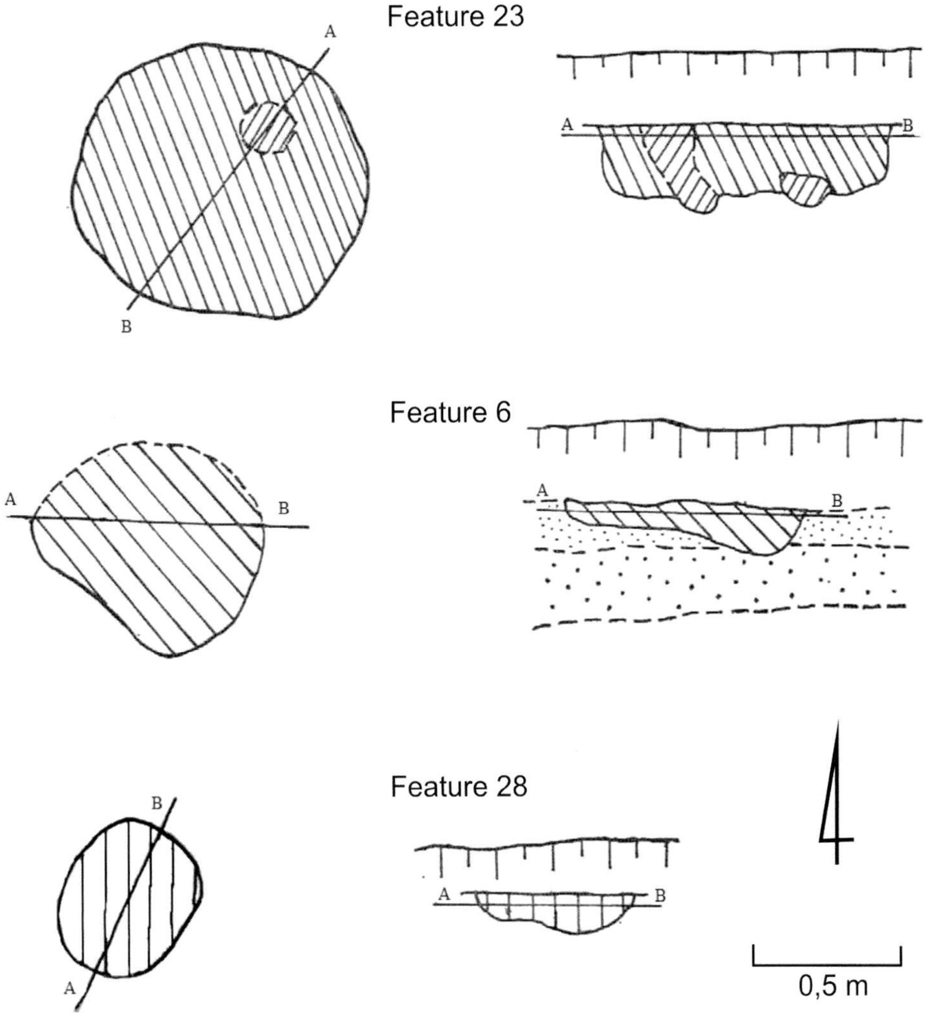

Figure 14.15: Smarglin, site 53, Kujawy-Pomerania voivodeship. Cross-section of Bell Beaker features (after Makarowicz 1993)

National Science Center of Poland project entitled: 'Late Neolithic/Early Bronze Age developments in the south-west Baltic Area (2500–1500 BC): why did the Bruszczew-Łęki Small type of power structures appear?' (2014/15/G/HS3/04720).

References

Bokiniec, A.Z., 1987.Schyłkowy neolit i wczesna epoka brązu na ziemi chełmińskiej. In Wiślański, T. (ed.), *Neolit i początki epoki brązu na ziemi chełmińskiej*, 207–21. Toruń: pod redakcją Tadeusza Wiślańskiego

Bokiniec, A.Z., 1989. Próba interpretacji kulturowej osady z przełomu neolitu i epoki brązu w Potoku, gm. Włocławek na podstawie ceramiki naczyniowej. Zeszyty Naukowe UMK, *Archeologia* 16, 45–71

Bokiniec, A.Z., 1995. Początki epoki brązu na Pomorzu Wschodnim, Warszawa, unpubl. PhD thesis

Bokiniec, A.Z. & Marciniak, M. 1987. Wstępne wyniki badań na wielokulturowym stanowisku Grudziądz-Mniszek 3, woj. toruńskie. In Wiślański, T. (ed.), *Neolit i początki epoki brązu na ziemi chełmińskiej*, 223–47. Toruń: pod redakcją Tadeusza Wiślańskiego

Bosch-Gimpera, P. 1926. Glockenbecherkultur. In Ebert, M. (ed.), *Reallexicon der Vorgeschichte,* B. 4 (2), 345–62. Berlin: de Gruyter

Budziszewski, J. & Włodarczak P., 2010. *Kultura pucharów dzwonowatych na Wyżynie Małopolskiej.* Kraków: Instytut Archeologii I Etnologii Pan, Oddział W Krakowie

Chachlikowski P. 2013. *Surowce eratyczne w kamieniarstwie społeczeństw wczesnoagrarnych Niżu Polskiego* (IV–III tys. przed Chr.). Poznań: Adam Mickiewicz University

Czebreszuk, J. 1996. *Społeczności Kujaw w początkach epoki brązu*, Poznań: Adam Mickiewicz University

Czebreszuk, J. 2000. Finds of archer's wristguards in the Baltic zone. In Kadrow, S. (ed.), *A Turning of Ages / Im Wandel der Zeiten. Jubilee Book Dedicated to Professor Jan Machnik on His 70th Anniversary*, 157–72. Kraków: Polish Academy of Sciences

Czebreszuk, J. 2001. *Schyłek neolitu i początki epoki brązu w strefie południowo-zachodniobałtyckiej (III i początki II tys. przed Chr.). Alternatywny model kultury*. Poznań: Adam Mickiewicz University

Czebreszuk, J. 2002. From Typochronology to Calendar. A Case Study: Society between Jutland and Kujawy in the 3rd Millennium BC. In Müller, J. (ed.), *Vom Endneolithikum zur Frühbronzezeit: Muster sozialen Wandels*, 235–44., Universitätsforschungen zur Prähistorischen Archäologie, 90. Bonn: Dr. Rudolf Habelt GmBH

Czebreszuk, J. 2003. Bell Beakers from West to East. In Bogucki, P. & Crabtree, P.J. (eds), *Ancient Europe 8000 BC – AD 1000: Encyclopedia of the Barbarian World*, 476–85. New York: Charles Scribner's Sons

Czebreszuk, J., Kośko, A., Makarowicz, P. & Szmyt, M. 2000. Podsumowanie. In Kośko, A. (ed.), *Archeologiczne badania ratownicze wzdłuż trasy gazociągu tranzytowego. Tom III. Kujawy, Część 4. Osadnictwo kultur późnoneolitycznych oraz interstadium epok neolitu i brązu: 3900 –1400/1300 przed Chr.*, 569–71. Poznań: Adam Mickiewicz University

Czebreszuk, J. & Kozłowska-Skoczka D. 2008. *Sztylety krzemienne na Pomorzu Zachodnim.* Szczecin: Muzeum Narodowe

Czebreszuk, J. & Krywaltsewitsch, M. 2003. Der Dolch aus Mesha, Nördliches Weissressland: Glockenbechereinflüsse in Osteuropa. *Archäologisches Korrespondenzblatt* 33 (1), 51–6

Czebreszuk, J. & Makarowicz P. 1995. Puchary dzwonowate. Zarys historii badań i współczesne kierunki refleksji. *Przegląd Archeologiczny* 43, 163–72

Czebreszuk, J. & Przybył A. 2002. *Osadnictwo neolityczne i protobrązowe w Smarglinie, woj. kujawsko-pomorskie, stanowisko 22.* Poznań: Adam Mickiewicz University

Czebreszuk, J. & Przybytek, M. 1997. Osadnictwo neolityczne na stanowisku 16 w Narkowie, gm. Dobre, woj. włocławskie. *Zapiski Kujawsko-Dobrzyńskie* 11, 53–65

Czebreszuk, J. & Szmyt, M. 1992. *Osadnictwo neolityczne i wczesnobrązowe w Dębach woj. włocławskie, stanowisko 29.* Poznań: Inowrocław

Czebreszuk, J. & Szmyt, M. 2008a. Bell Beakers and their Role in a Settlement Evolution during the Neolithic-Bronze Transition on the Polish Lowland. In Baioni, M., Leonini, V., Lo Vetro, D., Martini, F., Poggiani Keller, R. & Sarti, L. (eds), *Bell Beakers in everyday life*, 221–33. Firenze: Museo Fiorentino Di Preistoria 'Paolo Graziosi'

Czebreszuk, J. & Szmyt, M. 2008b. Siedlungsformen des III Jahrtausends v.Chr. in der polnischen Tiefebene (Kulturen der Trichterbecher, Kugelamphoren und Schnurkeramik). Stand und Perspektiven der Untersuchungen. In Müller, J. & Dörfler, W. (eds), *Umwelt – Wirtschaft – Siedlungen im dritten vorchristlichen Jahrtausend Mitteleuropas und Südskandinaviens,* 219–42. Neumünster: Offa-Bücher 84

Czebreszuk, J. & Szmyt, M. 2011. Identities, Differentiation and Interactions on the Central European Plain in the 3rd millennium BC. In Hansen, S. & Müller, J. (eds), *Sozialarchäologische Perspektive: Gesellschaftlicher Wandel 5000–1500 v. Chr. zwichen Atlantik und Kaukasus*, 269–291. Darmstadt

Czebreszuk, J., & Szmyt, M. 2012. Bell Beakers and the Cultural Milieu of North European Plain. In Fokkens, H. & Nicolis, F. (eds), *Background to Beakers. Inquiries into Regional Cultural Backgrounds of the Bell Beakers Complex*, 157–75. Leiden: Sidestone Press

Domańska, L. 2013. *Krzemieniarstwo horyzontu klasycznowióreckiego kultury pucharów lejkowatych na Kujawach.* Łódź: Uniwersytet Łódź

Furmanek, M. 2017. Box 3: Kornice, site 33. Bell Beaker culture burial ground and settlement. In Włodarczak 2017 (ed.), 323–4

Furmanek, M., Hałuszko, A., Mackiewicz, M., & Myślecki, B. 2015. New data for research on the Bell Beaker Culture in Upper Silesia, Poland. In Meller, H., Arz, H. W., Jung, R. & Risch, R. (eds), 2015. *2200 BC – Ein Klimasturz als Ursache für den Zerfall der Alten Welt? 7. Mitteldeutscher Archäologentag vom 23. bis 26. Oktober 2014 in Halle (Saale), 525–38.* Tagungen des Landesmuseum für Vorgeschichte 12/II. Halle/Saale: Landesamt für Denkmalpflege und Archäologie Sachsen-Anhalt

Jażdżewski, K. 1937. Ślady kultury pucharów dzwonowatych na Kujawach. *Z otchłani wieków* 12, 83–94

Józwiak, B. 2003. *Społeczności subneolitu wschodnioeuropejskiego na Niżu Polskim w międzyrzeczu Odry i Wisły.* Poznań: Wydawnictwo Poznańskie

Kadrow, S. 1995. *Gospodarka i społeczeństwo. Wczesny okres epoki brązu w Małopolsce.* Kraków: Instytut Archeologii

Kadrow, S. 2001. *U progu nowej epoki. Gospodarka i społeczeństwo wczesnego okresu epoki brązu w Europie Środkowej.* Kraków: Instytut Arxeikigii

Kamieńska, J., & Kulczycka-Leciejewiczowa, A. 1970. The Bell Beaker Culture. In Wiślański, T. (ed.) *The Neolithic in Poland*, 366-–83. Wrocław-Warszawa-Kraków: Instytut Historic Kultury Materialnaj

Kostrzewski, J. 1935. Przyczynki do poznania wczesnej epoki brązu. I. Kultura iwieńska. *Wiadomości Archeologiczne* 13, 75–94

Kośko, A. 1979. *Rozwój kulturowy społeczeństw Kujaw w okresach schyłkowego neolitu i wczesnej epoki brązu.* Poznań: Adam Mickiewicz University

Kośko, A. 1988. Rozwój kulturowy społeczeństw Kujaw w okresie późnego neolitu oraz interstadium epok neolitu i brązu w aspekcie recepcji egzogennych wzorców kulturotwórczych. In Cofta-Broniewska, A. (ed.), *Kontakty pradziejowych społeczeństw Kujaw z innymi ludami Europy*, 145–83. Inowrocław: Urząd Miejski

Kośko, A & Szmyt, M. 2007. Opatowice – *Wzgórze Prokopiaka, vol. II. Studia i materiały do badań nad późnym neolitem Wysoczyzny Kujawskiej* II. Poznań: Wydawnictwo Poznańskie

Kozłowski, L. 1920. Wielkopolska w epoce kamienia. Część II. *Przegląd Archeologiczny I* (II), 1–2, 1–51

Kulczycka-Leciejewiczowa, A. 1993. *Osadnictwo neolityczne w Polsce południowo-zachodniej.* Wrocław: Instytut Archeolgii i Etnologii

Kupryjanowicz, M., & Szal, M. 2015. Palinologiczne ślady osadnictwa prehistorycznego w centralnej części Puszczy Knyszyńskiej / Palynological traces of prehistoric settlement activity in the central part of the Knyszyn Primeval Forest. In Wawrusiewicz, A., Januszek, K., & Manasterski, D. (eds), 2015, 225–41

Machnik, J. 1979. Krąg kultur ceramiki sznurowej. In Hensel, W. & Wiślański, T. (eds), *Prahistoria ziem polskich, vol. II, Neolit*, 337–441. Wrocław-Warszawa-Kraków-Gdańsk: Instytut Historic Kultury Materialnaj

Makarowicz, P. 1993. Osada ludności z interstadium epok neolitu i brązu w Smarglinie, woj. włocławskie, stan. 53. *Sprawozdania Archeologiczne* 45, 113–46

Makarowicz, P. 1998. Kujawski nurt trzcinieckiego kręgu kulturowego – podstawy taksonomiczne. In Kośko,

A. & Czebreszuk, J. (eds), '*Trzciniec' – system kulturowy czy interkulturowy proces?*, 33–60. Poznań: Wydawnictwo Poznańskie

Makarowicz, P. 2000. Osadnictwo społeczności kultury iwieńskiej oraz trzcinieckiego kręgu kulturowego (2400–1400/1300 BC). In Kośko, A. (ed.), *Archeologiczne badania ratownicze wzdłuż trasy gazociągu tranzytowego, vol. III, Kujawy, part 4, Osadnictwo kultur późnoneolitycznych oraz interstadium epok neolitu i brązu: 3900 – 1400/1300 przed Chr.*, 457–550. Poznań: Wydawnictwo Poznańskie

Makarowicz, P. 2003. Northern and Southern Bell Beakers in Poland. In Czebreszuk, J. & Szmyt, M. (eds), *The Northeast Frontier of Bell Beakers. Proceedings of the symposium held at the Adam Mickiewicz University, Poznań (Poland), May 26–29 2002*. 39–49. Oxford: British Archaeological Reports International Series 1155

Makarowicz, P. 2010. *Trzciniecki krąg kulturowy – wspólnota pogranicza Wschodu i Zachodu Europy*. Poznań: Wydawnictwo Poznańskie

Makarowicz, P. & Czebreszuk, J. 1995. Ze studiów nad tradycją pucharów dzwonowatych w zachodniej strefie Niżu Polski. *Folia Praehistorica Posnaniensia* 7, 99–133

Makohonienko, M. 2008. Szata roślinna i etapy rozwoju krajobrazu kulturowego Kujaw w rejonie Pagórków Radziejowskich w okresie neolitu i epoce brązu. Podstawy palinologiczne. In Bednarczyk, J., Czebreszuk, J., Makarowicz, P. & Szmyt, M. (eds), *Na pograniczu światów. Studia z pradziejów międzymorza bałtycko-pontyjskiego ofiarowane Profesorowi Aleksandrowi Kośko w 60. rocznicę urodzin*, 353–70. Poznań: Wydawnictwo Poznańskie

Manasterski, D. 2009. *Pojezierze Mazurskie u schyłku neolitu i na początku epoki brązu w świetle zespołów typu Ząbie-Szestno*. Warszawa: Instytut Archeologii

Nowak, M. 2009. *Drugi etap neolityzacji ziem polskich*. Kraków: Instytut Archeologii

Papis, P. 2013. Źródła neolityczne ze stanowiska Zalesie 2, gm. Międzyzdroje, woj. zachodniopomorskie, Szczecin, unpubl. MA thesis

Piezonka, H. 2012. Stone Age hunter-gatherer ceramics of north-eastern Europe: new insights into the dispersal of an essential innovation. *Documenta Praehistorica* 39, 23–51

Rosiak, A. & Kałużna-Czaplińska, J. 2015. Analizy substancji organicznych zachowanych w masie ceramicznej / Analysis of organic substances preserved in the ceramic mass. In Wawrusiewicz, A., Januszek, K., & Manasterski, D. (eds), 2015, 273–82

Rzepecki, S. 2011. *The roots of megalithism in the TRB culture*. Łódź: Instytut Archeologii

Simonsen, J. 2017. *Daily Life at the Turn of the Neolithic. A comparative study of longhouses with sunken floors at Resengaard and nine other settlements in the Limfjord region, South Scandinavia*. Moesgaard: Jutland Archaeological Society Publications 98

Sobieraj, J. 2017. Beyond the world of farmers: the Subneolithic, 4000–2000 BC. In Włodarczak, P. (ed.), 337–60

Szmyt, M. 1996. *Społeczności kultury amfor kulistych na Kujawach*. Poznań: Fontes Archaeologici Posnaniensis 46

Szmyt, M. 2013. *Late Neolithic Landscapes on the Polish Lowland: people, culture and economy in Kujawy – 4th and 3rd millennia BC*. Poznan/Bonn: Studien zur Archäologie in Ostmitteleuropa / Studia nad Pradziejami Europy Środkowej 12

Szmyt, M. 2017. Collective graves, flint axes, and cows. The people of the Globular Amphora Culture on the Vistula and Odra. In Włodarczak, P., 211–73

Wawrusiewicz, A., Januszek, K. & Manasterski, D. 2015. *Obiekty obrzędowe pucharów dzwonowatych z Supraśla. Złożenie darów – przejęcie terenu czy integracja kulturowa? / Ritual features of Bell beakers in Supraśl. The offering – taking posession of the land or cultural integration?* Białystok: Muzeum Podlaskie w Białymstoku

Wierzbicki, J. 1999. Łupawski mikroregion osadniczy ludności kultury pucharów lejkowatych. Poznań: Adam Mickiewicz University

Włodarczak, P. 2006. *Kultura ceramiki sznurowej na Wyżynie Małopolskiej*. Kraków: Instytut Archaeologii

Włodarczak, P. (ed.) 2017. *The Past Societies. Polish Lands from the first evidence of human presence to the Early Middle Ages. Vol. 2. 5500 – 2000 BC*. Warszawa: Institute of Archaeology and Ethnology of the Polish Academy of Sciences

Włodarczak, P. 2017a. Battle axes and beakers. The Final Eneolithic societies. In Włodarczak, (ed.), 275–336

Włodarczak, P. 2017b. Towards the Bronze Age in south-eastern Poland (2300–2000 BC). In Włodarczak, (ed.), 377–97

Żurowski, J. 1932. Pierwsze ślady kultury puharów dzwonowatych w Polsce. *Wiadomości Archeologiczne* 11, 117–68

15

Bell Beaker settlements in Denmark

Torben Sarauw

Bell Beaker-inspired pottery has now been found at number of localities in Denmark, especially in Jutland, and these sites must predominantly be interpreted as settlements (Fig. 15.1). Since 2007, when a similar review was undertaken, the number of these sites has risen by *c.* 40% (Sarauw 2007a). This striking increase is a direct by-product of major activity in the construction industry during the last decade, and it reflects the many extensive open area excavations that have consequently been undertaken in Denmark. Another important observation is the steadily deteriorating state of preservation of the building remains from this period, as will become evident from the examples given below. Denmark is an intensively cultivated agricultural country, and many Late Neolithic house sites have therefore suffered heavy plough damage. As a result, it is often only the final remnants that are found in archaeological excavations. Fortunately, the story also has a positive side and the increased excavation activity, in conjunction with amendments to the Museums Act of 2003, has afforded excellent opportunities for radiocarbon dating and other scientific analyses. This has resulted, for example, in a greater number of finds of plant macro-remains being analysed and published (eg, Andreasen 2009; Jensen 2013).

Most of the known Beaker sites still consist of houses with a larger or smaller sunken part filled with cultural deposits that have provided good preservation conditions especially for pottery and flint (Table 15.1). Other incidences of large pits and cultural deposits have, furthermore, often previously been erroneously interpreted and therefore not recognised as the remains of poorly-preserved, plough-damaged house sites. It was first with the publication of the three Beaker houses at Myrhøj in western Himmerland that a greater awareness emerged of what the buildings of this time looked like and how persistent long-term ploughing could

Context	%	*No.*
Houses	57.3	51
Pits	9	8
Surface finds	7.9	7
Culture layer	13.5	12
Miscellaneous	12.4	11

Table 15.1: Contexts for finds of Bell Beaker pottery. Grave finds are omitted

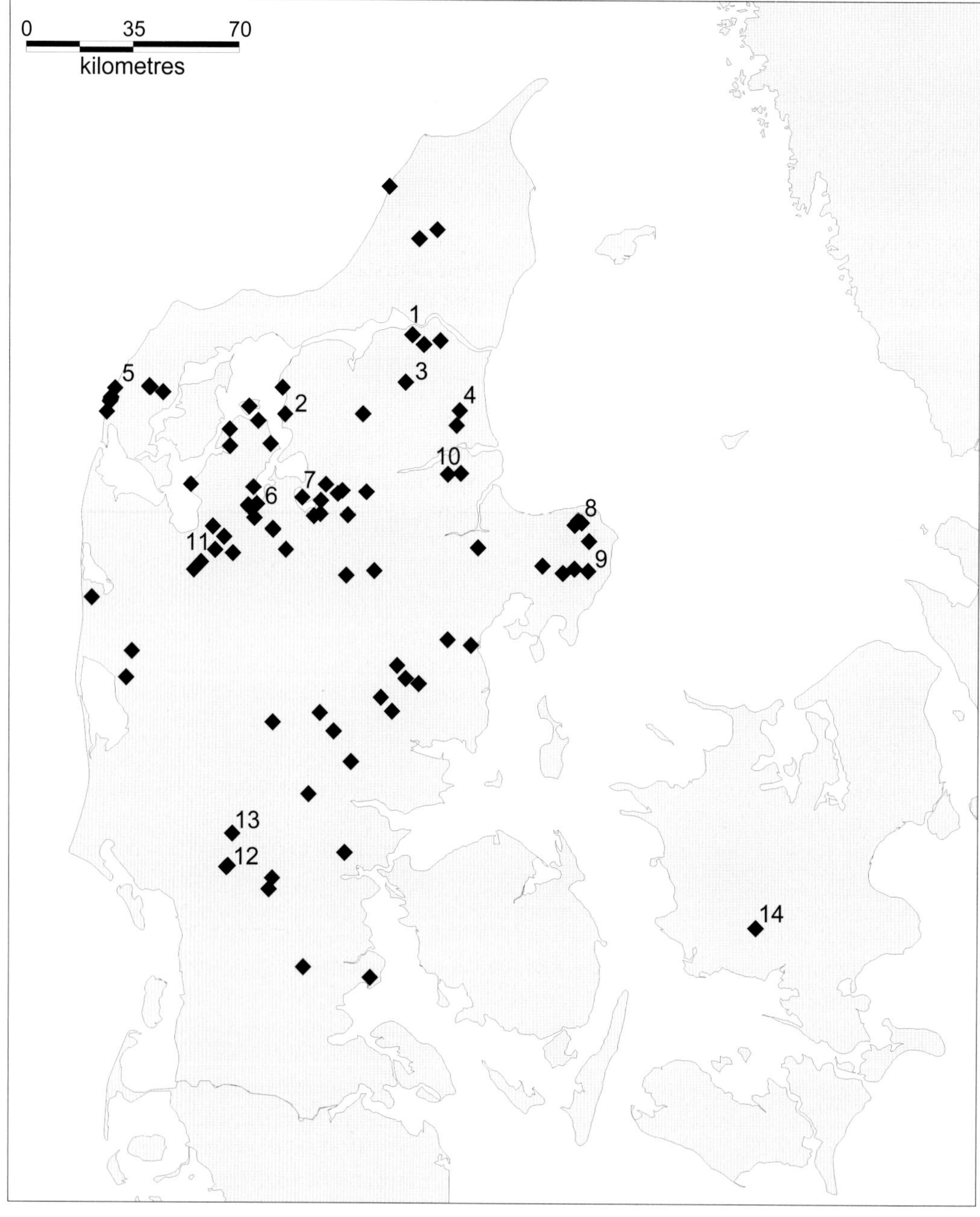

Figure 15.1: The distribution of sites with Bell Beaker material in Denmark (see Table 15.1). The most important sites mentioned in the paper are: 1 – Bejsebakken; 2 – Myrhøj; 3 – Støvring Ådale, Kronhjorten; 4 – Solbjerg; 5 – Lyngby; 6 – Glattrup IV; 7 – Skrubben; 8 – Hemmed Plantage & Kirke; 9 – Diverhøj; 10 – Sem Bakker; 11 – Stendis; 12 – Nørre Holsted III; 13 – Tørsiggård; 14 – Borup Riis

markedly change the appearance of the house remains, destroying all but the deep, sunken parts (Jensen 1973, 106). The contextual conditions presented in Table 15.1 should therefore be treated with some reservation because, given the often deficient or limited areas excavated, it is difficult to evaluate what the individual feature types or contexts actually represent. A good illustration of this is provided by a small but characteristic group of sites where intact or crushed Bell Beakers have been found in pits. One example is at Sem Bakker in eastern Jutland, where a private individual dug up two undecorated vessels and a Bell Beaker from what was possibly a pit (*AUD* 1992, no. 275; Hübner 2005, 209). Another is at Tørsiggård, in southern Jutland, where a Bell Beaker was found during the covering of a potato clamp (Kjersgaard 1965, 122): The vessel had originally been placed upside-down in a shallow pit. The question is whether finds like these represent ordinary settlement refuse pits or whether they should be interpreted as some form of votive feature. Bell Beakers have also been used in wetland offerings, as seen at Lyngby, south-west of Thisted in north-western Jutland, where a Bell Beaker was found at the foot of a coastal slope.[1] The vessel had apparently been placed in a hollow which, according to the finder, also contained peat. A fourth find, which is probably settlement related but difficult to perceive simply as a refuse pit, was encountered at Nørre Holsted between Kolding and Esbjerg: At the base of a 0.75 m deep oval pit measuring 2 × 1.4 m lay sherds from two or three Bell Beakers and 17 loom weights of fired clay (Rindel 1993, 21; Grundvad & Poulsen 2014). The pit fill also contained large quantities of charcoal. This feature was originally interpreted as a weaving pit but should probably be interpreted as some kind of votive arrangement located in the marginal zone of a settlement area (*ibid.*). Two other pits located a couple of hundred metres to the north in the same settlement area are also interesting in this respect as both showed traces of fire in the form of charcoal and red, burnt sand. One of them contained half a Bell Beaker while the other yielded a complete saddle quern and two straight-walled beakers (Grundvad & Poulsen 2013, 10; 2014, 17).

Another question that should be highlighted here is when can a settlement be ascribed to the Beaker complex and when should it simply be dated instead to the early part of the Late Neolithic (LN I), which is coeval with the Beaker complex in Denmark *c.* 2350–1950 BC (Vandkilde *et al.* 1996; Sarauw 2008b, 116)? More than 340 house sites from LN I, distributed across *c.* 160 localities, are now known from Denmark (Nielsen forthcoming).[2] Of these, almost 100, distributed across 48 localities, can be ascribed to the Beaker complex but the true number is probably much greater, as some of the Jutish two-aisled houses without a sunken part and with an early date (*c.* 2350–2000 BC) should perhaps also be assigned to this complex. Poorly-preserved two-aisled house sites with no associated pits or cultural deposits and the like, often contain no finds, which is why they are typically referred, either typologically or on the basis of radiocarbon dates, to LN I. There are, however, examples of house types with and without sunken parts occurring side by side at several localities in Jutland, for example at Bejsebakken and Glattrup IV, demonstrating that both types were known and used during this period (Sarauw 2006; Simonsen 2017, 130ff.). Nevertheless, it remains somewhat of a mystery why one house type was sometimes preferred to the other, and why houses at this time had sunken floors at all.

If we examine the distribution of the Beaker complex in Denmark, a new pattern appears to be emerging as the number of sites increases (Fig. 15.1). The distribution is no longer specifically associated with northern Jutland and Djursland (eg, Vandkilde 2001, fig. 9). On the contrary, marked concentrations have now become evident in the south-western Limfjord area and within a belt extending across eastern and central Jutland. It is however possible that the distribution map is biased by areas of archaeological responsibility associated with specific museums, for example around Thy and Skive, having museum staff with a particular interest in this period (eg, Liversage 1989; 2003; Simonsen 2017, 121ff.). Furthermore, it is striking that a 'Bell Beaker-free' area still exists between the southernmost locality in southern Jutland and the northernmost one in northern Germany (eg, Mertens 2003). There is also a remarkable absence of finds on the Danish islands: A Maritime Beaker turned up during the excavation of a medieval village at Borup Riis on Zealand, but there is no further information on its context (Ebbesen 2006, footnote 15), and there are five or six finds of Bell Beakers from Funen and Langeland, predominantly from passage graves. Several stray finds of classic Beaker pressure-flaked barbed and tanged arrowheads are recorded from Funen which, together with Bell Beakers found in graves, probably represent an early, more easterly orientated phase (eg, Ebbesen 2006, 80; Sarauw 2008b, 111).

Settlement structure and site continuity

If we take a closer look at the placing of the settlements in the landscape, in northern Jutland they are located especially on sandy soils on smaller or larger plateaus and often on south-facing terrain. They also frequently lie close to watercourses and meadowlands. The situation is similar elsewhere in Denmark, for example at Hemmed Kirke and Hemmed Plantage on Djursland, where the settlement lay on a sandy ridge above a former wetland area (Boas 1993, 128). A further example is provided by the settlement at Nørre Holsted in southern Jutland, which was situated on a sandy plateau with a large wetland area to the east and a stream to the north (Grundvad *et al.* 2015, 52). This clear preference for elevated terrain is further underlined by the discovery in several instances, for example at Hovergård and Diverhøj, of house sites underneath barrows (Jensen 1984; Asingh 1988). In a few fortunate cases, such as the Myrhøj and Hemmed settlements, house remains have also been sealed by shifting-sand deposits and with good preservation conditions (Jensen 1973, 64; Boas 1993, 119). Shifting sand may also be found in fill layers in the sunken part of the houses, and this could indicate that the surrounding landscape has been intensively cultivated.

It is difficult to make definitive statements about the settlement structure and the size of the settlements. Most investigations have taken the form of narrow linear trenches, and only minor fragments of the greater whole have therefore been exposed. In many cases, for example at Stendis near Holstebro or several of the Beaker sites in the Skive area, the settlements typically comprise one to three houses (Skov 1982; Simonsen 2017, 121ff.). Experience from localities where larger areas have been exposed does, however, often indicate greater complexity. This is true for example at Bejsebakken in northern Jutland, where, including trial trenches, an area of *c.* 9.5 hectares was uncovered and where it became evident that the Late Neolithic settlement was spread over a very large area (Sarauw 2006). The settlement traces here comprised 23 house sites of various types and several major occurrences of cultural deposits but there were relatively few pits given the size of the area. Analysis of the pottery, combined with the radiocarbon dates, showed that the settlement, which was grouped in three to four concentrations, covered a period of *c.* 200–300 years and had, in the form of two to three farms, moved around within a large resource area during this time (Sarauw 2008b, 103f.).

Another example that will be mentioned here, and to which we will return, is the Neolithic settlement complex in Støvring Ådale, where the Historical Museum of Northern Jutland has undertaken numerous investigations over the last decade. A total area of more than 63 hectares has been subjected to evaluation. Of this, the topsoil was removed from a total of 8.5 hectares in connection with the excavations. This resulted in the identification of five minor sites with houses dating from the Single Grave culture to the Late Neolithic. Ten houses have been investigated in total, of which four have sunken parts. One of these settlements is Kronhjorten (Fig. 15.2) where, within an area of 3500 m^2, the remains of two two-aisled houses and two houses with sunken floors were investigated and all dated to the early Late Neolithic. Three of the houses contained Beaker pottery. Two of the houses, one with and one without a sunken part, have been radiocarbon dated to the transition between the Single Grave culture and the Late Neolithic.

Similar large excavations have been undertaken at Nørre Holsted in southern Jutland where, over the course of several campaigns, a total area of ten hectares has been uncovered and 16 two-aisled houses have been excavated, of which ten have been dated to the Late Neolithic (Grundvad *et al.* 2015). In addition, there are 14 three-aisled longhouses from the Early Bronze Age. At least three of the houses have partly-sunken floors, and one of them can, together with some special pits mentioned above, be dated to an early part of the Late Neolithic, based on the Beaker pottery (Dollar 2013; Grundvad & Poulsen 2013; 2014). The area also included a small burial ground and at least one house from the Single Grave culture. There appears therefore to have been some form of site continuity over a longer period. Even though the total area excavated at the Hemmed settlements, including Egehøj from the Early Bronze Age, was very small, a similar site continuity is evident (Boas 1983; 1993). This means that, within a radius of 1 km, there were house sites from the end of the Single Grave culture to the middle of the Bronze Age (*ibid.*). Despite some gaps in the settlement, there also seems be an extended continuity of place, from an early part of the Late Neolithic to the Early Bronze Age, at Resengaard, near Skive, including the nearby settlement at Marienlyst Strand, where 27 sunken-floored houses have been investigated (Simonsen 2017, 363).

A partial conclusion from the above could be that the Beaker settlements should predominantly be seen as diffuse and labile: the farmsteads have often moved around within a large resource area. But there are also several examples of areas where several farms could theoretically be contemporaneous. One example is Myrhøj where, within an area

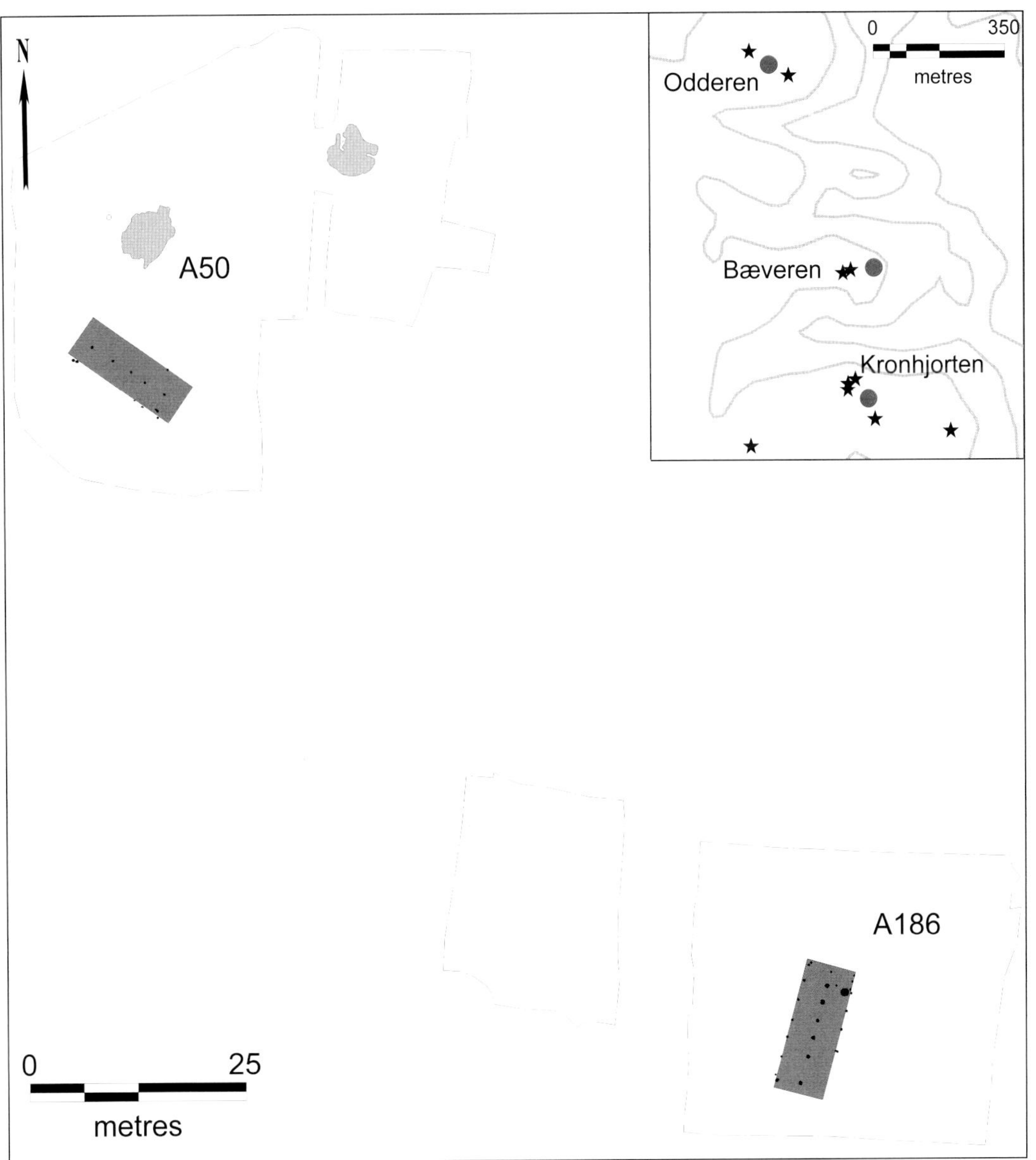

Figure 15.2: Kronhjorten in Støvring Ådale in Himmerland. Detailed drawings of houses A50 and A186 are shown in Figs 15.4 & 5. Both houses are radiocarbon dated to the transition between the Single Grave culture and the Late Neolithic. The small map insert shows all the houses (black stars) from the Single Grave culture and the Late Neolithic in Støvring Ådale, as well as the distances between the three localities of Bæveren, Kronhjorten and Odderen

of 500 m^2, there were the remains of three houses with no stratigraphical relationship to each other (Jensen 1973). At *c.* 43% of these settlements there are therefore at least two or more houses. However, it is very difficult to make definite statements about their contemporaneity unless there are special stratigraphical circumstances or a large number of radiocarbon dates are available.

Houses from the Late Single Grave culture

Before considering the houses from the early part of the Late Neolithic in more detail, it is necessary to consider selected houses from the final part of the Single Grave culture. As already outlined above, and as will be shown in both this and the following section, a form of continuity of place is evident at several localities, with settlement traces being present from both the Single Grave culture and the early Late Neolithic. The house types are also the same, even though they appear to vary somewhat in size. Moreover, in several instances it is difficult to determine whether a settlement should be ascribed to the Single Grave culture or the early Late Neolithic. This is true for example of the trapezoid post-built houses at Tandrupgård in western

Himmerland and in Støvring Ådale, described in the next section. The dating problems apply to both the material culture, where the finds assemblages point both backwards and forwards in time, and to the radiocarbon dates. As a result, several houses are dated to an overlapping period of about a century between the Single Grave culture and the Late Neolithic. The late single graves in central Jutland are therefore contemporary with the earliest settlements containing Beaker pottery (Vandkilde *et al.* 1996, 187; Hübner 2005, 750). The overlap extends from about 2350–2250 BC, although the transitional period was in reality probably shorter (Hübner 2005, 666f.; Sarauw 2008b, 111). These early Beaker settlements, or 'transitional settlements', are characterised by a mixture of Beaker-inspired pottery and traditions from the Single Grave culture, such as the use of straight-walled Beakers. The flint assemblages can similarly point in two directions, for example with the presence of both pressure-flaked arrowheads and D-arrowheads. A classic example of this is seen at Hemmed Plantage and Hemmed Kirke, where two houses are dated to around the transition between the Single Grave culture and the Late Neolithic (Boas 1993). At Hemmed Plantage, a house was partially excavated which had a sunken eastern end containing Beaker-inspired pottery (see next section). About 200 m to the west, at Hemmed Kirke, an E–W-oriented two-aisled house was investigated which measured *c.* 16 × 6 m, corresponding to an area of 94 m², and had a rectangular ground plan with rounded corners (Fig. 15.3,A).[3] The wall traces comprised oval post-holes spaced about 2 m apart. The roof-bearing construction consisted of three posts, and there was a further post in each gable. The cultural deposits over the house were found to contain both pottery and flint from the Late Single Grave culture / early Late Neolithic, including D-arrowheads and pressure-flaked arrows of several types (Boas 1993, 127f.). A house at Solbakkegård IV, in south-western Jutland, and one at Lille Torup, in Vendsyssel, can be dated typologically to the Late Single Grave culture (Siemen 2008, 73; Sarauw forthcoming). The house at Solbakkegård measured 5.7 × 12.2 m, corresponding to 64 m², and was oriented approximately E–W (Fig. 15.3,B). Its roof-bearing construction consisted of three posts. In addition to a further two-aisled house, the same locality also had flat graves dating from the Late Single Grave culture and a cremation grave containing a Bell Beaker and four pressure-flaked, barbed and tanged arrowheads (*AUD* 1999, no. 611). At Lille Torup, in addition to a house measuring *c.* 15 × 5 m (house C) with a rectangular ground-plan and traces of four roof-bearing posts, there were settlement traces from the Late Neolithic. A poorly-preserved two-aisled house was also found at Nørre Holsted where, as already mentioned, houses from the Late Neolithic and special pits containing Beaker pottery were also investigated (Dollar 2013, 46; Grundvad & Poulsen 2013). The house measured *c.* 13 × 5 m and six pottery vessels had been buried by the corner post to the north-east, stacked one on top of the other (*ibid.*). At Uglviggård near Esbjerg, a pottery vessel containing charred grains of naked barley was found in a post-hole belonging to a house from the Late Single Grave culture (Andreasen 2009, 37). Similar house offerings have also been discovered in early Late Neolithic houses, for example at Møsvrå near Kolding, where a Bell Beaker was found in a post-hole or pit that should probably be assigned to the building (Sarauw 2006, 53; Eisenschmidt 2014, 96f.; Nielsen forthcoming).

Most of the house sites from the Late Single Grave culture consist, however, of poorly-preserved remains of buildings with partly-sunken floors and in a few cases scattered post-holes that do not form any obvious pattern. This is true for example at Blegind near Skanderborg, Solbjerg house I in eastern Himmerland (Jensen 1973, 106ff.; Johansen 1986), Nørre Boris in north-western Jutland (Simonsen 1987, 141), Ørum on Djursland (Nielsen & Rasmussen 2012, 41) and several other places. A classic example is provided by two houses at Vorbasse, which were investigated in connection with a large Iron Age village (Fig. 15.3,C) (Hvass 1977; 1986). The Vorbasse locality is of further interest because a hoard containing tongued wedges was also investigated there, as well as a number of pits distributed over a *c.* 350 × 200 m area on the Iron Age site (Hvass 1986, 326). This gives an indication of the size of the resource area that was exploited. One of the houses was very poorly preserved, while the other comprised the remains of the sunken part and the presumed northern wall (Fig. 15.3,C). Its dimensions were a minimum of 4 × 6 m. In the same building, traces of a small hearth

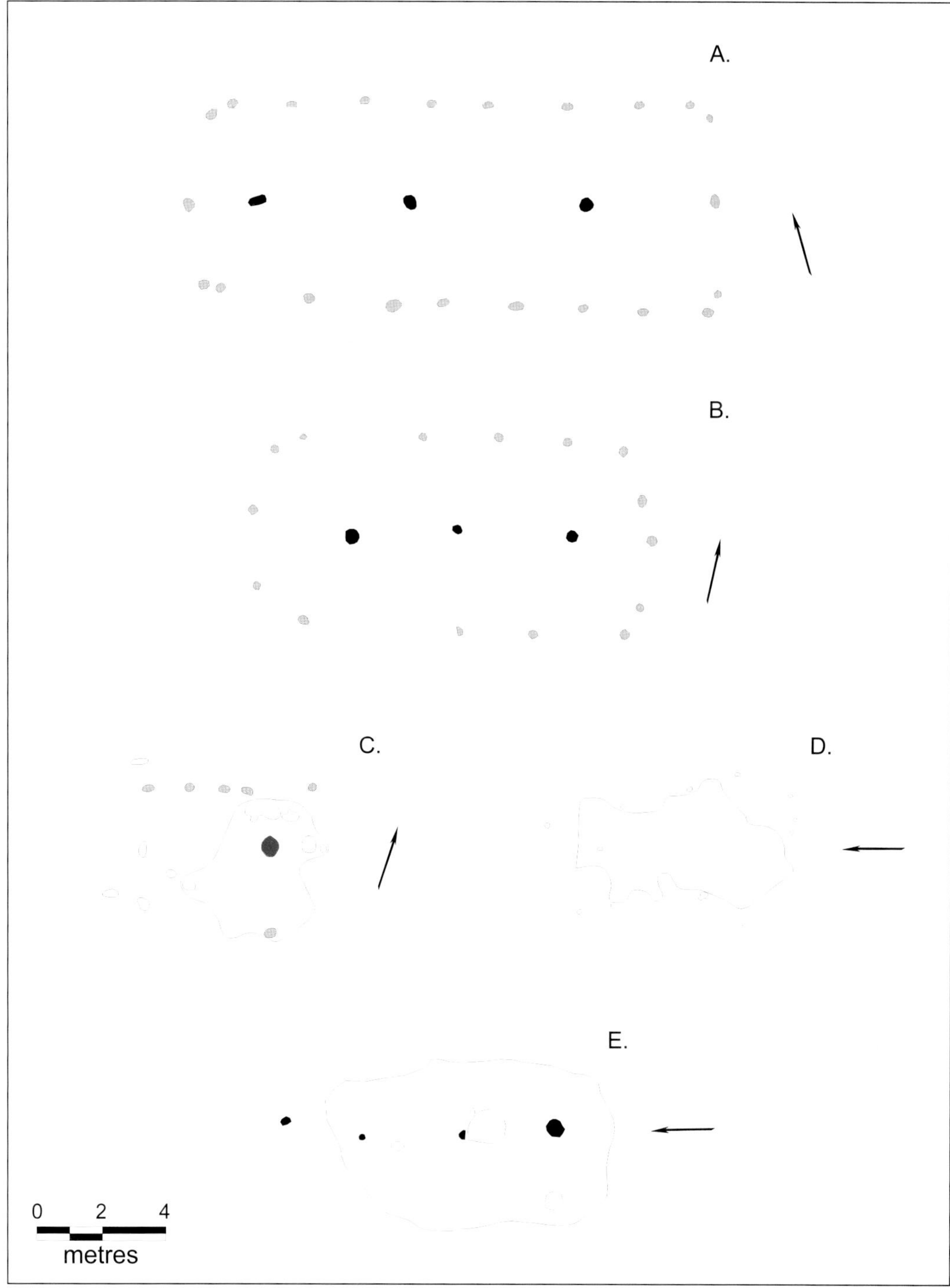

Figure 15.3: Houses from the Late Single Grave culture. Hearths and cooking pits are marked in red. The traces of roof-bearing posts are evident as black features. A – Hemmed Kirke house VI (after Boas 1993); B – Solbakkegård IV (after Siemen 2008); C – Vorbasse house XXII (after Hvass 1977); D – Sønder Novrup (after Siemen 2008); E – Støvring Ådale, Bæveren

were evident from the red colouration of the underlying subsoil sand. A presumed stone-set hearth was also found at the base of the sunken part of house I at Solbjerg, together with a charcoal-filled pit (Johansen 1986, 281). Larger and more regular sunken-floored houses are also known from Sønder Novrup near Esbjerg and Støvring Ådale, Bæveren, in Himmerland (Siemen 2008, 74). At Sønder Novrup, the house remains comprised a large, irregular sunken part, where there had been three roof posts, and scattered wall and gable posts (Fig. 15.3,D). The building measured *c.* 4–5 × 11 m and was oriented N–S. The house site at Bæveren in Støvring Ådale was also oriented N–S and had minimum dimensions of 5 × 10 m; it had traces of four roof-posts and a 0.7 m deep pit that possibly belongs to the building (Fig. 15.3,E). These house sites therefore point forwards in time and clearly underline the fact that sunken-floored Late Neolithic houses had their roots in the Jutish Late Single Grave culture. The houses did not become larger and more standardised in form until the Late Neolithic.

Bell Beaker houses

The Bell Beaker houses are specifically characterised by the eastern 40–60% of the building having a sunken floor. Houses of this type are mainly found in Jutland, but also occur sporadically on Funen and Zealand and in Scania. Similar houses are not known from other Beaker contexts outside Denmark and must therefore be perceived as a special tradition related to the Beaker complex in Jutland (but see Czebruszek & Szmyt this volume). The custom of having a sunken floor in part of the house continued into the Early Bronze Age (Boas 1983), when it disappeared, only to reappear in the Early Iron Age.

Like those of the Late Single Grave culture, the size of Beaker houses varies somewhat (Fig. 15.4). For example, house A643 at Bejsebakken, which is interpreted as a dwelling due to the presence of a hearth, measures only 9.5 × 4.5–5 m, corresponding to *c.* 43–47.5 m^2. Another house, A170, measures *c.* 14 × 4.3–5 m, corresponding to *c.* 70 m^2 (Fig. 15.4,B). This should be seen in relation to the fact that the average size of the longhouses at Bejsebakken, both with and without a sunken part, is 83 m^2 (Sarauw 2006, 47). The two-aisled houses without a sunken part at Bejsebakken are typically 15 m long and *c.* 5.6–6 m wide, corresponding to ground plans of 75–80 m^2 (Fig. 15.5,A).

At another locality, Glattrup IV in north-western Jutland, where five houses were investigated, three with and two without a sunken part, the length of the buildings varies from 12.8–16.5 m and the width from 4.5–7.1 m (Simonsen 2017, 68) (Figs 15.4,C & 15.5,C). There is great variation within the individual buildings, as several of the houses are trapezoid in ground-plan. There are, however, also records of larger houses, for example in the Viborg area. A settlement was investigated at Skrubben which had seven houses, six with a sunken part. One of the buildings was 21 m long and up to 6 m wide, corresponding to an area of 110 m^2 (Fig. 15.4,E) (Nielsen 2004, 26). Here too the ground-plan was trapezoid.

A common feature of the two house types ascribed to the early Late Neolithic is that they are often oriented E–W and resemble each other in size and construction. Both often contain traces of four to five roof-posts spaced 2–5 m apart, although exceptions do of course exist. It may be particularly difficult to identify the traces of the roof-bearing posts in the sunken parts because the original post-holes may have disappeared as a result of the particular activities that took place here. The character and degree of preservation of the wall traces may also vary somewhat. Consequently, many houses only have a few scattered post-holes associated with them, despite the fact that the fill layers in the sunken parts would be expected to have had a preservational effect on the traces of the wall construction. These traces may comprise both single and double rows of post, more or less regularly spaced. In some cases, for example Myrhøj house D in western Himmerland or Hemmed Plantage house III, the wall posts at either side of the building appear to have been placed opposite each other, suggesting that they were linked by a cross beam which stabilised the roof construction (Fig. 15.4,F & G). The sunken-floored houses at Resengaard and Glattrup IV are thought to have had 0.5 m wide turf walls supported by external posts and interior panels with stakes and posts (Simonsen 2017, 106ff.). No definite entrances have been identified, although several suggestions can be found in the literature (Boas 1993, 131; Simonsen 2017, 133).

The sunken part of the houses is often elongated or rectangular in plan and, as mentioned above, is often located to the east. Its width corresponds to the width of the house, unless the remains of the building have been severely plough-damaged (eg, Fig. 15.4,D). These sunken features may vary in depth from just a few centimetres to a metre and they therefore represent quite substantial earthworks. The sides usually slope steeply at the long sides and eastern gable. However, the situation is often difficult to decipher because the fill may have been disturbed or slipped during the demolition of the obsolete building or as a result of subsequent cultivation.

Towards the west, and the non-sunken part, the sunken floor slopes more evenly upwards so that the two parts of the house are naturally coupled together. It is often in this area that traces of hearths are found. The sunken parts are usually deepest in the middle and their base can appear relatively flat, albeit within a restricted area. This basal level does, however, often contain several local shallow pits (eg, Fig. 15.4,A & C), the function of which is difficult to explain: Were they intentionally made, or did they result from specific repeated activities such as mucking out?

The fill of the sunken parts may have a complex stratigraphy or be simpler and more homogeneous, thereby indicating a briefer period of accumulation. Definitive floor or dirt layers, arising from the building's period of use, are difficult to demonstrate because *in situ* finds of artefacts such as querns or complete pottery vessels are rare from the house interiors. Moreover, the house sites have often been ploughed through in all directions after they were abandoned, perhaps because these areas had a high soil-nutrient status and the settlement area was part of a larger resource area, within which the farmstead and its inhabitants moved around. An alternative interpretation is that the ploughing should be perceived as a combined practical and ritual act: a kind of rite of transformation from dwelling to field (Simonsen 2017, 393).

The fill layers of the houses, most of which are secondarily deposited, may be rich in finds, especially of pottery and flint, and therefore contain a wealth of information on the various settlement activities. Further to these are large quantities of secondarily deposited fire-cracked stones which, in some way or other, were originally involved in everyday activities such as cooking, heating water, drying grain etc. The pottery in the houses may be very fragmented and worn, but distribution analyses from selected houses at Bejsebakken have shown that the sherds can often be fitted together to make vessel sides, leading in some cases to the interpretation of the fill layers as homogeneous, coeval units (Sarauw 2008b, 91f.). Flint debitage deposited in the houses located in the flint-rich areas of northern Jutland contain a wealth of information on raw-material strategies and the production of for example flint daggers (Sarauw 2008a).

As mentioned above, many Bell Beaker houses contain pits and hearths, which is interesting in relation to how the layout and use of these buildings should be interpreted. In houses with a sunken eastern part there is a tendency for the hearths to lie to the west of this, or at the transition between the sunken and non-sunken parts. This is true for example of houses A170, A643 and A539 at Bejsebakken (Sarauw 2006, 55ff.) (Fig. 15.4,A & B). Similarly, house D at Myrhøj, Hemmed Plantage house III and Diverhøj house I all have hearths to the W (Fig. 15.4,F & G). Further to these are several of the houses at Glattrup IV, which may have one hearth in the sunken part and another just outside it (Simonsen 2017, 131f.) (Fig. 15.4,C). Different types of pits in houses with and without sunken parts bear witness to the various activities undertaken in these buildings. The pit in house A186 at Kronhjorten was 1 m in diameter and 0.2 m deep (Fig. 15.5,B), while several of the pits in the Glattrup houses, which lay close to the walls, were very deep: For example, the north-eastern pit in house 3 had a depth of 0.65 m (Fig. 15.4C). Clusters of pits were also evident in two-aisled house A214 at Bejsebakken and in Hemmed Plantage house III (Figs 15.4,G & 15.5,A). Some of these pits should perhaps be seen in relation to beer brewing (Simonsen 2017, 349). A few of the two-aisled houses that have been radiocarbon dated to the Late Single Grave culture or early Late Neolithic, for example at Visse Nygaard in Himmerland, have had some form of room division, indicating that these buildings had several different functions, despite their limited area of only *c.* 70 m^2 (Fig. 15.5,D). Room division is also seen in the so-called wall-trench houses in southern and central Jutland, which are otherwise typically dated to LN II and the Early Bronze Age (Hertz 1997; Poulsen & Grundvad 2015). The house at Visse Nygaard is atypical in various ways, as it is slightly trapezoid with closely-spaced wall posts and a rounded gable to the north. By the southern gable there are also traces of two roof-bearing posts in a three-aisled construction. Another atypical house was investigated in the settlement complex at Støvring Ådale mentioned above (Fig. 15.5,E). This building is oriented N–S, trapezoid in ground plan and measures 17.8 × 6–7.5 m, giving an area of 117 m^2. In addition to internal supporting posts for the closely-spaced wall posts, there were also four supporting posts

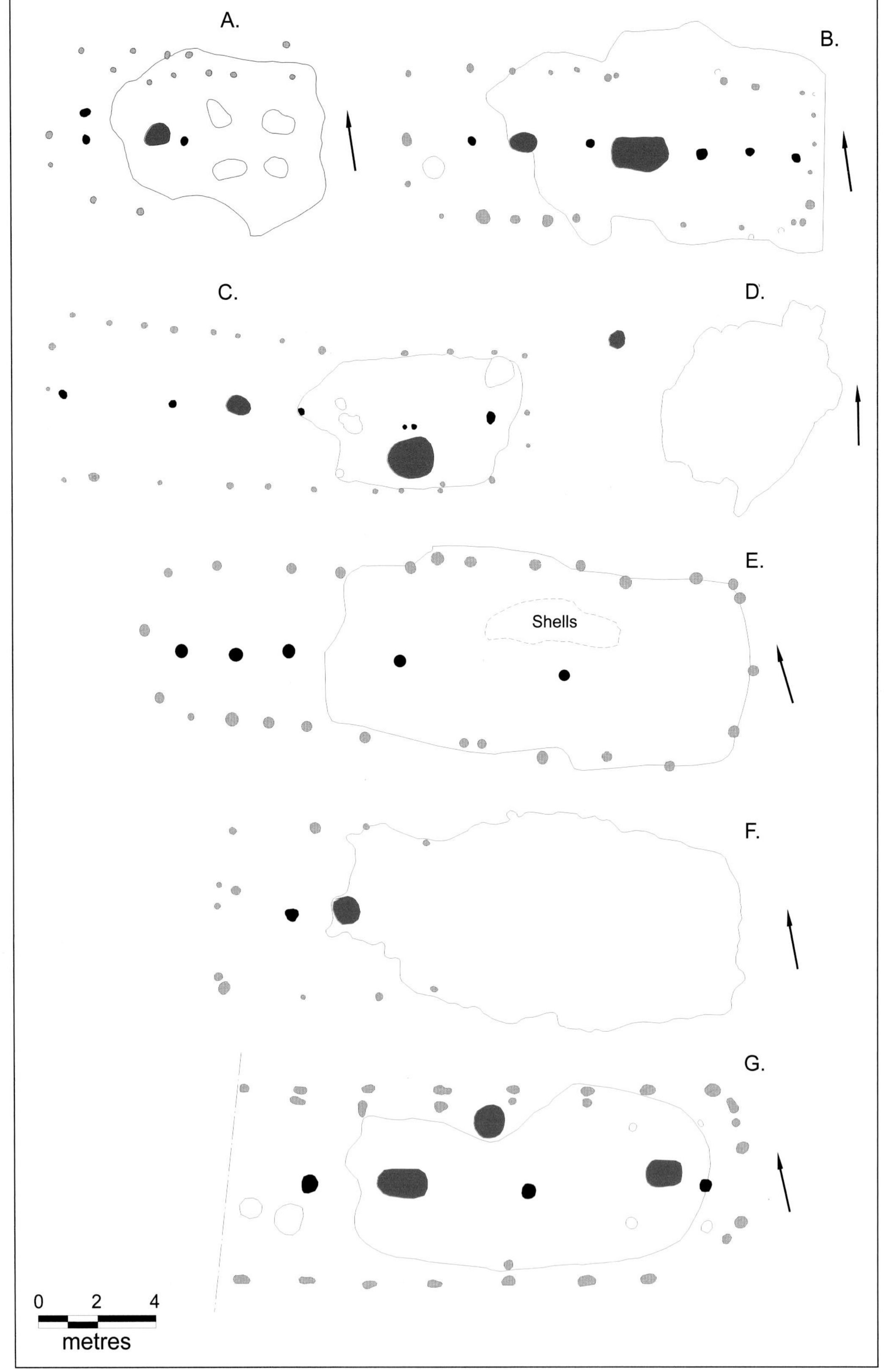

Figure 15.4: Two-aisled Beaker houses with a sunken eastern part. Same key as Fig. 15.3. A – Bejsebakken house A643 (after Sarauw 2006); B – Bejsebakken house A170; C – Glattrup IV house 3 (after Simonsen 2017); D – Kronhjorten house A50; E – Skrubben house I (after Nielsen 2004); F – Myrhøj house D (after Jensen 1973); G – Hemmed Plantage house III (after Boas 1993)

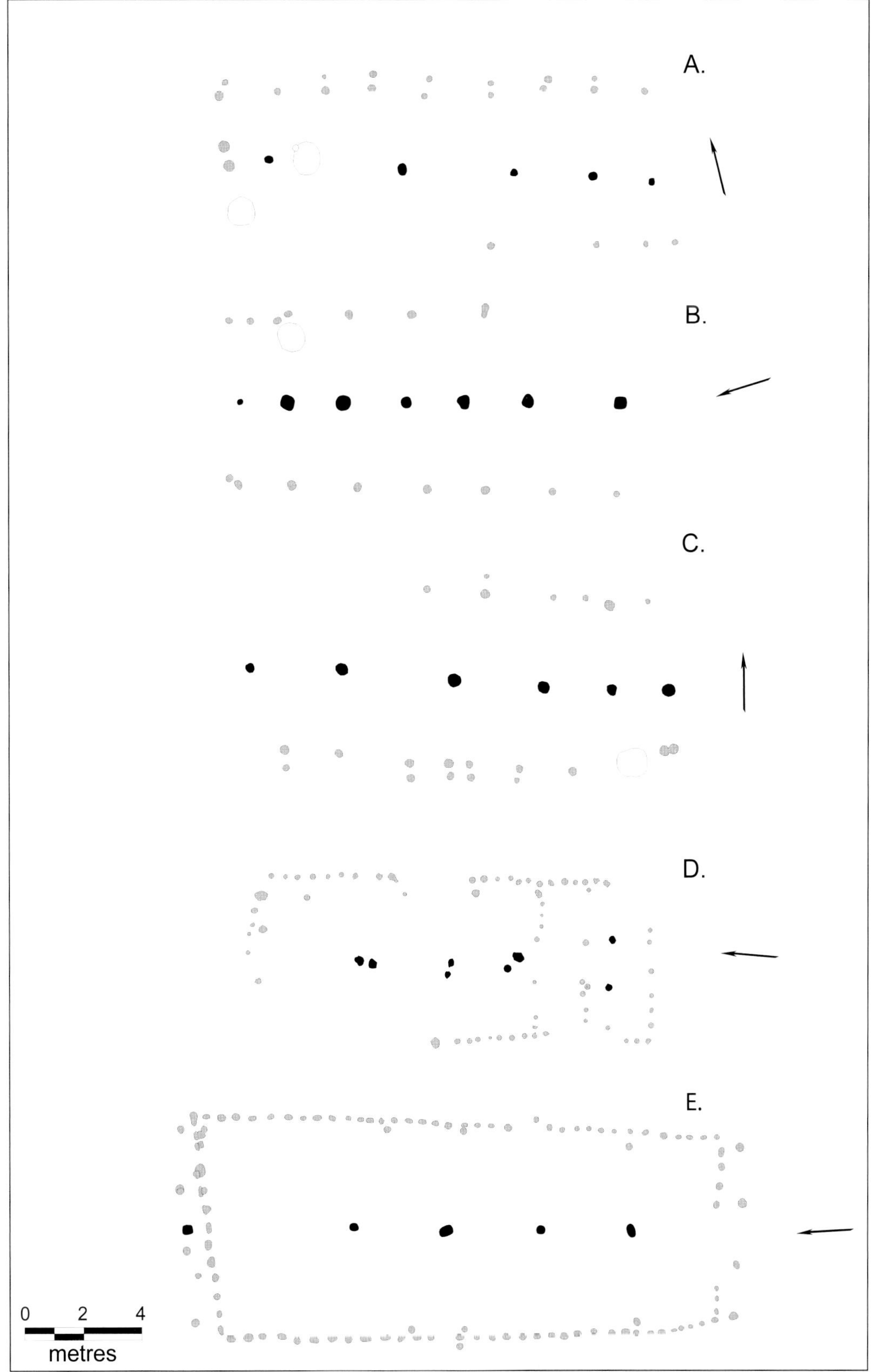

Figure 15.5: Two-aisled houses. A – Bejsebakken house A214 (after Sarauw 2006); B – Kronhjorten house A186, C – Glattrup IV house 4 (after Simonsen 2017); D – Visse Nygaard; E – Støvring Ådale, Odderen

in each gable. The northern roof-bearing post was, furthermore, positioned outside the gable, which resulted in a larger post-free space in the broad western end where the house's hearth was perhaps located. The building's entrances appear to have been to the southern end of the western side. Three radiocarbon dates place the house in the Late Single Grave culture/early Late Neolithic. About 100 m to the north-west lay another house of similar construction with an entrance to the south and an area of *c.* 178 m^2. A parallel to these two buildings is found at Tandrupgård in western Himmerland, where a trapezoid house was found with closely-spaced wall posts and a broad north-facing gable (Jensen 2010, 31). This house has been radiocarbon dated to the transition between the Single Grave culture and the Late Neolithic.

A major question in relation to sunken-floored two-aisled houses is, of course, why was so much energy expended on removing numerous cubic metres of earth, when the entire house could simply have been built above ground? There has also been much debate about the degree to which the sunken parts represented a kind of loose housing area for livestock, while the living quarters lay in the western, non-sunken end (Simonsen 1983, 88; Nielsen 1998, 16; Sarauw 2006, 56ff.). Recently, based on historical analogies, it has been proposed that there was perhaps no rigid division between dwelling and byre in early Late Neolithic houses, but that these buildings had a combined function as an animal shed and barn, where people and animals co-existed under the same roof at specific times of the year (Nielsen forthcoming). Based on the many feature and structure types, and the various activity traces, other researchers have proposed that the sunken parts should be seen as the primary activity areas for the human inhabitants (Simonsen 2017, 150ff.). Moreover, it is maintained, based on the evidence from the Resengaard houses, that there is a link between the sunken-floored construction and the choice of building materials, with the use of turf walls being the explanation for the sunken area (*ibid.*, 152). In other words, there was a desire to create greater headroom in a part of the building. Turf was chosen because it saved on timber and promoted a good indoor climate. Moreover, it is conceivable that the sunken floor provided the opportunity to construct a loft for storage.

In the interpretation of the sunken floors, several recently investigated sites should be highlighted as they contribute important information, even though some of them have rather late dates. Three houses with sunken parts, dating from LN II (1950–1700 BC), were encountered at Petersborg, in eastern Jutland, where several houses from the Late Neolithic – Early Bronze Age have been investigated. At the base of the sunken area in one of the buildings were three round cellar pits, each of which contained a large quantity of charred grain, apparently sorted by cereal species (Borup forthcoming). Large quantities of grain in what must be presumed to be a burnt-down house were also encountered at Hestehaven near Skanderborg (see also Robinson 2000; Møbjerg *et al.* 2007). There was 37 litres of charred grain at the base of the sunken part, perhaps representing part of the year's harvest. In some cases, it was sorted, but some of it had apparently become mixed, possibly due to the collapse of the loft in which it may have been stored (Jensen 2013). There was a house containing Bell Beaker pottery at the same locality. Several of the Resengaard houses also contained charred grain, and house 1 yielded *c.* 14 kg of threshed and processed/winnowed cereals (Henriksen 2001, 7f.; Simonsen 2017, 390). No traces of the containers in which the grain must have been stored were, however, found here. At Kronhjorten, in Støvring Ådale, more than 200 cereal grains were found within a limited area at the base of the sunken floor in a house dated to the Bell Beaker culture, based on the pottery and two radiocarbon dates (Andreasen 2017) (Figs 15.2 & 15.4,D). More interestingly, however, the sampled material was also found to contain straw/stems, rachis segments/glume bases, glumes and seeds, all of which lay heavily compacted directly on the sandy subsoil. The material is interpreted as threshing waste from the processing of emmer and barley, which was subsequently used as a kind of floor covering or litter in the sunken part (*ibid.*). There was no animal dung or hay mixed in with it this litter, but it did contain mouse faeces and a few hazel rods and small oak twigs. The hazel rods may have been part of a wattle construction, while the presence of small twigs of oak should perhaps be interpreted as remains of leaf fodder, even though there is nothing in the building to indicate that is was ever a byre. On the contrary, the sunken area had a large lower stone from a saddle quern and a polissoir at its base, together with a handful of other stones (Fig. 15.6).

It is clear from the above account that the sunken part of the buildings was not used as a byre. In several instances, including at Bejsebakken, this conclusion is supported by phosphate mapping data (Sarauw 2006, 59). Neither is there anything in the layout of the houses such as stall partitions, sturdy posts for the tethering animals or the like that supports the byre theory. Definite byres are first known in Denmark from period II of the Early Bronze Age (Rasmussen 1999, 283; Ethelberg 2000, 192ff.; Grundvad *et al.* 2015, 63). The function of the sunken part must therefore have been the same as in the Late Single Grave culture, when this tradition became established and when a form of consensus apparently emerged with regard to what a house should look like – a consensus that was probably based on the houses' functions and the requirements that people had with respect to layout, organisation and storage.

Conclusion and future perspectives

Important evidence for some form of continuity between the Single Grave and the Bell Beaker cultures is provided by the so-called 'transitional sites' such as Hemmed Kirke, Hemmed Plantage, Kronhjorten, Solbjerg etc., where the material culture, in the form of pottery and flint, suggests that this was the case. Several of these settlements also have traces that can be assigned to the Late Single Grave culture and the early Late Neolithic/Bell Beaker culture. At Solbjerg, in eastern Himmerland, where remains of three poorly-preserved houses with sunken parts were investigated, it is possible to trace how the material culture changes from the Late Single Grave culture to the early Late Neolithic (Jensen 1973, 107f.; Johansen 1986). The earliest house is dated to the Late Single Grave culture, based partly on vessels with a flat rim collar and straight-walled beakers ornamented with vertical lines. But there are also sherds with cross-hatched zones executed in toothed comb. A proportion of the pottery recovered from house II is dominated by sherds with horizontal stripes. The pottery assemblage in house III is of the same character as the Myrhøj pottery, for example sherds ornamented with horizontal, encircling furrows and distinct Bell Beaker motifs, including filled lozenges. Parallels to the pottery assemblage are seen at Kronhjorten in Støvring Ådale, where 260 sherds were found, representing at least 18 pottery vessels. There is ornamentation on 20% of the pottery, and toothed comb is by far the commonest form of decoration (Fig. 15.7). Remains were found of at least four different Bell Beakers, in both thin-walled and coarser wares. Several vessels are ornamented with zones in the Maritime style. In one case there are rows of horizontal lines executed in toothed comb, supplemented with zigzag patterns. There are also chevrons or contiguous triangles executed as furrows as well as a vessel with a flat rim collar decorated with toothed comb. Finally, there is a vessel decorated with vertical cockle impressions. The two-aisled house A186 at the same locality also contained a thin-walled rim sherd in the Maritime style. In addition to a quantity of flint debitage (390 flint waste flakes), a pressure-flaked arrowhead and a D-arrowhead were recovered (Fig. 15.8). Five flint flakes (bifacial thinning flakes) possibly originate from the production of pressure-flaked tools. The house site has been radiocarbon dated to 2460–2200 and 2460–2150 cal BC.[4]

As mentioned above, similar assemblages are evident at Hemmed Kirke and Hemmed Plantage. This underlines that there is some form of continuity and development in the range of available types, with respect to both flint and pottery. A fine example of this is provided by the straight-walled Beakers of the Single Grave culture, which are also found in the early Late Neolithic. The vessel form and ornamentation technique are the same, but Beaker-like ornamental designs have been added. In otherwords foreign elements have been adapted to the local context (Sarauw 2008b, 106). The 'transitional settlements' therefore demonstrate that it was the same family or group of people and their descendants who inhabited these localities but who, over time, adopted a new material culture consistent with the trends seen elsewhere in Jutland, and across north-western Europe as a whole. A corresponding development is evident in the burial customs, where battle axes were replaced by flint daggers, but where the graves were often placed in the barrows of the Single Grave culture (eg, Hübner 2005, 688f.; Sarauw 2007b, 68).

Figure 15.6: Basal level in the sunken-floored house A50, Støvring Ådale, Kronhjorten. The quern stone is seen in the foreground. Photo: Marie Vang Posselt

If we return to the settlements, the house types and the locations of the domestic sites are, as mentioned above, often the same in both periods. The settlements of the Late Single Grave culture do not, however, manifest themselves anywhere near as strongly as the Bell Beaker settlements in the archaeological record. They are fewer in number, and there is a tendency for the houses to be smaller and, if the trapezoid two-aisled houses from the transition between the two periods are excluded, perhaps of rather slighter construction. The latter applies in particular to the houses with sunken parts, as illustrated by the Vorbasse examples. These differences are unlikely to be the result of source-related factors. The degree of plough damage must have been approximately the same for both periods, although slighter and smaller buildings are presumably more difficult to detect and identify. There is, moreover, a tendency for the settlement patterns to change at the beginning of the Late Neolithic such that they became larger and there was greater continuity of place. This sees expression at several settlements, for example Bejsebakken, Glattrup IV and Myrhøj, where there are many more houses than on a typical settlement of the Single Grave culture. The more massive presence of settlements in the Late Neolithic should, however, not necessarily be explained in terms of a huge growth in population, or that new areas were taken into cultivation and settled (Apel 2004, 299; Siemen 2008, 71). If we take Hübner's distribution map for graves from phases 3a and 3b of the Late Single Grave culture, corresponding to *c.* 2450–2250 BC, (Hübner 2005, 659f.), and compare this with the distribution of the Bell Beaker settlements, there is great coincidence, which indicates that people were living in virtually the same areas (Fig. 15.9). An explanation for the observed changes should perhaps be sought instead in a major reorganisation of farming, such that arable agriculture became more diverse in the Late Neolithic, leading to greater stability in food resources (Andreasen 2009, 34; Iversen 2017, 367). While naked

Figure 15.7: Examples of Bell Beaker pottery from house A50, Kronhjorten

barley was the commonest cereal type in the Single Grave culture, wheat and barley were of almost equal importance in the Late Neolithic (Andreasen 2009, 17f.). In the Late Neolithic, people apparently cultivated several different cereal types at the same time, which reduced the risk of a failed harvest. The fact that people also exploited natural resources is demonstrated by one of the Vorbasse houses, where acorns, hazelnuts and apple pips were found (Jørgensen 1977). Similar material has been recovered at other localities from both the Single Grave culture and the Late Neolithic (Andreasen 2009, 24). A Late Neolithic house at Skrubben (Fig. 15.4,E) had a fill layer containing large quantities of cockle, mussel and oyster shells, showing that the fjord's resources were also being exploited (Nielsen 2004, 27). The importance of animal husbandry relative to arable agriculture during the Single Grave culture and the Late Neolithic is unfortunately an aspect that is very poorly illuminated, primarily because animal bones are very rarely preserved at the settlements of the time. This is also true of fishing and hunting for the same reason. New finds types in the

Figure 15.8: Pressure-flaked arrowhead and D-arrowhead from house A50, Kronhjorten

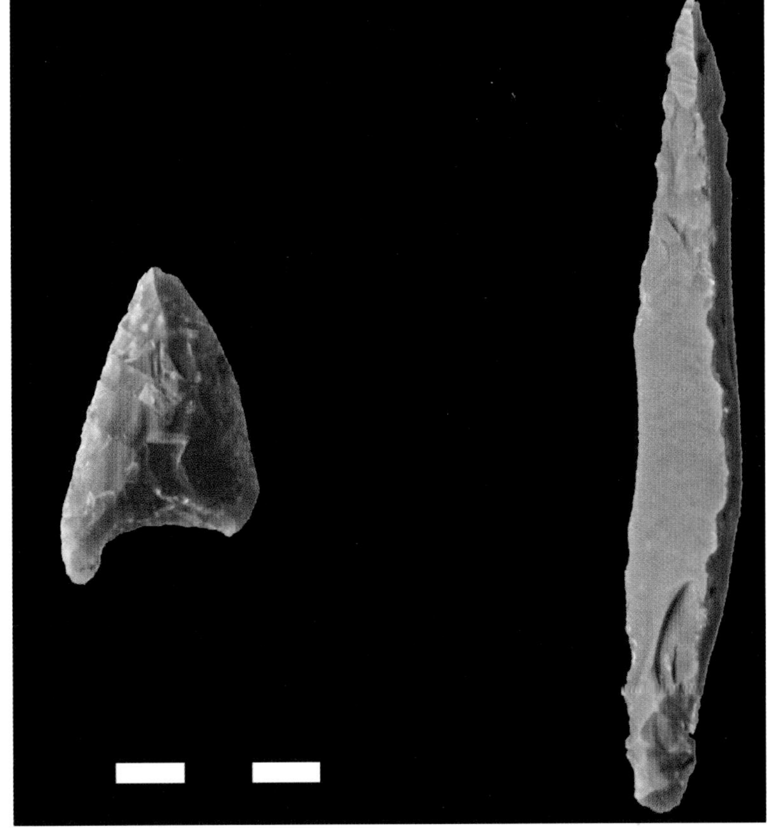

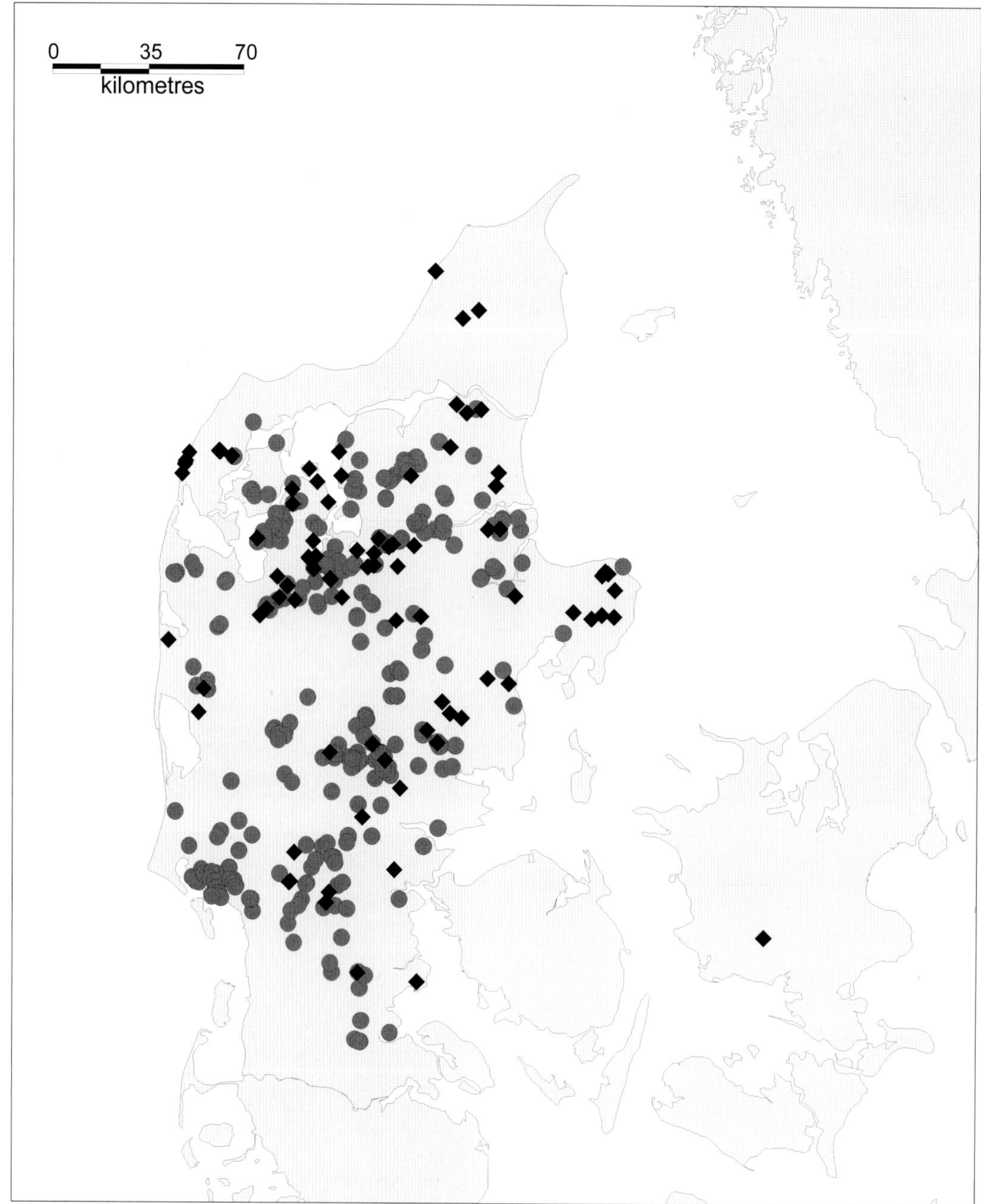

Figure 15.9: Graves (circles) from Hübner's phases 3a and 3b (2005, 659) and settlements (lozenges) with Bell Beaker pottery

early Late Neolithic, such as loom weights and strainers (for cheesemaking), show that animal husbandry must, however, have been of major significance (Jensen 1973, 90; Ebbesen 1977). Pollen analyses from Single Grave culture and the Late Neolithic contexts indicate, furthermore, the presence of extensive grazing areas, thereby underlining the fact that animal husbandry constituted a significant part of the economy (Andersen 1995, 75; Klassen 2008).

Notes

1. Museum Thy, THY 6013, parish code and record number 110105-116
2. The basis for the compilation is the author's catalogue from 2007. Further to this, examination of the Sites and Monuments database and the catalogue for Nielsen (forthcoming)
3. The houses have been surveyed precisely using the program MapInfo, taking account of rounded gables and variable building widths, which explains the frequent difference between

the cited area and that obtained by calculating length × breadth
4. 2σ, Poz-78902, Poz-78903

Acknowledgements

Thanks to valued colleagues at various Danish museums for assistance in collating the data. Thanks to Poul Otto Nielsen, National Museum of Denmark, and Lotte Sparrevohn, Kroppedal Museum, for access to unpublished material.

References

Adamsen, C. & Ebbesen, K. (eds), 1986. *Stridsøksetid i Sydskandinavien. Beretning fra et symposium 28.–30.X.1985 i Vejle.* København: Arkæologiske Skrifter 1

Andersen, S. Th. 1995. History of Vegetation and Agriculture at Hassing Huse Mose, Thy, Northwest Denmark, since the Ice Age. *Journal of Danish Archaeology* 11, 1992–93, 57–79

Andreasen, M.H. 2009. Agerbruget i enkeltgravskultur – Senneolitikum og ældre bronzealder i Jylland belyst ud fra plantemakrofossiler. *Kuml* 2009, 9–55

Andreasen, M.H. 2017. ÅHM 6499, Kronhjorten, etape 1 (FHM 4296/2037). Makrofossilanalyse af en prøve fra en forsænkning i et langhus fra Klokkebægerkulturen. Moesgård: Afdeling for Konservering og Naturvidenskab Moesgård Museum 5

Apel, J. 2004. From marginalisation to specialisation. Scandinavian flint-dagger production during the second wave of Neolithisation. In Knutsson, H. (ed.), *Coast to Coast – Arrival. Results and Reflections*, 295–308. Uppsala: Coast to Coast Book 10

Asingh, P. 1988. Diverhøj – A Complex Burial Mound and a Neolithic Settlement. *Journal of Danish Archaeology* 6, 1987, 130–54

AUD. Rigsantikvarens Arkæologiske Sekretariat (eds), 1984–2001. *Arkæologiske udgravninger i Danmark.* København: AUD

Boas, N.A. 1983. Egehøj. A Settlement from the Early Bronze Age in East Jutland. *Journal of Danish Archaeology* 2, 90–101

Boas, N.A. 1993. Late Neolithic and Bronze Age Settlements at Hemmed Church and Hemmed Plantation. *Journal of Danish Archaeology* 10, 1991. 119–35

Borup, P. forthcoming. Catalogue no. 395. In Kastholm *et al.* (eds), forthcoming

Czebreszuk, J. & Szmyt, M. (eds), 2003. *The Northeast Frontier of Bell Beakers. Proceedings of the symposium held at the Adam Mickiewicz University, Poznań (Poland), May 26–29 2002.* Oxford: British Archaeological Reports International Series 1155

Dollar, S.R. 2013. Hustomter fra senneolitikum og tidligste bronzealder i Vejen kommune. *Arkæologi i Slesvig* 14, 39–49

Dörfler, W. & Müller, J. (eds), 2008. *Umwelt – Wirtschaft – Siedlungen im dritten vorchristlichen Jahrtausend Mitteleuropas und Südskandinaviens.* Internationale Tagung Kiel 4–6 November 2005. Neumünster: Offa Bücher 84

Ebbesen, K. 1977. Sikar og klokkebægerkultur. *Holstebro Museum Årsskrift* 1977, 51–64

Ebbesen, K. 2006. *The Battle Axe Period.* København: Attika

Eisenschmidt, S. 2014. Vom Spätneolithikum in die vorrömische Eisenzeit – Grabhügel und Siedlung in Møsvrå bei Kolding. *Arkæologi i Slesvig* 15, 87–103

Ethelberg, P. 2000. Bronzealderen. In Ethelberg *et al.* (eds), 2000, 135–280

Ethelberg, P., Jørgensen, E. & Robinson, D. (eds), 2000. *Det Sønderjyske Landbrugs Historie. Sten- og bronzealder.* Haderslev Museum og Historisk Samfund for Sønderjylland. Haderslev: Winds Bogtrykkeri A/S

Grundvad, L. & Poulsen, M. E. 2013. Omvendte ofre. *Skalk* 2013, 4, 9–11

Grundvad, L. & Poulsen, M. E. 2014. Nordens ældste væv. *Skalk* 2014, 6, 16–17

Grundvad, L., Poulsen M.E. & Andreasen M.H. 2015. Et monumentalt midtsulehus ved Nørre Holsted i Sydjylland – Analyse af et langhus fra ældre bronzealder periode I. *Kuml* 2015, 49–65

Henriksen, P.S. 2001. *Arkæobotanisk undersøgelse af materiale fra fire bopladser fra dolktid til ældre bronzealder ved Skive.* NNU Rapport 11. København: Nationalmuseet

Hertz, E. 1997. Vestervang-huset fra sen bondestenalder – Et usædvanligt arkæologisk fund på motorvejen ved Vejen. *Mark og Montre* 1997, 21–5

Hübner, E. 2005. *Jungneolithische Gräber auf der Jütischen Halbinsel. Typologische und chronologische Studien zur Einzelgrabkultur.* København: Det Kongelige Nordiske Oldskriftselskab

Hvass, S. 1977. A House of the Single-Grave Culture Excavated at Vorbasse in Central Jutland. *Acta Archaeologica* 48, 219–32

Hvass, S. 1986. En boplads fra enkeltgravskulturen i Vorbasse. In Adamsen, C. & Ebbesen, K. (eds), 1986, 325–34

Iversen, R. 2017. Big-Men and Small Chiefs: The Creation of Bronze Age Societies. *Open Archaeology* 3, 361–75

Jensen, J.Aa. 1973. Myrhøj, 3 hustomter med klokkebægerkeramik. *Kuml* 1972, 61–122

Jensen, J.Aa. 1984. Boplads under højen. En bronzealderhøj og en ny hustomt med klokkebægerkeramik. *Fra Ringkøbings Amts Museer*, 51–68

Jensen, P.M. 2013. *Makrofossilanalyse fra SBM 1271, Hestehaven (FHM 4296/1059). Arkæobotanisk analyse af to neolitiske huse fra Skanderborg.* Moesgård: Afdeling for Konservering og Naturvidenskab Moesgård Museum 5

Jensen, ST. 2010. Huse fra bondestenalder i Vesthimmerland. Årbog 2010, 27–36. Vesthimmerlands Museum

Johansen, E. 1986. Tre bosættelser fra sen enkeltgravskultur /tidlig senneolitikum ved Solbjerg, Østhimmerland. In Adamsen, C. & Ebbesen, K. (eds), 1986, 280–5

Jørgensen, 1977. Acorns as Food-Source in the Later Stone Age. *Acta Archaeologica* 48, 233–8

Kastholm, O.T., Nielsen P.O. & Sparrevohn L.R. (eds), forthcoming. *Houses for the Living. Two-aisled houses from the Neolithic and Early Bronze Age in Denmark.* København: Det Kongelige Nordiske Oldskriftselskab

Kjersgaard, 1965. Glimt fra arbejdsmarken. *Nationalmuseets Arbejdsmark* 1963–65, 121–49

Klassen, L. 2008. Zur Bedeutung von Getreide in der Einzelgrabkultur Jütland. In Dörfler, W. & Müller, J. (eds), 2008, 49–65

Liversage, D. 1989. Radiometrisk datering og beaker bosættelse i en nordvestjysk biotop. In Larsson, L. (ed.), *Stridsyxekultur i Sydskandinavien. Rapport från det andra Nordiske symposiet om stridsyxetid i Sydskandinavien*, 219–25. Lund: Arkeologiska Inst., Lunds Universitet

Liversage, D. 2003. Bell Beaker Pottery in Denmark – Its Typology and Internal Chronology. In Czebreszuk, J. & Szmyt, M. (eds) 2003, 39–49

Mertens, K. 2003. Einflüsse der Glockenbecherkultur in Norddeutschland. In Czebreszuk, J. & Szmyt, M. (eds), 2003, 51–71

Møbjerg, T., Jensen, P.M. & Mikkelsen, P.H. 2007. Enkehøj. En boplads med klokkebægerkeramik og korn. *Kuml* 2007, 9–45

Nielsen, M. 2004. Klokkebægerhusene på Skrubben 10. Hvad 1200 m² sommerhusgrund gemte! *Viborg Bogen* 2004, 22–30

Nielsen, P.O. 1998. De ældste langhuse. Fra toskibede til treskibede huse i Norden. In Kyhlberg, O. (ed.), *Hus och tomt i Norden under förhistorisk tid*, 9–30. Stockholm: Bebyggelsehistorisk tidskrift 33

Nielsen, P.O. forthcoming. The Development of the two-aisled Longhouse during the Neolithic and Early Bronze Age. In Kastholm *et al.* (eds), forthcoming

Nielsen, T.B & Rasmussen L.W. 2012. Huse og høj ved Ørum Djurs. Årbog 2012 fra Museum Østjylland, 38–45

Poulsen, M.E. & Grundvad, L. 2015. Vestervang ved Vejen – væggrøftshuse fra overgangen mellem yngre stenalder og ældre bronzealder. *By, marsk og geest* 27, 20–35

Rasmussen, M. 1999. Livestock without bones. In Fabech, C. & Ringtved, J. (eds), *Settlement and landscape. Proceedings of a conference in Århus, Denmark, May 4–7 1998*, 189–204. Højbjerg: Jutland Archaeological Society

Rindel, F.O. 1993. Bønder fra stenalder til middelalder ved Nørre Holsted – nye arkæologiske undersøgelser på den kommende motorvej mellem Vejen og Holsted. *Mark og montre* 29, 19–27

Robinson, S.E. 2000. Det slesvigske agerbrug i yngre stenalder og bronzealder. In Ethelberg *et al.* (eds), 2000, 281–98

Sarauw, T. 2006. *Bejsebakken. Late Neolithic Houses and Settlement Structure.* København: Nordiske Fortidsminder Serie C

Sarauw, T. 2007a. On the outskirts of the European Bell Beaker Phenomenon – the Danish case. *www.jungsteinSITE.de*, 1–61

Sarauw, T. 2007b. Male Symbols or Warrior Identities? The 'Archery Burials' of the Danish Bell Beaker Culture. *Journal of Anthropological Archaeology* 26, 65–87

Sarauw, T. 2008a. Early Late Neolithic dagger production in northern Jutland: marginalised production or the source of wealth? *Bericht der Römisch-Germanischen Kommission*, 87, 2006, 215–72

Sarauw, T. 2008b. On the Outskirts of the European Bell Beaker Phenomenon. The settlement of Bejsebakken and the social organisation of Late Neolithic societies. In Dörfler, W. & Müller, J. (eds), 2008, 83–125

Sarauw, T. forthcoming. Neolithic and Early Bronze Age two-aisled houses in North Jutland. In Kastholm *et al.* (eds), forthcoming

Siemen, P. 2008. Settlements from the 3rd millennium BC in southwest Jutland. In Dörfler, W. & Müller, J. (eds), 2008, 67–82

Simonsen, J. 1983. A Late Neolithic House Site at Tastum, Northwestern Jutland. *Journal of Danish Archaeology* 2, 81–9

Simonsen, J. 1987. Settlements from the Single Grave Culture in NW-Jutland. A Preliminary Survey. *Journal of Danish Archaeology* 5, 1986, 135–51

Simonsen, J. 2017. *Daily Life at the Turn of the Neolitic. A comparative study of longhouses with sunken floors at Resengaard and nine other settlements in the Limfjord region, South Scandinavia.* Højbjerg: Jutland Archaeological Society

Skov, T. 1982. A Late Neolithic House Site with Bell Beaker Pottery at Stendis, Northwestern Jutland. *Journal of Danish Archaeology* 1, 39–44

Vandkilde, H. 2001. Beaker Representation in the Danish Late Neolithic. In Nicolis, F. (ed.), 2001. *Bell Beakers today, Pottery, people, culture, symbols in prehistoric Europe. Proceedings of the International Colloquium Riva del Garda (Trento, Italy) 11–16 May 1998, 333–60.* Trento: Provincia Autonoma di Trento, Servizio Beni Culturali Ufficio Beni Archeologici

Vandkilde, H., Rahbek, U. & Rasmussen, K.L. 1996. Radiocarbon Dating and the Chronology of Bronze Age Southern Scandinavia. In Randsborg, K. (ed.), Absolute Chronology. Archaeological Europe 2500–500 BC. *Acta Archaeologica* 67, 183–198

16

An overview of Bell Beaker house plans in the Netherlands

J.P. Kleijne and E. Drenth

In the Netherlands, the Late Neolithic Bell Beaker phenomenon (*c.* 2400–1900 BC) is well-known for its burial monuments which feature prominently in debates concerning pottery typochronology, continuity with the preceding Corded Ware Phenomenon (*c.* 2800–2400 BC) and funerary landscape developments. Regarding settlements, the picture is far sketchier and based on a problematic dataset. Previously, and among others, Lanting and Van der Waals (1976), Van der Waals (1984) and Drenth and Hogestijn (2001) have tried to summarise the evidence for Bell Beaker habitation. Several more recent studies (eg, Fokkens *et al.* 2016; Drenth *et al.* 2014; Kleijne in press) also contribute to this particular topic and Hogestijn and Drenth (2000; 2001) have summarised the Middle and Late Neolithic house plans from the Netherlands. Since these papers, further possible structural evidence has been found at Epse and Heiloo (see below) adding to the corpus. All authorities agree, however, that the dataset is meagre, consisting mainly of single features, clusters of features, various kinds of cultural layers and finds from the fills of natural gullies. From these features only a very small number of structures including house plans can positively be identified (Fig. 16.1). This contribution outlines and examines these supposed house plans from the Netherlands and the difficulties of interpretation that surround them.

Bell Beaker house plans – the problems

As mentioned above, over the past few decades, various authors have discussed the evidence for Bell Beaker habitation, presented Late Neolithic house plans, and started discussions concerning the validity of certain postulated structures. Some 18 years ago Hogestijn and Drenth (2000) had already scrutinised assertions made regarding Middle and Late Neolithic house plans from the Netherlands. More recently, this subject has been revisited (Drenth *et al.* 2014) and after a critical examination using similar criteria to the studies mentioned above, only those structures that are likely house plans are presented here but even these have been questioned by other authors. In that review article only one probable house plan is accepted for the Bell Beaker period and this is a discovery that was made long ago at Vlaardingen (Zuid-Holland) though even this site is not without its critics

Figure 16.1: Sites in the Netherlands discussed in the text

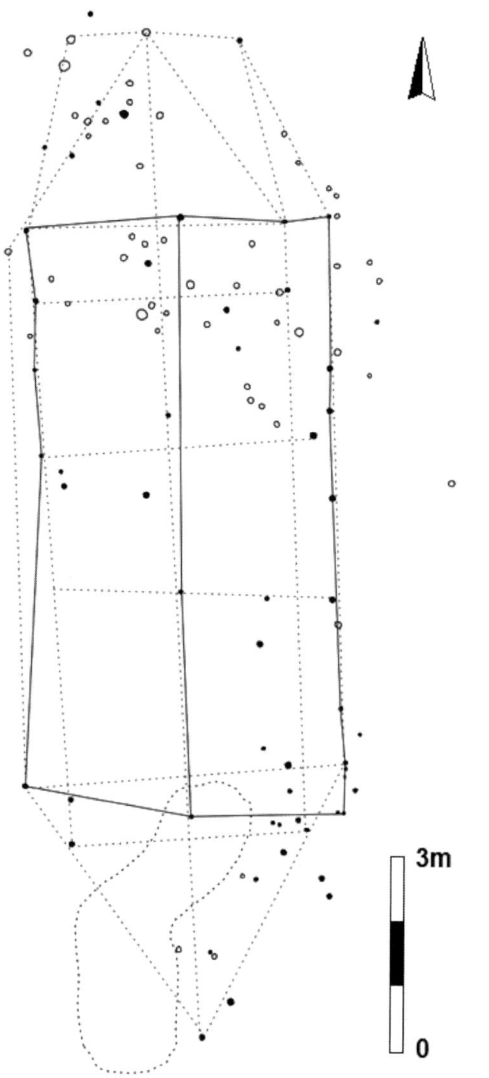

Figure 16.2: Barendrecht-Carnisselande site 3, possible house plan with two possible reconstructions (modified after Moree et al. *2010)*

(see below). Both of these studies make it clear that there are three main difficulties in identifying Late Neolithic houses. The first problem is that of the reliability or validity of the postulated structure. A second hurdle is the dating of the structure and finally there is the question of a structure's function: as a house, a shed or another kind of (roofed or open) structure. Any assumed function may also have been seasonal in nature.

With regard to the first problem, discussions are often based on a wide variety of either clearly or more loosely applied arguments. Arguments for positive identification usually include the regularity of post alignments, closely associated artefacts and/or radiocarbon dates, the presence of central roof-bearing posts or outer wall posts at equal distances, the presence of hearth structures or other internal features, the recognition of the house plan during excavation and the uniformity in depth, shape and filling of the features that make up the house plan. Exemplary is the work of Arnoldussen (2008, 167–74) on the possible Late Neolithic and Early Bronze Age house plans from the Dutch central river area. He critically examines settlements in terms of their dating evidence, associations and structural remains and in so doing he rejects, for example, the claim that the excavations at Meteren-De Bogen (Gelderland) have yielded Late Neolithic house plans citing '… unclear stratigraphical contemporaneity, high feature-density of uniform features, absence of datable material, lack of corroborating parallels elsewhere…' as the reasons for rejection (Arnoldussen 2008, Appendix, 63–75). While this holds true for the particular site of De Bogen, there are several other Late Neolithic settlements, such as at Barendrecht-Carnisselande (see below), where features are uniform and clear-cut (even wood is sometimes preserved), where parallels can be found in the methods of construction, where dating evidence is present and where stratigraphy seems less complicated. Other studies, for example Fokkens *et al.* (2016, 293–4), dismiss many of the proposed Late Neolithic and Early Bronze Age house plans as being 'too unstructured'. In their view, these proposed house plans contrast with house plans that have regular central posts and wall posts such as the typical three-aisled longhouses of the Middle Bronze Age.

In this respect, the supposed Bell Beaker 'house plan' of Barendrecht-Carnisselande site 3 should be mentioned here (Fig. 16.2) (Moree *et al.* 2010, 48–71). The settlement consists of several cultural layers built up on the top of a levee of a freshwater gully. The earliest occupation dates to the Vlaardingen group, whereas the later phases date to the Bell Beaker and Middle Bronze Age periods. Features from the Bell Beaker phase are associated with a substantial quantity of material culture, Bell Beaker, Potbeaker and Common Ware pottery as well as a small droplet of copper of probable British or Irish origin. Radiocarbon dates place this settlement well into the later phase of the 3rd millennium BC.

The house plan has been reconstructed from a general spread of post-holes some of which still preserved timber uprights and at least two possible reconstructions have been proposed, both of which are very irregular but appear to represent two-aisled buildings differing mainly in their straight or rounded ends (Fig. 16.2). The first reconstruction suggests a house plan with straight ends measuring 9.2 × 4.9 m. The second reconstruction suggests a house plan of 15.3 × 5 m. No internal structural elements were observed. The irregularity of the ground-plans and the widely-spaced yet well-preserved posts has led some to regard the reconstructions as unreliable (Fokkens 2016, 202–4; Drenth *et al.* 2014, 64).

Problems with dating are also significant largely due to the problems of horizontal stratigraphy and the certain association of dated features or material culture with the structures. The Bell Beaker houses excavated by Louwe Kooijmans have now been claimed as Bronze Age by the same authority (Louwe Kooijmans 1993, 88) and the stratigraphy of Meteren-De Bogen has also been disputed (Bourgeois & Fontijn 2008, 51–4; Lanting & Van der Plicht 2002, 198–201; Lohof 2003; Meijlink 2001). At Ottoland-Kromme Elleboog the range of material culture includes Bell Beaker to Hilversum pottery with no direct association of any ceramic style with the structure (Wassink 1981).

Regarding function, the wide-spaced posts at Vlaardingen-Arij Koplaan have been variously interpreted as a house, wind breaks or palisades (Van der Waals 1984, 10; Van Beek

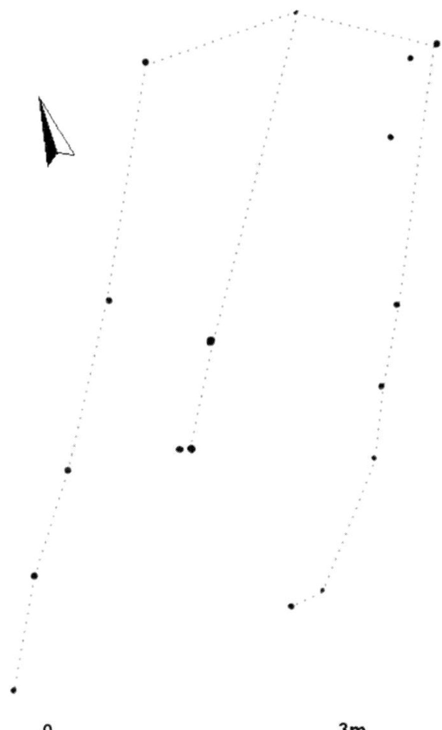

Figure 16.3: Vlaardingen-Arij Koplaan trench 15, northeast corner with a possible Bell Beaker house plan (modified after Van Beek 1990)

1990, 171–2; Lanting & Van der Plicht 2000, 82) and a funerary function has been suggested for Meteren-De Bogen (Meijlink 2001, 415, 417). For this reason, in many cases and as in Britain and Ireland (Gibson this volume) the word 'structure' may be preferable to 'house'.

These problems must be borne in mind when considering the corpus of possible Bell Beaker house plans and related structures in the Netherlands. Several old sites, and some recent excavations, have produced tentative structural evidence that have been previously ignored or discarded. The former sites have already been discussed (Hogestijn & Drenth 2000), but for the sake of transparency and clarity, they will be re-examined in this overview. Additionally, several house plans dating to the Late Neolithic/Early Bronze Age transition period, the closing centuries of the 3rd millennium BC and first centuries of the 2nd millennium BC, will also be described.

Critical overview of Bell Beaker structural plans

Vlaardingen-Arij Koplaan (Zuid-Holland), trench 15 (Fig. 16.3)

This settlement is usually known simply as Vlaardingen and the structure was first depicted

Figure 16.4: Molenaarsgraaf settlement (modified after Louwe Kooijmans 1974), possible house plans 1 and 2 (dark post-holes and dotted lines) and graves (dark pits)

in the PhD thesis of Van Beek (1990, fig. 98). A concentration of 17 post-holes was found on the top of the bank of a Late Neolithic creek and comprised three irregular rows of wooden posts orientated NE–SW. The structure measures at least 6 × 2.8 m and has a two-aisled plan, with possibly one rounded end and may have extended beyond the boundaries of the excavation trench. It has been alternatively interpreted as wind-breaks or palisades (Van Beek 1990, 171–72). The plan is attributed to the Bell Beaker period, but absolute dating evidence to support this claim is lacking and whilst a cultural layer containing Bell Beaker and Common Ware pottery, flint and burnt bone was observed in the same, north-eastern part of the trench, there are no radiocarbon dates for this layer and its relationship with the structure could not be firmly established.

Vlaardingen excavation trench 9 also provided Bell Beaker material associated with early radiocarbon dates of 386 ±110 BP (GrN-2481), 3910±30 BP (GrN-2158), 3850±50 BP (GrN-3097) and 3910±100 BP (GrN-2419). Bayesian modelling of these dates (together with a single stratigraphically separated Vlaardingen date) puts the Bell Beaker occupation between 2470–2140 cal BC (95.2% probability; Kleijne in press). This has been extrapolated to also assume an early date for the structure in trench 15 (Hogestijn and Drenth 2000, 62–3).

The interpretation of the Vlaardingen house is not without its critics, however and Lanting and van der Plicht question the interpretation of the post-hole arrangements due to their irregularity (Lanting and Van der Plicht 2000, 82).

Graafstroom-Molenaarsgraaf (Zuid-Holland) (Fig. 16.4)

This settlement, usually known as Molenaarsgraaf, was published as part of the PhD thesis of Louwe Kooijmans (1974, 169–339). It originally identified two outline house plans, house 1 and house 2, and several additional rows and concentrations of posts in both the eastern and western excavation trenches. Next to the structures, four graves were discovered (one cenotaph, one ox burial and two Bell Beaker crouched inhumations). Bell Beaker, Barbed Wire and Common Ware pottery and associated material was found in the cultural layer that covered the features, a peaty natural gully fill (to the east of the domestic activity) and from several pits on the settlement itself.

House 1 consists of an oval-shaped structure, orientated almost exactly E–W. The house is completely preserved and measures 20.5 × 6.2 m. The plan of this house is regular, with central posts more or less regularly spaced between 3.2–4.6 m apart, and with opposing wall posts, creating a two-aisled structure. In the west end of the house, a possible hearth was present and several pits along the northern long axis may be associated.

House 2 consists of a more convex-shaped structure, orientated WNW–ESE. The house is less well preserved at the southeast end but measures at least 18.8 × 6.8 m. The plan of this house is also fairly regular, with central posts between 2–5.4 m apart, and opposing wall posts once again creating two aisles. It differs from house 1 in having extra structural elements parallel with the central posts, creating some form of four-aisled rectangular partition.

Relative chronology is provided by the

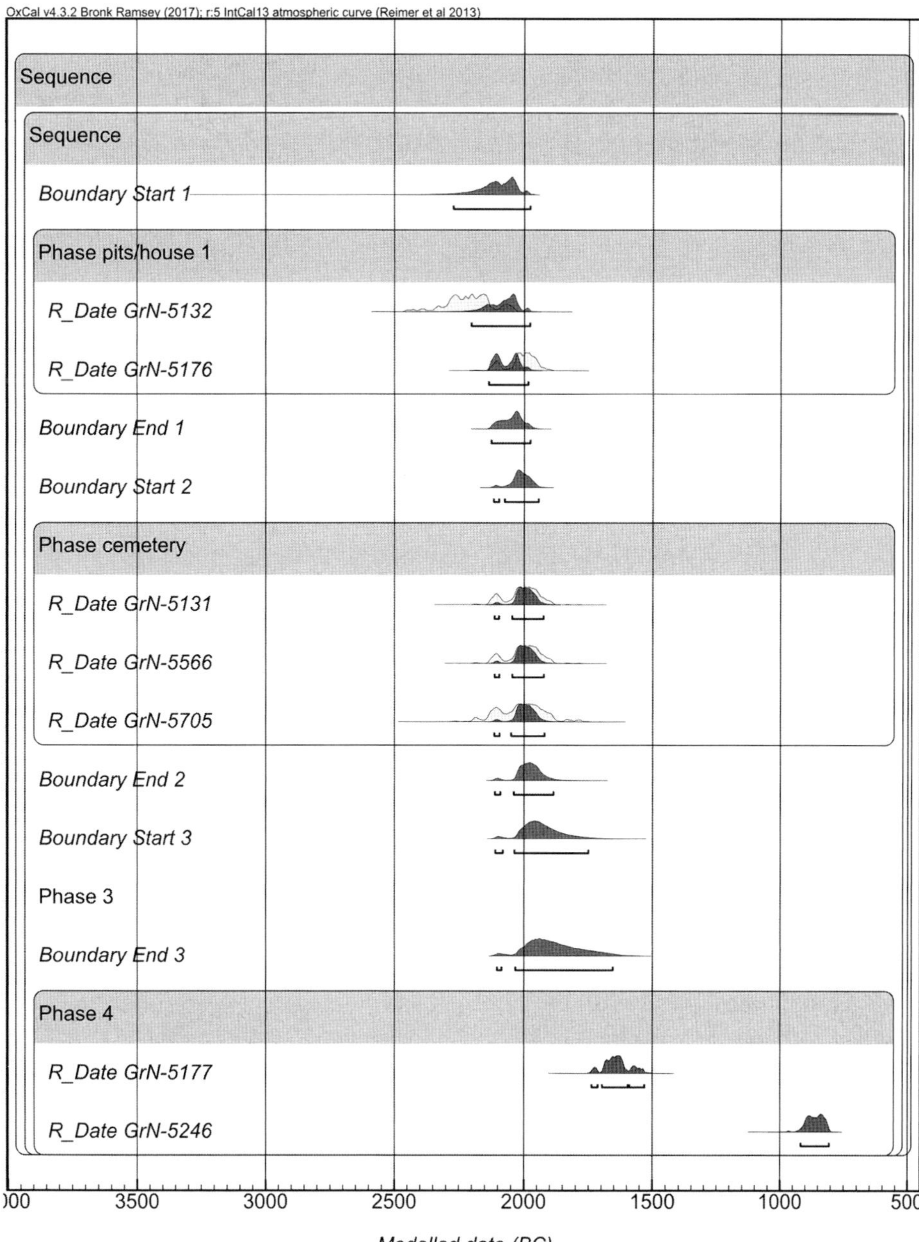

Figure 16.5: Bayesian model for the Molenaarsgraaf settlement

stratigraphic position of house 2, with several wall posts disturbing the ox burial and the pits that are associated with house 1. Reliable absolute dates are only available from several other pits and graves on the settlement and are not directly associated with these structures. Louwe Kooijmans proposed that the occupation history of the site comprised Phase 1 which included most of the pits, house 1 and the start of the cultural layer development. Phase 2 saw the development of the cemetery with its two Bell Beaker burials and Phase 3 consists of house 2 and the top of the gully deposits.

Based on this phasing, a Bayesian model was constructed (Fig. 16.5). Phase 1 started between 2490 cal BC and 2025 cal BC (95.4% probability) and lasted until between 2130–1980 cal BC (95.4% probability). A hiatus between the first occupation and the cemetery phase of 0–105 years (95.4% probability) was modelled then Phase 2, the cemetery, started between 2080–1940 cal BC (92.3% probability) and lasted until 2040–1880 cal BC (93.0% probability). Phase 2 and the second occupation phase were separated by an interval of between 0–175 years (95.4% probability). There are no dates

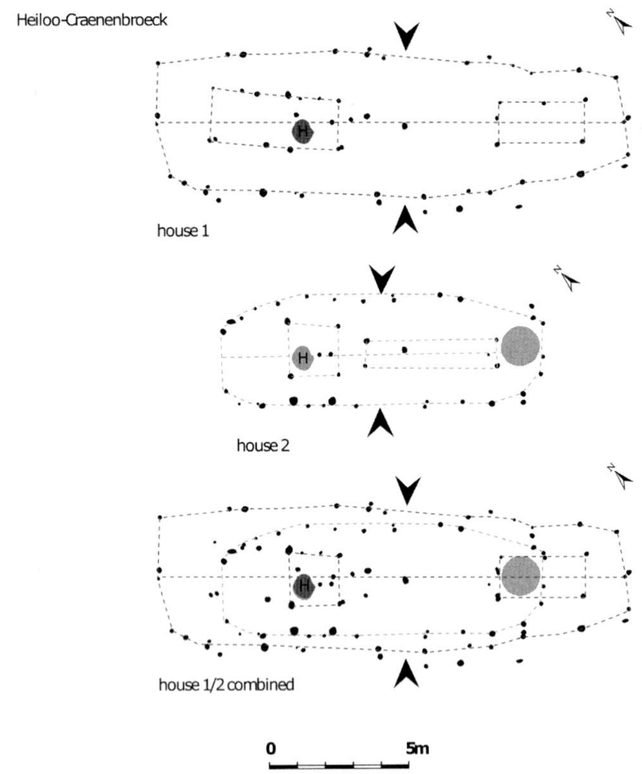

Figure 16.6: Heiloo-Craenenbroeck house plans 1 and 2 and house plan 1/2 combined. A hearth (marked by an H), a water pit (grey) and possible entrances are indicated (after De Koning & Drenth 2108)

from phase 3, but it probably started between 2040–1750 cal BC (93.3% probability) and ended between 2040–1650 cal BC (94.3% probability). A fourth phase was represented by limited Middle Bronze Age activity, before the settlement was sealed by a layer of peat.

The reconstruction of the Molenaarsgraaf structures has not been universally accepted and Van der Waals (1984) seriously questioned their validity seeing them as a 'drawing table exercise in joining dots' (van der Waals pers comm to Alex M. Gibson). Furthermore, though maintaining his original structural hypothesis, the excavator himself has since questioned the site sequence and particularly the position of the structures within that sequence (Louwe Kooijmans 1993, 88). In this article, Louwe Kooijmans preferred to see the houses as being very late in the sequence and fully Bronze Age in date associated with plain pottery characteristic of this period. Although the radiocarbon dates for phase 1 and the presence of Bell Beaker sherds on site suggest at least an origin for this settlement in the Beaker period, only new radiocarbon dates, associated with the house plans themselves, can further elucidate the phasing and nature of occupation at Molenaarsgraaf.

Heiloo-Craenenbroeck (Noord-Holland) (Fig. 16.6)

The settlement of Heiloo-Craenenbroeck has been recently excavated and published (De Koning 2016; De Koning & Drenth 2018). It consists of a large concentration of post-holes and pits and (at least partially younger) ard marks set in a coastal dune environment. Strangely enough, the only material remains from this settlement are three fragments of pottery, 11 flint artefacts, two worked stones and a small quantity of bones from domesticated animals. The concentration of post-holes lack horizontal stratigraphy in terms of intercutting features and is interpreted as either the remains of two possible house plans or a single house plan with a more complex internal structure.

House plan 1 is irregular in its structure, with only a low number of central posts present, two central rectangular four-post elements, and with clearly defined wall posts and possible entrances along the long axis. The house plan measures 16.6 × 4.9 m (max).

House plan 2 also has an irregular structure but is more oval in shape. Several central posts are present, but again mainly consists of wall posts and two central four-post elements. The house plan measures only 11.5 × 3.75 m.

The possible house plans overlie, but do not intersect, one-another and both consist of an oval to rectangular structure with an NW–SE orientation. Also there is only a single hearth in the NW part of both structures which might suggest a single-phased structure with an internal arrangement comparable to Molenaarsgraaf house 2 and Noordwijk-Bronsgeest (see below). A double row of wall posts and possible indications of internal phasing suggest possible repairs of a type that have been noted in Bronze Age house plans in the coastal dune area of the Western Netherlands (eg, house 1 at Velsen Westlaan 1 (Noord-Holland) Kleijne 2015, 44).

The house plans have been radiocarbon dated by several charcoal dates from a post-hole and the hearth, a single charcoal date from the arable field which covers the features, and an organic date from peat sealing the whole occupation level. A three-phase Bayesian analysis of this occupation

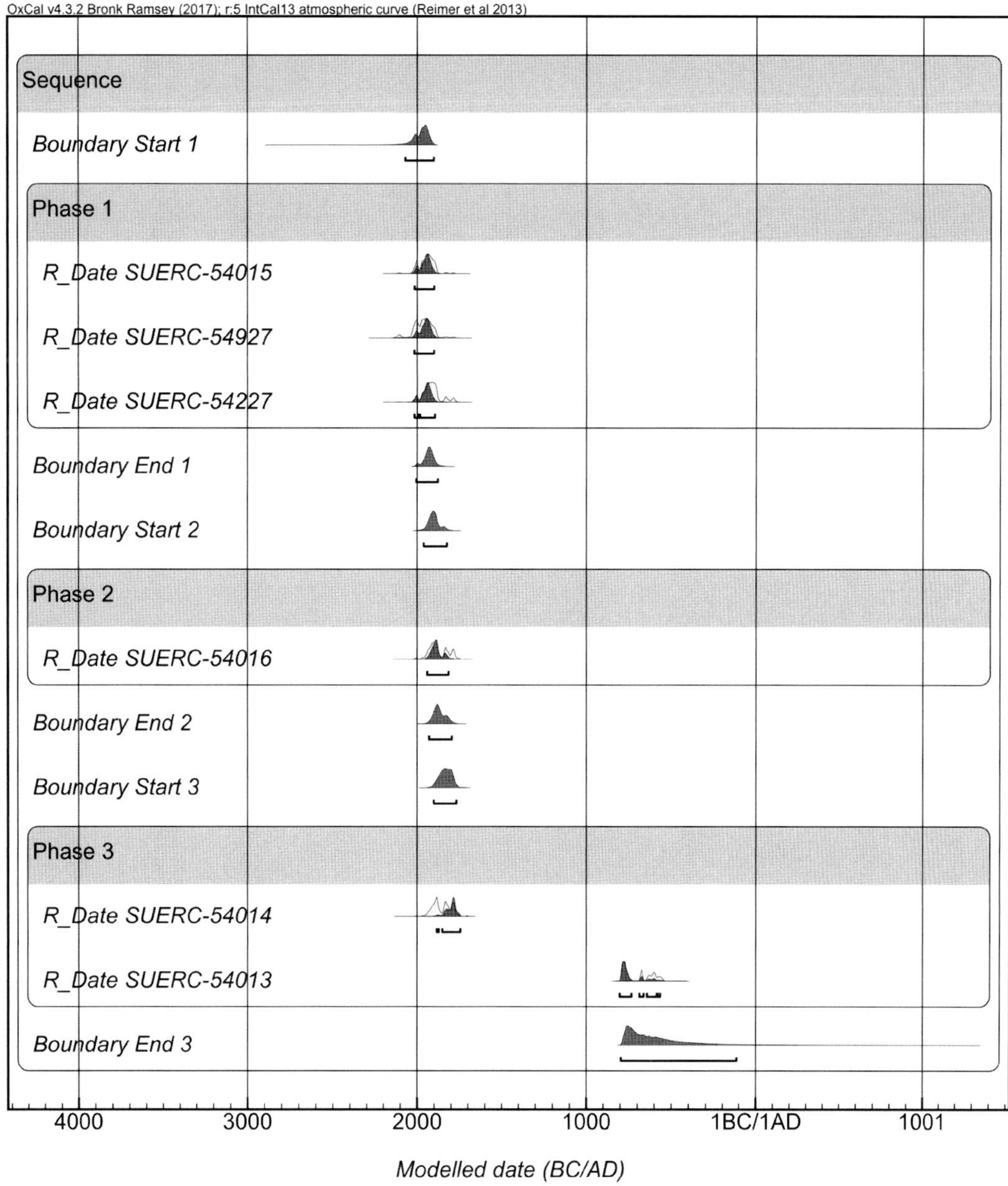

Figure 16.7: Bayesian model for the Heiloo-Cranenbroeck settlement

(Fig. 16.7) places the start of occupation phase between 2070–1900 cal BC (95.4% probability) and the end of the occupation phase between 2010–1880 cal BC (93.2% probability). A phase postdating the use of the house(s) is dated by a wooden object from a waterhole suspected as being later than the post-holes. The start of this second phase can be dated between 1970–1820 cal BC and ending between 1930–1790 cal BC (95.4% probability). The moment at which the coastal dune starts drowning because of the rising groundwater, is dated by the bottom of a peat sequence. This phase starts between 1910–1770 cal BC (95.4% probability).

Noordwijk-Bronsgeest (Zuid-Holland) (Fig. 16.9)

The settlement of Noordwijk-Bronsgeest was published by Van Heeringen *et al.* (1998 and Van Heeringen & Van der Velde 1999) and revised by Van der Velde (2008). Many features such as post-holes and pits were uncovered in this dune landscape, along with traces of agricultural activities (ard marks) and a water pit. The settlement was later covered

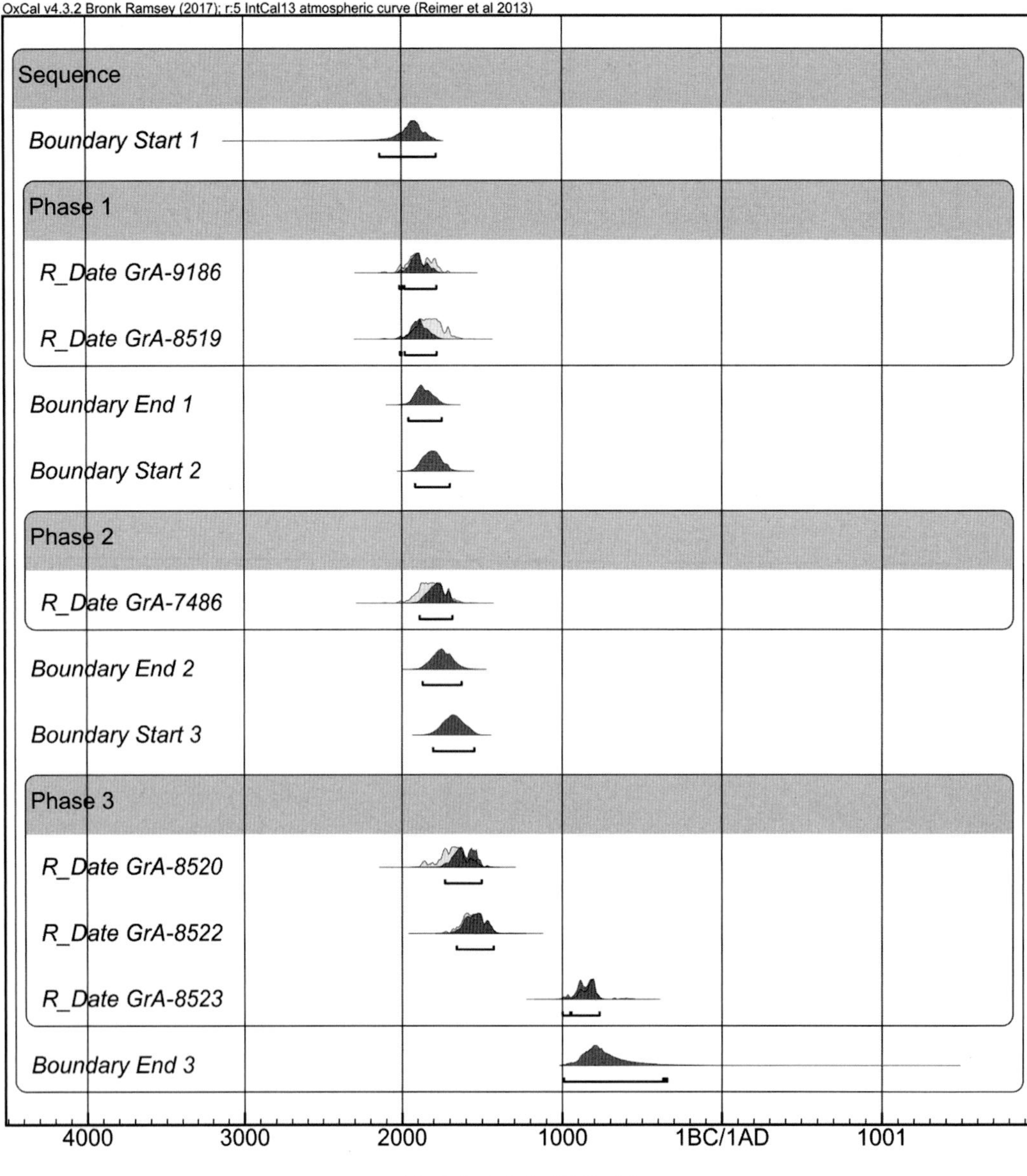

Figure 16.8: Bayesian model for the settlement of Nordwijk-Bronsgeest

by peat and dune sand. The house plan is two-aisled, with additional central structural elements, and possible entrances at both the short and long ends. The plan is oriented towards the NW–SE and measures 15 × 6 m. Associated pottery consists of Barbed Wire and nail/cord impressed Bronze Age pottery (Early Hilversum), the former suggesting that it *may* have its origins at the end of the Beaker period in the Netherlands whilst the six radiocarbon determinations firmly date this structure to the Early Bronze Age.

A Bayesian model (Fig. 16.9) was constructed based on the radiocarbon dates (Van Heeringen *et al.* 1998, 38) and dividing the settlement into three phases. Phase 1 consists of the house plan and primary occupation (Bronsgeest I and Bronsgeest II), phase 2 consists of the layer on top of the house (Bronsgeest VI), and phase 3 consists of a single peaty depression and the subsequent peat formed by rising ground water levels and sealing the settlement after occupation (Bronsgeest III, Bronsgeest IV and Bronsgeest V).

Phase 1 starts between 2140–1770 cal BC (95.4% probability) and ends between 1960–1740 cal BC (95.4% probability). Phase 2 starts between 1920–1690 cal BC (95.4% probability) and ends between 1870–1620 cal BC (95.4%

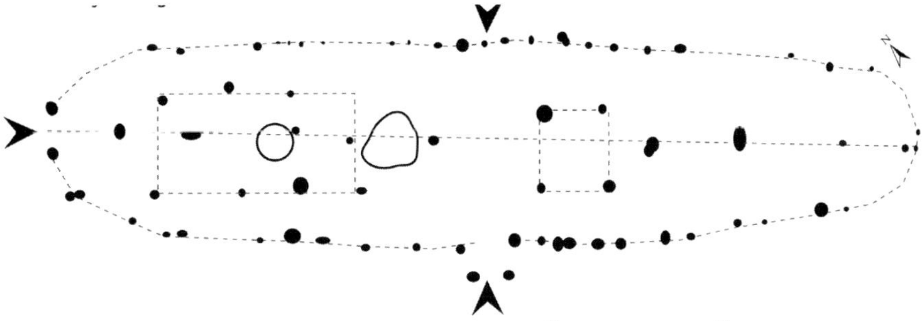

Figure 16.9: Noordwijk-Bronsgeest house plan 1, features and possible entrances are indicated

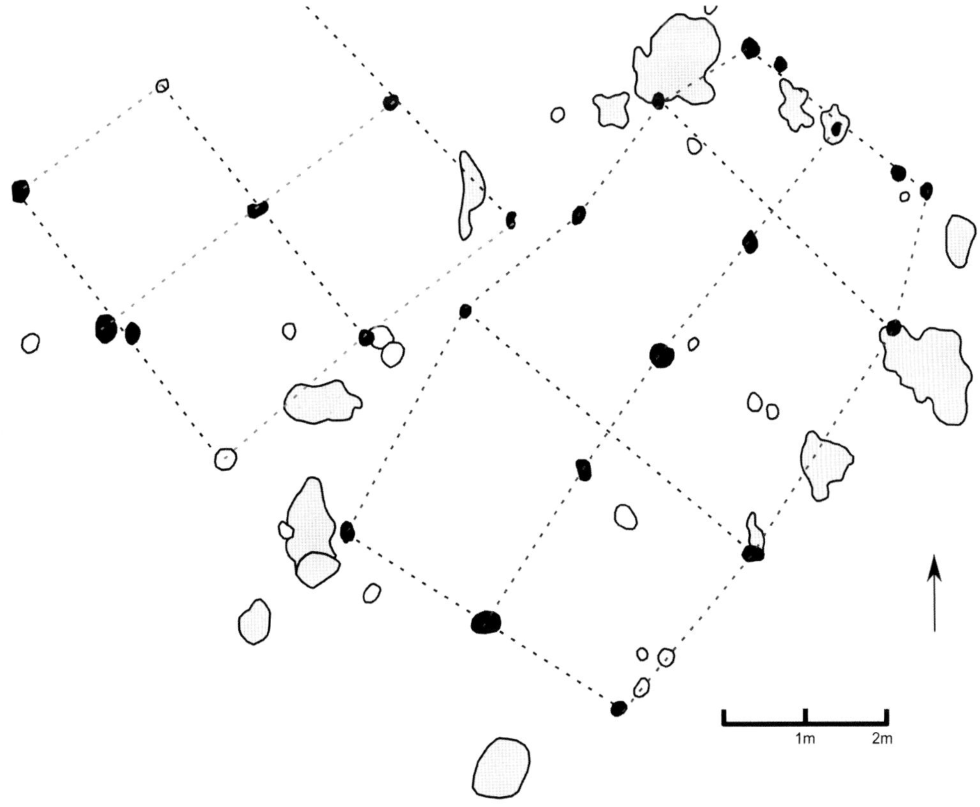

Figure 16.10: Ottoland-Kromme Elleboog, dark post holes (black) and pits (grey) and the two possible house plans (modified after Wassink 1981)

probability). Phase 3 starts between 1810–1540 cal BC (95.4% probability) and ends between 990–360 cal BC (95.1% probability). These dates suggest that this is in fact a Hilversum-dated structure perhaps built on an earlier Barbed Wire Beaker site.

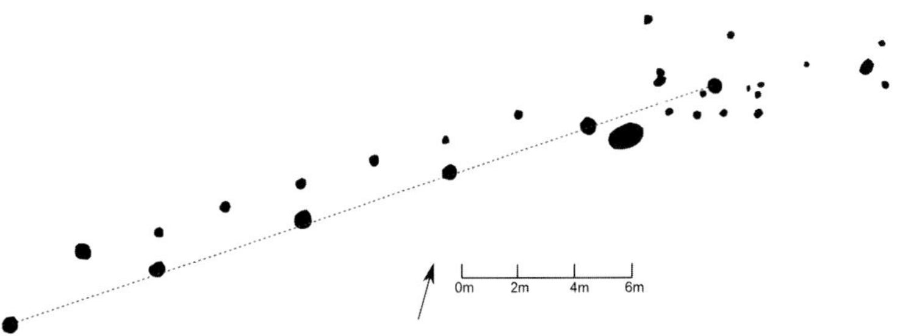

Figure 16.11: Ottoland Oosteind plane 4, post holes, pig grave and a possible house plan (modified after Deunhouwer 1986)

Ottoland-Kromme Elleboog (Zuid-Holland) (Fig. 16.10)

The settlement of Ottoland-Kromme Elleboog was excavated by Louwe Kooijmans and is only described in detail in a Masters thesis by Wassink (1981). The settlement consists of two possible house plans surrounded by a number of pits on the levee of a breakthrough channel, geologically similar to Molenaarsgraaf and Ottoland Oosteind (see below). Both houses are two-aisled with straight ends and orientated NW–SE. Neither of the house plans have any indications of internal structure. Bell Beaker and Barbed

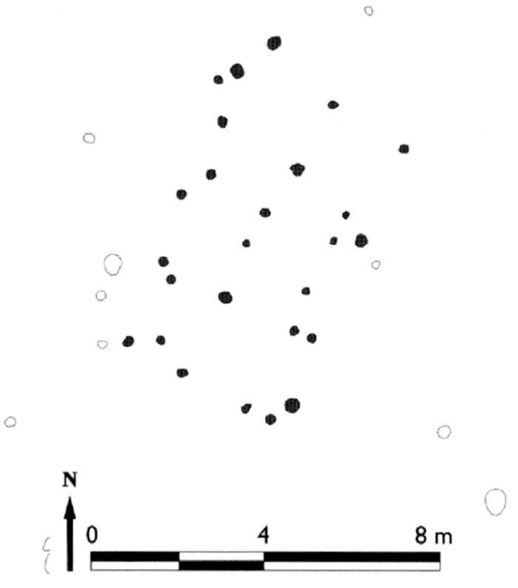

Figure 16.12: Deventer-Epse Noord, house 23 (Hermsen & Van der Wal 2016)

Wire pottery was found mainly in the (refuse?) pits in close proximity to the houses, but no radiocarbon dates are available. While house plan 1 is quite substantial and convincing, the configuration of house plan 2 remains obscure due to the low number of post-holes present and the limits of the excavation trench. House plan 1 measures 7.3 × 4.5 m (max). The possible house plan 2 cannot properly be measured due to the limited nature of the reconstruction.

Ottoland-Oosteind (Zuid-Holland) (Fig. 16.11)

The settlement of Ottoland-Oosteind was excavated by Louwe Kooijmans, and results have only been reported in a Masters thesis by Deunhouwer (1986). At this settlement, in plane 4 of the excavation, a straight line of substantial post-holes was uncovered, possibly the remains of the central post row of a house plan. Other features related to this house plan have not been found and its reconstruction as a two-aisled plan therefore must therefore remain highly speculative. The length of this row of central posts is 25.9 m, with the posts *c.* 5.5 m apart. A grave was discovered next to the line of posts containing the remains of a 2-year old domestic pig. Bell Beaker and Barbed Wire pottery suggests that this possible structure belongs to the second half of the 3rd millennium and the beginning of the 2nd millennium BC but no absolute dates are available.

Deventer-Epse Noord house 23 (Overijssel) (Fig. 16.12)

A recently published structure was excavated by the municipality of Deventer (Hermsen & Van der Wal 2016, 124–5). The reconstruction delineates a two aisled structure measuring *c.* 7 × 3.7–4 m and orientated NE–SW. The central posts and the wall posts are irregularly placed but do seem to be linked to one-another. Unfortunately, no material culture could be associated with the features of the structure and no radiocarbon dates were obtained and therefore its Bell Beaker date can only be assumed. The two-aisled, partly irregular lay-out finds parallel with the structure from Ottoland-Kromme Elleboog (see above). Similar arrangements of posts have come to light at the Middle and Late Neolithic settlements of Wateringen 4 (Zuid-Holland) (Raemaekers *et al.* 1997) and Haamstede-Brabers (Zeeland) (Verhart 1992).

Finally, there are several tentatively identified 'house plans' that should be mentioned, but that are not included in our overview because they all suffer from insufficient detail so that they are unconvincing or improbable (following Arnoldussen 2008, 171–4). The house plans of Tiel-Medel (Gelderland) (Ufkes 2005) and Rhenen-Remmerden (Utrecht) (Jongste 2001) have no uniform features and no radiocarbon dates associated with them. The house plan of Vasse (Overijssel) (Verlinde 1984) has no Late Neolithic material culture, no radiocarbon dates and no known parallels. The Zwolle-Windesheim and Regteren (Overijssel) (Van Beek & Wevers 1995) house plans have no associated material culture, no radiocarbon dates and are more similar to Middle Bronze Age B house plans. The Zwolle-Ittersummerbroek (Overijssel) (Waterbolk 1995) and Zutphen-Looërenk (Gelderland) (Bouwmeester 2008, 69–70) also have no associated material culture, no radiocarbon dates and no uniform features (regarding depth and fill).

Developments through time

This overview of the structures tentatively identified and associated with the Bell Beaker phenomenon in the Netherlands, has demonstrated the paucity of reliable data suggesting that despite the numerous and well-known Beaker burials in the Netherlands, structural evidence is even more rare and ambiguous than in nearby Britain and Ireland (Gibson this volume). Nevertheless, we can optimistically start to compare the different plans by looking at common features and differences and tentatively trace diachronic developments from the preceding Late Neolithic Vlaardingen/Stein group and local Funnel Beaker and Single Grave/Corded Ware phenomena.

One of the most remarkable features of several house plans discussed here is the two-aisled configuration, which in several cases has been expanded with an internal central post-setting either in the short ends of the building (Heiloo-Craenenbroeck, Noordwijk-Bronsgeest) or possibly continuous throughout the whole building (Molenaarsgraaf house 2). Houses that do not have this post-setting have been found at Vlaardingen, Barendrecht Carnisselande 3, Ottoland Kromme Elleboog and Molenaarsgraaf house 1. Interestingly, these internal post settings are also found in the large Stein house plans of Veldhoven-Habraken (Noord Brabant) (Van Kampen & Van den Brink 2013) and Oerle (Noord-Brabant) (Hissel 2012). Interestingly, Van der Velde (2008, 171) remarked that the Early Bronze Age plan of Noordwijk, with its internal structure, could well represent the transition from traditional two-aisled houses to well-known three-aisled houses of the Middle Bronze Age. A similar (if not identical) case was made by Louwe Kooijmans who suggested on the basis of his Bronze Age reinterpretation of the Molenaarsgraaf structures, that 'this very restricted evidence for housing in Late Beaker/Early Bronze Age times suggests that the Late Neolithic small-house tradition continued and that longhouses, implying cattle stalling, came into use not earlier than the end of this phase' (Louwe Kooijmans 1993, 88).

Could then these internal central post-settings be related to the activities carried out in the specific sandy landscapes of coastal dunes and the southern Netherlands' cover sand area, perhaps related to differences in how farming practices such as cattle stalling and manuring (sandy soils are naturally nutrient-poor) were undertaken? Or could the extra structural rigidity have been required because of the lower longevity of wooden posts in this area? Another interesting structural development is the disappearance of house plans defined by bedding trenches, which were relatively common in the Stein house plans of Veldhoven (Van Kampen & Van den Brink 2013), Funnel Beaker house plans such as the one from Flögeln (Lower Saxony) (Zimmermann 2008) or more recently Dalfsen (Overijssel) (Van den Beld and Van der Velde 2017) and even the recent Vlaardingen site of Den Haag-Wateringse Binnentuinen (Zuid-Holland) (Stokkel & Bulten 2017). None of the Single Grave or Bell Beaker house plans exhibit this characteristic.

Secondly, an interesting observation relates to finds assemblages in relation to Bell Beaker house plans. On some settlements, a wealth of material culture has been found (such as on Molenaarsgraaf, Barendrecht and the Noord-Holland Corded Ware settlements) whereas on other settlements, especially in the sandy Pleistocene or coastal dune areas (such as at Heiloo-Craenenbroeck, Veldhoven-Habraken and Oerle), material culture is notably lacking. Is this purely a preservation issue, with the Neolithic level absent on these settlements, or is there also a cultural reasoning behind this remarkable difference? When we delve deeper into the finds themselves, the research by Kleijne (in prep) shows a decrease in the quantity of Bell Beaker pottery throughout the second half of the 3rd millennium BC, and an increase in Barbed Wire pottery on Bell Beaker settlements. Alongside this, there is a small presence of Potbeakers but the majority of the pottery comprises thick-walled, undecorated Common Ware. Flint and stone artefacts are mostly made from local coastal, riverine and till sources and were used to conduct basic craft activities. An interesting find is the copper droplet from Barendrecht 3, signalling the earliest evidence for local copper working in the Netherlands. Isotopic analysis shows that the copper fragment itself came from a British or Irish ore. Ireland, of course, is well known as a region of origin for Bell Beaker copper in the British Isles (O'Brien 2012) and can now also be seen as possibly the source of (at least some) Bell Beaker copper in the Low Countries. This contrasts with the chemical signature from copper daggers which seem to be of Central European origin (Butler & Van der Waals 1966).

Thirdly, this overview makes clear that there exists a wide variety of opinions and arguments on what a house is and how it

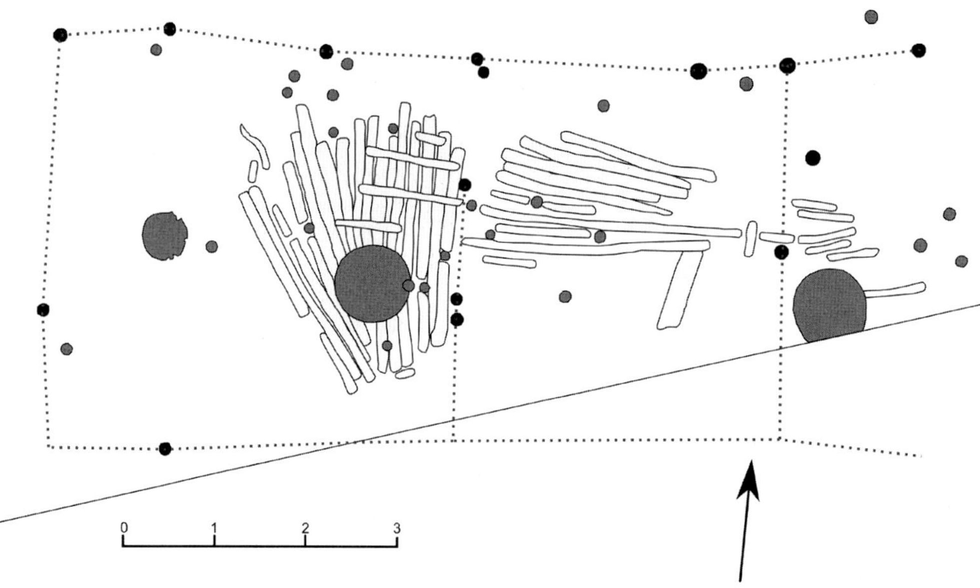

Figure 16.13: Plan of Hunte 1 house

should be defined as well as the inherent problems of dating. Whereas some authors strictly define houses based on structured elements and regularity, other scholars favour a more lenient approach taking internal structures, hearths and finds distributions into closer consideration – domestic structures rather than houses. This matter can also be approached functionally, relating house regularity to its function within a subsistence economy, and seasonal habitation in the Late Neolithic. Similarly, the lack of houses in Early Bronze Age Britain has been related to the development of a particular practice of residential mobility (Brück 1999) which can now also be associated with a rise in pastoralism at the expense of crop-based agriculture (Stevens & Fuller 2015). Much more research into the interdisciplinary subject of subsistence economy and residential mobility is needed before more definitive answers can be proposed for the Netherlands.

Most important is the observation already noted by Drenth *et al.* (2014, 63). It remains to be seen whether a regular lay-out is the indispensable criterion for the identification of a house plan. The Middle and Late Neolithic site of Hunte 1 (Lower Saxony) (Fig. 16.13) clearly illustrates this point. This site contains traces of habitation from the Funnel Beaker Culture and the Single Grave/Corded Ware and Bell Beaker phenomena (Kossian 2007). Here, next to a wide variety of bone, ceramic and stone artefacts, the vestiges of several structures within an irregular post setting were excavated in the 1930s/1940s. Interestingly, remains of worked construction wood and in several instances hearths and clay floors formed integral elements, indicating solid, roofed and habitable structures. A study by Nobles (2013) on the Single Grave Culture settlement of Mienakker (Noord-Holland) also questions the 'rule' of a regular post setting. In this case, the find distribution has been used convincingly to substantiate the claim for a house plan, despite the irregular arrangement of its constituent elements.

An optimistic interpretation of most of these structures as house plans therefore acceptable within the acknowledged limits of the data. It is hoped that further studies, both on new excavations and revisiting old excavation archives, combining features and finds distributions, will further elucidate the thorny problem of Dutch Bell Beaker settlement.

Acknowledgements

We would like to thank drs. I. Hermsen and drs. B. Vermeulen for drawing our attention to Epse and providing us with a digital plan of this possible structure, depicted here as Fig. 16.13. Thanks to Jan de Koning for discussing the stratigraphy of the Heiloo site in relation to the Bayesian model and the possibility of using his (re-)digitised plans for both Heiloo and Noordwijk. Jos Kleijne received funding from the Deutsche Forschungsgemeinschaft (DFG, German Research Foundation – Projektnummer 2901391021–SFB 1266).

References

Arnoldussen, S. 2008. *A Living Landscape. Bronze Age settlement sites in the Dutch river area (c. 2000–800 BC).* Leiden: Sidestone Press

Arnoldussen, S. & Fokkens, H. (eds), 2008. *Bronze Age settlements in the Low Countries.* Oxford: Oxbow Books

Bourgeois, Q.P.J. & Fontijn, D.R. 2008. Houses and barrows in the Low Countries. In Arnoldussen, S. & Fokkens, H. (eds), 2008, 41–57

Bouwmeester, H.M.P. 2008. Bronze Age occupation on coversand ridges of the Looërenk near Zutphen. In Arnoldussen, S. & Fokkens, H. (eds), 2008, 69–74

Brück, J. 1999. What's in a settlement? Domestic practice and residential mobility in Early Bronze Age southern England. In Brück, J. & Goodman, M. (eds), *Making places in the prehistoric world: themes in settlement archaeology*, 52–75. London: UCL Press

Butler, J.J. & Van der Waals, J.D. 1966. Bell Beakers and Early Metal-working in the Netherlands. *Palaeohistoria* 12, 41–139

De Koning, J. 2016. *Heiloo Craenenbroeck. Kennemerstraatweg 225–29. Een nederzetting uit de overgang van neolithicum naar bronstijd.* Zaandijk: Hollandia Rapport 570

De Koning, J. & Drenth, E. 2018. Heiloo-Craenenbroeck. A peat-covered Late Neolithic/Early Bronze Age site with one or two house-plans and ard-marks in the western coastal area of the Netherlands. In: Kleijne, J.P., Furholt, M. & Müller, J. (eds), T*hink global, act local. Bell Beakers in Europe. Proceedings of the Bell Beaker Workshop Kiel 2017, Kiel.* Journal of Neolithic Archaeology 20 Special Issue 4, 123–142

Deunhouwer, P. 1986. *Ottoland – Oosteind. Een grondsporen-aardewerkanalyse van een in 1969 opgegraven nederzetting in de Alblasserwaard, met bewoningssporen uit het Laat-Neolithicum en de Bronstijd.* Unpubl. MA thesis, Leiden University

Drenth, E. & Hogestijn, J.W.H. 2001. The Bell Beaker Culture in the Netherlands: the state of research in 1998. In Nicolis, F. (ed.) *Bell beakers today. Pottery, people, culture, symbols in prehistoric Europe. Proceedings of the International Colloquium Riva del Garda (Trento, Italy), 11–16 May 1998*, 309–32. Trento: Provincia autonoma di Trento, Servizio beniculturali, Ufficio beni archeologici

Drenth, E., Ten Anscher, T.J., Van Kampen, J.C.G., Nobles, G.R. & Stokkel, P.J.A. 2014. Huisplattegronden uit het Laat- en Midden-Neolithicum in Nederland. In Lange, A.G., Theunissen, E.M., Deeben, J.H.C., Van Doesburg, J., Bouwmeester, H.M.P. & De Groot, T. (eds), *Huisplattegronden in Nederland. Archeologische sporen van het huis*, 61–96. Groningen: Barkhuis

Fokkens, H., Steffens, B.J.W. & Van As, S.F.M. 2016. *Farmers, fishers, fowlers, hunters. Knowledge generated by development led archaeology about the Late Neolithic, the Early Bronze Age and the start of the Middle Bronze Age (2850–1500 cal BC) in the Netherlands.* Amersfoort: Nederlandse Archeologische Rapporten 053

Hermsen, I.C.G. & Van der Wal, M. (eds), 2016. *Drukte langs de Dortherbeek. Archeologisch onderzoek naar de nederzettingsresten uit de late prehistorie en de Romeinse tijd bij boerderij De Olthof in Epse-Noord (gemeente Deventer).* Deventer: Gemeente Deventer

Hissel, M. 2012. *Een inheems-Romeinse nederzetting in Oerle-Zuid (gemeente Veldhoven). Definitief archeologisch onderzoek in plangebied 'Zilverackers', gemeente Veldhoven, deelgebied Oerle-Zuid.* Amsterdam: Diachron Rapport 50

Hogestijn, J.W.H. & Drenth, E. 2000. The TRB culture 'house-plan' of Slootdorp-Bouwlust and other known 'house plans' from the Dutch Middle and Late Neolithic: A Review. In Kelm, R. (ed.), *Vom Pfostenloch zum Steinzeithaus. Archäologische Forschung und Rekonstruktion jungsteinzeitlicher Haus- und Siedlungsbefunde im nortwestlichen Mitteleuropa*, 126–154. Heide: AÖZA

Hogestijn, J.W.H. & Drenth, E. 2001. In Slootdorp stond een Trechterbeker-huis? Over Midden- en Laat-Neolithische huisplattegronden uit Nederland. *Archeologie* 10, 42–79

Jongste, P.F.B. (ed.), 2001. *Rhenen – Remmerden, AAO en DO.* Amersfoort: ADC Archeoprojecten

Kleijne, J.P. 2015. *Kennemerland in de Bronstijd.* Haarlem: Huis van Hilde. Noord-Hollandse Archeologische Publicaties 1

Kleijne, J.P. in press. Embracing Bell Beaker. Adopting new ideas and objects across Europe during the later 3rd millennium BC (c. 2600–2000 BC), Leiden: Sidestone Press (Scales of Transformation in Prehistoric and Archaic Societies 2)

Kossian, R. 2007. *Hunte 1. Ein mittel- bis spätneolithischer und frühbronzezeitlicher Siedlungsplatz am Dümmer, Ldkr. Diepholz (Niedersachsen). Die Ergebnisse der Ausgrabungen des Reichsamtes für Vorgeschichte in den Jahren 1938 bis 1940.* Hannover: Veröffentlichungen der Archäologischen Sammlungen des Landesmuseums Hannover 52

Lanting, J.N. & Van der Plicht, J. 2000. De ^{14}C-Chronologie van de Nederlandse pre- en protohistorie III: Neolithicum. *Palaeohistoria* 41/42, 1–110

Lanting, J.N. & Van der Plicht, J. 2002. De ^{14}C-chronologie van de Nederlandse pre- en protohistorie IV: bronstijd en vroege ijzertijd, *Palaeohistoria* 43/44, 117–246

Lanting, J.N. & Van der Waals, J.D. 1976. Beaker culture relations in the Lower Rhine Basin. In Lanting, J.N. & Van der Waals, J.D. (eds), *Glockenbecher Symposion Oberried 1974*, 1–80. Haarlem: Bossum

Lohof, E. 2003. Grafheuvel 'De Bogen' bij Meteren once more revisited. *ADC-info* 2003, 110–19

Louwe Kooijmans, L.P. 1974. *The Rhine/Meuse Delta, four studies on its prehistoric occupation and Holocene geology.* Leiden: Analecta Praehistorica Leidensia 7

Louwe Kooijmans, L.P. 1993. Wetland Exploitation and Upland Relations of Prehistoric Communities in the Netherlands. In Gardiner, J.P. (ed.), *Flatlands and Wetlands: Current Themes in East Anglian Archaeology*, 71–116. Norwich: Oxbow Books

Meijlink, B.H.F.M. 2001. The barrow of 'The Bogen'. In Metz, W.H., Van Beek, B.L. & Steegstra, H. (eds), *Patina. Essays presented to Jay Jordan Butler on the occasion of his 80th birthday*, 405–30. Groningen/Amsterdam: privately published

Moree, J.M., Bakels, C.C., Bloo, S.B.C., Brinkhuizen, D.C., Houkes, R.A., Jongste, P.F.B., Van Trierum, M.C., Verbaas, A. & Zeiler, J.T. 2010. Barendrecht-Carnisselande: bewoning van een oeverwal vanaf het Laat Neolithicum tot in de Midden-Bronstijd. In

Carmiggelt, A., Van Trierum, M.C. & Wesselingh, D.A. (eds), *Archeologisch onderzoek in de gemeente Barendrecht. Prehistorische bewoning op een oeverwal en middeleeuwse bedijking en bewoning*, 15–154. Rotterdam: BOOR

Nobles, G.R. 2013. Spatial analysis. In Kleijne, J.P., Brinkkemper, O., Lauwerier, R.C.G.M., Smit, B.I. & Theunissen, E.M. (eds), *A Matter of Life and Death at Mienakker (the Netherlands). Late Neolithic Behavioural Variability in a Dynamic Landscape*, 185–240. Amersfoort: RCE

O'Brien, W. 2012. The Chalcolithic in Ireland: a chronological and cultural framework. In Allen, M.J., Gardiner, J.P., Sheridan, J. A. & McOmish, D. (eds), *Is there a British Chalcolithic? People, Place and Polity in the late third millennium*, 211–25. Prehistoric Society Research Paper 4. Oxford: Oxbow Books

Raemaekers, D.C.M., Bakels, C.C., Beerenhout, B., Van Gijn, A.L., Hänninen, K., Molenaar, S., Paalman, D., Verbruggen, M. & Vermeeren, C.E. 1997. Wateringen 4: A Settlement of the Middle Neolithic Hazendonk 3 Group in the Dutch Coastal Area. *Analecta Praehistorica Leidensia* 29, 143–91

Stevens, C.J. & Fuller, D.Q. 2015. Did Neolithic farming fail? The case for a Bronze Age agricultural revolution in the British Isles. *Antiquity* 86, 707–22

Stokkel, P.J.A. & Bulten, E.E.B. (eds), 2017. *De Wateringse Binnentuinen Gemeente Den Haag. Een Vlaardingennederzetting in het Wateringse Veld.* Den Haag: Gemeente Den Haag

Ufkes, A. 2005. *Een nederzetting uit de Vroege Bronstijd te Tiel-Medel. Een archeologische opgraving te Tiel-Medel 'Oude Weiden', vindplaats 5, gemeente Tiel (Gld.).* Groningen: ARC Rapport 124

Van Beek, B.L. 1990. Steentijd te Vlaardingen, Leidschendam en Voorschoten. De vondstverspreiding in Laat-Neolithische nederzettingen in het Hollandse kustgebied. Unpubl. PhD thesis, Universiteit van Amsterdam

Van Beek, R. & Wevers, H. 1995. Twee woonstalhuizen uit de Vroege Bronstijd. Windesheim (Zwolle) en Rechteren (Dalfsen). *Archeologie en Bouwhistorie in Zwolle* 3, 106–21

Van den Beld, Y. & Van der Velde, H.M. 2017. Een grafveld uit de Trechterbekerperiode in Oosterdalfsen; spiegel van een complexe samenleving? *Paleo-aktueel* 28, 7–15

Van der Velde, H.M. 2008. The Early Bronze Age farmstead of Noordwijk. In Arnoldussen, S. & Fokkens, H. (eds), 2008, 67–174

Van der Waals, J.D. 1984. Bell Beakers in Continental Northwestern Europe. In Guilaine. J. (ed.), *L'Âge du cuivre européen. Civilisations à vases campaniformes*, 3–35. Paris: CNRS

Van Heeringen, R.M. & Van der Velde, H.M. 1999. Delta Talk: An Early Bronze Age House Plan and Field System in the Coastal Dunes near Noordwijk, the Netherlands. In Sarfatij, H., Verwers, W.J.H. & Woltering, P.J. (eds), *In Discussion with the Past. Archaeological studies presented to W.A. van Es*, 23–34. Zwolle/Amersfoort: SPA/ROB

Van Heeringen, R.M., Van der Velde, H.M. & Van Amen, I. 1998. *Een tweeschepige huisplattegrond en akkerland uit de Vroege Bronstijd te Noordwijk, prov. Zuid-Holland.* Amersfoort: Rapportage Archeologische Monumentenzorg 55

Van Kampen, J. & Van den Brink, V. 2013. *Archeologisch onderzoek op de Habraken te Veldhoven. Twee unieke nederzettingen uit het Laat Neolithicum en de Midden Bronstijd en een erf uit de Volle Middeleeuwen.* Amsterdam: Zuidnederlandse Archeologische Rapporten 52

Verhart, L.B.M. 1992. Settling or trekking? The Late Neolithic house plans of Haamstede-Brabers and their counterparts. *Oudheidkundige Mededelingen van het Rijksmuseum van Oudheden te Leiden* 72, 73–99

Verlinde, A.D. 1984. Bronstijd- en andere sporen in de opgraving van 1982 te Vasse, gem. Tubbergen. *'t Inschrien* 16, 7–16

Wassink, J.C.L. 1981. Ottoland – Kromme-Elleboog. Een Laat-neolithische – vroege-bronstijd nederzetting in de Alblasserwaard, provincie Zuid Holland. Unpubl. MA thesis, Leiden University

Waterbolk, H.T. 1995. De prehistorische nederzetting van Zwolle-Ittersumerbroek. *Archeologie en Bouwhistorie in Zwolle* 3, 122–73

Zimmermann, W.H. 2008. Phosphate mapping of a Funnel Beaker Culture house Flögeln-Eekhöltjen, district of Cuxhaven, Lower Saxony. In Fokkens, H., Coles, B.J., Van Gijn, A. L., Kleijne, J.P., Ponjee, H.H. & Slappendel, C.G. (eds), *Between Foraging and Farming: An extended broad spectrum of papers presented to Leendert Louwe Kooijmans*, 123–30. Leiden: Faculty of Archaeology, Leiden

17

Beaker domestic architecture in Britain and Ireland

Alex M. Gibson

Early in the second half of the 3rd millennium BC, the European Bell Beaker phenomenon reached Britain and Ireland appearing in graves around 2450 cal BC. Its arrival is paradoxical since in some ways the users of Beakers seriously affected the archaeology of the islands whilst in other ways they seem to have had remarkably little impact. Metallurgy and crouched burials were introduced (the latter re-introduced), yet ritual monuments seemed to have continued largely unchanged. This latter observation was the basis for Burgess and Shennan's Beaker Package hypothesis (Burgess & Shennan 1976) which marked a major shift in archaeologists' attitudes to the Beaker phenomenon. The idea of Beaker invasions had persisted in the archaeological literature for most of the late 19th and 20th centuries but in Burgess and Shennan's view, Beakers marked not a full-scale folk invasion, but elements of a widely accepted cult package involving a restricted set of paraphernalia (archery equipment, the distinctive ceramic type, individual crouched inhumation, early metallurgy) but little in the way of population movement – perhaps just a few 'missionaries' or prospectors. Certainly, 'The Beaker Folk' seemed to have had no effect on the monumental architecture already in vogue in these islands. They brought no visible European influences to bear on the stone, timber and earth circles that had already been in use in Britain for some 500 years and which continued to be used for almost another millennium. They also revisited earlier Neolithic causewayed enclosures and burial monuments such as long barrows, chambered tombs and passage graves. This prompted the present writer to develop the Beaker Veneer hypothesis in which it was suggested that many of the so-called Beaker burial practices had already existed in pre-Beaker contexts (Gibson 2004; 2007). An increased radiocarbon dataset, however, shows that some of these burials pre-date the Beaker arrivals by several centuries and the continuum that was originally envisaged is no longer tenable. Nevertheless, there seems to be a resurgence of Middle (not Late) Neolithic ways associated with later Beakers, Food Vessels and Urns after 2200 BC.

Isotopic evidence from the rich and early grave of the Amesbury Archer (Chenery & Evans 2011) re-opened the migration debate regarding European Beaker People though interestingly the terminology changed from invasion to migration. This instigated The Beaker People Project (Parker Pearson *et al.* 2016; 2019) involving the systematic radiocarbon dating of Beaker graves as well as the isotopic analysis of the skeletons and whilst there proved to be considerable mobility amongst the occupants of Beaker-associated graves, this mobility was chiefly within Britain: the Amesbury Archer and an individual from Bee Low, Derbyshire, and possibly the Boscombe Bowmen (Wiltshire) appear to have been exceptions to the rule (Parker Pearson *et al.* 2016; 2019). The Beaker People Project, however, examined all Beaker burials regardless of date and did not concentrate on the earliest graves so the results only give an overview of the Beaker population during a period of over half a millennium. Recent DNA analysis by contrast suggests that there was considerable population change with the advent of Beakers (Olalde *et al.* 2018). This makes the negligible Beaker effect on native monuments and customs even more curious (Gibson forthcoming).

Since the early antiquarians of the 18th and particularly the 19th centuries, Beaker graves have attracted considerable archaeological attention and, as Neolithic and Bronze Age archaeology generally continued to focus on burial monuments throughout the 19th and 20th centuries, it is hardly surprising that a considerable dataset was compiled. As at 2014 some 323 Beaker burials had been discovered in Britain (Heise 2014) and the number continues to rise with the increase in developer-funded projects. It is also hardly surprising that this highly visible dataset formed the main corpus for various studies including Clarke's (1970) reanalysis and the Beaker People Project already mentioned. But by focussing only on burials, the data become unavoidably self-selecting and biased.

An attempt was made to redress this in the present writer's PhD thesis of 1981 (Gibson 1982) in a study of Beakers from non-funerary contexts. Although the study was entitled Beaker Domestic Sites, in fact comparatively few sites provided much in the way of stratigraphic and/or contextual information so the term 'domestic' was interpreted liberally. Stray finds from land surfaces or from the turf in barrow mounds were interpreted as the result of pre-monument manuring processes, pit groups as the structured deposition of midden material and artefact spreads as attesting the proximity of settlements. Few settlement sites *per se* could be identified. One theme that did prove obvious was that Beaker was rarely found in strict association with other ceramic types despite the clear overlap in dates for Grooved Ware and Beakers at the end of the Neolithic and Beakers, Food Vessels and Collared Urns in the earlier Bronze Age. Even in artefact spreads, the presence of other ceramic types could be explained in terms of the revisiting of sites rather than contemporaneous use. In sealed contexts, Beaker domestic material was inevitably pure Beaker with a range of vessel sizes as well as a mix of fine and rusticated wares. This differed considerably from much of Continental Europe where reference was being made to other associated pottery types as 'Common Ware', 'Complimentary Ceramics' or *Begleitkeramik* (central European accompanying pottery) (*Inter alia* Benkovsky-Pivovarová, 2016; Besse 2004; Strahm 2004 and papers in this volume). These can be pejorative terms that suggest that this pottery was secondary in importance to the Bell Beaker wares. Indeed, on some domestic sites, the 'Common Ware' was by far the dominant ceramic tradition with Beaker representing a very small proportion of the assemblage. The Beaker Veneer hypothesis may be more pertinent to Continental Europe than it proved to be to Britain.

Settlement structures in the Later Neolithic

Structural evidence from the Neolithic and Bronze Age in Britain and Ireland, other than ritual and burial monuments, is comparatively rare and geographically restricted. In recent years, with the increase in developer-funded archaeology, the number of earlier Neolithic buildings (presumed houses) has increased dramatically (Smyth, 2014; Barclay & Harris, 2017; Gibson 2017). These tend to be rectangular in outline, based on modular construction and built in a variety of post-hole and bedding trench techniques. They form a loose 'type' that is now becoming increasingly recognisable even before excavation (Gibson 2017). Houses from the Middle Neolithic (*c.* 3500–3000 BC) remain almost unknown and the dating of some of the 'Middle Neolithic' houses from Shetland has recently been questioned by Sheridan (2014) who sees dates and ceramics as indicating a Chalcolithic or Early Bronze Age date. To these we shall return.

Later Neolithic (*c.* 3000–2500 BC) structures

Figure 17.1: Simplified plans of Grooved Ware associated Later Neolithic Houses in Orkney. 1 – Skara Brae House 1; 2 – Skara Brae House 7; 3 – Crossiecrown Grey House; 4 – inyo House G; 5 – Rinyo House A; 6 – Crossiecrown Red House,. Skara Brae after Childe (1931); Rinyo after Childe & Grant (1947); Crossiecrown after Card et al. *(2016)*

are best known in Orkney where the excellent building qualities of the tabular Caithness sandstone have ensured the remarkable preservation of a building type that comprises sub-square structures with internal fittings, alcoves built into the thickness of the wall and central stone-lined hearths (Fig. 17.1). The settlement at Skara Brae is well known and has become the archetypal 'Stone Age Village' but this iconic settlement is by no means unique in the Orcadian archipelago. In addition to Skara Brae (Childe 1931), Rinyo (Childe & Grant 1947), Barnhouse (Richards 2005) and the monumental enclosed site at Ness of Brodgar currently under excavation, other similar building plans have been recovered (Hunter *et al.* 2007; Richards & Jones 2016). The settlement at Crossiecrown (Card *et al.* 2016) was, like the other settlements, associated with Late Neolithic Grooved Ware pottery and radiocarbon dates span the first half of the 3rd millennium BC. Whilst there are undoubtedly differences in terms of detail amongst these buildings, they clearly belong to the same architectural tradition and develop into 'nucleated settlements' such as Skara Brae and Rinyo. Whilst double houses have been found at some sites, the ground floor area of the 'standard' single houses averages some 25 m^2 though not all this space was available when hearths and furniture are considered. These settlements ultimately last, but seriously decline, into the Beaker period (Bayliss *et al.* 2017). A similar scenario was encountered at Links of Noltland, Westray, (Clarke *et al.* 2016) and Toft's Ness, Sanday, (Dockrill *et al.* 2007). At the former site, Beaker-related pottery was dated to around 2270–1970 cal BC (95% probability)

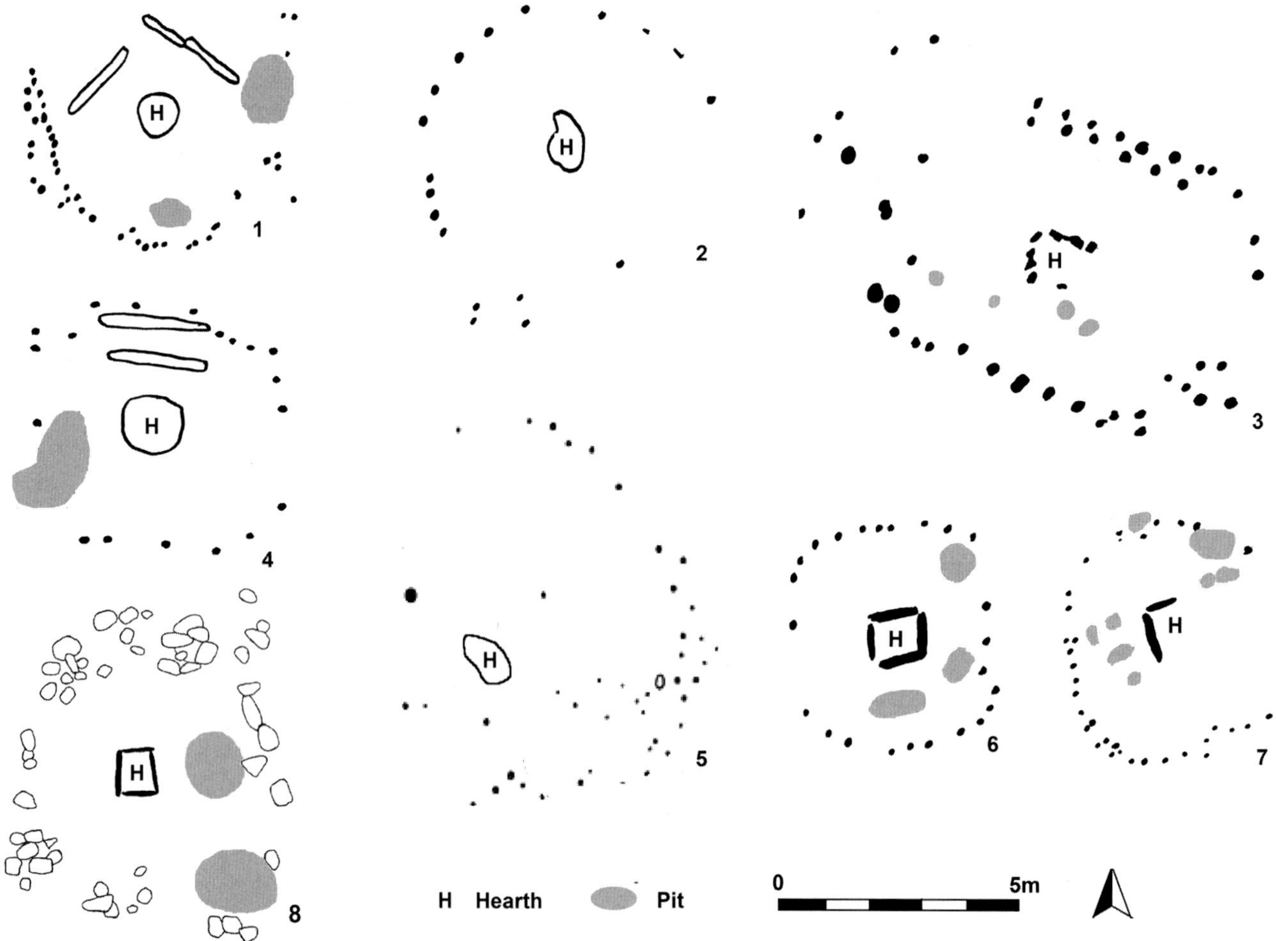

Figure 17.2: Simplified plans of stakehole defined late Neolithic structures. 1 & 4 – Durrington Walls (after Parker Pearson 2007); 2 & 5 – Upper Ninepence, Walton after Gibson 1999); 3 – Raigmore (after Simpson 1996); 6 & 7 – Trelystan (after Britnell 1982); 8 – Piperstown (after Smyth 2014)

after the period of major construction whilst at the latter site radiocarbon dates extend into the 2nd millennium though Beaker ceramics are absent.

Outside of the Orkney islands Grooved Ware houses are less easy to find and this may be due to their flimsy nature. This must have been a matter of choice as the large timber circles that date to this time clearly reflect the carpentry, joinery and architectural capabilities of Late Neolithic groups (Gibson 2005). In 1943 the incomplete ground-plan of a presumed rectangular house was excavated at Ronaldsway in the Isle of Man and dated to the middle of the 3rd millennium (Bruce *et al.* 1947; Burrow 1997). The house was defined by a slightly sunken floor and defined by earth-set stones and post-holes. There was a near central stone-lined hearth.

Most of the domestic structures that have been identified have been found within protected contexts, sealed and preserved by later monuments. In 1979, the excavation of two round barrows at Trelystan, Powys, Wales revealed two pre-barrow sub-rectangular structures each measuring around 4 m across and defined by light stake-built walls (Fig. 17.2). The structures had internal stone-lined hearths and pits containing fire-cracked stones. Being associated with Grooved Ware, the excavator concluded that the building type was 'without any very close parallel on Late Neolithic sites in Britain' (Britnell 1982, 185). In fact, the lay-out and the central stone-lined hearth made the Trelystan houses appear very similar to those of Skara Brae though lacking visible internal furnishings but given the lack of similar structures between these two widely separated sites, such an analogy was considered dangerous.

A similar structure (and incomplete traces of a second) was discovered, also below a round barrow, at Upper Ninepence, Walton, Powys some 50 km to the south of Trelystan (Gibson 1999). These were also associated with Grooved Ware pottery, had central hearths and stake-defined walls (Fig. 17.2). The stakes of Structure 1 in particular were more robust than those at Trelystan and the structure was more circular in outline but it had a similar size measuring some 6 m across. Destruction of the eastern side by a later feature precluded recovery of the full outline.

A post-hole structure was excavated in 1972–3 below a cairn at Raigmore, Highland, Scotland (Fig. 17.2). Though post-holes and pits were difficult to distinguish and the definitive plan of the structure was not recoverable, nevertheless, the features outlined a space some 14 × 6 m (Simpson 1996). Once again, the structure had a central hearth also defined by edge-set stones. Traces of possible human bone from this hearth suggested to the excavator that the structure may have been as much ritual as domestic though some of this bone may date to later use of the overlying cairn.

The latest excavations at the large Wessex enclosure of Durrington Walls have revealed the floor-plans of structures similar to Walton and Trelystan (Parker Pearson 2007). These small sub-square structures had beaten chalk floors and central hearths, stake supported walls and remarkable surface preservation suggested the outlines of furniture similar in design to the stone flagged furniture of the Orcadian sites (Fig. 17.2). Preserved beneath the bank of the super-henge, the exact numbers of these houses are not known but if the density of those within the excavated areas is multiplied around the circumference of the site then a considerable 'settlement' can be envisaged although the resurfacing of the chalk floors identified by soil micromorphology (inf. M Parker Pearson) suggests that the settlement was not permanently occupied but rather visited seasonally at major festivals. This settlement ended in the mid 3rd millennium BC, was slighted by a monumental, if short-lived, palisade enclosure and was then sealed by the material of the bank in the early part of the second half of the 3rd millennium BC coinciding with the arrival of Beakers (Parker Pearson & Gaffney 2016). Very similar structures with central stone-lined hearths have also been found at Piperstown in Co. Dublin with patchy, stone-defined outlines and associated with late Neolithic ceramics (Rynne & Ó hÉailidhe 1966). Smyth (2014, 93) has rightly compared these to the Trelystan structures.

The stake-hole defined walls, the central hearths and the floor areas being comparable to the Orcadian sites and ranging from 20–31 m^2 suggest the distinct possibility of a common Late Neolithic architectural tradition across large parts of Britain and Ireland based on the 'Skara Brae Model' and must be seen as further proof of the homogeneity of the Grooved Ware phenomenon extending beyond artefacts and ritual architecture. But in all areas there seems to be a dramatic change with the introduction of Beakers. The Durrington Walls settlement is sealed as the internal timber monuments are closed off by the giant earthwork and the Orcadian societies seem to have all but collapsed before Beaker appears. Times were changing, possibly dramatically so, but the reasons for this are beyond the scope of this paper.

Beaker structures

The general paucity of Beaker settlements in the British archaeological record was admirably summarised some time ago by Bradley (1970) and Simpson (1971). In 1978, Ashbee could still suggest that Beaker warriors may have been mobile and may have lived in the Chalcolithic equivalent of Romany caravans (Ashbee 1978, 139). This hypothesis was not particularly well received but serves to illustrate the frustration felt amongst prehistorians by the lack of positively identifiable domestic sites in spite of tantalising glimpses of 'settlement activity' and, of course, the substantial dataset provided by burial and ritual sites. In the present writer's own thesis (Gibson 1982), examples of Beaker domestic activity (interpreted liberally as Beaker from non-sepulchral contexts) were numerous, but houses were rare. Since then the corpus has grown slightly but Beaker settlements have continued to be elusive and it is interesting that the large infra-structural developments of Ireland, so responsible for the considerable increase in our knowledge of Neolithic house types, have not had a similar effect on our understanding of Beaker domestic architecture. As we shall see, this may be due to their flimsy nature. We are still, to a large degree, clutching at straws in our search for Beaker domestic sites and some of the evidence presented here can fairly be said to be 'structural evidence' rather than house or dwelling sites. Much of the evidence from lowland Britain and Ireland, as with the Later Neolithic Grooved Ware houses, suggests comparatively flimsy building techniques that are not conducive to preservation within an arable environment unless they lie within protected contexts such as beneath round barrows or below deposits of hillwash or colluvium (Allen 2005). Nor are they suited to discovery by aerial photography or geophysical prospection, techniques that are so heavily relied upon in developer-funded projects.

Starting on the fringes, the stone houses of Shetland have already been noted above. The longevity of these houses is still a matter of debate and radiocarbon dates are comparatively few or have questionable stratigraphic integrity (Sheridan 2014). To date, no Grooved Ware has been recognised in Shetland and the ceramics associated with some of these houses is peculiarly insular but some flat-based pottery is clearly Beaker influenced as demonstrated by the 'S'-shaped profiles of some pots as well as the zoned and geometric decorative motifs (Calder 1950; 1956). Much of this material is incised (a common technique on Beakers after 2200 BC) but some vessels from the houses at Ness of Gruting and Stanydale also utilise comb and shell impressions. The sherds from the anomalous 'Temple' at Stanydale are cord decorated in the style of AOC Beakers. To what extent this pottery will be found at other morphologically similar houses on Shetland is an unknown quantity dependant on excavation, but the later pottery from the double structure of the Benie Hoose (Calder 1961) demonstrates that caution must be exercised when dating by surface features and/ or constructional similarities alone.

The houses of Shetland (Fig. 17.3) have thick stone walls and elongated entrance passages in part dictated by the thickness of the walls but no doubt also to insulate against the harsh winds and climate of the islands. In such they are similar to the later Neolithic houses of Orkney but differ considerably in their internal arrangements. The stone-built furniture is missing and although there are alcoves in the wall, these are not as regular as those found in Orkney perhaps due in part to the more irregular nature of the building materials. The Stanydale and Ness of Gruting houses have similar internal areas (*c.* 30 m^2) but that from Scord of Brouster (House 1) is almost half the size (Whittle *et al.* 1986).

Evidence for roof structures is lacking except at the altogether much larger structure of the Stanydale 'Temple' so called because of its size, its similarity in outline to local Neolithic chambered cairns and its location (the sea cannot be seen from the site – a rare occurrence in Shetland). Here two large posts undoubtedly helped support a pitched roof that probably rested directly on the massive walls. Carbonised remains indicated that the wood of the posts was spruce – a non-native species – that must have been imported or at the very least to have represented the collection of driftwood. The internal architecture at the Stanydale 'Temple' also differs from the other houses as it has internal piers supporting corbelled side chambers. The cord decorated Beaker came from the top of the post-holes.

A wooden structure defined by gullies, stake-holes and post-holes lay below the Late Bronze Age and Iron Age phases of the North House at Sumburgh, Shetland (Downes & Lamb 2000). Due to the truncated nature of the remains, the excavators declined to suggest a reconstruction or firm outline, but a possible oval structure may be suggested. Radiocarbon dates attest occupation from just before 2000 BC to the middle of the 2nd millennium. Cord decorated and S-profiled pottery may suggest Beaker affinities but such decoration is also not out of place in local Bronze Age contexts.

The few radiocarbon dates from these sites suggest an earliest date of 2200 cal BC and in reality possibly later (Sheridan 2013). By this time (Needham's 'Fission horizon' – Needham 2005) a range of Beaker practices and artefacts had spread widely across Britain and were receiving local adaptations but these seem not to have been adopted in Shetland. Instead the pottery itself seems to have been the attraction to local groups and there was a clear attempt to emulate or replicate Beakers at a local level. What rites or ideologies may have driven this desire or need must for the time being remain conjecture.

On Orkney, as we have already seen, Beaker appears in the Grooved Ware settlements after they had entered a period of rapid decline described as the result of a catastrophe by Childe (1931, 64). Richards *et al.* (2016) have made a case for double houses spanning the 3rd and 2nd millennia BC, the best known being house 8 at Skara Brae or houses 1 and 6 at Barnhouse (Richards 2005). Whilst the double

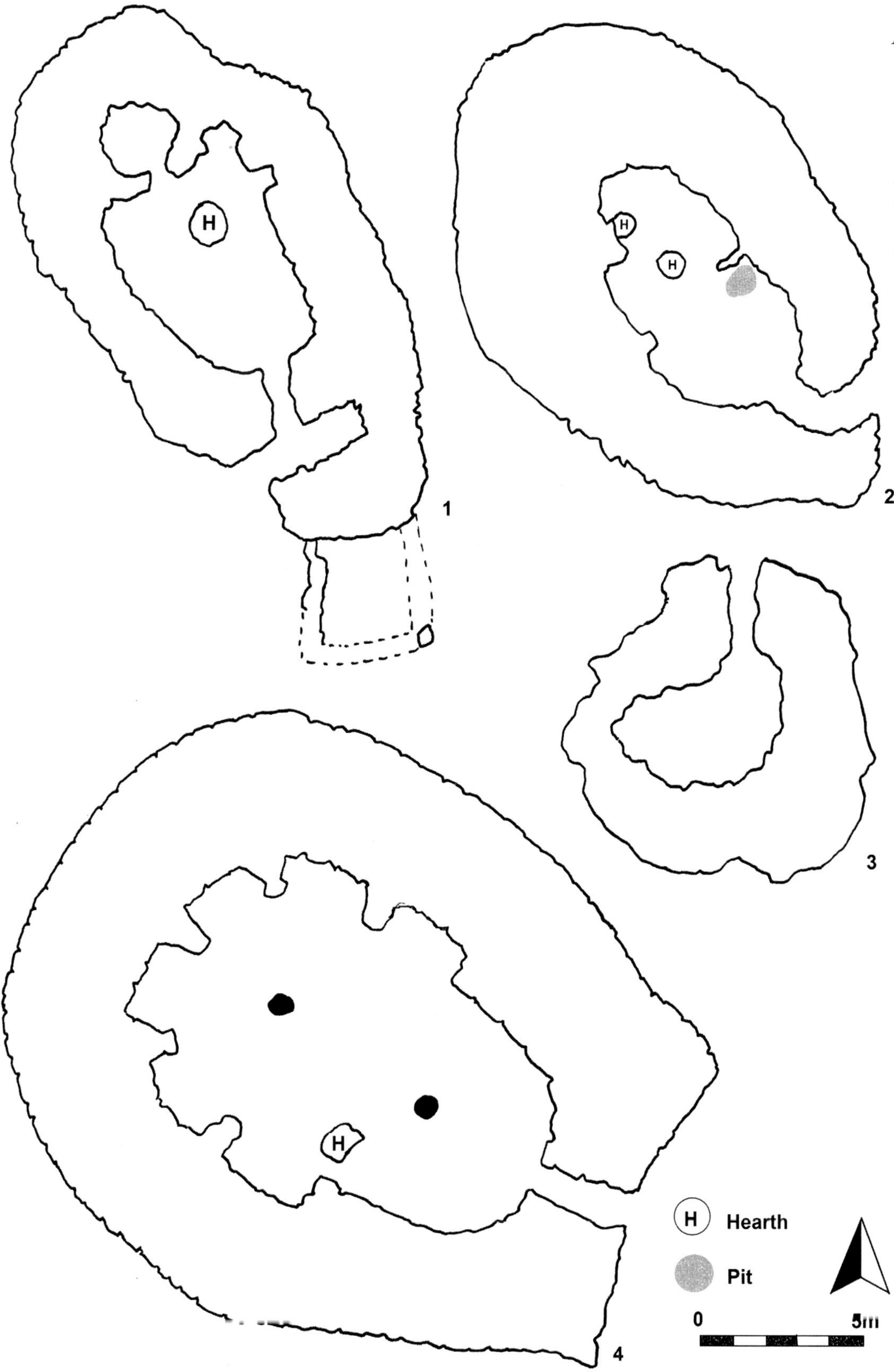

Figure 17.3: Simplified plans of Beaker associated structures in Shetland. 1 – Stanydale House; 2- Ness of Gruting; 3 – Scord of Brouster 1; 4 – Stanydale 'Temple'. 1 & 2 (after Calder 1956, 3, Whittle et al. *1986, 4 and Calder 1950)*

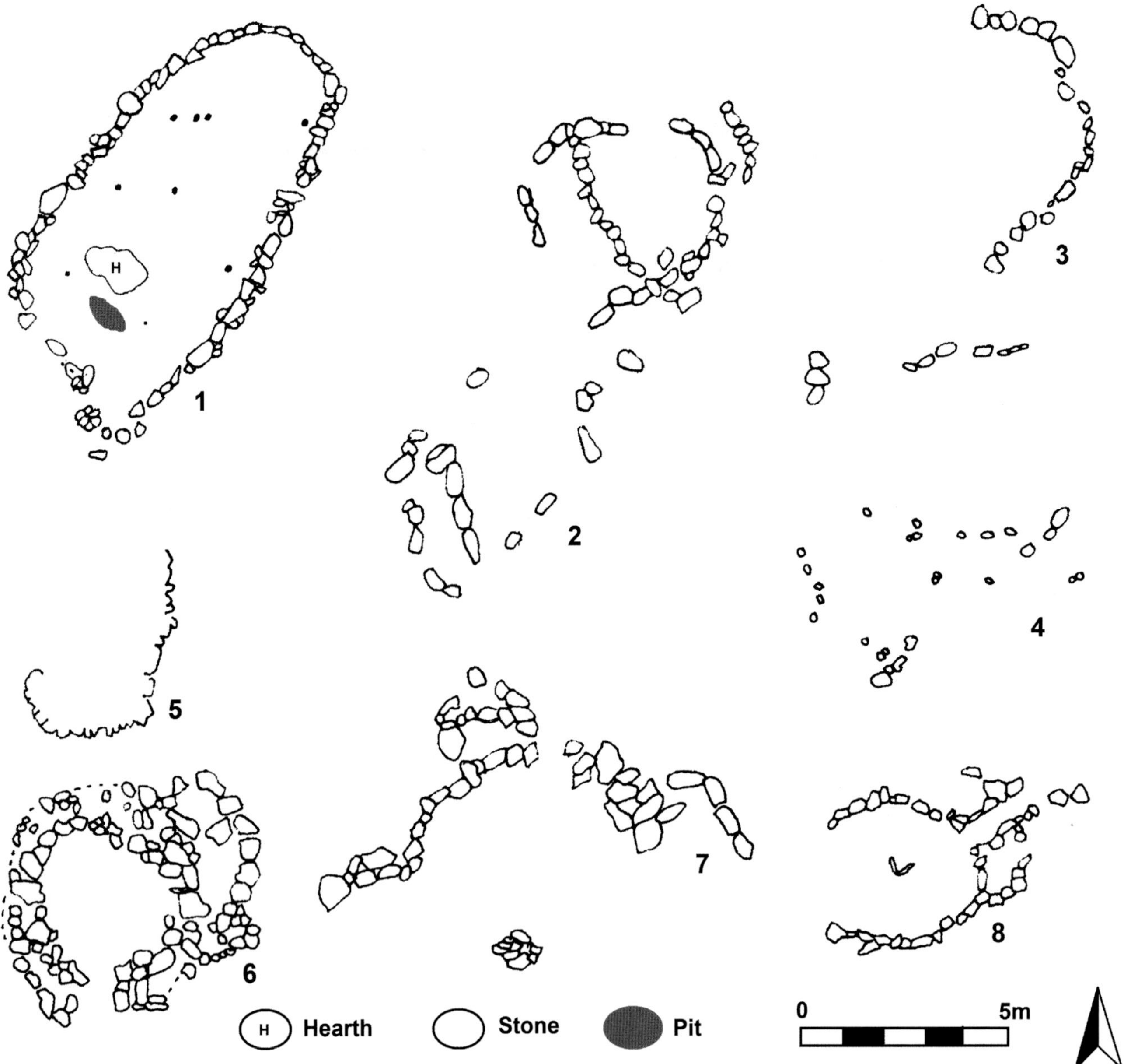

Figure 17.4: Simplified plans of Beaker-associated structures in the Hebrides. 1 & 2 – Northton (after Simpson et al. *2006); 3 – Sorrisdale (after Ritchie & Crawford 1978); 4 – Cill Donnain (after Sharples 2012); 5 – Rosinish (after Shepherd 1976); 6 – Allt Chrisal T19, 7 – Allt Chrisal T26 (both after Brannigan & Foster 1995), 8 – Dalmore (after Sharples 2009)*

houses are undoubtedly contemporary with the appearance of Beakers in Orkney, there are no direct Beaker associations and instead they seem to represent a regeneration or adaptation of the stone house tradition after Childe's 'catastrophic' collapse of the Grooved Ware-associated societies. This is undoubtedly driven by the suitability of the Caithness flagstone as an ideal building medium.

The eight Beaker-associated houses known so far in the Outer Isles do seem to suggest a certain homogeneity of architectural style although there are few complete examples (Fig. 17.4). House 1 at Northton, Isle of Harris, is by far the best preserved and was excavated into a sand dune and surrounded by midden material. The stone 'wall' appears to have been a low revetment course. House 2 was similarly situated. It was more ruined but it still seems to have had the same overall plan and dimensions (Simpson *et al.* 2006). Rather more stone here may suggest that the sand was held back to a greater height and the excavator has suggested that an upturned boat may have been used for the roof. This may also have been the case for the oval houses of Shetland where boats are still used to roof thick-walled buildings (Fig. 17.5). Sorrisdale, Coll and Rosinish, Benbecula,

Figure 17.5:Boathouse at Southvoe, Dunrossness, Shetland (photo by and reproduced by courtesy of Jenny Murray)

though incompletely excavated, also appear to have been built into the sand dunes and the curvature of the walls suggest dimensions similar to Northton (Ritchie & Crawford 1978; Shepherd 1976). Cill Donnain, South Uist is known only superficially from surface traces (Sharples 2012) and the exact form of the structure and its affinities must await excavation but its association with ard agriculture supports the domestic interpretation.

In Ireland, the structures that may be associated with Beaker pottery comprise a mixture of post construction, stake construction, bedding trenches, stone revetments and sunken features (Fig. 17.6). As mentioned above, it is notable that the large amount of rescue archaeology in Ireland, responsible for so many new Early Neolithic house discoveries, has failed to have a similar effect on our knowledge of Chalcolithic structures again suggesting their flimsy nature. The main contenders for Beaker houses remain at Monknewtown, Co. Meath and Knockadoon, Lough Gur, Co. Limerick (Sweetman 1976; Grogan & Eogan 1987). Structural evidence was also identified at the early copper extraction site at Ross Island, Co. Kerry (O'Brien 2004) and we shall examine these separately. Uncertainty clearly surrounds the Lough Gur structures which have produced not just Beaker but also earlier Neolithic and Late Bronze Age ceramics and direct association cannot be proven unequivocally. However Irish Neolithic houses, as we have already discussed, tend to be rectangular and modular in design and later Bronze Age houses tend to be more regularly circular and so differ considerably and significantly from the 6 circular or oval sites on Knockadoon. They also seem fairly uniform in their size and overall lay-out with approximate internal areas varying from 24–18 m^2. The exception is the house no. 2 from site D which has a stone-revetted oval form, similar to those in the Western Isles, but an approximate internal area of only around 14 m^2. To these sites may be added two similarly sized stake-hole structures at Graigueshoneen, Co. Waterford, and Rathwilladoon, Co. Galway) with areas of *c.* 19 m^2 and *c.* 18 m^2 respectively (Johnston *et al.* 2008; Lyne 2009). Both these sites were discovered during rescue excavations in advance of new developments and they are roughly circular in plan. Graigueshoneen has an internal hearth and part of the circumference at least comprised an inner and outer stake-hole ring.

Two smaller Beaker-associated structures have also been discovered during rescue excavations. An open rectangle defined by a bedding trench was located at Ahanaglogh, Co. Waterford and a small oval or subrectangular stake-hole arrangement was discovered at Cloghers, Co. Kerry (Johnston *et al.* 2008; Kiely 2003). They have estimated areas of 8 and 15 m^2 respectively and, like Lough Gur D2, are considerably smaller than the other sites. The sunken structure at Monknewtown, Co. Meath resembles the oval structures of the Western Isles in both form and size (Sweetman 1976) but once again contains ceramics other than Beaker so the exact affinity of the site is uncertain. Like Northton, the structure has

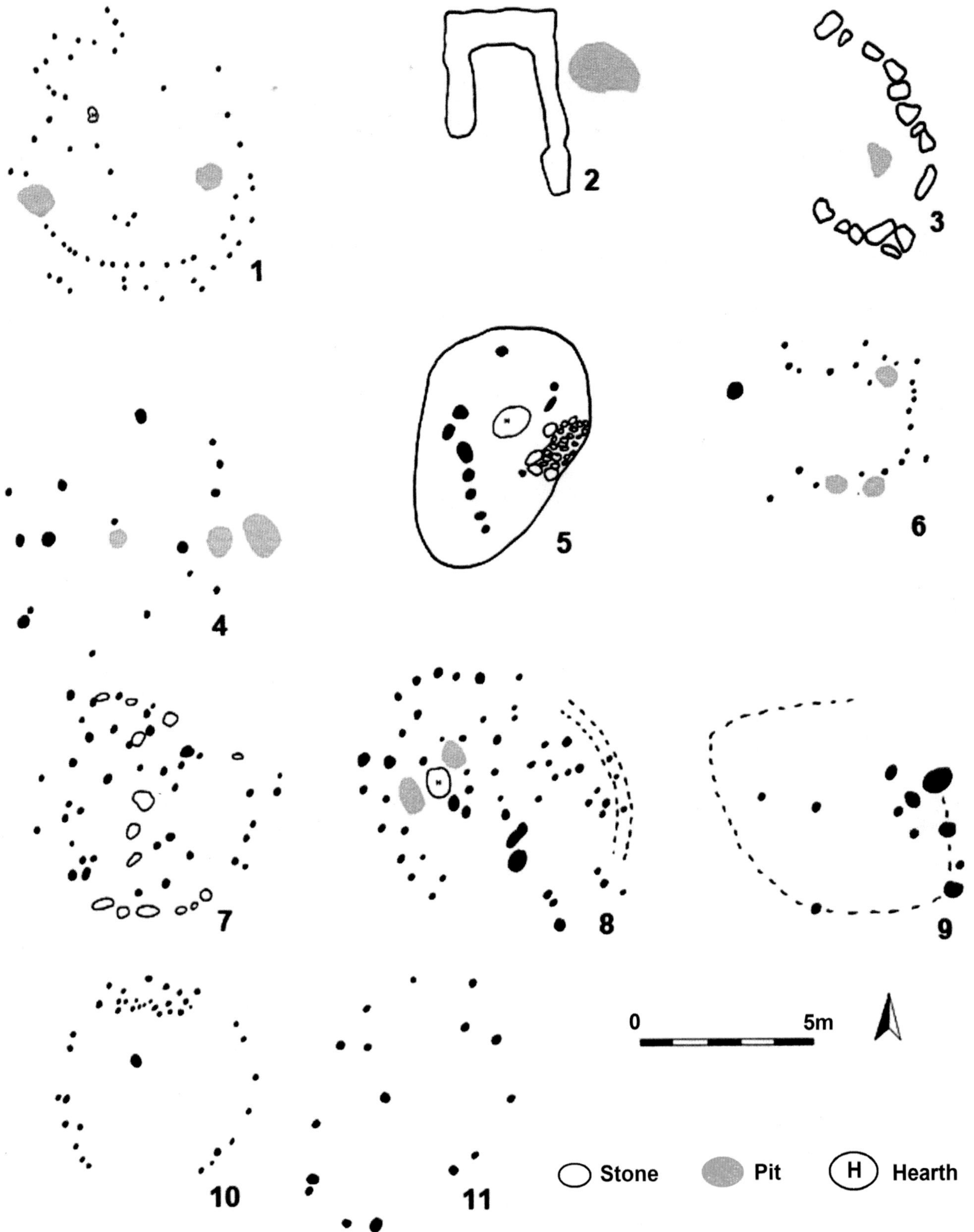

Figure 17.6: Simplified plans of Beaker associated structures in Ireland. 1 – Graigueshoneen; 2 – Ahanaglogh; 3 – Lough Gur D II; 4 – Rathwilladoon; 5 – Monknewtown; 6 – Cloghers; 7 – Lough Gur C I; 8 – Lough Gur C II; 9 – Lough Gur D III; 10 – Lough Gur C III; 11 – Lough Gur D II. Graigueshoneen & Ahanaglogh (after Johnston et al. *2008); Lough Gur (after Grogan & Eogan 1987); Rathwilladoon (after Lyne 2009); Monknewtown (after Sweetman 1976); Cloghers (after Kiely 2003)*

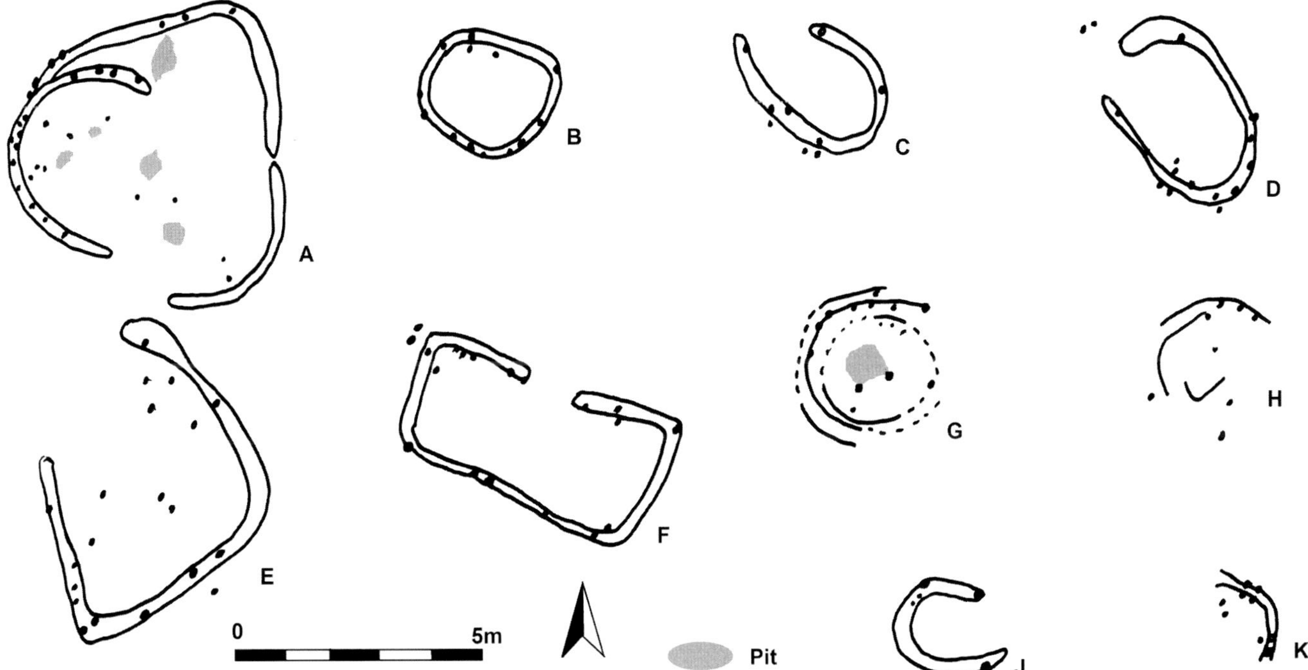

Figure 17.7: Simplified plans of the Beaker associated structures at Ross Island (after O'Brien 2004)

been sunk into the surrounding subsoil, has an internal hearth, and internal stake-holes are presumed roof supports.

All ten of the structures identified at Ross Island, Co Kerry (Fig. 17.7) are small and flimsy indeed and drawing the outlines of these structures makes them appear more certain than the descriptions in the excavation report suggest (O'Brien 2004). Structures A, E and F have areas of 17, 12 and 9 m^2 respectively and therefore do not vary too far from the average but the other sites have areas under 5 m^2 and would appear to have had functions other than habitation. O'Brien suggests that all these structures may have been temporary and/or associated with ore processing and certainly when compared to other structures, they appear enigmatic.

The evidence from England is also ambiguous (Figs 17.8 & 9). There are some clear circular or oval ground-plans of structures firmly associated with Beaker such as the floor deposit with surrounding stake-holes from Hockwold-cum-Wilton (Norfolk) (Bamford 1982) and oval post-hole structures from Sutton Hoo, Suffolk (Hummler 2005), Hunstanton, Norfolk (Bradley *et al.* 1993), and High Lea, Dorset (inf. John Gale; Darvill 2010, 175). An oval floor-plan associated with pits and hearths was also located at Beacon Hill, North Yorkshire (Moore 1964) once again associated with fine and rusticated Beaker and a broadly similar arrangement of pits and stake-holes was found at Gravelly Guy, Oxfordshire (Lambrick & Allen 2004). An elongated and a roughly circular post-hole arrangement were found at Belle Tout, Sussex (Bradley 1982) but their similarity to some of the Ross Island sites may suggest that they were flimsy and perhaps temporary structures. A circular stone-banked enclosure from Butley, Suffolk is known only from an unpublished typescript by S. West (1976) in Ipswich Museum and although there are internal hearths and pits the exact nature of the site (ritual or domestic) is not certain.

The plan of a large structure below Chippenham Barrow 5, Cambridgeshire (Leaf 1939) clearly resembles a later prehistoric round house. It has a double stake-hole outer wall with two large entrance pits in the north-east. There would also appear to have been a ring of internal roof-supporting posts. The numbers of 'hearths' in the interior and crossing the outer wall suggests that they are not purposeful hearths but rather patches of more intensive burning resulting from the destruction of the structure. Whilst the size of Chippenham would not be out of place in a later Prehistoric setting, it does clearly dwarf the other Beaker structures and the post and stake-hole rings may be more connected with

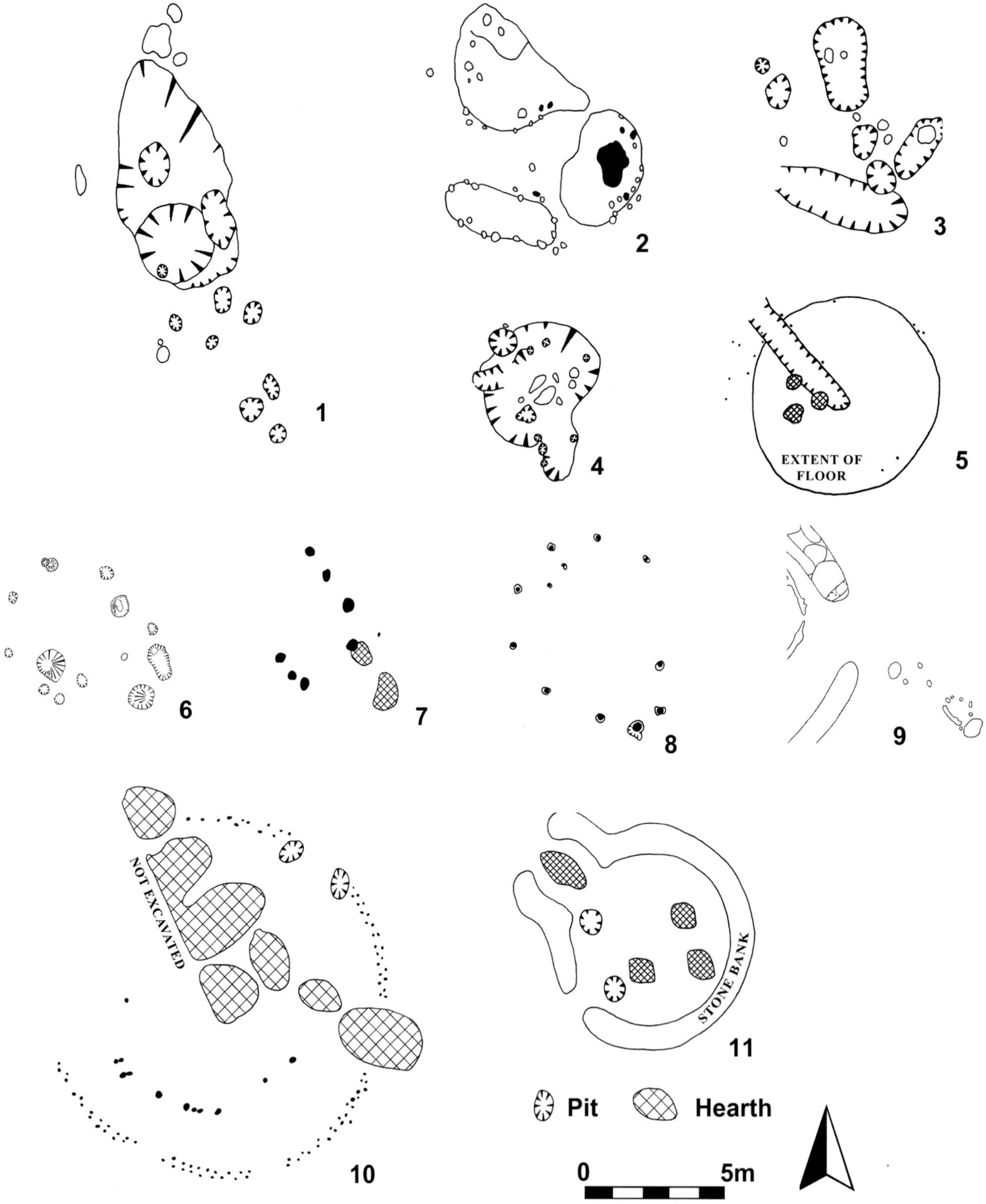

Figure 17.8: Simplified plans of Beaker associated structures in England. 1 – Cavenham 484; 2 – Cavenham 0482; 3 – Cavenham 0483; 4 – Cavenham 0485; 5 – Hockwold-cum-Wilton; 6 – Sutton Hoo; 7 – Beacon Hill; 8 – Hunstanton; 9 – Fengate; 10 – Chippenham Barrow 5; 11 – Butley. Cavenham (after Gibson & Gill 2013); Hockwold-cum-Wilton (after Bamford 1982); Sutton Hoo (after Hummler 2005); Beacon Hill (after Moore 1964); Hunstanton (after Bradley et al. *1993); Fengate (after Pryor 1993); Chippenham Barrow 5 (after Leaf 1939); Butley (after West unpubl.)*

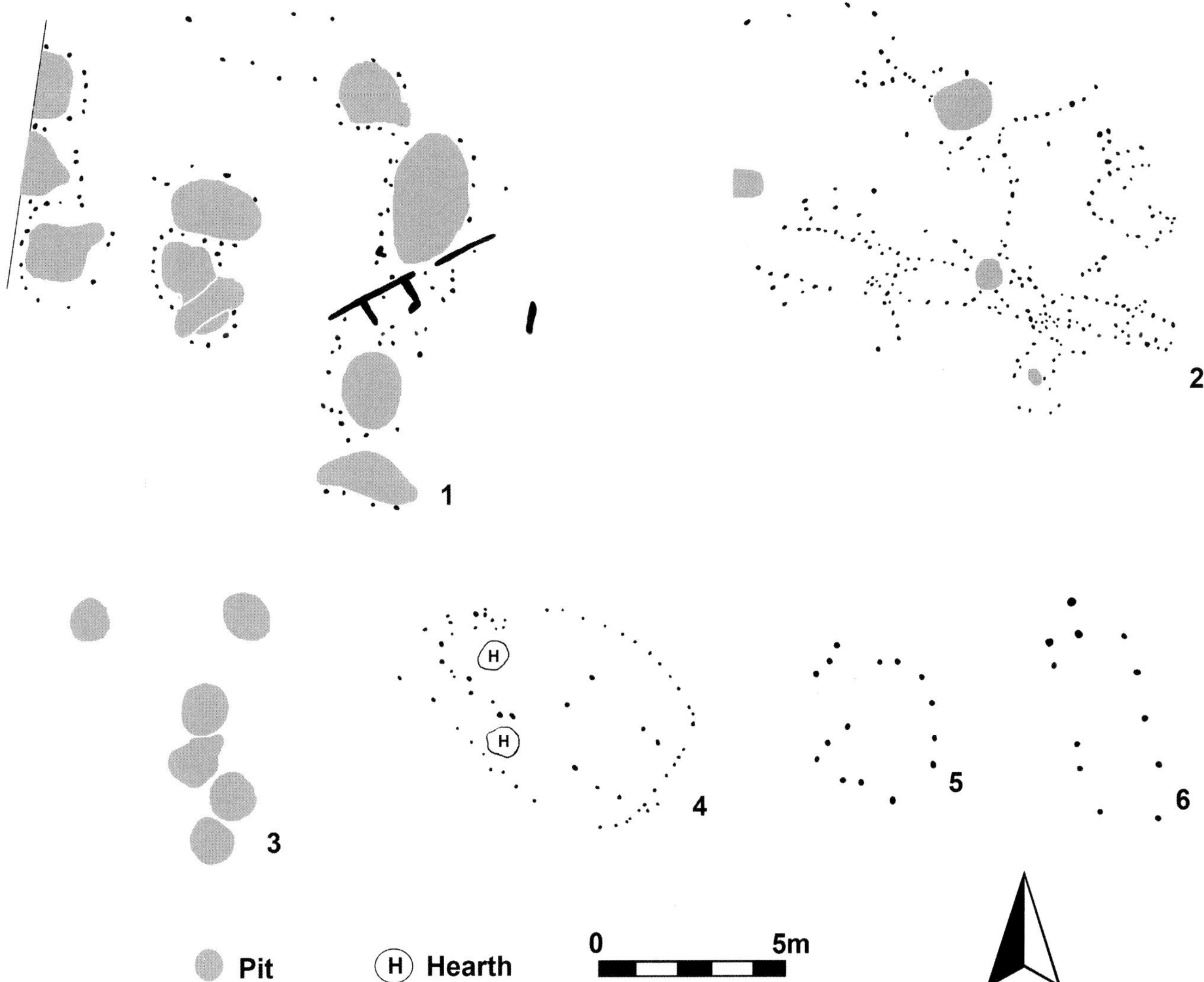

Figure 17.9: Simplified plans of Beaker associated structures in England. 1 – Easton Down (after Stone 1933); 2 – Swarkeston (after Greenfield 1960); 3 – Gravelly Guy (after Lambrick & Allen 2004); 4 – High Lea (after a plan generously supplied by John Gale); 5 – Belle Tout 1, 6 – Belle Tout 5 (both after Bradley 1982)

an early phase in the barrow's construction rather than with earlier habitation. That point having been made, however, the burning down of pre-barrow constructional features seems counterproductive and the partial plan of a circular structure from Fengate, Cambridgeshire (Fig. 17.8,9; Pryor 1993) would appear to have had similar proportions to Chippenham.

The other structures from England are much more enigmatic and may be described as structured or complex pits rather than dwellings. Pits associated with stake-holes have long been known at sites such as Easton Down, Wiltshire (Stone 1933) and more have recently been excavated at Cavenham, Suffolk (Gibson & Gill 2013). At both sites the pits were filled with Beaker domestic materials, both fine ware and coarser rusticated vessels. This may be a form of structured deposition with Beaker midden material 'closing' the pits after their primary period of use and if so, their direct association with domestic activity must remain uncertain (though clearly they were not sepulchral in origin). The pre-barrow stake-holes at Swarkeston, Derbyshire (Greenfield 1960) provide a tantalising glimpse of what may have been a more extensive area of domestic activity and the parallel stake-hole lines do suggest an element of structural intent even if no floorplans are immediately recognisable.

Non-structural domestic activity

The distribution of Beaker domestic structures in Britain and Ireland is uneven (Fig. 17.10) with large areas of southern Scotland and northern England being unrepresented. Neveretheless,

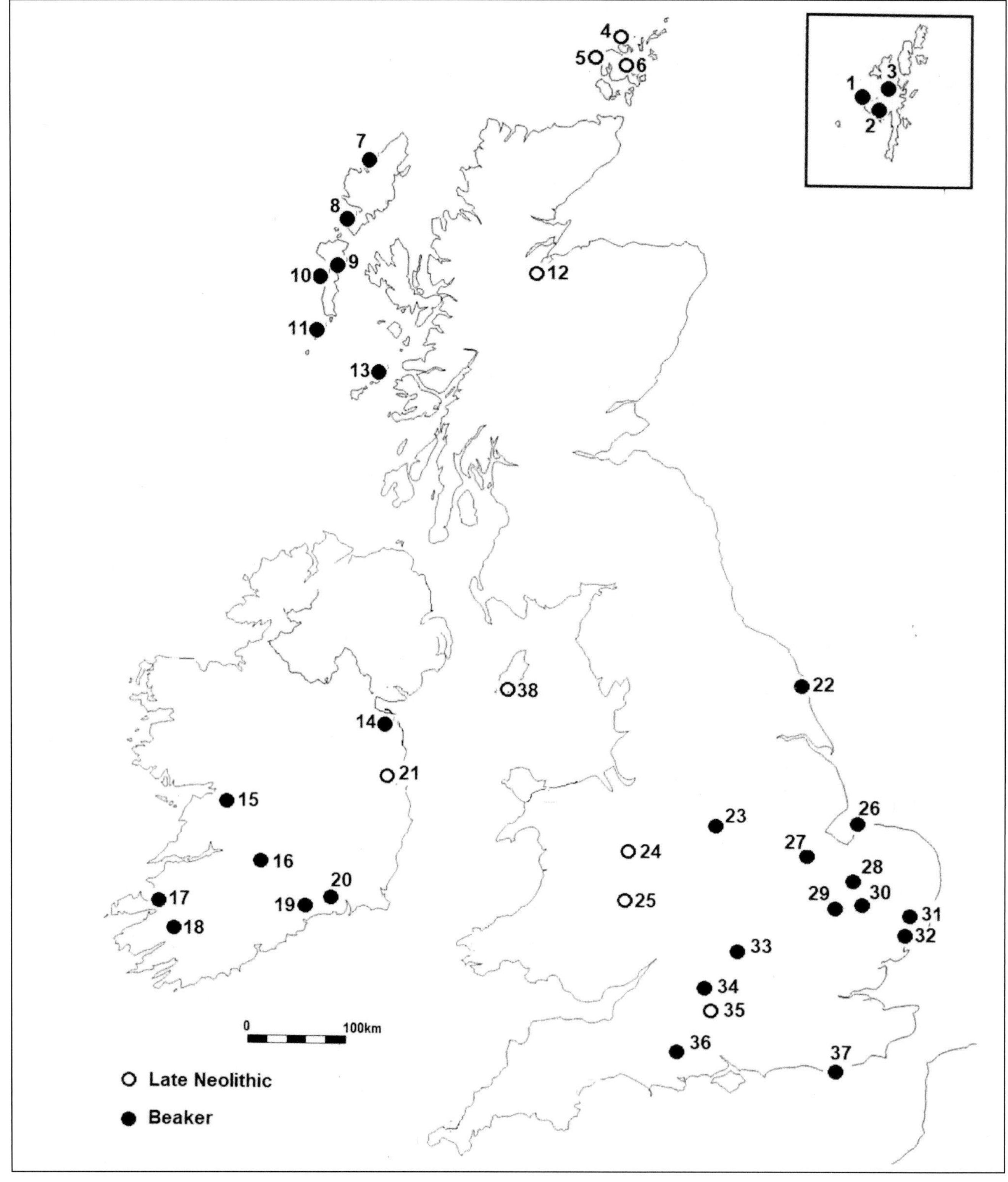

Figure 17.10: Late Neolithic and Beaker sites mentioned in the text. 1 – Scord of Brouster; 2 – Ness of Gruting; 3 – Stanydale; 4 – Rinyo; 5 – Skara Brae; 6 – Crossiecrown; 7 – Dalmore; 8 – Northton; 9 – Rosinish; 10 – Cill Donnain; 11 – Allt Chrisal; 12 – Raigmore; 13 – Sorrisdale; 14 – Monknewtown; 15 – Rathwilladoon; 16 – Lough Gur; 17 – Cloghers, 18 – Ross Island; 19 – Ahanaglogh; 20 – Graigueshoneen; 21 – Piperstown; 22 – Beacon Hill; 23 – Swarkeston; 24 – Trelystan; 25 – Walton; 26 – Hunstanton; 27 – Fengate; 28 – Hockwold-cum-Wilton; 29 – Chippenham; 30 – Cavenham; 31 – Butley; 32 – Sutton Hoo; 33 – Gravelly Guy; 34 – Easton Down; 35 – Durrington Walls; 36 – High Lea; 37 – Belle Tout; 38 – Ronaldsway

non-structural domestic contexts are known such as the coastal midden sites of the borderlands (compare the map of all 'domestic' activity in Gibson 1982, fig. 22) and in Cumbria, pits with domestic materials are currently emerging as chance finds. Intensive research in the Milfield Basin, Northumberland has also revealed tantalising traces of potential activity. The distribution map therefore represents structural evidence only and it is suspected that it will only be a matter of time before the blank areas become filled although, as mentioned above, this will probably rely on intensive research and chance discoveries.

Other evidence for Beaker settlement in lowland Britain comprises midden deposits and occupation spreads without structural elements (Gibson 1982) and the association of Beaker with plough marks at, for example, Rosinish and Ashcombe Bottom, Sussex (Allen 2005), the latter sealed by hillwash, suggests Beaker sherds being spread as part of a manuring process probably having been incorporated in midden material from a nearby settlement. Stray Beaker sherds in barrow mounds may have been similarly incorporated in turf and topsoil used to construct the barrow. In Kent, Beaker pottery and lithics have been found below peat deposits exposed by drainage gullies and other earthworks (Halliwell & Parfitt 1985) again, as in the Sussex dry valleys, offering only small windows into what may have been more extensive areas of occupation in the broadest sense. This has led Allen (2005) to suggest that Beaker occupation in agriculturally rich areas may lie buried below substantial deposits of hillwash and other deposits and certainly the majority of structural evidence that we have has been protected by mounds or sand dunes.

Economy

The economic bases of the Later Neolithic and Beaker period are difficult to estimate due to the paucity of unequivocal domestic sites and to the fact that most of the large ecofact assemblages come from monuments that have a clear ritual function such as Durrington Walls and Mount Pleasant (both Wiltshire) and where the faunal and floral data may be skewed by the activities that took place there. The overwhelming pig assemblage from Durrington Walls, for example, demonstrated the winter slaughter of young animals suggesting solsticial feasting events (Wright *et al.* 2014).

Curation of remains may also alter the picture and the 180 cattle skulls from the primary mound over the Beaker barrow at Irthlingborough, Northamptonshire is unlikely to represent a feasting event given the lack of meat-yielding bones but rather a structured deposit of selected skeletal parts, perhaps dismantled bucrania (Davis & Payne 1993; Harding & Healy 2007). This selection of curated material may also have been the explanation for the 300 cattle represented at Gayhurst, Buckinghamshire mostly by leg bones (Deighton & Halstead 2007). Though feasting events may have been responsible for this deposit, it is likely that those events were multiple and took place over a considerable period. (It is noteworthy that the so-called *Hecatombs*, literally the sacrifice of 100 bulls and associated feasting, at major religious festivals in Ancient Greece rarely involved figures anywhere near 100 and may even have been as few as 12 (Jones 1988)). The problem is further compounded by the acid and neutral soils that predominate in Britain so again the data are biased towards calcareous environments.

What data can be used suggest that cattle and sheep were the predominant domestic species with pig far less common (Bamford 1982; Simpson *et al.* 2006; Hay with Robinson 2011). This contrasts with the Grooved Ware associated Late Neolithic where pig appears to have been much more important. These data may be supplemented by lipid residue analysis of ceramics which seems to show a shift from porcine and ruminant adipose fats in the Late Neolithic (Mukherjee 2004) to dairy products with Beakers (Šoberl *et al.* 2009). The latter study focused principally on funerary ceramics so again the data may be skewed but the contrast with the beer residues that have been claimed for Iberian Bell Beakers (although not necessarily convincingly) is noteworthy and, unless fermented milk is envisaged, questions the Beaker = alcoholic beverage hypotheses that have frequently been proposed (*inter alia* Sherratt 1987). A large rusticated Beaker from a pit at Maxey Quarry (Cambridgeshire) (Gibson & Snape 2013) was found to have extensive internal carbon residues resulting from its use as a cooking vessel and analysis has shown that it contained ruminant as opposed to porcine adipose fats (Carl Heron pers. comm.) adding to the data for the shift from pig to cattle and sheep in Beaker domestic contexts.

Evidence for cereals is scarce but in the Thames Valley at least, there was a slight increase in cereal cultivation from the Late Neolithic when it was almost absent and six-row naked barley has been found as an impression in a Beaker from Eynsham (Oxfordshire) (Hey with Robinson 2011, 325). Barley was associated with Beaker-period ard cultivation at Cladh Hallan (Uist) (Parker Pearson *et al.* undated) and traces of similar ard marks were found at Rosinish (Benbecula) (Shepherd 1976) associated with grains of barley and oats indicating that Beaker-associated arable agriculture was being practised as far north as the Western Isles.

Discussion

As mentioned in the introduction to this chapter, the mechanics of the arrival of Beakers in Britain has been and still is a matter of debate from the mass migration of round-headed Beaker warriors to the less dramatic contact with Europe afforded by a few 'missionaries' bringing a new and attractive ideology (the Beaker Package – Burgess & Shennan 1976). Maritime and All Over Ornamented Beakers suggest contact with the whole coastline of Continental Europe and the Amesbury Archer (Chenery & Evans 2011) clearly demonstrates the movement of peoples although in what numbers remains uncertain. Although isotope analysis of Beaker burials as part of the Beaker People Project (Parker Pearson *et al.* 2016) has demonstrated considerable mobility within Britain there was little evidence for immigration from the Continent but it must be taken into account that the samples were not from uniformly early burials and so are unlikely to settle the 'first wave' issue. The recent DNA analysis of Neolithic, Beaker and Bronze Age populations by Olalde *et al.* (2018) has demonstrated a considerable population influx, emanating from northern Europe, apparently coinciding with the appearance of Beakers in Britain but there are few Late Neolithic samples in Olalde's database since most burials at this time were by cremation (although those few samples that do date to this 'Grooved Ware' phase are clearly native Neolithic in genetic make-up).

In the burial record, early Beakers are usually associated with crouched inhumations in pits below round barrows and with a distinctive set of artefacts as mentioned above. Strictly speaking, they RE-introduced crouched inhumations to Britain as we have a growing corpus of such burials in pre-Grooved Ware contexts. Some 200 years after these early burials, the rigidity of the burial mode and associations breaks down and we have a much greater variation in the burial record including practices and grave assemblages that have a distinctly Middle Neolithic feel. The users of Beakers seem to have had a less dramatic effect on the monumental record in Britain. Circles of wood, stone and earth originating at the start of the 3rd millennium continue throughout the Beaker and Early Bronze Age periods but there are some subtle changes. Timber circles may be replaced by stone towards the second half of the 3rd millennium and some timber and stone circles may have been 'closed off' by encircling banks and ditches at about the same time (Gibson 2012). This may be a response to the appearance of Beakers and Beaker-users may even have been responsible for at least some of these events, but whatever the mechanisms, there are certainly modification processes at work. After 2200 BC, these circular monuments take on a more sepulchral role suggesting a change in function and focus.

Archaeological attention has always been drawn to the richness of burials and the visibility of ritual monuments. Little attention has been paid to settlement archaeology outside of the Northern Isles due to the difficulty of identifying settlement sites. Those that have been discovered have been found by chance and in protected contexts sealed by sand dunes, hillwash or indeed later monuments. Nevertheless, there do seem to be a number of changes in the settlement record over time. The construction of substantial rectangular houses of the earlier Neolithic (Smyth 2014) seems to have declined in the 37th century cal BC when we then have a general gap in the settlement record equating to the Middle Neolithic. Later Neolithic houses, from *c.* 3000 cal BC, as we have seen, tend to be sub-rectangular whether defined by stone walls in the North or stake-holes in the South. Where the evidence survives, these Grooved Ware settlements seem to decline suddenly coinciding with the arrival of Beakers and this demise, particularly in the Northern Isles, has been termed catastrophic by Childe (1931). This happens in Orkney at the end of the 3rd millennium by which time Beakers have been in Britain for at least two to three centuries. It cannot therefore be invaders that close the Grooved Ware settlements. More likely it is the effect of the arrival of Beakers on the rest of Britain that has a knock-on effect on the Northern Isles perhaps restricting trade or contact with the mainland and, in effect, choking the life-supply of sites such as Rinyo, Skara Brae and the strongly fortified Ness of Brodgar.

Although no settlement structures associated with early Beakers have so far been discovered, other than the possible shelters at Ross Island, nevertheless there appears to be a general preference for oval structures with floor areas of roughly between 15 and 30 m^2 at the end of the 3rd and early 2nd millennia whether defined by stake-holes such as at High Lea, by revetment walls as at Northton, by sunken floors as at Monknewtown or by substantial walls as at Stanydale. Similarity with some of the Spanish and Breton oval structures cannot be denied (Nicolas *et al.* this volume) suggesting a maritime or Atlantic link. If this is the case, the use of boats in the roofing of these structures may gain added plausibility.

The admittedly scant evidence suggests scattered settlements as opposed to the nucleated Grooved Ware sites such as Skara Brae, Durrington Walls and, to a lesser extent, Trelystan and Upper Ninepence. After Needham's Fission horizon *c.* 2200 BC (Needham 2005) burial traditions become more varied and contemporary non-Beaker ceramics enter the archaeological record. These maintain a separation from Beakers. They always appear secondary to Beakers in burial mounds and on settlements there is considerable ceramic integrity with little if any mixing of Beaker and Bronze Age ceramic forms. On British Beaker settlements, terms such as *Begleitkeramik* do not apply as assemblages are 100% Beaker with vessels appearing in finer and coarser wares (Gibson 1982) and in a range of sizes from small, fine ware forms to large rusticated Potbeakers (Gibson & Snape 2013). Although the data have some problems of interpretation, Beakers also appear to mark an economic shift from a reliance on pigs to a more mixed economy with cattle and sheep: wild fauna are rare. There seems also to be an increase in cereal production marking the start of the marked increase in agriculture that we see in the Bronze Age.

Acknowledgements

The writer is grateful to Thor McVeigh (Galway) and Neil Carlin (Dublin) for providing information and for their views on the Irish material, to Alison Sheridan (National Museums Scotland) for allowing access to the pottery from Stanydale and Ness of Gruting and to Jenny Murray (Shetland Museums) for access to the Scord of Brouster pottery and providing Fig. 17.5.

References

Allen, M.J. 2005. Beaker settlement and environment on the Chalk Downs of southern England. *Proceedings of the Prehistoric Society* 71, 219–46

Ashbee, P. 1978. *The Ancient British.* Norwich: University of East Anglia

Bamford, H. 1982. *Beaker Domestic Sites in the Fen Edge and East Anglia.* Norwich: East Anglian Archaeology 16

Barclay, A.J. & Harris, O.J.T. 2017. Community building: houses and people in Neolithic Britain. In Bickle, P., Cummings, V., Hoffman, D. & Pollard, J. (eds), *The Neolithic of Europe. Papers in Honour of Alasdair Whittle,* 222–33. Oxford: Oxbow Books

Bayliss, A., Marshall, P., Richards, C. & Whittle, A. 2017. Islands of history, the late Neolithic timescape of Orkney. *Antiquity* 91 (359), 1171–88

Benkovsky-Pivovarova, Z., 2016. Zur Datierung der Begleitkeramik der Glockenbecherkultur. *Studia Archaeologica Brunensia* 21, (2), 61–74

Besse, M. 2004. Bell Beaker Common Ware during the third millennium BC in Europe. In Czebreszuk, J. (ed.), 2004, 127–48

Bradley, R., 1970. Where have all the houses gone? Some approaches to Beaker settlement. *Current Archaeology* 2, (10), 264–66

Bradley, R. 1982. Belle Tout – Revision and Re-assessment. In Drewett, P.L. *The Archaeology of Bullock Down, Eastbourne, East Sussex: the Development of a Landscape,* 12–20. Monograph 1. Lewes: Sussex Archaeological Society

Bradley, R., Chowne, P., Cleal, R.M.J., Healy, F. & Kinnes, I. 1993. *Excavations on Redgate Hill, Hunstanton, Norfolk, and at Tattershall Thorpe, Lincolnshire.* Norwich: East Anglian Archaeology 57

Brannigan, K. & Foster, P. 1995. *Barra: Archaeological Work on Ben Tangaval.* Sheffield: Sheffield Academic Press

Britnell, W. 1982. The excavation of two round barrows at Trelystan, Powys. *Proceedings of the Prehistoric Society* 48, 133–202

Bruce, J.R., Megaw, E.M. & Megaw, B.R.S. 1947. A Neolithic Site at Ronaldsway, Isle of Man. *Proceedings of the Prehistoric Society* 13, 139–60

Burgess, C. & Miket, R. (eds), 1976. *Settlement and Economy in the Third and Second Millennia BC.* Oxford: British Archaeological Reports 33

Burgess, C. & Shennan, S. 1976. The Beaker Phenomenon: some suggestions. In Burgess, C. & Miket, R. (eds), 309–31

Burrow, S. 1997. *The Neolithic Culture of the Isle of Man. A Study of Sites and Pottery.*. Oxford: British Archaeological Reports 263

Calder, C.S.T. 1950. Report on the excavation of a Neolithic Temple at Stanydale, in the parish of Standsting, Shetland. *Proceedings of the Society of Antiquaries of Scotland* 84, (1949–50), 185–205

Calder, C.S.T. 1956. Stone Age house sites in Shetland. *Proceedings of the Society of Antiquaries of Scotland* 89 (1955–56), 340–97

Calder, C.S.T. 1961. Excavations in Whalsay, Shetland, 1954–5. *Proceedings of the Society of Antiquaries of Scotland* 94, (1960–61), 28–45

Card, N., Downes, J., Richards, C., Jones, R., Challands, A., French, C.A.I. & Thomas, A., 2016. The settlement of Crossiecrown: the Grey and Red houses. In Richards, C. Jones, R. (eds), 2016. *The Development of Neolithic House Societies in Orkney. Investigations in the Bay of Firth, Mainland, Orkney (1994–2014),* 160–95. Oxford: Oxbow Books

Chenery, C.A. & Evans, J.A. 2011. A Summary of the Strontium and Oxygen Isotope Evidence for the Origins of Bell Beaker Individuals found near Stonehenge. In Fitzpatrick, A.P. *The Amesbury Archer and the Boscombe Bowmen: Bell Beaker Burials at Boscombe Down, Amesbury, Wiltshire.* 185–90. Salisbury: Wessex Archaeology Report 27

Childe, V.G. 1931. *Skara Brae. A Pictish Village in Orkney.* London: Kegan, Paul, Trench, Trubner & Co

Childe, V.G. & Grant, W.G. 1947. A stone age settlement at the Braes of Rinyo, Rousay, Orkney (second report). *Proceedings of the Society of Antiquaries of Scotland* 81, 16–42

Clarke, D.L. 1970. *The Beaker Pottery of Great Britain and Ireland.* Cambridge: Cambridge University Press

Clarke, D.V., Sheridan, A., Shepherd, A., Sharples, N., Armour-Chelu, A.,Hamlet, L., Bronk Ramsey, C., Dunbar, E., Reimer, P., Marshall, P. & Whittle, A. 2016. The end of the world or just 'goodbye to all that'? Contextualising the red deer heap from the Links of Noltland, Westray, within late 3rd-millennium cal BC Orkney. *Proceedings of the Society of Antiquaries of Scotland* 146, 1–33

Czebreszuk, J. (ed.), 2004. *Similar but Different: Bell Beakers in Europe.* Poznan: Adam Mickiewicz University

Darvill, T. 2010. *Prehistoric Britain* (2nd edn). London: Routledge

Davis, S. & Payne, S. 1993. A barrow full of cattle skulls. *Antiquity* 67, 12–22

Deighton, K. & Halstead, P. 2007. The cattle bone from Barrow 2. In A. Chapman, A Bronze Age barrow cemetery and later boundaries, pit alignments and enclosures at Gayhurst Quarry, Newport Pagnell, Buckinghamshire, 152–75. *Records of Buckinghamshire* 47, 83–211

Dockrill, S.J., Bond, J.M., Smith, A.N. & Nicholson, R.A. 2007. *Investigations in Sanday, Orkney. Vol 2: Toft's Ness, Sanday, An Island Landscape through 3000 years of Prehistory.* Kirkwall: The Orcadian Ltd & Historic Scotland

Downes, J. & Lamb, R. 2000. *Prehistoric Houses at Sumburgh in Shetland. Excavations at Sumburgh Airport 1967–74.* Oxford: Oxbow Books

Gibson, A.M. 1982. *Beaker Domestic Sites: A Study of the Domestic Pottery of the late Third and early Second Millennia BC in the British Isles.* Oxford: British Archaeological Reports 107

Gibson, A.M. 1999. *The Walton Basin Project: Excavation and Survey in a Prehistoric Landscape 1993–7.* Research Report 118. York: Council for British Archaeology

Gibson, A.M. 2004. Burials and Beakers: seeing beneath the veneer in Late Neolithic Britain. In Czebreszuk, J. (ed.), 2004, 173–92

Gibson, A.M. 2005. *Stonehenge and Timber Circles.* (2nd edn). Stroud: Tempus

Gibson, A.M. 2007. A Beaker Veneer? Some Evidence from the Burial Record. In Larsson, M. & Parker Pearson, M. (eds), *From Stonehenge to the Baltic. Living with Cultural Diversity in the Third Millennium BC,* 47–64. Oxford: British Archaeological Reports 1692

Gibson, A.M. 2012. An Introduction to the study of Henges: time for a change? In Gibson, A.M. (ed.), 2012, *Enclosing the Neolithic. Recent Research in Britain & Europe,* 1–20. Oxford: British Archaeological Reports International Series 2440

Gibson, A.M., 2017. Excavation of a Neolithic house at Yarnbury, near Grassington, North Yorkshire. *Proceedings of the Prehistoric Society* 83, 189–212

Gibson, A.M. forthcoming. Beakers in Britain: continuity and change in the later 3rd millennium BC. In Bailly, M. & Caraglio, A. (eds), *Identity? Prestige? What Else? Challenging views on the spread of Bell Beakers in Europe during the late 3rd millennium BC.* Archeologia Mediterrannée

Gibson, A.M. & Gill, D. 2013. Beaker occupation at Cavenham Quarry, Suffolk. In Prieto Martinez, P & Salanova, L. (eds), 2013. *Current Researches on Bell Beakers. Proceedings of the 15th International Bell Beaker Conference: from Atlantic to the Ural,* 251–64. Santiago de Compostella: Galician Archaeopots

Gibson, A. & Snape, N. 2013. Two Beaker Vessels from Maxey Quarry, Cambridgeshire. In Prieto Martinzez, M. P. and Salanova, L. (eds), *Current Researches on Bell Beakers. Proceedings of the 15th International Bell Beaker Conference From Atlantic to Ural, 5th–9th May, 2011, Poio (Pontevedra, Galicia, Spain),* 129–37. Santiago de Compostella: Galician Archaeopots

Greenfield, E. 1960. The excavation of Barrow 4 at Swarkeston, Derbyshire. *Derbyshire Archaeological Journal* 80, 1–48

Grogan, E. & Eogan, G., 1987. Lough Gur excavations by Sean P.O'Riordain: further Neolithic and Beaker habitations on Knockadoon. *Proceedings of the Royal Irish Academy* 87C, 7–506

Halliwell, G. & Parfitt, K. 1985. The prehistoric land surface in the Lydden Valley: an initial report. *Kent Archaeological Review* 82, 39–43

Harding, J. & Healy, F. 2007. *The Raunds Area Project: a Neolithic and Bronze Age Landscape in Northamptonshire.* London: English Heritage

Heise, M.E. 2014. Heads North or East? A Re-examination of Beaker Burials in Britain. Unpubl. PhD thesis, University of Edinburgh

Hey, G. with Robinson, M. 2011. Neolithic communities in the Thames Valley: the creation of new worlds. In

Morigi, A., Schreve, D., White, M, Hey, G., Garwood, P., Robinson, M., Barclay, A. & Bradley, P. (eds), *Thames Through Time. The Archaeology of the Gravel Terraces of the Upper and Middle Thames. Early Prehistory to 1500BC,* 221–60. Thames Valley Landscapes Monograph No32. Oxford: Oxford Archaeology

Hummler, M. 2005. Before Sutton Hoo. In Carver, M. (ed.), *Sutton Hoo: A Seventh Century Princely Burial Ground and its Context,* 392–458. Research Report 69. London: Society of Antiquaries of London

Hunter, J., Bond, J.M. & Smith, A.N. 2007. *Investigations in Sanday, Orkney. Vol 1: Excavations at Pool, Sanday, A Multi-period Settlement from Neolithic to Late Norse Times.* Kirkwall: The Orcadian Ltd & Historic Scotland

Johnston, P., Kiely, J. & Tierney, J. 2008. *Near the Bend in the River. The archaeology of the N25 Kilmacthomas realignment.* NRA Scheme Monograph 3. Dublin: National Roads Authority

Jones, P. 1988. *Homer's Odyssey: a companion to the English translation of Richmond Lattimore.* Bristol: Bristol Classical Press

Kiely, J. 2003. *Archaeology Excavation Report, Cloghers, Tralee, Co.Kerry.* Inishannon: Eachtra Archaeological Projects.

Lambrick, G. & Allen, T. 2004. *Gravelly Guy, Stanton Harcourt, Oxfordshire. The Development of a Prehistoric and Romano-British Community.* Thames Valley Landscapes Monograph 21. Oxford: Oxford Archaeology

Leaf, C.S. 1939. Further excavations in Bronze Age barrows at Chippenham, Cambridgeshire. *Proceedings of the Cambridge Antiquarian Society* 39, 29–68

Lyne, E. 2009. *N18 Gort to Crusheen Road Scheme.* Bray: Irish Archaeological Consultancy.

Moore, J.W. 1964. Excavations at Beacon Hill, Flamborough Head. *Yorkshire Archaeological Journal* 41, 191–202

Mukherjee, A.J. 2004. The Importance of Pigs in the Later British Neolithic: Integrating Stable Isotope Evidence from Lipid Residues in Archaeological Potsherds, Animal Bone, and Modern Animal Tissues. Unpubl. PhD thesis, University of Bristol

Needham, S. 2005. Transforming Beaker Culture in north-west Europe; processes of fusion and fission. *Proceedings of the Prehistoric Society* 71, 171–218

O'Brien, W. 2004. *Ross Island. Mining, Metal and Society in Early Ireland.* Bronze Age Studies 6. Galway: National University of Ireland Galway

Olalde, I. *et al.* 2018. The Beaker Phenomenon and the genomic transformation of north-west Europe. *Nature* 555, (7695), 190–96

Parker Pearson, M. 2007. The Stonehenge Riverside Project: excavations at the east entrance of Durrington Walls. In Larsson, M. & Parker Pearson, M. (eds), 125–44

Parker Pearson, M. & Gaffney, V. 2016. 'Ground-truthing Durrington Walls', *British Archaeology*, November-December 2016, 26–31

Parker Pearson, M., Chamberlain, A., Jay, M., Richards, M., Sheridan, A., Curtis, N., Evans, J., Gibson, A., Hutchison, M., Mahoney, P., Marshall, P., Montgomery, J., Needham, S., O'Mahoney, S., Pellegrini, M., & Wilkin, N. 2016. Beaker People in Britain: migration, mobility and diet. *Antiquity* 90, 620–37

Parker Pearson, M., Sheridan, A., Jay, M., Chamberlain, A., Richards, M.P. & Evans, J. 2019. *The Beaker People; isotopes, mobility and diet in prehistoric Britain.* Prehistoric Society Research Paper 7. Oxford: Oxbow Books

Parker Pearson, M., Marshall, P., Mulville, J. & Smith, H. Undated. The Prehistoric Village at Cadh Hallan. https://www.sheffield.ac.uk/archaeology/research/cladh-hallan/index. Accessed April 2018

Pryor, F.M.M. 1993. Excavations at Site 11, Fengate, Peterborough, 1969. In Simpson, W.G., Gurney, D.A., Neve, J. & Pryor, F.M.M. (eds), *The Fenland Project No7. Excavations in Peterborough and the Lower Welland Valley 1960–1969,* 127–40. Peterborough: East Anglian Archaeology 61

Richards, C. (ed.), 2005. *Dwelling Among the Monuments: The Neolithic Village of Barnhouse, Maes Howe Passage Grave and surrounding Monuments at Stennes, Orkney.* Cambridge: McDonald Institute Monograph

Richards, C. & Jones, R. (eds), 2016. *The Development of Neolithic House Societies in Orkney. Investigations in the Bay of Firth, Mainland, Orkney (1994–2014).* Oxford: Oxbow Books

Richards, C., Downes, J., Gee, C. & Carter, S. 2016. Materialising Neolithic house societies in Orkney, introducing Varme Dale and Muckquoy. In Richards, C. & Jones, R. (eds), 2016, 224–53

Ritchie, J.N.G. & Crawford, J. 1978. Recent work on Coll and Skye. (i) Excavations at Sorisdale and Killunaig, Coll; (ii) Notes on prehistoric and later artefacts from Coll; (iii) Beaker pottery from Skye. *Proceedings of the Society of Antiquaries of Scotland* 109, 1977–78, 75–103

Rynne, E. & Ó hÉailidhe, P. 1966. A group of prehistoric sites at Piperstown, Co. Dublin. *Proceedings of the Royal Irish Academy* 64, 61–84

Sharples, N. 2009. Beaker settlement in the Western Isles. In Allen, M.J., Sharples, N. & O'Connor, T. (eds), *Land and People: papers in memory of John G. Evans*, 147–58. Oxford: Oxbow Books

Sharples, N. 2012. The Beaker-period and Early Bronze Age settlement at Sligeanach, Cill Donnain. In Parker Pearson, M. (ed.), *From Machair to Mountains,* 215–58. Sheffield Environmental and Archaeological Research Campaign in the Hebrides Vol 4. Oxford: Oxbow Books

Shepherd, I.A.G. 1976. Preliminary results from the Beaker settlement at Rosinish, Benbecula. In Burgess, C. & Miket, R. (eds), 209–19

Sheridan, A. 2013. *Plus ça change…?* . Developments in Shetland, *c.*2500 to 1800 BC. In Mahler, D.L. (ed.), *The Border of Farming – Shetland and Scandinavia,* 47–72. Copenhagen: National Museum of Denmark

Sheridan, A. 2014. Shetland, from the appearance of a 'Neolithic' way of life to c.1500 BC: a view from the 'mainland'. In Gulløv, H.C. (ed.), *Northern Worlds – Landscapes, Interactions and Dynamics*, 67–94. Studies in History & Archaeology Vol 22. Copenhagen: National Museum

Sherratt, A. 1987. Cups that Cheered. In Waldren W.H. & Kennard R.C. (eds), *Bell Beakers of the Western Mediterranean. Definition, interpretation, theory and new site data,* 81–114. Oxford: British Archaeological Reports International Series 331

Simpson, D.D.A. 1971. Beaker houses and settlements in Britain. In Simpson, D.D.A. (ed.), *Economy and Settlement in the Neolithic and Early Bronze Age in Britain and Europe,* 131–52. Leicester: Leicester University Press

Simpson, D.D.A. 1996. Excavation of a kerbed funerary monument at Stoneyfield, Raigmore, Inverness, Highland, 1972–3. *Proceedings of the Society of Antiquaries of Scotland* 126, 53–86

Simpson, D.D.A., Murphy, E.M. & Gregory, R.A. 2006. *Excavations at Northton, Isle of Harris.* Oxford: British Archaeological Reports 408

Smyth, J. 2014. *Settlement in the Irish Neolithic. New Discoveries at the Edge of Europe.* Prehistoric Society Research Paper 6. Oxford: Oxbow Books, the Prehistoric Society and the Heritage Council, Ireland

Šoberl, L., Pollard, J. & Evershed, R. 2009. Pots for the afterlife: organic residue analysis of British Bronze Age pottery from funerary contexts. *PAST* 63, 6–8

Stone, J.F.S. 1933. Excavations at Easton Down, Winterslow, 1931–32. *Wiltshire Archaeological and Natural History Magazine* 46, 225–42

Strahm, C. 2004. Die Glockenbecher-Phänomen aus der Sicht der Komplimentär-Keramik. In Czebreszuk, J. (ed.), 2004, 101–26

Sweetman, P.D. 1976. An earthen enclosure at Monknewtown, Slane, Co. Meath. *Proceedings of the Royal Irish Academy* 76C, 25–72

West, S.E. 1976. Archaeology of the Butley Region. Unpubl. typescript in Ipswich Museum

Whittle, A.W.R., Keith-Lucas, M., Milles, A., Noddle, B., Rees, S. & Romans, J.C.C, 1986. *Scord of Brouster. An Early Agricultural Settlement on Shetland.* Oxford: Oxford University Committee for Archaeology

Wright, E., Viner-Daniels, S., Parker Pearson, M. & Albarella, U. 2014. Age and season of pig slaughter at Late Neolithic Durrington Walls (Wiltshire, UK) as detected through a new system for recording tooth wear. *Journal of Archaeological Science* 52, 497–514

18

The introduction of the Bell Beaker culture in Atlantic France: an overview of settlements

Clément Nicolas, Quentin Favrel, Lolita Rousseau, Vincent Ard, Stéphane Blanchet, Klet Donnart, Nicolas Fromont, Lorraine Manceau, Cyril Marcigny, Pablo Marticorena, Théophane Nicolas, Yvan Pailler and Julien Ripoche

Atlantic France played an important role in the Bell Beaker 'world'. Mainly known from burials, developer-led and research archaeology have revealed reliable domestic assemblages so that we now have a significant settlement corpus, some associated with radiocarbon dates. These advances have shed much light on the regional Bell Beaker Culture, its appearance, its relationship with existing local cultures, its cultural expressions and the lifestyles at that time. Data concerning subsistence economies are still under-represented. Aquitaine, Poitou-Charentes, Pays de la Loire, Brittany, and Normandy do not form an homogeneous area but are different landscapes united by the Atlantic seaways. They have not been equally well researched and whilst the Late Neolithic Artenac culture has been well studied, elsewhere the contemporary cultural groups are poorly defined or even unidentified due to the lack of consistent and unambiguous contexts (Fig. 18.1).

The beginnings of the Bell Beaker culture are not precisely dated. Typologically, the initial stage (including Maritime, All-Over-Corded & All-Over-Ornamented styles) is mainly known from collective and a few individual burials, all without reliable radiocarbon dates, though the different regional chronologies place this around the mid-3rd millennium BC (Fig. 18.2). The increasing numbers of domestic sites make it now possible to question the impact of Bell Beakers on the local Late Neolithic societies. We will examine the domestic architecture, ceramics and lithic production, considering firstly the Late Neolithic 1 societies (*c.* 2900–2500 BC) and secondly the Bell Beaker period (*c.* 2550–1950 BC). Finally, metalwork will be examined from a settlement perspective.

Domestic architecture

*The Late Neolithic 1 (*c.* 2900–2500 BC)*

Over 50 buildings are known for the local Late Neolithic period (Figs 18.3–18.5) and 16

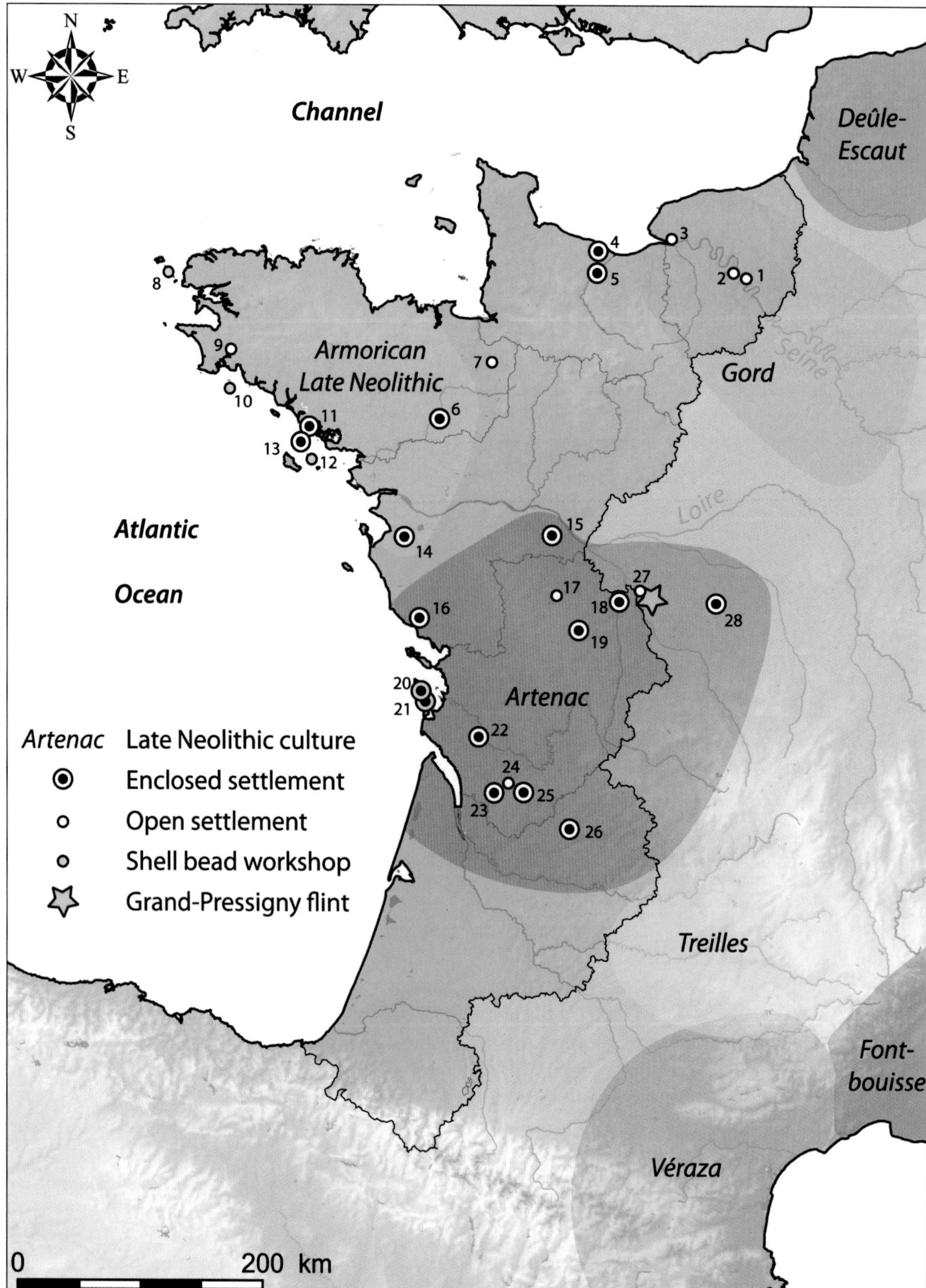

Figure 18.1: Map of the Late Neolithic 1 cultures in Atlantic France and the main related sites mentioned in the text.
1. Vivier-Le Clos-Saint-Quentin;
2. Port-au-Chanvre;
3. La Mare-des-Mares;
4. La Campagne;
5. La Delle du Poirier;
6. La Hersonnais;
7. La Barrais;
8. Beg ar Loued;
9. Kervouyec;
10. Saint-Nicolas;
11. Le Lizo;
12. Er Yoh;
13. Groh Collé;
14. Les Prises;
15. Les Choffaux;
16. Rue des Menhirs;
17. Fief Baudoin;
18. La Croix-Verte;
19. Les Chavis;
20. La Perroche;
21. Ponthezières;
22. Diconche;
23. Les Limousines;
24. Les Graves;
25. Le Camp;
26. Beauclair;
27. Le Fond d'Arrêt;
28. Les Vaux.

reach up to 100 m long. They have various shapes, being rectangular (a ubiquitous form), rectangular with rounded corners (south of the Loire) or apse-ended (north of the Loire). This division is also expressed in the orientations of the buildings: NE–SW towards the south, and NW–SE towards the north. Small and medium-sized buildings, generally represented by a few post-holes, are between 4 and 27 m long and 3.7 to 10.5 m wide with an area of 14–240 m² (Fig. 18.3). Half of them (16) were excavated within the La Rue des Menhirs enclosure, Avrillé, Vendée (Fromont *et al.* 2014a; Fig. 18.3,3). A further 4 were found at La Mare des Mares, Saint-Vigor-

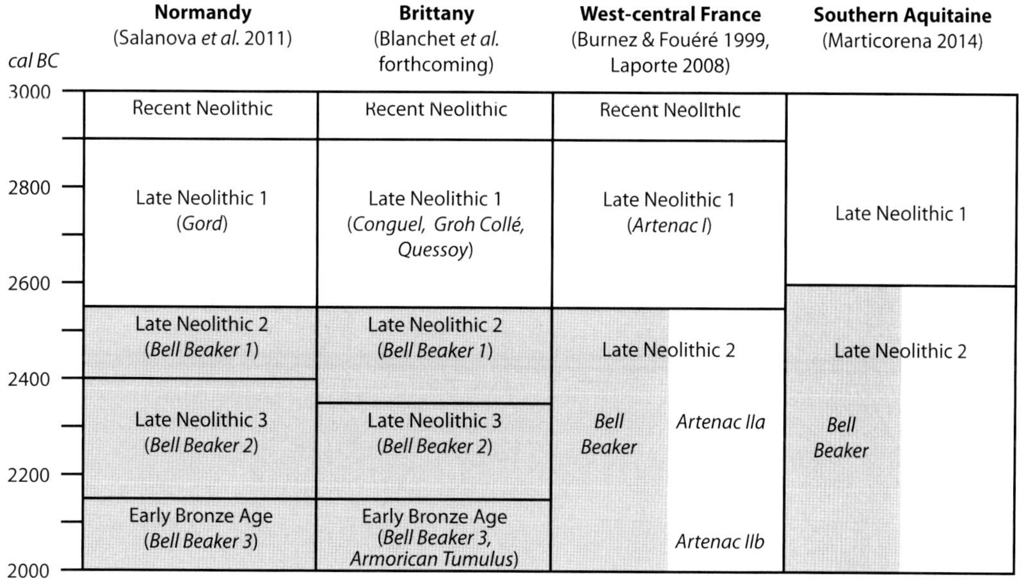

cal BC	Normandy (Salanova *et al.* 2011)	Brittany (Blanchet *et al.* forthcoming)	West-central France (Burnez & Fouéré 1999, Laporte 2008)	Southern Aquitaine (Marticorena 2014)
3000	Recent Neolithic	Recent Neolithic	Recent Neolithic	Late Neolithic 1
2800	Late Neolithic 1 (*Gord*)	Late Neolithic 1 (*Conguel, Groh Collé, Quessoy*)	Late Neolithic 1 (*Artenac I*)	
2600	Late Neolithic 2 (*Bell Beaker 1*)	Late Neolithic 2 (*Bell Beaker 1*)	Late Neolithic 2	Late Neolithic 2
2400	Late Neolithic 3 (*Bell Beaker 2*)	Late Neolithic 3 (*Bell Beaker 2*)	*Bell Beaker* / *Artenac IIa*	*Bell Beaker*
2200	Early Bronze Age (*Bell Beaker 3*)	Early Bronze Age (*Bell Beaker 3, Armorican Tumulus*)	*Artenac IIb*	
2000				

Figure 18.2: Chronological framework of the 3rd millennium BC in Atlantic France

d'Ymonville, Seine-Maritime (Lepaumier *et al.* 2005). Among the latter, three are clearly two-aisled with ridge beam posts and one is surrounded by bedding-trenches open to the NE, representing a possible porch (Fig. 18.3,1). The two apse-ended houses from La Delle du Poirier, Saint-André-sur-Orne, Calvados, are built with two lateral load-bearing walls comprising six large post-holes (Fig. 18.3,2) (Ghesquière *et al.* forthcoming) and similar buildings have been excavated in the Grand-Pressigny area (Laroche *et al.* 2014).

The largest buildings are usually delimited by a foundation trench (Figs 18.4–18.5) and an axis of load-bearing post-holes, sometimes in pairs, is set up along the inner walls. The ridge beam is generally borne by large posts with post-holes exceeding 1 m in diameter and up to 2 m deep and it has been suggested that the depth of the post-holes might be related to the presence of an upper floor (Fouéré 1998; Ghesquière *et al.* forthcoming). One of the two building types is narrow and very long (54–103 × 9–16 m) covering an area of 480–1584 m². The other is wider and shorter (45–66.5 × 16.8–18 m) providing an internal area of 675–1043 m² (Fig. 18.6).

Interruptions in the bedding trenches show that there were generally several entrances except at La Hersonnais, Pléchâtel (Ille-et-Vilaine), whose four buildings have an axial entrance towards the east preceded by a trapezoidal courtyard although other entrances may have existed (Tinévez 2004). On this same site, two buildings have a perpendicular wing (27–40 m long) on the north-east. South of the Loire, a courtyard bounded by a ditch is associated with the buildings.

The largest buildings may be surrounded by a fence forming a circular to sub-rectangular enclosure *c.* 1100–25,000 m² in area and internal radiating lines of post-holes divided the inner space. At La Rue des Menhirs, Avrillé, the site lies at a confluence and is bounded by ditches and palisades, enclosing an area of *c.* 4 hectares (Fromont *et al.* 2014a). At Le Camp, Challignac, the two buildings are within an area of 18 hectares surrounded by chalky ramparts (Burnez 2010; Louboutin 2014). At the Recent/Late Neolithic site at La Campagne, Basly (Calvados), a burnt oak fence defended a spur and was associated with dozens of arrowheads, often burned, illustrating that at least some enclosures were defensive (Fromont *et al.* 2014b; (Fig. 18.7).

Some of the largest buildings have evidence for re-building. At La Hersonnais, Pléchâtel, the four houses had at least two phases, and the buildings may have operated in pairs (Tinévez 2004; Fig. 18.4,1 & 2), whereas in Beauclair, Douchapt, two houses overlap (Fouéré 1998). If some seem isolated, others are surrounded by smaller buildings and might be considered villages. At Les Chavis, Vouillé, aerial surveys have revealed two large buildings with a dozen smaller ones inside and outside the fenced enclosures (Maitay *et al.* 2018; Fig. 18.5,2).

Radiocarbon dates for these largest buildings

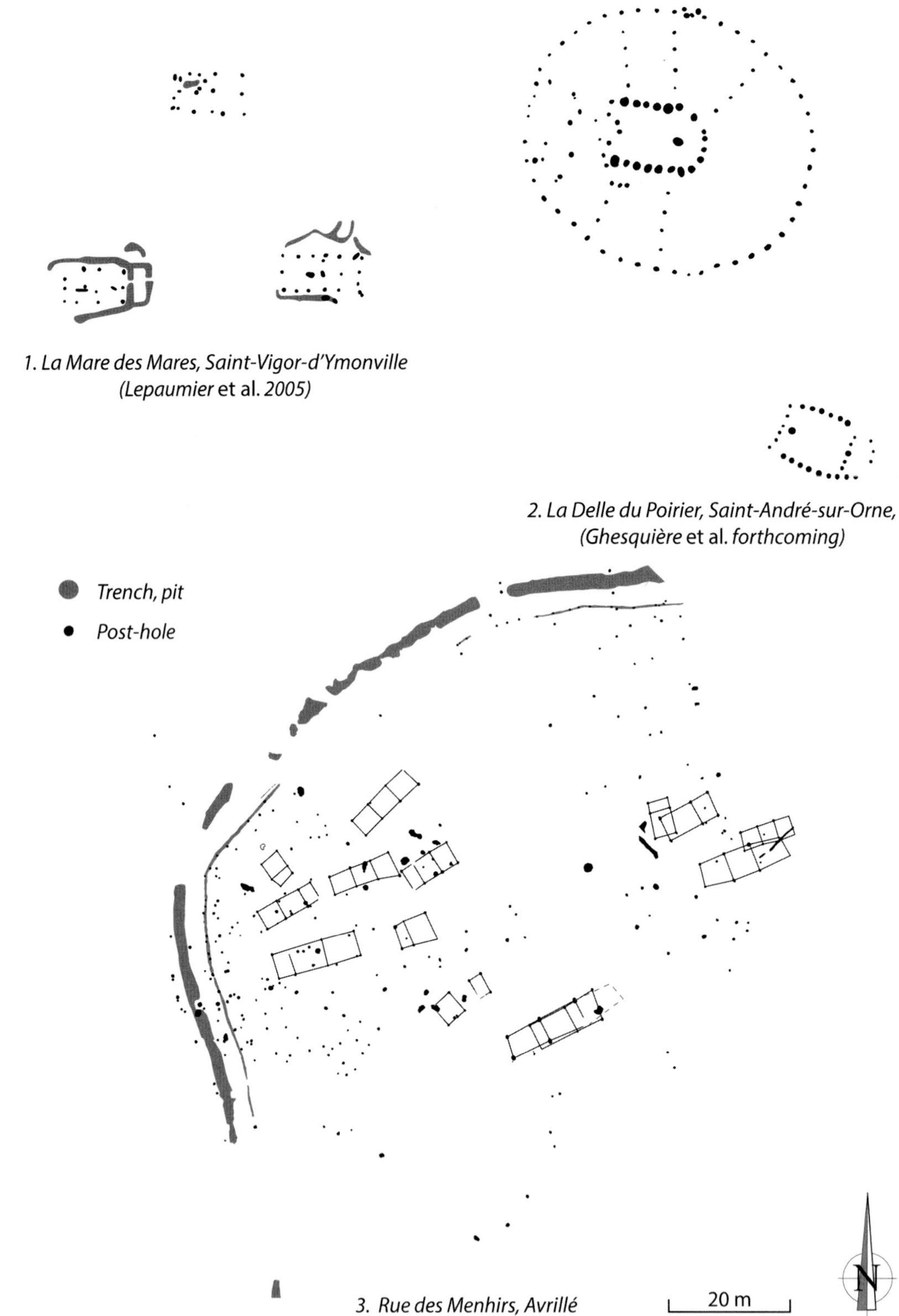

Figure 18.3: Medium-sized Late Neolithic houses in Atlantic France

point towards the first half of the 3rd millennium BC. However, some of them, dated between *c.* 2630–2280 cal BC (Beauclair, Douchapt and maybe Le Camp, Challignac) might have been contemporary with the earliest Bell Beakers (Fouéré 1998; Burnez 2010).

Different medium-sized buildings might also be contemporary, as at La Delle du Poirier,

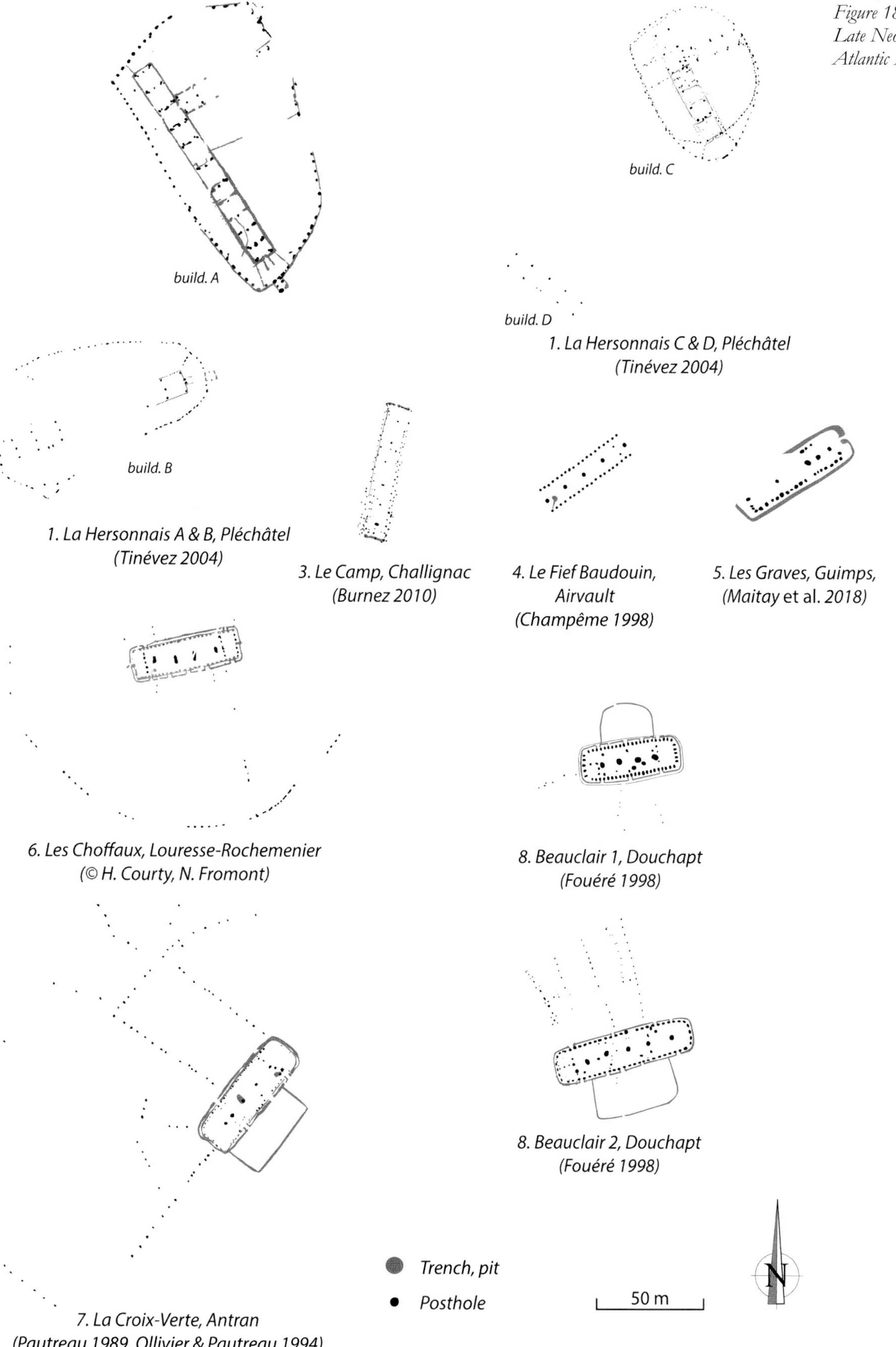

Figure 18.4: Larger Late Neolithic houses in Atlantic France

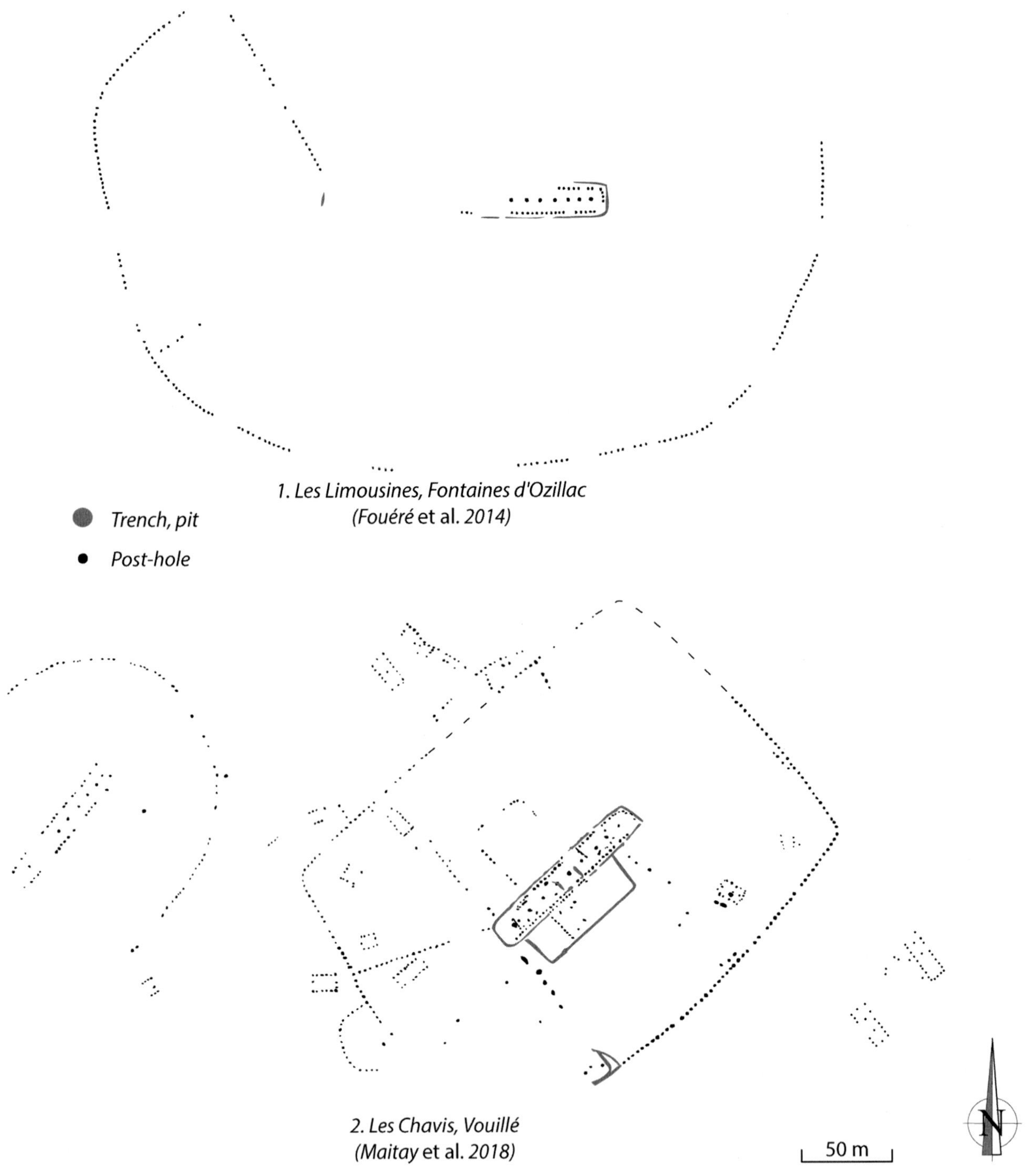

Figure 18.5: The largest Late Neolithic houses in Atlantic France

Saint-André-sur-Orne (Ghesquière *et al.* forthcoming; Fig. 18.3,2) or at La Mare des Mares, Saint-Vigor-d'Ymonville (Lepaumier *et al.* 2005; Fig. 18.3,1). At La Rue des Menhirs, Avrillé, nine certain and seven possible buildings have been recognised but not all are contemporary (Fig. 18.3,3)

On the coast, small buildings are made of wood, stone or earth. Whithin the Ponthezières enclosure, Saint-Georges d'Oléron (Charente-Maritime), small post-hole structures (< 5 m^2) sometimes with stone-based walls have been excavated (Laporte 2009) and similar structures occur in Le Camp du Lizo enclosure, Carnac (Le Rouzic 1933). This site is enclosed by stone, wooden and earthern ramparts, 5–12 m wide

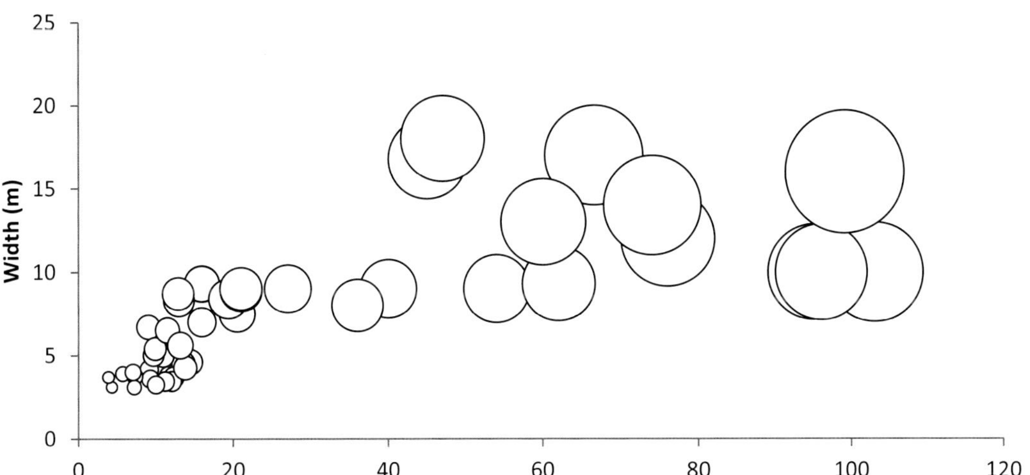

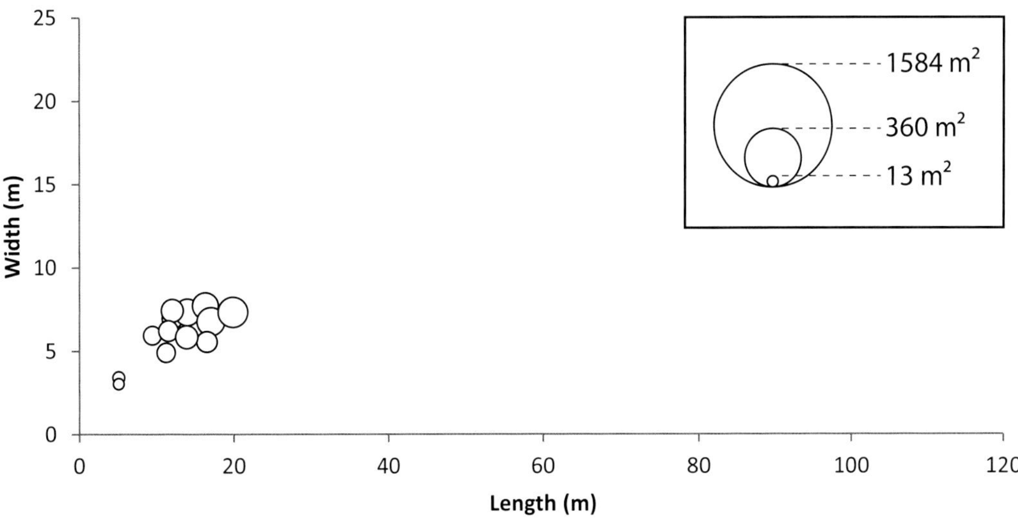

Figure 18.6: Diagram of length, width and surface of Late Neolithic 1 and Bell Beaker houses

and at least 1 m high. Within it, the buildings are circular or angular in shape, of various sizes (*c.* 2–15 m^2) and walled by flat or upright slabs. In some cases, these structures are contiguous and interconnected. Fired daub suggest that the superstructures were of wattle and daub construction.

This overview demonstrates the diversity of domestic architecture during the Late Neolithic 1. There are both open and enclosed sites. All sizes of buildings are present and presumably not all were houses. The largest buildings occur on both sides of the River Loire but it is still difficult to appreciate their status (Tinévez 2004). Did they act as a central place, or house a 'village community' (Tinévez 2004, 164) of several families? Whatever the explanation, we can see a trend towards nucleated settlement, with large and clusters of smaller houses or a combination of both.

The Bell Beaker period

In western France, more than 100 Bell Beaker domestic sites and nearly 300 graves are known (Fig. 18.8). Around 20 Bell Beaker buildings are known in western France (Blanchet *et al.* 2012 & forthcoming) but most of them lack firm evidence of domestic use. The majority are almond-shaped (Fig. 18.9) and their areas range between 36–95 m^2, the largest reaching 20 m

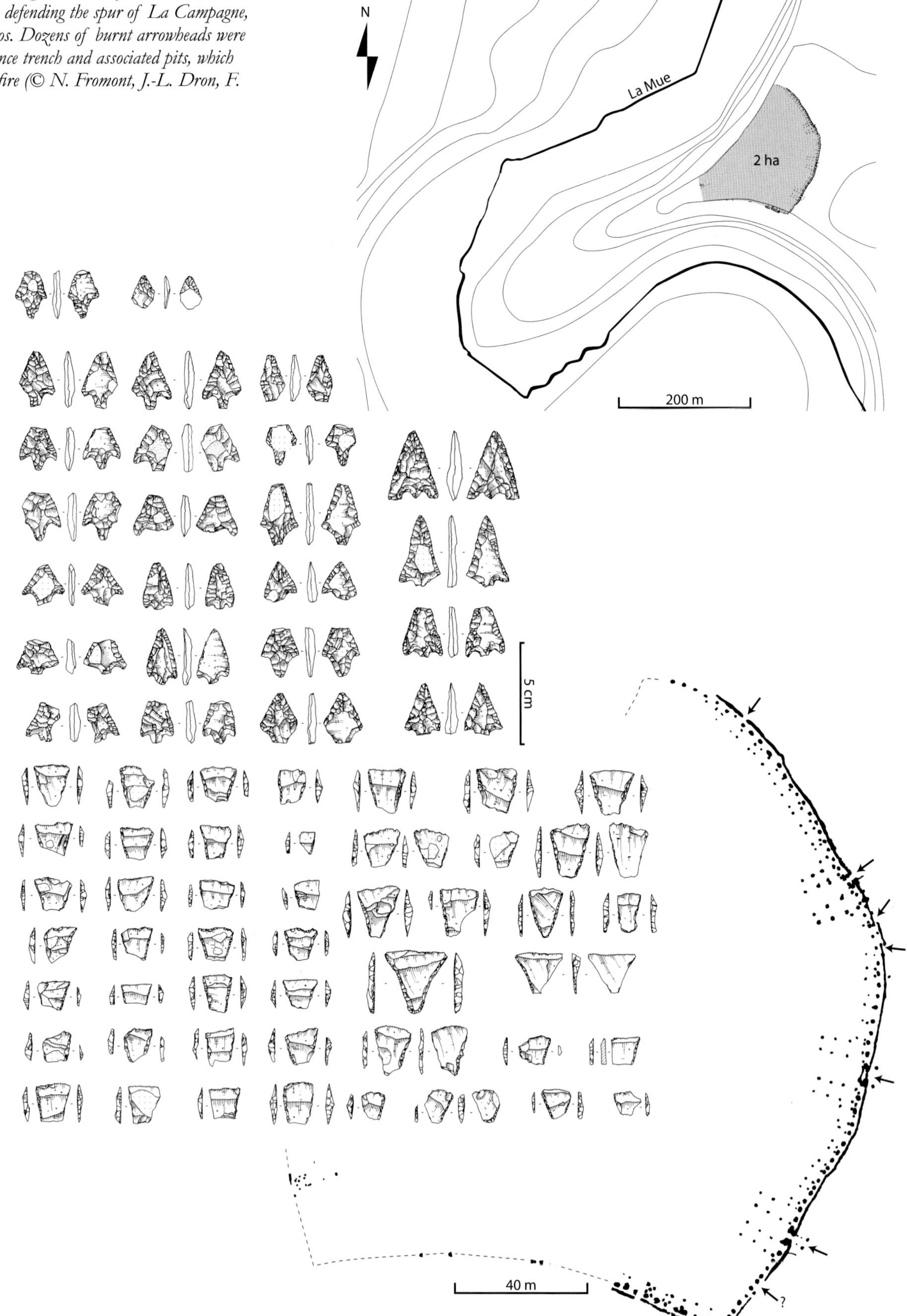

Figure 18.7: Setting and detail of the Recent/Late Neolithic fence defending the spur of La Campagne, Basly, Calvados. Dozens of burnt arrowheads were found in the fence trench and associated pits, which show signs of fire (© N. Fromont, J.-L. Dron, F. Charraud)

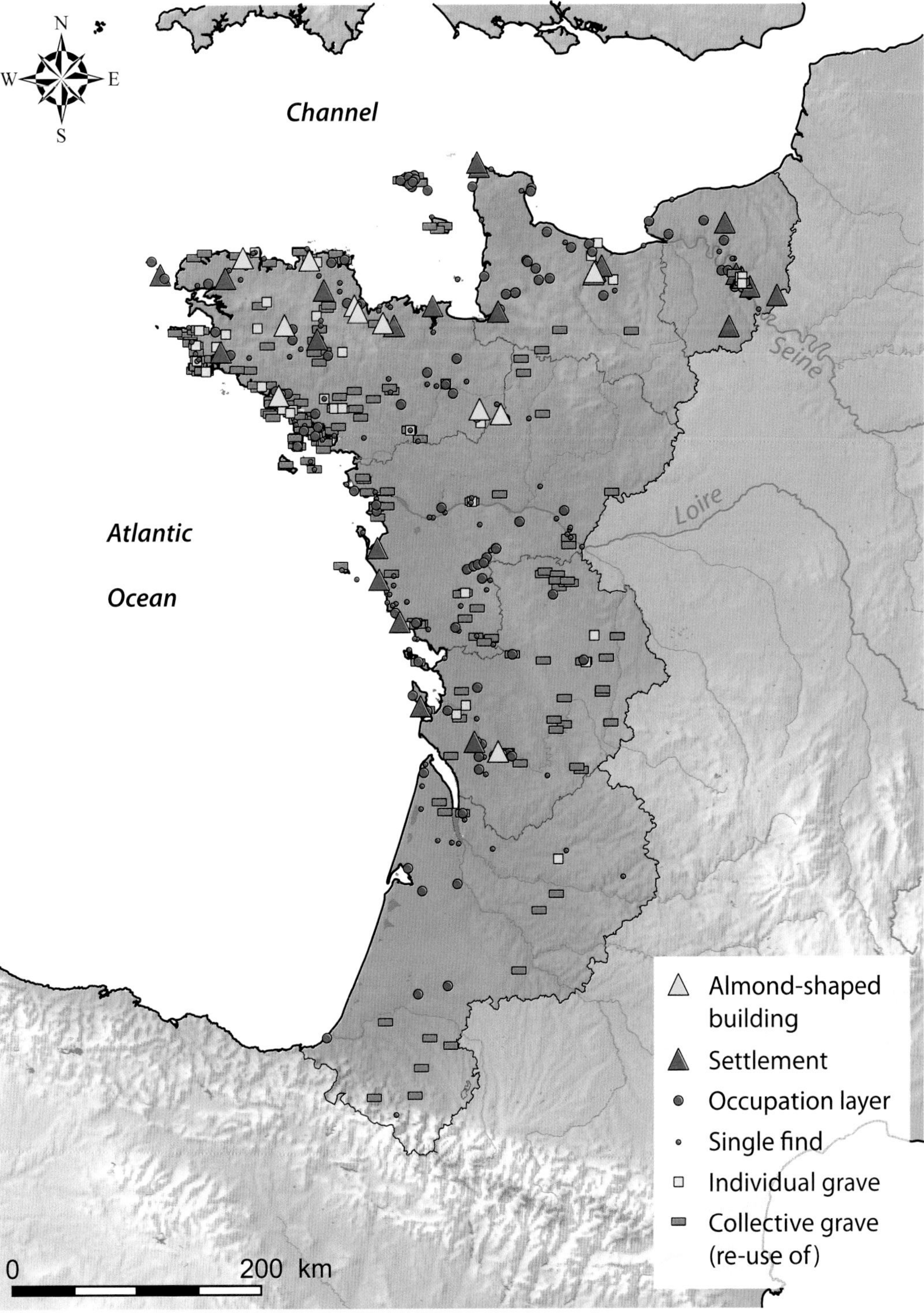

Figure 18.8: Distribution map of the Bell Beaker culture in Atlantic France and in the Channel slands (after Gadbois-Langevin 2013; Favrel 2015; Rousseau 2015; Nicolas 2016 with updates; P. de Jersey pers. comm.)

long at Bourg Saint-Pair, Bais, Ille-et-Vilaine (*ibid.*; Fig. 18.9,10). Some are more or less trapezoid, with the wider end (*c.* 7.5 m) towards the SE and the narrower (> 2.5 m) towards the NW. The walls are marked by bedding-trenches averaging 0.3 m wide. Internal posts probably served to support the wooden frame and the entrance, mainly towards the wider end, is usually marked by two larger post-holes.

These buildings produced few artefacts, at best some sherds (including Bell Beakers) and a few stone implements. The radiocarbon

Table 18.1: Radiocarbon dates for almond-shaped Bell Beaker houses

Site	*Date BP*	*Cal BC (95.4 %)*	*Lab. no.*	*References*
Bourg Saint-Pair, Bais	3820±40	2460–2140	Ly-7151	Blanchet *et al.* forthcoming
	3790±40	2410–2040	Ly-7150	
Chemin des Prés, Ars-en-Saintonge	3810±30	2400–2140	Beta-472436	Lemaire & Bosc-Zanardo 2018
Kergorvo, Carhaix	3840±35	2460–2200	Poz-47986	Blanchet *et al.* forthcoming
	3820±40	2460–2140	Beta-293514	
La Delle du Poirier, Saint-André-sur-Orne	3860±30	2470–2210	Beta-424681	Ghesquière *et al.* forthcoming
La Tourelle, Lamballe	4035±35	2840–2470	GrA-38015	Blanchet *et al.* forthcoming
Le Coin des Petits Clos, build. 1, Trémuson	4203±28	2900–2670	UBA-37060	Toron *et al.* 2018
	3980±30	2580–2450	Beta-444995	
Le Coin des Petits Clos, build. 2, Trémuson	3685±33	2200–1960	UBA-37062	

dates are from charcoal from the bedding trenches or post-holes and might be intrusive or have an 'old wood' effect. Nevertheless, most range between 2430–2150 cal BC, in the middle of the Bell Beaker period (Blanchet *et al.* forthcoming; Table 18.1). Two earlier dates from La Tourelle, Lamballe (Côtes-d'Armor; Blanchet *et al.* 2012) and Le Coin des Petits Clos 1, Trémuson (Côtes-d'Armor; Toron *et al.* 2018) might suggest an earlier appearance between 2660–2460 cal BC (Table 18.1, GrA-38015 & Beta-444995). The earliest date, obtained from building 1 at Le Coin des Petits Clos, of 2900–2680 cal BC, is probably too old (Table 18.1; UBA-37060 & Beta-444995). Finally from the same site, a radiocarbon date from building 2 might suggest that this architecture persists until the end of the 3rd millenium (Table 18.1, UBA-37060).

These almond-shaped structures are associated with very few, if any, other domestic features such as outhouses, pits or post-holes and are frequently isolated. Some buildings are truncated (La Tourelle at Lamballe, Bourg Saint-Pair at Bais) and this may explain their apparent isolation, but where the bedding-trench is well preserved and the truncation is limited, it is conceivable that the occupation did not affect the subsoil (Blanchet *et al.* forthcoming). Three sites yielded several houses. The radiocarbon dates for the two at Le Coin des Petits Clos suggest that they are not contemporary but on the two other sites, the structures could be synchronous. At Creac'h ar Vrenn, Cléder (Finistère), three almond-shaped buildings, *c.* 60 m apart share the same orientation (Nicolas 2015; Fig. 18.9,6) and at Le Haut-Brétorin, Le Pertre (Ille-et-Vilaine), two buildings, spaced 15 m apart, were recognised during trial trenching (Leroux 2013). These buildings seem to share a common architectural tradition and although the corpus is quite large, questions remain regarding the scarcity of artefacts and ecofacts. What is their precise chronology? How long was their occupation? How were they occupied? What was their environmental setting?

Initially recognised in Brittany, these almond-shaped buildings are now found in a wide area of western France: in Normandy at La Delle du Poirier, Saint-André-sur-Orne (Ghesquière *et al.* forthcoming) and in Charente close to Cognac at Le Chemin des Prés, Ars-en-Saintonge (Lemaire & Bosc-Zanardo 2018; Fig. 18.9,7 & 9).

From a regional perspective, the Bell Beaker almond-shaped buildings are distinctly different from the Late Neolithic 1 houses, although there are some shared features. For north-western France, they have nearly the same orientation (NW–SE) with the main entrance towards the south-east. In both periods, bedding-trench construction is used. The dimensions of Bell Beaker buildings correspond to those of the Late Neolithic 1 medium-sized houses. Houses may appear in small clusters of two or three possibly contemporary buildings but Bell Beaker monumental buildings (30–100 m long) are still unknown. Nevertheless, Bell Beakers mark an architectural inovation and until evidence is found to the contrary, the most striking fact is the lack of large,

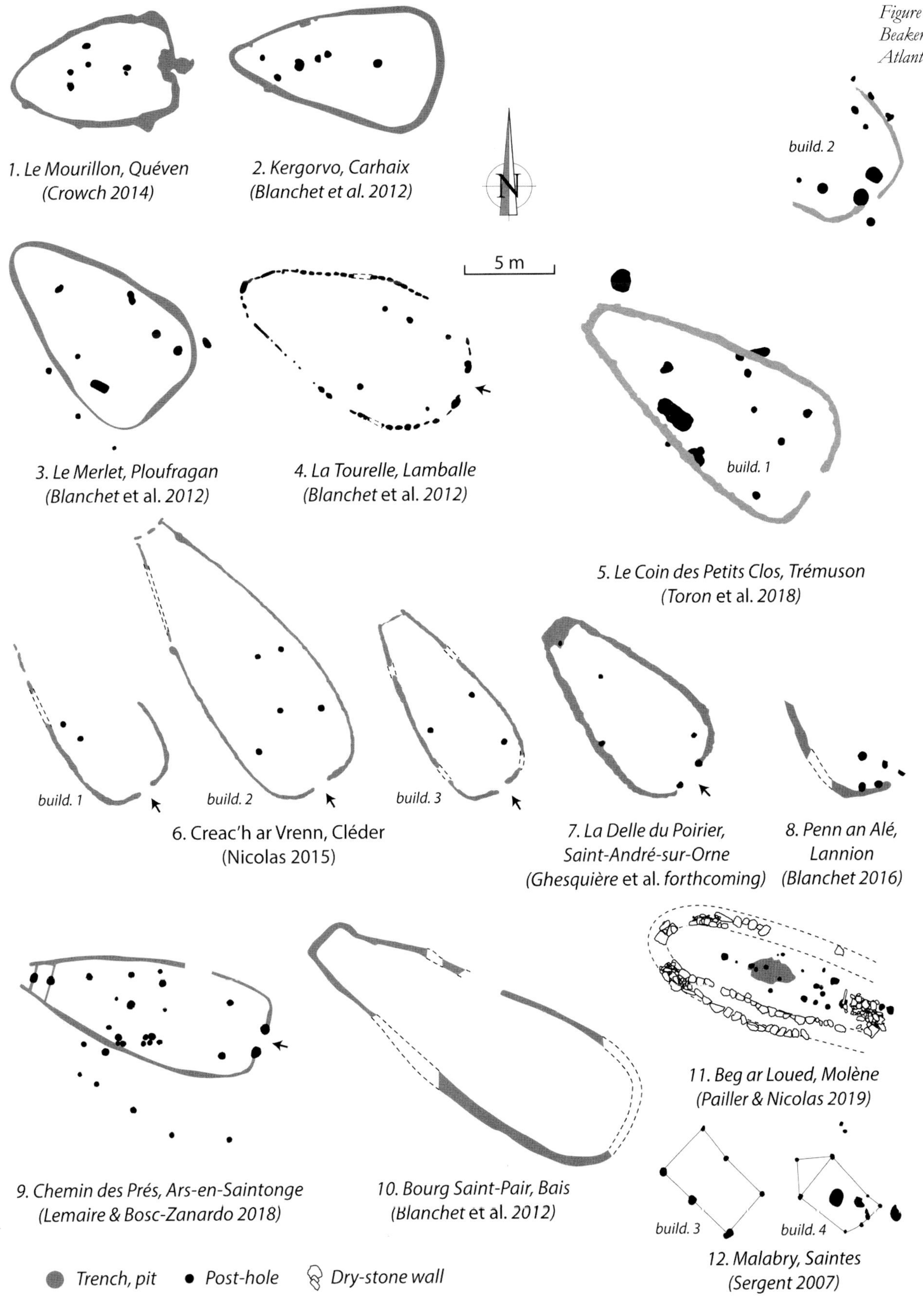

Figure 18.9: Bell Beaker houses in Atlantic France

enclosed buildings suggesting changes in socio–economic organisation and land use.

Smaller post-hole structures are known at Malabry, Saintes (Charente-Maritime). These two buildings (3 and 4), located 14 m apart, are likewise oriented NW–SE, measure 5 × *c.* 3 m and have an area of 13–16 m². One is rectangular, while the other, quite similar, ends with an axial post-hole to the north-west (Fig. 18.9,12). A pit 0.5 m from building 4, contained coarse ware and two Maritime sherds, suggesting a Bell Beaker attribution for these two analogous buildings (Sergent 2007).

In coastal areas there is some occupation of La Hague rock shelters, such as La Jupinerie, Omonville-la-Petite, Manche (Marcigny *et al.* 2005) but there are also stone structures though mostly poorly preserved (see Laporte 2009, Rousseau 2015). Although late (*c.* 2150–1950 cal BC), the only well-preserved site is Beg ar Loued on Molène Island (Finistère), where a dry-stone house with an apsed western end was found though the eastern part is largely destroyed (Fig. 18.9,11). The dry-stone walls are at least 0.75 m high with outer facings of upright slabs and the house measures 16.5 × 5.5 m (*c.* 45 m²). Ridge beam posts and stakes supported the wooden frame and the interior was paved with small stones and had a hearth-pit. This dry-stone architecture is unique for western France but is similar to those in northern Scotland (Pailler & Nicolas 2019; Gibson this volume).

Metalworking evidence in Bell Beaker settlements

The first metalworking occurred during the Bell Beaker period and in the Pyrenees, the first copper mines seem to be opened at that time (Beyrie & Kammenthaler 2008). Metalworking remains are found on several settlements in the form of small copper items (ore, slags or nodules) as at Les Florentins, Val-de-Reuil, Eure (Billard 1991), Le Vivier/Le Clos-Saint-Quentin, Poses, Eure (Billard *et al.* 1994), La Passe de l'Écuissière, Dolus-d'Oléron, Charente-Maritime (Laporte 2009) and maybe at Beg ar Loued, Molène Island, Finistère (Gandois *et al.* in Pailler & Nicolas 2019). The most complete site is undoubtedly La République, Talmont-Saint-Hilaire (Vendée), which has yielded pits likely to be related to metalworking, as well slags and crucibles (Gandois *et al.* 2016). Furthermore, an ingot mould and Bell Beaker pottery have been found at Crec'h Choupot, Trédarzec, Côtes-d'Armor (Nicolas 2014). More exceptional is a surface find following a storm on La Plage de la Roussellerie, Saint-Brévin-les-Pins/Saint-Michel-Chef-Chef (Loire-Atlantique) which, after sieving, produced several Bell Beaker gold sheet ornaments, a copper chisel and, above all, a tiny chiselled gold bar. The latter is likely a small ingot used for making sheet ornaments. Moreover, gold flakes and prills of molten gold were found at the same place, attesting to the local exploitation of alluvial deposits (Tessier & Bernard 1995).

Ceramic production

The Late Neolithic 1 north of River Loire (c. 2900–2500 BC)

In north-western France, the characterisation of ceramic productions in the first half of the 3rd millennium BC is not easy due to the scarcity of settlement contexts and sufficiently large assemblages. Therefore, any approach to providing a detailed chronology and cultural dynamics is limited. In Brittany, a number of studies have led to the identification of several cultural groups or specific styles: Conguel, Kerugou, Groh Collé, Quessoy (see Blanchard 2017). Their chronology, largely based on megalithic contexts, is still imprecisely established to such an extent that there are several conflicting models. From settlements, the assemblages from La Barrais at Saint-Sauveur-des-Landes, Ille-et-Vilaine (Hinguant & Laporte 1997) and from Kervouyec, Quimper, Finistère (Nicolas 2013) are characterised by barrel shapes, flat or flanged flat bases, handles (horizontal lugs), spindle whorls and spoons (Fig. 18.10). The pottery assemblage from La Hersonnais, Pléchâtel, Ille-et-Vilaine (Tinévez 2004), dated to the 27th century cal BC, show influences of the Conguel style (bowls) and the Artenac culture (decorative patterns), as well as shapes without regional counterparts (Fig. 18.10).

In Normandy, the Recent and Late Neolithic 1 pottery is still poorly understood. Besides the ubiquitous straight-sided shapes, some specific trends are related to the Late Neolithic 1 pottery such as the greater diversity in shapes, profiles with a slight inflection even a carination, increasing number of plastic elements and a

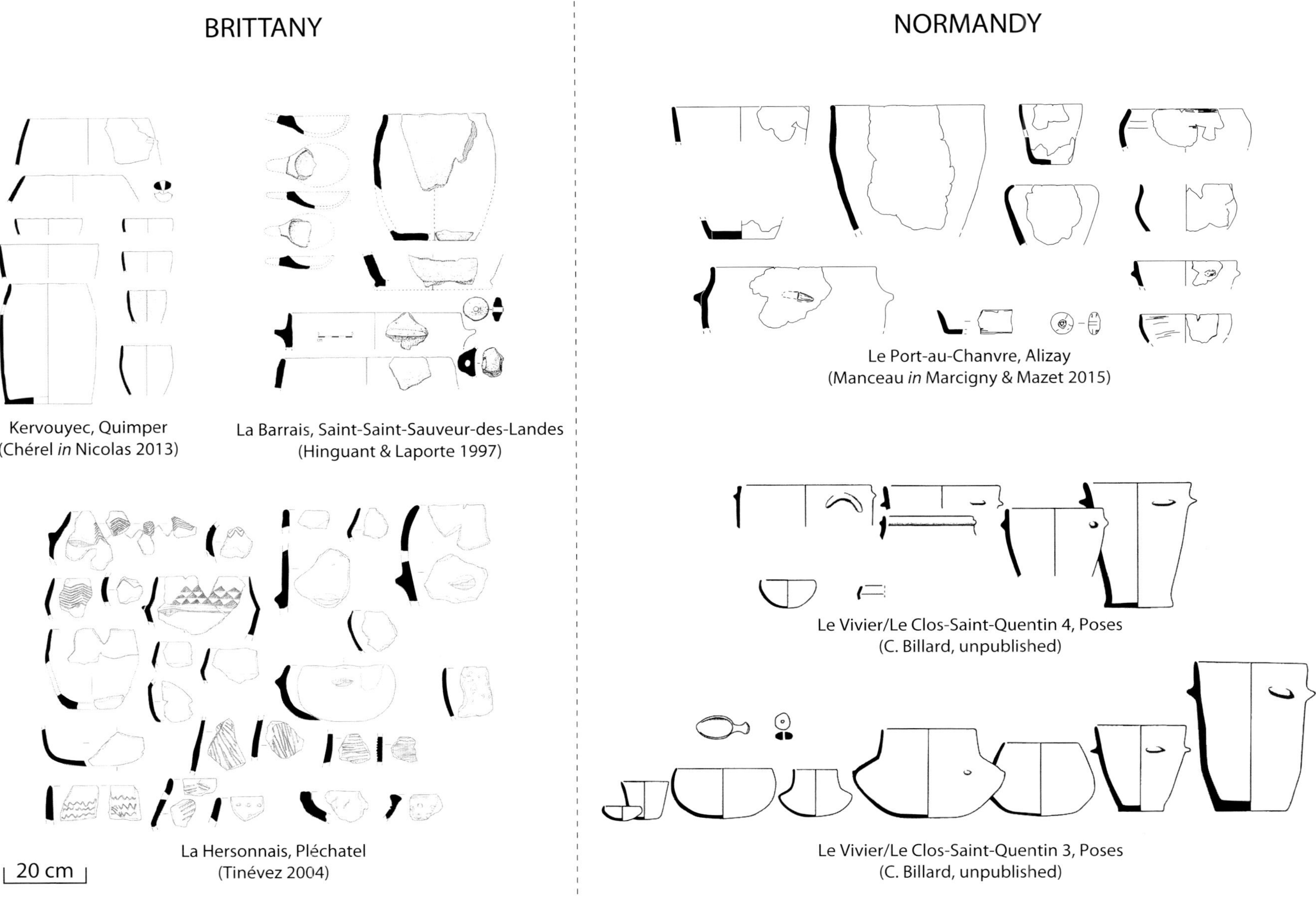

Figure 18.10: Late Neolithic 1 domestic pottery in northern Atlantic France (c. 2900–2500 BC). (CAD A.-F. Chérel,. L. Manceau, T. Nicolas)

greater care in clay preparation and surface treatment (Fig. 18.10). The Late Neolithic 1 sees the reappearance of low and open shapes such as bowls (sometimes with plastic knobs) and low-carinated cups though closed shapes, low or high, also exist. The inflection is generally located a few centimetres below the rim. The bases are flat, little or non-flanged and handles consist of plastic knobs and horizontal lugs. Spindle whorls are also part of the pottery sets. Similar features are found in the Gord culture defined in the Paris Basin (Salanova *et al.* 2011). Shapes with a high inflection are peculiarly frequent in the Deûle-Escaut group in northern France (Bostyn *et al.* 2014) but they are also known in Brittany (Tinévez 2004). Low-carinated cups are found equally in the Artenac culture.

The Late Neolithic south of River Loire (c. 2900–2150 BC)

In west-central France and northern Aquitaine, the Artenac Culture appears and expands during the 3rd millennium. Three main stages can be identified: Artenac I (pre-Bell Beaker), Artenac IIa (synchronous with International or Maritime-Derived Bell Beakers), Artenac IIb (contemporary with late Bell Beaker or later). Within the fine ware, globular ceramics are gradually replaced by low-carinated and closed shapes during stages IIa and IIb (Figs 18.11–18.12). During these stages, there is an increasing number of smoothed nose-like lugs, sinuous carinations or ornamented panels (Burnez & Fouéré 1999). This pottery is always associated with flat-based coarse ware, inherited from Recent Neolithic traditions and stylistic transfers between Bell Beaker and Artenac pottery have been highlighted (Cormenier 2009). Finally, a paint-like red slip appears on some Artenac ceramics and might be related to Bell Beaker pottery.

In southern Aquitaine, a great homogeneity of shapes and styles is observed before and during the Bell Beaker period. A main feature is the flat base, sometimes slightly flanged, beside which round bases are found, and the first carinated shapes appear. Plastic ornaments and handles are scarce and include in particular a set of two horizontal superimposed lugs, which suggests influences from the Véraza group (Languedoc & Catalonia) and the Treilles group (Southern Massif Central). A row of three cordons below the rim finds parallel in the Crosien group. Bell Beaker pottery appears from its early stage (Chopin, pers. comm.). In the meanwhile, local pottery shapes already in use during the first half of the 3rd millennium are found together with Bell Beaker common ware (especially multi-perforated rims – Besse 2014, type 7) and sometimes proper Bell Beakers. Preliminary studies suggested that the use of grog might have been introduced during the later 3rd millennium but shapes and styles seem unchanged.

The Bell Beaker period (c. 2550–2150 BC)

The legacy of the Late Neolithic 1

Beaker is indubitably the most characteristic ceramic of the later 3rd millennium, but other contemporary types are known from settlements. These mostly comprise pottery with a smooth under-rim cordon (Besse 2014, types 5 & 6). Such cordoned pottery is quite abundant but finds few parallels outside northern France before the Bell Beaker period. It might originate from some Late Neolithic 1 coarse ware, as both share similar morphologies, in particular trunconic and barrel-shaped vessels. A smooth under-rim cordon becomes the main plastic ornament to the detriment of horizontal lugs during the later 3rd millennium when Bell Beakers appear (Favrel 2015; Fig. 18.13) possibly as a result of a local evolution of an existing ceramic tradition.

The local development of the Bell Beaker culture

In this section we use the terminology used by Needham (2005) and Besse (2014) as a descriptive tool but not necessarily for implying specific stylistic connections. For north-western France, nearly 450 sites have yielded Bell Beaker pottery, solely or within assemblages and around 30 of them have been radiocarbon dated. A seriation on the main assemblages (*c.* 60) allow the identification of three stages between 2550–1950 cal BC (Favrel 2015; Blanchet *et al.* forthcoming; Fig. 18.13).

Stage 1 (*c.* 2550–2350 cal BC) sees the appearance of the Bell Beaker phenomenon and a relatively quick and significant renewal of the pottery assemblage previously in use. The lack of reliable radiocarbon dates does not facilitate a chronological framework, except by extra-regional comparisons. Stage 1 is featured by Maritime Beakers, a few AOO and AOC

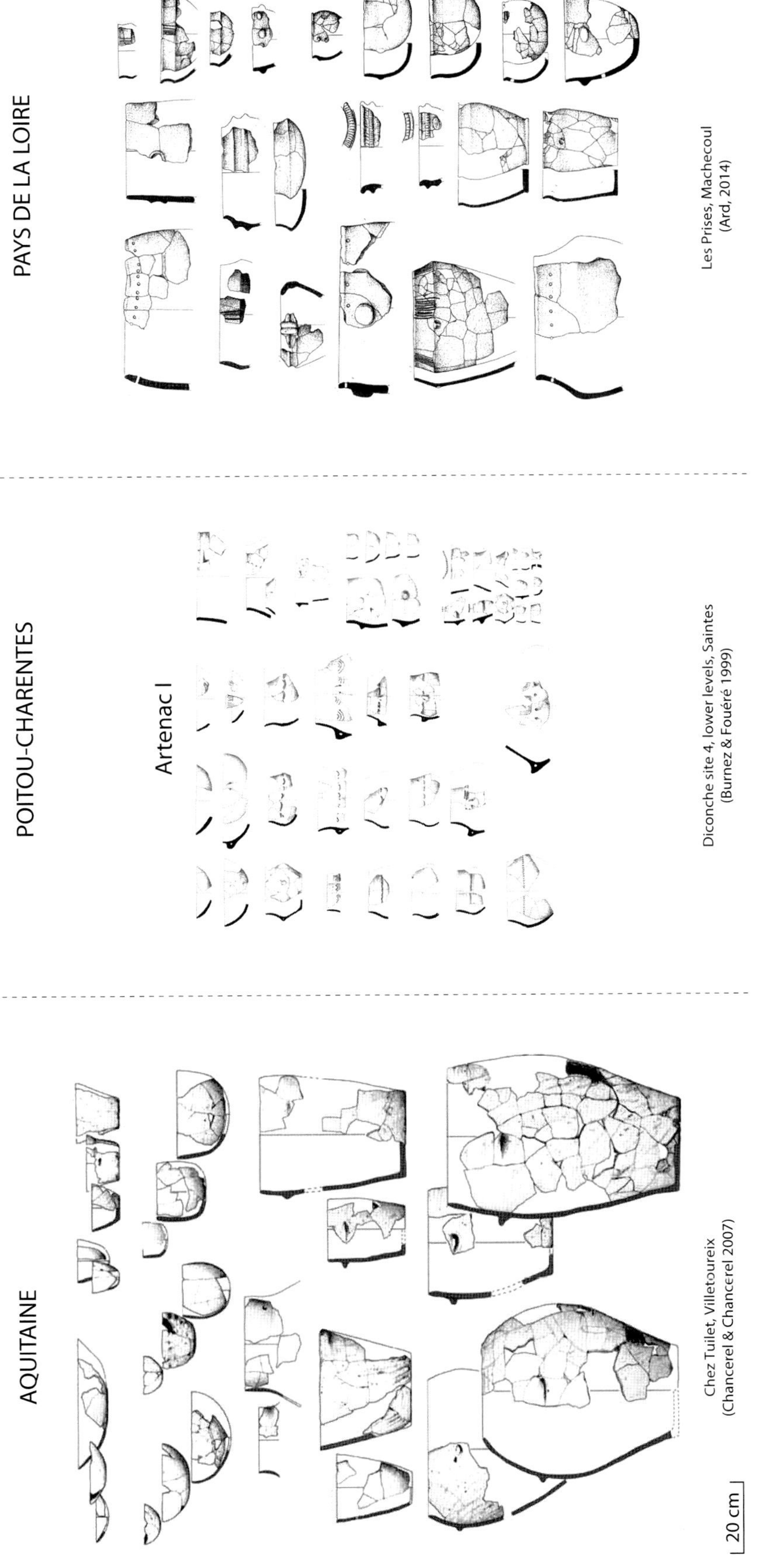

Figure 18.11: Late Neolithic 1 domestic pottery in southern Atlantic France (c. *2900–2500 BC*). *Brittany according to Blanchet* et al. *(forthcoming); Normandy (according to Noël 2008; Marcigny 2016 and Manceau (in Marcigny & Mazet 2015)) (CAD T. Nicolas, C. Marcigny, E. Ghesquière)*

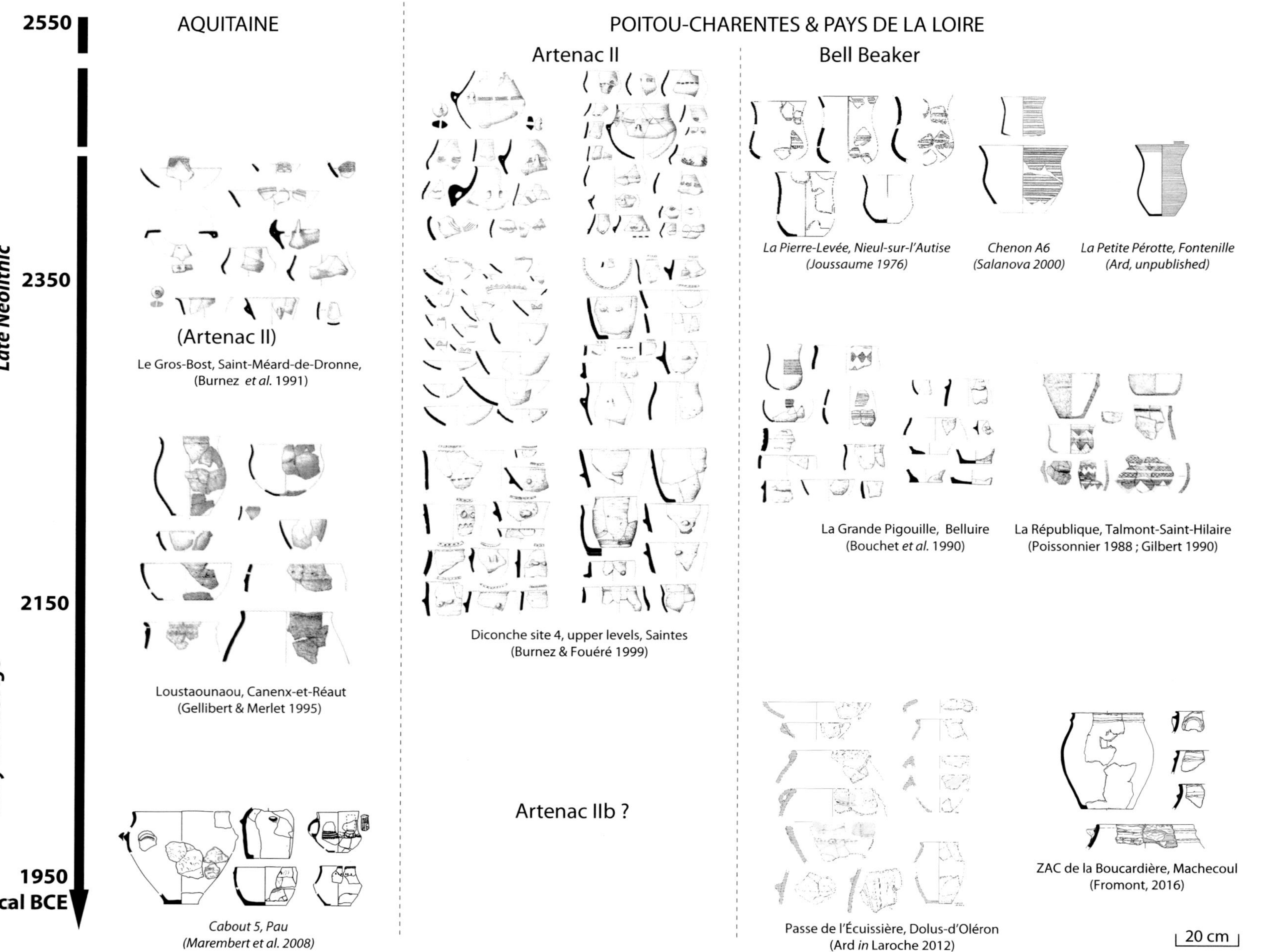

*Figure 18.12: Bell Beaker pottery and contemporary ceramics in southern Atlantic France (*c. *2550–1950 BC)., burial contexts. Shaded surfaces indicate red slip on ceramics. Brittany according to Blanchet* et al. *(forthcoming); Normandy (according to Noël 2008, Marcigny 2016 and Manceau (in Marcigny & Mazet 2015)) (CAD T. Nicolas, C. Marcigny, E. Ghesquière)*

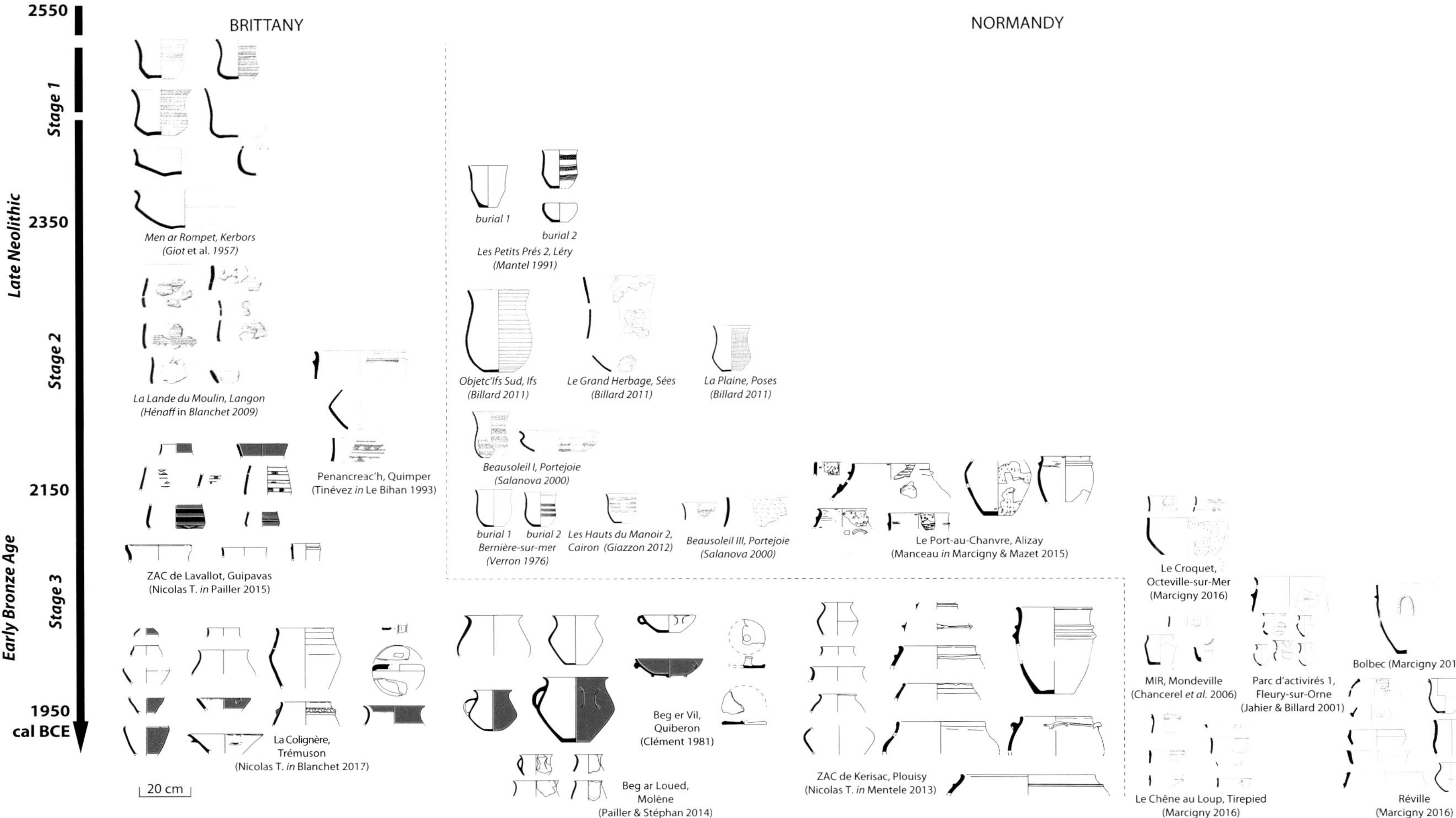

Figure 18.13: Bell Beaker pottery in northern Atlantic France (c. 2550-1950 BC), burial contexts. Shaded surfaces indicate red slip on ceramics. Brittany according to Blanchet et al. *(forthcoming); Normandy, according to Noël 2008, Marcigny 2016 and Manceau (in Marcigny & Mazet 2015) (CAD T. Nicolas, C. Marcigny, E. Ghesquière)*

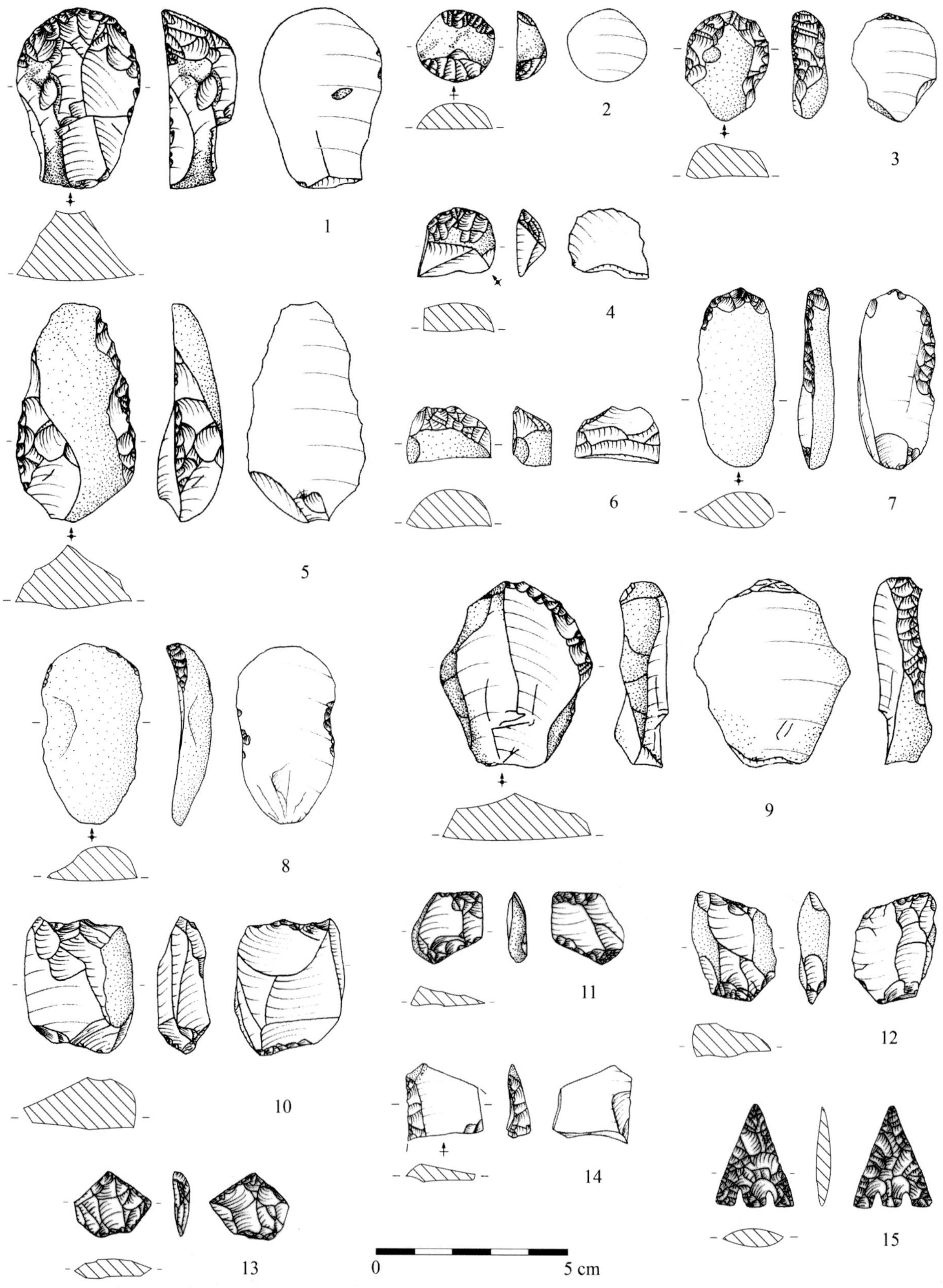

Figure 18.14: An example of Bell Beaker flint industries from the settlement of La République, Talmont-Saint-Hilaire, Vendée. 1–9 – Scrapers; 10–13 – Splintered pieces; 14 – retouched flake; 15 – Arrowheads with squared barbs and tang (Drawings L. Rousseau)

Beakers, as well as hybrid types, such as Cord-Zoned Maritime (CZM) Beakers, which seem to occur over a few generations (Lanting & Van der Waals 1976; Salanova 2000). Beakers with All-Over-Horizontal ornamentation or banded horizontal lines are associated with the Maritime Beakers. Coarse ware includes low-bellied and S-profile pots and ceramics with an under-rim cordon. Open shapes or forms with a wide mouth prevail.

Maritime Beakers from Brittany closely match those in Portuguese Extremadura (Salanova 2000) and, to a lesser extent, in Galicia (Prieto Martinez & Salanova 2009). However, a significant difference can be noticed on the Beaker bases, which are overwhelmingly omphalos bases in Brittany, but frequently flattened or round in Iberia (Veiga Ferreira 1966). Some corded decoration and slender-profiled Beakers might suggest influences from the Rhine valley (L'Helgouac'h 1975). Petrographic studies carried out on numerous series in Brittany and Normandy have shown that a large part of the pottery is locally made (Salanova *et al.* 2016). Therefore, the introduction of new pottery types requires the movement of potters (Salanova 2000). Few Maritime Beakers with a tempering of a volcanic nature might have been imported.

Stage 2 (*c.* 2350–2150 cal BC) is defined by occurrences of Beakers with dotted or incised geometrical patterns. Open carinated shapes such as shallow bowls and basins appear, as well as finger-nail decorated pots. The use of red slip and white inlays have been recognised. Coarse ware consists of S-profile pots with straight or everted rims and an under-rim cordon.

During stage 3 (*c.* 2150–1950 BC), fine ware includes the late Bell Beakers and S-profile Beakers with a higher belly (mid-bellied), handled or not. No unquestionable association exists for both Beaker types, however, they are found with the same coarse ware, dominated by closed shapes with a concave neck and smooth cordons. Narrowing rims are frequent. Horizontal cordons are located lower on the pots than previously and frequently paired and associated with horizontal lugs. An arciform cordon was also very common at this time. Red slip and white inlays are still in use. The end of the Bell Beaker phenomenon seems to merge into the beginnings of the Early Bronze Age and the rise of the Armorican Tumulus Culture in the last century of the 3rd millennium (Nicolas 2016).

Bell Beaker stone industries

During the Bell Beaker period, the main Late Neolithic 1 workshops (axeheads made of type A metadolerite from Plussulien or flints from Saintonge, Bergerac area or the plain of Caen, Grand-Pressigny blades and daggers) ceased to be exported or, at best, continued at a reduced scale (Fouéré & Dias-Merinho 2008; Ihuel *et al.* 2015; Nicolas *et al.* 2015). On settlements, the occasional exogenous stones are generally fragmented and might result from the re-use of Neolithic items. Flint procurement is mainly done close to settlements, even if the quality is poor. Substitute rocks, like quartz, quartzite, Eocene sandstone or microquartzite, are also exploited. This exclusively local supply might be seen as different to the previous period and suggestive of reduced trade networks in high quality flint (Ghesquière & Guyodo 2008).

In the Armorican Massif, Grand-Pressigny flint is very scarce in Bell Beaker settlements (Rousseau 2015) and those artefacts that do occur might derive from old or recovered items. The individual burial from La Folie, Poitiers (Vienne), produced a distal end of a *livre-de-beurre* blade with a Rhine-like AOO Beaker. Radiocarbon dates suggest that this is quite late, *c.* 2400–2200 cal BC (Ihuel *et al.* 2015). Similar discoveries of Grand-Pressigny daggers on blades with AOC Beakers have been made in two further graves in northern France and are probably related to the diffusion of Grand-Pressigny products towards the Netherlands (*ibid.*). In Brittany, an end-scraper/strike-a-light on a short thick blade made of Grand-Pressigny flint has been found with an AOC Beaker and two Maritime Beakers in a stone-cist at Kerallant, Saint-Jean-Brévelay, Morbihan (Nicolas *et al.* 2013). Except for these early blades, Grand-Pressigny flakes (as well other high-quality flints) seem to have been used throughout the Bell Beaker period mainly for arrowheads (Nicolas 2016).

Regarding polished artefacts, several axe-heads in Bell Beaker contexts might be residual (Rousseau 2015). In Brittany, Le Roux (2011) has argued for the late use of type A metadolerite outcrop. Black and purple slates, schistic sandstone, type A metadolerite and several indeterminate metamorphic rocks were used for wristguards and ornaments (Nicolas 2016). In the Aquitaine Basin, slate and cementstone have been used (Rousseau 2015). Considering macro-lithic tools, the procurement is strictly local.

Except in specialised workshops, there are few differences in flint knapping between the Late Neolithic 1 and the Bell Beaker period: the technique involved (hard direct percussion or anvil percussion) is similar and their proportions vary according to the date and the geographical areas (Rousseau 2015). During the Bell Beaker period, knapped tools are less varied and mainly include scrapers and retouched flakes; to which can be added side scrapers, borers (in decline compared to the Late Neolithic 1) and unretouched flakes (Fig. 18.14). In southern Aquitaine, unretouched and intensively used flakes are very frequent (Marticorena 2014).

In western France, Bell Beaker arrowheads from burials include mainly the type with squared barbs and tang and its derivatives (with pointed or rounded tang or with slanted barbs) and such arrowheads are also found in settlements coexisting with cruder barbed-and-tanged types and some leaf-shaped types (perhaps rough-outs). Different levels of skill are involved in producing arrowheads, from marginally retouched blanks to more fancy products (Nicolas 2016) but a main trend is the use of high quality, sometimes imported, flint, while the remaining flint industries are sourced locally.

The locally sourced macro-lithic tools persist from the Neolithic and are used for almost all activities, like knapping (hammers, anvils) or grinding (querns, grinders, crushers). The typology of these implements does not change greatly over time, except querns of which the 'basin' type seems to be limited to the second half of the 3rd and the first half of the 2nd millennium (Donnart 2015). Metalworking led to a greater variety of macro-lithic tools for use in the extraction and processing of ores (Cert 2005; Hamon *et al.* 2009). These tools are generally absent from western France, due to the lack of copper mines, except for that at Le Causiat in the Pyrenees (Beyrie & Kammenthaler 2008). However, a few open stone or clay moulds for objects or ingots might date to the Bell Beaker Culture (Nicolas 2014; Gandois *et al.* in Pailler & Nicolas 2019). Metal shaping is carried out with anvils and hammers on a polished active surface and most of these tools are reused polished axeheads, whose cutting edge has been blunted. Over 50 of them have been found in north-western France but almost all are stray finds (Boutoille 2012) however one was associated with sherds of a Maritime vessel in a possible ruined stone-cist in the middle of the alignment at Le Moulin, Saint-Just, Ille-et-Vilaine (Le Roux *et al.* 1989). 'Cushion stones' are scarce but a piece was found in a stone-cist at Lesconil, Plobannalec, Finistère, together with a tanged copper dagger (Nicolas *et al.* 2013).

The introduction of the Bell Beaker culture in western France

The introduction of the Bell Beaker culture to Atlantic France is likely to have happened in many ways, and regionally. On the one hand, the Bell Beakers seem to be widely imposed or adopted north of River Loire and evidence for Late Neolithic 1 cultures continuing into the second half of the 3rd millennium is still lacking. On the other hand, some local communities in west-central France (Artenac IIa & b) or in southern Aquitaine seem to be fairly unreceptive to Bell Beakers and it seems they coexisted in quite close proximity. Local cultures borrow some ceramic decorative patterns or some common ware shapes but continue to make their own pottery.

Quite radical changes can be seen in settlements. The large enclosed sites built during the Late Neolithic 1 can be limited by quite massive defences or take advantage of naturally protected places. In several cases, such sites have produced Bell Beaker pottery but mainly in late, or insecure contexts and there is no unequivocal evidence for them being maintained by Beaker users. Meanwhile, there are several open and small-sized Beaker settlements marking a new way of land-use and possibly a new socio-economic regime. The almond-shaped house, first identified in Brittany (Blanchet *et al.* 2012) but now been extended to Normandy and west-central France, is a real novelty breaking with Late Neolithic 1 traditions. Regarding burial, megalithic graves are still used during the Bell Beaker period but specific burial customs seem to be different and more individual (Salanova 2007).

The introduction of the Bell Beaker fine

ware, is obvious. The earliest have close parallels with Iberia and, to a lesser extent, the Rhine valley and the Artenac copying of some Bell Beaker motifs illustrates their significance to local communities. In the meanwhile, some Late Neolithic 1 coarse ware types seem to be adopted and adapted by Bell Beaker users and there would seem to have been reciprocal acculturations between these groups.

The common stone tools remain roughly the same but are more restricted. They also show some acculturations, like the arrowhead type with squared barbs and tang attested from the Late Neolithic 1 in western France and included in the Bell Beaker 'set'. Nevertheless, stone industries reflect economic changes, with diminished flint supply networks and the appearance of new metalworking tools. The concomitant decline of Grand-Pressigny daggers and the first copper daggers around the mid-3rd millennium is probably not a coincidence. New metal artefacts might have made specialised flint production less attractive and even have jeopardised the economic balance.

The evidence suggests that local Late Neolithic 1 communities contributed to the Bell Beaker culture in Atlantic France. Considering the cultural significance of pottery shapes (and presumably the related pottery traditions), the persistence of some Late Neolithic 1 coarse ware suggests that the Bell Beaker culture might have been partly adopted by local communities, as suggested for south-eastern France (Lemercier *et al.* this volume). The new Bell Beaker ideology and material culture could have been spread more easily thanks to shared values, like the social worth of warriorhood and its related artefacts (arrowheads, daggers). However, the Bell Beaker culture was not equally successful everywhere and some local communities seem to have developed in their own way. Despite some Late Neolithic 1 legacies, the introduction of the Bell Beaker culture in Atlantic France resulted in radical changes in land use, architecture, burial customs, fashions and presumably in socioeconomic organisation.

Acknowledgements

We are grateful to several peoples, who have provided us with different sets of unpublished data stemming in particular from development-led archaeology: Cyrille Billard (SRA Normandie/ UMR 6566 CReAAH), François Charraud (UMR 8215 Trajectoires), Anne-Françoise Chérel (Inrap/UMR 8546 AOrOc), Hélène Courty (SRA Pays de la Loire), Aurélie Crowch (SDAM/UMR 6566 CReAAH), Jean-Luc Dron (Éducation nationale), Pierrick Fouéré (Inrap/UMR 5608 Traces), Raphaël Gadbois-Langevin (Cégep de Limoilou/ Université du Québec), Emmanuel Ghesquière (Inrap/ UMR 6566 CReAAH), Xavier Hénaff (Inrap/UMR 8167 Orient & Méditerranée), Philip de Jersey (Guernsey Museum), Roland Le Guévellou (Inrap), Alexandre Lemaire (Archeodunum/ UMR 5608 Traces), Éric Nicolas (Inrap), Eddie Roy (Inrap), Frédéric Sergent (Inrap/UMR 5608 Traces), Sébastien Toron (Eveha/UMR 6566 CReAAH). We thank Bob Rowntree and Alex M. Gibson for improving the English version of this article.

References

Ard, V. 2014. *Produire et échanger au Néolithique. Traditions céramiques entre Loire et Gironde au IVe millénaire avant J-C. Paris: CTHS*

Besse, M. 2014. Bell Beaker common ware during the third millennium BC in Europe. In Czebreszuk, J. (ed.), *Similar but different. Bell Beakers in Europe*, (2nd edn) 127–48. Leiden: Sidestone Press

Beyrie, A. & Kammenthaler, É. 2008. Aux origines de l'activité minière dans les Pyrénées occidentales: l'exploitation du cuivre, du fer, de l'or et de l'argent. *Archéopages* 28–33

Billard, C. 2011. Les sépultures individuelles campaniformes de Normandie. In Salanova, L. & Tchérémissinoff, Y. (eds), *Les sépultures individuelles campaniformes en France,* 37–46. Suppl. *Gallia Préhistoire* 41. Paris: CNRS Éditions

Billard, C., with collaboration of Bourhis, J.-R., Desfossés, Y., Evin, J., Huault, M.-F., Lefebvre, D. & Paulet-Locard, M.-A. 1991. L'habitat des Florentins à Val-de-Reuil (Eure). *Gallia Préhistoire* 33(1), 140–71

Billard, C., Aubry, B., Blancquaert, G., Bourhis, J.-R., Habasque, G., Marinval, P., Pinel, C. & Ropars, A. 1994. Poses – Le Vivier – Le Clos Saint Quentin (Eure). L'occupation de la plaine inondable au Néolithique et au début de l'Age du Bronze. *Revue Archéologique de l'Ouest* 11, 53–113

Blanchard, A. 2017. *Néolithique récent de l'ouest de la France: IVe–IIIe millénaires avant J.-C. Productions et dynamiques culturelles.* Rennes: Presses universitaires de Rennes

Blanchet, S. (ed.), 2009. *Langon "La Lande du Moulin/ La rue des Demoiselles" (Ille-et-Vilaine – Bretagne).* Inrap Grand-Ouest. Rennes: SRA Bretagne

Blanchet, S. (ed.), 2016. *Côtes-d'Armor, Lannion, Penn an Alé: occupations rurales de l'âge du Bronze et antiques.* Inrap Grand-Ouest. Rennes: SRA Bretagne

Blanchet, S., Nicolas T. & Toron S. 2012. Des constructions inédites à la transition Néolithique final-Bronze ancien en Bretagne: premier bilan. *InterNéo* 9, 135–45

Blanchet, S., Favrel, Q., Fily, M., Nicolas, C., Nicolas, T., Pailler, Y. & Ripoche, J. forthcoming. Le Campaniforme et la genèse de l'âge du Bronze ancien en Bretagne: vers une nouvelle donne. In Buchez, N., Lemercier, O., Praud, I. & Talon, M. (eds), *Session 5: La fin du Néolithique et la genèse du Bronze ancien dans l'Europe du Nord-Ouest*, Congrès préhistorique de France, 30 mai–4 juin, Amiens. Paris: Société Préhistorique Française

Bostyn, F., Beugnier, V., Martial, E., Médard, F., Monchablon, C. & Praud, I. 2014. Habitat et économie au Néolithique final, l'exemple du site de Raillencourt-Sainte-Olle (Nord) entre activités domestiques et productions artisanales. *Bulletin de la Société Préhistorique Française* 111 (4), 679–726

Bouchet, J.-M., Burnez, C. & Fouéré, P. 1990. La grande Pigouille à Belluire (Charente-Maritime). *Bulletin de la Société Préhistorique Française* 87 (5), 153–60

Boutoille, L. 2012. L'outillage lithique utilisé dans la cadre de la déformation plastique des métaux. Premier aperçu des découvertes françaises. *Bulletin de l'Association pour la Promotion des Recherches sur l'Âge du Bronze* 10, 95–98

Burnez, C. 2010. *Le Camp à Challignac (Charente) au IIIe millénaire av. J.-C. Un établissement complexe de la culture d'Artenac dans le Centre-Ouest de la France.* Oxford: British Archaeological Reports International Series 2165

Burnez, C. & Fouéré, P. (eds), 1999. *Les enceintes néolithiques de Diconche à Saintes (Charente-Maritime), une périodisation de l'Artenac.* Mémoire 25. Paris: Société Préhistorique Française

Burnez, C., Fischer, F. & Fouéré, P. 1991. Le Gros-Bost à Saint-Méard-de-Drône (Dordogne). *Bulletin de la Société Préhistorique Française* 88(10/12), 291–340

Cert, C. 2005. Les outils de métallurgiste du site du Néolithique final de La Capitelle du Broum (Péret, Hérault). In Ambert, P. & Vaquer, J. (eds), *La première métallurgie en France et dans les pays limitrophes*, 109–15. Mémoire 37. Paris: Société Préhistorique Française

Champême, L.-M. 1998. Le Bâtiment sur poteaux du Fief Baudoin (Airvault, Deux-Sèvres). In Gutherz, X. & Joussaume, R. (eds), *Le Néolithique du Centre-Ouest de la France*, 297–306. Mémoire 14. Chauvigny: Association des Publications Chauvinoises

Chancerel, A. & Chancerel, G. 2007. Villetoureix – Chez Tuilet. *Archéologie de la France – Informations*

Chancerel, A., Ghesquière, E., Marcigny, C. 2006. L'enclos du Néolithique récent/Bronze ancien du MIR (Mondeville). In Chancerel, A., Marcigny, C. & Ghesquière E., (eds), *Le plateau de Mondeville (Calvados), du Néolithique à l'âge du Bronze*. Documents d'Archéologie Française 99, 100–110. Paris: Éditions de la Maison des Sciences de l'Homme

Clément, M. 1981. Les débuts de l'âge du Fer dans le domaine vénète armoricain. Unpubl. PhD thesis. Paris: Université de Paris I Panthéon-Sorbonne

Cormenier, A. 2009. Les interactions entre Artenacien et Campaniforme dans le Centre-Ouest de la France – L'apport des décors céramiques. In Laporte, L. (ed), *Des premiers paysans aux premiers métallurgistes sur la façade atlantique de la France (3500–2000 av. J.-C.)*, 314–28. Mémoire 33. Chauvigny: Association des Publications Chauvinoises

Crowch, A. (ed.), 2014. *Commune de Quéven (N° Insee: 56185). Extension de la zone du Mourillon Ouest, 'Park an Denved'*. Service départemental d'Archéologie du Morbihan. Rennes: SRA Bretagne

Donnart, K. 2015. Le macro-outillage dans l'Ouest de la France: pratiques économiques et techniques des premières sociétés agropastorales. Unpubl. PhD thesis. Rennes: Université Rennes 1

Favrel, Q., 2015. Le Nord-Ouest de la France à travers le prisme du Campaniforme: analyses fonctionnelles, chronologiques et spatiales de la céramique de la deuxième moitié du troisième millénaire avant notre ère. Unpubl. Master 2 thesis. Rennes: Université de Rennes 2

Fouéré, P. 1998. Deux grands bâtiments du Néolithique final artenacien à Douchapt (Dordogne). In *Rencontres méridionales de Préhistoire récente (deuxième session),* 311–28 Arles, 1996. Antibes: APDCA

Fouéré, P., Dias-Meirinho, M.-H. 2008. Les industries lithiques taillées des IVe et IIIe millénaires dans le centre-ouest de la France. In Dias-Meirinho, M.-H., Léa, V., Gernigon, K., Fouéré, P., Briois, F. & Bailly, M. (eds), In M.-H. Dias-Meirinho, V. Léa, K. Gernigon, P. Fouéré, F. Briois & M. Bailly (eds), *Les industries lithiques taillées des IVe et IIIe millénaires en Europe occidentale*, Colloque international, Toulouse 7–9 avril 2005, 231–258. Oxford: BAR International Series, 1884

Fouéré, P., Rousseau, J., Vacher, S. & Durand, G. 2014. Un bâtiment néolithique de type Antran aux Fontaines d'Ozillac (Charente-Maritime). *Archéaunis* 41, 14–19

Fromont, N. (ed.), 2016. *Machecoul 'ZAC de la Boucardière' (Loire-Atlantique). Des occupations protohistoriques, antiques, médiévales et modernes au bord du Marais breton.* Inrap Grand-Ouest. Nantes: SRA Pays de la Loire

Fromont, N., San Juan, G., Dron, J.-L. & Besnard, M. 2014a. L'enceinte du Néolithique récent/final de Basly 'La Campagne' (Calvados): un habitat groupé, ostentatoire et défensif. In Joussaume, *et al.* (eds), 149–61

Fromont, N., Forré, P., Ard, V., Donnart, K. 2014b. Les bâtiments sur poteaux plantés de l'enceinte de la fin du Néolithique à Avrillé « rue des Menhirs » (Vendée). In Joussaume *et al.* (eds), 201–14

Gadbois-Langevin, R. 2013. Le Campaniforme en France: étude spatiale de l'évolution d'un territoire, un ensemble divisé ? Unpubl. Master 2 thesis. Dijon: Université de Bourgogne

Gandois, H., Gehres, B., Querré, G. & Rousseau, L. 2016. Quelques nouveaux éléments concernant le site de la République, Talmont-Saint-Hilaire (Vendée): une datation sur caramel de cuisson et des indices supplémentaires pour une activité métallurgique domestique campaniforme. In Boulud-Gazo, S. (ed.), *Le Campaniforme et l'âge du Bronze dans les Pays de la Loire, Projet collectif de Recherche, Bilan d'activités, année 2015*, 189–207. Nantes: SRA Pays de la Loire

Gellibert, B. & Merlet, J.-C. 1995. L'habitat chalcolithique de Loustaounaou à Canenx-et-Réaut (Landes). *Archéologie des Pyrénées occidentales et des Landes* 14, 141–59

Ghesquière, E. & Guyodo, J.-N. 2008. Les industries lithiques taillées des IVe et IIIe millénaires avant J.-C. dans le quart nord-ouest de la France. In Dias-Meirinho, M.-H., Léa, V., Gernigon, K., Fouéré, P., Briois, F. & Bailly, M. (eds), *Les industries lithiques taillées des IVe et IIIe millénaires en Europe occidentale,* 113–33. Oxford: British Archaeological Reports International series, 1884

Ghesquière, E., Charraud, F., Giazzon, D., Hachem, L., Manceau, L., Marcigny, C., Mougne, C., Nicolas, C. & Seignac, H. forthcoming. Grands bâtiments du Néolithique final à St-André-sur-Orne (Calvados). In Buchez, N., Lemercier, O., Praud, I. & Talon, M. (eds), *Session 5: La fin du Néolithique et la genèse du Bronze ancien dans l'Europe du Nord-Ouest. Congrès préhistorique de France, 30 mai–4 juin, Amiens.* Paris: Société Préhistorique Française

Giazzon, D. (ed.), 2012. *Cairon (Calvados), Les Hauts du Manoir 2: évolution d'un parcellaire à l'âge du Bronze ancien.* Inrap Grand-Ouest. Caen: SRA Basse-Normandie

Gilbert, J.-M. 1990. *Talmont-Saint-Hilaire (Vendée), La République 2 (85.288.008), Fouille de Sauvetage, avril 1990.* Nantes: SRA Pays de la Loire

Giot, P.-R., Briard, J. & L'Helgouac'h, J. 1957. Fouille de l'allée couverte de Men-ar-Rompet à Kerbors (Côtes-du-Nord). *Bulletin de la Société Préhistorique Française* 54(9), 493–515

Hamon, C., Ambert, P., Laroche, M., Guendon, J.–L., Rovira, S. & Bouquet, L. 2009. Les outils à cupules, marqueurs de la métallurgie du district de Cabrières-Péret (Hérault) au Chalcolithique. *Gallia Préhistoire* 51, 179–212

Hinguant, S. & Laporte, L. 1997. L'occupation Néolithique final de La Barrais à Saint-Sauveur-des-Landes (Ille-et-Vilaine). *Revue Archéologique de l'Ouest* 14, 17–26

Ihuel, E., Mallet, N., Pelegrin, J. & Verjux, J. 2015. The dagger phenomenon: circulation from the Grand-Pressigny region (France, Indre-et-Loire) in Western Europe. In Prieto Martínez, M. P. & Salanova, L. (eds), *The Bell Beaker transition in Europe: mobility and local evolution during the third millennium BC,* 113–26. Oxford: Oxbow Books

Jahier, I. & Billard, C. 2001. Fleury-sur-Orne, ZAC Parc d'activités 1 (bâtiment protohistorique). *Bilan scientifique de la Région Basse-Normandie* 2000, 33–5

Joussaume, R., Large, J.-M., Corson, S., Le Meur, N., Tortuyaux, J.-P. (eds). 2014. *Enceintes néolithiques de l'Ouest de la France, de la Seine à la Gironde.* Mémoire 48. Chauvigny: Association des Publications chauvinoises

Le Gall, V. (ed). 2016. *Glomel (Côtes d'Armor), Roc'h Lédan: un habitat de l'âge du Bronze et une occupation médiévale.* Rapport de diagnostic archéologique, Inrap Grand-Ouest. Rennes: SRA Bretagne

Lanting, J.N. & Van der Waals, J.D. 1976. Beaker culture relations in the Lower Rhine basin. In Lanting, J.N. & Van der Waals, J. D. (eds), *Glockenbecher symposion, Oberried 1974,* 1—80. Haarlem: Bossum.

Laporte, L. 2008. Du Néolithique final au tout premier Bronze ancien dans le Centre-Ouest de la France et plus généralement sur sa façade atlantique; des données encore très lacunaires pour la seconde moitié du IIIe millénaire av. J.-C. *Bulletin de la Société Préhistorique Française* 105(3), 555–576

Laporte, L. (ed.) 2009. *Des premiers paysans aux premiers métallurgistes sur la façade atlantique de la France (3500–2000 av. J.-C.).* Mémoire 33. Chauvigny: Association des Publications Chauvinoises

Laroche, M. (ed.), 2012. *Le gisement 18 passe de l'Écuissière à Dolus-d'Oléron (Charente-Maritime). Une occupation du Bronze ancien en milieu littoral.* Communauté de Communes Nord du Bassin de Thau. Poitiers: SRA Poitou-Charentes

Laroche, M., G. Broux & Lethrosne, H. 2014. Un habitat du Néolithique final à Pussigny 'le Fond d'Arrêt' et 'la Pierre Levée', *Archéologie en Région Centre* 5(3), 1–11

Le Bihan J.-P., Robic, J.-Y. & Tinévez, J.-Y. (eds), 1993. *Un habitat de transition Néolithique – âge du Bronze, Quimper 'Penancreach' (Finistère).* Rennes: SRA Bretagne

Lemaire, A. & Bosc-Zanardo, B. 2018. Un bâtiment 'en amande' hors de la péninsule armoricaine : le bâtiment bat1023 d'Ars (Charente) 'Chemin des Prés'. *InterNéo* 12, 170–178

Lepaumier, H., Marcigny, C. & Ghesquière, E. 2005. L'architecture des habitats protohistoriques de Normandie: quelques exemples de la fin du IIIe millénaire au début du second âge du Fer. In Buchsenschutz, O. & Mordant, C. (eds), *Architectures protohistoriques en Europe occidentale du Néolithique final à l'âge du Fer,* 231–64. Paris: CTHS

Leroux, G. (ed.), 2013. *Le Pertre (Ille-et-Vilaine), LGV, secteur 4, phase 3, Le Haut-Brétorin – La* Grée. Inrap Grand-Ouest. Rennes: SRA Bretagne

Le Roux, C.-T. 2011. Une 'production de masse' dès le Néolithique: les ateliers de Plussulien (Côtes-d'Armor) et les haches polies en métadolérite du type A. *Bulletin de la Société Géologique et Minéralogique de Bretagne* 9, 3–33

Le Roux, C.-T., Lecerf, Y. & Gautier, M. 1989. Les mégalithes de Saint-Just (Ille-et-Vilaine) et la fouille des alignements du Moulin de Cojou. *Revue Archéologique de l'Ouest* 6, 5–29

Le Rouzic, Z. 1933. Premières fouilles au Camp du Lizo. *Revue Archéologique* 6 (2), 189–19

L'Helgouac'h, J. 1975. Informations archéologiques. Circonscription des Pays de la Loire. *Gallia Préhistoire* 18 (2), 541–61

Louboutin, C. 2014. Challignac, Le Camp. *Bilan Scientifique Régional de la Région Poitou-Charentes* 2013, 41–3

Maitay, C., Maguer, P. & Ard, V. 2018. Architecture des bâtiments du Néolithique à l'âge du Bronze dans le Centre-Ouest de la France. In Lemercier, O., Sénépart, I., Besse, M. & Mordant, C. (eds), *Habitations et habitat du Néolithique à l'âge du Bronze en France et ses marges. Actes des secondes Rencontres Nord/Sud de Préhistoire récente,* APRAB/RMPR/Internéo, Dijon, Novembre 2015, 637-656. Toulouse: Archives d'Écologie Préhistorique

Mantel, E. 1991. Les sépultures des Petits Prés et du Chemin des Vignes à Léry (Eure): étude archéologique. *Gallia Préhistoire* 33, 185–92

Marcigny, C. 2016. Peuplement et échanges culturels sur les rivages de la Manche à l'âge du Bronze: l'exemple normand. Unpubl. PhD thesis. Toulouse: EHESS

Marcigny, C. & Mazet, S. (eds), 2015. *Au bord de l'eau ! Les occupations humaines d'une berge de la Seine du Tardiglaciaire à nos jours, Le Postel, Le Pré Rompu, le Chêne, Le Port au Chanvre, Les Diguets, Alizay, Le Fort, Les Limais, Igoville (Eure).* Inrap Grand-Ouest. Rouen: SRA Normandie

Marcigny, C., Juhel, L. & Ghesquière, E. 2005. L'abri sous roche de la Jupinerie à Omonville-la-Petite (50). *Revue de la Manche* 47 (190), 38–9

Marembert, F., Dumontier, P., Davasse, B. & Watter, J. 2008. La transition Néolithique final / Bronze ancien sud Aquitaine à travers les tumulus de Cabout 4 et 5 de Pau. *Archéologie des Pyrénées Occidentales et des Landes* 27, 77–112

Marticorena, P. 2014. *Les premiers paysans de l'ouest des Pyrénées: synthèse régionale à la lumière des haches de pierre polie.* Baigorri: Université populaire du Pays basque

Mentelé, S. (ed.), 2013. *Bretagne, Côtes d'Armor, Plouisy ZAC de Kerisac: Des implantations successives de l'âge du Bronze.* Rapport de diagnostic, Inrap Grand-Ouest. Rennes: SRA Bretagne

Needham, S. 2005. Transforming Beaker Culture in North-west Europe; Processes of Fusion and Fission. *Proceedings of the Prehistoric Society* 71, 171–218

Nicolas, C., Rousseau, L. & Donnart, K. 2015. La pierre à l'aube de la métallurgie, de la sphère domestique au monde funéraire: l'exemple du grand nord-ouest de la France. In Nordez, M., Rousseau, L. & Cervel, M. (eds), *Recherches sur l'âge du Bronze, Nouvelles approches et perspectives.* Suppl. *Bulletin de l'APRAB*, 1, 103–37

Nicolas, C. 2016. *Flèches de pouvoir à l'aube de la métallurgie, de la Bretagne au Danemark (2500–1700 av. n. è.).* Leiden: Sidestone Press

Nicolas, C., Pailler, Y., Stéphan, P. & Gandois, H. 2013. Les reliques de Lothéa (Quimperlé, Finistère): une tombe aux connexions atlantiques entre Campaniforme et âge du Bronze ancien. *Gallia Préhistoire* 55, 181–227

Nicolas, E (ed.), 2013. *Finistère, Quimper, Kervouyec: Kervouyec II. De multiples occupations protohistoriques.* Inrap Grand-Ouest. Rennes: SRA Bretagne

Nicolas, E. (ed.), 2015. Cléder et Plouescat, Finistère Creac'h ar Vrenn. *Des bâtiments de la transition entre le Néolithique final et l'âge du Bronze ancien. Une nécropole du Bas-Empire.*

Nicolas, T. 2014. Les lingotières de Trédarzec 'Crec'h-Choupot' (Côtesd'Armor) et de Bédée 'ZAC des Gabrielles' (Ille-et-Vilaine). Des indices de métallurgie de la fin du IIIème millénaire av. J.-C. en Bretagne. *Bulletin de l'APRAB* 12, 134–6

Noël, J.-Y. 2008. In terra incognita: le Campaniforme normand, synthèse préliminaire du mobilier céramique. *Bulletin de la Société Préhistorique Française* 105 (3), 577–93

Ollivier, A. & Pautreau, J.-P. 1994. Une construction de type Antran: les chavis à Vouillé (Vienne). *Bulletin de la Société Préhistorique Française* 91 (6), 420–1

Pailler, Y. (ed.), 2015. *Guipavas (Finistère), ZAC nord Lavallot. Occupations diachroniques du plateau léonard: des premiers agriculteurs à la libération de Brest.* Inrap Grand-Ouest. Rennes: SRA Bretagne

Pailler, Y. & Nicolas, C. (eds), 2019. *Une maison sous les dunes: Beg ar Loued, île Molène, Finistère. Identité et adaptation des groupes humains en mer d'Iroise entre les IIIe et IIe millénaires avant notre ère.* Leiden: Sidestone Press

Pailler, Y. & Stéphan, P. 2014. Landscape Evolution and Human Settlement in the Iroise Sea (Brittany, France) during the Neolithic and Bronze Age. *Proceedings of the Prehistoric Society* 80, 105–39

Pautreau, J.-P. 1989. Pérennité d'un sanctuaire: la Croix-Verte à Antran. In Mohen J.-P. (ed.), *Le temps de la Préhistoire*, 1, 109–11. Paris: Société Préhistorique Française

Poissonnier, B. (ed.), 1988. *Talmont-Saint-Hilaire (Vendée), La République 2, Fouille de sauvetage urgent, avril-mai 1988.* Nantes: SRA Pays de la Loire

Prieto Martinez, P. & Salanova, L. 2009. Coquilles et Campaniforme en Galice et en Bretagne: mécanismes de circulation et stratégies identitaires. *Bulletin de la Société Préhistorique Française* 106 (1), 73–93

Rousseau, L. 2015. Des dernières sociétés néolithiques aux premières sociétés métallurgiques: productions lithiques du quart nord-ouest de la France (IIIe–IIe millénaires av. notre ère), Unpubl. PhD thesis. Nantes: Université de Nantes

Salanova, L. 2000. *La question du Campaniforme en France et dans les îles Anglo-normandes: Productions, chronologie et rôles d'un standard céramique.* Paris: CTHS

Salanova, L. 2007. Les sépultures campaniformes: lecture sociale. In Guilaine, J. (ed.), *Le Chalcolithique et la construction des inégalités, Tome 1, Le continent européen,* 213–28. Séminaire du Collège de France. Paris: Errance

Salanova, L., Brunet, P., Cottiaux, R., Hamon, T., Langry-François, F., Martineau, R., Polloni, A., Renard, C. & Sohn, M. 2011. Du Néolithique récent à l'âge du Bronze dans le Centre Nord de la France: les étapes de l'évolution chrono-culturelle. In Bostyn, F., Martial, E. & Praud, I. (eds), *Le Néolithique du Nord de la France dans son contexte européen: habitat et économie aux 4e et 3e millénaires avant notre ère. Revue Archéologique de Picardie*, special no. 28, 77–99

Salanova, L., Prieto-Martínez, M.P., Clop-García, X., Convertini, F., Lantes-Suárez, O. & Martínez-Cortizas, A. 2016. What are large-scale archaeometric programmes for? Bell Beaker pottery and societies from the third millennium BC in western Europe. *Archaeometry* 58 (5), 722–735

Sergent, F. (ed.), 2007. *Saintes 'Malabry'.* Inrap Grand-Sud-Ouest. Poitiers: SRA Poitou-Charentes

Tessier, M. & Bernard, J. 1995. La Roussellerie-l'Ermitage en Saint-Michel-Saint-Brévin (Loire-Atlantique): un site d'occupation continue du Néolithique final au Bronze final. *Bulletin de la Société Préhistorique Française* 92 (4), 479–98

Tinévez, J.-Y. (ed.), 2004. *Le site de la Hersonnais à Pléchâtel (Ille-et-Vilaine): un ensemble de bâtiments collectifs du Néolithique final.* Travaux 5. Paris, Société Préhistorique Française.

Toron, S., Donnart, K. & Favrel, Q. 2018. Trémuson (22) 'Le Coin des Petits Clos', un site du Néolithique moyen et final aux composantes continentale et atlantique. *InterNéo* 12, 116–126

Veiga Ferreira, O. da. 1966. *La culture du vase Campaniforme au Portugal.* Memoria nova serie 12. Lisbonne: Serviços Geologicos de Portugal

Verron, G. 1976. Les civilisations néolithiques en Normandie. In J. Guilaine (ed.), *La Préhistoire française, II, Les civilisations néolithiques et protohistoriques*, 387–401. Paris: éd. du CNRS

19

Where have all the houses gone? Or times they are a changin'

Alex M. Gibson

This title, parodying *Where Have all the Flowers Gone?* a protest song originally written in 1955 by Pete Seeger and which was popular in the 1960s, was used by Richard Bradley almost 50 years ago to lament the lack of Beaker domestic sites in Britain following his excavations and identification of possible structures at Belle Tout, Sussex (Bradley 1970a; 1970b). In this popular article Bradley stressed the flimsy nature of the Bell Beaker structures located at Belle Tout and the consequent problems of their survival. That some of these structures have subsequently been reinterpreted as periglacial features reinforces the difficulty of the quest for Beaker domestic architecture (Bradley 1982). Eight years later, the same lack of houses led Paul Ashbee (1978) to suggest that the 'Beaker People' may have lived itinerant lives in the Chalcolithic equivalent of Romany caravans and on the other side of Bell Beaker Europe, Vencl (1994) could suggest a similar scenario to explain the lack of Corded Ware sites in central Europe. As an undergraduate student at Newcastle University I remember my prehistory tutor, Prof. George Jobey, joking that the Beaker People never lived anywhere, they were only content to die. These examples, academic, fanciful and jocular, serve to illustrate the general frustration felt by archaeologists in their search for Neolithic and Bronze Age domestic structures generally and it is a frustration that still, to an extent, persists not only in Britain. It is a common theme running through the regional syntheses in this volume.

The second title, by Bob Dylan (released 1964) refers to another common theme obvious throughout the volume and addressed in the second part of this section, namely that whatever Beakers represent, they appear at a time of change though whether catalyst or consequence is more difficult to determine. In all regions of this study, they lay the foundations for the Early Bronze Age, a time of continuity and prosperity, of individual importance, trade and communal construction.

In fact, and again as stressed throughout this volume, it is not a lack of Beaker domestic activity that is the problem. All the contributors write of pits or layers of occupation material. Pits, possibly originally for storage but later receiving cultural debris or even shallower single fill pits designed to receive midden material as a ritual, perhaps regenerative act, preserve domestic debris albeit in a secondary and perhaps even selective context. Cultural layers, on the other hand, probably represent actual midden sites from which much of the pit fills were derived and attest settlement on site, or at least in the immediate vicinity. The settlement may have been episodic, short-lived, seasonal, transient but settlement it was.

As well as these negative and sometimes ephemeral features, environmental data can be used to reconstruct settlement. Palynology can reconstruct the green environment. The study of plant macrofossils can shed light on plant exploitation. Faunal analysis from insects to mammals can answer questions of stock rearing, animal exploitation and living conditions in past societies. Bioanthropology can assess the general health of the population as well as identifying potential sub-strates within society. Lipid and other absorbed residue analyses of ceramics can help reconstruct diet, isotope analyses can also answer dietary and mobility questions and microwear analysis of lithics can paint a picture of everyday domestic activities as well as materials exploitation. These are by no means all the scientific techniques that can be used to reconstruct past societies and whilst not all avenues will be able to be explored on every site depending on, for example, preservation conditions, nevertheless they serve to indicate that we can today glean more from the archaeological record than ever before in the history of archaeology and all are relevant, as the papers in this volume make clear, to the study of settlement. Settlement archaeology extends far beyond house plans.

At my own site of Upper Ninepence in the Walton Basin in Wales, preservation of bone was non-existent and only carbonised plant macrofossils survived in terms of conventional palaeoenvironmental data (Gibson 1999). The site comprised a cluster of pits and stake-holes below a later round barrow and the ceramics suggested two distinct phases of activity, one associated with Impressed Ware of the Middle Neolithic and the other associated with Grooved Ware of the Later Neolithic. Two circular domestic structures belonged to this later phase (Gibson – undated references refer to this volume). To what extent, if any, did these phases overlap? The radiocarbon dates for both phases suggested two distinct periods of occupation: the earlier lay between the 35th and 30th centuries BC whilst the Grooved Ware phase fell between the 29th and 26th centuries BC. There was no mixing of ceramic traditions in the pits, each contained chronologically and culturally distinct assemblages.

Microwear analysis of the lithics from the pits indicated that the artefacts had suffered post-use damage, perhaps from being trampled, suggesting that they had already been discarded, perhaps in a midden environment, before they were selected for final deposition. But the use wear traces identified in the two periods proved very different. In the middle Neolithic, a full range of agricultural activities seems to have been undertaken, whilst in the Grooved Ware phase, meat cutting and hide preparation were by far the dominant activities.

Lipid analysis of the pottery also provided very different results. Ruminant fats were found in the Impressed Ware whilst the Grooved Ware vessels contained purely porcine adipose fats. The vessels from both traditions were predominantly made from local clay though some of the Impressed Ware may have been imported from sources up to 50 km away.

Pollen did not survive in the well-drained acidic soils but charcoals and plant macrofossils indicated cereal cultivation and the exploitation of hazel and a mixed range of scrubland species in the Middle Neolithic suggesting an environment comprising grassland, scrubland and cultivated areas. The Grooved Ware taxa also suggested grassland but cereal evidence was much rarer and there was an overwhelming preponderance of oak in the charcoal samples. Acorns were also found perhaps complementing the conclusions drawn from the lipid analysis suggesting a change from a ruminant to pig-based economy and, of course, exploitation of oak woodland as opposed to scrubland.

Though the data were admittedly limited, and whilst the site did not have a Beaker phase, nevertheless we were able to demonstrate a complete change of economy between the Middle and Later Neolithic phases as well as a complete change in ceramic assemblage suggesting a real cultural hiatus, cultural replacement and an archaeological schism. It demonstrates the value of an holistic approach to settlements and much more work of this kind needs to be undertaken on sites with later Neolithic and Beaker phases not just in Britain but across Europe more generally.

Nevertheless, the work undertaken so far in Europe does suggest a real change heralded by the appearance of Beakers at least in some areas. In Britain, the sub-square Grooved Ware houses of the Later Neolithic gave way to more oval forms some slightly sunken, others constructed of stakes. The structures from both phases are comparatively flimsy outside of the Orcadian and Shetland archipelagos and especially in lowland areas. Beaker house sites are still rare and are likely to remain so for, as a result of their flimsy nature, they are unlikely to be detected by geophysical prospection in developer-funded projects. Their discovery, as in the past, will largely result from chance discoveries and the excavation of protected contexts.

In the neighbouring Netherlands, pre-Beaker and Beaker houses are equally as rare as they are in Britain and the desire to identify them has led to some erroneous or tentative interpretations (Kleijne & Drenth). The limited data, however, suggest a change from the small rectangular Vlaardingen type house to the advent of two- and then three-aisled buildings that develop into the longhouses of the Early Bronze Age. Beaker sites with traces of later occupations suggest that a period of greater stability and more permanent settlements, perhaps resulting from a change in economic regime, are heralded by the arrival of Beakers. Proceeding eastwards, the scenario is slightly different in Denmark (Sarauw) where change is not envisaged on such a scale but rather native populations can be seen to adopt a slowly changing material culture perhaps for reasons of display and prestige. Early houses have a mix of Corded Ware and Beaker but as the Beaker period progresses, houses become larger, more robust, aisled and with a partly sunken floor. The environmental data attest a mixed economy but increased and more varied cereal production suggests greater stability. This scenario can also be demonstrated in Poland where there was a greater emphasis on cereal production in the Beaker period, when houses again become more robust than those of the preceding Neolithic and when the numbers of pits and the amount of domestic debris increases (Czebreszuk & Szmyt). Once again it suggests the on-set of more permanent settlement and greater economic stabilty.

In these northern lands, the transition from Corded Ware to Bell Beaker appears smooth with some Corded Ware appearing on Beaker domestic sites. This is unlike the scenario in Britain where, in a domestic context, Grooved Ware and Beakers are not found in strict association, Beaker domestic assemblages are pure Beaker with a range of fine and rusticated forms. Beaker (but not Grooved Ware) then goes on to influence Early Bronze Age forms. It suggests that the arrival of Beakers coincides with the collapse of Grooved Ware societies across Britain and not only in Orkney

In Central Germany, the transition appears somewhat similar to the British picture (Spatzier & Schunke). The Beaker domestic pottery is very different to the preceding Corded Ware tending to have Beaker shapes, sometimes with handles and everted and cordoned rims that herald the Early Bronze Age Únětice forms. Whilst aisled rectangular buildings are known from both the preceding Schönefeld and Corded Ware Cultures, the Beaker houses were sited away from the earlier settlements, become larger, often two-aisled trapezoid structures once again anticipating the more formalised longhouses of the Únětice. Nucleated settlements point towards greater stability and an increased focus on arable agriculture that also continued into the Early Bronze Age. In southern Germany, by contrast, the domestic pottery is derived from Corded Ware forms (Strahm) but domestic architecture changes. Pre-Beaker settlement is mainly represented by pits and spreads but with Beakers two-aisled rectangular houses appear representing a Beaker innovation that once again developed into the Early Bronze Age longhouse forms. The mechanics of the arrival of Beakers in these two areas seem very different with adaption and adoption in the south but with potential replacement in the north.

In Bohemia and Moravia, despite the richness of Beaker burials in this area, domestic evidence is rare beyond the usual pits and cultural layers. Sill-beam construction may have been employed in domestic architecture as blank areas can often be detected within artefact-rich spreads suggesting the ghosts of buildings (Turek). Rare post-hole-constructed bowed walled structures mark a Beaker innovation but whereas Corded Ware settlements tend to be avoided by Bell Beaker users in central Germany, in Bohemia and Moravia, and as in southern Germany, there is very much a sense of continuity. Environmentally there seems to be a greater emphasis on cattle in the Beaker period but also much richer and larger cereal and pulse assemblages. Interestingly, pig predominates in grave deposits but not on settlement sites. The associated domestic pottery is derived from local pre-Beaker traditions again demonstrating fusion rather than schism.

The pottery belonging to pre-Beaker groups in Hungary also forms part of the Beaker domestic assemblage (Reményi *et al.*) but the large rectangular buildings that preceded Beakers were replaced with bowed-wall, boat-shaped structures, some with sunken floors. Beaker groups, particularly of the Csepel group, seem to have operated alongside existing populations (Nagyrev Culture) and even communicated and interacted with each other but there is no mixing in the cemeteries or on the settlements indicating a degree of cultural differentiation. Once again, an increase in arable agriculture can be documented with the arrival of Beakers signalled by an increase in plant diversity, woodland clearance and an increase in animal husbandry, changing from a pre-Beaker cattle and sheep economy to predominantly cattle and horses.

Despite the richness and quantity of Beaker burials in Hungary and the Czech Republic, in neighbouring Austria, Beaker is poorly represented and regional ceramics form the domestic basis of Beaker assemblages. Despite this there is a slight change in settlement structure at this time. The hilltop and defended sites of some Neolithic cultural groups are abandoned in favour of valley and open locations more favourable for arable agriculture (Kern *et al.*). Rectangular post-built houses were constructed by the preceding Neolithic populations and continue into and through the Beaker period but they appear to become more varied including rectangular, trapezoid and boat-shaped structures. Some buildings had sunken floors in both the pre- and Beaker phases and, as in Germany and central Europe, the rectangular houses continued and developed into the Earlier Bronze Age. Environmental data are scarce but horses appear with Beakers, probably via the Danube from neighbouring Hungary.

In Switzerland and central-eastern France, lakeside pile dwellings, and subrectangular, slightly oval structures (Upper Rhône) common amongst late Neolithic groups, are abandoned in favour of rectangular dryland sites (Besse *et al.*) but despite this shift in settlement location, there is continuity manifested in the Beaker-associated domestic pottery that is derived from local forms. As in the Czech Republic, sill-beam houses leaving no surface traces appear to have been used and are represented by 'empty areas' within layers of domestic debris, the richness of which demonstrates that these were not short-lived settlements so despite leaving few traces, the houses may have been permanent and substantial. The house layout did not change much from the preceding period. It was still predominantly rectangular, sometimes substantially constructed and with apsidal ends, but located in different environments. Once again, the environmental data suggest increased cereal cultivation and plant exploitation.

Turning to Atlantic, southern and Mediterranean Europe, in north-western France, the local pre-Beaker pottery influences domestic assemblages but there appears to have been a change in settlement types (Nicolas *et al.*). The large, elongated timber aisled buildings of the Late Neolithic, often enclosed or in defended positions, give way to smaller oval or almond-shaped buildings constructed from both wood and stone depending on topography. These small undefended buildings do not share the large range of sizes seen in the later Neolithic and appear to represent settlement structures designed for small family units rather than the earlier large, communal longhouses. They bear a close comparison to the oval structures found in Britain and Ireland, and especially those of the Northern and Western Isles (Gibson). They are open settlements and represent a dramatic change in land-use and settlement strategies.

In north-western Iberia there again appears to be a dramatic social break with the appearance of Bell Beakers and although the local Penha-type pottery and Bell Beaker types co-existed for some 200 years, their distributions appear to have been exclusive and used by different groups (Prieto-Martinez). Beaker can be found at some of the defended sites such as walled or ditched settlements and with small oval to circular houses but only in the latest levels and these give way to unenclosed settlements with oval to boat-shaped houses often arranged in groups. Settlements increase in size and longhouses appear towards the end of the Beaker period. These larger settlements suggest greater stability, and extensive woodland clearance in turn suggests more expansive agriculture. As we have seen elsewhere, the

Beaker longhouses presage Early Bronze Age settlement types.

In Portugal Beakers are found at the earlier walled enclosures but only after the walls have been decommissioned (Valera *et al.*) reminiscent of a social collapse as suggested for the stone houses at Skara Brae (Gibson). In the case of the large ditched enclosures, In the Alentejo some of the ditches had silted before Beakers appear whilst in the south, they continued to be constructed. Drystone circular houses are often grouped around a similar structure with more massive walls suggesting a tower. They are often built over the walls of the abandoned fortified sites and the robustness of their construction suggests their intended permanency. Beakers appear at time when there is a fast-developing social trajectory involving the need for prestigious display in terms of artefacts and constructions yet they form only one facet of this display network to the extent that sites on which they are found can be claimed as sites with Beakers but not exclusive Beaker sites.

The picture is similar, but with some differences in central Spain (Garrido-Pena). Domestic ceramic assemblages comprise local globular forms which later develop into Early Bronze Age types and decorated Bell Beaker can account for as little as 1% of the total ceramic assemblage. Beaker settlements continue the tradition of circular to oval huts with sunken floors and wattle and daub superstructures. Whilst preceding sites can be open or enclosed, the Beaker sites tend to be open (except in the southern Meseta), command wide vistas and lie on important communications routes such as river valleys. As in other areas, Beakers coincide with a developing trend in more intensive agriculture including increased forest clearance, more widespread cereal cultivation and larger herds of cattle and pig.

To the south of the Iberian peninsula, in Andalusia, and as in southern Portugal, the large ditched enclosures continue to be used and Beakers appear in the later phases. The richness and exotic nature of some other artefacts from these sites suggest that Beakers are playing their part in this need for display and prestige as suggested for neighbouring Portugal. However, at some of the large stone-walled Neolithic settlements, Beakers arrive after they had reached their peak and mark the serious decline, contraction or even the destruction of these sites (Lazarich). Beaker houses are circular to oval, often with stone foundations and wattle and daub superstructures and some may have sunken floors. Stability is suggested by the increase in the number of settlements at this time. They exploit good agricultural land, are close to permanent water supplies, and there is an expansion of agricultural production marked by larger and more abundant storage pits and an increase in soil erosion. This seems to come to an end with a period of greater aridity leading to increased territorial competition.

In neighbouring Mediterranean France, local Late Neolithic groups do not appear to have been replaced by Beaker users, but rather to have lived alongside them and nearly all Maritime Beakers are found on existing Neolithic sites (Lemercier *et al.*). Nevertheless, the appearance of Beakers does represent a new cultural identity and Beakers do not evolve out of Late Neolithic ceramics. Later Neolithic settlements do not seem to have favoured any particular topographical position but in the Beaker period coastal locations and lower river valleys seem to have been preferred though elevated positions were also occupied and occasionally defended in the later Beaker period. As with Atlantic and Mediterranean Iberia, some of the defended settlements of the later Neolithic were already in decline before the arrival of Beakers. Beaker houses are rare but the elongated oval houses of some of the defended sites seem to change in favour of more oval, almost lenticular forms in the Beaker period. Post-hole-defined aisled structures have been found further inland in the lower Rhone Valley suggesting the influence of both coastal and central European inland traditions the latter presumably moving southwards using the communications routes afforded by the main river valley. Copper artefacts also suggest an Iberian influence at this time and in terms of subsistence, there is an increase in both arable agriculture and animal husbandry in keeping with the picture in other parts of Europe. Interestingly, there appears to be an increase in hunting activity associated with Beaker though this appears locally specific and is not really noted elsewhere except Sardinia (see below).

In both Sardinia and Sicily, Beaker ceramics are associated with those of the local existing cultures but interestingly, in Sicily, Beakers have a different petrology and is more similar to the succeeding Early Bronze Age forms (Melis). In Sardinia, settlements are often defended but also sited on low lying ground and gentle slopes and the internal structures often have sunken floors. They tend to be trapezoidal but numbers are few. In the Beaker period, trapezoidal structures persist, often with stone walls and occasionally with an apsidal end. There seems to have been increased competition for land at this time with increased stock farming and, as in neighbouring France, a reliance on hunting. In Sicily, elongated oval huts of the pre-Beaker settlements give way to more circular forms with Beaker associations although there are no exclusively Beaker sites. Nevertheless, and as can be seen elsewhere, Beakers mark a period of change. There is increased stability within the settlement record, a shift to higher ground more suited to stock rearing, evidence for increased woodland clearance and increased cereal production. The apparent competition for land gave rise to local elites and Beakers may have played a part in the need for prestigious display items. Contrary to Mediterranean France and Sardinia, there seems to have been a reduction in hunting.

To the North in the central and northern Italian peninsula, Beakers again mark a period of change though interaction with preceding local groups is attested by much of the domestic pottery which has its origins in local forms and continued to develop into Early Bronze Age types (Baioni *et al.*). At many sites the circular Chalcolithic house plans are replaced by rectangular timber-framed buildings often with wattle and daub walls and they are occasionally flimsy in construction. Elsewhere sunken oval-floored and elliptical structures persist. Sites seemed to have preferred open, well-drained land in river valleys and on communications routes though all terrains were utilised including upland locales and terraced settlements. Unusually, Beaker can often be associated with short-lived settlements but this contradicts the environmental evidence for marked woodland clearance and a corresponding increase in cereal cultivation and a shift from earlier sheep herding to cattle and pig breeding. The horse also makes an appearance at this time suggesting links to the grasslands to the north of the region.

The Beaker artefact package comprising the pot itself and associated artefacts centred around archery has been well discussed in modern literature but too much similarity or uniformity has, perhaps, been accredited to this. The associated crouched inhumation makes a reappearance in the British archaeological record, but not so elsewhere. In much of northern Europe Beaker inhumations more or less continue those of the preceding Single Grave Culture groups. In southern Europe, multiple inhumations in pits and hypogea are adopted by Beaker users and there is much more of a sense of continuity in Continental Europe than in Britain. Even in Ireland we see a resurgence of megalithic traditions associated with Beaker pottery.

In the domestic sphere, the regional syntheses in this volume show that Beakers appear at a time of change and, in many ways, herald the Early Bronze Age and the stability that particularly marks that period of prehistory. Almost all areas demonstrate the start of a more stable economy, renewed woodland clearance and stock and arable intensification. In some regions this would seem to have followed a period of collapse seen in the demise of the Orcadian 'villages' and ritual monument construction in Britain, in the decline of the long communal houses and defended sites of Atlantic France, and in the contraction of the large fortified enclosures of Iberia, particularly in the southern part of the peninsula. Whether Beaker users were the catalyst for this collapse or whether they exploited any vacuums that resulted from these troubled times must remain speculative.

In terms of house plans, in areas where there is little change in the geometry of the houses (Netherlands, Denmark, Poland, Switzerland, Iberia, Sardinia) nevertheless the structures become larger, often with the development of aisles, and are more robustly constructed. Even in Switzerland and the Czech Republic, house 'ghosts' represented by relatively clean, rectangular areas within occupation spreads suggest permanent stable settlement given the extent of the domestic detritus in which they are situated. The authors of the papers in this volume also see a continuous development from the Beaker period into the full Early Bronze Age.

In other areas Beaker-associated houses exhibit a different geometry from oval to rectangular in the Rhone Valley and parts of

Italy, from elongated oval to almost lenticular in Atlantic France and from circular to oval to rectangular in northern Iberia. These represent a real change in domestic architecture and it is difficult not to attribute this to a cultural shift. In Central Europe, the appearance of longhouses with externally bowed walls can certainly be identified as a Beaker introduction differing from the earlier rectangular forms particularly in Hungary, and forming an element of Beaker house types in neighbouring Austria and in Bohemia and Moravia. These also mark a real change in domestic architecture and in Hungary especially the siting of Beaker settlements away from those of the preceding Neolithic again represents real social change.

As concisely stated by Valera *et al*, the majority of sites discussed in all areas covered by this volume represent sites with Beakers rather than Beaker sites. But there are two exceptions. In Britain, Beakers are only found with the Late Neolithic Grooved Ware on ritual sites such as henge monuments and stone and timber circles but the association of the two ceramic types can rarely be demonstrated and can, in many cases, be seen to belong to clearly different periods of activity. In the domestic sphere, there are few early Beaker settlements. Beakers appear with burials before they manifest themselves in domestic assemblages but when they do appear, these assemblages can be demonstrated to be pure Beaker with a range of sizes and fabrics and with an element of undecorated and rusticated wares. This scenario can also be detected in the Corded Ware areas of northern Europe in particular. Pottery rusticated with 'crowsfoot' impressions ('ungulate' impressions in Iberia) formed by pairs of fingernails may be influenced by Atlantic assemblages. In Britain, Beaker goes on to influence Early Bronze Age Food Vessels and Collared Urns whose forms mark a re-emergence of Middle Neolithic types. In Germany, Zwenkau pottery forms the main component of Beaker domestic assemblages and has only fairly recently been recognised as such (Spatzier & Schunke) as it was formerly considered proto-Únětice as, like in Britain, it influences later forms. These Beaker-shaped vessels with handles and cordons below the rims do not have ready parallels in the preceding ceramic assemblages. These two regions stand apart from the rest of Europe.

Bell Beakers spread over large areas of Europe in a comparatively short time bringing with them new and prestigious artefacts that are clearly adopted and adapted by local populations but the mechanics of this are still not fully understood. Recent DNA analyses suggest an element of folk movement (Olalde *et al.,* 2018) in some areas, principally from the Steppe and the Yamnaya horse-rearing communities. It is tempting to see this represented by the rectangular and broadly rectangular houses of Central and Northern Europe, but the DNA suggest that this migration also affected Britain where the oval houses have much more in common with Atlantic and Mediterranean Europe. Whilst a Dutch origin has been suggested for British Beakers (Sheridan 2008), the dissimilarity of domestic structures, especially given the uncertainty regarding Molenaarsgraaf (Kleijne & Drenth) is worthy of note.

The eastern and western split between oval (including almond-shaped) and rectangular houses does, to a certain extent also mirror the split in the burial record with single grave burials sharing broadly the same distribution as the rectangular houses and with multiple inhumations more common in western and southern Europe. Again Britain represents an anomaly as one of the earliest Beaker mortuary deposits, The Boscombe Bowmen burial, comprises a multiple deposit that is very northern French in character yet single inhumations are also re-introduced at this time (Fitzpatrick 2011). Beaker burial practices become much more varied after 2200 BC. The artefacts of the Beaker phenomenon, therefore, exhibit an ability to be included in and adopted by existing local practices.

In overview, the Bell Beaker phenomenon appears to be plural in scale and in terms of adoption, adaption and interaction. Regional variations can be expressed in artefact assemblages, the settlement record, burials and, of course in the Beakers themselves and their associated domestic ceramics. This can be likened to the regional differences in a wide-spread religion where similar artefact assemblages are recognisable but where local differences in practices can be dramatic. The religion may not be adopted in all areas depending on the strength of pre-existing traditions and this also seems true of the patchy nature of the Bell Beaker distribution across Europe. While distinct changes can be detected in some areas, in others adoption and adaption is very much the key to the deposition of the artefactual phenomenon but what does seem universal is the coincidence of the spread of Beakers with increased farming, a more settled economy, perhaps territorial jealousies, and the need for the emerging elite to adopt more and varied means of display to maintain and build on their positions of power.

References

Ashbee, P. 1978. *The Ancient British*. Norwich: University of East Anglia

Bradley, R. 1970a. Where have all the houses gone? Some approaches to Beaker settlement. *Current Archaeology,* 2 (10), 264–66

Bradley, R. 1970b. The excavation of a Beaker settlement at Belle Tout, East Sussex, England, *Proceedings of the Prehistoric Society* 36, 312–79

Bradley, R. 1982. Belle Tout – revision and re-assessment. In Drewett, P.L. (ed.), *The Archaeology of Bullock Down, Eastbourne, East Sussex: the Development of a Landscape,* 12–20. Monograph 1. Lewes: Sussex Archaeological Society

Fitzpatrick, A.P. 2011. *The Amesbury Archer and the Boscombe Bowmen. Bell Beaker Burials at Boscombe Down, Amesbury, Wiltshire.* Salisbury: Wessex Archaeology.

Gibson, A.M. 1999. *The Walton Basin Project: Excavation and Survey in a Prehistoric Landscape 1993–7.* Research Report 118. York: Council for British Archaeology.

Olalde, I. *et al.* 2018. The Beaker Phenomenon and the Genomic Transformation of Northwest Europe. *Nature,* 555, No. 7695, 190–6

Sheridan, A. 2008. Upper Largie and Dutch-Scottish Connections during the Beaker Period. In Fokkens, H., Coles, B., Van Gijn, A.L., Kleijne, J.P., Ponjee, H.H. & Slappendel, C.G. (eds), *Between Foraging and Farming. An Extended Broad Spectrum of Papers Presented to Leendert Louwe Kooijmans,* 247–60. Leiden: Analecta Praehistorica Leidensia 50

Vencl, S. 1994. K problému sídlišť kultur s keramikou šňůrovou – Some comments on the problem of Corded-Ware culture settlement sites. *Archeologické Rozhledy* 46, 3–24

INDICES

Numbers in *italics* refer to pages with illustrations, 't' indicates a table

Index of sites

General index